DI011403

*A Critical Bibliography of
French Literature*

A Critical Bibliography of French Literature

D. C. CABEEN
General Editor

VOLUME II

THE SIXTEENTH CENTURY
Edited by
ALEXANDER H. SCHUTZ
Ohio State University

SYRACUSE UNIVERSITY PRESS
1956

Second printing, September 1966

Printed in the United States of America

To the memory of
ROBERT V. MERRILL

GENERAL INTRODUCTION

" Qui scit ubi scientia sit, ille est proximus habenti."
Ferdinand Brunetière, *Manuel de l'histoire de
la littérature française (Avertissement)*

THERE EXISTS TODAY no adequate guide for the selection of the best articles or books of scholarly criticism devoted to French literature.   Most of the existing bibliographies, whether they cover a single author, a literary movement, or a larger period, aim to achieve completeness.   They thus impose upon the user a difficult choice among the numerous items they list, and, in the absence of qualitative indications, he must often make such a selection intuitively.

The present bibliography is doubly critical.   First, it is selective, for it gathers together only that information which is essential to the specialist, the advanced student, or the cultivated amateur of French literature.   Every item listed is, in the opinion of the compilers, valuable to anyone undertaking further studies.   Secondly, the bibliography is critical in form, since each collaborator has briefly appraised the books or articles with which he deals.   The object has consistently been to point out what still remains valid and important in a work of whatever date.

A bibliography whose guiding principle is that of critical selectivity must be objective. In so far as possible, each author or subject has been treated by a scholar who is known in the United States for his interest in that author or subject.   But no collaborator has worked in a vacuum : his judgments have been influenced by consultation with the individual Volume Editors and with the General Editor.   And yet, everyone who has taken part in this enterprise knows that it must inevitably be marred by errors and omissions, which the Editors earnestly beg all users of the bibliography to call to their attention.   Such a complex work as this can always bear improvement.

It is hoped that this bibliography will prove to be a constructive force, suggesting by implication which subjects have been comparatively neglected or inadequately treated and which aspects of a writer, a group, or a period require reinterpretation today.   In the future, scholarly writing can hardly fail to benefit from a critical bibliography which obviates the need for many of the preliminary explorations hitherto necessary.   Under normal circumstances, indeed, the bibliography should so stimulate new works as to be itself soon outdated—and no result could more deeply gratify the compilers.

Finally, it is especially significant that the present work is at once American in inspiration and co-operative in nature.   Undertaken in the United States when Europe was being shaken by the first clashes of a devastating war, continued in spite of the difficulties and delays of uneasy later years, this *Critical Bibliography* bears witness to the conviction of its American and French contributors that French literature is the common heritage of the civilized world.

THE EDITORS

GENERAL EDITOR'S NOTE

THE BIBLIOGRAPHICAL forms adopted for this volume, as well as for the series as a whole, have been selected with a view to giving the greatest amount of information compatible with clearness and brevity. To this end, the forms of the H. W. Wilson Company, with some slight modifications, were chosen for periodicals, and those of the Library of Congress for books.

The strongest argument for the use of the Library of Congress forms and spellings is that its catalogue is the one source available to all collaborators working on this project.

In many cases, the General Editor (who compiled the Index) would have liked to give in more detail the information used in the Library of Congress catalogue in identifying authors and other proper names appearing in an entry. Often this information is priceless and is not available elsewhere, since it has been obtained by literary, historical, and genealogical research which has never been equaled in a large-scale research project for scope, thoroughness, and precision. But the need to economize on space forbids complete reproduction of much of this valuable material.

A somewhat more detailed explanation of the Index than the brief note which heads it seems called for. Any index so simple and obvious as to need no explanation would be the easiest to compile, but in a volume like this would be too cumbersome to use to the best advantage. The great proportion of the indexed subjects appear less than three times, and it is not difficult for the reader to look up three or fewer serial numbers to find the one needed. However, the presence of an identifying word or so before the serial numbers of items which appear more than three times will unquestionably save a substantial amount of trouble if the user will take the few moments necessary to understand the mechanics of the Index. Thus : the entry " Villey-Desmeserets, Pierre Louis Joseph " illustrates a number of the principles which have guided the compilation of this Index. The name of this scholar is given in the Index in full, as it appears in the LC catalogue. However, in annotations the name " Villey " alone is used, both for reasons of brevity and because other scholars habitually employ the shorter form. Under his name appears " Bédier & Hazard," with the serial numbers 94, *1785*; the annotation of item no. 94 mentions the fact that Villey was a contributor to the 16th century section of this history of French literature by these

ix

two authorities.   Since, however, Villey's name does not head the entry, the number 94 is not italicized here.   The number 94 is, of course, italicized under the indexed names of both Joseph Bédier and Paul Hazard.   No. *1785* is here italicized, since Villey is the author who heads the entry of the item *1785*, which is a section of some eleven pages on Montaigne and his *Essays* in *Bédier & Hazard*. No. 1785 appears twice under the Montaigne index-heading: once under *Criticism* and once under the *Essais*, but not in italics.

However, innumerable items do not lend themselves so neatly to brief identification, even by specialists on the given subject, but the loss of time devoted to consulting the item itself seemed hardly sufficient to justify the substantial amount of printing required for more complete identification.   Based on the idea that if a name is worth mentioning in an analysis, it should be listed under that item, the Index attempts to be as complete as possible.   In a few cases this leads to an excessively large number of references under some items, but this was unavoidable.

In general, subject headings in the Index are given in English, except in cases in which a translation would be inadequate or too lengthy (e.g., *Ligue*, *mignons*). Non-English words and titles of studies, or abbreviations of such titles, are italicized.

In the main body of this volume there has been no effort to eliminate duplicate titles. In fact, many items appear several times.   Usually the first appearance of the study carries the full entry, and subsequent ones only the title, with a cross-reference to the first mention.   Usually also the annotations of items after the first occurrence offer material of further interest.   Even when nothing new is presented, the mere presence of an item in a given section adds something to the subject by acting as a significant reminder.   In the Index, however, it was not found practicable to indicate a distinction between the main item and cross-references to it.

Last names of sixteenth-century writers are abbreviated to an initial only in sections devoted to them and so indicated by a heading or a sub-heading.   When a book was published in Paris, no place of publication is given.

I wish here to express my sincere thanks to the Committee on research activities of the Modern Language Association of America, whose generous grant has rendered great service to this volume, and to the Graduate School of Ohio State University, which also made a substantial contribution.   The project as a whole is greatly in-debted to the Editors of the Syracuse University Press for the difficult and often thankless task of proof reading.   Finally, I am most grateful to the Reference Department of the New York Public Library, and particularly to MM. A. P. De Weese and James Tobin for their valuable assistance upon many knotty problems. Scholarship in the United States owes an immense debt to Reference Librarians for their patience, courtesy, tenacity of purpose, and high degree of ingenuity and of skill in research techniques which enables them to discover solutions for the most difficult problems.

DAVID C. CABEEN

FOREWORD

THE PRESENT VOLUME was begun and much of the preliminary work carried on under the editorship of Robert V. Merrill, of the University of California at Los Angeles. Among the " seiziémistes " in the United States, he was clearly indicated for the task by his administrative ability, his firm grounding in the Classics and a succession of important studies dealing mainly with the impact of Platonic and Neo-Platonic ideas on the Pléiade, a topic which was the major concern of his scholarly career.

The series would have been happily augmented by a volume on Neo-Platonic themes and imagery in sixteenth century literature, representing the results of many years of research and which was unfinished at the time of his death (January 1, 1951). The manuscript has been entrusted to Professor R. J. Clements of New York University, who expects to bring it to conclusion.

Robert Valentine Merrill was born in Middletown, Connecticut, on November 24, 1892. His father was at the time Professor of Latin at Wesleyan University and was ordained in 1895 to the Episcopal priesthood. He later became a distinguished professor of Latin at the University of Chicago. His mother likewise has been interested in the ancient Classics, adding to this knowledge a keen appreciation of French literature as well.

Robert Merrill entered the University of Chicago in 1910. In 1913 he went as a Rhodes scholar to Balliol College, Oxford, where, in 1916, he received his A.B. degree. In the true Renaissance manner, he extended his interests to include athletics. Captain of the varsity fencing team during his undergraduate years at Chicago, he continued his activity at Oxford, where he was a member of the all-University team. On his return to Chicago as a member of the faculty, he coached the team for some time.

Terminating his war service as a First Lieutenant in 1919, he taught for a year at the University of Minnesota, returning then to Chicago, where he received his doctorate in Romance Languages in 1923, remaining on the staff until January, 1947 and serving also for extended periods as Executive Secretary of the Department and Head Marshal of the University. It was at the University of Chicago that the present writer, later to take over the editorship of this volume, came to know him.

Professors, colleagues, and former classmates remember him for his many qualities. He was an excellent student, with a wide diversity of knowledge and an amazing memory that enabled him to retain long literary passages, even, at times to parody them with a combination of rare wit and keen penetration.   He was a capable musician who, at Oxford, had been for three years a member of the Bach choir and, at Chicago, enthusiastically devoted himself to the Renaissance madrigal.   Members of Professor Wilkins' Dante class recall not merely his academic participation, but also his renditions of the Wolfe-Ferrari settings to the *Vita Nuova.* He was, in other words, representative, as few have been in our day, of the period to which he devoted his scholarly activities. But most of all, those who knew him remember his warm friendship and profound humanity.   It was felt by those of his friends who were consulted in the making of this Foreword, that an impersonal account could not do him justice.

Called to the University of California at Los Angeles in 1947, he served for three years as Chairman of the Department of French.   He was quickly recognized in his new post as a man of judgment, complete moral integrity, and high scholastic standards. From the beginning he was called upon to serve on several important Boards and Committees of the University, extending his influence beyond the departmental lines to the campus at large.   Short though his stay was there, he left a deep imprint.   It is thus in every way fitting that this volume be dedicated to his memory.

*　　*　　*

In our day, the French sixteenth century, long neglected in this country, is attracting workers in increasing numbers.   By no means an easy field, it is full of by-ways and complexities.   To understand the Renaissance, a good background is required in the Greek and Latin classics.   By the same token, the direct relationship between the " Middle Ages " and the " Renaissance " in France has not yet been sufficiently explored.

For these purposes there are still many gaps.   As Monseigneur Grente points out in the *Indications Bibliographiques* which form part of the Introduction to his *Diction-naire des Lettres (Seizième Siècle)*, essential tools are lacking: " Les historiens des lettres françaises ne disposent pour le seizième siècle d'aucun répertoire bibliographique."

In spite of the aid furnished by the indispensable bibliographies of Lanson and of Mademoiselle Giraud, several areas of the Renaissance present special difficulties, especially in what this volume refers to as Background.   Fortunately, contributors outside of the Romance literatures have also come to our aid.

During the Renaissance, the riches of many European nations were brought together in a common interest.   Humanism is, by its very nature, international.   Yet it is well to point out that there was also a French Renaissance of distinctive character, in which the nation, barely emerging from the trials of the Hundred Years' War, played a decisive role, developing European materials along the lines of a long and powerful national tradition.   We who today believe in the continued flowering of French culture may take heart from this historic parallel.

ALEXANDER H. SCHUTZ
Ohio State University

BIBLIOGRAPHY OF ROBERT V. MERRILL

THE TITLES ARE here listed in the order of their appearance. The fact that eight of the thirteen studies are important enough to be included in this critical bibliography is a measure of their scholarly value.

The platonism of Joachim du Bellay. Chicago, University of Chicago Press, 1925, 150 p. (741, 1268, 2575, i.e. three different mentions)

A note on the Italian genealogy of Du Bellay's Olive, Sonnet CXIII. MP 24:163-66, 1926-27 (1267, 2698).

Platonism in Petrarch's Canzoniere. MP 27:161-74, 1929-30.

Lucian and Du Bellay's Poète courtisan, MP 29:11-20, 1931-32 (1266).

Considerations on Les amours de I. du Bellay. MP 33:129-38, 1935-36 (1263).

Jean Lemaire, Du Bellay and the second Georgic. MLN 51:453-55, 1936 (1265).

Platonism in Pontus de Tyard's Erreurs amoureuses (1549). MP 35:139-58, 1937-38 (783).

Three sonnets of the sun. MP 36:247-53, 1938-39.

Ronsard and the burning grove. MP 37:337-41, 1939-40.

Eros and Anteros. Spec 19:265-84, 1944 (740).

Du Bellay's Olive CXII and the Rime diverse. MLN 60:527-30, Dec. 1945 (1264).

The Pléiade and the Androgyne. CL 1:97-112, 1949.

Molière's exposition of a courtly character in Don Juan. MP 19:33-55, 1921-22, the outgrowth of a highly original paper in Professor Nitze's seminar.

ABBREVIATIONS USED IN VOLUME II

AA	Ausgaben und Abhandlungen aus dem Gebiete der romanischen Philologie
AAB	Académie nationale des sciences, belles-lettres et arts de Bordeaux, Actes
AAF	Archives de l'art français
AAGP	*See* AA
AAP	Archivos argentinos de pediatria
AASF	Annales Academiae scientiarum fennicae
AB	Art bulletin
Acad	Academy
ACHF	Archives curieuses de l'histoire de France
ACUJ	Acta et Commentationes Imp. Universitatis Jurievensis (olim Dorpatensis)
ADB	Académie delphinale, Bulletin
AESC	Annales : économies, sociétés, civilisations
Aevum	Aevum
AFR	Anglo-French review
AHR	American historical review
AHS	Annales d'histoire sociale
AHSR	Archives historiques et statistiques du Rhône
AIBL	Institut de France. Académie des inscriptions et belles-lettres. Comptes rendus des séances
AIV	Istituto veneto di scienze, lettere ed arti, Atti
AJJR	Société Jean Jacques Rousseau (Geneva), Annales
ALAM	Annales littéraires et artistiques du Maine
ALG	Archiv für Literaturgeschichte
AM	Annales du Midi
AMD	Academia de ciencias morales y políticas, Madrid, Discursos
AMH	Annals of medical history
AMP	Institut de France. Académie des sciences morales et politiques. Séances et travaux. Compte rendu
AMS	Folger Shakespeare Library, Washington, D.C. Joseph Quincey Adams memorial studies. Washington, 1948
AMT	Archives médicales de Toulouse
AnP	L'année philosophique
APC	Annales de philosophie chrétienne
Aph	Archiv für Philosophie
APSR	American political science review
AR	Archivum romanicum
Archiv	Archiv für das Studium der neueren Sprachen

Aréthuse	Aréthuse
ARG	Archiv für Reformationgeschichte
ASHF	Société de l'histoire de France, Annuaire-bulletin
ASI	Archiviio storico italiano
ASL	Archivo storico lombardo
ASNP	Italy. Reale scuola normale superiore, Pisa. Annali ... Filosofia filologia
ASS	Archivio di storia della scienza (Archeion)
Aht	Athenaeum; studi periodici di letteratura e storia
AthL	Athenaeum (London)
ATR	Anglican theological review
AUB	Annales des universités de Belgique
AUL	Lyons. Université. Annales
AUP	Paris. Université. Annales
AWV	Akademie der Wissenschaften, Vienna. Philosophisch-historische Klasse, Sitzungsberichte
BA	Books abroad
BAGB	Bulletin de l'Association Guillaume Budé
BAHM	Academia de la historia, Madrid, Boletín
BARB	Académie royale des sciences, des lettres et des beaux-arts de Belgique. Classe des lettres et des sciences morales et politiques. Bulletins
Baudrier	Baudrier, H. Bibliographie lyonnaise; recherches sur les imprimeurs, librairies, relieurs et fondeurs de lettres de Lyon au 16e siècle. Lyons, Brun, Picard, 1895-1921. 12 v.
BB	Bibliophile belge
BBB	Bulletin du bibliophile et du bibliothécaire
BBRP	Berliner Beiträge zur romanischen Philologie
BCA	Bibliothèque classique de l'amateur
BCHM	Bulletin de la Commission historique et archéologique de la Mayenne
BCBA	Académie royale de Belgique. Classe des beaux-arts. Bulletin
Bcr	Bulletin critique
BDC	Bibliothèque d'un curieux
BDV	Bulletin d'histoire ecclésiastique et d'archéologie religieuses des diocèses de Valence, Gap, Grenoble et Viviers
BE	Bibliothèque elzévirienne
BEC	Bibiliothèque de l'École des chartes
BEFR	Bulletin de l'École française de Rome
Bel	Belfagor
BEP	Bulletin des études portugaises et de l'Institut français au Portugal
Beibl	Beiblatt zur Anglia
BFAA	Biblioteca di filosofia diretta da Antonio Aliotta
BFL	Bibliothèque de la Faculté de philosophie et lettres de l'Université de Liége
BGHD	Bulletin géographique historique et descriptive
BH	Bulletin hispanique
BHAP	Bulletin de la Société historique et archéologique du Périgord
BHM	Bulletin of the history of medicine
BHren	Bibliothèque d'humanisme et renaissance
BI	Bulletin italien
BibP	Bibliothèque de la Pléiade
BL	Bookman, London

BLCR	Boletín de la Liga argentina contra el reumatismo
BLE	Institut catholique de Toulouse. Bulletin de littérature ecclésiastique
BLR	Bibliothèque de la renaissance
BLS	Strasbourg. Université. Lettres, Faculté des, Bulletin de la Faculté des lettres de Strasbourg
BM	British museum library
Bman	Bookman, London
Bméd	Bruxelles-médical
BMJ	British medical journal
BMLA	Bulletin of the Medical library association
BMP	Padua, Museo civico, Bolletino
BN	Bibliothèque nationale
BNYAM	Bulletin of the New York academy of medicine
BP	Bibliothèque de la Pléiade
BPH	France. Comité des travaux historiques et philosophiques. Bulletin philologique et historique (jusqu'en 1715)
BPI	Biblioteca pedagogica antica e moderna italiana e straniera
BRCC	Bibliothèque de la Revue des cours et conférences
BRLC	Bibliothèque de la Revue de littérature comparée
Brunet	Brunet, Jacques Charles. Manuel de l'amateur de livres. Didot, 1860-65. 6 v.
BS	Bollingen series
BSA	Shakespeare association. Bulletin
BSAHL	Bulletin de la Société archéologique et historique du Limousin
BSAL	Société académique de Laon, Bulletin
BSAM	Société des amis de Montaigne, Paris, Bulletin
BSAW	Sächsische Akademie der Wissenschaften, Leipzig. Berichte über die Verhandlungen. Philosophisch-historische Klasse
BSB	Société d'émulation du Bourbonnais. (Lettres, sciences et arts. Moulin.), Bulletin
BSBA	Bulletin de la Société scientifique et littéraire des Basses-Alpes
BSHE	Bibliothèque de la Société d'histoire ecclésiastique de la France
BSHM	Bulletin de la Société française de l'histoire de la médecine
BSHP	Bulletin de la Société de l'histoire du protestantisme français
BSLP	Bulletin de la Société de linguistique de Paris
BSLS	Bulletin de la Société d'agriculture, sciences et arts de La Sarthe
BSNL	Société nivernaise des lettres, sciences et arts, Bulletin.
BSP	Société historique et archéologique du Périgord, Bulletin
BSPI	Bulletin de la Société de l'histoire de Paris et de l'Ile-de-France
BSPS	Bollettino della Società pavese di storia patria
BSV	Bulletin de la Société archéologique, scientifique et littéraire du Vendômois
BTP	Bibliothèque des textes philosophiques
BUAT	Toulouse, France. Université. Bulletin de l'Université et de l'Académie de Toulouse
ca	*circa* (about)
Cabeen	D. C. Cabeen, General Editor, A critical bibliography of French literature (Syracuse, N.Y.) Syracuse University Press, 1947-51, v. 1, 4
CB	Cabinet du bibliophile
CC	Civiltà cattolica
CCM	Collection des chefs-d'œuvre méconnus

CDA	Courrier de l'art
CDF	Les cours des facultés
CDHF	Collection des documents inédits sur l'histoire de France
CET	Collection Écrivains de toujours
CGOM	Collection : Les grands ordres monastiques et instituts religieux, dirigée par E. Schneider
CFI	Cahiers français d'information
ch	chapter
CH	Church history
CHR	Catholic historical review
Chris	Christendom
CL	Comparative literature
CLE	Collection Les chefs-d'œuvre expliqués
CLM	Collection des langues du monde
ClR	Classical review
Comm	Commerce
COI	Les chefs-d'œuvre inconnus
Con	Convivium
Corr	Le correspondant
CPF	La collection La Pléiade françoise
Cph	Collection philosophes
CPl	Collection de la Pléiade
CPMP	University of California publications in modern philology
Cr	Critique
Crit	La critica
Criterion	Criterion
CSCG	Collection Selecta des classiques Garnier
CSCL	Columbia university studies in comparative literature
CSCP	Cornell studies in classical philology
CSE	Collection " Savoir et enseigner "
CSRPL	Columbia university studies in Romance philology and literature
CTEH	Collection de textes pour servir à l'étude et à l'enseignement de l'histoire
Cult	La cultura
CW	Catholic world
DH	Documents d'histoire
DLit	Deutsche Literaturzeitung
DR	Dublin review
DSGJ	Deutsche Shakespeare-Gesellschaft, Weimar. Jahrbuch
DTC	Dictionnaire de théologie catholique
DV	Deutsche Vierteljahrsschrift für Literaturwissenschaft und Geistesgeschichte
EB	Elizabethan bibliographies
EC	Études classiques, Les
Edda	Edda
EF	Études françaises
EHR	English historical review
EI	Études italiennes
EJ	Economic journal
ELBA	Ecclesiae Londino-Batavae Archivum
ELEC	Études de littérature étrangère et comparée

EPM	Études de philosophie médiévale
EQ	Evangelical quarterly
ER	Educational review
Eras	Erasmus
ES	Englische Studien
Esp	Esprit
EssAF	Essays, Albert Feuillerat. New Haven, Yale University Press, 1943
Est	English studies
ET	Expository times
EtGP	Études romanes dédiées à Gaston Paris, Bouillon, 1891
ETR	Études théologiques et religieuses
Études	Études
Eur	Eurydice
fasc	fascicule
FestET	Festschrift, Ernst Tappolet. Basil, Schwabe, 1935
FestEW	Festschrift für Eduard Wechssler. Jean, Gronau, 1929
FestJV	Festschrift, Johannes Vahlen, Berlin, Reimer, 1900
FFBN	Fonds français, Bibliothèque nationale
FL	Figaro littéraire
FMLS	French men of letters series
Fmod	Le français moderne
FortR	Fortnightly review
FR	French review
FS	French studies
GA	Les grands artistes
GBA	Gazette des beaux-arts
GCFI	Giornale critico della filosofia italiana
GEF	Grands écrivains français series
GEL	Les grands événements littéraires
GELF	Grands écrivains de la France series
GGA	Göttingische Gelehrte Anzeigen
Gl	Glanes
Gno	Gnomen
GP	Les grands philosophes
Grässe	Grässe, J.G.T. Trésor des livres rares et précieux. Dresden, Kuntze, 1859-1869. 7 v.
GR	Grande revue
Greg	Gregorianum
Grev	Germanic review
Griv	La grive
GRM	Germanisch-romanische Monatschrift
GSLI	Giornale storico della letteratura italiana
GSR	Graduate school record (Ohio State University)
HB	The historical bulletin
Hisp	Hispania
Hist	History
HJ	Historisches Jahrbuch
HLB	Huntington Library bulletin
HLQ	Huntington Library quarterly

HLR	Harvard law review
HomEM	Hommage à Ernest Martinenche. Éditions d'Artrey, 1939?
Hren	Humanisme et renaissance
HSRL	Harvard studies in romance languages
HTB	New York Herald Tribune books
HTM	History teachers magazine (Historical outlook)
HTR	Harvard theological review
HTS	Harvard theological studies
HZ	Historische Zeitschrift
ICC	Intermédiaire des chercheurs et curieux
ICS	Italia che scrive
IJE	International journal of ethics
IL	Information littéraire
Ill	L'illustration
Inter	Interpretation
IP	Collection : Les idées pédagogiques
Isis	Isis
ISLL	Illinois. University. University of Illinois studies in language and literature
Ital	Italica
IUHS	Iowa University humanistic studies
JAMA	Journal of the American Medical Association
JAn	Journal d'Ancenis
JCL	Journal of comparative literature
Jdéb	Journal des débats
JE	Journal des économistes
JEGP	Journal of English and Germanic philology
JGIL	Journal général de l'imprimerie et de la librairie
JHI	Journal of the history of ideas
JHSR	Johns Hopkins studies in romance literatures and languages
JLW	Jahrbuch für Liturgiewissenschaft
JMH	Journal of modern history
JP	Journal of philosophy
JPE	Journal of political economy
JR	Journal of religion
JREL	Jahrbuch für romanische und englische Sprache und Literatur
JS	Journal des savants
JSCMA	Journal of the South Carolina medical association
JWI	London University. Warburg institute. Journal of the Warburg Institute
KJRP	Kritischer Jahresbericht über die Fortschritte der romanischen Philologie
KS	Kantstudien
LAS	Leben und ausgewählte Schriften der Vater und Begründer der reformierten Kirche
LC	Library of Congress
LE	Collection Le livre de l'étudiant
LF	Literarhistorische Forschungen
LGRP	Literaturblatt für germanische und romanische Philologie
LH	Lettres d'humanité
Libr	The Library, a quarterly review of bibliography
LL	Life and letters and the London Mercury
Logos	Logos

LR	Lettres romanes
LRS	Leipziger romanistische Studien. Sprachwissenschaftliche Reihe
LZD	Literarisches Zentralblatt für Deutschland
MAB	Maatschappij der antwerpsche Bibliophilen
MAC	Académie nationale des sciences, arts et belles-lettres de Caen. Mémoires
MAH	Mélanges d'archéologie et d'histoire, École française de Rome
MAI	Institut de France. Académie des inscriptions et belles-lettres. Mémoires
MAM	Académie des sciences, lettres et beaux-arts de Marseille. Mémoires
MARB	Académie royale des sciences, des lettres et des beaux-arts. Brussels. Classe des lettres et des sciences morales et politiques. Mémoires
MASA	Michigan academy of science, arts and letters
MAT	Académie des sciences, inscriptions et belles-lettres de Toulouse, Mémoires
MAV	Academie de Versailles; Mémoires de la Société des lettres et des arts de Seine-et-Oise
MBP	Münchner Beiträge zur romanischen und englischen Philologie
MC	Minerva chirurgica
MCH	Monographs in church history
MCMP	Michigan University. The University of Michigan contributions in modern philology
MDL	Collection : Maîtres des littératures
MélAJ	Mélanges, Alfred Jeanroy. Droz, 1928
MélAL	Mélanges, Abel Lefranc. Droz, 1936
MélBrunot	Mélanges, Ferdinand Brunot. Société nouvelle de librairie et d'édition. 1904
MélEC	Mélanges, Émile Chatelain. Champion, 1910
MélEH	Mélanges, Edmond Huguet. Boivin, 1940
MélEP	Mélanges, Émile Picot. Damascène Morgand, 1913
MélGL	Mélanges, Gustave Lanson. Hachette, 1922
MélHC	Mélanges, Henri Chamard. Nizet, 1951
MélHH	Mélanges, Henri Hauvette. Les presses françaises, 1934
MélHW	Mélanges, Henri Weil. Fontemoing, 1898
MélJV	Mélanges, Joseph Vianey. Les presses françaises, 1934
MélMR	Mélanges, Mario Roques. Didier, 1950
MélPC	Poitiers. Université. Faculté des lettres. Mélanges littéraires et historiques publiés à l'occasion du centenaire de sa restauration, 8 octobre, 1945. Poitiers, Université de Poitiers, 1946
MélPL	Mélanges, Paul Laumonier. Droz, 1935
MerF	Mercure de France
MFCL	Facultés catholiques de Lille, Mémoires et travaux
Mfran	Muse française
MGW	Manchester guardian (Weekly edition)
MisLK	Miscellany, L. E. Kastner. Cambridge, (Eng.), Heffer, 1932
Mlat	Medicina latina
MLJ	Modern language journal
MLN	Modern language notes
MLQ	Modern language quarterly (Seattle)
MLQL	Modern language quarterly (London)
MLR	Modern language review
MMP	Musée pédagogique et Bibliothèque centrale de l'enseignement primaire. Mémoires et documents scolaires

MP	Modern philology
MPLL	University of Michigan, publications in language and literature
MRAI	Mémoires de littérature tirés des registres de l'Académie royale des inscriptions et belles-lettres
MSA	Société académique d'agriculture, des sciences et belles lettres du département de l'Aube. Mémoires
MSHP	Société de l'histoire de Paris et l'Ile de France. Mémoires
MSNA	Mémoires de la Société nationale d'agriculture, sciences et arts d'Angers
MT	Medical times, Journal of the American medical profession
Mus	Museum, Maanblad voor philologie en geschiedenis, Leiden
MW	Medical world
NAK	Nederlandsch Archief voor Kerkgeschiedenis
NC	Nineteenth century
NCSCL	University of North Carolina studies in comparative literature
NCSR	University of North Carolina. Studies in the Romance languages and literatures
nd	No date of publication given
NDHC	Nouveau dictionnaire historique et critique
NEJM	New England journal of medicine
Néo	Néophilologus
NEQ	New England quarterly
NF	Neue Folge
NJGL	Neue Jahrbücher für das klassiche Altertum, Geschichte und deutsche Literatur und für Pädagogik
NL	Les nouvelles littéraires
NM	Neuphilologische Mitteilungen
NMBS	The University of New Mexico bibliographical series
NNY	The nation, New York
np	No place of publication given
NPR	Neue philologische Rundschau
NRC	Nouvelle revue critique
NRE	Nouvelle revue encyclopédique
NRF	Nouvelle revue française
Nrev	Nouvelle revue
ns	New series
NS	Neueren Sprachen
NSN	New statesman and nation
NYU	New York University
Occ	L'occident
OCLL	Ohio. State university, Columbus. Contributions in languages and literature
OMLP	Oregon. University of Oregon monographs. Studies in literature and philology
Osiris	Osiris
OSLP	See OMPL
p.,	page, and pages
Par	Paru
PBA	British academy, Proceedings
PBAA	Papers of the Bibliographical association of America
PCHM	Publicaciones de la cátedra de historia de la medicina
PEC	Peuples et civilisations series
PEL	Periods of European literature series

PERF	Publications de l'École roumaine en France
PF	Pléiade françoise
PFI	Publications de la Faculté des lettres de l'Université d'Istanbul
PFLA	Publications de la Faculté des lettres d'Alger
PFS	Strasbourg, Faculté des lettres, Publications
PFSS	Poésie française au xvie siècle
PGMJ	Post graduate medical journal
PGRG	Publikationen der Gesellschaft für Rheinische Geschichtskunde
PJ	Philosophisches Jahrbuch
PL	Poet lore
PMAS	Papers of the Michigan academy of science, arts and letters
Pméd	Le progrès médical
PMFS	Publications of the University of Manchester. French series
PMLA	Publications of the Modern language association of America
Poly	Polybiblion, partie littéraire
PPRL	University of Pennsylvania, publication of the series in Romance languages and literatures
PQ	Philological quarterly
PRR	Presbyterian and reformed review
PSAB	Publications de la Société archéologique de Bordeaux
PSB	Princeton seminary bulletin
PSCF	Publications de la Société calviniste de France
QR	Quarterly review
RAA	Revue anglo-américaine
RABM	Revista de archivos, bibliotecas y museos
RAHM	Revista argentina de historia de la medicina
RAI	Reale accademia d'Italia, studi e documenti
RAL	Revue de l'Amérique latine
RAM	Revue d'ascétique et de mystique
RAn	Revue de l'Anjou
RarB	Raretés bibliographiques
RB	Revue bleue, *see* RPL, Revue politique et littéraire
RBA	Revue des beaux-arts
RBelgique	Revue de Belgique
Rbib	Revue des bibliothèques
RBP	Revue belge de philologie et d'histoire
RCC	Revue des cours et conférences
RClL	Revue critique des idées et des livres
RCLJ	Revue critique de législation et de jurisprudence
Rcon	Revue contemporaine
Rcr	Revue critique d'histoire et de littérature
RCSS	Records of civilization : sources and studies
RDB	Revue des bibliothèques
RDM	Revue des deux mondes
RDP	Revue du droit publique et de la science politique en France et à l'étranger
REH	Revue des études historiques
REHF	Revue des études hongroises et finno-ougriennes
REI	Revue des études italiennes
Ren	Renaissance

REL	Revue des études latines
RenN	Renaissance news
RER	Revue des études rabelaisiennes
RES	Review of English studies
Rev	La revue (La revue mondiale, ancienne Revue des revues)
RevH	Revista de historia (Lisbon)
RevHM	Revue hommes et monde
RFN	Rivista di filosofia neo-scolastica
RFor	Romanische Forschungen
RFrance	Revue de France
RG	Revue germanique
RGE	Collection Le roman des grandes existences
Rgén	Revue générale (Brussels)
RHAM	Revue historique et archéologique du Maine
RHB	Revue historique de Bordeaux
RHDF	Revue historique de droit français et étranger
RHE	Revue d'histoire ecclésiastique
Rheb	Revue hebdomadaire
RHEF	Revue d'histoire de l'église de France
RHFr	Revue d'histoire franciscaine
Rhisp	Revue hispanique
Rhist	Revue historique
RHL	Revue d'histoire littéraire de la France
RHM	Revue d'histoire moderne et contemporaine
RHPC	Revue d'histoire politique et constitutionnelle
RHph	Revue d'histoire de la philosophie (till 1931); continued in 1933 as : Revue d'histoire de la philosophie et d'histoire générale de la civilisation
RHPR	Revue d'histoire et de philosophie religieuse
RI	Rivista d'Italia
RIFD	Rivista internazionale di filosofia del diritto
Rin	Rinascità
RIPB	Revue de l'instruction publique en Belgique
RivI	Rivista d'Italia
RLA	Revue des livres anciens
RLC	Revue de littérature comparée
RLH	La revue : littérature, histoire, arts et sciences des deux mondes
RLille	Revue de Lille
RLJ	Revue de législation et de jurisprudence
RLM	Rivista di letterature moderne
RLR	Revue des langues romanes
RM	Revue de Marseille
Rmois	Revue du mois
Rmus	Revue musicale
RNS	Revue néo-scolastique (Louvain)
Rom	Romania
RP	Romance philology
RPar	Revue de Paris
RPB	Revue philomathique de Bordeaux et du Sud-Ouest
Rpéd	Revue pédagogique

RPF	Revue de philologie française et provençale; after 1897 becomes Revue de philologie française et de littérature
RPFE	Revue philosophique de la France et de l'étranger
Rph	Revue de philosophie
RPL	Revue politique et littéraire. Revue bleue
RPLH	Revue de philologie, de littérature et d'histoire anciennes
RPol	Revue de Pologne
Rpor	Revista portuguesa de filosofia
RPP	Revue politique et parlementaire
RQH	Revue des questions historiques
RR	Romanic review
Rren	Revue de la renaissance
Rrét	Revue rétrospective
RSB	Romanische Studien, hrsg. von Eduard Boehmer. Bonn, Weber
RSE	Romanische Studien, hrsg. von Emil Ebering
RSI	Rivista storica italiana
RSPT	Revue des sciences philosophiques et théologiques
RSS	Revue du seizième siècle
Rsyn	Revue de synthèse
RTAM	Recherches de théologie ancienne et médiévale
RTP	Review of theology and philosophy
RTPh	Revue de théologie et de philosophie
RU	Revue universitaire
RUC	Revista da universidade de Coimbra
Runiv	Revue universelle
RUSE	Rutgers University studies in English
RYF	Razón y fe
SAQ	South Atlantic quarterly
SAWW	Akademie der Wissenschaften, Vienna. Philosophisch-historische Klasse. Sitzungsberichte.
SBA	Bayerische Akademie der Wissenschaften, Munich. Sitzungsberichte der philosophisch-philologischen und der historischen Classe
SBN	Société des bibliophiles normands
SBW	Studien der Bibliothek Warburg
Ser	Serapheum
SFL	Sächsische Forschungsinstitut in Leipzig
SFR	Studj di filologia romanza (1885-1903) Studj romanza, 1903-date
SHAF	Société de l'histoire de l'art français
SHF	Société de l'histoire de France
SHR	Scottish historical review
SJ	see DSGJ
SKGV	Sprache und Kultur der germanisch-romanischen Völker
SL	Special libraries
SM	Studi medievali
Soleinne	Soleinne, Martineau de. Bibliothèque dramatique de monsieur de Soleinne. Catalogue by P.L. Jacob, bibliophile. (pseud.) Administration de l'Alliance des arts, 1843-45. 8 v. in 4
SoR	Southwest review (Texas review)
SP	North Carolina, University. Studies in philology

Spec	Speculum
Spectator	Spectator, a weekly review of politics, literature, theology and art
SR	Sewanee review
SQ	Shakespeare quarterly
SRB	Société rouennaise de bibliophiles
SRL	Saturday review of literature
SRPL	Saturday review of politics, literature, science and art (London)
STFM	Société des textes français modernes
StGR	The French mind; studies in honor of Gustave Rudler. Oxford, Clarendon Press, 1952
SWI	Studies of the Warburg institute
Symp	Symposium
Syn	Synthèses
TBR	New York Times book review
Tchemerzine	A. Tchemerzine, Bibliographie d'éditions originales et rares d'auteurs français des xve, xvie, xviie, et xviiie siècles
TEH	Theologische Existenz Heute
TF	Les textes français. Collection des universités de France, publiées sous les auspices de l'Association Guillaume Budé
TFM	see STFM
THR	Travaux d'humanisme et renaissance
TLF	Les textes littéraires français
TLS	The Times literary supplement (London)
Tmod	Les temps modernes
t.p.	Title page
TPQ	Theologisch-praktische Quartalschrift
TR	Theologische Rundschau
trans	translation by
TSK	Theologische Studien und Kritiken
TT	Theology today
TVR	Tidjschrift voor Rechtsgeschiedenis
UIHS	University of Iowa humanistic studies
UMS	University of Missouri studies
UTQ	University of Toronto quarterly
V. and v.	volume, and volumes
VHI	Collection des Vies des hommes illustres
VW	Volk im Werden
WBEP	Wiener Beiträge zur englischen Philologie
WR	Westminster review
WUS	Washington University (St. Louis) studies
YFS	Yale French studies
YR	Yale review
YSE	Yale studies in English
ZFSL	Zeitschrift für französische Sprache und Literatur (v. 1-10, 1879-88 called Zeitschrift für neufranzösische Sprache und Literatur)
ZGJD	Zeitschrift für die Geschichte der Juden in Deutschland
ZHT	Zeitschrift für die historische Theologie
ZKG	Zeitschrift für Kirchengeschichte
ZMP	Zeitschrift für Mathematik und Physik

ZPPK   Zeitschrift für Philosophie und philosophische Kritik
ZRP   Zeitschrift für romanische Philologie
ZVL   Zeitschrift für vergleichende Literaturgeschichte

CONTRIBUTORS TO VOLUME II *

DON CAMERON ALLEN
Johns Hopkins University

NEWTON S. BEMENT
University of Michigan

MORRIS BISHOP
Cornell University

WILLIS HERBERT BOWEN
University of Oklahoma

DAVID C. CABEEN
Formerly of Vanderbilt University

PHILIP MACON CHEEK
University of North Carolina

ROBERT J. CLEMENTS
New York University

LANCASTER E. DABNEY
University of Texas

DAVID DAVIES
The Honnold Library
Claremont, California

WOLFGANG BERNARD FLEISCHMANN
University of North Carolina

DONALD MURDOCH FRAME
Columbia University

WERNER P. FRIEDERICH
University of North Carolina

LOYAL NORMAN GOULD
University of North Carolina

HÉLÈNE HARVITT
Brooklyn College

J. WOODROW HASSELL
University of South Carolina

HELMUT A. HATZFELD
Catholic University of America

JAMES HUTTON
Cornell University

PAUL OSKAR KRISTELLER
Columbia University

HARRY KURZ
Queens College

J. CORIDEN LYONS
University of North Carolina

ALBERT DOUGLAS MENUT
Syracuse University

EDWARD F. MEYLAN
University of California, Berkeley

* Names are given here in most cases as in the MLA " List of Members " as of September, 1954.

xxix

OLIN HARRIS MOORE
Ohio State University

NANCY OSBORNE
Anderson College

JAMES S. PATTY
University of Colorado

ELIZABETH SKIDMORE SASSER
Texas Technological College

ALEXANDER HERMAN SCHUTZ
Ohio State University

GEORGE OTTO SEIVER
University of Pennsylvania

ISIDORE SILVER
University of Connecticut

NORMAN B. SPECTOR
Northwestern University

STERLING A. STOUDEMIRE
University of North Carolina

RICHARD R. STRAWN
Wabash College

OLIVER TOWLES
Formerly of New York University

GEORGE BYRON WATTS
Davidson College

WILLIAM LEON WILEY
University of North Carolina

SAMUEL FREDERIC WILL
Indiana University

TABLE OF CONTENTS

VOLUME II

CHAPTER I. BACKGROUND MATERIALS

(Nos. 1-619)

NEWTON S. BEMENT, DAVID DAVIES, DONALD M. FRAME, HELMUT A. HATZFELD, PAUL O. KRISTELLER, HARRY KURZ, ALBERT D. MENUT, ELIZABETH S. SASSER, ALEXANDER H. SCHUTZ

Bibliographies
(Nos. 1-39)

DAVID DAVIES

Anglo-French and Franco-American studies, a current bibliography. RR: 29:343-72; 30:151-86; 31:114-46; 32:17J-98; 33:132-56; 34:154-72; 35:186-202; 36:161-90; 37:105-26; 38:97-116; 39:181-203, 1938-1948. Continued in FrAR 2:203-32; 3:79-119, 1949. 1

An annual bibliography inaugurated by Donald F. Bond who acknowledged in first and subsequent issues collaboration of J. F. McDermott, E. D. Seeber, and J. E. Tucker. In later issues of the RR, J. M. Carrière also collaborated. Issues appearing in FrAR compiled by J. M. Carrière, J. F. McDermott, H. C. Rice, and J. E. Tucker.

Although bulk of the books, articles, and reviews listed fall in later periods, nevertheless the renaissance student will find it quite useful.

Baldensperger, Fernand. Bibliography of comparative literature, by F. Baldensperger and W. P. Friederich. Chapel Hill, University of North Carolina Press, 1950. 701 p. (NCSCL, no. 1). 2

Classified bibliography of books and articles. Entries and references quite brief and not annotated. Very few cross references; it does not appear that any entry is in more than one classification. No index. *See* 2661.

Besterman, Theodore. A world bibliography of bibliographies and of bibliographical catalogues, calendars, abstracts, digests, indexes, and the like. 2d ed. rev. and greatly enlarged throughout. London, privately published by the author, 1947-49. 3 v. 3

Classified bibliography of more than 63,000 separately published bibliographies. Third volume is an index. As in the case of Bohatta *(q.v.)* the student will not

find these volumes useful in the main field of his interest, but where his studies take him into unknown regions, they may help him to orient himself.

"Biblio," catalogue des ouvrages en langue française dans le monde entier. Service bibliographique des Messageries Hachette, 1933-. 4

French national bibliography analogous to the *Cumulative book index.* Published monthly since October 1933 with annual cumulations. Each book entered under author, title, and subject; complete bibliographical information given under author or main entry only. Work aims to include also all books in French published outside of France. In the first years some theses, society publications, and official publications were included. Beginning with the 1936 volume, all theses sustained in French universities in letters and science have been included. Immediately following the war, the annual volumes included works omitted from volumes for the war years.

Bibliographic index ; a cumulative bibliography of bibliographies. 1937-. New York, Wilson, 1938-. 5

Cumulative register of bibliographies either published separately, in periodicals, or as parts of other works. Extremely useful. 1000 to 1500 periodicals examined regularly for bibliographies. An idea of its coverage is indicated by the fact that whereas Besterman *(q.v.),* taking all of time for his province, lists approximately 64,000 bibliographies, the first volume of this work covering the years 1937-42 lists approximately 50,000.

Bohatta, Hanns, and Franz Hodes. Internationale Bibliographie der Bibliographien, ein Nachschlagewerk unter Mitwirkung von Walter Funke. Frankfurt-am-Main, Klostermann, 1950. 652 p. 6

Voluminous list of bibliographies, given without critical comment, listing works varying widely in excellence. Although the student will not find here bibliographical material on French sixteenth-century literature which is not listed elsewhere, the volume is useful in pointing out bibliographies which may be useful when dealing with background, or relationship of other areas of study to literature. Present volume lists subject bibliographies only. Subsequent volume will list personal bibliographies. Unlike similar work by Besterman *(q.v.)* this listing includes bibliographies appearing in periodicals or as parts of other works.

British Museum. Dept. of printed books. Short-title catalogue of books printed in France and of French books printed in other countries from 1470 to 1600 now in the British museum. London, printed by order of the Trustees, 1924. 491 p. 7

" In the present catalogue it has been found possible ... to register nearly twelve thousand editions.... Considerable as the collection is, it represents probably not much more than a fifth of the editions known to have been printed at Paris, and less than a sixth of the output of the French provinces." Preface. An author list without indices. Useful as a guide to BM holdings and for verifying bibliographical details, but of no use to one needing a subject bibliography.

The British national bibliography. London, The Council of the British national bibliography, 1950-. 8

Cumulative bibliography published weekly and quarterly in the year. In last issue for each month is a full index of authors, titles, and subjects for the month. Valuable subject guide to British books. Each volume has three parts : classified list arranged by Dewey decimal numbers, author and title index, and subject index. British equivalent of our Cumulative book index. Work is compiled in the British Museum where copies of all new books are deposited by law.

Brunet, Jacques C. Manuel du libraire et de l'amateur de livres. 5th ed. Didot, 1860-1865. 6 v. *See* 2417. 9

Annotations for 16th-century books frequently valuable. *See* note to no. 13, 18th-century volume in this series.

Calot, Frantz, and Georges Thomas. Guide pratique de bibliographie. 2e édition refondue avec le concours de Clément Duval. Delagrave, 1950. 278 p. 10

Useful and convenient guide to reference books. Only a small part of the volume directly useful to students of French literature, but items included well chosen and annotations succinct and pertinent.

Fisher, John H. Serial bibliographies in the modern languages and literatures. PMLA 66:138-56, April, 1951. 11

Extremely important and well done guide to bibliographies appearing in journals. Preliminary discussion of the scope of these bibliographies interesting and valuable. Author aimed to include for each bibliography the following items of information : 1) Place, dates of publication, and publisher; 2) Price; 3) How the bibliography is sponsored and how bibliographers are chosen; 4) When and where it was started; 5) Its scope and special features; 6) Names of present, or most recent, complete staff. Following classified list of bibliographies are a Subject Index and an Index of Bibliographers.

Giraud, Jeanne. Manuel de bibliographie littéraire pour les XVIe, XVIIe et XVIIIe siècles français, 1921-1935. Vrin, 1939. 304 p. 12

See Cabeen's note in the volume on the 18th century this series p. 4, 30B.

Continuation of Lanson, listing books and articles published in 1921-1935. Author has listed also theses, and articles appearing in publications of learned societies and *festschriften.* She has not tried to make listings comprehensive and complete; warns that provincial learned society publications have been unavoidably slighted.

Reviews : J. Bonnerot in BBB ns 18:281-282, 1939; J. Lavaud in Hren 6:380-81, 1939.

Guigue, Albert. La Faculté des lettres de l'Université de Paris depuis sa fondation (17 mars 1808), jusqu'au 1er janvier, 1935. Alcan, 1935. 371 p. Liste des thèses de doctorat ès lettres depuis le 14 février 1810 jusqu'au 1er janvier 1935 : p. 57-184. Liste des thèses de doctorat d'université du 30 mai 1899 au 1er janvier, 1935 : p. 207-32. 13

The theses are on a variety of subjects and listed chronologically, not by subject. Earlier lists of theses, those by Maire, Mourier, and Deltour, are more usefully arranged.

Index bibliographicus; catalogue international des bibliographies courantes. 2e éd. mise à jour et considérablement augm. Publiée par Marcel Godet et Joris Vorstius. Matériaux fournis par la Bibliothèque de l'Etat à Berlin et par 37 pays. Berlin et Leipzig, De Gruyter, 1931. 420 p.   14

Guide to bibliographies currently appearing in periodicals and to other bibliographies published at intervals. Student will find nothing on his subject which cannot be found elsewhere; useful in orienting oneself in allied fields.

Lancaster, H. Carrington. American bibliography. French language and literature. 1921-, in PMLA 1922-.   15

Annual bibliography of books and articles by American scholars. First issue edited by George L. Hamilton. Subsequent issues through 1953 edited by H. Carrington Lancaster. First four issues were bibliographical essays. Subsequent issues have been lists classified by subject. Mode of publication has varied. Early issues appeared in the March number of PMLA. Later bibliographies appeared annually in an undated supplement; most recent bibliographies appear in the April issue of PMLA. Originally the policy was to cover the bibliography of the year preceding publication of the list. Later bibliographies covered the year in which the bibliographies were issued. Recently there has been a return to the original practice.

Lanson, Gustave. Manuel bibliographique de la littérature française moderne, xvie, xviie, xviiie et xixe siècles. Nouv. éd. rev. et cor. Hachette, 1939. 1820 p.   16

The best known and most generally useful bibliography for French literature. *See* the note to No. 40 in the volume on the 18th century, *Critical bibliography of French literature.* This printing is identical with the 1931 edition.

Le Petit, Jules. Bibliographie des principales éditions originales d'écrivains français du xve au xviiie siècle. Quantin, 1888. 583 p.   17

Elaborate bibliographical descriptions and reproductions of title-pages of original editions of important literary works. Items arranged chronologically with author and title indices at end of volume. Less than one fifth of the volume devoted to 16th century. Useful for identifying editions, but not a guide for the scholar in any other sense. 1927 edition is a photo-lithographic reissue of the 1888

edition and reproductions are often not as clear as in latter edition.

Leroy, Emile. Guide pratique des bibliothèques de Paris. Editions des Bibliothèques nationales, 1937. 284 p.   18

There are a large number of Parisian libraries which the research worker might overlook. Present volume gives general information on contents of these and mentions specifically notable collections. Library hours, terms of admission, and other useful information also given.

La librairie française, catalogue général des ouvrages en vente. Cercle de la librairie, 1931-1952. 10 v.   19

A " national bibliography " inasmuch as it seeks to list all books in print, or all books published in France in successive periods. For years 1930-1945, arrangement is by author with a title index; only useful in verifying bibliographical details about particular volumes. For the books published in the years 1946-1951, arrangement is by subject and hence for the period is an immensely useful tool to the student. Author and title indices are provided for this period.

The Library of Congress subject catalog, a cumulative list of works represented by Library of Congress printed cards. 1950-. Washington, The Library of Congress.   20

" The Library of Congress subject catalog is designed to serve as a continuing and cumulative subject bibliography of works currently received and cataloged by The Library of Congress and other American libraries participating in its cooperative cataloging program...." The catalog is issued in three quarterly issues and an annual cumulation.

Lonchamp, Frédéric C. Manuel du bibliophile français (1470-1920). Paris and Lausanne, Librairie des bibliophiles, 1927. 2 v.   21

V. I contains excellent survey of the history of the book arts; especially good for book illustration.

Maire, Albert. Répertoire alphabétique des thèses de doctorat ès lettres des universités françaises 1810-1900 avec table chronologique par université et table détaillée des matières. Picard, 1903. 226 p.   22

Theses listed alphabetically by author. Also a listing of authors by university, arrangement here being chronological under the university. Also an index of authors and subjects which makes the volume quite useful.

Malclès, Louise N. Les sources du travail bibliographique. Geneva, Droz; Lille, Giard, 1950. 2 v. in 3. 23
V. I is devoted to general bibliographies and V. II to special bibliographies.

A guide not only to bibliographies but to reference books in general. Student will find both volumes useful; in the second there is a section devoted to French language and literature, p. 230-302; in the first are sections on bibliographies of bibliographies, national bibliography, theses, printing history, and library catalogues.

Mourier, Athénaïs, and Félix Deltour. Notice sur le doctorat ès lettres suivie du catalogue et de l'analyse des thèses françaises et latines admises par les facultés des lettres depuis 1810, avec index et table alphabétique des docteurs; quatrième édition corrigée et considérablement augmentée. Delalain, 1880. 442 p. 24

There are earlier editions of the work; present edition covers years 1810-80. There were annual supplements from 1880-81 to 1901-02. Theses arranged chronologically and under each year by faculty. Description of contents of each thesis given in most cases and there is a subject index.

Neveux, Pol Louis, and Emile Dacier. Les richesses des bibliothèques provinciales de France. Éditions des bibliothèques nationales de France, 1932. 2 v. 25

In addition to other information, work indicates special collections and notable individual works to be found in larger provincial libraries, with mention of notable collections in smaller provincial libraries (those containing less than 10,000 volumes). University and other well-known research collections also described.

Palfrey, Thomas R., Joseph G. Fucilla, and William C. Holbrook. A bibliographical guide to the Romance languages and literatures. Evanston, Chandler, 1951. 4th ed. 85 leaves. 26

Valuable and conveniently arranged guide to reference books for students of Romance languages. Bibliographical items generally not annotated.

Peyre, Henri. Ouvrages français parus depuis la guerre. (September, 1939-September, 1942) RR 34:97-108, 1943. 27

A list put together with difficulty during war years; useful in piecing together bibliography for period indicated.

Quérard, Joseph M. Les supercheries littéraires dévoilées. Galerie des écrivains français de toute l'Europe qui se sont déguisés sous des anagrammes, des astéronymes, des cryptonymes, des initialismes, des noms littéraires, des pseudonymes facétieux ou bizarres, etc. Seconde édition considérablement augmentée, publiée par MM. Gustave Brunet et Pierre Jannet suivie 1° du Dictionnaire des ouvrages anonymes par Ant.-Alex Barbier. 3ᵉ éd., rev. et augm. par Olivier Barbier. Duffis, 1869-70. 7 v. 28

This work and that of Barbier, here joined, most useful of dictionaries of anonymous and pseudonymous literature. Annotations on books listed.

Lebègue, Raymond. Renaissance. *In:* Reports concerning French literary and linguistic studies in the period 1940-1945. MLR 41:280-85, 1946. 29

Bibliographical essay on more important books and articles appearing in period. Bibliography for war years may be constructed by using the present essay, the list by Peyre, and standard bibliographies such as *Biblio* and *La librairie française.*

Revue de littérature comparée. 30

Each issue of first six volumes carried a classified list of books and articles in comparative literature. Beginning with volume seven, one number of each volume usually dedicated to a particular phase of comparative literature; this number did not have the bibliography, there being in such cases only three bibliographical sections per volume. Publication suspended during war; since then usua l practice has been to publish, as in the earlier volumes, a bibliographical section in each number. The review has published two analytical indices of its own contents covering the period 1921-30, and 1931-50. Mˡˡᵉ Giraud combed the review for items for her bibliography. Editors or compilers of bibliographical section are not indicated.

Schneider, Georg. Handbuch der bibliographie. Leipzig, Hiersemann, 1930. 674 p. 31

Critical bibliography of bibliographies within limited areas, indicated in contents, and listings of encyclopedias and biographical dictionaries. Compiler's section, *Allgemeine nationale Bibliographien,* is for practical purposes an enumeration of bibliographies useful to literary students. Although now more than twenty years old, students will find work valuable since it lists in addition to bibliographies, literary histories which contain valuable bibliographical sections.

Tchemerzine, Avenir. Bibliographie d'éditions originales et rares d'auteurs français des xve, xvie xviie, et xviiie siècles. Plée, 1927-1934. 10 v. 32

Like Le Petit *(q.v.)* work intended primarily for the bibliophile, bookdealer, or scholar seeking to identify a particular edition of a work by a well-known author. Whereas Le Petit arranged items chronologically, they are here arranged alphabetically by author. Author gives fulldress bibliographical descriptions and reproductions of title pages. *See* 2428.

Les thèses de lettres à Paris depuis 1939. RHL 48:110-12, 183-90, 285-88, 372-80, 1948. 33

These listings of theses in French literary history follow the order of Giraud bibliography. It will be remembered that that volume lists theses.

Torossian, Araxie. Liste des thèses soutenues devant les Universités françaises Paris et Provinces en 1948 et 1949. AUP 20:69-92, 1950. 34

List arranged by year and university.

United Nations Educational, Scientific and Cultural Organization. Répertoire des bibliothèques de France, Bibliothèques des départements. Édité par l'Organisation des Nations Unies pour l'éducation, la science et la culture [et] la Direction des services des bibliothèques de France. [Bibliothèque nationale.] 1950. 470 p. 35

Description of provincial libraries. In addition to giving library hours, name of library, and library history, a general description of the book stock is given with titles of catalogues issued by library and of other works describing library collection. Analytical index of collections indicating where collections on special subjects or individuals may be found. Should be used in conjunction with Neveux et Dacier, *Richesses des bibliothèques provinciales de France* (no. 25). Present volume is second in a series; the other two are concerned with libraries of Paris and with centers of documentation.

Varillon, François. Bibliographie élémentaire de littérature française; choix méthodi-que d'éditions et d'études critiques. Gigord, 1936. 300 p. At head of title : F. Varillon and H. Holstein. 36

Authors intend the volume first of all for students desirous of consulting a handy elementary bibliographic guide before going to more erudite, but more cumbersome works; it is in fact quite useful for this first contact with a new area. Work also intended to be useful to librarians and professors to some degree as a handy compendium and ready reference volume.

Will, Samuel F. A bibliography of American studies on the French renaissance (1500-1600). Urbana, The University of Illinois Press, 1940. 151 p. (ISLL, v. 26, no. 2). *See* 331. 37

Lists principally books and articles produced by Americans and Canadians in period 1886-1937. Includes works in theology, navigation, exploration, history, political science, and medicine in addition to literature. 1895 items in 12 classifications with index.

— French literature. MLQ 2:439-64, 1941. 38

Bibliographical essay on important books for the renaissance. Comments on books; indicates areas where literature is thin or non-existent.

Wiley, W. L., and S. F. Will. French bibliographies and general works. *In:* Recent literature of the renaissance. SP 36:334-51, 1939. 39

Lists material in this field for 1938. Appears annually in April issues of this periodical. From 1939 to 1943 inclusive, bibliography edited by Samuel F. Will and William Leon Wiley. From 1944 until 1946, work carried on by Prof. Will; since then has again been the joint effort of the two original editors.

History of Printing

(Nos. 40-87)

David Davies

Baudrier, Henri. Bibliographie lyonnaise; recherches sur les imprimeurs, libraires, relieurs et fondeurs de lettres de Lyon au 16e siècle. Publ. et contin. par J. Baudrier. Lyon, Paris, 1895-1950. 13 v. Tables by Georges Tricou. Geneva, Lille, 1950-52. 40

Works begun by H. Baudrier, carried on by his son, J. Baudrier; twelfth volume published by the latter's brother-in-law, H. de Terrebasse, who notes in this volume that a quantity of interesting material remains to be published. These volumes contain bibliographies of Lyons printers, biographical material, and documents on men in the book trades at Lyons. *See* 2415.

Bernard, Auguste J. Histoire de l'imprimerie royale du Louvre. Impr. impériale, 1867. 311 p.   41

List of books printed at *Imprimerie royale du Louvre*, 1640-1736, preceded by a *Précis historique* and followed by a list of types belonging to the press. Fuller treatment for sixteenth century (prehistory) is in Duprat (no. 60).

— Geoffroy Tory, peintre et graveur, premier imprimeur royal, réformateur de l'orthographie et de typographie sous François Ier. 2e éd., entièrement refondue. Tros, 1865. 410 p.   42

Standard work on Tory. First edition appeared in 1857. English translations appeared in 1899, and 1909, George B. Ives translating the latter edition. Bernard was more enthusiastic than critical and work should be used with care. *See* 2590.

Bigmore, Edward C. A bibliography of printing with notes and illustrations. Comp. by E. C. Bigmore and C. W. H. Wyman. London, Quaritch, 1880-86. 3 v.   43

Only attempt at a comprehensive bibliography of printing. Outdated; not particularly good for French printing, nevertheless useful. Work reproduced by photo-offset, New York, Duschnes, 1945. 2 v.

Bouchot, Henri F. X. M. The book; its printers, illustrators, and binders from Gutenberg to the present time, with a treatise on the art of collecting and describing early printed books, and a Latin-English and English-Latin topographical index of the earliest printing places. Edited by H. Grevel. Containing one hundred and seventy-two facsimiles of early typography, book illustrations, printers' marks, bindings, numerous borders, initials, head and tail pieces, and a frontispiece. London, Grevel, 1890. 383 p.   44

Third chapter is a concise and general view of printing in Europe in 16th century. English version of Bouchot's *Le livre* contains much material not in original edition; omits some material.

Brun, Robert. Les beaux livres d'autrefois, le xvie siècle. Babou, 1931. 32 p. 40 pl.   45

Remarkable series of plates. Text contains much material found in author's *Le livre français* (Larousse 1948) Chapter II. Brun also contributed the third chapter on the 15th and 16th centuries to André Lejard, *The art of the French book*. London, Elek, 1947. 166 p.

— Le livre illustré en France au xvie siècle, avec 32 planches hors texte. Alcan, 1930. 336 p.   46

Brief but worthwhile survey of history of book illustration in period. Nearly two-thirds devoted to a catalogue of principal illustrated books of period. Catalogue is annotated; notes pertinent and valuable.

Calot, Frantz; Louis Marie Michon; Paul J. Angoulvent. L'art du livre en France des origines à nos jours; préface de Pol Neveux. Delagrave, 1931. 301 p. 47

Third chapter is on 16th century printing. Profusely illustrated. Short bibliography, p. 288. Work concerned primarily with development of book design and illustration.

Cartier, Alfred. Bibliographie des éditions des de Tournes, imprimeurs lyonnais, mise en ordre avec une introduction et des appendices par Marius Audin et une notice biographique par E. Vial. Édit. des Bibliothèques nationales de France, 1937-. 735 p. 48

Cartier gathered material over more than forty-year period. Work published after his death. One of most important works for history of the press at Lyons. Contains discussion of the de Tournes as printers, biographical sketches, chronological catalogue of de Tournes imprints, description and reproductions of typographical material of the press.

Chassaigne, Marc. Étienne Dolet; portraits et documents inédits. Michel, 1930, 348 p.   49

Chapters 3 and 4 concern Dolet's activities as printer and publisher; outline his difficulties with his fellow master printers at Lyons.

Claudin, Anatole. Histoire de l'imprimerie en France au xve et au xvie siècle. Imprimerie nationale, 1900-14. 4 v.   50

First two volumes devoted to Paris printers; second two to those of Lyons. Work replete with illustrations and type facsimiles. Although Claudin gives material on printers who worked in 16th century, he is only interested in describing such books as they printed in 15th. A supplement to the four volumes published in 1926 by Maggs Brothers, London, reproducing 721 facsimiles on 346 plates.

— Les origines et les débuts de l'imprimerie à Bordeaux. Claudin, 1897. 116 p.   51

" Extrait de la *Revue catholique de Bordeaux*. Tiré à cent exemplaires." One of a large number of articles and monographs by the author on beginnings of printing in the provinces. Present work devoted almost entirely to 16th century printers; reproductions of their works given.

— Origines et débuts de l'imprimerie à Poitiers. Bibliographie des premiers livres imprimés dans cette ville (1479-1515) avec notes, commentaires, éclaircissements et documents inédits. Claudin, 1897.   192, LXXVI p.   52

Careful account of first presses of the city. A companion atlas with title *Monuments de l'imprimerie à Poitiers. Recueil de facsimilés des premiers livres imprimés dans cette ville (1479-1515)*. Contains 258 facsimiles on 182 plates, reproducing title-pages, illustrations, text, and printers' marks of period. Work supplemented by author's *Nouvelles recherches. In:* BBB, April, 1898, p. (171-94), also issued separately.

Clément-Janin, Michel H. Les imprimeurs et les libraires dans la Côte-d'Or. 2e éd., avec portrait et facsimilé. Dijon, Darantière, 1883. 238 p.   53

Although there is some mention of printers and booksellers in other cities, this is principally an account of printers and booksellers in Dijon from introduction of printing into 19th century.

Corrard de Breban. Recherches sur l'établissement et l'exercice de l'imprimerie à Troyes, contenant la nomenclature des imprimeurs de cette ville depuis la fin du XVe siècle jusqu'à 1789 et des notices sur leurs productions les plus remarquables, avec facsimilé et marques typographiques. Chossonnery, 1873. 200 p.   54

Short account of the press at Troyes, followed by biographical dictionary of printers who worked in the city during period indicated.

Courboin, François et Marcel Roux. La gravure française; essai de bibliographie. Le Garrec, 1927-28. 3 v.   55

In V. I, section XIV, p. 262-98, is a useful bibliography of the illustrated book.

Delalain, Paul A. Essai de bibliographie de l'histoire de l'imprimerie typographique et de la librairie en France. Picard, 1903. 47 p.   56

Although fifty years old this is one of the few bibliographies available for history of French printing and publishing.

Delisle, Léopold V. Catalogue des livres imprimés ou publiés à Caen avant le milieu du XVIe siècle; suivi de recherches sur les imprimeurs et les libraires de la même ville. Caen, Jouan & Delesques, 1903-04. 2 v.   57

First volume is a catalogue of books published in the city within period indicated; second contains biographical information on Caen booksellers and printers, and many documents.

Didot, Firmin. Observations littéraires et typographiques sur Robert et Henri Estienne. *In his:* Poésies de Firmin Didot, suivies d'observations littéraires et typographiques sur Robert et Henri Estienne. Didot, 1834. p. 291-323.   58

Interesting study from a specialist's viewpoint of Henri Estienne, great 16th century editor, author, and printer, by the 19th century inventor of stereotypy, who was also a type engraver, printer, and *littérateur*.

Dumoulin, Joseph. Vie et œuvres de Fédéric Morel, imprimeur à Paris depuis 1557 jusqu'à 1583. Dumoulin, 1901. 288 p.   59

In many ways a model monograph on a French printer. Meticulous in detail; lacks any breadth of view. Contains biography of Morel; an account of his literary works; reproductions of his types, title pages, and printers' marks; *pièces justificatives*; and a bibliography of his press.

Duprat, François A. B. Histoire de l'Imprimerie impériale de France; suivie des spécimens des types étrangers et français de cet établissement. Imprimerie impériale, 1861. 578 p.   60

The first two chapters give sixteenth-century prehistory of the press, before its formal establishment in 1640.

Giraudet, Eugène. Les origines de l'imprimerie à Tours (1467-1550) contenant la nomenclature des imprimeurs depuis la fin du xve siècle jusqu'en 1850. Tours, Rouillé-Ladevèze, 1881. 130 p.   61

Biographical information on Tours' first printers and bibliographical notes on the product of their presses.

Harrisse, Henry. Excerpta Colombiniana. Bibliographie de quatre cents pièces gothiques, françaises, italiennes & latines du commencement du xvie siècle non décrites jusqu'ici; précédée d'une histoire de la Bibliothèque Colombine et de son fondateur. Welter, 1887. 316 p.   62

Introduction works out interesting conclusions concerning techniques and customs of 16th century printers and publishers. Author illustrates possibilities of establishing identity of printers of 16th-century books by analyzing form of capital T in fonts employed, producing evidence to show that this is the letter whose form varies most widely.

Internationale Bibliographie des Buch- und Bibliothekswesens. Mit besonderer Berücksichtigung der Bibliographie. N. F. bearb. von Rudolf Hoecker und J. Vorstius. Leipzig, Harrassowitz, 1928-41. 15 v.   63

Annual bibliography covering period 1926-40. Contains a section on printing history. Publication is successor to *Bibliographie des Bibliotheks- und Buchwesens* which appeared as *Beihefte* to *Zentralblatt für Bibliothekswesen* where bibliographies appeared for years 1904-12, 1922-25.

Jadart, Henri, i.e. Charles Henri. Les débuts de l'imprimerie à Reims et les marques des premiers imprimeurs, 1550-1650. Reims, Impr. de l'Indépendant rémois, 1893. 118 p.   64

First 28 pages contain running account of first printing at Rheims, particularly concerned with Nicolas Bacquenois. P. 29-46 contain *documents inédits*; remainder largely occupied with bibliographies of works published by individual printers.

La Caille, Jean de. Histoire de l'imprimerie et de la librairie, où l'on voit son origine et son progrès, jusqu'en 1689. Divisée en deux livres. La Caille, 1689. 322 [26] p.   65

Book one is concerned with history of printing in Europe up to 1500. Book two is concerned with history of printing in Paris to 1689, giving for most part disconnected notes on printers of the peroid.

Lacroix, Paul, Édouard Fournier, et Ferdinand Seré. Le livre d'or des métiers. Histoire de l'imprimerie et des arts et professions qui se rattachent à la typographie comprenant l'histoire des anciennes corporations et confréries depuis leur fondation jusqu'à leur suppression en 1789. Librairie historique, archéologique et scientifique de Seré, 1852. 160 p.   66

Practically ends at end of 16th century; the account of that century is a history of French printing. With a number of imperfections, the work still has value in tracing out main aspects of typographic history in the epoch.

Lepreux, George. Gallia typographica; ou, Répertoire biographique et chronologique de tous les imprimeurs de France depuis les origines de l'imprimerie jusqu'à la révolution. Champion, 1909-1914. 5 v.   67

Four volumes devoted to provincial printers. Author's plan for Parisian printers not completed; first volume of *Série parisienne* devoted exclusively to *imprimeurs du roi*. Each volume has two parts, biographies of printers, and documenta. Valuable part of each volume is author's discussion of his sources in the introduction. In volume on Paris this feature amounts to a critical bibliographical essay.

Levasseur, Émile. Histoire des classes ouvrières et de l'industrie en France avant 1789. 2e éd. (entièrement refondue). Rousseau, 1900-1901. 2 v.   68

There is some danger of mistaking for restrictions on the press, regulations and restrictions which were common to industry generally. Second volume of this work will assist in assigning printing to its place among other industries.

Lexikon des gesamten Buchwesens, herausgegeben von Karl Löffler und Joachim Kirchner unter Mitwirkung von Wilhelm Olbrich. Leipzig, Hiersemann, 1935-37. 3 v.   69

Useful, concise encyclopedia of printing, publishing, and allied subjects; bibliographies of varying quality at end of articles.

Lhote, Amédée. Histoire de l'imprimerie à Châlons-sur-Marne. Notices biographiques et bibliographiques sur les imprimeurs-libraires, relieurs et lithographes (1488-1894) avec marques typographiques et illustrations. Châlons-sur-Marne, Martin, Claudin, 1894. 232 p.   70

Biographical dictionary of printers and booksellers drawn principally from municipal and departmental archives. Contains numerous bibliographical references and lists of works published by the individual printers. Arranged chronologically. *Pièces justificatives*, p. 167-213.

Macfarlane, John. Antoine Vérard. London. Printed for the Bibliographical society at Chiswick Press, Sept. 1900 for 1899. 143 p. (Half-title : Illustrated monographs [issued by the Bibliographical society] no. VII.) 71

Best known work on Vérard. Introduction gives facts on Vérard's life and work, bibliography of his publications, p. 1-26, and 83 reproductions from his books.

McKerrow, Ronald B. An introduction to bibliography for literary students. Oxford, Clarendon, 1927. 359 p. 72

First part describes printing methods of 16th and 17th centuries. Renaissance printing methods described from French sources found in Don Cameron Allen's *Some contemporary accounts of renaissance printing methods.* (*In* Libr 17:167-71, Sept., 1936.)

Maignien, Edmond A. L'imprimerie, les imprimeurs et les libraires à Grenoble du xve au xviiie siècle. Grenoble, Dupont, 1884. 603 p. 73

Historical sketch of printing and bookselling at Grenoble, followed by biographical information on printers and booksellers arranged chronologically. Foregoing occupies cxiv pages. Main body of work is *Bibliographie grenobloise*, 1490-1788, being books published at Grenoble.

Maittaire, Michael. Historia typographorum aliquot parisiensium vitas et libros complectens. London, 1717. 2 v. in 1. 74

Contains sketches of the lives of Simon de Colines, Michel de Vascosan, Guillaume Morel, Adrien Turnèbe, Fédéric Morel, Jeanne Bienné.

Mellottée, Paul. Histoire économique de l'imprimerie. Tome I, L'imprimerie sous l'ancien régime 1439-1789. Hachette, 1905. 531 p. 75

Concise history of economic aspects of printing—laws governing publishing, organization of the industry, working conditions, guilds. Best single-volume treatment of subject. Bibliography p. 481-517.

Nisard, Charles. Histoire des livres populaires, ou de la littérature du colportage depuis le xve siècle jusqu'à l'établissement de la commission d'examen des livres du colportage (30 novembre, 1852). Amyot, 1854. 2 v. 76

An examination of literature only on foremost printers gives one a distorted view of the book trade. Work gives a glimpse of the type and quality of a considerable part of the printing of the age.

Pansier, Pierre. Histoire du livre et de l'imprimerie à Avignon du xive au xvie siècle. Avignon, Aubanel, 1922. 3 v. 77

Second volume devoted to 16th century; volume three contains *pièces justificatives et tables*, about half of the former applicable to 16th century. Contains a bibliography.

Paris. Bibliothèque nationale. Département des manuscrits. Inventaire de la collection Anisson sur l'histoire de l'imprimerie et la librairie, principalement à Paris [du xiiie au xviiie siècle]. (Manuscrits français 22061-22193) par Ernest Coyecque. Leroux, 1900. 2 v. 78

Relatively few documents in collection concerned with 16th century but these are valuable.

Pasquier, Émile, and Victor Dauphin. Imprimeurs & libraires de l'Anjou. Angers, Éditions de l'Ouest, 1932. 403 p. 79

Printers and booksellers are arranged alphabetically under their cities; pertinent facts given concerning them; not confined to 16th century.

Pichon, baron Jérôme F., et Georges Vicaire. Documents pour servir à l'histoire des libraires de Paris, 1486-1600. On y a joint des renseignements sur quelques bibliophiles, sur des doreurs sur cuir, enlumineurs, imprimeurs, fondeurs de caractères, papetiers, parcheminiers, relieurs de cette même époque. Techener, 1895. 294 p. 80

Great number of individuals included, but material on them is scanty. Authors intended to make available material for history of printing and book making but not to produce such a history. Documents not given *in extenso*; most concern printers, letter founders, and booksellers.

Porcher, R. Notice sur les imprimeurs & libraires blésois du xvie au xixe siècle. 2e éd. revue, corrigée et augmentée. Blois, Migault, 1895. 292 p. 81

Sketches of printers and booksellers at Blois in period indicated arranged chronologically.

Renouard, Antoine A. Annales de l'imprimerie des Estienne; ou, Histoire de la famille des Estienne et de ses éditions. Renouard, 1843. 585 p. 82

Bibliography of publications issued by various members of Estienne family, followed by biographies of printers. Still best single volume on Estiennes as printers.

Renouard, Philippe. Bibliographie des impressions et des œuvres de Josse Badius Ascensius, imprimeur et humaniste, 1462-1535. Paul et Guillemin, 1908. 3 v. 83

Contains biographical sketch of Badius, an account of his writings and editorial work, documents concerning himself and his family, and " bibliographie des ouvrages édités, commentés ou imprimés par Josse Badius Ascensius." In the preface Renouard reviews the literature on Badius up to the time he wrote.

— Documents sur les imprimeurs, libraires, cartiers, graveurs, fondeurs de lettres, relieurs, doreurs de livres, faiseurs de fermoirs, enlumineurs, parcheminiers et papetiers ayant exercé à Paris de 1450 à 1600. Recueillis aux Archives nationales et au Département des manuscrits de la Bibliothèque nationale, par Ph. Renouard. Champion, 1901. 84

Documents concerned with private lives of men in book trades—marriages, apprenticeships, wills, quarrels, arrests—and not with their trades or with business life in the period. Generally only extracts or pieces of documents given.

— Imprimeurs parisiens, libraires, fondeurs de caractères et correcteurs d'imprimerie, depuis l'introduction de l'imprimerie à Paris (1470) jusqu'à la fin du xvie siècle. Rbib 32:19-86, 251-82; 33:201-32, 395-424; 34:159-210; 36:29-76; 41:235-93; 42:256-322; 44:351-76, 418-41, 1922-34. 85

Series of articles constitutes an augmented edition of this work, first edition appeared in 1898; based on manuscript sources and material previously published by Pichon et Vicaire, Coyecque, and others.

Tilley, Arthur A. A Paris bookseller of the sixteenth century, Galliot Du Pré. Libr ns 9:36-65, Jan., 1908, 143-72, Apr., 1908. 86

Author analyses Du Pré's publications as a reflection of the reading of the educated public. Of value not only for information on Du Pré and his publications, but also for description of bookselling and publishing in period. Paul Delalain published two articles on Du Pré in JGIL, Dec. 6, 1890 and Oct. 3, 1891; also published separately. *See also: Galliot Dupré et sa famille, documents inédits*, BHren 4:427-35, 1944.

Vereeniging ter Bevordering van de Belangen des Boekhandels. Amsterdam. Bibliotheek. Catalogus. 's Gravenhage, Nijhoff, 1920-1949. 6 v. 87

Catalogue of library of Dutch association of booksellers and publishers among best general bibliographies of literature of printing.

Principal Periodicals Dealing with the Renaissance

(Nos. 88-93)

A. H. Schutz

Bibliothèque d'humanisme et renaissance. Travaux et documents, 1941-. 88

Same publisher as Hren. Change of title dictated by war conditions, although it seems that emphasis is on what might be termed " basic research " in the sense that more attention is paid to documents, wills, inventories, and the like. Reviews scarce, gathered in certain volumes only.

Humanisme et renaissance. 1-7, 1934-40, no more. Droz. 89

Continues RSS but with broader base, in that it goes farther back into Middle Ages and at same time takes up more marginal aspects of renaissance movement in all of Europe.

Revue des études rabelaisiennes. Publication trimestrielle consacrée à Rabelais et à son temps. Champion, 1903 through 1912. 90

Visible workshop of Abel Lefranc and his co-workers of the critical edition. Raw materials, model pieces and scaffoldings of that still unfinished structure. Long articles and short notes in profusion; considerable part of any Rabelais bibliography may be said to be concentrated there; opposite of selective. Continued by RSS.

Revue de littérature comparée. Boivin, 1921-. 91
Renaissance being so largely "comparatiste," a periodical of this kind would be important. Hac many articles of value, yet index from 1931-50 reveals not a single item concerning either Ronsard or Du Bellay.

Revue de la renaissance. v. 1-14, 1901-1913. No more published. 92
Founded as a monthly; became bimonthly and then quarterly. Edited by Léon Séché. Illustrated. Editor was frequent contributor, as were Paul Laumonier and Pierre Villey.

Revue du seizième siècle. Champion, 1913-33, no more. 19 v. 93
Enlarges scope of RER. Takes in many more articles on French renaissance outside of Rabelais than its predecessor. Reviews useful.

Histories of Literature
(Nos. 94-124)

Donald M. Frame

Bédier, Joseph, et Paul Hazard. Histoire de la littérature française illustrée. Larousse, 1923-24. 2 v. 94
Standard work by excellent scholars in large format, beautifully illustrated. 16th century part (I, 126-213) by Jean Plattard (first half); Pierre de Nolhac, Henry Bidou, and Pierre Villey (second half). *See* 1785. Good selective bibliographical materials. Superseded by revised edition.
Reviews : H. Buffenoir in Rcr ns 91:477-78, Dec. 1, 1924; K. Glaser in ZFSL 49:183-86, 1927; F. Strowski in RCC 26¹:574-76, 1925.

— Littérature française. Revised ed. directed by Pierre Martino, Larousse, 1948-49. 2 v. 95
Excellent revision by Pierre Jourda, Jean Baillou, and Raymond Lebègue, follows original in general but improves and brings it up to date. Excellent new selective bibliographical materials.. Admirably planned and executed.
Reviews : L. G[uérin] in Par 52:54-55, July, 1949; F. Vial in FR 23:410-11, 1949-50.

Braunschvig, Marcel. Le xv1ᵉ siècle. *In his :* Notre littérature étudiée dans les textes. Colin. V. 1, 8th ed., 1933. p. 125-327. 96

V. 1 covers Middle Ages, Renaissance, and 17th century. Good skeleton of facts goes with selections from each author. Generally good sampler for individual figures, better for minor than major writers, less useful for currents and periods. Sound bibliographical materials.
Reviews : H. Buffenoir in Rcr ns 88:100, Mar. 1, 1921; K. Glaser in ZFSL 49²:198, 1927.

Cons, Louis. Anthologie littéraire de la renaissance française. New York, Holt, [c1931]. 318 p. 97
Mainly an introductory anthology for American students; work offers 100 pages of superb, sensitive, critical scholarship in Introduction (p. vii-xxxii) on spirit of the age and in presentations of individual authors.
Review : M. E. Coindreau in MLN 47:416-17, 1932.

Darmesteter, Arsène. Le seizième siècle en France. Tableau de la littérature et de la langue, by A. Darmesteter and Adolphe Hatzfeld. Delagrave, 1878. 16th ed., 1934. 301 p. plus 384 p. *See* 610. 98
First part includes *Tableau de la littérature* (p. 1-182) and *Tableau de la langue* (183-301); second part, *Morceaux choisis* (384 p.). Best is the remarkable section on the language. First part more informative than critical, with useful notices on incredible number of writers but meager and disappointing treatments of men like Montaigne and Rabelais. Same is true of second part, though broad sampling is generally good. Despite its age, book as a whole remains a very valuable compendium.
Reviews : P. T[amizey] de L[arroque] in Poly 1:334-35, 1878; O. Ulbrich in ZRP 3:289-97, 1879.

Dictionnaire des lettres françaises. Le seizième siècle. Publié sous la direction de mgr. Georges Grente. (Assistant directors, Albert Pauphilet, Louis Pichard, Robert Barroux.) Fayard, 1951. 718 p. 99
First complete volume of long-planned series to appear; one fascicule on Middle Ages came out in 1939. Magnificent achievement, indispensable. Handsome folio volume containing about 2000 articles (and excellent cross-references) on literary men and subjects by a large team of topnotch scholars. Rich substantial articles on major figures and works. Bibliographies almost ignore foreign work, but extremely good and rich for French scholarship. *See* 127, 315, 1808.

Reviews : D. M. Frame in RR 44:295-97, 1953; D. P. Walker, R. E. Asher and M. A. Sereech, in BHRen 16:267-72, 1954.

Faguet, Émile. Le xvıᵉ siècle (1500-1610). *In his :* Histoire de la littérature française. 8th ed., Plon, 1900-01. v. I, p. 247-467.   100

Except for poetry, treatment entirely by genres, not periods. Best parts are those handled in his *Seizième siècle* (no. 101); also interesting portraits of minor writers; good illustrative excerpts.

— Seizième siècle; études littéraires. Lecène, Oudin, 1894. 5th ed., 1894. 425 p. *See* 647.   101

Essays on eight leading writers, always readable, nearly always worth reading, not always reliable. Generally best on prose-writers (Rabelais, Montaigne); also good on Marot.

Reviews : C. Dejob in Rcr ns 37:131-34, Feb. 12, 1894.

Haedens, Kléber. Une histoire de la littérature française. Julliard, [1945]. 473 p.   102

Written by a young man for young readers. At times unreliable, anecdotal gallery of picturesque sketches of men and works; refreshing, original, readable, with many fine insights.

Reviews : M. Blanchot in Jdéb, Sept. 22, 1943, p. 3; Simone David in FR 19:453-54, 1945-46.

Hervier, Marcel. Les écrivains français jugés par leurs contemporains. Mellottée, 1911-39. v. 1 (Le 16ᵉ et le 17ᵉ siècle), [c1911]. 676 p.   103

Useful collection of contemporary opinions about leading writers : Marot, Du Bellay, Ronsard, Rabelais, Montaigne, Régnier, d'Aubigné.

Jaloux, Edmond. Introduction à l'histoire de la littérature française. Le xvıᵉ siècle. Geneva, Cailler, [c1947]. 359 p.   104

The 31 chapters offer excellent portraits of individual writers; sometimes scanty treatment of the works. Sketchy on currents and periods, not always reliable for facts; stimulating, fresh, sympathetic appraisals.

Jasinski, René. Seizième siècle. *In his :* Histoire de la littérature française. Boivin, 1947. V. 1, p. 109-252.   105

Excellent history reflecting recent scholarly findings; makes good use of grouping

by generations. Rather short treatment of 16th century and its greatest writers; abundant sketches of minor figures. Lucid, well-informed, well-organized.

Reviews : L. A. Bisson in MLR 43:118-19, 1948; M. Françon in FR 22:128-35, 1948-49; Hélène Harvitt in *ibid.* 21:508-09, 1947-48; H. Lacroix in Par 35:66-67, Oct., 1947; R. Mortier in RBP 27:783-87, 1949; S. de Sacy in MerF 301:523-26, Nov. 1, 1947; P. Van Tieghem in RLC 22:592-94, 1948.

Jeanroy, Alfred. De l'avènement à la mort de François Iᵉʳ (1515-1547). *In :* Hanotaux, Gabriel. Histoire de la nation française. Société de l'histoire nationale, and Plon, 1923. v. 12, p. 539-76.   106

Presentation popular, but intelligent, acute, well-informed.

Review : C. Ruutz-Rees in RR 17:149-54, 1926.

La Croix du Maine, François Grudé, sieur de. Bibliothèque. L'Angelier, 1584. *In :* La Croix du Maine et Du Verdier : Les bibliothèques françoises. Éd. by Rigoley de Juvigny, Saillant et Nyon et al, 1772-73, 6 v. V. 1-2. (V. 3-6 contain Du Verdier's Bibliothèque.)   107

Contemporary literary *Who's who*, sometimes useful for details on minor figures, otherwise superseded.

Lanson, Gustave. Le seizième siècle. *In his :* Histoire de la littérature française. Hachette, 14th ed., 1920. p. 221-356. 108

Still best one-volume history of French literature. Excellent critically as well as historically. Especially valuable on Montaigne and currents of thought and style. Appendix and many footnotes show modifications of author's original views.

Review : H. de Curzon in Rcr ns 38:511-15, Dec. 24, 1894.

— Le seizième siècle. *In his :* Histoire illustrée de la littérature française. 2nd ed., Hachette, 1923, v. 1, p. 167-263.   109

Excellent illustrations, large format; same text as original history (no. 108).

Reviews : H. Buffenoir in Rcr ns 90:456-57, Dec. 1, 1923; K. Glaser in ZFSL 49:183-86, 1927.

— **et Paul Tuffrau.** Le xvıᵉ siècle. *In their :* Manuel illustré d'histoire de la littérature française. Hachette, 1929. 1949 ed., Hachette, and Boston, Heath. p. 99-160.   110

Abridgement of original Lanson (no. 108) for less advanced students. Rather short on 16th century, but well cut : leaves out minor writers except to summarize trends they represent; gives excellent full picture of major writers. Admirable introductory manual.

Mönch, Walter. Frankreichs Literatur im XVI. Jahrhundert. Eine nationalpolitische Geistesgeschichte der französischen Renaissance. (*Added to title page :* Grundriss der romanischen Philologie, begründet von Gustav Gröber. nf. Geschichte der französischen Literatur, 5) Berlin, De Gruyter, 1938. 333 p. 111

Competent treatment, despite surprising omissions from bibliography; designed among other things to bring Morf (no. 113) up to date. Emphasis indicated by the subtitle, on thought rather than form, rather heavy ; Marguerite de Navarre, Calvin and Bèze treated better than Rabelais, Ronsard, Montaigne.

Review : H. W. Lawton in MLR 34:273-74, 1939.

Morçay, Raoul. La renaissance. Gigord, 1933-35. 2 v. (Histoire de la littérature française pub. sous la direction de J. Calvet, II, III). 112

Best full treatment of subject, despite some weaknesses like comparatively meager and disappointing treatment of Montaigne. Thoughtful, judicious, reliable. Excellent critical bibliographies at end of each chapter.

Reviews : P. Jourda in Rcr ns 101:311-16, 1934; R. Marichal in Hren 2:70-73, 1935; 3:330-34, 1936.

Morf, Heinrich. Geschichte der französischen Literatur im Zeitalter der Renaissance. 1898. 2nd ed., Strasbourg, Trubner, 1914. 267 p. (*Added to title page :* Grundriss der romanischen Philologie, begründet von G. Gröber. NF 1. Französische Literatur, 4.) 113

Very good short treatment; solid, thoughtful. Good selective bibliographies at end of each section.

Reviews : R. Radouant in RHL 6:472-75, 1899; L. R[oustan] in Rcr ns 80:215-17, Oct. 2, 1915.

Nitze, William Albert. A history of French literature from the earliest times to the great war. By William A. Nitze and E. Preston Dargan. New York, Holt, 1922. 781 p. 3rd ed., A history of French literature from

earliest times to the present. New York, Holt, [c1938]. 852 p. 114

Challenging arrangement. Part II (the renaissance) includes 16th century (by Nitze) and most of 17th. Very good treatment, best and most recent in English; judicious, readable, informative. Minor figures subordinated so that major ones have space enough to come to life. Especially good on Calvin, Rabelais, Pléiade. Useful, selective, minimum bibliography.

Reviews : M. P. Brush in FR 2:85-87, 1928-29; C. Gauss in MLN 39:35-45, 1924; K. Glaser in ZFSL 51:473-74, 1928; H. C. Lancaster in MLN 43:211-12, 1928; A. Schinz in MP 21:215-20, 1923-24.

Patterson, Warner Forrest. Three centuries of French poetic theory; a critical history of the chief arts of poetry in France (1328-1630). Ann Arbor, University of Michigan Press, 1935. 2 v. (MPLL, v. 14, 15). 115

The 16th century is treated in I, 176-978 and parts of II, which comprises chronological lists of treatises (1-56) and an illustrative anthology by genres of verse (57-452). A bit too bent on rehabilitating the *Rhétoriqueurs*; sometimes unnecessarily heavy and detailed; valuable, solid source book. See 323, 1054A.

Reviews : L. Cons in MLN 52:122-24, 1937; R. Guiette in RPB 17:942-44, 1938.

Petit de Julleville, Louis. Histoire de la langue et de la littérature françaises des origines à 1900. V. III, Seizième siècle. Colin, 1897. 864 p. 116

Volume consists of 12 chapters on 16th century by leading specialists. Excellent work ; now outdated by 16th century research done since. Bibliographies useful for 19th century scholarship. F. Brunot's chapter (XII) on language especially good.

Reviews : E. Bourciez in Rcr ns 43:472-74, June 14, 1897; E. Stengel in ZFSL 20²:14-21, 1898.

Plattard, Jean. La renaissance des lettres en France de Louis XII à Henri IV. Colin, 1925. 2nd ed., 1931. 220 p. 117

Very good short handbook by a solid scholar with a wide range of competence. Treatment of first half of century often resembles that in original Bédier and Hazard (no. 94); arranged more for reading, less for reference.

Reviews : L. Delaruelle in RSS 13:150-52, 1926; J. Hombert in RBP 5:1025-26, 1926.

Saintsbury, George E. B. A short history of French literature. 7th ed., Oxford, Clarendon, 1882 [1937]. 638 p.   118

More useful for minor than major figures or currents or periods; often outdated; keen, critical, masterful. Materials in some cases enlarged and revised in 11th ed. of *Encyclopaedia Britannica* (1910-11) in articles on French literature, Montaigne, Rabelais, Ronsard, and others. Partial shorter treatment in European context in *The earlier renaissance*. Edinburgh, Blackwood, 1901. 423 p.

Saulnier, Verdun L. La littérature française de la renaissance (1500-1610). Presses universitaires de France, 1942. 127 p.   119

Remarkable achievement in clear condensation, offering no textual samples but excellent tables and economic and political notes; good full treatment of major writers. Makes good use of grouping by generations. Fresh, enthusiastic, critical, well-informed.

Spingarn, Joel E. A history of literary criticism in the renaissance. New York, Macmillan, 1899. 6th impression, Columbia University Press, 1924. 350 p.   120

Study of development of classic spirit in Italy, France, and England. Finds Italian sources for all ideas in other two countries. Valuable for backgrounds, critical attitudes, questions, influences. Part II (p. 171-250) deals with France. Italian translation by Antonio Fusco (*La critica letteraria nel Rinascimento*, Bari, Laterza, 1905) includes additional material.

Reviews : C. Bastide in Rcr ns 48:305-07, 1899; (Italian tr.) K. Vossler in ZFSL 29²:142, 1906.

Strowski, Fortunat. De Ronsard à Montaigne. *In:* Hanotaux, Gabriel. Histoire de la nation française. Société de l'histoire nationale, and Plon. 1923. v. 13:1-74. 121

Presentation popular, particularly intelligent, acute, well-informed.

Review : C. Ruutz-Rees in RR 17:149-54, 1926.

Tilley, Arthur. The dawn of the French renaissance. Cambridge University Press, 1918. 636 p.   122

Valuable broad, rich treatment of visual arts as well as literature in approximately first third of 16th century. Part II (p. 183-372) deals with renaissance in letters.

Reviews : J. Plattard in RSS 6:294-97, 1919.

— The literature of the French Renaissance. Cambridge University Press, 1904. 2 v.   123

Old but still useful treatment of period 1525-1610. More generous than selective toward minor writers, sometimes lacking in relief; perceptive, well-informed, humane, readable. Bibliographical materials valuable for earlier scholarship, though now outdated.

Reviews : J. Plattard in RER 3:87-93, 1905; H. Schneegans in ZFSL 29²:132-41, 1906.

Wright, C. H. Conrad. A history of French literature. New York, Oxford University Press, 1912. Revised ed., 1925. 990 p.   124

Good thorough treatment, well-informed and well balanced, generally still valid.

Reviews : L. Roustan in Rcr ns 74:454-55, Dec. 7, 1912; O. Schultz-Gora in ZFSL 43²:65-71, 1915; A. Terracher in MLN 28:121-24, 1913; A. Tilley and H. Oelsner in MLR 8:121-30, 277, 1913.

Renaissance and Humanism
(Nos. 125-139)

HARRY KURZ and A. H. SCHUTZ

Allen, Percy Stafford. The age of Erasmus. Oxford, Clarendon Press, 1914. 303 p.   125

Reports with factual detail life of period from about 1475 to 1530. Many quotations from memoirs, correspondence, books; work draws a fascinating picture in its ten chapters on the life of pupils in schools, texts and teachers, then universities, curricula, examinations, wanderings of faculties and students. One chapter traces life and activities of Erasmus. Others report on monasteries, prevalence of fraud and force by military bands and pirates, manners of the age, superstitions impeding progress, regular pilgrimages to Jerusalem and Venice. Manner of presentation lively and period lives again in many quotations. Final chapter, *Transalpine renaissance*, portrays Erasmus at zenith of his glory, 1517, guests he received at Basle, Louvain, Antwerp; now outmoded in its point of view that the renaissance in the North was a transfusion of culture from Italy. Whole work a valuable scholarly contribution based on realistic details culled from Erasmus and a host of his contemporaries.

Reviews : Anon in AthL 143:785-86, June 6, 1914; Anon in CW 99:686-87, 1914; Anon in NNY 99:286-87, Sept. 3,

1914; Anon in SRPL 117:744, June 6, 1914.

Bibliothèque nationale, Paris. Collection Picot. MS fr. 23, 192-276.   126

Some 200,000 unpublished slips, containing a wide variety of notes and bibliographic references on renaissance life and letters, collected in a number of large volumes and arranged alphabetically. Of utmost value for research in period; has not been exploited to its fullest possibilities; difficult of access, unless in Paris.

Champion, Pierre. Vue générale du XVIᵉ siècle. *In:* Dictionnaire des lettres françaises. *See* 99, p. 3-23.   127

Excellent *étude générale* (so the author refers to it on p. 22); in some respects a *tour de force*, so tightly packed is material in these few pages.

Ferguson, Wallace Klippert. The renaissance in historical thought. Boston, Houghton, Mifflin, 1948.   429 p.   128

Important attempt to trace through five centuries various significances attached to the term renaissance, ideas concerning the movement rather than its factual content. From earliest traditions in Italy, to the period of Erasmus in the North; from 17th century humanistic concepts to rationalistic applications of 18th and Romantic rehabilitation of the 19th. Manifestations in art and literature leading to the Burckhardtian interpretation of the Italian phase. Chap. IX is the central point, examining the renaissance in its European aspects and leading in modern times to its re-attachment to the Middle Ages. A closely reasoned synthesis of a cultural phenomenon, with avoidance of fragmentation of its essential continuity.

Reviews : H. Baron in AHR 55:864-66, 1949-50; W. F. Church in Spec 24:431-33, 1949; F. R. Johnson in MLQ 12:108-10 1951; P.O.K. in JP 47:129-32, Feb. 16, 1950; V. L. Saulnier in BHren 13:212-13, 1951; J. W. Swain in JEGP 49:252-54, 1950; C. Trinkaus in RenN 3:1-4, Spring, 1950; W. W. J. Wilkinson in CHR 35:322-23, Oct., 1949.

Hall, Vernon. Renaissance literary criticism. New York, Columbia University Press, 1945.   260 p.   129

Study of Italy, France, England under identical chapter headings : *Fight for the vernacular, Theories of the drama, Theories of the epic, Scorn for the people, Decorum*

and minor genres, The poet and his purpose. Discusses social aspects of critical thought of the age, as evidenced in rising national feeling, defense of vernacular, adhesion to aristocratic diction in favored literary forms. Italy, disunited, cannot follow pattern of the others. Original and debatable points of view make this a stimulating work, with clear contrasts between three countries. French section (p. 82-152) a useful analysis of literary ideals of a society in transition toward absolutism.

Reviews : J. W. H. Adkins in MLR 41:429-30, 1946; H. Craig in AHR 51:493-495, 1945-46; F. M. Krouse in MLN 61:135-36, 1946; E. Sweeting in RES 23:68-69, 1947.

Hannay, David. The Latin renaissance. New York, Scribner, 1898.   381 p. (PEL).   130

An especially valuable feature is the thorough treatment of Spanish literature of the renaissance (p. 1-184). Second part has three chapters on Elizabethan writers and one on Italy. Two chapters on France (p. 290-351) deal succinctly with poets and prose writers of latter half of 16th century. Author shows insight, clarity, and stimulating summation. All major and many minor writers are discussed wisely and often with wit.

Haydn, Hiram. The counter-renaissance. New York, Scribner, 1950.   705 p.   131

Discusses philosophic background of 16th century trends in renaissance thought. Treats classical revival of 14th and 15th centuries as a prologue, scientific awakening of 17th as an epilogue. Between these and overlapping he sets the counter-renaissance, a reprise of the ancient duel between faith and reason. Fuses in sympathetic focus such diverse champions as Luther, Machiavelli, Calvin, Montaigne, and Bacon; shows how the Reformation and assertion of faith is not an isolated religious phenomenon but a phase of the duel fought between the reason of humanism and distrust of it among thinkers of the counter-renaissance. Light thrown on Montaigne's Raymond Sebond marks the *Essais* more strikingly as a segment of a vast European current of thought. Imparts a sense of design and meaning to a confused, angry, disputative phase of the renaissance, leading eventually to ultimate triumph of reason under a God of universal purpose manifesting in a Nature of law and order.

Lefranc, Abel. La civilisation intellectuelle en France à l'époque de la renaissance. 132
RCC, as follows :

18²:58-68, 1909-10. État des études sur la renaissance.
18²:145-54. Les divisions du xvie siècle.
18²:481-94. Diverses définitions de la renaissance.
18²:721-39, 817-27. Les origines : les rapports intellectuels du Moyen-Age et de la renaissance.
19¹:49-60, 1910-11. Indépendance intellectuelle au Moyen-Age.
19¹:97-105. La fin du Moyen-Age; La révolution du xive siècle.
19¹:145-54. Le xve siècle : civilisation et littérature.
19¹:193-202. Le xve siècle : les romans.
19¹:241- 49. Le Petit Jehan de Saintré.
19¹:289-300. Les romans et les farces au xve siècle.
19¹:337-45. Les poètes au xve siècle.
19¹:345-55. Les humanistes; l'imprimerie.
19¹:433-53. La renaissance italienne; les guerres d'Italie; La renaissance en Allemagne.
19¹:481-91. La renaissance aux Pays-Bas; Erasme; Les grands rhétoriqueurs.
19¹:529-39. Leçon d'ouverture.
19¹:625-33. La société et les arts à la fin du xve siècle.
19¹:673-82. L'art à la fin du xve siècle et au commencement du xvie siècle; les grandes divisions de la renaissance.
19¹:721-30. Les grands rhétoriqueurs.
19¹:769-777. Jean Lemaire de Belges.
19²:97-106. Jean Lemaire (suite).
19²:145-54. Jean Lemaire (fin). Jean Parmentier.
19²:223-30. Jean Parmentier (fin). La chanson au xve et au xvie siècle.
19²:289-96. Jean Bouchet.
19²:385-96. Le théâtre au xve siècle.
19²:481-91. L'hellénisme et l'orientalisme en France au début de la renaissance.
19²:529-39. Josse Bade et Jérome Aléandro.
19²:673-83. Le mysticisme de Lefèvre d'Étaples.
20:1-10, 1911-12. Guillaume Budé.
20:49-58. Guillaume Budé (suite).
20:145-54. Guillaume Budé (fin); Louise de Savoie.
20:289-301. La jeunesse de François Ier.
20:337-344. François Ier.
20:500-09. Considérations générales.
20:545-54. Le roi et la cour.
The titles are self-explanatory.

Lectures are at times too oratorical to be helpful; often crowded with valuable bibliography (unfortunately, authors rather than complete entries), plus many provocatively new ideas. Subsequent scholarship could have followed up more fruitfully than it has his development of continuity between Middle Ages and renaissance. Amazing familiarity with MS book inventories, through researches of Coyecque, whose work he estimates at its proper value, qualitatively, but fails to appraise the small percentage which even that extraordinary pioneer in notarial researches was able to handle, in the nature of the case, there being so much.

— Grands écrivains français de la renaissance. Champion, 1914. 414 p. *See* 663, 714, 737, 738, 739, 2569.   132A
Still of considerable interest and value, often cited.

— La vie quotidienne au temps de la renaissance. Hachette, 1938. 253 p.   133
An attempt, by copious quotations and commentary, to recreate the experience of living and working in France during latter half of 16th century. Sources are correspondence, memoirs, literature, much of it unedited material. Daily activities of large and small-town social classes are reported, from the King, through ministers, poets, country noblemen, bourgeois, students, even peasants and artisans, ladies and their salons, including favorite books and topics of conversation. Gives rich and varied detail, but only an informed and imaginative reader could get the feel of living from its pages. Author's warmth is appealing; number of quotations transform the work into a source book rather than an interpretive portrait of a nation at work.

Pater, Walter Horatio. The renaissance. 2nd ed., London, Macmillan, 1877. 225 p.   134
An impressionistic series of essays beginning with Amis et Amile and Aucassin and Nicolette as proofs of a continuity between Middle Ages and renaissance. Author has gift of insight and style which make his studies dance lightly but truly where the scholar treads cautiously. Pico della Mirandola shares the task of reconciling Gods of Greece with Christianity. Similarly, the sculptural forms of Michelangelo are in the tradition of the ideality and abstraction of ancient art. Chapters on Botticelli, Luca della Robbia, Da Vinci, Giorgione, are followed by a study of DuBellay to show that the French

renaissance is in him a marriage between medieval French forms and Italian interpretation. Pater's intuitional vision has prophetic values later substantiated by research. *See* 1281.

Renaudet, Augustin. Préréforme et humanisme à Paris pendant les premières guerres d'Italie (1494-1517). Champion, 1916. 739 p. (Diss., Paris). 2nd ed. 1954.   135

If this masterly book bears to a very large extent upon the Reformation, treatment is on such a scale that it is essential for a comprehension of the intellectual movement in the whole of the early French renaissance, as distinguished from the Italian and other cosmopolitan forces. A large work, worth attentive reading, which cannot fail to raise many questions and offer a vast stock of information. *See* 162, 197.

Review : P. Villey in RHL 25:321-25, 1918.

Simone, Franco. Le moyen âge, la renaissance et la critique moderne. RLC 18:411-35, 1938.   136

How the terms have been appraised by the critics... "nous avons voulu rechercher l'origine de la conception d'une rupture entre le Moyen Age et la renaissance et montrer la conséquence qui en dérivait: l'oubli dans lequel était plongé le xvᵉ siècle." (p. 421) A different approach to a problem which leads, however, to a conclusion somewhat like that of Lefranc (whom he does not cite), namely, that there must be no scission either between the two historical epochs, which lead into each other naturally, nor between an Italian and a French renaissance, since the French used the Italian influences in their own particular way and for their own particular purposes. Very good article, full of substance, a ticklish thesis well argued.

Spingarn, J. E. A history of literary criticism in the renaissance. *See* 120.   137

Author revised second edition and added some footnotes in later imprints. Recommends Italian translation by Antonio Fusco (Bari, 1905) as best for additions not used in American versions. Work important as a contribution on development of classical tenets in Italian criticism from Dante to Tasso, in French from Du Bellay to Boileau, in English from Ascham to Milton. Best section is the study of critical thought in Italian humanism. French study (p. 171-250) reviews literary thinking of Du Bellay, Scaliger, and

Vauquelin de La Fresnaye, poetic art as seen by Peletier and Ronsard, and theories of drama in these critics and others such as Grévin, Jean de La Taille, Pierre de Laudun. Emphasis throughout on preeminence of Italian writers in shaping the classical ideal in Europe.

Thompson, James Westfall; Ferdinand Schevill; George Sarton; George Rowley. The civilization of the renaissance. Chicago, University of Chicago Press, n.d. (1929), 130 p.   138

The Mary Tuttle Bourdon Lectures at Mount Holyoke. In order of authorship (which is the book order); *Exploration and discovery during the renaissance, The society of the Italian renaissance, Science in the renaissance* and *The art of the renaissance.* Brilliant and informative chapters, written independently, yet make a real synthesis. First especially modern in showing how voyages of discovery of 13th century operated like those of late 15th on minds of men and enlarged their horizons. Sarton's lecture shows renaissance not to have been a great period for scientific investigation, natural sciences being too dependent on ancient authority.

Toffanin, Giuseppe. Storia dell'umanesimo (dal XIII al XVI secolo.) Naples, Perrella [1933]. 339 p.   139

Deals mainly with Italy; excellent for general renaissance background. Abstruse in style; penetrating in thought and highly original in the type of facts gathered together. One may not always agree with author's opinions, but they must be carefully considered and treated with respect.

Review : L. Tonelli in ICS 17:13, 1934. Two other reviews mentioned in SP 32:382, 1935.

Renaissance and Reformation
(Nos. 140-186)

HELMUT A. HATZFELD

Political and Cultural Aspects
(Nos. 140-144)

Reusch, Franz H. Der Index der verbotenen Bücher, ein Beitrag zur Kirchen und Literaturgeschichte. Bonn, Cohen, 1883-85. 2 v.   140

Fundamental work on national and pontifical indexes from about 1500 and particularly on the *Index librorum prohibitorum* established by the Council of Trent.

Fliche, Augustin, and Victor Martin. Histoire de l'église depuis les origines jusqu'à nos jours. Bloud, 1936 ff. v. 16 : É. de Moreau, P. Jourda et P. Janelle. La Crise religieuse du xvie siècle. Bloud, 1950. 460 p.   141

Important, reliable work.

Hulme, Edward Maslin. The renaissance, the Protestant revolution, and the Catholic reformation in continental Europe. New York, Century, 1914. 589 p. Revised ed. 1917. 589 p.   142

Popular narrative, plenty of details.

Review : G. C. Sellery in AHR 20:393-94, 1914-15. " For advanced college classes."

Mourret, Fernand. Histoire générale de l'église. Bloud et Gay, 1920-28. 8 v. V. 5 : La renaissance et la réforme. 1921. 604 p.   143

Classical work from French and Catholic viewpoint.

Review : W. S. in CHR 17:249, 1931-32. " Standard history, balanced, comprehensive, sufficiently detailed."

Ritter, Gerhard. Die Neugestaltung Europas im 16. Jahrhundert; die kirchlichen und staatlichen Wandlungen im Zeitalter der Reformation und der Glaubenskämpfe. Berlin, Tempelhof, 1950. 381 p.   144

Most recent and fine orientation, with good bibliography for France, from a viewpoint both German and Protestant.

History of the Popes

(Nos. 145-146)

Pastor, Ludwig, *freiherr* von. The history of the popes, from the close of the middle ages. Drawn from the secret archives of the Vatican and other original sources. Edited by Ralph Francis Kerr, F. I. Antrobus, E. Graf and E. F. Peeler. Saint Louis, Herder, 1891-1950. 36 v.   145

Translation of the German monumental work : *Geschichte der Päpste seit dem Ausgang des Mittelalters.* Each German volume is split in two. Work includes all popes of reformation and counter-reformation, starting with Martin V (1417-31). This is the distribution of the popes of importance for 16th century over the different volumes : V : Innocent VIII (1484-92), v. VI : Alexander VI (1492-1503), Julius II (1503-13), v. VII-VIII : Leo X (1513-21), v. IX-X : Adrian VI (1522-23), Clement VII (1523-34), v. XI-XII : Paul III (1534-49), v. XIII : Julius III (1550-55), v. XIV : Marcellus II (1555), and Paul IV (1555-59), v. XV-XVI : Pius IV (1559-65), v. XVII-XVIII : Pius V (1560-72), v. XIX-XX : Gregory XIII (1572-85), v. XXI : Sixtus V (1585-90), v. XXII : Sixtus V and Innocent IX (1591), v. XXIII-XXIV : Clement VIII (1592-1605).

Reviews : Anon CC 662:204-10, Apr. 17, 1915 on v. 11-12; F. S. Betten in CHR 19:203-05, 1933-34 reports on v. 21-24 without strictly critical remarks; A. Giorgetti in ASI 85:102-07, 1927 on v. 21-22; A. Giorgetti in ASI 81:286-316, 1923 on v. 15-16; C. A. Kneller in TPQ 88:113-20, 1935; W. Platzhoff in HZ 138:375-80, 1928 on v. 19-20; P. Richard in RHE 16:431-43, 1921 on v. 13-14; P. Richard in RHE 19:588-93, 1923 on v. 17-18; J. Schmidlin in HJ 28:366-72, 1907, and 30:588-98, 1909 on v. 7-8; 33:604-10, 1911 on v. 9-10.

Ranke, Leopold von. The ecclesiastical and political history of the popes of Rome during the sixteenth and seventeenth centuries. Philadelphia, 1840-41, 5 v.; 4th ed. in 3 v., London, 1866.   146

Translation of *Die römischen Päpste* (1834). Still important as powerful historiography of one of the greatest historians. Therefore 12th German edition in 2 v., 1923, still used as standard work. Put on the *Index librorum prohibitorum*, 1841.

Religious Orders and Congregations

(Nos. 147-154)

General

Heimbucher, Max Josef. Die Orden und Kongregationen der katholischen Kirche. Paderborn, Schöningh, 1896-97; 3rd ed. 1933-34. 2 v.   147

Most complete, authentic, and best known survey of monastic and spiritual organizations prior and posterior to counter-reformation, with rich bibliography, 1:33-60. New orders of 16th century like the Barnabites (1530), Capuchins, Camillians, Hospitalers, Jesuits, Theatines (1524), Oratorians (1564), Ursulines, etc. are duly considered.

Review : R. M. Huber in CH 10:24, 1941.

Camillians

Der hl. Kamillus von Lellis und sein Orden, von deutschen Kamillianerpatres. Freiburg, Herder, 1914. 358 p. 148
History of the Order of the " Ministers of the sick " founded in 1582.
Review : G. Krüger in HTR 17:45-48, 1924.

Hospitalers

Monval, Jean. Les frères hospitaliers de St. Jean de Dieu. Grasset, 1936. 250 p. (CGOM, v. 22). 149
Gives full information of purpose of this " Maltesian " order, founded to hospitalize and care for the poor in their sickness.

Jesuits

Boehmer, Heinrich. Die Jesuiten. Leipzig, Teubner, 1904, 164 p.; 4th ed. 1921. 109 p. 150
Protestant appraisal of achievements of Jesuits, written with great sympathy. There exists a French translation of first edition. Colin, 1910. 304 p. English translation appeared in Philadelphia, Castle Press, 1928. 192 p.
Review : W. Koehler in HZ 126 (3rd ser. 30):167-68, 1922 (praises revised 4th ed.).

— Studien zur Geschichte der Gesellschaft Jesu. V. I. Bonn, Falkenroth, 1914. 435 p. 151
Inquiry into less known formative years of the order during lifetime of Saint Ignatius.
Review : G. Krüger in HTR 17:45-46, 1924.

Campbell, Thomas Joseph. The Jesuits, 1534-1921 : a history of the Society of Jesus from its foundation to the present time. New York, Encyclopedia Press, 1921. 2 v. 152
Outside story of the order, very accurate, comprehensive and rich in details, by one of its members.
Review : P. Guilday in AHR 28:304-05, 1922-23.

Fouqueray, Henri. Histoire de la Compagnie de Jésus en France des origines à la suppression, 1528-1762. 5 v. Picard, 1910-24. V. I : Les origines et les premières luttes 1528-1572 (1910). 698 p. V. II : La ligue et le banissement. (1913). 745 p. 153

Extensive, well-documented description of vicissitudes of the Society of Jesus in France. Too apologetic.
Review : G. L. Burr in AHR 15:845-47, 1909-10, and 19:143-45, 1913-14. " Industrious compilation " ... " Avid of miracle."

Missions

Lesourd, Paul. Histoire des missions catholiques. Libraire de l'Arc, 1937. 491 p. 154
Participation of the orders in 16th century missions is given in an excellent survey on p. 62-70. Main division according to continents. Many illustrations.

History of Piety
(Nos. 155-157)

Autin, Albert. L'échec de la réforme en France au XVIe siècle; contribution à l'histoire du sentiment religieux. Colin, 1918. 286 p. 155
Drawing heavily on literature, author tries to prove that French spirit of measure was incompatible with puritanistic exaggerations of secular austerity.
Review : M. Viller in RHE 18:140-44, 1922. " Une synthèse psychologique et dans les grandes lignes suffisamment exacte."

Brémond, Henri. Histoire littéraire du sentiment religieux en France depuis la fin des guerres de religion à nos jours. Bloud et Gay, 1914-33, 11 v.; v. I-III (1916-33). 156
First volumes mainly concerned with Richeome, St. Francis of Sales and movement called " humanisme dévot."
Review : H. Hatzfeld in JLW 14:523-43, 1934.

Hyma, Albert. The Christian renaissance : a history of the " Devotio moderna." Grand Rapids, Mich., The Reformed Press, 1924; 2nd ed. New York, Century, 1925. 501 p. 157
Scholarly and original attempt at explaining Dutch spirituality from Ruysbroeck to Gerard Groote and Erasmus, centering around Brethren of the Common Life (1380-1520), as a stepping stone to the reformation. A particular chapter on *The Christian renaissance in France* and a worthwhile bibliography p. 477-94.
Review : E. W. Miller in AHR 30:346-48, 1924-25.

General Trends Towards a Reformation
(Nos. 158-159)

Hauser, Henri, et Augustin Renaudet. Les débuts de l'âge moderne. La renaissance et la réforme. Alcan, 1938. 651 p. (PEC, v. 8). 158
Respectable presentation.

Pourrat, Pierre. La spiritualité chrétienne. Gabalda, 1927-31. 4 v. V. III : Les temps modernes. Première partie. De la renaissance au jansénisme, 1927. 617 p. 159
A first attempt at an ecclesiastical history which is concerned with prayer, asceticism and mysticism of the spiritual giants and saints rather than with organizational and institutional problems of the Church. Here is condensed what in Brémond's work is lavishly expanded and illustrated.
Reviews : L. Christiani in RHEF 11:537-43, 1925; J. de Guibert in RAM 6:412-17, 1925.

Reformation
(Nos. 160-162)

Hearnshaw, Fossey John Cobb. The social and political ideas of some great thinkers of the renaissance and the reformation. New York, Barnes and Noble, 1925. 215 p. 2nd ed. 1949. 160
Excellence illustrated by contributions from first class British scholars : I. Introductory. The renaissance and the reformation by the editor, 9-31; I : Nicholas of Cusa by E. J. Jacob, 32-60; III : Sir John Fortescue by Miss A. E. Levett, 61-86; IV : Niccolò Machiavelli by the editor, 87-122; V : Sir Thomas More by A. W. Reed, 123-148; VI : Desiderius Erasmus by J. A. K. Thomson, 149-70; VII : Martin Luther by J. W. Allen, 171-92; VIII : John Calvin by Rev. W. R. Matthews, 193-215.
Review : J. Dickinson in APSR 21:164-68, 1927. " Fresh and suggestive interpretation."

Lucas, Henry Stephen. The renaissance and the reformation. New York, Harper, 1934. 765 p. 161
Contains : Book I : The renaissance, 3-416; book II : The reformation, 417-747. Stresses the *Devotio moderna* based on the *Imitatio Christi* as a high lay spirituality, entrenched in Northern Humanism, defending as its classics : St. Jerome, St. Ambrose, St. Chrysostome, St. Au-

gustine. It is the fundamental attitude of the biblical humanists represented first by Wessel Gansfort, 1489, so called by J. Lindeboom, *Het Bijbelsch Humanisme in Nederland*, Leiden, 1913.

Renaudet, Augustin. Préréforme et humanisme à Paris pendant les premières guerres d'Italie (1494-1517). See 135, 197. 162
Excellent study of conditions in Paris, Meaux and elsewhere short of the reformation which stirred Lefèvre d'Étaples, Briçonnet, and other early humanists to scriptural studies versus theological speculations. Rich bibliography p. XI-XLVIII. *See* 158.
Review : C. Pfister in Rhist 123:-336-42, Sept.-Dec., 1916.

Luther
(Nos. 163-164)

Febvre, Lucien Paul Victor. Un destin; Martin Luther. Rieder, 1928. 314 p. 163
Popular but scholarly introduction to German reformer by famous French literary historian saw different translations into English, among which that by Roberts Tapley. New York, Dutton, 1929. 329 p. Febvre's point is understanding of Luther's " tragedy " as a personal plight and its catastrophic impact on concepts and policy of the German state. Original, but typically French viewpoint.
Review : A. Renaudet in Rhist 159:372-75, Sept.-Dec., 1928.

Moore, Will Grayburn. La réforme allemande et la littérature française; recherches sur la notoriété de Luther en France. Strasbourg, La Faculté des lettres à l'Université, 1930. 512 p. (PFS, facs. 52) (Diss., Strasbourg). 164
Based on rather unknown texts, tries to trace all possible influences of Luther on 16th century French literature. First gives a survey of Luther himself as a literary figure and of Frenchmen who, living in Germany, knew his writings, namely François Lambert and Guillaume Dumolin. Lists French translation of Luther's works at different epochs (before 1523; after 1550). Tries to show that practically all the *humanistes chrétiens* are somewhat under his influence (?). Very precious bibliography of 586 items. *See* 772, 1931.
Reviews : A. Renaudet in Rhist 165:359-61, Nov.-Dec., 1930; W. S. in CHR 17:249, 1931-32.

Reformation in Europe
(Nos. 165-168)

Gagnebin, Ferdinand Henri. Études historiques sur la réformation au seizième siècle en Allemagne, en Suisse et en France. Second ed. Lausanne, La Concorde, 1936. 203 p. 165
Readable short history of the reformation in Central and Western Europe from a strictly orthodox Protestant viewpoint.

Lindsay, Thomas Martin. A history of the reformation. New York, Scribner, 1906-07, 2 v. 166
Only second volume deals with France, from a fair but definitely Protestant viewpoint as far as doctrine and policy are concerned. Religious trends not interwoven with general intellectual trends of century.
Review : W. W. Rockwell in AHR 12:874-76, 1906-07. " Interpretation has its barriers."

Herzog, Johann Jakob, ed. Realencyklopädie für protestantische Theologie und Kirche. Ed. by Johann J. Herzog, Gustave L. Plitt and Albert Hauck. 3rd rev. ed., Leipzig, Hinricks, 1896-1913, 24 v. 167
Rich information on all aspects of Reformation. Objective insofar as reformation is exclusively in hands of Protestant scholars, but Catholics were requested to contribute to Counter-reformation problems.

Smith, Preserved. The age of the reformation. New York, Holt, 1920. 861 p. 168
Scholarly and stylistically appealing presentation with rich bibliography, currents, undercurrents, and individual reformers.
Review : E. M. Hulme in AHR 26:765-67, 1920-21.

Reformation in France
(Nos. 169-174)

Baudrillart, Alfred. The Catholic church, the renaissance and Protestantism. London, Paul, 1908. 331 p. 169
Translation by Mrs. Philip Gibbs of a series of lectures on influence of the renaissance, on Catholicism and Protestantism, from French original, L'église catholique, la renaissance, le protestantisme (1904).
Review : F. R. in DR 144:428-29, 1909 : "... lack of restraint...."

Charbonnel, Mme Josephe (Chartrou). La réforme et les guerres de religion. Colin, 1936. 222 p. 170
Condensed explanation of the situation with a short, good bibliography and a chapter on interrelations between reformation and literature (p. 202-14).
Review : A. Fliche in RHE 33:904-05, 1937 : " Tout en ne cachant pas sa sympathie pour les réformateurs, Madame Chartrou a su conserver une objectivité et une impartialité de bon aloi."

Imbart de La Tour, Pierre. Les origines de la réforme. 4 v. Tome I : La France moderne (1905); tome II : L'église catholique, La crise et la renaissance (1909); tome III : L'évangélisme, 1521-1538 (1914); tome IV : Calvin et L'institution chrétienne (1935). Hachette, 1905-35; second editions with recent bibliography : Melun, D'Argences, 1944 (v. II) and 1948 (v. I). 171
Attraction here is in the detailed description of the first serious struggle between principles of a theocratic and those of a national concept of the state, as well as in the analysis of the tension between an intellectual-scholastic and a lively, humanistic concept of religion. The way to the compromise solution to be expected, which only France found at end of 16th century made visible from outset, when Leo X favored Christian humanists, while radicals, led by Luther, were incapable of understanding political problem involved : " L'ère des réformes pacifiques est close; celle des révolutions va s'ouvrir." The new edition of v. I was made by Jean de Pins, that of v. II by Mlle. Yvonne Lanhers.
Reviews : M. François in BEC 105:281-82, 1944 (v. II); H. Hauser in Rhist 90:354, 1906 (v. I) and 103:317, 1910 (v. II); L. Hogu in RHEF 5:519-25, 1914 (v. III); R. N. C. Hunt in EHR 51:332-35, 1936 (v. IV); A. Lang in TSK 107:148-63, 1936 (v. IV); also P. Richard in RHE 6:852-57, 1905 (v. I): " Pas familiarisé avec les Archives du Vatican " and 12:548-53, 1911 (v. II): " Puissante structure et rigoureux enchaînement."

Kelly, Caleb Guyer. French Protestantism, 1559-1562. Baltimore, 1918. 186 p. (Diss., Johns Hopkins.) 172
Stresses sociological shift from peasants to nobility in tendency to embrace Protestantism after 1555.

Nürnberger, R. Die Politisierung des französischen Protestantismus. Calvin und

die Anfänge des protestantischen Radikalismus. Tübingen, Mohr, 1948. 146 p. 173

Interpretations based on Protestant
material exclusively, not on new sources,
drive at the persuasion that the French
structure of State was bound to produce
an activistic Protestant party which falsified Calvin's original concept of relations
between Church and State. See 1933.

Review : O. Vasella in Eras 3:776-78,
1950 : "Manche Darstellungen hinter-
lassen einen zwiespältigen Eindruck."

Viénot, John. Histoire de la réforme française des origines à l'édit de Nantes. Fischbacher, 1926-34. 2 v. 174

Popular, but reliable, particularly for
period after 1538 as still contained in v. I.
Protestant viewpoint.

Review : J. Dagens in RHE 24:918-20,
1928 : " Cette histoire est aussi un plai-
doyer."

Counter-reformation
(Nos. 176-186)

General Trends

Dictionnaire de théologie catholique,
contenant l'exposé des doctrines de la
théologie catholique, leurs preuves et
leur histoire. Ed. A. Vacant, E. Mangenot,
E. Amann et al. Tomes I-XV. Letouzet,
1899 ff.; troisième tirage 1930-1950. 176

First-class encyclopedia of religious subjects; Counter-reformation and modern
times are stressed; highly scholarly and
reliable, some articles outstanding, e.g.
one on Jesuits, V. VIII, 1012-1108 by
Pierre Bouvrier, S.J.

Reviews : in ET 15:361-62, 1903-04 :
"first hand acquaintance." For references
to the detailed reviews of almost all the
fascicles made at the moment of their
appearance see RHE, Tables générales I
(1928), 49; and II (1946), 58.

Jourdan, George Vivillers. Movement
towards Catholic reform in the early 16th
century. London, Murray, 1914. 367 p. 177

Deals with reform attempts before and
opposed to Luther by men like Lefèvre
d'Étaples, Érasmus, St.Thomas More, etc.

Maurenbrecher, Wilhelm. Geschichte der
katholischen Reformation. V. I. Nörd-
lingen, Beck, 1880. 417 p. 178

Scholarly presentation from the Catholic
viewpoint.

Review: H. Baumgarten in HZ ns 10:154,
1881.

Philippson, Martin. Les origines du catho-
licisme moderne; la contre-révolution religieuse au XVIᵉ siècle. Brussels, Merzbach,
1884. 618 p. 179

An impartial survey of Catholic reformation.

Review : P. Frédericq in Rhist 34:316,
May-Aug., 1887.

Schnurer, Gustav. Katholische Kirche
und Kultur in der Barockzeit. Paderborn,
Schöningh, 1937. 804 p. 180

Modern approach at embodying counter-
reformation with Baroque culture. Broad
and interesting bibliography, p. 767-90.

Review : E. de Moreau in RHE 35:334-
39, Apr., 1939.

Council of Trent

Dejob, Charles. De l'influence du Concile
de Trente sur la littérature et les beaux
arts chez les peuples catholiques. Thorin,
1884. 413 p. 181

Deals with first direct and articulate
interference of the Church with secular
literary activities of members; excellent
guide for understanding literature of late
16th century.

Denzinger, Heinrich Joseph Dominik.
Enchiridion symbolorum, definitionum et
declarationum de rebus fidei et morum quod
a Clemente Bannwart denuo compositum
iteratis curis edidit Johannes Bapt. Umberg,
S.J. Editio 21-23. Freiburg, Herder, 1937.
695 p. 182

Contains in abridgment, but well sufficient for literary student, decrees of Fifth
Lateran Council (1512-17) and Council of
Trent (1545-63) as well as all important
pronouncements of popes of 16th century.

Review : R. M. Huber in CH 10:5-6,
1941 : " No ... student could afford to be
without this handy manual."

Jedin, Hubert. Geschichte des Konzils von
Trient. I : Der Kampf um das Konzil.
Freiburg, Herder, 1949. 644 p. 183

Planned in 4 volumes, this will become
the long expected critical history of the
Council which decided the face of counter-
reformatory Catholicism. Nothing done
of this kind in the last 300 years, since
works of Sarpi and Pallavicino.

Review : R. Draguet in RHE 45:790-93,
1950.

— Das Konzil von Trient; ein Überlick über die Erforschung seiner Geschichte. Rome, Edizioni di "Storia e letteratura," 1948. 225 p. 184

Survey by one of most competent scholars in matters Tridentine.

Censorship

Gotwald, William Kurtz. Ecclesiastical censure at the end of the fifteenth century. Baltimore, Johns Hopkins Press, 1927. 87 p. (Diss., Johns Hopkins). 185

Matter of fact survey of first appearances of *Indices librorum prohibitorum. See* 140.

Review : E. Jourdan in Rhist 162:132, 1929 : " Il s'agit seulement de censures promulguées par le Saint Siège."

Putnam, George Haven. The censorship of the church of Rome and its influence upon the production and the distribution of literature. New York, Putnam, 1906-1907. 2 v. 186

Important; v. I, is a kind of combination of Dejob and Reusch with considerations on censorship in general, Protestant and secular, in historical perspective.

Review : D. M. McIntyre in RTP 3:225-29, 1907-08 : " full story of the Ecclesiastical Censorship based on Reusch."

Philosophy
(Nos. 187-311)

PAUL O. KRISTELLER

NOTE : I wish to thank Prof. Alma LeDuc, who did some preliminary work for this section, and made her material available to me when I took it over. Some entries, contributed entirely by her, are marked with her initials (A.L.).

General Studies

Baillou, Jean. L'influence de la pensée philosophique de la renaissance italienne sur la pensée française : état présent des travaux relatifs au XVIᵉ siècle. REI 1:116-53, 1936. 187

Comprehensive survey article with numerous references. *See* 2663.

Busson, Henri. Les sources et le développement du rationalisme dans la littérature française de la renaissance. (1533-1601). Letouzet & Ané, 1922. XVII, 685 p. (Thèse principale présentée, pour le Doctorat ès lettres, à la Faculté des lettres de l'Université de Paris). (BSHE) 188

By rationalism author means application of rational methods to religious subjects. After discussing some ancient and Italian sources, and their transmission to France, he describes rationalistic elements in a great number of French philosophers, theologians, and poets of 16th century, examining in particular their attitude toward such basic religious problems as providence, immortality, miracles, and divinity of Christ. Concludes that the *Libertin* movement of 17th century is a direct continuation of 16th century rationalism. Classifications, judgments, and statements on sources and influences often too vague, and the label " rationalism " is too readily applied. Invaluable source of information not otherwise available, based on practically all previous scholarly studies on the subject as well as on a first-hand study of text materials. Careful bibliography, quotations, and summaries. Another work by same author *(La pensée religieuse française de Charron à Pascal, see* 1835) deals primarily with 17th century; also contains valuable information for influence of 16th century thought in 17th century; this work, much more mature and cautious, helps to correct the first volume. *See* 1552, 2051, 2666.

Reviews : J. Charbonnel in RSS 11:289-301, 1924; A. Renaudet in RHL 31:536-46, 1924; J. S. Will in RR 17:157-59, 1926.

Capitolo, Guido. La filosofia stoica nel secolo XVI in Francia. Naples, Perrella, 1931. 63 p. (BFAA). 189

Superficial sketch of 16th century Stoicism, with a more detailed treatment of Montaigne, Lipsius, and Charron.

Carriere, Moriz. Die philosophische Weltanschauung der Reformationszeit in ihren Beziehungen zur Gegenwart. 2nd ed. Leipzig, Brockhaus, 1887. 2 pts., 419 and 319 p. 190

Comprehensive though antiquated account of renaissance thought : Ramus, Lipsius, Montaigne, Charron, Sanchez, Bodin.

Cassirer, Ernst. Das Erkenntnisproblem in der Philosophie und Wissenschaft der neueren Zeit. Berlin, Bruno Cassirer, 1906, v. 1, 608 p. 191

Thorough, well-documented history of early modern epistemology. Covers Bovillus, Ramus, Montaigne, Charron, Sanchez, and La Mothe le Vayer.

Reviews : A. Buchenau in KS 14:278-82, 1909; W. Kinkel in DLit 27:1169-75, 1906; 32:965-74, 1911.

— Individuum und Kosmos in der Philosophie der Renaissance. Leipzig-Berlin, Teubner, 1927. 458 p. (SBW, 10)   192

Extensive discussion of philosophy of Bovillus (p. 93 ff.) and in appendix (p. 299-412) a critical edition of his *Liber de sapiente*, prepared by Raymond Klibanski. Reviews : H. Levy in Logos 17:367-74, 1928; D. Mahnke in KS 35:316-17, 1930; F. Medicus in DLit 49:2047-52, 1928; I. Pusino in ZKG 47:117-19, 1928; A. Renaudet in Rhist 160:136-38, 1929.

Charbonnel, J. Roger. La pensée italienne au XVIe siècle et le courant libertin. Champion, 1917. 720 p. (Thèse principale pour le Doctorat ès lettres).   193

Four chapters deal with thought of various Italian thinkers, whereas ch. 1 and 6 illustrate their influence in France and other countries up to 18th century. Only a small part concerns French authors of 16th century, such as Gentillet, Henri Estienne, Noël du Fail, De Thou, Bodin, and others. Interesting for fortune of the Italian thinkers, especially in 17th and 18th centuries. Bibliography and quotations most careless. Style and arrangement confused and confusing. The very concept of " libertins " as used by author lacks clarity. Treats as a unit a number of divers authors and ideas that have nothing in common except their supposed or real opposition to Christian orthodoxy, and is too much inclined to take at face value all charges of atheism and the like launched by controversial writers of the time. Quotes liberally from previous scholarly studies, not always giving full credit to sources of information. Should be used with greatest caution. *See* 2667. Review : H. Busson in RSS 6:122-27, 1919.

Fremy, Edouard. L'Académie des derniers Valois. Académie de poésie et de musique. 1570-1576. Académie du Palais. 1576-1585. Leroux, 1887. 399 p.   194

Good material on *académies* of Baïf and Pibrac, which Fremy agrees with Sainte-Beuve in considering forerunners of *Académie française* (p. 390).

Contains unedited discours by members of *Académie du Palais* which show its philosophical trend : informative, but a certain amount of intellectual bias must be taken into account, as well as a not too

closely knit critical method of approach. Review : J. Madeleine in Nrev 53:577-88, 1888.

(A.L.)

Kristeller, Paul Oskar. Marsilio Ficino e Lodovico Lazzarelli : contributo alla diffusione delle idee ermetiche nel rinascimento. ASNP ser 2, 7:237-62.   195

Discusses role of Le Fèvre d'Étaples and of Symphorien Champier as editors and commentators of Hermetic writings translated by Ficino and Lazzarelli.

Owen, John. The skeptics of the French renaissance. London, Swan Sonnenschein, 1893. p. 421-830.   196

Continuation of similar work on Italian sceptics; discusses Montaigne, Ramus, Charron, Sanchez, La Mothe le Vayer, and Pascal. Popular treatment in the form of a dialogue. *See* 1696.

Renaudet, A. Préréforme et humanisme à Paris pendant les premières guerres d'Italie (1494-1517). *See* 135.   197

Rich, scholarly, and important work contains much information on Lefèvre, Clichtove, Bovillus, Champier and their contemporaries as well as bibliographies of their writings. Well indexed. *See* 162. Reviews : P. S. Allen in EHR 33:112-13, 1918; E. Milano in RSI 34:326-29, 1917; C. Pfister in Rhist 123:336-43, 1916; R. in Rcr 51 (ns 84):308-12, 1917.

Zanta, Léontine. La renaissance du stoïcisme au XVIe siècle. Champion, 1914. 367 p.   198

Broad treatment of influence of Stoic ideas in 16th century France, with some consideration of ancient and contemporary Italian and German sources, and of more or less successful efforts to harmonize Stoic and Christian ideas. Second part is more detailed study of life and works of Justus Lipsius and of Guillaume Du Vair. Suffers from vagueness of certain conceptions, but remains indispensable for its subject. *See* 2283. Review : J. Plattard in RSS 6:131-33, 1919.

Charles de Bouelles

(Nos. 199-203)

Bouelles, Charles de (Carolus Bovillus). Il sapiente. Ed. Eugenio Garin. Turin, Einaudi, 1943. 189 p.   199

Italian version of B.'s *Liber de sapiente*, based on both the early edition and on modern text of Klibansky. Short introduction discusses influence of Florentine platonists in France.

Brause, Karl Hermann. Die Geschichtsphilosophie des Carolus Bovillus. Borna-Leipzig, Noske, 1916. 89 p. (Diss., Erlangen). 200

Discusses B.'s views on history as contained in his *Aetatum mundi supputatio* and *Quaestionum theologicarum libri septem*.

Dippel, Joseph. Versuch einer systematischen Darstellung der Philosophie des Carolus Bovillus nebst einem kurzen Lebensabrisse. Ein Beitrag zur Geschichte der Philosophie des 16. Jahrhunderts. Würzburg, Thein, 1865. 256 p. 201

Biography based on older secondary works; book contains only extant comprehensive analysis of B.'s philosophical thought, based on all his printed works; analysis clear and detailed, though somewhat pedestrian.

Groethuysen, Bernhard. Die kosmische Anthropologie des Bovillus. Aph 40:66-89, 1931. 202

Analyzes B.'s conception of man against the background of the Italian Platonists and Aristotelians of the renaissance. *See also* the author's *Anhang : Der mystische Mensch in Frankreich : in :Handbuch der Philosophie*, Munich and Berlin, 1931. 3, p. 145-49.

Michel, Paul-Henri. Un humaniste Picard: Charles de Bouelles. REI 1:176-86, 1936. 203

Sketchy survey of life and influence of B. Not documented.

Symphorien Champier
(Nos. 204-207)

Champier, Symphorien. Le myrouel des apothicuaires et pharmacopoles. (Le miroir des apothicaires.) New ed. by P. Dorveaux. Preface by Gustave Planchon. Welter, 1895. 56 p. *See* 431. 204

Text accompanied by biographical and historical introduction, footnotes and an index.

Review : C. J. in Rcr 32 (ns 46):207-09, 1898.

Allut, P. Étude biographique et bibliographique sur Symphorien Champier. Lyon, Scheuring, 1859. 431 p. *See* 461. 205

Detailed and documented biography of C.; accurate description of his printed works; reprints of : *L'ordre de chevalerie*; *Petit dialogue de noblesse*; *L'antiquité origine et noblesse de Lyon*; *L'antiquité de Vienne*.

Ballard, J. F., and M. Pijoan. A preliminary check-list of the writings of Symphorien Champier, 1472-1539. PMLA 28: 182-88, 1939-40. 206

Lists 99 editions of C.'s works, arranged alphabetically by titles. Corrects older bibliography by Allut. No library locations given.

Moench, Walter. Die italienische Platonrenaissance und ihre Bedeutung für Frankreichs Literatur-und Geistesgeschichte. Berlin, Ebeling, 1936. 399 p. (RSE, 40). 207

Contains a long chapter on Platonic writings of C. (p. 212-300). *See* 743.

Reviews : A. Buck in Gno 13:622-24, 1937; P.O. Kristeller in GCFI 18:205-07, 1937.

Josse Clichtove
(Nos. 208-213)

Clichtove, Josse. De bello et pace opusculum, christianos principes ad sedandos bellorum tumultus et pacem componendam exhortans. Ed. by Marqués de Olivart. Madrid, Revista de derecho internacional y política exterior, 1914. 51 fols. 208

Facsimile reproduction of original edition published by Simon Colinaeus, 1523, 149 p.

Chérot, H. La société au commencement du XVIe siècle d'après les homélies de Josse Clichtove (1472-1543). RQH ns 13:533-44, 1895. 209

Surveys information concerning people, students, and clergy of the time as contained in the sermons of C. (1534).

Clerval, J. A. De Judoci Clichtovei Neoportuensis doctoris theologi Parisiensis et Carnotensis Canonici vita et operibus (1472-1543). Picard, 1894. 151 p. (Diss., Paris). 210

Only available monograph on this author. Detailed, accurate account of his life, works, and learned activities, amply documented from printed and manuscript sources. Position and development of this neglected but influential author treated in a most judicious and impartial manner. Introduction contains full and valuable bibliography of C.'s works,

including several unpublished manuscripts.
Review : L. D. in BEC 56:371-72, 1895.

Christiani, L. Josse Clichtove et son Antilutherus (1524). RQH 89 (ns 45):120-34, 1911. 211
Analyzes main points and arguments contained in C.'s treatise against Luther.

Haeghen, Ferdinand van der. Bibliotheca belgica. Ser. 1, v. 4, Ghent, 1880-90.
212
Pages not numbered, arrangement alphabetical. Contains detailed and accurate bibliography of works of C., with a short but documented biography. One addendum found in ser. 2, v. 3, Ghent, 1891-1923.

Salembier, A. Josse Clichtove, Docteur en Sorbonne, Curé de Wazemmes en 1519. RLille 27 (ser. 3, v. 3):419-31, 1908-09. 213
Documented account of an episode in C.'s life, with a general emphasis on antiLutheran controversies of his later years.

Robert Gaguin
(Nos. 214-217)

Gaguin, Robert. Epistolae et orationes. Ed. Louis Thuasne. Bouillon, 1903 (on cover 1904). 2 v. (BLR, 2-3). 214
Excellent critical edition of G.'s letters with a detailed biography, rich historical notes, appendix of other texts and documents, and adequate index.
Review : F. Flamini in AIV 64 (ser. 8, v. 7²):1-12, 1904-05.

Simone, Franco. Robert Gaguin ed il suo cenacolo umanistico, I:1473-1485. Aevum 13:410-76, 1939. 215
Rich and documented study of G.'s humanistic activities and relations, with special emphasis on his connections with Italy. Continuation apparently was never published.

Thuasne, Louis. Le Curial d'Alain Chartier et la traduction de Robert Gaguin : note sur un manuscrit nouvellement acquis par la Bibliothèque nationale. RDB 11:13-19, 1901. 216
Shows, on the basis of manuscripts, that Latin version of Alain Chartier's *Curial*, previously attributed to Ambroise de Cambray, was actually a work of G. plagiarized by Ambroise. Prefaces of both versions published at end of article.

Vaissière, Pierre de. De Roberti Gaguini ministri generalis ordinis sanctae trinitatis vita et operibus, 1425-1501. Chartres, Durand, 1896. 102 p. (Diss., Paris). 217
Detailed and documented study of G.'s life and works.
Review : Y. in BEC 57:443-44, 1896.

Amadis Jamyn
(No. 218)

Graur, Theodosia. Un disciple de Ronsard, Amadis Jamyn, 1540 (?)-1593; sa vie, son œuvre, son temps. Champion, 1929. 350 p. 218
Generally accepted standard life of J., well-documented, scholarly, precise. Not useful for study of the *Discours philosophique*, to which it contributes only a few lines. A number of references to philosophical aspects of his poems, and chapter on connection of the poet with *Académie du Palais* fairly detailed. *See* 1372, 2543.
Review : Françoise de Borch in RSS 17:171-73, 1930.
(A.L.)

Pierre de La Primaudaye
(Nos. 219-222)

Anderson, Ruth Leila. Elizabethan psychology and Shakespeare's plays. Iowa City, The University, 1927. 182 p. (UIHS, v. 3, no. 4). 219
" John Davies' 'complete system of psychology ' is derived from the *Academy* of La Primaudaye (p. 230)," writes R. L. Anderson. Convincing but a little scant as to detail.
References : R. L. Anderson, *A French source for John Davies of Hereford's system of psychology.* PQ 6:57-66, 1927; D. T. Starnes, *The French Academie and the Wits commonwealth. See* 222. R. W. Battenhouse, *Marlowe's Tamburlaine, a study in renaissance moral philosophy. See* 221.
(A.L.)

Ballu, C. Curiosités poétiques du xvɪᵉ siècle : Pierre de La Primaudaye. Rren 7:110-14, 1906. 220
Two pages of notes on L. family, and on Pierre's *Quatrains* followed by three pages of *Quatrains* (Latin) with their French translation by Nicolas Viret. Slender contribution, with certain factual interest.
(A.L.)

Battenhouse, Roy W. Marlowe's Tamburlaine; a study in renaissance moral philosophy. Nashville, Vanderbilt University Press, 1941. 266 p.   221

Accepts familiar opinion that L.'s comment on Tamburlaine, in chapter on Pride, in his French academy, translated into English in 1586, by T. B., is one of Marlowe's sources for that play (p. 13). Contribution not detailed, but shows extent to which L.'s work was read in England.

Starnes, D. T. The French academie and Wits commonwealth. PQ 13:211-14, 1934.   222

Short parallel passages reveal " the close dependence of the compiler of *Wits commonwealth* upon the French *Academie* for many of his definitions " (p. 212).

Pierre de La Ramée (Ramus)
(Nos. 224-260)

NOTE: In the interest of uniformity of bibliographical procedure, this author is listed alphabetically under the name by which he is carried in the LC catalogue, " La Ramée." However, since he is commonly spoken of by scholars as " Ramus," he will be referred to in the annotations in this section as " R."

La Ramée, Pierre de. Basilea : eine Rede an die Stadt Basel aus dem Jahre 1570, ed. Hans Fleig. Bâle, Basilisk-Verlag, 1944. p. 1-23, fol. 24-57, p. 58-77.   224

Edition of Latin text of R.'s oration, with German version on opposite pages. Edition accompanied by biographical introduction, historical notes, and indices.

Barroux, Robert. Pierre de La Ramée et son influence philosophique; essai sur l'histoire de l'idée de la méthode à l'époque de la renaissance. École nationale des chartes, positions des thèses. 1922. p. 12-20.   225

Summary of an unpublished thesis in which R. is discussed as center of a methodological and epistemological tradition which begins with Roger Bacon and Petrarch, and leads to Francis Bacon and Descartes.

Bement, Newton S. Petrus Ramus and the beginnings of formal French grammar. RR 19:309-23, 1928. *See* 570.   226

Discusses historical significance of R.'s French grammar, against background of his Latin grammar.

Bernus, A. Pierre Ramus à Bâle. BSHP 39:508-30, 1890.   227

Detailed study of an episode in R.'s life, accompanied by text of his letter to R. Gwalter and Ludwig Lavater, in Latin and French.

Bertrand, J. Jacques Charpentier est-il l'assassin de Ramus? RDM 51 (3rd per. 44):286-322, Mar. 15, 1881.   228

Tries to defend Charpentier against charge made by Waddington that he was responsible for the murder of R.

Birkenmajer, L. A. Nikolaj Kopernik. Cracow, Spolka Wydawniczej Polskiej, 1900. 711 p.   229

Fundamental monograph on Copernicus contains text of R.'s correspondence with Rheticus (p. 603-06).

Cantor, Moritz. Petrus Ramus, Michael Stifel, Hieronymus Cardanus, drei mathematische Charakterbilder aus dem 16. Jahrhundert. ZMP 2:353-76, 1857.   230

Discusses life of R. and especially content and significance of his mathematical works. (p. 354-62).

— Ramus in Heidelberg. ZMP 3:133-43, 1858.   231

Detailed account of R.'s stay in Heidelberg, based on unpublished and other university records.

Carrière, Victor. Pierre de La Ramée et la principalité du Collège de Presles. RHEF 26:238-42, 1940.   232

Unfriendly note which documents some details of R.'s life between 1563 and 1570.

Chagnard, Benjamin. Ramus et ses opinions religieuses. Strasbourg, Heitz, 1869. 36 p. (Diss., Strasbourg).   233

Short analysis of *Commentariorum de religione christiana libri quattuor*, with biographical introduction.

Coring, Gustav. Das Gymnasium zu Dortmund und die Pädagogik des Petrus Ramus. Emsdetten, Lechte, 1933. 53 p. (Diss., Cologne).   234

Discusses educational program of R. and its influence on the college of Dortmund during 16th and 17th centuries. Useful bibliography.

Craig, Hardin. A contribution to the theory of the English renaissance. PQ 7:321-33, 1928.   235

Mentions the influence of R.'s logic in England, among other facts.

Delcourt, Marie. Une lettre de Ramus à Joachim Rheticus (1563). BAGB 44:3-15, 1934. 236

Critical text, with French version, of R.'s famous letter concerning principles of astronomy.

Desmaze, Charles. XVIᵉ siècle: P. Ramus professeur au Collège de France, sa vie, ses écrits, sa mort (1515-1572). Cherbuliez, 1864. 137 p. 237

Biography of R., accompanied by a few texts and documents, such as the letter to Rheticus. Revised from the BSAL, 1853.

Duhamel, Pierre Albert. The logic and rhetoric of Peter Ramus. MP 46:163-71, 1948-49. 238

Shows that R. was a conservative reviser and adapter of Aristotelian logic and rhetoric and that his contribution lay in simplification and popularization rather than in the theory of logic. Well documented.

Freudenthal, J. Beiträge zur Geschichte der englischen Philosophie. Aph 4:450-77, 1891; 5:1-41, 1892. 239

Discusses in great detail controversy between Everard Digby and Sir William Temple, which resulted from introduction of Ramism into Cambridge by latter author.

Funke, Otto, ed. Grammatica anglicana von P. Gr. (1594). Vienna and Leipzig, Braumueller, 1938. 39 p. (WBEP, 60). 240

Introduction deals with R.'s grammatical theories, and with his influence in England.

Review : B. von Lindheim in Beibl 49:331-34, 1938.

Gmelin, Hermann. Das Prinzip der Imitatio in den romanischen Literaturen der Renaissance. RFor 46:83-360, 1932. 241

Has a section on R., his ideal of eclectic imitation, and his controversies (p. 337-43).

Graves, Frank Pierrepont. Peter Ramus and the educational reformation of the sixteenth century. New York, Macmillan, 1912. 227 p. (Diss., Columbia). 242

Broad account of background, life, and educational program of R. Most detailed study of R. in English; bibliography, index.

Reviews : F. E. Farrington in ER 46:193-94, 1913; P. Van Dyke in AHR 18:581-82, 1912-13.

Grunwald, M. Miscellen. Aph 9:310-36, 1896. 243

Publishes a letter (p. 335) to R. from C. J. Curio.

Guggenheim, M. Beiträge zur Biographie des Petrus Ramus. ZPPK 121:140-53, 1903. 244

Discusses R.'s relations to Sturm, Beza, and Zurich reformers.

Johnson, Francis R., and Sanford V. Larkey. Robert Recorde's mathematical teaching and the anti-Aristotelian movement. HLB 7:59-87, 1935. 245

Emphasizes parallelism between Recorde and R., without assuming a direct influence of one upon the other.

Lenient, C. F. De Ciceroniano bello apud recentiores. Joubert, 1855. 74 p. 246

Discusses R.'s attitude toward Cicero (p. 50 ff.).

Lobstein, Paul. Petrus Ramus als Theologe; ein Beitrag zur Geschichte der protestantischen Theologie. Strasbourg, Schmidt, 1878. 88 p. 247

Clear and detailed analysis of R.'s theological views, as expressed in his *De religione christiana*, against the background of his philosophy.

Maurat-Ballange, Albert. Ramus et Dorat. BSAHL 63:5-27, 1913. Reprinted : Limoges, Ducourtieux & Gout, 1913, 26 p. 248

Discusses relations between R. and his enemies, Charpentier and Dorat.

Miller, Perry. The New England mind; the seventeenth century. New York, Macmillan, 1939. 528 p. 249

Emphasizes influence of Ramism on logical and rhetorical theories and practices of Puritan theologians in 17th century America. Appendix (p. 493-501) on *The literature of Ramus' logic in Europe*.

Reviews : G. L. Abernethy in Ethics 51:109-11, 1940-41; C. Bridenbaugh in AHR 45:887-89, 1939-40; H. A. Larrabee in JP 37:79-80, 1940; W. W. Sweet in JR 20:290-92, 1940.

Nelson, Norman E. Peter Ramus and the confusion of logic, rhetoric, and poetry. Ann Arbor, University of Michigan Press, 1947. 22 p. (MCMP, 2). 250

Lively and provocative attack against R. and against importance attributed to his logic by recent literary historians. Although the point that R. confused logic and rhetoric as traditionally understood is well taken and nobody will take R.'s attacks on Aristotle at their face value, author treats R. too much as a scapegoat for certain features of contemporary literature which he dislikes, and fails to see him against the background of his own period.

Petersen, Peter. Geschichte der aristotelischen Philosophie im protestantischen Deutschland. Leipzig, Meiner, 1921. 542 p.
251

Discusses also R.'s influence in Germany.

Reviews : A. Schneider in DLit 43:599-601, 1922; E. Spranger in HZ 128:111-14, 1923.

Prantl, Carl von. Über Petrus Ramus. SBA 2:157-69, 1878.
252

Valuable and detailed survey of R.'s logical writings, in the caustic style that characterizes the author's famous history of logic.

Rácz, Lajos. La logique de P. de La Ramée en Hongrie. REHF 2:199-201, 1924.
253

Discusses a case of Ramist influence in Transylvania in 17th century.

Radouant, René. L'union de l'éloquence et de la philosophie au temps de Ramus. RHL 31:161-92, 1924.
254

A substantial study; discusses union of eloquence and philosophy as a widespread slogan of renaissance humanism, which received a more specific meaning in R.'s desire to combine logic and rhetoric.

Rosen, Edward. The Ramus-Rheticus correspondence. JHI 1:363-68, 1940.
255

Interprets a passage in R.'s letter to Rheticus and stresses historical significance of R.'s demand for elimination of hypotheses from astronomy, which should be limited to observations only.

Stern, A. Deux lettres de Ramus à Tremellius. Rcr 16 (ns 13):295-96, 1882.
256

Publishes two letters of R. (1570 and 1571) to Immanuel Tremellius, Professor of Hebrew at Heidelberg.

Tuve, Rosemond. Elizabethan and metaphysical imagery: renaissance poetic and twentieth-century critics. Chicago, University of Chicago Press, (1947). 442 p.
257

Chs. 11-13 discuss in detail influence of Ramist logic upon imagery of English poetry in 16th and 17th centuries. *See also* article by same author, *Imagery and logic: Ramus and metaphysical poetics.* JHI 3:365-400, 1942.

Voigt, Georg. Über den Ramismus an der Universität Leipzig. BSAW 40:31-61, 1888.
258

Documented account of introduction of Ramism at University of Leipzig during second half of 16th century, and of resultant controversies.

Waddington, Charles Tzaunt. De Petri Rami, vita, scriptis, philosophia. By C. Waddington-Kastus. Joubert, 1848. 205 p. (Diss., Paris).
258-A

Largely superseded by same author's later book, (259) though section on R.'s doctrine seems more concise in this thesis.

Review : H. Ritter in GGA 2:1268-71, 1849.

— Ramus (Pierre de La Ramée), sa vie, ses écrits et ses opinions. Meyrueis, 1855. 480 p.
259

Still the fundamental monograph on R. Contains a detailed and documented account of his life, works, and influence. Treatment of his thought less satisfactory.

Reviews : L. Feugère in his : *Les femmes poètes au XVIe siècle.* Didier, 1860, p. 375-91; E. Saisset in RDM 26:50-60, Mar.-Apr., 1856; also in his : *Précurseurs et disciples de Descartes.* Didier, 1862, p. 59-79. Anon in BSHP 4: 167-72, 1856.

Wuerkert, Johannes Georg. Die Encyclopaedie des Petrus Ramus. Ein Reformversuch der Gelehrtenschule des 16. Jahrhunderts. Leipzig-R., Schmidt, 1898. 57 p. (Diss., Leipzig).
260

Discusses in detail and in a systematic arrangement by topics changes in curriculum and in method of teaching, proposed by R. in his various writings.

Loys Charondas Le Caron
(Nos. 261-264)

Carolus-Barré, Louis. Le contrat de mariage de Louis Le Caron dit Charondas avec Marie de Hénault. BHren 7:252-57, 1945.
261

Publishes the document of 1568, with a biographical introduction in which the more important previous studies on L. are referred to.

Digard, Anicet. Études sur les jurisconsultes du seizième siècle : Louis Le Caron, dit Charondas. RHDF 7:177-92, 1861. 262

A documented study of his life and works.

Gohin, Ferdinand. De Lud. Charondae (1534-1613) vita et versibus. Leroux, 1901. 115 p. (Diss., Paris). 263

Life and verse of a minor poet and jurist whose connections with literary movements of the times are evaluated by Gohin. Traces through L.'s intellectual activities important tendencies of 16th century. Indispensable for study of an author for whom there is no *travail d'ensemble.* Useful bibliography.

Pinvert, Lucien. Louis le Caron, dit Charondas (1536-1613). Rren 2:1-9, 69-76, 181-88, 1902. 264

A documented study of his life and works.

Jacques Le Fèvre d'Etaples

(Nos. 265-278)

Barnaud, Jean. Jacques Lefèvre d'Étaples. ETR 11:3-29, 98-129, 135-59, 203-37, 1936. 265

A study of L.'s background, life and intellectual development down to his controversy with Noël Béda. These articles, along with the one published in the BSHP during the same year, were reprinted with added cover and table of contents, but without a title page (Montpellier, 1936; *see* the announcement in the BSHP 86-216, 1937).

— Jacques Lefèvre d'Étaples; son influence sur les origines de la Réformation française. Cahors, Coueslant, 1900. 121 p. 266

Survey of his life and work, with special emphasis on his religious opinions and controversies.

Douen, O. La Bible française avant Lefèvre d'Étaples. BSHP 40:541-52, 1891. 267

Discusses previous versions of the Bible and compares L.'s translation with that of Jean de Rely.

— La Bible française Lefèvre d'Étaples. BSHP 43:318-24, 1894. 268

Discusses the version of the Bible by Jean de Barro.

— La Réforme française est-elle la fille de la Réforme allemande ? BSHP 41:57-92, 1892. 269

Emphasizes Protestant elements in L.'s commentaries on the Gospels and on St. Paul.

Graf, Charles Henri. Essai sur la vie et les écrits de Jacques Lefèvre d'Étaples. Strasbourg, Schuler, 1842. 130 p. (Diss., Strasbourg). 270

Most important older monograph on L. Solid and documented account of his life, works, and theological opinions. Gives little attention to L.'s contributions to philosophy, mathematics, and other fields of secular learning.

— Jacobus Faber Stapulensis; ein Beitrag zur Geschichte der Reformation in Frankreich. ZHT 1852:3-86; 165-237. 271

Detailed and documented monograph on L.'s life and religious views. Chronological list of his works added at the end; not found in earlier French edition of this study.

Imbart de La Tour, Pierre. Lefèvre d'Étaples. Corr 253 (ns 217):240-69, Oct. 25, 1913. 272

Authoritative, undocumented essay; stresses mysticism of L. and transitional character of his religious views.

Kunze, Horst. Die Bibelübersetzungen von Lefèvre d'Étaples und von P. R. Olivétan verglichen in ihrem Wortschatz. (LRS, 11). Leipzig, Romanisches Seminar, and Paris, Droz, 1935. 236 p. Also printed as thesis, Leipzig, Dittert, 1935. 237 p. 273

Linguistic comparison between two French versions of the Bible, made respectively by L. and by Olivétan.

Reviews : G. Gougenheim in BSLP (no. 114) 38:93-94, 1937; E. Lerch in ZRP 57:610-16, 1937; E. Poppe in Archiv 171:96-99, 1937; H. Rheinfelder in LGRP 58:398-400, 1937.

Laune, Alfred. Des secours dont Lefèvre d'Étaples s'est servi pour sa traduction française de l'Ancien testament. BSHP 50 (4th ser.) 10:595-607, 1901. 274

Since L. knew little Hebrew, author investigates various Latin and French versions and interpretations of Old Testament accessible to him, illustrated through parallel passages.

— La traduction de l'Ancien testament de Lefèvre d'Étaples. Le Cateau, Roland, 1895.

48 p. (Diss., Faculté de théologie protestante de Paris.) 275

Describes various editions of L.'s version of Old Testament, compares his translation in detail with preceding Latin and French versions, discussing differences between various editions of L.'s translation. Author concludes that L. for his later editions used Robert Estienne's edition of 1532.

Massebieau, L. Une acquisition de la Bibliothèque du Musée pédagogique. Rpéd ns 6:414:32, 1885. Also printed separately as fascicule 2 in : MMP, nd, 19 p. 276

Describes an edition of L.'s dialogue and introduction to Aristotle's *Physics* and discusses content and significance of these works One of the rare studies dealing with the non-theological part of L.'s writings.

Quiévreux, Paul. La traduction du Nouveau Testament de Lefèvre d'Étaples. Le Cateau, Roland, 1894. 55 p. (Diss., Faculté de théologie protestante de Paris.) 277

Compares L.'s version in its various editions with preceding Latin and French editions of New Testament; concludes it is based on Latin rather than on Greek text.

Spiess, Karl. Der Gottesbegriff des J. Faber Stapulensis : ein Beitrag zum Verständnis der religiösen Eigenart Johann Kalvins. Marburg, Hamel, 1930. 187 p. (Diss., Marburg). 278

Short biography of L., then a more detailed analysis of his religious views, with a comparison between L., Luther, and Calvin; discussion of L.'s influence on Farel, Calvin, and others.

Jean de L'Espine

(No. 279)

Hogu, Louis. Jean de L'Espine, moraliste et théologien (1505?-1597); sa vie, son œuvre, ses idées. Champion, 1913. viii, 184 p. 279

Study of one of lesser ministers of French Reformation whose activities led to a better understanding of background of movement (p. 15). Hogu's contribution has its value, even though curiously uneven.

Review : R. Sturel in RHL 21:445-48, 1914.

Guillaume Postel

(Nos. 280-290)

Postel, Guillaume. Les très-merveilleuses victoires des femmes du Nouveau-monde, suivi de la Doctrine du siècle doré, avec une notice biographique et bibliographique par Gustave Brunet. Turin, Gay, 1869. 115 p. 280

Reprint of edition of Paris of 1553, with a short note on life and writings of P. and on background of this work.

Bainton, Roland H. Wylliam Postell and the Netherlands. NAK ns 24:161-72, 1931. 281

Discusses links between P. and David Joris's circle, on basis of Joris's papers in Basel. Publishes a few letters and excerpts.

Butler, Sir Geoffrey. William Postel, world peace through world power. *In his :* Studies in statecraft, being chapters, biographical and bibliographical, mainly on sixteenth century. Cambridge University Press, 1920. p. 38-64. Bibliography of William Postel, in same work, p. 117-31. 282

Essay on P.'s life and works, with emphasis on his view of international law. Bibliography lists editions of his works found in British libraries. For other such bibliographies, *see also :* E. G. Vogel, *Verzeichnis der Originalausgaben von Wilhelm Postels Schriften auf der Königl. öffentlichen Bibliothek zu Dresden.* Serapeum 14:363-78, 1853. Émile Picot, *Les Français italianisants du XVIe siècle,* 2566, v. 1, p. 313-24.

Desbillons, François Joseph Terrasse, Nouveaux éclaircissements sur la vie et les ouvrages de Guillaume Postel. Liège, Tutot, 1773. 161 p. 283

Most important older biography of P. with a discussion of his works, collection of testimonies, and catalogue of his printed works.

Kvacala, Jan. Postelliana; urkundliche Beiträge zur Geschichte der Mystik im Reformationszeitalter. ACUJ 23 no. 9 pt. 3, 1915. XX, 88 p. 284

Indispensable for critical study of P. Publishes a number of short treatises and letters of P., mostly from manuscript sources. Other letters of P. or addressed to him in the following publications : Jacques George de Chaufepié, NDHC 3:215-36, Amsterdam, 1753. *Correspondance de Christophe Plantin,* ed. M. Rooses,

v. 1, MAB (Uitgave no. 12, Antwerp, 1883), p. 80-89; 154-55; 189-91. *Briefe von Andreas Masius und seinen Freunden 1538 bis 1573*, ed. Max Lossen, PGRG 2, Leipzig 1886, p. 160-65. *Abrahami Ortelii (Geographi Antverpiensis) et virorum eruditorum ad eundem et ad Jacobum Colium Ortelianum (Abrahami Ortelii Sororis filium) Epistulae ELBA*, ed. Joannes Henricus Hessels, Cambridge, 1887, p. 42-49; 186-92. *See also: Corpus Schwenckfeldianorum 13* (Leipzig 1935) 713 ff.; 14 (1936) 981 ff.; 1026 ff. Postel's *Apologia pro Serveto* was published by Johann Lorenz von Mosheim, *Anderweitiger Versuch einer vollständigen und unpartheyischen Ketzergeschichte*, Helmstaedt, 1748, p. 455-99. Excerpts from it had been published previously in Mosheim's *Historia Michaelis Serveti*. Helmstaedt, 1727, p. 141-47. Two letters to Conrad Pellicanus are mentioned by Ludwig Geiger, *Zur Geschichte des Studiums der hebräischen Sprache in Deutschland während des sechzehnten Jahrhunderts*. ZGJD 4:125-26, 1890.

— Wilhelm Postell; seine Geistesart und seine Reformgedanken. ARG 9:285-330, 1911-12 ; 11:200-27, 1914 ; 15:157-203, 1918.   286

Detailed account of P.'s life and religious opinions; with special emphasis on his idea of tolerance. Valuable for extensive and partly new sources. References inaccurate. Analysis of P.'s thought lacks clarity and coherence.

Lefranc, Abel. La détention de Guillaume Postel au prieuré de Saint-Martin-des-Champs (1562-81). ASHF 28:211-30, 1891.   287

Biography of P., with special emphasis on last years. Publishes his will and several other documents.

Sallier, Abbé Claude. Éclaircissements sur l'histoire de Guillaume Postel. MRAI 24:325-38, 1743.   288

Discusses P.'s life, his prophetic writings and a Paris manuscript containing his *Rétractions*.

Schweizer, J. Ein Beitrag zu Wilhelm Postels Leben und zur Geschichte des Trienter Konzils und der Inquisition (1547-48). RQ 24 : Geschichte p. 94-106, 1910.   289

Discusses P.'s relations to Jesuits, Inquisition, and Council of Trent, partly on basis of new material. Publishes two tracts addressed by P. to the Council.

Weill, George. De Guilielmi Postelli vita et indole. Hachette, 1892. 127 p. (Diss., Paris)   290

Detailed and well documented account of P.'s life and learned activities. His religious opinions treated, but shortly and with moderation. Appendix gives several previously unpublished letters and documents. Although supplemented or superseded by work of Kvacala and of other scholars, this monograph still indispensable.

Francisco Sánchez

(Nos. 291-311)

Bullón y Fernández, Eloy. Francisco Sánchez. *In his :* De los orígenes de la filosofía moderna. Los precursores españoles de Bacon y Descartes. Salamanca, Rodríguez, 1905. p. 153-91.   291

Analysis of S.'s thought, preceded by a short biography.

Cazac, H. P. Le lieu d'origine et les dates de la naissance et de la mort du philosophe Francisco Sánchez. BH 5:326-48, 1903. 292

Most important biographical study on S. in which crucial documents concerning his origin, birth, academic career, and death are published for first time.

— El lugar de origen y las fechas de nacimiento y de defunción del filósofo Francisco Sánchez. RABM 3rd ser. 11:1-12, 159-76, 1904.   293

Spanish version of important article first published in French, with scattered revisions and with addition of some plates and of an important new document concerning S.'s birthplace.

— Le philosophe Francisco Sánchez le Sceptique (1550-1623) et les Maisons galiciennes de Castro. BAHM 53:55-119, 1908.   294

Detailed and documented account of various episodes in life of S., especially of his relations with members of Castro family and with Giulio Cesare Vanini. Appendix reprints among other documents the prefaces of S.'s poem *De cometa* and of his treatise *Quod nihil scitur*.

Ciribini Spruzzola, Ada. Il problema del metodo e l'empirismo pseudo scettico nel pensiero di Fr. Sanchez. RFN 35:71-94, 1943.   295

Analysis of S.'s philosophical thought, with an emphasis on its non-sceptical elements.

Coralnik, A. Zur Geschichte der Skepsis. I. Franciscus Sanchez. Aph 27 (ns 20):188-222, 1914. 296

Sketchy analysis of S.'s philosophy.

Gerkrath, Ludwig. Franz Sanchez, Ein Beitrag zur Geschichte der philosophischen Bewegungen im Anfange der neueren Zeit. Vienna, Braumüller, 1860. 145 p. 297

Short biography, and detailed discussion of philosophical doctrine of S.; ample quotations and frequent references to Bacon and Descartes. Earliest substantial monograph on S., on which many later students have drawn.

Giarratano, Cesare. Il pensiero di Francesco Sanchez. Naples, Pierro, 1903. 105 p. 298

Short survey of S.'s life and works; author analyzes his philosophical thought. To the negative, sceptical ideas of S. he opposes his positive conceptions as found especially in his medical writings; thus finds reasons for removing S. from company of other renaissance sceptics and for considering him as a forerunner of Bacon and Descartes.

Review : G. Gentile in Crit 2:323-24, 1904.

Iriarte-Ag., J. Francisco Sánchez, el autor de Quod nihil scitur (Que nada se sabe), á la luz de muy recientes estudios. RYF 110:23-42, 157-81, 1936. 299

Discusses the fortune and philosophic doctrine of S., summarizing results of Iriarte-Ag.'s German thesis. Contains an analysis of S.'s poem De cometa.

— Francisco Sánchez el escéptico disfrazado de Carneades en discusión epistolar con Cristóbal Clavio; un autógrafo inédito y una revalorización de su doctrina. Greg 21:413-451, 1940. 300

Author publishes from a ms. of Università Gregoriana in Rome a letter addressed to Christophorus Clavius and dealing with geometrical problems, which is signed Carneades and attributed by the editor on good grounds to S. The important piece not only throws light on S.'s mathematical studies and interests but also adds weight to sceptical strand in his thought which had been too much discounted by most recent scholars. Letter was reprinted, with a Portuguese version, in Rpor 1:294-305, 1945.

— Kartesischer oder Sanchezischer Zweifel? Ein kritischer und philosophischer Vergleich zwischen dem kartesischen Discours de la méthode und dem Sanchezischen Quod nihil scitur. Bottrop i. W., Postberg, 1935. 147 p. (Diss., Bonn) 301

Detailed analysis of philosophical thought of S., with ample quotations. Comparison between S. and Descartes, not always convincing. Of special value is the extensive discussion of S.'s influence and reputation during following centuries.

Review : B. Jansen in PJ 50:370-72, 1937.

Menéndez y Pelayo, Marcelino. De los orígenes del criticismo y del escepticismo y especialmente de los precursores españoles de Kant. Discursos de recepción y de contestación leídos en la Junta pública de 15 Mayo de 1891. AMD 6:79-198, 1891-94. (Especially p. 149-82). Also in his: Ensayos de crítica filosófica. Madrid, Rivadeneyra, 1892. p. 193-366. (Especially p. 293-341); 2nd ed., Madrid, Suárez, 1918. p. 119-221. (Especially p. 178-206) 302

Important study of Spanish scepticism contains a substantial section on the thought of S.

Moreira de Sá, Artur. Francisco Sanches, filósofo e matemático. Lisbon, 1947. 2 v. (Diss., Lisbon) 303

Detailed study of S.'s life, works, philosophy, geometry, and influence, accompanied by documents and a bibliography. (Not seen.)

Review : S. T(avares) in Rpor 4:72-77, 1948.

Pimenta, Alfredo. O Filósofo Francisco Sánchez. In his: Estudos filosóficos e críticos. Coimbra, Imprensa da universidade, 1930. p. 83-96. 304

Critical review of S., Que nada se sabe, Spanish translation with a preface by Menéndez y Pelayo, (Madrid), Gil-Blas, (1923?), and a short evaluation of S.'s thought.

Review : RTAM 4:102-03, 1932.

Rocha Brito, A. da. O português Francisco Sanches, Prof. de filosofia e de medicina nas universidades de Mompilhér e Tolosa. BEP ns 7:1-71, 1940. 305

Documented biography, with many illustrations, including a facsimile of S.'s birth record (Braga 1551), and a Portuguese version of the contemporary biography by Delassus.

4

Senchet, Emilien. Essai sur la méthode de Francisco Sanchez professeur de philosophie et de médecine à l'Université de Toulouse. Giard & Brière, 1904. 170 p. (Diss., Toulouse)   306

Study of S.'s thought in which his positive views are emphasized and in which he is considered both as a continuator of ancient scepticism and as a forerunner of modern critical philosophy. Introduction contains documented biography partly based on unpublished sources. Appendix gives preface of the *Quod nihil scitur* in Latin and French, and the genealogy of S.'s family from data given to the author by Cazac.

Review : J. Barbot in AMT 10-11:313-20, 341-48, 367-71, 1904 (with several new documents on S.'s medical career.)

Ciribini Spruzzola, Ada. Francesco Sanchez alla luce delle ultime recerche. By Ada Spruzzola. RFN 28:372-91, 1936. 307

Detailed and documented study of S.'s life, based on preceding literature as well as on manuscript notes assembled by H. P. Cazac for his unfinished study of S., accessible to author at *Institut catholique* of Toulouse.

Tavares, Severiano. A data de composiçao do Quod nihil scitur. Rpor 1:386-91, 1945.   308

Argues that S.'s chief philosophical treatise was composed in 1575.

— Francisco Sanches e a critica. Rpor 2:165-76, 1946.   309

Surveys opinions of previous scholars on S.'s scepticism.

— Francisco Sanches e o problema da sua nacionalidade. Rpor 1:63-76, 1945. Cf. also 392-94; 2:81-86, 1946.   310

Argues unconvincingly for Portuguese birth of S. Valuable for bibliographical references.

Vasconcellos, Basilio. Que nada se sabe, Traduçao da obra Quod nihil scitur de Francisco Sanches. RevH 2:122-27; 187-199; 272-92, 1913; 3:159-66; 240-45, 1914; 4:45-56; 169-84; 362-77, 1915; 5:61-70, 1916.   311

Latin text and Portuguese translation, with footnotes, of S.'s major philosophical work.

Science and Travel
(Nos. 312-488)

ALBERT DOUGLAS MENUT

General

Brunet, Pierre. Table chronologique du 16ᵉ siècle concernant la France. ASS 24:198-216, 1942.   312

Tabular presentation of principal scientific achievements in France during 16th century.

Brunot, Ferdinand. Histoire de la langue française des origines à 1900. Tome II, Le seizième siècle. Colin, 1906. 504 p. *See* 609.   313

Chapter V, *Le français dans les sciences médicales*, p. 36-55, and chapter VI, *Le français dans les sciences mathématiques*, p. 56-61, present excellent survey of growth of use of French in these subjects, with copious bibliographical references. Chapter VII, *Le français dans la philosophie*, p. 62-71, includes references to natural science, chemistry, and physics. Not exhaustive, but extremely useful. *See* 609.

Castiglione, Arturo. History of medicine. Translated from Italian E. B. Krumbhaar, ed. New York, Knopf, 1941. 1013 p. 314

Copiously illustrated work of general reference, excellent bibliography, well indexed. Section on 16th century medicine superior to Garrison. (318, 319)

Dictionnaire des lettres françaises. Le seizième siècle. *See* 99.   315

Work of very uneven value owing to typographic errors and careless editing. Bibliographies often incomplete or antiquated. Serviceable if used with caution. *See* 127, 1808.

Duhem, Pierre. Études sur Léonard de Vinci. Hermann, 1906-13. 3 v. 316

Extensive survey of Léonard de Vinci's theories in later Middle Ages and early Renaissance. Indispensable, but must be used cautiously; author often hasty, prejudiced or careless of facts.

— Le système du monde : histoire des doctrines cosmologiques de Platon à Copernic. Hermann, 1913-17. 5 v. 317

Five additional volumes originally contemplated by the author have never been published.

Garrison, Fielding Hudson. The period of the renaissance, the revival of learning, and the reformation (1438-1600). *In his:* An introduction to the history of medicine. Philadelphia, Saunders, 1914. p. 131-75. 318

Well indexed and illustrated.

— The medical literature of France. BNYAM 9:267-93, 1933. 319

Résumé, all too brief, of significant contributions to medical science in France from the Middle Ages, by a distinguished authority.

Hanotaux, Gabriel, ed. Histoire des sciences en France. *In his:* Histoire de la nation française. Plon-Nourrit, 1924. V. 14, 15. 320

Best and fullest account, though somewhat general in treatment and out of date with respect to details. V. XIV : *Histoire des mathématiques, de la mécanique et de l'astronomie,* p. 3-163; *Histoire de la physique,* p. 165-418; *Histoire de la chimie,* p. 419-610. V. XV : *Histoire des sciences biologiques,* p. 33-56; *Histoire de la philosophie,* p. 347-74.

Lefèvre de La Boderie, Gui. La Galliade ou de la révolution des arts et sciences. Chaudière, 1578. 131 ff. 321

Interesting résumé of scientific and artistic advances under François Ier by a distinguished orientalist and poet of following generation. *See* 1376.

Niceron, Jean Pierre. Mémoires pour servir à l'histoire des hommes illustres dans la république des lettres, avec un catalogue raisonné de leurs ouvrages. Briasson, 1727-1745. 43 v. 322

Invaluable source of primary information concerning European writers both biographical and bibliographical. Should be checked with modern sources. Especially rich in 16th and 17th century items.

Patterson, Warner F. Three centuries of French poetic theory; a critical history of the chief arts of poetry in France (1328-1630). *See* 115. 323

Useful manual containing numerous *Arts de seconde rhétorique,* with examples of French verse in every genre of period, analyses of theories and historical development of same. *See* 1054A.

Plattard, Jean. Le système de Copernic dans la littérature française au xvie siècle. RSS 1:220-37, 1913. 324

Excellent summary of literary references by a distinguished authority.

Recueil de voyages et de documents pour servir à l'histoire de la géographie depuis le XIIIe siècle jusqu'à la fin du XVIe siècle. Charles Schefer and Henri Cordier, ed., Leroux, 1882-1923. 24 v. 325

Well edited, with notes, glossary and index for each work. Last three volumes plates, maps, etc. *See* under Geography items pertinent to this bibliography.

Sainéan, Lazare. L'histoire naturelle et les branches connexes dans l'œuvre de Rabelais. RSS 3:187-277, 1915; 4:36-104, 203-306, 1916; 5:28-74, 1918; 6:84-113, 1919; 7:1-45, 185-205, 1920; 8:1-41, 1921. *Reprinted,* Champion, 1921. 449 p. 326

Author's purpose primarily lexicographical and etymological, but covers admirably scientific knowledge of period as well as of Rabelais, indicating latter's sources. Invaluable for detailed information, copiously indexed. *See* 895, 2112.

Schmidt, Albert Marie. La poésie scientifique en France au seizième siècle : Peletier, Ronsard, Scève, Baïf, Belleau, du Bartas, les cosmologues, les hermétistes; de l'influence des sciences et des méthodes de pensée sur la création poétique (1555-1610). Michel, 1940. 378 p. 327

"La poésie scientifique ... réserve à l'étude attentive l'émouvant spectacle d'esprits préoccupés à imposer un ordre conceptuel au chaos des pensées de la Renaissance. Ces poètes demeurèrent étrangers à l'activité créatrice des sciences de leur temps; ils se contentèrent des conceptions surannées du monde que perpétuaient les manuels scolaires ou les poèmes néo-latins." (p. 15). Definitive work, based upon extensive knowledge of science of the time as well as on pertinent writings of 16 individual poets. *See* 1176, 1347.

Smith, David E. Medicine and mathematics in the 16th century. AMH 1:125-140, 1917. 328

Excellent mise-au-point regarding contribution of period to permanent body of scientific knowledge.

Thorndike, Lynn. A history of magic and experimental science. V. V and VI. The sixteenth century. New York, Columbia University Press, 1941. 695, 766 p. 329

Distinguished work, stressing scientific errors and pseudo-science of period, mine of information indispensable for French as well as Latin, German, English, Italian, and Spanish contributions.

Wickersheimer, Ernest. La médecine et les médecins en France à l'époque de la renaissance. Welter, 1905. 575 p.   330
Invaluable reference work, well indexed. Companion volume to same author's *Dictionnaire biographique des médecins en France au moyen-âge*, Droz, 1936, 2 v.

Will, Samuel F. A bibliography of American studies on the French renaissance (1500-1600). *See* 37.   331
Chapter X, *Sixteenth-century French navigations and discoveries in the new world* (p. 86-100) only portion of this useful bibliography pertinent to science.

Yates, Frances A. The French academies of the sixteenth century. London, Warburg Institute, University of London, 1947. 377 p.   332
Study of sources in Italian precedents, with special reference to Dorat, Baïf, Pontus de Tyard and the *Académie d'Henri III*. Of interest to scientific history is the chapter *Natural philosophy in the academies*, p. 95-104.

Agriculture

(Nos. 333-340)

Béroalde de Verville, François. L'histoire des vers qui filent la soye. En cette Serodokinomasie, ou recherche de ces vers, est discouru de leur naturel, gouvernement, utilité, plaisir et profit qu'ils rapportent. Tours, Sifleau, 1600. 60 p. unnumbered.
333
300 ten-syllable quatrains, half-serious satire which led to a series of rejoinders defending the silk-worm. *See* Henri Clouzot, *La sériculture dans Béroalde de Verville.* RSS 3:281-86, 1915. Most recent estimate of Béroalde is by V. L. Saulnier, *Etude sur Béroalde de Verville*, BHren 5:209-326, 1944.

Estienne, Charles. Agriculture et maison rustique. Dupuys, 1564. 252, 40 p.   334
Translation of Estienne's *Praedium rusticum* (1554) by Jean Liébault, with additions by the translator. Frequently reprinted until superseded by the *Théâtre d'agriculture* of Olivier de Serres in 1600.

Gohory, Jacques. Devis sur la vigne, vin et vendanges, d'Orl. de Suave, auquel la façon ancienne du plant, labour et garde est decouverte et reduitte au present usage. Sertenas, 1550. 104 p.   335
On the attribution to Gohory, *see* W. H.

Bowen, *The earliest treatise on tobacco*, Isis 28:349-63, 1938.

Gorgole de Corne. Quatre traictéz utiles et delectables d'agriculture. Corrozet, 1560. 127 p.   336
Revision of *Le Livre des prouffits champestres et ruraulx* translated for Charles V from Latin of Pietro Crescenzi, *Duodecim libri ruralium commodorum* (ca. 1300) and first published in French by Vérard in 1486. *See* Cabeen, v. 1, item 408. Arranged in four books as follows : (1) *La maniere de planter, arracher, labourer, semer et emonder les arbres sauvages*, par G. de C. (2) *La maniere d'enter, planter et nourrir arbres et jardins, par G. de C.* (3) *La manière de semer et faire pépinières de sauvageaux, par F. Dany.* (4) *L'art d'enter, planter et cultiver jardins, par Nicolas Du Mesnil.* Another edition, L'Angelier, 1560. 127 p.

Laffémas, Barthélemy. Les propriétés des muriers en leur bois, fruicts et racines. Monstroeil, 1599. 8 p.   337
Early attempt at scientific description of mulberry tree reflects keen interest in sericulture manifested by Henri IV and Sully, in whose service Laffémas was a tireless pamphleteer. Reprinted in *La façon de faire et semer la graine des muriers*, 1604, 36 p.; also in *Instruction du plantage des muriers*, 1605.

Mizauld, Antoine. Le jardinage. Item, comment il faut les enter et les rendre medicinaux. Lertout, 1578. 399 p.   338
Doctor of medicine, Mizauld offered his readers advice regarding medical virtues of vegetables as well as directions for their cultivation.

Serres, Olivier de. Theatre d'agriculture et mesnage des champs. Metayer, 1600. 1004 p. *See* 2032.   339
Illustrated work; enjoyed great authority throughout the 17th century, was reprinted eight times before the author's death in 1619. Legend has it that Henri IV had passages read to him daily after dining. Latest complete edition, Société d'agriculture de la Seine, *See* 2032. *Pages choisies, illustrées*, Firmin-Didot, 1941. 325 p. Not a critical edition. *See* Lavondès, A., *Olivier de Serres, seigneur du Pradel* (1539-1619). Carrières-sous-Poissy, La Cause, 1936. 311 p.

— La cueillette de la soie par la nourriture des vers qui la font. Metayer, 1599. 118 p.   340

Work included at end of most editions of *Theatre d'agriculture* subsequent to first. German and English translations published in 1603 and 1607, respectively.

Architecture

(No. 341)

Bullant, Jean. Reigle generalle d'architecture des cinq manieres de colonnes, a sçavoir : tuscane, dorique, ionique, corinthe et composite. Marnef et Cavellat, 1568. 60 p. 341
Member of a famous family of architects, author constructed tombs of Montmorency, Henri II, and Catherine de Médicis and drew the plans of the Tuileries.

Astronomy, Astrology, Witchcraft, Black Arts, Etc.

(Nos. 342-364)

Beauvoys de Chauvincourt, sieur de. Discours de la lycanthropye ou de la transmutation des hommes en loups. Rezé, 1599. 32 p. 342
Apparently only contribution of this country squire to science.

Boaistuau, Pierre. Histoires prodigieuses les plus memorables qui ayent esté observees depuis la nativité de Jesus Christ jusques a nostre siecle; extraictes de plusieurs fameux autheurs Grecz et Latins, sacréz et prophanes : mises en nostre langue par P. Boaistuau, surnommé Launay, natif de Bretaigne, avec les pourtraictz et figures. Brière, 1560. 173 p. 49 gravures sur bois. 343
Contains : *Prodiges de Sathan; des enfantements monstrueux; de la generation des monstres; prodiges de fouldres, tonnoires et tempestes; des pierres precieuses; des poissons estranges; des cometes, dragons, flambeaux; amours prodigieuses, serpents monstrueux, etc.*
Miscellany indicative of cultural lag common to every age; especially noteworthy in age of transition. Several editions.

Bodin, Jean. De la demonomanie des sorciers. Jacques du Puys, 1580. 556 ff. 344
Precursor of modern political theorists was also a rigorously fanatical champion of magic, especially witchcraft. *Decipimur specie recti. See* Roger Chauviré : *Jean Bodin, auteur de la République,* nos. 2054, 2078.

Du Moulin, Antoine. Physionomie naturelle, extraicte de plusieurs philosophes anciens et mises en françois. Lyon, Tournes, 1550. 151 p. 345
Anthology of Greek, Latin and Arabic writings.

Fine, Oronce. La sphere du monde proprement ditte cosmographie, composee nouvellement en français et divisee en cinq livres, comprenant la premiere partie de l'astronomie et les principes universels de la geographie et de l'hydrographie. Colines, 1530. 64 ff. 346
Fine was first to occupy chair of mathematics at Collège de France; succeeded by Ramus. Vascosan published a 2nd ed. of this work in 1551, including also reprint of author's *Epistre exhortative, see* under Mathematics. On Fine's limitations, *see* Thorndike, *History of magic,* etc., v. 5, p. 285-86.

— La theorique des cielz, mouvemens et termes pratiques des sept planetes redigee en français. Pierre, 1528. 45 ff. 347
Apparently author's translation from a Latin original. Frequently reprinted.

Focard, Jacques. Paraphrase de l'astrolabe, contenant les principes de geometrie, la sphere, l'astrolabe ou declaration des choses celestes; le miroir du monde ou explication des parties de la terre. Lyon, Tournes, 1546. 187 p. 348
2nd ed. *revue et augmentée* par J. Bassentin, *escossais, avec une amplification en l'usage de l'astrolabe par lui-mesme ajoustee.* Lyon, Tournes, 1555. 192 p. Work shows considerable advance over *La sphere du monde* of Oronce Fine.

Fontaine, Jacques. Discours de la puissance du ciel sur les corps inferieurs. Gorbin, 1581. 141 p. 349
Doctor of medicine from St. Maximin (Var), Fontaine was an ardent defender of astrology and occult beliefs. *See* Thorndike, *History of magic,* etc., v. 6, p. 188-90.

Grévin, Jacques. Discours sur les vertus et facultéz de l'antimoine, contre ce qu'en a escrit maistre Loys de Launay. Wechel, 1566. 34 ff. 350
Grévin continued his argument in a *Second discours,* Du Puys, 1568. 127 ff. *See* Thorndike, *History of magic,* etc., v. 5, p. 477-79. Standard biography of Grévin is by Lucien Pinvert, no. 1371 : *Jacques Grévin (1538-1570), étude biographique et littéraire.*

Jacquinot, Dominique. L'usage de l'astrolabe avec un traicté de la sphere. Gazeau, 1545. 84 ff.   351
Frequently reprinted—1558, 1559, 1573, 1598, 1617—work based on 13th century treatise on sphere by Sacrobosco.

L'Apostre, Georges. Le septenaire ou louange du nombre sept. A très vertueux et docte personnage Georges de Maubuisson, son Mecene. Pinocier, 1585. 63 ff.   352
Original French works on chiromancy, oneiromancy and arithmancy are notably rare in the 16th century, although several such were translated from Latin or Italian. Work touches upon arithmancy, but deals principally with examples of magic effects wrought by the number seven.

La Taille, Jean de. La geomance abregee … pour sçavoir les choses passees, presentes et futures ensemble le blason des pierres precieuses, contenant leurs vertus et propriétés en prose et en vers. Breyer, 1574. 50 18 ff.   353
Curious excursion into black arts by author of Saül furieux.

La Taysonnière, Guillaume de. La geomance, par laquelle on peut prevoir, deviner et predire de toutes choses douteuses et incertaines. Lyon, Rigaud, 1575. 115 p.   354
Example of extreme credulity of a country gentleman. See Thorndike, no. 329, v. 6, p. 472-73.

Le Loyer, Pierre. Discours et histoires des spectres, visions et apparitions des esprits, anges, demons et ámes se monstrans visibles aux hommes. Angers, 1586. In 4 parts, 178 p.   355
2nd ed., augmentée, Buon, 1605. 976 p. Classic of demonology, widely quoted and later widely ridiculed.

Massé, Pierre. De l'imposture et tromperie des diables, devins, enchanteurs, sorciers, noueurs d'esguilletes, chevilleurs, necromanciens, chiromanciens et aultres qui par telle invocation diabolique, arts magiques et superstitions abusent le peuple. Poupy, 1579. 250 ff.   356
Title deceptive : author only halfheartedly against magical arts. See Thorndike, History of magic, etc., 6:524-25.

Mesmes, Jean Pierre de. Les institutions astronomiques. Vascosan, 1557. 314 p.   357
See Thorndike, History of magic, etc., 6:20-22.

Node, Pierre. Declamations contre l'erreur execrable de maleficiers, sorciers, enchanteurs et semblables observateurs des superstitions, lesquels pululent maintenant couvertement en France. Carroy, 1578. 78 p.   358
Includes Les articles et erreurs touchant ceste matiere condamnéz a Paris par la faculté de theologie, avec une tres chestienne et docte preface faicte a ceste censure par Jehan Gerson et les docteurs de la droicte faculté. This early 15th century item follows a powerful attack against black arts using traditional arguments of the Church. Node was a Franciscan friar.

Perréal, Jean. La complainte de nature a l'alchimiste errant. Guillard et Warancore, 1561. 75 ff.   359
Another edition of same year bears title : De la transformation metallique, trois anciens tractez en rithme françoise asçavoir : La fontaine des amoureux de science, par J. de La Fontaine; Les remonstrances de nature à l'alchimiste errant, avec la response dudict alchymiste, par J. de Meung. See A. Vernet, Jean Perréal, poète et alchimiste. BHren 3:214-52, 1943.

Tyard, Pontus de. Mentice ou discours de la verité de divination par astrologie. Galiot du Pré, 1573. 114 p.   360
2nd edition, augmentée. First edition appeared at Lyons, 1558 and was second of Pontus's prose works published after he abandoned poetry for theology. Excellence of style lifts work above banalities of its substance. See Thorndike, History of magic, etc., v. 6, p. 107-08. Pontus was mildly opposed to astrology, in spite of the title.

— Premier discours de la nature du monde et de ses parties. Le premier curieux. Lyon, Tournes et Guil. Gazeau, 1557. 156 p. 361
Having turned from poetry to the Church, Pontus wrote two treatises on the universe, of which this is the first. Work opens with a noble hymn to science and poses a number of primary questions regarding man's place in the world; reviews astrology, physics, and meteorology.

— Second discours de la nature du monde et de ses parties. Le second curieux. Lyon, Tournes et Guil. Gazeau, 1558. 123 p. 362
See John C. Lapp, The universe of Pontus de Tyard : a critical edition of L'Univers, Ithaca, Cornell University Press, 1950, 201 p. Introduction, bibliography, and

text of *Le premier curieux* and *Le second curieux* from third revised edition, Lyons, L'Angelier, 1587. *See* 776.

Review : S. F. Baridon in BHren 12:411-19, 1950.

Prieur, Claude. Dialogue de la lycanthropie ou transformation d'homme en loup, vulgairement dits loupsgaroux et si telle se peut faire. Louvain, Maes, 1596. 72 ff.   363

Author cites numerous examples in support of lycanthropy. *See* Thorndike, *History of magic*, etc., v. 6, p. 547.

Thibault, Jean. Apologie de maistre J. T., astrologue de l'imperiale majesté et de Madame, et contre les invectives d'aulcuns pronostiqueurs avec demonstrations comment la personne est semblable au ciel, terre, mer et a toutes creatures, et que une eclipse a plus d'effect avant le point eclyptique qu'apres, etc. Antwerp, 1530. 234 p.   364

The " imperial majesty " was Charles V. Author produced several prognostications and calendars and a famous *Thrésor du remède*, q.v. under Medicine, no. 454.

Biological Sciences
(Nos. 365-374)

Bauhin, Johann. Histoire notable de la rage des loups, advenue l'an 1590 avec les remedes pour empecher la rage. Montbéliard, 1591. 91 p.   365

Pioneer in botany with his *Historia plantarum universalis*, Bauhin was doctor of medicine to Count of Montbéliard. His observations on course of *la rage* are minute and long served as a model.

— Traité des animaux aians ailes qui nuisent par leurs piqueures ou morsures, avec les remedes : oultre plus une histoire de quelques mouches ou papillons non vulgaires apparus l'an 1590 qu'on a estimees fort venimeuses. Montbéliard, 1593. 90 p.   366

Earliest entomological study in French.

Belon, Pierre. L'histoire de la nature des oyseaux avec leurs descriptions et naïfs portraicts retiréz du naturel, escripte en sept livres. Corrozet, 1555. 382 p.   367

Highly esteemed by Buffon, Belon's works remained in vogue throughout 17th century. He was on occasion capable of acute observation of natural objects; not without a love of mystification and readily accepted tall tales. Attached to a mission sent to the Levant by Francis I in 1546, he spent three years of travel in that region

and later traveled extensively in England, Germany, and Italy. *See* Paul Delaunay, *L'aventureuse existence de Pierre Belon du Mans*, no. 2107. Extensive bibliography and scholarly account of Belon's works.

— L'histoire naturelle des estranges poissons marins, avec la vraie peincture et description du daulphin et de plusieurs aultres de son espece, observee par Pierre Belon. Chaudière, 1551. 116 p.   368

First work of its kind in French, highly praised by Buffon.

— La nature et diversité des poissons, avec leurs pourtraicts representéz au plus pres du naturel. Estienne, 1555. 448 p.   369

Work retains much of preceding item on sea fish, employing same wood-cuts; adds extensive treatment of fresh-water fish.

— Les observations de plusieurs singularitéz et choses memorables trouvees en Grece, Asie, Judee, Egypte, Arabie et autres pays estranges, redigees en trois livres. Corrozet, 1553. 212 ff.   370

Translated into Latin by Carolus Clusius for Plantin, Antwerp, 1589. 495 p.

— Portraicts d'oyseaux, animaux, serpens, herbes, arbres, hommes et femmes d'Arabie et d'Egypte, observéz par Pierre Belon. Le tout enrichy de quatrains, pour plus facile cognoissance des oyseaulx et autres portraicts. Cevellat, 1557. 123 p.   371

Popularization of the preceding item; purpose praiseworthy, but verse very mediocre.

— Les remonstrances sur le default du labour et culture des plantes et de la cognoissance d'icelles. Corrozet, 1558. 80 ff.   372

Translated into Latin by Carolus Clusius, Antwerp, Plantin, 1589. 87 p.

Gohory, Jacques. Instruction sur l'herbe petum, ditte en France l'herbe de la royne, ou medicee, et sur la racine mechiocan. (16 ff.) Seconde partie contenant un brief traité de la racine mechoacan, venue de l'Espagne nouvelle, traduit d'espagnol de Monardes, de Seville, en françois par J.G.P. (15 ff.) Du Pré, 1572. 31 ff.   373

See W. H. Bowen : *The earliest treatise on tobacco*. Isis 28:349-63, 1938.

Rondelet, Guillaume. L'histoire entiere des poissons, composee premierement en latin par maistre G. Rondelet, maintenant traduite en françois par Laurent Joubert

avec leurs pourtraicts au naïf. Lyons, Bonhome, 1558. 2 v. in 1. 374
Besides writing about fish, Rondelet wrote on mathematics—in Latin. *See* estimate of his works by E. W. Gudger, Isis 22:8-30, 1934 *see* 2108; also extracts from mathematical writings, Osiris 3:165-92, 1937, pt. 1. On the translator, *see* below under Medicine.

Cryptography
(No. 375)

Vigenère, Blaise de. Traité des chiffres ou secretes manieres d'escrire. L'Angelier, 1586. 343 p. 375
Apparently the earliest treatise in French. *See* Denyse Métral. *Blaise de Vigenère, archéologue et critique d'art* (1523-1596), no. 2592.

Economics
(Nos. 376-379)

Cole, Charles Woolsley. French mercantilist doctrines before Colbert. New York, Smith, 1931. 243 p. (Diss., Columbia) 376
Analysis of 16th century theorists : Bodin (p. 47-57), Laffémas (p. 63-112), Montchrétien's *Traité de l'œconomie politique, See* 2132, p. 113-61.

Bodin, Jean. Discours de Jean Bodin sur le rehaussement et diminutions des monnoyes tant d'or que d'argent et le moyen d'y remedier; responce aux Paradoxes de M. de Malestroict. Dupuys, 1566. 63 p. 377
Published together with *Paradoxes* of Malestroict and *Paradoxe* of Garrault, Dupuys, 1578.

Laffémas, Barthélemy. Reiglement general pour dresser les manufactures en ce royaume et couper le cours des draps de soie, et autres marchandises qui perdent et ruynent l'estat. Monstroeil et Richer, 1597. 210 p. 378
Another edition : Rouen, 1597. Important work proposing economic program after religious wars. *See* above, C. W. Cole and also same author's *Colbert and a century of French mercantilism*, New York, Columbia University Press, 1939, I : p. 28-39; v. II : Bibliography.

Malestroict, Jehan Cherruyt de. Paradoxes du seigneur de Malestroict ... sur le fait des monnoyes, presentés a sa majesté au mois de mars. Vascosan, 1566. 22 p. 379

Another édition : *Les remonstrances et paradoxes.* Poitiers, Noscereau, 1566. 14 p. Only title page different. *See* George A. Moore, *Response of J. Bodin to Paradoxes of Malestroict and the Paradoxes.* Translated from 2nd French ed., 1578. Washington, Country Dollar Press, 1946. 90 p. Excellent introduction presents background of debate and summarizes current ideas on monetary theory and practice. *Also :* J. Y. Le Branchu, *Ecrits notables sur la monnaie, XVIe siècle.* Alcan, 1934. v. 1.

Geography, Exploration and Travel
(Nos. 380-411)

Atkinson, Geoffroy. La littérature géographique française de la renaissance; répertoire bibliographique. Description de 524 impressions d'ouvrages publiés en français avant 1610 et traitant des pays et des peuples non-européens que l'on trouve dans les principales bibliothèques de France et de l'Europe occidentale. Picard, 1927. 563 p. Supplément, Picard, 1936. 88 p. 380
Invaluable guide to a vast field of scientific and pseudo-scientific literature still largely unexplored. Completeness of bibliography makes it unnecessary to repeat here any except outstanding items of this immense literature. *See* 2895.

— Les nouveaux horizons de la renaissance française. Droz, 1935. 502 p. 381
Contains a helpful *Liste chronologique des ouvrages géographiques de la renaissance*, p. 433-72, and also a unique *Liste alphabétique des ouvrages portant dates fausses*, p. 473-79. *See* 2895.

Barré, Nicolas. Copie de quelques lettres sur la navigation du chevallier de Villegaignon es terres de l'Amerique oultre l'aequinoctial, jusques soubz le tropique de Capricorne; contenant sommairement les fortunes encourues en ce voyage, avec les meurs et façons de vivre des sauvages du pais : envoyee par un des gens dudict seigneur. Martin Le Jeune, 1557. 38 p. 382
First of several books and pamphlets concerning French expedition to and settlement at Fort Coligny near Rio de Janeiro, led by royal admiral Villegagnon, 1555-57, with Protestant participation. Failure of enterprise led to publication of several vituperative attacks against Villegagnon, who apparently wrote nothing himself in defense. Above item attributed to N. Barré, who published the following

year a *Discours sur la navigation du Ch. de Villegagnon en Amerique*, Le Jeune, 1558. In 1561 appeared anonymously *L'histoire des choses memorables advenues en la terre du Bresil ... sous le gouvernement de M. de V. depuis l'an 1555 jusqu'a l'an 1558*; in 1565, also anonymously, the *Brief recueil de l'affliction et dispersion de l'eglise des fideles au pays de Bresil, ou est contenue sommairement le voyage et navigation faicte par M. de V. et de ce qui est advenue*. The final and fullest account of this unhappy affair was the *Histoire d'un voyage fait en la terre du Bresil*, by the Protestant Jean de Léry, Geneva, 1578, several times reprinted. *See below* under Léry.

Bonnaffé, Ernest. Voyages et voyageurs de la renaissance. Leroux, 1895. 172 p. 383

Semi-popular work, useful synopsis including English, Spanish, and Portuguese travels as well as French.

Bonnerot, Jean. Les routes de France. Laurens, 1921. 167 p. 48 plates. 384

Semi-popular work, treating sentimentally historical events connected with principal highways of France. Plates excellent.

Chinard, Gilbert. L'exotisme américain dans la littérature française au XVIe siècle. Hachette, 1911. 246 p. 385

Basic study of penetration of voyage and exploration accounts into current of ideas. Favorably reviewed by Pierre Villey, RHL 33:207-12, 1912.

Fordham, Sir Herbert George. Les routes de France : étude bibliographique sur les cartes-routières et les itinéraires des guides-routiers de France, suivie d'un catalogue des itinéraires et guides-routiers, 1552-1850. Champion, 1929. 106 p. 51 pl. 386

Comprehensive survey of road-guide literature, historical introduction, bibliographical list, and facsimiles of charts. Definitive work, portions of which were published previously in several periodicals.

Gassot, Jacques. Le discours du voyage de Venise a Constantinople, contenant la querele du grand Seigneur contre le Sophi; avec elegante description de plusieurs lieux, villes et citez de la Grece. Le Clerc, 1550. ff. 34. 387

Nephew of royal secretary, Gassot was sent on a mission to Sultan by Henri II. Travelled in Persia, Turkey and Greece, but his " elegant description " deals

mostly with last named, where he was delighted with ancient monuments. Later editions : Paris, 1606; Bourges, 1674.

Julien, Charles André. Les Français en Amérique pendant la première moitié du XVIe siècle; textes des voyages de Gonneville, Verrazano, J. Cartier et Roberval. Ed. by C. A. Julien, R. Herval and T. Beauchesne. Presses universitaires, 1946. 223 p. 388

Handy collection of principal voyages, well edited with introduction and notes. Based upon original editions.

Alfonce, Jean. La cosmographie, avec l'espère et régime du soleil et du Nord, par Jean de Fonteneau, dit Alfonse de Saintonge, capitaine-pilote de François Ier, publiée et annotée par Georges Musset. Leroux, 1904. 516 p. 389

Published from original ms. in Bibl. Nat. Fonteneau was with Roberval in Canada in 1542-44. Work essentially a pilot guide.

— Les voyages aventureux du capitaine Jean Alfonce. Poitiers, Marnef, 1559. 136 p. 390

Photostatic reproduction, Boston, Massachusetts Historical Society, no. 10, 1920, from copy in Huntington Library. Work probably edited by Mellin de Saint-Gelais. Alphonce was prototype of Xenomanes in Rabelais : *see* Abel Lefranc, *Les navigations de Pantagruel*, Leclerc, 1905, p. 73. *See also* Georges Musset, *La vérité sur Alphonse de Saintonge*, BGHD, 1906, p. 120-27.

Cartier, Jacques. Brief recit et succincte narration de la navigation faite es ysles de Canada, Hochelage, Saguenay et aultres et particulierement des mœurs, langages et ceremonies d'habitants d'icelles. Roffet, 1545. 187 p. 391

The best critical edition of Cartier's voyages is : *The voyages of Jacques Cartier, published from the originals with translations, notes and appendices*, by H. P. Biggar. Ottawa, Acland, 1924. 330 p. Reproduces manuscript copy of first voyage (1534) and first edition of *Voyages* (1545).

Chesneau, Jean. Le voyage de Monsieur d'Aramon, ambassadeur pour le Roy en Levant. Ed. Charles Schefer in Recueil de voyages, VIII, Leroux, 1887. 296 p. 392

Published from the original ms., written by the royal secretary from the official report of the ambassador. D'Aramon was in Constantinople from 1542-55.

Cognet, Michel. Instruction des points plus excellens et necessaires touchant l'art de naviguer, ensemble un moyen facile et tres sur pour naviguer Est et Oest. Antwerp, Heinrick, 1581. 221 p. 393

Compendium of practical rules for handling sailing vessels as well as for navigating, with charts and tables.

Estienne, Charles. Les fleuves de France. Estienne, 1552. 72 p. 394

Published with *La guide des chemins de France* in 1554 edition and frequently thereafter. Published in 1553 with *Les voyages de plusieurs endroits de France*, etc.

— La guide des chemins de France. Estienne, 1552, 207 p. 395

Frequently reprinted, often with addition of *Les fleuves de France*, above. *See* Abel Lefranc, *La guide des chemins de France de Ch. Estienne.* RSS 1:19-27, 1913. Critical ed., Jean Bonnerot, Champion, 1936, 2 v.

— Les voyages de plusieurs endroits de France et encores de la Terre Saincte, d'Espaigne, d'Italie et autrès pays. Les fleuves du royaulme de France. Estienne, 1553. 113, 6 p. 396

Most ambitious of Estienne's travel guides, including both items above, plus main routes to Palestine, Spain, and Italy.

Hoyarsabal, Martin de. Les voyages aventureux du capitaine M. de H., habitant de Cubiburu, contenant les reigles et enseignemens necessaires a la bonne et seure navigation. Bordeaux, Chouin, 1579. 114 p. 18. 397

Textual similarities between this pilot guide and *Voyages aventureux* of Jean Alfonce suggest strongly that work was plagiarized in part from earlier text. *See* Ch. de La Roncière, BEC 65:116-25, 1904. Photostatic reproduction of this first edition, Massachusetts Hist. Soc., no. 253, Boston, 1930. Frequently reprinted; revised ed., Bordeaux, Millanges, 1633, "augmentée de la declinaison du soleil, qui a esté faite suivant la reformation du calendrier de l'an 1582." Voyages to Asia, Africa and Newfoundland.

Léry, Jean de. Histoire d'un voyage fait en la terre du Bresil, autrement dite Amerique. Geneva, Chuppin, 1578. 424 p. 398

See critical edition with introduction by Charly Clerc, Payot, 1927. 319 p. " avec gravures d'un anonyme du 16ᵉ siècle." *See* 382.

Nicolay, Nicholas de. Les quatre premiers livres des navigations et peregrinations orientales de N. de Nicolay Dauphinois, seigneur d'Arefeuille, varlet de chambre et geographe ordinaire du roy. Lyon, Roville, 1568. 181 p., et figures hors texte. 400

Work translated to English and published, London, 1585; to Italian, Antwerp, 1577, Venice, 1580. Two later French editions published in Antwerp, 1576 and 1586. Author, geographer to Charles IX, travelled in Turkey, Palestine, and Egypt. Appeal of work certainly enhanced by numerous " belles et mémorables histoires advenues en nostre temps " and by " figures au naturel, tant d'hommes que de femmes selon la diversité des nations." First 16 pages not numbered; following a five-page *lettre dédicatoire* to Charles IX, there is a two-page *Elégie* by Ronsard.

Pigafetta, Antonio. Le voyage et navigation faict par les Espaignolz es isles de Mollucques, des isles qu'ilz ont trouvé audict voyage, des roys d'icelles, de leur gouvernement et maniere de vivre, avec plusieurs aultres choses. Colines, 1522. 22 ff. Translated by J.-A. Fabre. 401

Best edition : Jean Denucé. *Relation du premier voyage autour du monde par Magellan, 1519-1522. Edition du texte français d'après les manuscrits de Paris et de Cheltenham.* Antwerp, Janssens, 1923. 290 p. Published also as v. 24 in *Recueil de voyages* (q.v.), Leroux, 1923.

Possot, Denis. Tres ample et abondante description du voyage de la Terre saincte dernierement commencé l'an de grace 1532, commençant le dict voyage depuis la ville de Nogens sur Sene jusqu'à la saincte cité de Hierusalem, escrit par D. P. et continué par Ch. Philippe, seigneur de Champarmoy. Chaudière, 1536. 128 p. gothic. 402

Account of travels of a priest of Coulommiers through Turkey and Palestine, arranged by month and year as a journal. Ed. by Ch. Schefer, *Recueil de voyages*, v. II, Leroux, 1890. 67 p. 153.

Postel, Guillaume. Des merveilles du monde, et principalement des admirables choses des Indes et du nouveau monde, histoire extraicte des escripts tres dignes de foy, tant de ceulx qui encores peu paravant en sont retournez. Et y est monstré le lieu du Paradis terrestre. 1553. Ff. 96. 403

Descriptions derived from Italian, French, and Latin sources, dealing with Asia, Africa and America.

— De la republique des Turcs, et la ou l'occasion s'offrera, des meurs et loy de tous Muhamedistes, par G. P. cosmopolite. Poitiers, Marnef, 1560. 3 v. 404

Work by erudite royal professor of oriental languages at Paris contains 3 sections : p. 1-127, *De la republique des Turcs*; p. 1-57, *Histoire et consideration de l'origine, loy et coustume des Tartares, Persiens, Arabes, Turcs...*; p. 1-88, *La tierce partie des orientales histoires, ou est exposee la condition, puissance et revenu de l'empire turquesque*. Polygraph in Latin, French, and Italian, Postel authored more than 50 books on geography, astronomy, history, travel, languages, and politics; took part in famous " querelle des femmes." *See Dictionnaire des lettres françaises, XVI*e *siècle.*

Le routier de la mer jusques au fleuve de Jourdain, nouvellement imprimé à Rouen. Rouen, Le Forestier, s.d. 29 ff. 405

At end : " Cy finissent les jugemens de la mer, des maistres, des marchans et de tout leur estre." Printed between 1500-1520. Probably earliest French book on navigation.

Terraube, Galard de. (Abbé de Boillas.) Discours des choses les plus necessaires et dignes d'estre entendues en la cosmographie. Morel, 1566. 40 ff. 406

Popular tract on cosmography, astronomy, and the continents, including Americas. Later editions : 1567, 1569, and 1575.

Thenaud, Jean. Le voyage et itineraire de oultre mer faict par Frère Jehan Thenaud, maistre es ars, docteur en theologie, gardien des freres mineurs d'Angoulesme. Et premierement du dict lieu d'Angoulesme jusques au Cayre. Sergent, 1530. Ff. 64, gothic. 407

Brunet, *Manuel*, indicates an edition of 1512, also of 64 ff.; since voyage was made in 1511, this is entirely possible. Date not given on title-page, but Ch. Schefer concludes in his introduction to his edition, *Recueil de voyages, V* Leroux, 1884, that this very rare work was not printed before 1530. Travels in Egypt, Turkey, Persia, Tartary, and Palestine.

Thevet, André. Cosmographie du Levant. Lyons, Tournes, 1554. 184 p. 408

Description of a trip by land and sea to Constantinople and Palestine. An Antwerp edition by Jean Richart, 1556, repeats text of first edition. 2nd ed., *revue et augmentée*, Lyons, Tournes, 1554. 218 p.

— Cosmographie muscovite par A. T., recueillie et publiée par le prince Augustin Galitzin. Techener, 1858. 179 p. 409

Selections from Thevet's *Cosmographie universelle*, with interesting preface by an amateur but well-informed scholar.

— La cosmographie universelle, illustree de diverses figures des choses plus remarquables. L'Huillier, 1575. 2 v. 410

Most ambitious work of century, covering astronomy and geography. Substantially dependable for those parts of Europe and Near East which Thevet visited ; illustrations represent often fantastic descriptions in text. V. 2, pt. 4 contains descriptions of America, with numerous drawings of cannibals.

— Les singularitéz de la France antartique, autrement nommee Amerique. La Porte, 1557. 166 ff. 411

Descriptions derived from relations of French, Spanish, and Portuguese explorers. Translated into English and Italian. New edition : Paul Gafferel, Maisonneuve, 1878. 459 p. Notes and introduction, illustrations.

Mathematics
(Nos. 412-428)

Boissière, Claude de. L'art d'arythmetique contenant toute dimension, tres singulier et commode, tant pour l'art militaire que autres calculations. Brière, 1554. 68 ff. 412

Work of a scholarly amateur impelled by a fascination for numbers.

— Le tres excellent et ancien jeu pythagorique, dit Rithmomachie, pour obtenir vraye et prompte habitude en tout nombre et proportion, nouvellement illustré. Brière, 1554. 36 ff. 413

Curious revival of Pythagorean mysticism of numbers. Under same inspiration, De Boissière wrote an *Art de la musique,* 1554.

Bouvelles, Charles de. Geometrie en françoys. Cy commence le livre de l'art et science de geometrie avecquez les figures sur chascune rigle au long declarees, par lesquelles on peult entendre et facilement comprendre le dit art et science de geometrie. Henri Estienne, 1511. 40 ff. 414

This earliest geometry in French frequently revised and augmented throughout century. Edition of 1547, by Colines, 70 ff., represents final form of text.

Cathalan, Jean. Arithmetique et maniere d'apprendre a chiffrer et a compter par la plume et par les jects. Lyon, Payan, 1555. 237 p.   415

Like all the arithmetical texts of century, this is a practical guide, a compilation of rules for changing money, reckoning measures, and calculating sums ; more theoretical works were still written in Latin.

Chauvet, Jacques. Les methodiques institutions de la vraye et parfaicte arithmetique. Marnef, 1578. 304 p.   416

Many editions. Frequently published in 17th century.

Fine, Oronce. Epistre exhortative, touchant la perfection et commodité des arts liberaulx mathematiques, composees soubz le nom et tiltre de la tres antienne et noble princesse Dame Philosophie. Et puis nagueres presentee au tres chrestien Roy de France. Leber, 1531. 8 ff.   417

Highly florid defense of study of mathematics, couched in allegorical form. Reprinted in Vascosan's edition (1551) of Fine's *La sphere du monde.* 64 ff. *See* Astronomy.

— La composition et usage du quarré geometrique, par lequel on peut mesurer fidelement toutes longueurs, hauteurs et profunditéz, tant accessibles comme inaccessibles, que l'on peut appercevoir à l'œil; le tout reduit nouvellement en françois, escrit et pourtraict par O. F., Gourbin, 1556. 28 ff.   418

Much revised edition of work published by Gourbin, 1570, 64 ff., entitled : *La pratique de geometrie d'Oronce, professeur du roy es mathematiques, en laquelle est comprins l'usage du quarré geometrique et de plusieurs autres instruments servans a mesme effet; ensemble la maniere de bien mesurer toutes sortes de plans et quantités corporelles, avec les figures et demonstrations; revue et traduite par Pierre Forcadel.*

Forcadel, Estienne. L'arithmetique entiere et abregee. Marnef et Cavellat, 1573. 197 p.   419

Professor of mathematics at *Collège de France,* Forcadel, one of first to lecture in French. First ed. of *Arithmetique* appeared in 1556; followed by *Second livre* in 1557 and *Troisième livre* in 1558. He published an *Arithmetique par les gects* in 1559. First ed. of *L'arithmetique entiere* printed by Périer in Paris, 1565.

Fustel, Martin. L'arithmetique abregee, conjointe a l'unité des nombres. Orry, 1588. 128 p.   420

Frequently republished in 17th century.

La Roche, Etienne de. L'arithmetique nouvellement composee par maistre Estienne de la Roche dict Villefranche, natif de Lyon sus le Rosne, divisee en deux parties. Lyon, Huyon, 1520. 230 ff.   421

Second edition, Lyons, Huguestan, 1538, 226 ff., contains a treatise on algebra, oldest known in French and also a notation of exponents which Descartes popularized a century later in his geometry.

Merliers, Jean de. L'art ou instruction pour mesurer toutes superficies de droite ligne. Denis du Pré, 1568. 157 p.   422

Textbook of trigonometrical measurements for surveyors.

— L'usage du quarré geometrique, descrit et demontré. Gourbin, 1568.   423

Merliers was a disciple of Fine, his work largely derived from latter's *Composition et usage du quarré geometrique,* above.

Peletier, Jacques. L'algebre de Jacques Peletier du Mans, departie en 2 livres. Lyon, Tournes, 1554. 237 p.   424

First extensive treatise on algebra in French. *See* J. M. Thureau, *Peletier, mathématicien manceau du 16ᵉ siècle,* Laval, 1935. 27 p.

Savonne, Pierre de. Arithmetique. Du Chemin, 1565. 192 p.   425

Popular work; seven editions published before 1600.

Stevin, Simon. La disme. Leyden, Plantin, 1585. 72 p.   426

Treatise on decimals included in *L'arithmetique de S. Stevin, aussi l'algèbre ... encore un livre particulier de la practique d'arithmetique contenant entre autres, les tables d'interest, la disme et un traicté des incommensurables grandeurs.* Leyden, Plantin, 1585. 2 v. This important work is an author's translation from original Flemish. *La disme* regarded as earliest explanation of decimal fractions and measures. *See* George Sarton, Isis 23:153-244, 1935.

Trenchant, Jean. L'aritmétique de Ian Trenchant, departie en trois livres ensemble un petit discours des changes avec l'art de calculer aux getons. Lyon, Trenchant, 1558. 375 p.   427

With several revisions and additions, work printed sixteen times during following century. *See* George Sarton, *Isis* 21:207-09, 1934.

Vinet, Elie. L'arpenterie, livre de geometrie enseignant a mezurer les champs. Bordeaux, Millanges, 1577. 183 p. 428

Practical treatise on surveying by a distinguished humanist, professor at Bordeaux, best known as philologist and historian. 2nd ed., 1583 with addition of *La maniere de faire les solaires et cadrans*, originally printed separately, Poitiers, 1564.

Medicine

(Nos. 429-457)

Besson, Jacques. De absoluta ratione extrahendi olea et aquas e medicamentis simplicibus.... L'art et moyen parfait de tirer huyles et eaux de tous medicamens simples et oleagineux premierement receu d'un certain empirique qu'on estimait alleman, et depuis confirmé par raisons et experience, nouvellement corrigé et augmenté d'un second livre par Jacques Besson, Dauphinois, professeur de mathematiques. Du Pré, 1571. 24 ff. Latin and French texts parallel. 429

Original Latin of *Livre I* published by Gessner, Zürich, 1559. *See* Thorndike, *History of magic*, v. 5, p. 588-96. *See* Besson under Technology.

Cabral, Barthélemy. Alphabet anatomic, auquel est contenue l'explication exacte des parties du corps humain et reduites en tables selon l'ordre de dissection ordinaire avec l'osteologie et plusieurs observations particulieres. Tournon, Michel et Linocier, 1594. 110 p. 430

Practical guide for students, frequently republished.

Champier, Symphorien. Le myrouel des appothiquaires et pharmacopoles, par lequel il est demonstré comment apothiquaires communement errent en plusieurs simples médecines contre l'intention des Grectz, etc. Lyon, Mareschal, 1524. 64 ff. Gothic letter. *See* 204. 431

This defense of Galen had at least 4 editions; primarily remarkable as first of critical medical discussions in French. Ed. with notes and glossary, Dr. P. Dorveaux, Welter, 1894. 56 p.

Colin, Sébastien. Declaration des abuz et tromperies que font les apothicaires fort utile a ung chascun studieux et curieux de sa santé, par Lisset Benancio (author's anagram). Tours, Bourgea, 1553. 55 ff. 432

Edited with notes and glossary by Paul Dorveaux, Welter, 1901. 88 p. Reprinted three times in French, twice in Latin in 17th century.

Du Breil, André. La police de l'art et science de la medicine, contenant la refutation des erreurs et insignes abus qui s'y commettent pour le jour d'huy. Cavellat, 1580. 151 p. 433

Among errors is prognostication by the stars.

Du Puis, Guillaume. Phlebotomie artificielle. Lyons, Rose et Monnier, 1536. 115 p. 434

First specialized treatise in French on bleeding.

Estienne, Charles. Dissection des parties du corps humain. Colines, 1546. 406 p. 435

Author's translation of Latin original, 1545. Illustrated. First 'complete' coverage of anatomy in French.

Eusèbe, Jean. La philosophie rationale, vulgairement appelee dialectique, pour les chirurgiens françois et autres amateurs de la langue françoyse, nouvellement dressee par maistre J. E., bourbonnays. Lyon, Saugrain, 1556. 346 p. 436

Elaborate directions for questioning patient to reach diagnosis.

— La science du poulx, le meilleur et plus certain moyen de juger des maladies. Lyon, Saugrain, 1568. 186 p. 437

Professor at Montpellier, Eusèbe was first to write on symptoms in French.

Fontaine, Jacques. Traitté de la varicelle. Aix-en-Provence, 1596. 104 p. 438

See Thorndike, *History of magic*, etc., 6:553-55. *See* Fontaine under Astronomy, no. 349.

Franco, Pierre. Traité des hernies, contenant une ample declaration de toutes leurs especes et autres excellentes parties de la chirurgie, assavoir de la pierre, des cataractes des yeux et autres maladies. Lyon, Falconet, 1556. 380 p. 439

Huguenot, Franco was driven by Waldensian massacres to Switzerland. Physician to Francis II, he rivalled Paré in putting operations for hernia, stone, and cataract upon a dignified and definite basis. *See La chirurgie de Pierre Franco, composée en 1561. Nouvelle édition avec une introduction historique, une biographie et l'histoire du Collège de chirurgie,* par E. Nicaise, Alcan, 1895. 546 p.

Grévin, Jacques. Deux livres des venins. Antwerp, Plantin, 1567-68. 334 p.   440

Successful playwright at twenty *(Jules Cesar,* 1560), Grévin turned to medicine during ten remaining years of his life. Major work was his translation of Vesalius, *Anatomes,* Wechel, 1569. *See* 1371, Lucien Pinvert, *Jacques Grévin (1538-1570),* ... *étude biographique et littéraire.*

Guido, Jean. Traicté et remedes contre la peste, utiles et salutaires a gens de tous estaz. 1545. 8 ff.   441

Typical of several similar treatises, showing no appreciable advance over those of preceding century. On latter, *see* A. C. Klebs and E. Droz, *Remèdes contre la peste,* Droz, 1925. 95 p. For additional 16th century examples, *see* Garrison, *Introduction to the history of medicine,* no. 318, p. 246-58; also Brunet, *Manuel, Supplément,* s.v. *peste*; also list in Brunot, *Histoire de la langue française,* 2:49, n. 5.

Guillemeau, Jacques. Traité des maladies de l'œil. Massé, 1585. 102 ff.   442

First treatise in French devoted exclusively to eyes. Author's *Tables anatomiques,* Charron, 1586, enjoyed wide popularity. Disciple of Paré.

Houël, Nicolas. Traicté de la theriaque et mithridat, contenant plusieurs questions generales et particulieres ... pour le profit et utilité de ceux qui font profession de la pharmacie, et aussi fort propre à ceux qui sont amateurs de la medecine. Bordeaux, 1573. 151 ff.   443

Frequently republished in 17th century.

Joubert, Laurent. Erreurs populaires au fait de la medicine et regime de santé. Bordeaux, 1570. 352 p.   444

In five books, reprinted by S. Millanges, Bordeaux, 1578, 603 p., and several times thereafter. Italian translation of 1592 and one in Latin of 1660. A *Segonde partie des erreurs populaires,* Brayer, 1580, reprinted and issued together with *Erreurs,* Méard, 1587, and frequently later. *See* E. Wickersheimer, *La médecine et les médecins en France à l'époque de la renaissance,* 497-542. *Also:* Dr. Barbillon, *A propos d'un scandale littéraire et médical, au 16e siècle; le livre des erreurs populaires de Laurent Joubert.* BSHM 26:193-203,

1932. On the life and works of Joubert, see P. Amoreux, *Notice historique et biliographique sur la vie de Laurent Joubert.* Montpellier, Tournel, 1814, 105 p.

— La pharmacopee de M. Laur. Joubert, ensemble les annotations de J. Paul Zangmeister. Lyon, 1579. 337 p.   445

Reprinted, Lyons, 1581 and 1588. First extensive pharmacopeia in French.

Le Baillif de La Rivière, Roch. Petit traité de l'antiquité et singularités de Bretagne armorique, en laquelle se trouve bains curans le lèpre, podagre, hydropisie, paralisie, ulcères et autres maladies. Rennes, Le Bret, 1578. 190 p.   446

Leader of Paracelsian school, Le Baillif was a tireless pamphleteer, winning vindication with his appointment as court physician under Henri IV.

Lefournier, André. La decoration d'humaine nature et aournement des dames, ou est montree la maniere et receptes pour faire savons, pommes, poudres et eaues delicieuses et odorantes pour laver et nettoyer tant le corps que les habillemens. Saint-Denys et Longis, 1530. 56 ff.   447

Regent of faculty of Paris, produced one of earliest works in French on personal hygiene.

Massé, Jean. L'art veterinaire avec annotations des dictions medicales plus difficiles. Périer, 1563. 184 ff.   448

Notable improvement upon first French veterinary treatise by Lozenne, Lyons, ca. 1500, 12 ff., entitled *Remèdes et medicines des chevaux.* (Cabeen, I, item 410).

Mizauld, Antoine. Le jardin medicinal, enrichi de plusieurs et divers remedes et secrets. Lertout, 1558. 462 p.   449

Based on earlier herbals, several times republished, for last time as a supplement in Elie Vinet et A. Mizauld, *La maison champestre et agriculture, divisee en 5 parties, avec le jardin medicinal et la façon d'user de la vertu des herbes,* Fouel, 1607. 811 p.

— Singuliers secrets et secours contre la peste, souventes fois experimentéz et approuvéz tant en certaine preservation que parfaicte guerison. Breuille, 1562. 304 p.   450

Mizauld was compiler of orthodox theories and recorded little that was original. Did much to perpetuate medical superstitions and magic.

Palissy, Bernard. Declaration des abus et ignorance des medecins, par Pierre Brailleur (pseud. of Bernard Palissy). Lyon, Jove, 1557. 63 p. 451

See Palissy under Technology. The attribution is doubtful.

Paré, Ambroise. Les œuvres d'Ambroise Paré, divisées en 27 livres, avec les figures et pourtraicts, tant d'anatomie que des instruments de chirurgie et de plusieurs monstres, reveuz et augmentéz par l'auteur pour la 2ᵉ edition. Buon, 1579. 3 v. 452

First ed. in 2 v., Buon, 1575; copy in Bibl. de Ste. Geneviève. Latest critical annotated edition by J.-F. Malgaigne, Baillière, 3 v., 1840-41, see 2028. See Francis R. Packard, *Life and times of Ambroise Paré* (1510-1590), with a new translation of his apology and an account of his journeys in diverse places. See 2030. Excellent bibliography.

Rousset, François. Traitté nouveau de l'hysteromotokie ou enfantement cesarien. Du Val, 1581. 228 p. 453

Earliest treatise in French on the caesarean operation.

Thibault, Jean. Le thresor du remede, preservatif et guerison bien experimentee de la peste et fievre pestilentielle, avec declaration dont procedent les goutes naturelles et comme elles doibvent retourner. Et aussi aucunes allegations et receptes sus le mal caduque, pleuresies et apoplexies et ce que il appartient a un parfaict medecin, etc. Antwerp, Martin l'Empereur, 1531. 122 ff. 454

See Thibault under Astronomy, no. 364. Most widely read of the medical compendiums.

Tolet, Pierre. Paradoxe de la faculté du vinaigre. Lyon, Tournes, 1549. 182 p. 455

See C. A. Mayer, *Pierre Tolet and the Paradoxe de la faculté du vinaigre*. BHren 13:83-88, 1951.

Une joyeuse medicine pour les dents. 456

Farcical poem inserted at end of *Le débat de l'homme et de la femme*, 2nd edition of works of Guillaume Alexis, 1520. See Curt Proskauer, *A merry medicine for the teeth ca. 1520*, BHM 21:102-09, 1947.

Vallambert, Simon. Cinq livres de la maniere de nourrir et gouverner les enfans dez leur naissance. Poitier, Marnef et Bouchet, 1565. 348 p. 457

In his preface, author states this is first of its kind in French. Began his career with a translation of Plato's *Crito*, published in 1542. His work on surgery, *De la conduite du fait de chirurgie*, Vascosan, 1558, shows influence of Paré.

Political Theory
(Nos. 458-464)

Albon, Claude d'. De la majesté royalle, institution et preeminence, et des faveurs divines particulieres envers icelle. Lyon, Rigaud, 1575. 178 p. 458

Tract in support of divine right theory, based upon theologic argument.

Béroalde de Verville, François. L'idee de la republique. Jouan, 1584. 102 ff. 459

Poem in decasyllables, divided into seven books, presenting a Utopian political organization with obvious indebtedness to both More and Bodin. Reprinted twice in twenty years.

Bodin, Jean. Les six livres de la republique. Du Puy, 1576. 759 p. 460

Frequently reprinted. See Roger Chauviré, *Jean Bodin auteur de la République*, no. 2054.

Budé, Guillaume. Le livre de l'institution du prince. Foucher, 1547. 192 p. 460A

Written in 1520, printed three times in 1547 under different titles : (1) as above; (2) *De l'institution du prince, reveu par missire Jean de Luxembourg*, Abbaye de l'Arrivour, 1547, 204 p.; (3) *Tesmoignage de temps ou enseignemens et exhortemens pour l'institution d'un prince*, Lyon, Gazeau, 1547, 104 p. See F. Brunot, *Histoire de la langue française*, 2:76.

Champier, Symphorien. La nef des princes et des batailles. Lyon, 1502. 38 ff. 461

Early work of Lyonais doctor of medicine and humanist, in tradition of *Speculum principis* genre. See Paul Allut, *Etude biographique et bibliographique sur Symphorien Champier*. See 205.

Gentillet, Innocent. Discours sur les moyens de bien gouverner et maintenir en bonne paix un royaume ou autre principauté...contre Nicolas Machiavel. Geneva, 1576. 639 p. 462

Work delighted Montaigne; effective answer to *Prince* and most significant contribution to political theory before Bodin's *République*. No definitive study of Gentillet exists. See 2658.

La Boétie, Estienne de. Discours de la servitude volontaire, suivi du Mémoire touchant l'Édit de janvier 1562 et d'une lettre de m. le conseillier de Montaigne. Introduction et notes de Paul Bonnefon. Bossard, 1922. 214 p. *See* 1405-10; 1457-1487.   463

Discours, written in 1548, not published in full until 1576 in v. III of *Mémoires de l'état de la France sous Charles IX*. Discovered by Paul Bonnefon in 1917, *Mémoire* first published by him in RHL 24:1-33, 307-19, 1917. *Œuvres complètes d'Estienne de La Boétie réunies pour la première fois et publiées avec des notes par Léon Feugère*, Delalain, 1846, 532 p., in general superior to later edition by Paul Bonnefon, 1892.

Saint-Thomas, François de. La vraye forme de bien et heureusement regir et gouverner un royaume ou monarchie; ensemble le vrai office d'un bon prince. Lyon, Saugrain, 1569. 149 p.   464

Example of anti-Machiavellian tract, in tradition of *Speculum principis* genre. Nothing known of author.

Prognostications, Almanacs and Ephemerides

(Nos. 466-478)

(This list includes only items of known authorship. *See* the article *Pronostication* by Robert Barroux in *Dictionnaire des lettres françaises, le seizième siècle*, no. 99, p. 579-580, for an extensive list of items of unknown authorship.)

Alegnos, Germain. La grant prenostication nouvelle pour ceste presente annee Mil CCCCC xix. 1519. 4 ff.   466

Like most of the pre-Rabelaisian prognosticators, Alegnos makes strong claim for absolute veracity of his predictions. *See* Thorndike, *History of magic*, etc., 5:283.

Benoit, Guillebaud. La pronostication du siecle advenir. Lyon, Arnoullet, 1533. 34 ff.   467

Published only a year after Rabelais' *Pantagrueline prognostication*; shows influence of latter in its satirical intention.

Des Périers, Bonaventure. La prognostication des prognostications, non seulement de ceste presente annee MD. xxxvii, mais aussi des aultres a venir, voire de toutes celles qui sont passees, composee par maistre Sacromoros, natif de Tartarie, et serf du tres

illustre et tres puissant roy de Cathai, serf des vertus. Morin, 1537. 12 p.   468

Reproduced in A. de Montaiglon, *Recueil de poésies françaises des XVe et XVIe siècles*, Jannet, 1855-78. v. 5, p.224-33.

Fine, Oronce. Les canons et documens tres amples touchant l'usage et pratique des communs almanachz que l'on nomme ephemerides; briesve et isagogique introduction sur la judicaire astrologique des choses advenir, avec un traité d'Alcabice nouvellement adjouté, touchant la conjonction des planetes en chascun des douze signes. Colines, 1543. 37 ff.   469

A work of serious intention by a distinguished savant.

La Taysonnière, Guillaume de. Le compost aritmetical, lequel montre a trouver le nombre d'or, l'epacte, l'indiction, lettre dymenchale. Sans lieu, Crèche, 1567. 53 p.   470

Native of Dombes, La Taysonnière dabbled in verse; wrote a regional history. *See also* under Astrology. Author of *Briefve arithmetique*, Lyons, Rigaud, 1570, and *Les principaux fondemens d'arithmetique*, Lyons, Rigaud, 1571.

Le Maistre, Edmond. Advertissement et presage fatidique pour six ans, contenant au long la prediction des signes célestes ... necessaire pour tous oeconomistez, laboureurs et autres menagers; le tout preveu selon la science astronomique par E. le M., provençal, mathematicien tres expert. Lastre, 1583. 16 ff.   471

Author otherwise unknown; work of serious intention.

Mizauld, Antoine. Les ephemerides perpetuelles de l'air, autrement l'astrologie des rustiques. Kerver, 1554. 288 ff.   472

Rudimentary conception of role of air currents applied to agriculture, medicine and, in conjunction with astrology, to human affairs. *See also* under Agriculture.

— Secretz de la lune, opuscule non moins plaisant que utile, sur le particulier consent et manifeste accord de plusieurs choses du monde avec la lune. Morel, 1571. 24 ff.   473

Besides a lunar calendar, summarizes most of astrological cant about lunar influences.

Rabelais, François. Pantagrueline prognostication. Lyon, Juste, 1532. 4 ff.   474

Facsimile reproduction, ed. Pierre-Paul Plan, Rueil, Chahine, 1922. 8 ff. Frequently reprinted in 19th century editions of Rabelais.

Turrel, Pierre. Fatale prevision par les astres. Lyon, 1528. 24 ff. 475
Book of rules for aspiring prognosticator, by a professional astrologer about whom nothing apparently is known.

— La grant pronostication avec l'almanach bien au long calculee pour l'an Mil ccccc et xxiii. Lyon, 1523. 12 ff. 476
See Thorndike, *History of magic,* etc., v. 5, p. 307-11.

— Le periode, c.a.d. la fin du monde contenant la disposition des choses terrestres par la vertu et influence des corps celestes. Lyon, 1531. 28 ff. 477
Curious exercise in eschatology mingled with astrological computations.

Vostet, Jean. Almanach ou prognostication des laboureurs reduite selon le kalendrier gregorien, avec quelques observations particulieres sur l'annee 1588, de si long temps menacee, par J. V., breton. Richer, 1588. 72 p. 478

Technology and Invention
(Nos. 479-488)

Besson, Jacques. L'art et science de trouver les eaux et fontaines cachees sous terre. Orléans, Trepperel, 1569. 85 p. 479
Professor of mathematics at Orléans, Besson produced several works containing designs and descriptions of machines, based largely on principle of pulley. Practicality of these " inventions " was slight, but drawings afford considerable interest; probably earliest technical designs published in France.

— Le cosmographe, instrument adjoint en la partie superieure du cosmolabe au lieu de l'atlas lequel sert particulierement pour la chorographie. Rouille, 1569. 104 ff. 480
Device for measuring land altitudes, serving the making of regional maps; with mathematical guide for its use.

— Le cosmolabe ou instrument universel. Rouille, 1567. 267 p. 481
Illustrated description of Besson's instrument for triangulation for cartographical uses.

— Description et usage du compas euclidien. DuPré, 1571. 128 p. 482
Describes both the dry-point and quarter-circle compass, with rules for their use.

— Theatre des instrumens mathematiques et mechaniques de Jacques Besson, dauphinois, docte mathematicien, avec l'interpretation des figures d'iceluy par François Beroald (de Verville). Lyon, Vincent, 1579, 40 p. 60 pl. 483
Translation of original Latin *Theatrum instrumentorum,* Orléans, 1569, with additional notes by Béroalde. French version, translated into Latin by J. Paschal, Lyon. 1582. French version frequently reprinted.

Bullant, Jean. Petit traicté de geometrie et d'horologiographie pratique. Cavillat, 1562. 28 p. 484
Application of geometrical rules essential to solar horometry.

— Recueil d'horologiographie. Sertenas, 1561. 143 p. 485
Famous architect of Tuileries, Bullant devised ingenious methods for measuring more accurately the time registered on sundials.

Fine, Oronce. Description de l'horloge planetaire faite par l'ordre de M. le cardinal de Lorraine de l'invention d'Oronce Fine en 1553. 1554. 10 ff. 486
Operated by a complex system of gears and pulleys, this planetary clock was exhibited in library of Sainte-Geneviève until 1846, then dismantled. *See* Fine under Astrology and Mathematics.

Palissy, Bernard. Les œuvres, publiées avec une notice historique et bibliographique et une table analytique par Anatole France. Charavay, 1880. 500 p. 487
Palissy's approach to ceramics and geology was experimental and his best writings are simple accounts of his trials and errors in evolving successful solutions to technical problems. *See* Ernest Dupuy, *Bernard Palissy,* no. 2160. *See* 2022.

Vinet, Emile. La maniere de faire des solaires, que communement on appelle quadrans. Poitiers, Marnef, 1564. 116 p. 488
Eminent humanist, principal of Collège de Guienne at Bordeaux, interested himself in horometry along with history, archeology, and philology. *See also* under Mathematics.

5

Art

(Nos. 489-545)

ELIZABETH S. SASSER

NOTE : In this contribution the arrangement is as follows : General works on the fine arts; Architecture; Emblems; Painting; Sculpture; Tapestry. Within each of these sections the order is that established by the Contributor.

General Editor

Fine Arts (General)

Sixteenth century France presents one of the rare moments in history when common purposes, sources of inspiration, and patronage effect a conscious unity of literature and the fine arts. The arts drew their inspiration from antique learning, yet continued French traditions and sustained the characteristics of national temperament. The fountainhead of creative enterprise was the court. Monarchs, abandoning the etiquette and prejudice of the times, lavished honorary titles upon men of letters and of the arts. The right to approach the king, the privilege of following in the royal company was conferred. The result was a realization of the dignity of the artist. Together poet and artist moved freely in the courtly milieu. Their aims were never more closely allied.

Art and literature eulogized the nobleman in verse or portraiture. The " triumphs," births, deaths, and coronations were celebrated by pageants and poems of such poets as Ronsard and Dorat, translated into magnificent spectacles by the foremost artists and architects. At Fontainebleau the classical decorations designed by Nicolas Labbé and Germain Pilon were under the direction of the writers Jamyn, Dorat, and Ronsard. The common interests of art and literature were forcefully united in the popularity of the emblem and the devise. The influence of the symbolic caprice extended to such diverse forms as Maurice Scève's Délie and the cryptic designs in paint and stone, such as those described by Symeoni at Anet or those at Dampierre derived from Alciati.

Just as the painter and sculptor drew heavily upon the motifs of literature, rich in classical embellishment and allegory, so the poet sought imagery from the painter and architect. La Grotte de Meudon was celebrated in Ronsard's Troisième églogue, Joachim du Bellay and Mellin de Saint Gelays described the beauties of the gardens and buildings at Anet, and Rabelais created the Abbey of the Thelemites in the guise of a renaissance château. Personal esteem or rivalry existing between artist and writer was perpetuated in verse. Ronsard's poem on Lescot constitutes nearly all that is known of the architect's life. De l'Orme was bitterly attacked by Ronsard, while Janet was eloquently dealt with in the Elegy beginning, " Pein-moy, Janet, pein-moy." Dorat praised Pilon, addressing him as, " Pilon, qui craindroit un Scopas en sculpture."

An exploration of the 16th century in France serves therefore a variety of purposes. The close relationship between authors and artists is disclosed in their collaborations and friendships. The symbolism discovered among the emblems and descriptions of " triumphs " may be of help in the interpretation of literary passages, or it may lead to the correction of curious misinterpretations of painted decorations. A knowledge of art forms enriches literature by supplying the ability to recreate visually, whether it be the face of a court personage, a classical design, or an architectural figure.   489

Michel, André. Histoire de l'art. Colin, 1905-25. 18 v. V. 4, part 2 : L'architecture de la renaissance en France; La sculpture en France de Louis XI à la fin des Valois; La médaille et l'art monétaire en France de Charles VII à Henri IV; La peinture en France depuis l'avènement de Charles VII jusqu'à la fin des Valois; Le vitrail français au xve et au xvie siècle. p. 491-814. V. 5, part 1 : L'émaillerie à Limoges, p. 448-61; Faïences fines du temps des Valois et Faïence de Bernard Palissy, p. 471-81. V. 5, part 2 : L'architecture en France sous le règne de Henri IV; La sculpture en France sous Henri IV; La médaille française au temps de Henri IV et de Louis XIII; La peinture en France sous le règne de Henri IV. p. 701-92. Also in v. 5, part 2, La tapisserie et le mobilier au xvie siècle, p. 887-945. 490

Essential work. Excellent text by specialists, each an authority in field about which he writes. Valuable bibliographies follow each chapter; articles from periodicals listed. Adequate photographs.

Laborde, Léon Emmanuel Simon Joseph, marquis de. Les comptes des bâtiments du roi (1528-1571). Baur, 1877-80. V. 1, 422. V. 2, 510 p. (SHAF)   491

Importance of Laborde cannot be overemphasized. His research forms a primary source for numerous books on French renaissance art appearing in the last quarter of 19th century. *Les comptes des bâtiments* was begun in 1856; not published, however, until after Laborde's death. Task of writing an introduction and editing the manuscript undertaken by J. J. Guiffrey. First volume and second to p. 198 given over to reproduction of a manuscript of *Bibliothèque nationale, Les Comptes des bâtiments royaux depuis 1528 jusqu'en 1570.* Manuscript believed to be an abridgment dating a century and a half after first years of the accounts. Portions concerning masonry, carpentry, and pure construction seem to have been somewhat shortened, while greatest attention is centered on works of art. Heading page one of manuscript is signature " J. F. Félibien," son of André Félibien, both of whom wrote numerous works on art. It is thought that the record of building was composed for the father and passed on to the son. Original from which it was taken is lost. Second volume of Laborde's study ends with reports of a diverse nature, drawn from documents in *Archives nationales.* General index at end of v. II. No illustrations.

Müntz, Eugène. La renaissance en Italie et en France à l'époque de Charles VIII. Didot, 1885. 560 p. 492

Five chapters of Book III present beginnings of renaissance in France to time of Charles VIII. Excellent background provided for development of 16th century art forms. Emphasis placed not solely upon Italian contributions to the French, but upon French contributions to Italy in field of music as well as in painting, architecture, and minor arts. Case established is notable for enthusiasm, rather than strength. Illustrations limited.

Dilke, Emilia Francis (Mrs. Mark Pattison). The renaissance of art in France. London, Kegan, Paul, 1879. 2 v. 493

Despite quaint style and slight moral trepidations of Victorian period, volumes make pleasant and informative general reading. First volume devoted to sculpture, architecture, and painting. Second treats subjects of painting on glass, engraving on wood and metal, enamellers of Limoges, and pottery. Result neither a comprehensive history, nor a work rich in original research. Attention should be called to v. I, in which there are references to relationships between artists and literary

figures, for example, Ronsard's friendships with Pierre Lescot and Janet. Chronological survey at end of v. II, but no bibliography. Nineteen illustrations on steel of little interest.

Bancel, E. Catalogue des livres précieux et des manuscrits avec miniatures composant la bibliothèque de M. E. M. B. Labitte, 1882. 303 p. 494

A sale catalogue in which items describing " triumphal entries " of 16th century are of considerable interest.

Taylor, Francis Henry. The school of Fontainebleau. *In his:* The taste of angels. Boston, Little, Brown, 1948. p. 185-99. 495

Brief but admirable introduction to art collections of French renaissance.

Laborde, Léon Emmanuel Simon Joseph de. La renaissance des arts à la cour de France. Potter. 2 v. 1,088 p. 496

Key source for subsequent writing on renaissance painting. Study based upon royal accounts, inventories, correspondence, contracts with artists, etc. Included are sections devoted to Clouets, to "painters to the King," chronologically arranged, to painters employed by the court, accounts of building with details concerning works of art executed in royal residences and tombs of Saint Denis. Index at end of v. I. No illustrations.

Roy, Maurice. Artistes et monuments de la renaissance en France. Champion, 1929-34. 2 v. 497

Series of brilliant essays derived from hitherto unedited documents and other new materials. Of special interest in v. 1 is the speculation upon acquaintanceship of Joachim du Bellay and " les deux Jehan Cousin " at Sens, the part played by Philibert Delorme in designing the triumphal entry of Henri II and Catherine de Medici into Paris in 1549, interesting facts about Château at Anet with descriptions by Symeoni of *devises* used as architectural ornament. General index and bibliography at end of v. 2. Illustrations.

Kernodle, George R. Renaissance artists in the service of the people. AB 25:59-64, 1943. 498

Political tableaux and street theatres in France, Flanders, and England. Barely touches surface of a rich field of research, yet stimulating introduction.

Architecture

(Nos. 499-508)

Champollion-Figeac, Jacques Joseph. Le palais de Fontainebleau. Imprimerie impériale, 1866. 648 p.   499
Provides one of best sources for a detailed study of Fontainebleau. Ch. 10 through 15 take up the building projects of Francis I, Henry II, Francis II, Charles IX, Henry III, and Henry IV. Accounts thoroughly documented. Lists of sculpture, tapestries, paintings, and art objects given. A section devoted to Benvenuto Cellini at Fontainebleau (p. 171-80).

Dan, Pierre. Le trésor des merveilles de la maison royale de Fontainebleau.... Cramoisy, 1642. 355 p. *See 524.*   500

Dimier, Louis. Fontainebleau. Laurens, 1911. 168 p.   501
Authoritative study of Fontainebleau written for general reader. Fact is conscientiously separated from fiction. First two chapters devoted to 16th century building program. Photographs of no great interest.

— Le château de Fontainebleau et la cour de François Ier. Calmann-Lévy, 1930. 234 p.
502
Fontainebleau described against background of historical and social events of period of Francis I. Material not new and presentation seems somewhat dull. No index, illustrations, or bibliography.

Lesueur, Frédéric et Pierre. Le château de Blois. Longuet, 1914-1921. 313 p.   503
Ch. II, III, and IV take up problems of 16th century construction. A few illustrations. Bibliography.

Clouzot, Henri. Philibert de l'Orme. Plon-Nourrit, 1910. 198 p.   504
Biography of the " Master Architect " to Francis I and Henry II. Discussion of the animosity held by Ronsard for Philibert. Bibliography. Well illustrated.

Gebelin, François. Les châteaux de la renaissance. Les beaux arts, 1927. 306 p.
505
One of best general surveys of renaissance châteaux. Sections taking up renaissance style of building, important architects, and history of each château. Photographs and comments on La Possonière interesting from literary standpoint. Bibliography. Excellent photography, as

well as reproduction of many of Androuet du Cerceau's designs.

Berty, Adolphe. La renaissance monumentale en France. Morel, 1864. 2 v.   506
Plates in each volume preceded by descriptions of structures illustrated. Illustrations in form of drawings of elevations, architectural details, and ornament. Few perspectives included.

Palustre, Léon. L'architecture de la renaissance. Quantin, 1892. 352 p.   507
Section II contains a short survey of French renaissance architecture by a 19th century authority. Meagerly illustrated.

Blomfield, Reginald. A history of French architecture. London, Bell, 2 v.   508
Interestingly written history of French renaissance architecture from reign of Charles VIII to death of Mazarin. V. 1 devoted to architecture of first three quarters of 16th century and includes a chapter on sculpture. First three chapters in v. 2 take up architecture and influences of last portion of 16th century. Both photographs of buildings and reproductions of architectural drawings used to illustrate volumes.

Emblems

(Nos. 509-524)

a. Bibliography

b. Sources

Praz, Mario. Studies in seventeenth-century imagery. London, University of London, 1947. v. 2, 209 p. (SWI, v. 3)   509
Extensive and valuable bibliography. As title implies, study primarily concerned with emblem books of 17th century; but many 16th century volumes also listed. Libraries where emblem books may be found are mentioned.

Alciati, Andrea. Emblematum libellus. Wechelus, 1534. 119 p. *See 2465-67.* 510
Emblem book appeared first in Italy in 1531. Both form and title were contribution of the distinguished lawyer, Andrea Alciati. Popularity of new literary expression, embellished with its appropriate woodcuts, produced innumerable editions of Alciati, printed by foremost presses of Europe, and gave rise to a fad for the curious literary pattern, which extends in varied forms throughout next four centuries. First Paris edition of Alciati comes from

year 1534. Contains 111 woodcuts of emblems, possibly by wood-engraver, Mercure Jollat. Facsimile reprint of this is *The first Paris edition of the Emblems of Alciat*, 1534, in Libr ser. 4, v. 4:326-31, 1923-24. For special bibliographical material *see* Henry Green, *Andrea Alciati and his books of emblems*. London, Trübner, 1872. 344 p.

Horapollo. Orus Apollo, de Aegypte, de la signification des notes hieroglyphiques des Aegyptiens. Kerver, 1543. sm. 511

Influence of writings of Horapollo upon origin of emblem literature makes this a source of utmost importance. First edition of interpretation of hieroglyphs was published in Venice by Aldus in 1505; first Paris edition in 1521. First French translation is that mentioned above; contains 197 woodcuts. *See also The Hieroglyphics of Horapollo*, trans. by George Boas. New York, Pantheon, 1950. 134 p. (BS 23). Very few reproductions of early illustrations included.

L'Anglois, Pierre, *sieur* de Bel-Estat. Discours des hiéroglyphes aegyptiens, emblemes, devises, et armoiries. L'Angelier, 1583. ff. 112. 512

Interesting for material relating popular hieroglyphics and emblem literature. Without figures. *See* Praz (509), p. 92.

Corrozet, Gilles. Hecatomgraphie. Janot, 1540. ff. 104 not numbered. 513

Contains 100 woodcuts of emblems; joins names of two important persons : Corrozet, the Platonist, and Jean Cousin, sculptor, painter, and engraver. Emblematic designs sometimes attributed to Cousin. Doubt cast upon this attribution by Didot in his study of Jean Cousin (531) p. 157-59. Reprint of *Hecatomgraphie* with introduction and notes by Ch. Oulmont, Champion, 1905.

Cousin, Jean. Le livre de fortune, recueil de deux cents dessins inédits de Jean Cousin publié d'après le manuscrit original de la Bibliothèque de l'Institut par Ludovic Lalanne. Rouam, 1883. 39, cciv p. 514

Original manuscript dated 1568. Jean Cousin referred to in nearly every work on French painting as a figure of importance; yet documentation verifying his accomplishments uncertain. To him is attributed the painted glass at Chapel of Vincennes, glass at Sens Cathedral, tomb of Admiral Chabot. As a painter, his surname was "the French Michaelangelo." Born about 1500,

death date uncertain; usually placed between 1583 and 1595. *Le livre de fortune* provides a possible source for study of elusive Cousin and links an important personage in field of art with long list of emblem makers. For a detailed account of Cousin with emphasis given to probable attribution to him of various book illustrations consult Didot (531).

Scève, Maurice. Délie. Ed. by E. Parturier. Hachette, 1916. 347 p. (TFM) 515

From literary standpoint this is certainly most interesting emblem source in 16th century France. It is, as Praz points out, rarely included among lists of emblem volumes; yet is in every sense an emblem book and one of few that possess real value as literature. Many of emblems apparently are result of Scève's personal fancy; but such emblems as " the viper who sacrifices herself in giving birth to her young " (CCXL), " the moth and the candle " (XXXI), and " the man attempting to stem the speed of a raging bull " (XXXIII) are found throughout emblem collections.

Paradin, Claude. Devises heroïques. Lyon, Tournes and Gazeau, 1557. 262 p. 516

Contains 182 woodcuts of devices with explanatory text. Unlike many emblems of Alciati and Sambucus, these woodcuts are not pictures with story-telling intent, but symbols. Should be especially helpful in explaining devices chosen by members of French court. Many designs seem to be directly related to sculpture and to architectural decoration of a heraldic nature. Similarities between the devices and those found in *Délie* evident.

Coustau, Pierre. Petri Costalii pegma. Lyon, Bonhomme, 1555. 336 p. 517

Contains 95 woodcuts. French translation : *Le pegme de Pierre Coustau, mis en Françoys par Lanteaume de Romieu gentilhomme d'Arles.* Lyons, Bonhomme, 1555. *See* Praz, no. 509, p. 43.

Nestor, Jean. Histoire des hommes illustres de la maison de Medici. C. Perrier, 1564. 236 p. 518

Woodcuts illustrate devices of different members of house of Medici. *See* Praz, no. 509, p. 117.

La Perrière, Guillaume de. Le theatre des bons engins. Janot, 1539. 519

Emblems illustrated with 101 woodcuts; dedication to " Madame Marguerite de

France." For further information concerning publications of Janot, Didot (no. 531) offers useful material. *See* p. 147-52.

Simeoni, Gabriele. Les devises ou emblemes heroiques et morales. Lyon, Roville, 1559. 52 p.   520

Simeoni's emblems published again in 1561. In this later edition they were coupled with emblems of Paolo Giovio, one of most popular of 16th century emblematists. Volume is *Dialogue des devises d'armes et d'amours*, translated from the Italian by S. Vasquin Philieul. To these are added *Les devises heroïques et morales du seigneur Gabriel Syméon*. Lyons, Roville, 1561. 255 p.

Sambucus, Joannes. Les emblèmes du Signeur Iehan Sambucus. Antwerp, Plantin, 1567.   521

Emblems of Sambucus closely related in style to those of Alciati. Woodcuts elaborate and somewhat complicated in manner. *See* 2505.

Guéroult, Guillaume. Le premier livre des emblemes. Lyons, Arnoullet, 1550. 72 p. Seconde livre de la description des animaux, contenant le blason des oyseaux. Lyons, Arnoullet, 1550. 62 p.   522

First book contains 28 woodcuts and second supplied with 60. Cuts are simple and rather crude. First series of emblems similar to those of that arbiter of emblematic taste, Alciati. Second group illustrations of fables rather than emblems. Modern reprint: introduction and notes by DeVaux de Lancey, Rouen, Lainé, 1937. 72 p. (SRB)

Montenay, Georgette de. Emblemes, ou devises chrestiennes. Lyons, Marcorelle, 1571. 8 preliminary leaves, 100 ff., and 8 leaves at the end.   523

Portrait and 100 copperplate engravings by Pierre Woeiriot. For an account of Woeiriot's career *see* Didot (no. 53) p. 281-303.

Dan, Pierre. Le tresor des merveilles de la maison royale de Fontainebleau. *See* 500.   524

Early and important source of information concerning Fontainebleau, its gardens, and fountains. Seven of the fountains illustrated by copperplate engravings of Abraham Bosse. Book also occupies itself with emblems. Devices and emblems are described but not illustrated.

Painting
(Nos. 525-540)

Dimier, Louis. Histoire de la peinture de portrait en France au XVIᵉ siècle. Paris & Brussels, Van Oest, 1924-1926. 3 v.   525

Monumental study by one of most prolific and scholarly writers on French renaissance art and architecture. V. I is a history of the portrait in crayon, oil paint, miniature, enamel, tapestry, and medallion. Is one of finest works of its kind in field of art history. Illustrations numerous, brilliantly selected, and a triumph of skill in reproduction. V. II and III provide a catalogue of all known examples of portraiture in crayon, oil, miniature, and enamel produced in France during 16th century.

— French painting in the sixteenth century. London, Duckworth, 1904. 330 p.   526

Best work on subject in English. Comprehensive and detailed treatment. Critical opinions expressed in regard to precursors of French renaissance painting possess a strong personal bias and of doubtful merit in light of contemporary appraisals. Dimier leans toward theory of French dependence upon Italian school of painting and in consequence places less stress on native French contributions to renaissance arts. No attempt made to expand work with accounts of tapestry, glass painting, or enamelling. No bibliography. 46 illustrations.

Bancel, E. M. Jehan Perréal. Launette, 1885. 248 p.   527

Provides useful and scholarly study of Perréal (born between 1460 and 1463—died c. 1529) as well as a correlation of the painter's life with political history and background of the times. Included among the illustrations are those attributed to Perréal, of a book made for Anne of Brittany, *Poeme de Jehan Demarest de Caen dit Jehan Marot sur la guerre de Gênes faite par le roi Louis XII*. Jehan Marot is the father of the more famous Clément Marot.

Bouchot, Henri. Les Clouet et Corneille de Lyon. Librairie de l'art, 1892. 62 p.   528

Little known of life of Jean, also called Janet, Clouet except that he was of Flemish origin and court painter under Louis XII and François I. Clouet's son François was born c. 1516 and died c. 1572. He succeeded to his father's title of " painter to the King "; served during reigns of François I, Henri II, François II, and

Charles IX. Through work of the Clouets an intimate glimpse is given of faces and personalities of French court in one of its most brilliant periods. Bouchot presents a cautious and scholarly analysis of attributions of paintings and drawings to Clouets. Comments upon François Clouet's friendship with poets of court are filled with interest. Third chapter taken up with a study of Corneille de Lyon. Ch. IV given over to followers of Clouet. Few reproductions and those not always satisfactory. Bibliography included.

Clouet, François. Three hundred French portraits, representing personages of the courts of Francis I, Henry II, and Francis II. Auto-lithographed by Lord Ronald Gower. London and Paris, Hachette, 1875. 2 v. 529

Short preface precedes drawings. Three hundred plates auto-lithographed from originals at Castle Howard, Yorkshire. Actual size adhered to except in cases of plates 36 and 126; these are somewhat reduced. Original drawings are black, red, and yellow chalk; reproduced in monochrome. From standpoint of historical interest and literary association, portraits in v. I perhaps most rewarding. Likenesses of such persons as Francis I, Henri II, Henri's children, Coligny, Mary Stuart, Jeanne d'Albret, and others of equal fame.

Germain, Alphonse. Les Clouet. Laurens, 1907. 128 p. (Half-title: Les grands artistes.) 530

Popular, but apparently sound. Material documented. Twenty-four well-chosen plates. No bibliography.

Didot, Ambroise Firmin. Étude sur Jean Cousin. Didot, 1872. 306 p. 531

Authoritative and valuable work. Gathers together known facts and well-documented evidence concerning Cousin's life and career. Portions of biographies of painter, written closest to Cousin's lifetime, reproduced, i.e., Félibien (1666), Piles (1699), Dezalliers d'Argenville (1745), and others. Careful discussion of Cousin's contribution in painting, sculpture, illustration, and glass-painting. Especially noteworthy is the section of book entitled *Gravure sur bois* (p. 125-214), which considers in some detail printers and engravers of period. Chapter on Pierre Woeiriot. Illustrated only by several likenesses.

Réau, Louis. School of Fontainebleau, p. 31-34; Portraits at the court of the Valois, p. 34-36. *In his:* French paintings in the XIVth, XVth and XVIth centuries. New York, London & Paris, Hyperion press, 1939. 41 p. 96 plates in black and white. 12 plates in color. 532

In addition to brief written accounts, book provides photographic plates of some excellence in both black and white and in color. Bibliographies of painters.

Dimier, Louis. Le Primatice. Leroux, 1900. 595 p. 533

Exhaustive study of Italian painter with emphasis on his work in France. Because of literary and allegorical nature of the paintings at Fontainebleau, Primatice is a figure of importance to students of 16th century literature. Rivalries of Primatice with Cellini and Delorme considered. Detailed descriptions of Primatice's paintings given, but not illustrated. Chronology of work. Bibliography. Index.

Lavedan, Pierre. Léonard Limosin et les émailleurs français. Laurens, 1913. 128 p. (GA) 534

First half of book occupied with history of enamel and medieval workers in the craft. Second portion devoted to Léonard Limosin (born 1505-d. c. 1577). Art of enamelling important literarily because of choice of subject frequently drawn from field of myth and allegory.

Ritchie, Andrew Carnduff. Léonard Limosin's triumph of the faith with portraits of the house of Guise. AB 21:238-50, 1939. 535

Interesting Catholic document with important family portraits. Points out usefulness of Paradin's *devises* as a method of identification, as well as value of a careful study of renaissance enamels from other than aesthetic viewpoint. Illustrated.

Félibien, André. Entretiens sur la vie et sur les ouvrages des plus excellents peintres. Trevoux, 1725. 6 v. 536

Published originally in 1666-88, one of the earliest compilations of facts concerning French painters. Lives of painters by " French Vasari " possess interesting, though not always accurate, fund of information.

Dezalliers d'Argenville, Antoine Joseph. Abrégé de la vie des plus fameux peintres. Bure, 1762. 4 v. 537

Useful references to renaissance painters from 18th century point of view.

Mariette, Pierre Jean. Abecedario. Dumoulin, 1851-53, 1859-60. 6 v.   538
Essential source for study of lives and works of French renaissance painters, though recent research discloses inaccuracies and points out new facts.

Vasari, Giorgio. Lives of the most eminent painters, sculptors and architects. Trans. by Mrs. Jonathan Foster. London, Bohn, 1850-1907. 6 v.   539
Concerning Italian painters, travelling to France to work, their contemporary, Vasari, supplies a colorful account. Though gossipy and often factually in error, the *Lives* remains an indispensable source of biographical detail.

Van Marle, Raimond. The development of the Italian schools of painting. The Hague, Nijhoff, 1923-36. 19 v.   540
One of finest modern studies of Italian renaissance painters and paintings. Painters' lives scrupulously documented; paintings carefully catalogued. Many splendid reproductions, excellently printed in black and white.

Sculpture
(Nos. 541-544)

a. General Treatment
b. Specific Sculptors

Koechlin, Raymond. La sculpture à Troyes. By Raymond Koechlin and Jean J. Marquet de Vasselot. Colin, 1900. 421 p.   541
Thorough and extensive, stressing transition from Gothic to renaissance sculpture at Troyes. Beginning at p. 157, renaissance figures of 16th century treated more specifically. Well illustrated. Bibliography.

Vitry, Paul. Jean Goujon. Laurens, 1927. 128 p. (GA)   542
Career and sculpture of Goujon (born c. 1510-died between 1563-68) discussed in able and pleasant fashion. Discriminating choice of photographs. No bibliography.

Babelon, Jean. Germain Pilon. Les beaux-arts, 1927. 150 p.   543
Careful investigation of sculptor's life (born c. 1536—died c. 1589) and works. Attention given to collaboration of Ron-

sard, Dorat, and Pilon for triumphal entry of Charles IX into Paris in 1571. Splendid photographs of Pilon's sculpture. Valuable bibliography.

Cellini, Benvenuto. Autobiography of Benvenuto Cellini. Trans. by John Addington Symonds. Garden City, N. Y., Garden City Publishing Co., 1927. 403 p.   544
Book 2, ch. IX-LI recount lively adventures of Cellini at court of Francis I.

Tapestry
(No. 545)

Baschet, Jacques. Tapisseries de France. Nouvelles éditions françaises, 1947. 93 p.   545
Section devoted to 16th century tapestries. Brief text; magnificent illustrations in full color.

Language
(Nos. 546-619)
NEWTON S. BEMENT
Contemporary Works

Barton, John. Donait françois pour briefment entroduyr les Anglois en la droit language du Paris et de pais la d'entour fait aus despenses de Johan Barton par pluseurs bons clercs du language avandite. Ca. 1400 (before 1409).   549
English-born author and "escolier de Paris," in order to promote easier communication between good people of England and France, and because French is language of "beaucoup de bones choses" besides being of practical value in law, undertakes to improve its use in England by providing short chapters on its alphabet, pronunciation, nouns (including number and gender), adjectives, adverbs, moods (including their usage), and parts of speech (including their identification), along with conjugation of *aymer* and *estre* plus a random list of other verb forms (Latin to French).
Reprinted with commentary, by E. Stengel in ZFSL 1:25-40, 1879.

Anonymous. Un petit livre pour enseigner les enfantz de leur entreparler comun françois. Early 15th century.   547
Substantially a contemporary book of manners, illustrating forms and syntax. Thirteen paragraphs of assorted vocabulary and phrases, frequently colorful (e.g., *Alez de cy, senglent filz de putaigne* or *Damoiselle, n'aves vous point nul amy?*).

Divisions of time; numerals and currency; asking one's way; quarrels and insults; how to address ladies, servants, demand hotel service, approach respectable persons, bargain in a market, pass time of day with all comers.

Reprinted in great part by E. Stengel in ZFSL 1:10-15, 1879.

Barcley, Alexander. Introductory to wryte and to pronounce Frenche, compyled by Alexander Barcley, compendiously at the commaundement of the ryght hye excellent and myghthy prynce Thomas, duke of Northfolke. London, Robert Copland, Mar. 22, 1521. 548

Barcley, in his "youth and hytherto accustomed & excercysed in two langages of Frenche and Englysshe," and having seen "the draughtes of other (treatyses) made before my tyme," trusts to "make the same more clere, playne, & easy," because his sponsor "hath thought it expedyent that our people ... sholde not be bitterly ignorant in the frenche tunge : whiche in times past hath ben so moche set by in Englande," especially in view of the present reconciliation and confederation.

Reprinted in part by A. J. Ellis, On early English pronunciation, London, Asher, 1869-89, v. 3, p. 803-14, and E. Stengel in ZFSL 1:23-24, 1879.

Palsgrave, John. Lesclarcissement de la langue françoyse composé par maistre Jehan Palsgrave Angloys natyf de Londres et gradué de Paris. London, Haukyns, 1530. 889 p. 549

Most complete compilation of period. Written in English, contains vast amount of bilingual material which has made it invaluable to lexicographers.

Divided into three books, third being, chapter by chapter, a continuation of second. I, Pronunciation, p. 1-64; II, General treatment of nine parts of speech (one being the participle), p. 65-150; III, Detailed treatment of each part of speech, with alphabetical lists of examples, p. 151-889.

Organization, which scholars have criticized without noting its pedagogical soundness, resulted from fact that Palsgrave, after having presumably completed his work (actually, the first two books), decided that he could distinguish it from those of his predecessors only by adding a third book. He then further distinguished his work from their two-division models by patterning his third book after Theodorus Gaza's Greek grammar.

While thus delayed in the process of adding a third book, Palsgrave was anticipated in fulfilling royal demand for a textbook by his rivals, Barcley, Giles Du Guez, and Petrus Vallensys. In the end, however, he was much pleased to find that he had used, as sources, authors recommended by Geoffroy Tory in latter's *Champ-Fleury* (1529). By the same token, some of the forms given by Palsgrave were already slightly antiquated.

Reprinted by F. Génin, with an introduction of 38 pages, in CDHF, Imprimerie nationale, 1852.

Dubois, Jacques. Iacobi Sylvii Ambiani in linguam gallicam Isagωge, una cum eiusdem Grammatica Latino-gallica, ex Hebraeis, Graecis et Latinis authoribus. Cum privilegio. Estienne, 1531. 159 p. 550

First French or Latin-French grammar published in France. In two parts : I, Introduction, p. 1-90, deals with phonetics and etymology; II, Grammar, p. 90-159, deals with morphology of eight parts of speech and is historical re-latinization which author found difficult to moderate (e.g., p. 113 : *Sed quo feror? grammatica Latina scribo, non Gallica*).

This first French grammar in France contains no study of syntax, and although title of second book of La Ramée's *Grammaire* of 1572 is *Touchant la syntaxe*, the subject as modernly understood was scarcely touched before first edition of Maupas's grammar appeared in 1607.

Guez, Giles du. An Introductorie for to lerne to rede, to pronounce and to speke French trewly, compyled for the right high, exellent and most vertuous lady, the Lady Mary of Englande, doughter to our most gracious soverayn lorde Kyng Henry the Eight. London, 1532. Godfray. 187 p. 551

In two parts : I, Pronunciation and morphology; II, Examples, with interlinear translation, of letters and dialogues on sundry subjects selected in view of royal usage.

Reprinted by F. Génin in the same volume with Palsgrave, cited above, no. 549, p. 891-1079.

Estienne, Robert. Dictionaire françois-latin. Robert Estienne, 1539. Corrigé et augmenté, 1549, 1564, 1572, 1584. 552

Ancestor of Nicot's *Thresor* of 1606, cited below, and therefore of Cotgrave's dictionary of 1611, cited below, as well as of most French-Latin dictionaries that appeared in the interim.

Meigret, Louis. Le tretté de la grammęre françoęze fęt par Louis Meigręt Lionoęs. Wechel, 1550. 144 p. 553

Earliest example of method later illustrated by Vaugelas. Meigret detects and respects good usage and logical construction, unmindful of Latin. However, his use of emancipated orthography and display of tendencies diametrically opposed to those of Dubois, resulted in great part from his ignorance both of etymology and historical background of subject. Work presents essential elements of French grammar, excepting syntax, of which only occasional traces are found.

Reprinted by W. Foerster, Heilbronn, Henninger, 1888. 211 p.

Pillot, Jean. Gallicae linguae institutio, latino sermone conscripta. Groulleau, 1550. 108 p. 554

Reprinted seventeen times by 1631, possibly because it is a clear, brief, and uninquisitive *résumé* of works of Pillot's predecessors. Latter part *(mots invariables)* frankly borrowed from Estienne's dictionary. Section on conjugations appears indebted either to Estienne's *La maniere de tourner en langue françoise les verbes*, of 1535 (BN X1327), or to his *De Gallica verborum declinatione*, of 1540. Pillot's work has been subject of research by Loiseau, cited below, and by E. Stengel in ZFSL 12:257-83, 1890.

Estienne, Robert. Traicté de la grammaire françoise. Robert Estienne, 1557. 110 p. Reprinted in Latin, 1558, and in both languages, 1569. 555

Honest, commercial plagiarism of Meigret and Dubois. People have complained, says Estienne, of Meigret's orthography and Dubois' use of so many words from his native Picardy. Therefore, " ... nous ayans diligemmẽt leu les deux susdicts autheurs, avons faict un recueil, principalement de ce que nous avons veu accorder à ce que avions le temps passé apprins des plus sçavãs en nostre langue, qui avoyent tout le temps de leur vie hanté és Cours de Frãce ... esquels lieux le langage s'escrit & se prononce en plus grãd pureté qu'en tous autres."

Collection having been organized " in the manner of the Latin grammars," manual's sole novelty lies in its having been extremely well printed.

Garnier, Jean. Institutio gallicae linguae in usum iuventutis germanicae ad illustrissimos iuniores principes Landtgravios Haessiae conscripta. Geneva, Crispin, 1558. 78 p. (v. Stengel, no. 618). (v. Livet, p. 270, cited below, 579). 556

Most noteworthy example since Palsgrave of grammars composed abroad to serve as textbooks rather than as contributions to the subject.

La Ramée, Pierre de. Gramere. Wechel, 1562. 126 p. Unsigned (BN X1920). *See* continuation in 1572, cited below, no. 560. 557

Although novel in that they are printed with reformed spelling and numerous special characters, La Ramée's works on French grammar are a sort of extension into French of his previous works on Latin grammar. His development of both fields is outlined by Bement, cited below.

Sotomayor, Baltazar de. Grammatica con reglas mvy prouechosas y necessarias para aprender a leer y escriuir la lengua Francesa. Alcalá de Cornellas, 1565. 96 p. 558

Probably first French grammar published in Spain. Production of French grammars abroad was greatest in England, Holland, and Germany.

Sainliens, Claude de, alias Holyband, Claudius. The French Littleton. A most easie, perfect and absolute way to learne the frenche tongue. London, Vautrollier, 1566. iiij-Qiv. *See* 561. 559

Despite presumptuous title, there is but a modicum of internal evidence of superiority complex of the native-born (author was native of Moulins in parish of Saint-Lians); Littleton, in preceding century, had authored the foundation work on English jurisprudence.

Apparently a pocket-size rearrangement of first edition of his *Schoolemaister* of 1573 (cited below). As such, it reverses traditional order of presentation (phonetics, grammar, exercises), and offers some refinement and development of extremely sparse grammatical theory borrowed from Garnier and called *règles de syntaxe*.

La Ramée, Pierre de. Grammaire de P. de La Ramée, Lecteur du Roy en l'Université de Paris, A La Royne, Mere du Roy. Wechel, 1572. 211 p. *See* 557. 560

Printed in duplicate columns, one in ordinary and other in reformed orthography, beginning with page 57. For tables of contents of La Ramée's grammars, see RR 19:315-19, 1928.

Advanced metamorphosis of traditional *methodis grammatices* inherited from Aelius Donatus and Priscian, as expanded by author's analytical method. More concerned with method than with material, although La Ramée, whose own lectures in French were famous, concurs with Robert Estienne in recommending observance of court usage.

Sainliens, Claude de, alias Holyband, Claudius. The French Schoolemaister, wherin is most plainlie shewed the true and most perfect way of pronouncinge of the French tongue, without any helpe of Maister or teacher : set foorthe for the furtherance of all those whiche doo studie privatly in their owne study or houses : Unto the which is annexed a Vocabularie for al such woordes as bee used in common talkes :   by M. Claudius Hollybande, professor of the Latin, Frenche and Englishe tongues. Dum spiro, spero.   Imprinted at London, by William How : for Abraham Veale, 1573. *See 559.* 561

Of twelve editions this is second; first is missing. Dedicated to Robert Sackville, by whose father Sainliens was employed as secretary or tutor, and at the request of whose grandfather Roger Ascham's *Schoolmaster* of 1570 was written for this same Robert during years 1564-68. Both its content and form follow tradition established by Palsgrave and Du Guez.

Sainliens' works in lexicography, *A dictionarie French and English* (London, 1593) and especially *The treasurie of the French tong* (London, 1580), appear to stand directly in the line of descent between Robert Estienne's French-Latin dictionary of 1539 and the works of Nicot and Cotgrave, cited below.

Estienne, Henri. Proiect dv livre intitulé De la precellence du langage François. Par Henri Estienne.   Le liure au lecteur, Ie suis ioyeux de pouuoir autant plaire Aux bons François, qu'aux mauuais veux desplaire. Patisson, 1579.   295 p.   La précellence du langage françois.   Réimprimée avec des notes, une grammaire et un glossaire par Edmond Huguet.   Colin, 1896.   434 p. 562

In this disordered and digressive *Proiect* which took the place of the book because Estienne's notes for latter had been left behind in his hasty departure from Geneva, author confines himself to grammar, omitting discussion of literature, and in a bantering conclusion admits Italian to second place.

Although largely devoid of philological science, work shows author to be better informed than Du Bellay or Pléiade with regard to true resources of French language.   *See 2119.*

Estienne, Henri. Hypomneses de gallica lingua, peregrinis eam discentibus necessariae : quaedam vero ipsis etiam Gallis multum profuturae.... Auctore Henr. Stephano : qui et Gallicam patris sui Grammaticen adjunxit...   Geneva, 1582.   335 p. 563

Contains best commentaries to date on article, syntax of pronouns, and such matters as effect of position on meaning of adjectives. Insufficient, however, to justify author's reputation of best grammarian of century, except possibly when taken in conjunction with other contributions scattered throughout his *Traicté de la conformité du langage françois avec le grec* (Paris, 1565), his *Deux dialogues du nouveau langage françois italianizé* (Geneva, 1578), and his *Précellence*, cited above.

Malherbe, François de. Commentaire sur Desportes.   *In:*   Œuvres de Malherbe, Hachette, 1862, 4:249-473. (GELF) 564

Not merely an applied *art poétique*, but a minutely critical examination of Desportes' diction and syntax. Similar examination of Malherbe's correspondence reveals that his practice did not invariably adhere to correction imposed on work of Desportes, which would have been equally applicable to language of Desportes' contemporaries.

Nicot, Jean. Thresor de la langue françoyse. Douceur, 1606.   666 p. 565

French words explained in French. Nicot cites examples of usage and their authors. Despite Cotgrave's mildly caustic reference to this procedure (quoted below), Nicot appears to have been one of Cotgrave's most carefully consulted sources.

Cotgrave, Randle. A dictionarie of the French and English tongues.   Compiled by Randle Cotgrave.   London, Islip, 1611. 956 double-column pages, plus appendix, 10 p., entitled : Briefe directions for such as desire to learne the French tongue. 566

French-English dictionary which will remain indispensable at least until completion of Huguet's dictionary cited below. *See 613.*

French readers are assured, in the preface, that words unknown to them were not invented by author, but merely collected by him, and that " Il pouvoit bien citer le nom, le livre, la page, & le passage; mais ce n'eut plus icy eté vn Dictionaire, ains vn Labirinte." To the sources thus implied may be added, according to internal evidence, Sainliens' *Treasurie* of 1580, his *Dictionarie* of 1593, and Nicot's *Thresor* of 1606.

Maupas, Charles. Grammaire et syntaxe françoise. Bacot, 1625. Signed at Blois, 1618, 360 p. This is the third edition of Grammaire françoise. Blois, Philippes Cottereau, 1607. 567

Textbook addressed to foreigners at a time when tradition of manuals addressed to them in Latin was still strong. Joannes Serreius' *Grammatica gallica* (Strasbourg, 1598), for instance, had been reprinted eleven times by 1648. Hence significance of title of Maupas's third edition. Although it was almost immediately outmoded owing to rapid development of the language, Maupas's work, motivated by a desire to provide better instruction in use of French, as distinguished from mere teaching of nomenclature or elaboration of grammatical theory, opened a new period. Marked beginning of practical study of syntax.

Oudin, Antoine. Grammaire françoise rapportée au langage du temps. Billaine, 1632. 2nd ed., Sommaville, 1640. 320 p. 568

Oudin's primary intention was to revise and develop Maupas's grammar cited above, but he found that it contained too many *antiquailles* from 16th century. Therefore utilized best of it, but drew examples from later sources, beginning with Malherbe's commentaries. On many points he anticipated Vaugelas' work. By breaking with sources from preceding literary period he became forerunner of Vaugelas and latter's contemporaries in study of current usage. His own forerunners in this tendency had been Meigret and Robert Estienne.

Modern Studies of Sixteenth Century Works on the Language

Beaulieux, Charles. Histoire de l'orthographe française. Champion, 1927. 2 v. 569

Shows incidentally that consistency of modern French spelling had its origins in 16th century.

Robert Estienne's system prevailed against contemporary reformers owing to powerful instrumentality of his dictionary, and continued to prevail because it had introduced into orthography then commonly in use a uniformity based on Latin tradition (1:210-361).

Bement, Newton S. Petrus Ramus and the beginnings of formal French grammar. *See* 226. 570

Relationship of La Ramée's Latin and French grammars. How he developed each grammar by expanding the one previously published and adhering to a single personal theory throughout the series.

— The problem of the French verb system, at home and abroad. MLJ 34:604-15, 1950. 571

Includes a survey and summary of multiple solutions offered by 16th century French grammarians in their attempts to classify French verbs. Conclusion notes incidentally that two sole " regular " conjugations recognized by present-day textbooks used in France are identical with only two regular conjugations which Pierre de La Ramée was able to discern in 1562. In view of recent history of the subject, La Ramée's solution was ultra-modern, as was also method he proposed to his students (quoted, p. 605) for working at such problems.

Benoist, Antoine. De la syntaxe française entre Palsgrave et Vaugelas. Thorin, 1877. 231 p. (Diss., Paris) 572

Deals with period 1530-1647. I, Synthesis of chief grammarians from Palsgrave to Henri Estienne; II, Comparisons between modern syntax and that of examples drawn chiefly from Amyot and frequently from Calvin and Coeffeteau; III, Review of Vaugelas' work. No index or bibliography of sources.

Review : O. Ulbrich in ZRP 1:579-81, 1877.

Brandon, Edgar E. Robert Estienne et le dictionnaire français au XVIe siècle. Baltimore, Furst, 1904. 133 p. (Diss., Paris) 573

Substantial history and treatment of Robert Estienne and his dictionaries, which has been harshly criticized owing to faulty editing or printing.

Reviews : E. Stengel in ZFSL 29:18-21, 1906; A. Thomas in Rom 33:618-21, 1904; J. Vianey, in RLR, 48:381-82, 1905.

Brunot, Ferdinand. La doctrine de Malherbe d'après son commentaire sur Desportes. Masson, 1891. 605 p. (AUL, v. 1) 574

Exposition of problems attending definition of " good usage " during pre-classical interim, with some attention to inconsistency of Malherbe's criticism and practice, and an appraisal of his effect on history of language and especially on contemporary and later lyric poetry. *See* 2268.

Clément, Louis. Henri Estienne et son œuvre française. Picard, 1898, 1899. 540 p, (Diss., Paris)   575

Second part, p. 197-455, offers a detailed and thorough study entitled : *Henri Estienne grammairien français. See* 969, 1971, 2121.

Farrer, Lucy E. La vie et les œuvres de Claude de Sainliens alias Claudius Holyband. Champion, 1908. 115 p. (Diss., Paris)   576

Essential, well-made book which presents much factual evidence concerning history of Holyband's grammars and composition of dictionaries at close of 16th century.

Reviews : E. Bourciez in Rcr ns 67:76, Jan. 28, 1909; H. Heiss in KJRP 11²:167, 1907-08.

Génin, F. L'éclaircissement de la langue française par Jean Palsgrave, suivi de la grammaire de Giles du Guez. Publiés pour la première fois en France par F. Génin. Imprimerie nationale, 1852. Introduction, 38 p. (CDHF)   577

Génin's introduction gives most complete picture of historical background of these two grammars, together with a comparative evaluation which attempts to minimize their extreme inequality, and a certain amount of apt linguistic comment.

Lambley, Kathleen. The teaching and cultivation of the French language in England during Tudor and Stuart times. University of Manchester Press, 1920. New York, Longmans, Green, 1920. 438 p. 578

Well-documented historical account of rise and decline of Anglo-French and French in England, with an introductory chapter on 13th and 14th centuries. Appendices, p. 403-28, provide chronological and alphabetical lists of manuals for teaching French to the English. *See* 2799.

Livet, Charles-Louis. La grammaire française et les grammairiens du xviᵉ siècle. Didier, 1859. 536 p.   579

First *ouvrage d'ensemble* in field. Offers fairly complete accounts, including ample

quotation, grouped thus : 1, Dubois; 2, Meigret, Pelletier, Des Autels; 3, Ramus; 4, Garnier, Pillot, Mathieu; 5, Robert Estienne, Henri Estienne ; appendices; Claude de Saint-Lien, Théodore de Bèze. No index.

Loiseau, Arthur. Étude historique et philologique sur Jean Pillot et sur les doctrines grammaticales du xviᵉ siècle. Saint-Cloud, Belin, 1866. 144 p. (Diss., Paris)   580

History of French grammar in 16th century, in which Pillot (1550, cited above) is made the central figure. Stengel supports Loiseau with regard to importance of Pillot. Brunot disagrees with Loiseau and appears to be justified in his opinion.

Millet, Adrien. Les grammairiens et la phonétique, ou l'enseignement des sons du français depuis le xviᵉ siècle jusqu'à nos jours. Monnier, 1933. 197 p.   581

For 16th century *see : Première partie,* ch. II, p. 26-40; *Deuxième partie,* ch. II, p. 133-44.

Starnes, Dewitt T. Bilingual dictionaries of Shakespeare's day. PMLA 52:1005-18, Dec., 1937.   582

P. 1015-17 show that Cotgrave frequently borrowed the English portions of his definitions from Thomas Thomas' *Dictionarium linguae Latinae et Anglicanae,* 5th ed., 1596 (1st ed., ca. 1588).

Thurot, Charles. De la prononciation française depuis le commencement du xviᵉ siècle, d'après les témoignages des grammariens. Imprimerie nationale, 1881-1883. 2 v.   583

V. I, p. xxii-lxxxvii, contains a bibliography of grammars and dictionaries of period 1521-1878. Whole no less useful for study of morphology than for study of pronunciation.

Reviews : E. Koschwitz in ZFSL 4²:87, 1882; P. Lallemand in Bcr, Feb. 15, 1882, p. 371.

Specialized References

Bastin, J. Le participe passé avec *avoir* au xviᵉ siècle. RPF 9:237-40, 1895.   584

Contrary to Brunot's belief, Marot's rule for agreement of past participle was not commonly observed. Writers of 16th century, including Marot, and even those of early 18th century, used either variable or invariable form of participle when the direct object preceded. When it followed, they generally used the invariable form.

Bement, Newton S. The conditional sentence from Commynes to Malherbe. New York, Institute of French studies, 1931, 26 p. (Supplement to the RR.)   585

Language of period was extremely rich in conditional sentence formulas. Usage became gradually restricted, however, to few which had been longest and most fully favored.

— The subjunctive in relative clauses from Commynes to Malherbe. PQ 10:294-306, 1931.   586

Classification of relative clauses, within whose varied categories are examined differentia which correspond to differences in mood usage.

— The French imperfect subjunctive and present conditional in the sixteenth century. PMLA 47:992-1011, Dec., 1932.   587

Summary of syntactical evidence of differentiation of senses and uses of these moods which occurred during course of the century.

— Some phonological, orthographical, and syntactical aspects of the persistence of the French present subjunctive endings -ons and -ez. PMAS 18:505-24, 1932.   588

Documented historical treatment up to end of 16th century, during which the yod came to be quite generally represented in orthography, or even duplicated, as, in Cotgrave's optative form : nous voyons and voyions (Table, fol. 4).

Adoption of endings -ions and -iez resulted from an intention to distinguish subjunctive from imperative mood. Modernly so-called imperative forms were left isolated and distinguishable when -ions and -iez were adopted in hypotactic construction but not in parataxis.

— French modal syntax in the sixteenth century. Ann Arbor, University of Michigan Press, 1934. 168 p. (MPLL, no. 11) 589

Study of one modern, four pre-16th century, and twelve 16th century authors. Basically factual. Status, developments, and changes observed by statistical method. Complete index of expressions, constructions, and mood usage.

Review : E. Bourciez in Rcr ns 102:141-43, 1935.

Borlé, Edouard. Observations sur l'emploi des conjonctions de subordination dans la langue du XVIe siècle, étudié spécialement dans les deux ouvrages de Bernard Palissy. Les belles lettres, 1927. 261 p.   590

Covers period from Commynes to Saint François de Sales, with a statistical method, abundant tables, and an alphabetical index. In author's words : " ... un travail qui ne vise qu'à être un répertoire aussi complet que possible des conjonctions de subordination employées par les prosateurs français du XVIe siècle." The claim is much too modest.

Categorically wrong in one conclusion : " ... la langue du XVIe siècle ne se servait jamais de ... pour que... " (p. 243). See 2157.

Review : A. M[eillet] in BSLP 30:144, 1930.

Fay, Percival B. Elliptical partitiv usage in affirmativ clauses in French prose of the fourteenth, fifteenth and sixteenth centuries. Champion, 1912. 87 p. (Diss., Johns Hopkins)   591

Much depends on the sense given to the definite article forming a part of the elliptical partitiv (i.e., the partitive article), that is, whether it indicates a determinate or an indeterminate totality. In the Heptaméron and later texts Fay inclines to view it as having the second sense.

Reviews : E. Bourciez in Rcr ns 76:16-17, July 5, 1913 ; E. Lerch in LGRP 36:86-87, 1915.

Gay, Lucy M. Studies in Middle French. MLN 22:104-09, 1907.   592

Author questions certain statements made by Darmesteter and Hatzfeld (no. 610). Refutes statement that use of ce for impersonal il is major practice; shows that de does occur after rien, quelque chose, etc., before adjectives.

Guerlin de Guer, Charles. La langue d'Amyot. Fmod 5:1-10, 127-41, 231-42, 1937.   593

Study of differences between first and later editions of Amyot's works shows that his corrections of orthography place him in Meigret's camp of reformists, his tendency was to simplify and modernize his style, his preference was for the syntax or constructions most commonly used in his time.

— Sur la langue du Picard Jean Calvin. Fmod 5:303-16, 1937.   594

Review of criticisms of Calvin's style, followed by a critical appreciation of its origins and qualities.

Field a fertile one, since linguistic range of Calvin's work is superior to that of any contemporary.

Huguet, Edmond. Étude sur la syntaxe de Rabelais comparée à celle des autres prosateurs de 1450 à 1550. Hachette, 1894. 460 p.   595

Foremost study of 16th century French prose among those which appeared near turn of century. *See* 911.

Reviews : L. Frankel in ZFSL 17:168-73, 1895; H. Schneegans in ZRP 19:118-31, 1895.

— Le langage figuré au seizième siècle. Hachette, 1933. 256 p.   596

Selected examples studied under two headings : origins and uses.

Reviews : E. Bourciez in Rcr ns 100:459-61, Oct.-Dec., 1933; A. Dauzat in Fmod 2:165-67, Mar.-Apr., 1934.

Lamb, William W. The syntax of the Heptameron. New York, 1914. 178 p. (Diss., NYU)   597

Investigation based on comparison with modern usage. Materials and results presented in serviceable form.

Mellerio, Louis. Lexique de Ronsard précédé d'une étude sur son vocabulaire, son orthographe et sa syntaxe. Plon, 1895. 251 p. (BE)   598

One of typical studies of its time, now largely superseded by works which have synthesized their results.

Review : E. Droz in Rcr ns 39:324-32, 1895.

Régnier, Adolphe. Lexique de la langue de Malherbe avec une introduction grammaticale. Hachette, 1869. 680 p. (GELF, v. 5)   599

Unusually extensive grammatical introduction : p. xvii-lxxxiv. Whole comparable to Mellerio's work, cited above.

Roumiguière, Henriette. Le français dans les relations diplomatiques. Berkeley, Calif., University of California Press, 1926. p. 259-340. (CPMP, v. 12, no. 4). (Diss., California)   600

Ch. I, *Le latin au XVe et XVIe siècle.* Brantôme, Pasquier. Ch. III, *Pourquoi le français devint-il la langue internationale de l'Europe?* Influence of 15th and 16th century events. Ch. IV, *Qualités particulières attribuées à la langue française et refusées aux autres langues.* Discussion of Brantôme, Henri Estienne, Charpentier, and Ronsard.

Review : P. Fouché in RLR 65:125-26, 1927.

Sainéan, Lazare. La langue de Rabelais. Boccard, 1923. V. I (1922), Civilisation de la renaissance; 508 p. V. II (1923), Langue et vocabulaire; 579 p.   601

Investigation of probable sources underlying Rabelais' prose creation. *See* 915.

Schoenfelder, Willibald. Die Wortstellung in den poetischen Werken Pierre de Ronsards. Gera, Buhr and Draeger, 1906. 80 p. (Diss., Leipzig.)   602

Since 1905 the production of studies of this type has declined noticeably in favor of studies covering a broader field and attempting to discern the course of syntactical evolution.

Smalley, Vera E. The sources of A dictionarie of the French and English tongues, by Randle Cotgrave (London, 1611). Baltimore, The Johns Hopkins Press, 1948. 252 p.   603

Thorough study of renaissance lexicography and of conditions which led to production of series of dictionaries stemming from Robert Estienne's dictionary of 1539, cited above. Best account of relationship of dictionaries which appeared during period 1539-1611.

Vaganay, Hugues. De Rabelais à Montaigne; les adverbes terminés en -ment. RER 1:166-87, 1903; 2:11-18, 173-89, 258-74, 1904; 3:186-215, 1905.   604

Two thousand adverbs; nine hundred still in use.

— Le vocabulaire français du seizième siècle; deux mille mots peu connus. ZRP 29:579-601, 705-36, 1904; 29:72-104, 177-213, 1905.   605

Words used in 16th century but found neither in Godefroy's *Supplément* nor in Cotgrave.

Vogels, J. Der syntaktische Gebrauch der Tempora und Modi bei Pierre de Larivey im Zusammenhang der historischen französischen Syntax. Bonn, Weber, 1880. p. 445-556. (RSB, no. 5)   606

Substantial, grammatically classified catalog of examples.

Voizard, Eugène. Étude sur la langue de Montaigne. Cerf, 1885. 308 p. (Diss., Paris).   607

Detailed study of Montaigne's orthography, grammatical forms, syntax, vocabulary, and style, plus notations concerning his influence abroad. Author concludes that linguistically, despite influence of

Latin, Montaigne is well in step with his time, so that the most distinctive feature of his writing is his style.

Titles cited in bibliography are in some instances approximations. Linguistically, Montaigne was in some respects ahead of his time. See 1796.

Wind, Bartina H. Les mots italiens introduits en français au xvie siècle. Deventer, Kluwer, 1928. 222 p. (Diss., Amsterdam) 608

Begins with a study of borrowing as a linguistic phenomenon, and of the effect of Italianism according to contemporary opinion. Attempts to discern limits of borrowing; studies vocabulary actually borrowed (word list not intended to be exhaustive) and its distribution among the various fields (art, science, professional, amusements, household, etc.). Offers over-all view of subject and provides a well-organized analysis of impact and result.

Review : A. Dauzat in RPF 41:209-11, 1929.

General Studies

Brunot, Ferdinand. Le seizième siècle. *In his:* Histoire de la langue française des origines à 1900. Colin, 1906. See 313.   609

Most serviceable single volume on subject, for either general or specific reference purposes. Although not a *tableau de la langue*, nor even exhaustive in many of its varied divisions, is most widely documented *ouvrage d'ensemble* and work of greatest range of content.

Unusual attention given to struggle against Latin and to general influences contributing either deliberately or unconsciously to development of French, which occupies first half of volume. Second half devoted to historical grammar.

At time of publication there was disappointment on the part of some critics, that a scholar so eminently qualified should have chosen to contribute merely a historical grammar instead of a critical appreciation, a psychological investigation, or some philosophical treatment of the subject. Such criticism was presumably nullified by publication of Brunot's *La pensée et la langue*, Masson, 1922.

Reviews : E. Bourciez in Rcr ns 63:225-27, Mar., 1907; H. Chatelain in RHL 13:742-46, 1906; A. Jeanroy in AM 19:437-438, 1907.

Darmesteter, Arsène. Le seizième siècle en France. Tableau de la littérature et de la langue, by A. Darmesteter and Adolphe Hatzfeld. 7th ed. Delagrave [1901 ?] 2 v. in 1. See 98.   610

First edition, 1878, one of earliest textbooks in the field. Darmesteter was instrumental in placing the study of historical syntax in curriculum. Subject became part four of his *Cours de grammaire historique de la langue française, publié par les soins de L. Sudre et E. Muret*, Delagrave, 1891-97. Like most pioneer works, these have been subjected to numerous corrections of detail.

Dauzat, Albert. Où en sont les études de français ? Bibliothèque du français moderne, 1935. 344 p.   611

Essential contributions by Dauzat, Fouché, Gougenheim, Esnault, Bloch, and Guerlin de Guer, consisting of history, bibliography, and review. Little account taken of American bibliography. No index of books and articles reviewed or mentioned.

For 16th century see, chiefly, p. 35-55, 87-111, 141-56, 233-62.

— Les étapes de la langue française. Presses universitaires de France, 2nd ed., 1948. 134 p.   612

Views period 1340-1610 as a single *étape*, p. 69-90.

Gougenheim, Georges. Grammaire de la langue française du seizième siècle. Lyons, IAC, 1951. 258 p. (CLM, v. 7)   612A

Utilizes works cited herein, of Brunot (no. 609), Darmesteter and Hatzfeld, (no. 610) and Huguet (no. 613), but is based directly upon texts by thirty-one authors of the period. Divisions : I. *Les sons*, based on Thurot's work (no. 583), and on contemporary grammars; II. *Les formes et leur emploi*; III. *Syntaxe des fonctions*. Substantially a grammar of differences between present-day and 16th century French, intended to serve as a reference and guide for uninitiated student. Most serviceable introduction to language of period in general. Satisfactorily indexed.

Huguet, Edmond. Dictionnaire de la langue française du seizième siècle. Champion, 1925-. See 566.   613

In 1953 available in the United States as far as MARR. (*Tome quatrième, fascicul- 42*), Didier, 1946.

Nyrop, Kristoffer. Grammaire historique de la langue française. Copenhagen, Gyldendal. Paris, Picard, New York, Stechert, 1899-1930. 6 v. 614
In field concerned, may be ranked next to Brunot's second volume, cited above.

Wartburg, Walter von. Évolution et structure de la langue française. Leipzig, Teubner, 1934. 256 p. 2nd ed., Chicago, University of Chicago Press, 1937. 290 p. 615
" Nous le destinons (ce livre) aux gens cultivés qui voudraient s'informer sur les grandes lignes de l'évolution de la langue française sans s'égarer dans les broussailles d'une terminologie spéciale." (Préface)
Ch. V, *Le seizième siècle*, p. 131-56. Brief treatment; author well fulfills avowed purpose.

Bibliographies

Bement, Newton S. A selective bibliography of works on the French language of the sixteenth century. PQ 26:219-34, 1947. 616
Divisions : I, *Bibliographies*, indicates the sources of a complete bibliography; II, *Works of the period*; III, *Modern articles and books on the works of the period and their authors*; IV, *Modern articles and books on 16th century French*; V, *General works partially devoted to 16th century French*.

Contains most items cited in present chapter, plus some which are not, with descriptions and commentaries.

Horluc, Pierre, and Georges Marinet. Bibliographie de la syntaxe du français (1840-1905). AUL ns II, droit, lettres, fasc. 20. Reprinted : Lyons, Rey, and Paris, Picard, 1908. 320 p. XVIᵉ siècle, p. 29-37, items 257-333. 617
Divisions : I, *Études générales, Grammaire comparée, Les théories*; II, *Les écrivains* (in chronological order). Entries described. Related material and reviews cited.

Bibliography continued through 1910 by Thurau, cited below.

Summaries of its most important items given by Dauzat, *Où en sont les études de français*, (611, p. 87-110).
Review : H. Yvon in RPF 23:65-66, 1909.

Stengel, Edmund. Chronologisches Verzeichnis französischer Grammatiken vom Ende des 14. bis zum Ausgange des 18. Jahrhunderts, nebst Angabe der bisher ermittelten Fundorte derselben. Oppeln, Franck, 1890. 150 p. 618
Years 1500-1600 : items 4-42, p. 19-31. Indispensable. Lists 603 items, years 1400-1799. Indexed : I, *Liste der Verfasser*; II, *Liste der Titel*; III, *Liste der Verlagsorte*. Entries complete, include variations in titles of successive editions; revisions by original or another author.

Corrections : (1) Item 15, De Trou, is mistakenly dated 1556 instead of 1656. (2) The title of item 36, De La Mothe, dated 1592, is incorrect according to the copy in the Library of Congress, whose title is approximated by the title given by Stengel for the edition of 1595.

Stengel's work supplemented by a few titles included for that purpose in present bibliography, and also, notably but not extensively, on cited pages of following three works :

Brunot, Ferdinand. *Histoire de la langue française des origines à 1900*. No. 313. II, 124, footnote 1.

Telle, J. A. *Les grammairiens français depuis l'origine de la grammaire en France jusqu'aux dernières œuvres connues*. 2ᵉ éd.

Thurot, Charles. *De la prononciation française depuis le commencement du XVIᵉ siècle, d'après les témoignages des grammairiens*. Imprimerie nationale, 1881-82. I, xxii-xliv.

Thurau, G. Historische französische Syntax, 1896-1910. KJRP 11¹:343-406, 1907-1908. 619
See note under Horluc and Marinet (617).

CHAPTER II. CLÉMENT MAROT

(Nos. 620-696)

HÉLÈNE HARVITT

Villey, Pierre. Tableau chronologique des publications de Marot. RSS 7:46-97, 206-234, 1920; 8:80-110, 157-211, 1921. 620
Definitive list of dates and works.

— Recherches sur la chronologie des œuvres de Marot. BBB 1920, p. 185-209, 238-49; 1921, p. 49-61, 101-17, 171-88, 226-52, 272-87; 1922, p. 263-71, 311-17, 372-88, 423-32; 1923, p. 48-54. 621
Examination and correction of previous chronologies. Indispensable.

Marot, Clément. Œuvres complètes. Ed. by N. Lenglet-Dufresnoy, The Hague, Gosse et Neaulme, 1731. 4 v. 622
According to Henri Guy " inexact et fantaisiste." Yet this must be credited as first annotated and critical edition of M.'s works; its erroneous chronology adopted by subsequent editions.

— Œuvres, annotées, revues, sur les éditions originales et précédées de la vie de Clément Marot par Charles d'Héricault. Garnier, 1867. 422 p. 623
Selected works. M. biography unreliable.

— Œuvres complètes, revues sur les éditions originales, avec préface, notes, et glossaire par Pierre Jannet. Picard, 1868. Lemerre, 1873-76. 4 v. 624
Reproduces Lenglet-Dufresnoy chronology, together with apocrypha which 1731 edition attributed to M.

— Œuvres choisies, accompagnées d'une étude sur la vie, les œuvres et la langue de ce poète, avec des variantes, des notes philologiques, littéraires, et historiques, et un glossaire, par Eugène Voizard. Garnier, 1908. 460 p. 625
Biography is above all a condensation of Guiffrey's. Good selection from every type of M.'s work.

— Les Œuvres de Clément Marot de Cahors en Quercy, éd. Georges Guiffrey. 626

V. I — C'est la vie de Clément Marot. Schemit, 1911.
Biography, written by G. Guiffrey, published posthumously by Robert Yve-Plessis, who revised and completed certain chapters. Has been used as a source-book for most contemporary scholarship on M.; many errors have been corrected and many statements amplified.

V. II — Claye, 1875.
Published during Guiffrey's lifetime. Contains the *Opuscules*.

V. III — Quantin, 1881.
Published during Guiffrey's lifetime. *Epîtres*.

V. IV — Schemit, 1929.
Introduction by Jean Plattard : editor has omitted such statements left by Guiffrey as are contradicted by more modern scholarship; certain poems accepted by Guiffrey as M.'s are today of doubtful authenticity. *Epigrammes, Estrennes, Epitaphes, Cimetière, Complainctes, Oraisons*.

V. V — Schemit, 1931.
Contains some *poèmes inédits* found by Gustave Mâcon. Several poems, from Guiffrey's original notes, are today of questionable authenticity. *Elegies, Ballades, Chants divers, Rondeaux, Chansons, Psaumes, Œuvres posthumes, Œuvres inédites*.

— Poésies inédites, éditées par Gustave Mâcon. BBB 1898, 157-70, 233-48. 627
Valuable contribution to M. scholarship. Mâcon discovered some very important and moving verses written by M. in his best manner; they are authentic and shed new light on M.'s stay at Ferrara and Venice.

Argus, Elisabeth. Clément Marot und Margarete von Valois, Herzogin von Alençon, Königin von Navarra. Borna-Leipzig, Noske, 1918. 62 p. (Diss., Munich) 628

M.'s biographical and literary relations with Marguerite. She gradually turned his interest towards the Bible and her encouragement is in part responsible for the translation of the Psalms. Any Platonism in M.'s work due to Marguerite's influence. Good discussion of M.'s influence upon Marguerite's technique.

Bailey, John Cann. Marot. *In his:* The claims of French poetry. London, Constable, 1907. p. 47-78. 629

Non-scholarly, pleasant, acute personal estimate of M.'s verse. Sees a very genuine religious strain of Protestant bent in the poet, refers to *Le riche en pauvreté*, *Complaincte d'un pastoureau chrestien*, and to *Le balladin* as proof.

Bayet, Jean. La source principale de l'Églogue de Clément Marot au Roy soubs les noms de Pan et Robin. RHL 34:567-71, 1927. 630

Takes Guiffrey to task for depending upon this poem for biographical data concerning M.'s childhood. Rustic pleasures suspiciously resemble those of Priam and Hecuba taken from a page of the *Illustrations de Gaule* by Jean Lemaire.

Becker, P. A. Clement Marots Liebeslyrik. SAWW, v. 184, 5th Abhandlung, 1917. 179 p. 631

Traces M.'s sentimental life through his poetry; an anthology (69-179) traces evolution of his love lyrics from conventional to personal and subjective expression of love.

— Clement Marots Psalmenübersetzung. BSAW, Bd. 72, I Heft, 1921. 44 p. 632

M. used Latin rather than Hebrew sources for his translation of the Psalms. Was mainly aided by commentaries and explanations of Martin Bucer; might also have been aided by Olivétan's translation of the Bible. Good analysis of liberties M. took with texts. M.'s translation opens a new era of lyrical poetry.

— Marots Leben. ZFSL 41:186-232; 1913; 42:87-139, 141-207, 1914. 633

Very thorough and penetrating study of M.'s life. Definitive.

— Die Versepistel von Clément Marot. *In his:* Aus Frankreichs Frührenaissance. — Kritische Skizzen. Leipzig, Selbstverlag des Romanischen Seminars; Droz, 1927. p. 47-85. (SFL) 634

Scholarly and readable survey of poets who wrote and developed verse-epistle until it reached highest form with M.

Bonnefon, Pierre. Le différend de Marot et de Sagon. RHL 1:103-38, 259-85, 1894. 635

Most complete account of Marot-Sagon controversy. Bonnefon shows how most of poetic world entered into the quarrel.

Bonnet, Jules. Clément Marot à la cour de Ferrare. BSHP 21:159-68, 1872. 636

Best for a description of court society at Ferrara. Mistakes Diane de Poitiers as the cause of M.'s flight from France.

— Clément Marot à Venise et son abjuration à Lyon. BSHP 34:289-303, 1885. 637

Bonnet's thesis is that M. was persecuted for a cause which was not really his: Protestantism.

Borland, Lois. The influence of Marot on English poetry of the sixteenth century. Chicago, University of Chicago, 1913. 107 p. (M. A. thesis) 638

Similarity of forms used by M. and Wyatt. Influence on Sir David Lyndsay, Alexander Montgomerie. Detailed comparison between M.'s *De Mme Louise de Savoie, mère du Roi, Eglogue au Roi*, and Spenser's November and December *Eclogues* of the *Shepherd's calendar*. Some *Amoretti* sonnets borrowed in part from *Elegies* of M., and small portions of *Faerie queene* resemble M.'s work.

Bullock, Walter L. The first French sonnets. MLN 39:475-78, 1924. 639

Corrects Clement's article. (641) *See* 2721.

Charlier, Gustave. Sur l'enfance de Marot. RHL 34:426-28, 1927. 640

Same thesis as Bayet. (630)

Clement, N. H. The first French sonneteer. RR 14:189-98, 1923. 641

First regular sonnet in France composed by M. in 1528-31.

Colletet, Guillaume. Notices biographiques sur les trois Marot, précédemment transcrites d'après le manuscrit détruit dans l'incendie de la bibliothèque du Louvre, le 24 mai 1871, et publié pour la première fois par Georges Guiffrey. Lemerre, 1871, 61 p. 642

Considers Jean Marot more important as Clément's father than as a poet in his own right. Extols Clément for having added grace to what was almost a barbaric language; many factual mistakes and naïvetés. Valuable paragraph p. 29-30 contains description of physical appearance of Clément Marot.

Cons, Louis. Marot. *In his:* État présent des études sur Villon. Les belles lettres, 1936. p. 28-30.   643

On M. as a pioneer critic and evaluator of Villon.

Douen, Orentin. Clément Marot et le psautier huguenot; étude historique, littéraire, musicale, et bibliographique, contenant des mélodies primitives des psaumes et des specimens d'harmonie de Clément Jannequin, bourgeois, etc. Imprimerie nationale, 1878-79.   2 v.   644

Longwinded and pedantic. Main thesis : M. was ardent pietist and reformer; the witty, gay aspects of M.'s work brushed aside. Wishes to whitewash the later M. from all suspicion of frivolity and misconduct. Lists editions of psalms and continuers of M.

Droz, Eugénie, and P. P. Plan. Les dernières années de Clément Marot. BHren 10:7-68, 1948.   645

Fréd. Chavannes's *Notice sur un manuscrit du XVIᵉ siècle appartenant à la Bibliothèque cantonale. Poésies inédites de Clément Marot, de Catherine de Médicis et de Théodore de Bèze,* (Lausanne, Bridel, 1844) " repris et complété."

Eckhardt, Alexandre. Marot et Dante. RSS 13:140-42, 1926.   646

Influence of Dante's *Inferno* in several lines of *L'enfer. See* 2716.

Faguet, Emile. Clément Marot. *In his:* Seizième siècle. Boivin, 1936. p. 35-75. *See* 101.   647

M. gave to French poetry vigor and tone. First of the three classicists, Marot, Ronsard, Malherbe, to mould the language.

Fromage, Robert. Clément Marot, son premier emprisonnement—Identification d'Isabeau et d'Anne. BSHP 59:52-71, 122-29, 1910.   648

Isabeau neither Diane de Poitiers, as Lenglet-Dufresnoy conjectures, nor the Catholic Church—theory of O. Douen; she was the wife of an official, who avenged herself upon M. for some insulting verses he had written.

Fromage's theory (endorsed by Emmanuel Philipot, RHL 19:59-74, 1912) that the mysterious Anne was Anne de Beauregard has been disproved by Abel Lefranc.

— Poésies inédites de Clément Marot. BSHP 58:44-50, 129-41, 225-42, 1909. 649

Most of the poems disclosed in these articles non-authentic (cf., Jean Plattard in RER 10:68-71, 1912, or BSHP 61:278-80, 1912).

Glauning, Friedrich. Syntaktische Studien zu Marot, ein Beitrag zur Geschichte der französischen Syntax. Nordlingen, Beck, 1873.   50 p.   650

M.'s syntax compared with Montaigne's.

Green, F. C. Marot's Preface to his edition of Villon's works. MP 22:69-77, 1924-25.   651

M. undertook task at Francis's request. M.'s estimate of Villon's artistic merit accurate; has been substantiated by posterity.

Guy, Henry. Clément Marot et son école. Champion, 1926.   337 p.   V. II of Histoire de la poésie française au XVIᵉ siècle.   652

Vivid and humanized account of M.'s life and character. Good reading; very little technical discussion of M.'s work. Has destroyed certain myths concerning the poet, e.g., his fighting at Pavia.

— Les sources françaises de Ronsard. RHL 9:217-56, 1902.   653

Ronsard bears strong traces of M.'s influence.

Harrisse, Henry. La Colombine et Clément Marot. Protat, 1886.   38 p.   654

Investigations into the Colombine Library at Seville disclosed unauthorized edition of M. published by Olivier Arnoullet, and publication, under separate cover, of a translation of sixth psalm which scholars had hitherto thought made its first appearance in print appended to Marguerite's *Miroir de l'âme pécheresse.*

Harvitt, Hélène J. Eustorg de Beaulieu, a disciple of Marot. Lancaster, New Era Printing Co., 1918.   164 p.   655

Only monograph that has appeared so far on the man; thorough investigation into life and works of Beaulieu, who like M. was one of the strong exponents of Calvinism and one of chief contributors to song book of the Reformation.

Hawkins, R. L. The books of reference of an adversary of Marot. RR 7:221-23, 1916. 656

Grande généalogie, in one section, contains in a few interesting lines a brief catalogue of authors and books popular during early renaissance in France.

Jourda, Pierre. Marguerite d'Angoulême, duchesse d'Alençon, reine de Navarre (1492-1549); étude biographique et littéraire. Champion, 1930. 2 v. (1184 p.) (BLR v. 19, 20). *See* 764. 657

Indispensable study of Marguerite's relations with M. and his school.

— Marot, l'homme et l'œuvre. Boivin, 1950. 167 p. 658

Appeared in series *Le livre de l'étudiant*. Professor Jourda of University of Montpellier has published many studies on French renaissance. Studies M.'s life, evolution of his work, debt to the *Rhétoriqueurs*, his role as an official poet, personal poetry, his art and influence. Good bibliography at end.

Karl, Louis. Une découverte bibliographique à propos de la chronologie marotique. RSS 10:107-10, 1923. 659

Recueil de vraye poésie françoyse, published in 1543, which escaped Villey's attention in his chronology.

Kinch, Charles E. La poésie satirique de Clément Marot. Boivin, 1940. 286 p. 660

Well-documented, serious study of M.'s satire.

Lebègue, Raymond. La source d'un poème religieux de Marot. MélAF, p. 58-74. 661

Detailed comparison between *L'oraison contemplative devant le crucifix mise de latin en françois* and *Ennea ad sospitalem christum* of Nicolas Barthélémy which was the model for the former poem.

Lee, Sir Sidney. The French renaissance in England. Oxford, Clarendon Press, 1910. 494 p. 662

P. 111-15, M. and his school well known to Wyatt and Surrey. P. 120-26 : many of Wyatt's lyric measures reflect rhythms of the M. school. Other scattered references. *See* 1148, 1658, 2800.

Lefranc, Abel. Le roman d'amour de Clément Marot. *In his:* Grands écrivains français de la renaissance. *See* 132A, p. 1-61. 663

Proves incontestably that the real Anne was Anne d'Alençon, daughter of Charles d'Alençon's illegitimate brother. M.'s love for her may be set alongside the Platonic loves of Dante for Beatrice, Petrarch for Laura. It was she who provided inspiration for his finest poetry.

Lerber, Walther de. L'influence de Clément Marot au XVIIe et XVIIIe siècles. Champion, 1920. 126 p. 664

History of M.'s reputation; contains valuable lists of famous judgments on M. Discussion of M.'s influence on La Fontaine, Voiture, Sarrazin, Scarron, Benserade, J. B. Rousseau, etc.

Mathorez, J. Un apologiste de l'alliance franco-turque au XVIe siècle, François Sagon. BBB, 1913. p. 105-20. 665

Interesting highlights in the career of M.'s arch enemy.

Mégret, Jacques. La Déploration de France sur la mort de Clément Marot. BBB, 1926. p. 85-89. 666

Description of the four editions of a plaquette containing four tributes to M. after his death.

Mensch, Joseph. Das Tier in der Dichtung Marots. MBP, v. 36. 667

M.'s treatment of animals in his work.

Morley, Henry. Clément Marot and other studies. London, Chapman and Hall, 1871. 2 v. V. I, p. 1-316; V. II, p. 1-64. 668

Best for full account of historical background of M.'s life and work. Good discussion of Jean Marot's work. Emphasis on romance and pageantry of court life, noble genealogies, international politics, and religious strife. Like so many early critics of M., he takes Ysabeau to be the personification of the unreformed Church.

Pannier, Jacques. Les portraits de Clément Marot. BHren 4:144-70, 1944. 669

Iconographical notes.

Parmenter, C. E. The authorship of La grande généalogie de Frippelippes. MP 23:337-48, 1925-26. 670

Through a very ingenious analysis of anagrams and allusions, author proves the *Grande généalogie* to be from the hand of Macé Vaucelles.

Pauphilet, Albert. Sur des vers de Pétrarque. MélHH, p. 113-21. 671

Some of Petrarch's poetry imitated by both M. and Ronsard. Especially good comparison made in this study of M.'s treatment of *O passi sparsi* with Ronsard's.

Picot, Émile. Querelle de Marot et de Sagon; pièces réunies par Emile Picot et Paul Lecombe. Introduction par Georges Dubosc. Rouen, Lainé, 237 p.   (SRB) 672

Introduction does not sufficiently stress professional jealousy as a motive for Sagon's rancor. Facsimile reproductions of all of the attacks launched by both sides.

Plattard, Jean. Comment Marot entreprit et poursuivit la traduction des Psaumes de David. RER 10:321-55, 1912.   673

Comparison of M.'s Psalms with *Les heures de Nostre Dame* of Gringoire. M. initially encouraged to do this work by Marguerite; he followed it up through the trials of his later life. Refutes Douen's stand that M. was an apostle of Protestantism.

— Marot, sa carrière poétique, son œuvre. Boivin, 1938. 227 p.   674

M. continues medieval tradition, that of *Roman de la rose* of Villon, of the *grands rhétoriqueurs*, yet may be considered a precursor of the Pléiade because he freed the lyric from artificial complications of *rhétoriqueurs* and brought to it simplicity and naturalness of the popular song.

Pratt, Waldo Selden. The music of the French Psalter of 1562; a historical survey and analysis, with music in modern notation. New York, Columbia University Press, 1939. 213 p.   675

Most valuable for a reproduction of traditional French tunes in modern notation, based primarily upon one of first editions of *Completed Psalter* by M. and Bèze, " A Paris, par Adrien le Roy & Robert Ballard, Imprimeurs du Roy, M. D. LXII." (p. 79).

— The significance of the old French Psalter begun by Clément Marot in 1532. New York, The hymn society, 1933. 16 p.   676

Sketchy and brief. Adds nothing new.

Prévot, Georges. Clément Marot est-il Normand? GR 112:293-306, Aug., 1923.   677

M. neither Normand nor Quercinois by temperament, but French.

Rahir, Edouard. La première édition des œuvres de Clément Marot.   MélEP, v. 2, p. 635-45.   678

M. issued his Aug. 12, 1532 edition to counteract errors of unauthorized editions.

Roedel, Alfred. Studien zu den Elegien Clément Marots. Meiningen, 1898. 107 p.   679

Discussion of context of elegies, grouped according to subject matter, of M.'s predecessors in this genre (Ovid, Tibullus), and of M.'s metrics. Dating unreliable.

Rose, Hermann. Der Einfluss Villons auf Marot. Trychopoli, Augustin, 1877. 34 p. (Inaug. diss., Greifswald.)   680

Seeks out traces of Villon's spirit, thought, and language in M. Points out parallels between Villon's *Requeste à Monseigneur de Bourbon* and M.'s *Epistre au roi pour avoir esté dérobé*, Villon's *Débat du cœur et du corps* and M.'s *Epigramme à Pierre Vayard*, and many others. Both poets sang of their loves and imprisonment; *style marotique* derives from Villon's bantering tone.

Ruutz-Rees, Caroline. Flower garlands of poets; Milton, Shakespeare, Spenser, Marot, Sannazaro. MélAF, p. 75-90.   681

Flower garlands, not uncommon in the classics, dropped out of fashion, to be revived by Sannazaro and M. From these sources they found their way into Spenser and Milton.

Sainte-Beuve, Charles Augustin. Marot. *In his :* Tableau de la poésie française au xvie siècle. Lemerre, 1876. 2 v.   682

Scattered references. Considers M. a descendant of Jean de Meung, Guillaume de Lorris, Alain Chartier, Villon. Not a poet of genius.

Scherer, Edmond. Clément Marot. *In his :* Études sur la littérature contemporaine. Calmann-Lévy, 1885. v. 8, p. 1-18.   683

Praises Guiffrey's edition. M.'s work most important historically.

Sebillet, Thomas. Art poétique françoys; édition critique, avec une introduction et des notes publiées par Félix Gaiffe. Droz, 1932. 226 p. (Diss., Paris) (STFM) 684

To illustrate his theories, Sebillet quoted amply from M. and his school. *See* 2344.

Shipley, Joseph T. First of the moderns. PL 35:626-31, 1924. 685

Several good translations into English.

Van Roosbroeck, G. L. Un débat sur Marot au xviiie siècle. RSS 9:281-85, 1922. 686

The debate was between Hamilton, Chaulieu, and La Fare. A defense of M. by La Fare against Hamilton has remained unnoticed until revealed here.

Vianey, Joseph. L'art du vers chez Clément Marot. MélAF, p. 44-57. 687

Metrics.

— La Bible dans la poésie française depuis Marot. RCC 23¹:485-95, 598-604, Feb. 28, 1922. 688

First article discusses faults and virtues of M.'s psalms. Second concerns itself with Bèze.

— Les Épîtres de Marot. Malfère, 1935. 176 p. 689

M. loosened up and diversified possibilities of the epistle, thus establishing it as a literary genre of artistic value. Good analysis of purposes for which M. used the epistle and metrical devices he employed.

— Les origines du sonnet régulier. Rren 4:74-93, 1903. 690

Origins of the popular sonnet form used by French poets go back to M.

Villey-Desmeserets, Pierre. A propos d'une édition de Marot. RSS 15:156-60, 1928. 691

An *Adolescence Clémentine* published July 12, 1533, discovered at the Munich

Library by Hämel (ZFSL 50:131, 1927); rectifies Villey's *Tableau.*

— Encore une édition inconnue de Marot. RSS 16:331-34, 1929. 692

Edition of Psalms discovered by Jacques Pannier, BSHP 78:238-40, 1929.

— Introduction à l'explication des pièces de Marot. RCC 33²:111-20, 229-47, 1932. 693

P. 111-20. One cannot fully appreciate M. unless one considers the progressive evolution of his work from early poetasting to a poetry of high inspiration and art.

P. 229-47. Precautions one must take in establishing a M. text.

— Marot et le premier sonnet français. RHL 27:538-47, 1920. 694

Does not settle the question : who wrote first French sonnet? *See* 2741.

— Marot et Rabelais. Champion, 1923. 431 p. (BLR v. 11) 695

Whereas Guiffrey, Becker and Guy are primarily interested in M. the man, Villey's emphasis is on M. the poet. Villey's main thesis seems to be that M. was merely a witty poet before his misfortunes; his personal sufferings enriched and matured his poetry.

Wagner, Albert. Clément Marot's Verhältnis zur Antike. Leipzig, Seele, 1906. 100 p. (Diss., Leipzig) 696

Influence of classics on M.; his translations; knowledge of Latin and ignorance of Greek. Through a scrutiny of M.'s poetry, author judges classical literature. M. not as far from the aims of Pléiade as later 16th century poets were led to believe.

CHAPTER III. MISCELLANEOUS WRITERS
(Nos. 697-731)

HÉLÈNE HARVITT

Eustorg de Beaulieu
(No. 697)

Becker, Ph. Aug. Eustorg de Beaulieu. *In:* Aus Frankreichs Frührenaissance : — Kritische Skizzen. Leipzig, Selbstverlag des Romanischen Seminars. Droz, 1927. p. 140-54. (SFL)   697
Mainly biographical; article based on book by Harvitt, no. 655. B. started in tradition of *rhétoriqueurs* and underwent influence of Marot; but as a religious song-writer, he may stand alone.

Victor Brodeau
(Nos. 698-699)

Jourda, Pierre. Un disciple de Clément Marot : Victor Brodeau. RHL 28:30-59, 208-27, 1921.   698
Was first and foremost a courtier; a poet only at odd times. Work divided into two parts—light verse, imitative of Marot and Saint-Gelais, and religious verse, which is of far greater importance; in this genre he ranks with Marot and Marguerite as one of first to essay religious poetry in 16th century. Although style is steeped in that of the *rhétoriqueurs*, sobriety and occasional grandeur of religious verse entitle him to the place of precursor to Corneille and Racine (rather far-fetched conclusion of the author).

— Lettres inédites de Victor Brodeau. MélAL, p. 155-60.   699
Seven letters to Montmorency show what information B. was anxious to have while he was away from court.

Claude Chappuys
(No. 700)

Roche, Louis P. Claude Chappuys (?-1575). Les belles lettres, 1929. 194 p. 700
P. 26-32 discuss fully the friendship between Marot and C., which dated from 1534.

Antoine du Moulin
(No. 701)

Cartier, Alfred, and Adolphe Chenevière. Antoine du Moulin, valet de chambre de la reine de Navarre. RHL 2:469-90, 1895; 3:90-106, 218-44, 1896.   701
Very scholarly biography with facts culled carefully from lives of D.'s contemporaries; D. was important as a friend of Marot, Beaulieu, Fontaine. *See* 2577.

Charles Fontaine
(Nos. 702-706)

Becker, Ph. Aug. Charles Fontaine. *In:* Aus Frankreichs Frührenaissance : — Kritische Skizzen. Droz, 1927. p. 155-66. (SFL)   702
Summary of Hawkins' material. F.'s work is a point of transition between Marot and the Pléiade.

Frank, Grace. The early work of Charles Fontaine. MP 23:47-60, 1925-26.   703
75 poems (uncovered after appearance of Hawkins's book), mostly composed by F. before age 23 are curiously religious in tone; point to fact that as a young man F. probably belonged to a group of *esprits éclairés* including Vatable and Calvin. Shows that early F. was gloomy, thoughtful; shared Marot's religious convictions.

Hawkins, Richmond Laurin. Maistre Charles Fontaine, parisien. Cambridge, Harvard University Press, 1916. 281 p. (HSRL)   704
Most complete work on F. Ch. II discusses F.'s part in Marot-Sagon controversy. Proves that F. not inimical to members of the Pléiade; not author of the *Quintil Horatian*; in fact, F. anticipated Du Bellay's teachings (Ch. VIII). *See* 734.

Roy, Émile. Charles Fontaine et ses amis. RHL 4:412-22, 1897.   705

72

F. the polemist studied through his defense of Marot and authorship of the *Contr'amye*. *See* 1298.

Ruutz-Rees, Caroline. Charles Fontaine's Fontaine d'amour and Sannazaro. MLN 27:65-68, 1912.   706

The *Fontaine* was constructed out of impressions gained during travels in Italy. *See* 2790.

François Habert
(Nos. 707-709)

Franchet, Henri. Le philosophe parfaict et Le temple de vertu de François Habert nouvellement remis en lumière avec notice et notes par Henri Franchet. Champion, 1923. 60 p.   707

Edition of two of H.'s most important works, with biography and chronology of publications of the poet.

Leykauff, August. François Habert und seine Übersetzung des Metamorphosen Ovids. Leipzig, Deichert, 1904. 123 p. (MBP)   708

Discusses other translations of Ovid before H.'s, and also H.'s sources. How H.'s translation of Ovid differs from Marot's and how both differ from the original. Comparison of their respective translations line by line, word by word.

Théret, Auguste. François Habert. *In his*: Littérature du Berry, poésie; les XVIᵉ, XVIIᵉ et XVIIIᵉ siècles. Laur, 1898. p. 9-147.   709

Contains no bibliographical material, yet a very good analysis of every type of H.'s poetry. Ch. I noteworthy for a discussion of H.'s literary indebtedness to Marot. P. 131-45 contain biographical notes on poets with whom H. had relations.

Antoine Héroët
(Nos. 710-714)

Arnoux, Jules. Un précurseur de Ronsard, Antoine Héroët, néo-platonicien et poète (1492-1568). BSBA, 15:209-33, 270-94, 305-36, 361-91; 1911-12. *Reprinted*: Digne 1912. 122 p.   710

Most comprehensive and detailed discussion of pre-H. Platonism. Minor works of H. analyzed in some detail and discussion of Book III of the *Parfaicte amye* better than Kerr's, 713. Indicates affinities between H.'s theories of love and

those of later poets—du Bellay, Ronsard, d'Aubigné, Lamartine, Vigny. *See* 748.

Gohin, Ferdinand. Œuvres poétiques d'Héroët. Cornély, 1909. 174 p. (STFM)   711

Full biography followed by a bibliography of H.'s complete works. H. was outstanding champion of Platonic love in early renaissance. Valuable discussion of circumstances which led to *Querelle des femmes*. *See also* Introduction of *Œuvres de François Rabelais*, Champion, 1913-31, v. 5, Ch. 2, p. xxx-lxix for a discussion of importance of *La parfaicte amye* in this controversy, and a discussion of this poem in relation to analogous works of other writers.

Grou, Lucien. La famille d'Antoine Héroët. RHL 6:277-82, 1899.   712

Details on Jehan Héroët, Antoine's father, on his two brothers and two sisters—especially on Marie, of whom Marguerite gives some information in *Heptameron* xxiii. *See* 750.

Kerr, W. A. R. Antoine Héroët's Parfaicte amye. PMLA 20 ns 13:567-83, 1905.   713

Makes mistake of thinking *L'amye de cour* was answer to *La parfaicte amye* instead of vice versa. Background of the *Querelle des femmes* and H.'s life discussed very cursorily. Each book of the *Parfaicte amye* analyzed separately. *See* 751.

Lefranc, Abel. Le Platonisme et la littérature en France à l'époque de la renaissance. *In his*: Grands écrivains français de la renaissance. *See* 132A, p. 63-137.   714

H.'s importance as a precursor of the Pléiade; roles played by La Borderie and Fontaine in the *Querelle des femmes*. *See* 737, 738, 2569.

Bertrand de La Borderie
(No. 715)

Livingston, Charles H. Un disciple de Clément Marot : Bertrand de La Borderie. RSS 16:219-82, 1929.   715

Sketchy biography. Points out similarity between L.'s *Discours du voyage à Constantinople* and Claude Chappuys' *L'épistre d'une navigation*. Proves definitely that L.'s *Amye de cour*, and not Héroët's *Parfaicte amye* caused the *Querelle des femmes*, for the first book of the *Parfaicte amye* is nothing more than a systematic refutation of *Amye de cour*. Appends L.'s versification of *Decameron* xviii.

Jean Salmon Macrin; *see* Jean Salmon, called Macrin

Charles de Sainte-Marthe

(Nos. 716-717)

Becker, Ph. Aug. Charles de Sainte-Marthe. *In:* Aus Frankreichs Frührenaissance : — Kritische Skizzen. Droz, 1927. p. 119-39. (SFL)   716

Fills in lacunae in Ruutz-Rees's book by mass of detail on S.'s friends, travels. Sees in poet a synthesis of Marot and Jean Bouchet; agrees that he did nothing to advance French poetry. Shows that although he remained Catholic from motives of prudence, was a decided protagonist of Reformed Church.

Ruutz-Rees, Caroline. Charles de Sainte-Marthe (1512-1555). New York, Columbia University Press, 1910. 664 p. (CSRPL)   717

S. a disciple of Marot; p. 232-52 maintain that S. followed Marot closely in manner and subject, even to point of imitating specific poems.

Mellin de Saint-Gelais

(Nos. 718-726)

Saint-Gelais, Mellin de. Œuvres complètes, avec un commentaire inédit de Bernard de La Monnoye, des remarques de Emm. Philippes-Beaulieux, R. Dezeimeris, etc. Edition revue, annotée et publiée par P. Blanchemain, Daffis, 1873. 3 v.   718

P. 32-42 list old editions used in arranging this one. After each poem occur transcriptions of erudite marginal notes left by B. de La Monnoye, together with commentaries by Philippes-Beaulieux and Blanchemain for comparison and contrast.

Blanchemain, Prosper. Melin de Sainct-Gelays. *In his :* Poètes et amoureuses; portraits littéraires du xvie siècle. Willem, 1877. v. I, p. 117-47.   719

Mere biography; erroneously believes S. to have been first to naturalize Petrarchian sonnet in France.

Frank, Grace. A MS of Mellin de Saint-Gelais' works. MLN 40:61, 1925.   720

Calls attention to a Vatican MS of S.'s works.

Jourda, Pierre. Sur quelques poésies faussement attribuées à Saint-Gelais. RHL 31:303-05, 1924.   721

Blanchemain edition of S. attributes to the poet some poems probably not his.

Lanson, Gustave. 1556, au château de Blois. Sophonisbe, de Mellin de Saint-Gelais. RHL 10:196, 1903.   722

Establishes date of first performance of S.'s play as 1556.

Longnon, Henri. Les déboires de Ronsard à la cour; les outrages de Melin de Saint-Gelais. BHren 12:60-70, 1950.   723

More information on rivalry of S. and Ronsard. *See* 1152.

Molinier, H. J. Mellin de Saint-Gelais. Picard, 1910. 614 p. (Diss., Toulouse) 724

Most thorough study of S., whose place is fixed between Marot and Ronsard. Definitive biography and astute appraisal of poet's importance. *See* 2388.

Ruutz-Rees, Caroline. A note on Saint-Gelais and Bembo. RR 1:427-29, 1910. 725

A *huitain* taken from Bembo. *See* 2775

Wagner, Ernst Winfred. Mellin de Saint-Gelays. Ludwigshafen, Lauterborn, 1893. 149 p. (Diss., Heidelberg)   726

Above all a detailed grammatical study of S.'s work. Narrow, technical, dull; no help in understanding S. as man or poet. Best part of book concerns itself with Italian influence on S.

Hugues Salel

(Nos. 727-729)

Salel, Hugues. Un précurseur de la Pléiade; Hugues Salel de Cazals-en-Quercy. Ed. by Louis Alexandre Bergougnioux Guitard, 1929. 342 p.   727

Definitive biography and edition of S.'s works. Marot's influence : p. 65-73

Harvitt, Hélène. Les Triomphes de Pétrarque; traduction en vers français par Simon Bougouyn, valet de chambre de Louis XII. RLC 2:85-89, 1922.   728

Attributed to S. by printed catalogue of the manuscripts of the *Fonds français de la Bibliothèque nationale. See* 2632, 2731.

Hulubei, Alice. Étude sur quelques œuvres poétiques d'Hugues Salel (1504-1553). Hren 2:122-46, 1935.   729

Contains material not found in Bergougnioux's volume.

Jean Salmon, called Macrin or Maigret
(No. 730)

Boulmier, Joseph. Salmon Macrin, l'Horace français. BBB 1870-71, p. 498-508.   730

Marot translated this contemporary from Latin into French. Short biography; poets of the Pléiade did in French what S. did in Latin.

Maurice Scève
(No. 731)

Saulnier, V. L. Maurice Scève. Klincksieck, 1948-49. 2 v.   731

Professor Saulnier of Sorbonne presents very scholarly study of S. the man and poet. Places S. in setting of Lyons of 16th century. Critical edition of work of S. to follow shortly. See 798.

CHAPTER IV. THE PLATONIC MOVEMENT
(Including Marguerite de Navarre)
(Nos. 732-784)

EDWARD F. MEYLAN

Generalities

Crane, Thomas F. Italian social customs of the sixteenth century and their influence on the literatures of Europe. New Haven, Yale University Press, 1920. 689 p. 732
> Best repertory of material on social background of Platonic movement. Minor authors such as Yver and Pasquier receive special attention because of their historical significance.

Festugière, [A. M.] Jean. La philosophie de l'amour de Marcile Ficin et son influence sur la littérature française au XVIe siècle. RUC 8:396-564, 1922. *Reprinted:* EPM 31:1-168, 1941. 733
> Most comprehensive work, beginning with an analysis of medieval courtly love, including all important French poets as well as several prose writers, up to 1560. Lengthy and sometimes confused, but excels in tracing sources. Original edition lacks table of contents, index, sub-titles; badly printed typographical errors. Sections on Sainte-Marthe, Tyard, Corrozet excellent. *See* 2783.
> Review : J. Lavaud in RSS 12:175-77, 1925.

Hawkins, Richmond L. The Querelle des amies; the Platonism of Charles Fontaine. *In his:* Maistre Charles Fontaine, parisien. *See* 704, p. 70-119. 734
> Re-statement of " querelle " with original information about one of foremost participants. Very clear analysis of the *Contr'amye.* Somewhat uncertain on subject of sources; ignores Leone Ebreo.

Huit, Charles. Le Platonisme en France. APC ns 36:418-34, 1897; 37:155-83, 421-34, 579-89, 1897-98. 735
> Last four articles in a series entitled *Le Platonisme pendant la renaissance.* Paying special attention to Dolet, Ramus, Le Roy, Serres, author looks into Lefranc's contention that Platonism dominated the " rénovation universelle " in XVIth century. Finds that, while it was hardly accepted by French philosophers, Platonism fared much better in literature, although it took on various other idealistic elements (as in Marguerite). Articles act as an antidote to tendency of characterizing the " spirit " of a period according to some of its literary production.

Kerr, W. A. R. Le cercle d'amour. PMLA 19:33-63, 1904. 736
> Shows relationship between literary Platonism and another form of idealism, mysticism of the " libertins spirituels." One of clearest articles on the subject. Importance of Mariolatry in France debatable.

Lefranc, Abel. Le platonisme et la littérature en France à l'époque de la renaissance (1500-1550). RHL 3:1-44, 1896. *Also in his :* Grands écrivains de la renaissance. *See* 132A, p. 63-137. 737
> Pioneer study, now obsolescent. Brilliant and comprehensive, but too brief for material involved. Fails to give definition of literary Platonism and to explain transformations it underwent at hands of Italians. Best as an outline of the diffusion of " Platonic " works, but should be used with caution and supplemented with more recent studies. *See* 714, 2569.

— Marguerite de Navarre et le Platonisme de la renaissance. BEC 58:259-92, 1897; 59:712-57, 1898. *Also in his:* Grands écrivains français de la renaissance. *See* 132A, p. 139-249. 738
> In this article all manifestations of 15th and 16th century idealism are affiliated with Platonism, or rather Neoplatonism. This broad philosophical conception of term " Platonism " may be defended, but it constitutes such a departure from literary premise of preceding article by same

76

author that reader is left confused. A more accurate title would have been : *The idealism of Marguerite and its relation to Platonism.* In this respect the article is excellent and has not been superseded. *See* 714, 737, 769, 2569.

— Le tiers livre du Pantagruel et la querelle des femmes. RER 2:1-10, 78-109, 1904. *Also in his:* Grands écrivains français de la renaissance. *See* 132A, p. 251-303. 739
Additional information which adds considerably to value of two preceding articles by same author. Literary Platonism appears less superficial or ridiculous when bound with story of feminism. *See* 737, 738.

Merrill, Robert V. Eros and Anteros. Spec 19:265-84, 1944. 740
Detailed history of myth of Eros's younger brother, with various meanings attached to it. Explains its numerous classical sources and its uses by 16th century poets.

— The Platonism of Joachim du Bellay. Chicago, University of Chicago Press, 1925. 150 p. 741
Full study, half of which is devoted to a detailed exposition of Platonistic concepts in works of Du Bellay. Author's conclusion that Du Bellay's Platonism was of the spirit rather than of the word indicates extent to which this manner of thinking pervaded the literary atmosphere. Introduction contains a useful list of Platonistic works published in France in 16th century. Value of the book would have been enhanced by an analytic table of contents. *See* 1268, 2574.

Meylan, Edward F. L'évolution de la notion d'amour platonique. Hren 5:418-442, 1938. 742
Describes steps through which Plato's original conception became the modern idea of "Platonic love" (Ficino, Pico, Bembo, Castiglione, Héroët).

Moench, Walter. Die italienische Platonrenaissance und ihre Bedeutung für Frankreichs Literatur- und Geistesgeschichte (1450-1550). *See* 207. 743
From standpoint of history of ideas the most searching study on subject. Systematic analysis of Italian sources (Pletho, Bessarion, Ficino, Pico) and of Champier, a would-be vulgarizer of Platonism in France. Relatively few pages devoted to lyric poets (Marguerite, Héroet, Scève).

Space given to Champier may seem unjustified because of small influence he wielded on literature, but an analysis of his works was needed.

Shorey, Paul. Platonism and French literature. *In his:* Platonism, ancient and modern. Berkeley, University of California Press, 1938. p. 146-74. 744
Excellent bird's-eye view; reveals simply and clearly various aspects of the question. It might well serve as an introduction to the subject.

Tracconaglia, Giovanni. Femminismo e platonismo in un libro raro del 1503 : La nef des dames di Symphorien Champier. Lodi, Dell'Avo, 1922. 72 p. 745
Short but valuable study, illustrating the blending of feminism and Platonism in literature.

Antoine Héroet
(Nos. 747-751)

Héroet, Antoine. Œuvres poétiques. Édition critique publiée par Ferdinand Gohin. Cornély, 1909. LXIX, 174 p. (STFM) 747
Contains *La parfaicte amye, L'androgyne,* mnior poems, biographical and bibliographical notices, Colletet's life of H., variants, glossary. A precise edition and monograph combined. Critical apparatus and factual introduction leave little to be desired. Literary appraisal, however, too " historical " and superficial.
Review : H. Hauvette in BI 10:273-75, 1910.

Arnoux, Jules. Un précurseur de Ronsard, Antoine Héroet, néo-platonicien et poète (1492-1568). *See* 710. 748
Local homage to most illustrious of bishops of Digne. Offers nothing new, except perhaps a painstaking analysis of H.'s poems.

Gohin, Ferdinand. Une poésie inédite d'Antoine Héroet : description d'une femme de bien. RHL 17:823-24, 1910. 749
Better and more complete text of one of the poems *(L'honneur des femmes)* included in his edition of H.'s Œuvres poétiques.

Grou, Lucien. La famille d'Antoine Héroet. *See* 712. 750
Interesting episode in life of H.'s sister Marie, which was used by Marguerite for one of her *Heptaméron* stories.

Kerr, W. A. R. Antoine Héroët's Parfaicte amye. *See* 713.   751

Clear analysis of the *Parfaicte amye*, with proper references to Platonic theories. Still valuable.

Marguerite d'Angoulême, Queen of Navarre
(Nos. 753-774)

Marguerite d'Angoulême, *queen* **of Navarre.** Les Marguerites de la Marguerite des Princesses. Texte de l'édition de 1547, publié avec introduction, notes et glossaire par Félix Frank. Librairie des bibliophiles, 1873. 4 v.   753

Includes both the *Marguerites* and the *Suyte des Marguerites*. Follows princeps edition with minor emendations from 2nd edition (1554). Sound introduction (with description of early editions), 30 pages of miscellaneous notes (insufficient), 500 word glossary. While this contains the bulk of M.'s lyric poetry, attention should be called to *Les dernières poésies* (*see* no. 25) and to the *Dialogue en forme de vision nocturne* reprinted by P. Jourda in RSS 13 : 1-49, 1926.

— Les dernières poésies de Marguerite de Navarre, publiées pour la première fois avec une introduction et des notes par Abel Lefranc. Colin, 1896. 461 p.   754

This collection escaped attention of most scholars for three centuries; does more than complete the *Marguerites*, for it brings to light the author's most ambitious attempt, namely, philosophical poem entitled *Les prisons*. While introduction is adequate as such, it raises certain questions of interpretation, about which *see* Jourda no. 657, v. I, p. 614-17.

Reviews : P. Courteault in Rcr ns 41:505-10, 1896; H. Hauser, ibid., 510-13; G. Lanson in RHL 3:292-98, 1896; G. Paris in JS, 1896:273-88, 356-68.

— Théâtre profane, édité par Verdun L. Saulnier. Droz, 1946. 357 p.   755

Contains seven plays with detailed commentaries. For textual criticism, however, see same author's *Etudes critiques sur les comédies profanes de Marguerite de Navarre* in BHren 9:36-77, 1947.

— Œuvres, Comédies. Ed. by E. Schneegans. Strasbourg, Heitz [1924 ?], XXVII, 247 p.   756

Four biblical and two spiritual dramas, reprinted from *Marguerites* and *Dernières*

poésies. Convenient, but not in conformity with scholarly standards.

— Comédie de la nativité de Jésus Christ; texte établi et présenté par P. Jourda. Boivin, 1939. 107 p.   757

Not one of M.'s best works, but edition is noteworthy for its comments on sources, syntax, vocabulary, and versification.

— Lettres de Marguerite d'Angoulême, publiées d'après des manuscrits de la Bibliothèque du roi par François Génin. Renouard, 1841, 485 p.   758

See the following item.

— Nouvelles lettres de la reine de Navarre, adressées au roi François Ier, publiées par François Génin. Renouard, 1842. 303 p.   759

Transcription of about half of M.'s letters. Faulty and incomplete reading of mss. Still useful, but should be checked with Jourda's *Répertoire*, no. 765. 146-page notice of first volume obsolete. In the 24-page supplementary notice of second volume the editor, misled by M.'s exalted phraseology, lends credence to the legend of her incestuous love for her brother.

Becker, Philip-August. Marguerite, duchesse d'Alençon, et Guillaume Briçonnet, évêque de Meaux, d'après leur correspondance inédite (1521-1524). BSHP 49:393-477, 661-67, 1900.   760

Documentary evidence of decisive role played by evangelistic bishop in formation of M.'s mysticism. Running commentary very helpful.

Clements, Robert J. Marguerite de Navarre and Dante. Ital 18:37-50, 1941.   761

Demonstrates conclusively that, contrary to common belief, M. owed very little to Dante. Even possible that she did not read beyond *Inferno*, V. Clearly composed and brilliantly written. *See* 2715.

Febvre, Lucien. Autour de l'Heptaméron; amour sacré, amour profane. Gallimard [1944]. 295 p.   762

Concerned with more than just the *Heptaméron*. Defends thesis that apparent dualism between M.'s idealism and her realism not due to a split personality but can be explained by her broad and transcendent concept of religion and morals. Covers somewhat same ground as Telle (774); approach, however, less formal, more lively, perhaps too petulant. *See* 982.

Review : M. Bataillon in BHren 8:245-253, 1946 (excellent).

Jourda, Pierre. Tableau chronologique des publications de Marguerite de Navarre. RSS 12:209-55, 1925. 763
Lists all printed poems which may be attributed to M. No attempt at description of early editions. Not usable for the *Heptaméron*.

— Marguerite d'Angoulême, duchesse d Alençon, reine de Navarre (1492-1549); étude biographique et littéraire. *See* 657. 764
V. 1 deals with life and poetry of M., v. 2 with the *Heptaméron* and sundry questions. Extremely detailed monograph, taking all previous publications into account. Presents all known facts and evaluates theories in their light, author himself remaining cautious in his judgments. Lends itself better to study of specific chapters than to acquisition of a clear *vue d'ensemble*. A more specific index would have made the book less unwieldy.
Reviews : J. Plattard in RSS 18:175-78, 1931; A. Renaudet, ibid., 272-308 (*Marguerite de Navarre, à propos d'un ouvrage récent*. More extensive than a conventional review.)

— Répertoire analytique et chronologique de la correspondance de Marguerite d'Angoulême. Champion, 1930. 265 p. (BLR ns t. XXI) 765
List of 1143 letters written by or addressed to M. Drawn from ms. as well as printed sources. Summary of each letter, some transcriptions. Most letters dated. Interest more historical than literary.

— Le mécénat de Marguerite de Navarre. RSS 18:253-71, 1931. 766
Impressive list of dedications and testimonials, showing M.'s great popularity in France and Italy.

— Une princesse de la renaissance : Marguerite d'Angoulême, reine de Navarre. Brouwer, 1932, 288 p. 767
Popular biography, not to be confused with scholarly study published by same author in 1930. With historical details kept to a minimum, M.'s personality stands out clearly and vividly. In this sense the book can well serve as a companion to its predecessor.

Lefranc, Abel. Les idées religieuses de Marguerite de Navarre d'après son œuvre poétique. BSHP 46:7-30, 72-84, 137-48, 295-311, 418-42, 1897. 768
On the basis of a painstaking analysis author avers that M. was a pre-Calvin "Protestant," a broad concept that flows naturally into the spiritualism of her last years. Fundamentally true, but M.'s religious beliefs have been more accurately defined since appearance of this pioneer study.
Review : H. Hauser in Rcr ns 46:252-56, 1898.

— Marguerite de Navarre et le Platonisme de la renaissance. BEC 58:259-92, 1897; 59:712-57, 1898. *Reprinted in his* : Grands écrivains de la renaissance, Champion, 1914. p. 139-249. 769
See 738.

Marichal, Robert. La Coche de Marguerite de Navarre. Hren 5:37-99, 247-96, 1938. 770
Complete study of one of M.'s best poems : mss., sources, composition, ideas, date, language, and versification. Model of thoroughness, except in regard to M.'s thought, which remains nebulous.

Meylan, Edward F. La date de l'Oraison de l'âme fidèle et son importance pour la biographie morale de Marguerite de Navarre. MLN 52:562-68, 1937. 771
Brief statement of conflicting theories. Sees evolution from evangelism to spiritualism.

Moore, Will Grayburn. Les grands esprits : Marot et Marguerite. *In his* : La Réforme allemande et la littérature française; recherches sur la notoriété de Luther en France. *See* 164. 772
Proves that the *Pater noster* published by Parturier in connection with his article on M.'s mysticism (773) partly a translation from Luther. Insists also on several similarities between various passages in M.'s poems and Luther's treatise on Christian freedom. *See* 1931.

Parturier, Eugène. Les sources du mysticisme de Marguerite de Navarre; à propos d'un manuscrit inédit. Rren 5:1-16, 49-72, 1904. 773
The ms. (printed in same volume, 108-114, 178-90, 273-80) that of the *Pater noster faict en translation et dialogue par la Royne de Navarre*. Parturier points out M.'s affinities with mysticism of Eckhart,

Tauler, Suso, and their followers, but he does not sufficiently recognize the fact that Marguerite gained access to some of these ideas through Luther. *See* Moore (772).

Telle, Emile V. L'œuvre de Marguerite d'Angoulême, reine de Navarre, et la querelle des femmes. Toulouse, Lion, 1937. 416 p.   774

Interpretation in light of social movements, e.g., *Les amours d'alliance, La réhabilitation du mariage par le mouvement réformiste, Les mariages clandestins.* Excellent background material, clearly presented, but organization open to criticism. Bibliography constitutes a good supplement to that of Jourda (763). *See* 986.

Reviews : M. Bataillon in BHren 8:247-48, 1946; H. W. Lawton in MLR 35:103-104, 1940; R. Marichal in Hren 5:183-87, 1938; E. F. Meylan in MLN 53:608-10, 1938.

Pontus de Tyard

(Nos. 774A-784)

Tyard, Pontus de. Les œuvres poétiques de Pontus de Tyard, *seigneur* de Bissy, avec une Notice biographique et des Notes par Ch. Marty-Laveaux. Lemerre, 1875. 266 p.   (PF, v. 4)   774A

Complete poetic works with extracts from prose works. Biography based on Jeandet. List of early editions with title-pages and other valuable information. Literary analysis sober but adequate, except for sources.

— Le Solitaire premier de Pontus de Tyard, édition critique par Silvio F. Baridon. Geneva, Droz, 1950.   84 p.   775

An adequate edition of most literary of T.'s discourses (subtitle : *Discours des muses et de la fureur poëtique*).

Review : A. Armand-Hugon in BHren 12:420, 1950.

— The Universe of Pontus de Tyard, a critical edition of L'univers, with introduction and notes by John C. Lapp. *See* 362.   776

Reprint of two cosmological discourses better known as *Le premier curieux* and *Le second curieux.* Small literary value. Analysis and critical apparatus woefully insufficient.

Review : S. F. Baridon in BHren 12:411-19, 1950. Gives a large number of variants neglected by Lapp.

Baridon, Silvio F. Pontus de Tyard (1521 ?-1605). Milan, Editrice Viscontea, 1950.   306 p.   777

Thoroughly documented monograph (in Italian). Contains an excellent analysis of T.'s thought, which is of some historical importance. Lacks bibliography.

Review : A. Armand-Hugon in BHren 12:422-23, 1950.

Chamard, Henri. Pontus de Tyard et ses Erreurs amoureuses (1549-1551). *In his:* Histoire de la Pléiade, Didier, 1939.   1:241-250; 2:124-30, 3:144-62.   780

There would be enough material in these scattered pages to form a condensed but well-rounded monograph. Particularly valuable for analysis of the *discours philosophiques* and for literary background. Rather critical but fair estimate.

Flamini, Francesco. Du rôle de Pontus de Tyard dans le pétrarquisme français. Rren 1:43-55, 1901.   781

Sees T.'s activity in France as similar to that of Cariteo and Tebaldeo in Italy. This first " rapprochement " now superseded by Vianey's studies. *See* 2725.

Jeandet, J. P. Abel. Pontus de Tyard, *seigneur* de Bissy, depuis évêque de Châlon. Aubry, 1860.   240 p.   782

One of earliest monographs with scientific approach and scholarly basis. Original and abundant documentation, due to fact that author's interest was primarily biographical. Literary analysis sketchy, sometimes faulty; bibliographical material not clearly presented.

Merrill, Robert V. Platonism in Pontus de Tyard's Erreurs amoureuses (1549). MP 35:139-58, 1937-38.   783

Thorough analysis, showing that T.'s Platonism for the most part formal rather than felt.

Vianey, Joseph. Les Erreurs amoureuses de Pontus de Tyard (1549). *In his:* Pétrarquisme en France, 2740. Goulet, p. 119-29.   784

Brief study of sources and influence. Notes that T.'s imitations and adaptations not slavish.

CHAPTER V. THE POETIC CIRCLE OF LYONS

(Nos. 785-816)

EDWARD F. MEYLAN

Generalities

Aynard, Joseph. Les poètes lyonnais précurseurs de la Pléiade. Maurice Scève, Louise Labé, Pernette du Guillet. Bossard, 1924. Introduction : 70 p.; text : 201 p. (CCM)   785

Convenient anthology, containing 4 *blasons*, 43 *dizains*, *la Saulsaye*, prefatory sonnet of the *Microcosme* by Scève, 5 poems and chansons by P. du Guillet, reprint of the 1556 edition of the *Œuvres* of L. Labé. Introduction largely based on Baur and Boy. Insists on distinction between the three poets and questions validity of the term " école lyonnaise."

Review : J. Plattard in RSS 12:188-89, 1925.

Baur, Albert. Maurice Scève et la renaissance lyonnaise. Champion, 1906. 131 p.   786

Life of the poet sketched on background of literary life in second city of France. Solidly documented and well composed; lacks bibliography and index. Does not contain an analysis of the *Délie*, which was to be the subject of a later work (it never appeared). Extensively and favorably reviewed. Remains standard general work on literary renaissance in Lyons. On Scève's life, however, it is corrected and completed by Guégan.

Reviews : J. Boulanger in RER 4:400-402, 1906; L. Delaruelle in RHL 15:355-357, 1908; J. L. Gerig in MLN 23:229-31, 1908.

Maurice Scève

(Nos. 787-800)

Scève, Maurice. Œuvres poétiques complètes de Maurice Scève ... réunies pour la première fois par Bertrand Guégan et publiées avec une introduction, un glossaire, des notes et une bibliographie. Garnier, 1927. 333 p. (CSCG)   787

Contains : *Délie, Arion, Saulsaye, Microcosme, Poésies diverses, Poésies latines.*

Best short biography. Bibliography includes works by S. only. Title-page misleading : no notes on text. This serious omission detracts greatly from usefulness of the book. Editions followed and variants indicated in bibliography.

— Délie object de plus haulte vertu. Edition critique avec une introduction et des notes par Eugène Parturier. *See* 515.   788

Introduction does not include a biography. List of books mentioned in notes contains references to the latter (excellent device). Cross-references throughout. Emblems of original edition reproduced. Glossary adequate. Possible sources and similarities listed in excessive number and should have been clearly distinguished from definite sources. *See* his corrections in RHL 24:483-86, 1917.

Review : J. Marsan in RHL 26:157-58, 1919.

— Sixty poems of Scève. Introduction; translation and comment by Wallace Fowlie. New York, The Swallow Press and William Morrow, 1949. 150 p. *See* 803.   789

Literal prose translations and suggestive commentaries most helpful to those who approach S.'s poetry for the first time.

Becker, Philipp August. Maurice Scève. ZVL 17:225-38, 1907-09.   790

Biographical information which lay somewhat scattered in Baur's book here brought together in compact form. In addition, emphasis is placed on S.'s reputation with other poets of 16th century.

Brugmans, Hendrik. Littérature et réalité dans la Délie de Maurice Scève. Hren 2:388-401, 1935.   791

Defends S.'s originality and literary merit, but misses the truly poetic element.

Brunetière, Ferdinand. Un précurseur de la Pléiade, Maurice Scève. *In his :* Études critiques, sixième série, Hachette, 1899. p. 79-95.   792

Explains S. as a " poète de transition," important only from the historical viewpoint. Finds him too obscure to be worth reading. *See* Larbaud's criticism. (794)

Gerig, John L. The family of Maurice Scève. PMLA 24:470-75, 1909.   793
Notes designed to fill some gaps in Baur's work. Taken mostly from the *Archives communales de Lyon.*

Larbaud, Valéry. Notes sur Maurice Scève. A l'enseigne de la Porte étroite, 1925. 38 p.   794
Pamphlet against " official " treatment of S. as an obscure poet (*see* Brunetière, 792). Illustrates : 1) popularity of S. with modern French poets, 2) revulsion against historical method in esthetic matters.
Preceded by *Notes sur Maurice Scève* in *Commerce, Cahier* V, Autumn, 1925, by Valéry Larbaud.

Lyons, J. C. A neglected manuscript : Guillaume Colletet's Essay on Maurice Scève. MP 28:13-27, 1930-31.   795
Short introduction and notes.

Parturier, Eugène. Maurice Scève et le Petit œuvre d'amour de 1537. RSS 17:298-311, 1930.   796
Defends attribution of this work to S., at least as a collaborator.

Saulnier, Verdun L. Des corrections aux textes de Maurice Scève. BHren 8:266-276, 1946.   797
Rejects most emendations suggested by Parturier, and to a lesser extent by Guégan.

— Maurice Scève. (ca. 1500-1560). *See* 731.   798
Exhaustive study of most challenging poet of the century. V. 1 contains text, v. 2 notes and bibliography. Best feature is explanation of baffling Scevian devices; *see* particularly sections titled *L'obscurité scévienne, Le symbolisme, Les parasites de l'obscurité concertée, Le beau vers* (p. 288-307). Many interesting side-lights on literary life in Lyons. A bold claim is made for modernity of S. : " *Le cimetière marin* et *Délie* sont de la même famille de mains et d'esprit." (p. 573) Brilliant style, marred only by some cumbersome sentences.
Review : P. Jourda in BHren 11:277-82, 1949. Worth reading as an introduction to the book.

Schmidt, Albert Marie. Maurice Scève, poète scientifique. *In his :* Poésie scientifique en France au seizième siècle, *see* 327. p. 109-66.   799
Best analysis and discussion of the *Microcosme.* Shows distinctly scholastic and Platonic inspiration of the poem. Somewhat verbose; sub-titles lacking, but analytic table of contents helpful.
Review : M. Raymond in Hren 7:241-244, 1940.

Vianey, Joseph. L'influence italienne chez les précurseurs de la Pléiade. BI 3:85-117, 1903.   800
Sees in S. an imitator of Serafino, although he admits that S. did more than copy and translate. Further discussion of sources in his *Pétrarquisme en France,* no. 2740, p. 58-80. *See* 2683.

Pernette du Guillet
(Nos. 801-806)

Du Guillet, Pernette. Poésies de Pernette du Guillet. Lyons, Perrin, 1830. 132 p.   801
Text collated on Lyons (1545) and Paris (1546) editions. Contains also Colletet's notice and Du Moulin's prefatory epistle. Re-edited in 1856 with small additions from a 1552 edition. For criticism *see* Saulnier, no. 806, p. 118.

Aynard, Joseph, *See* no. 785.   802

Baur, Albert. Pernette du Guillet et les femmes de la renaissance lyonnaise. *In his :* Maurice Scève et la renaissance lyonnaise. *See* 789. p. 77-90.   803
Same theory as in Buche. Interesting discussion of moral standards of the period. Baur believes that both D. and Louise Labé tried to emulate the Italian *cortegiane oneste* (on this point *see also* Miss O'Connor's book, no. 813).

Buche, Joseph. Pernette du Guillet et la Délie de Maurice Scève. *In :* MélBrunot, p. 33-39.   804
Convincing defense of thesis that *Délie* is none other than D.

Guégan, Bertrand. Pernette du Guillet and Maurice Scève. *In :* Œuvres poétiques complètes de Maurice Scève. *See* 785, p. xxiii-xxxiii.   805
This section of Guégan's introduction presents short but specific narrative of the

affair between D. and Scève, based on a careful analysis of the *Rymes*.

Saulnier, Verdun L. Étude sur Pernette du Guillet et ses Rymes, avec des documents inédits. BHren 4:1-119, 1944. 806

Long awaited monograph, with luminous analysis of D.'s poetry (ideas and form). Does not add greatly to her scanty biography. Takes issue with Baur on the question of the *cortegiana onesta* (D. did not resemble Louise Labé). Description of editions on p. 116-19.

Louise Labé
(Nos. 807-816)

Labé, Louise. Œuvres de Louise Labé, publiées avec une étude et des notes par Prosper Blanchemain. Librairie des bibliophiles, 1875. 220 p. 807

Unreliable study; incomplete notes.

— Œuvres de Louise Labé publiées par Charles Boy. Lemerre, 1887. 2 v. 808

V. I : *Œuvres, bibliographie, notes et variantes*; v. II : *Recherches sur la vie et les œuvres de Louise Labé, glossaire*. Text is that of 1556 edition. Solid documentation, sound judgment.

Aynard, Joseph. *See* no. 788. 809

Blanchemain, Prosper. Louise Labé. *In his:* Poètes et amoureuses : portraits littéraires du XVIe siècle. Willem, 1877. p. 177-219. 810

Well written and entertaining, but unreliable on points of fact. Contains Colletet's notice.

Koczorowski, Stanislaw. Louise Labé; étude littéraire, by Stanislas-Pierre Koczorowski. RPol 1:469-91, 1924; 2:219-50, 1924. *Reprinted*, Champion, 1925. 51 p. 811

Fairly good literary study, with facts taken from Boy. Points out similarities with Marot, Petrarch and Second, but fails to convince that these were actual models.

Review : H. Chamard in RHL 33:266-268, 1926.

Larnac, Jean. Louise Labé, la belle cordière de Lyon (1522?-1566). Didot, 1934. 214 p. 812

Reconstruction of Louise's life in the form of a novel. In spite of some gratuitous assumptions (unavoidable in this sort of book), it should not be confused with other fanciful historical novels. In last analysis, however, one is either for or against this type of work.

Review : P. Jourda in RHL 41:617-18, 1934.

O'Connor, Dorothy. Louise Labé, sa vie et son œuvre. Les presses françaises, 1926. 177 p. 813

Previous research made available in convenient form. Findings of predecessors verified with original documents; Boy corrected on several minor points. Presents an original theory of Louise's love affair with Magny. Befuddled on subject of morals (Was Louise a *cortegiana onesta* or a *courtisane publique?*). Bibliography and index.

Review : P. Jourda in RSS 14:177-80, 1927.

Sainte-Beuve, C. A. Louise Labé. *In his:* Portraits contemporains. Calmann-Lévy, 1876, 5:1-38, and Nouveaux lundis, Calmann-Lévy, 1885, 4:289-317. 814

Written before appearance of Boy's edition, no. 808, these essays have no value other than to point out literary value of L.'s sincerity.

Tracconaglia, Giovanni. Une page de l'histoire de l'italianisme à Lyon : à travers le Canzoniere de Louise Labé. Lodi, Dell'Avo, 1915-17. 115 p. 815

Wealth of possible Italian sources and reminiscences. For the rest, superseded by O'Connor.

Review : F. Neri in GSLI 74:149-52, 1919.

Tricou, Georges. Louise Labé et sa famille. BHren 5:60-104, 1944. 816

New biographical information drawn from various archives in or about Lyons. Supplements O'Connor (813).

CHAPTER VI. FRANÇOIS RABELAIS
(Nos. 817-916)

ALEXANDER H. SCHUTZ

Rabelais, François. Œuvres de Rabelais, Édition variorum, augmentée de pièces inédites, des songes drolatiques de Pantagruel, ouvrage posthume, avec explication en regard; des remarques de Le Duchat, etc. et d'un nouveau commentaire historique et philologique, par Esmangart et Eloi Johanneau. Dalibon, 1823. 9 v.   817

Venerable old work, mainly of historic interest, but of which the notes are still not without value. Editors apparently first to point out Gargantua is a popular hero. The *variorum* negligible. Allusions to other editions scattered and erratic.

— Œuvres de François Rabelais; édition critique publiée par Abel Lefranc ... Jacques Boulenger, Henri Clouzot, Paul Dorveaux, Jean Plattard et Lazare Sainéan. Champion, 1912-31. 5 v.   818

A model for future editions of great works, as near to definitive as such a thing can be. Unfortunately not complete, extending only to end of Bk. III. Bk. IV due soon. There are, in the nature of the situation, no indices to correlate all this scattered material found in the elaborate introduction and notes, so that existing monographs on specialized subjects like medicine are still useful.

Reviews : E. Bourciez in Rcr sn 77:381-384, 1914; Lucy M. Gay in MLN 28:55-59, 1913; F. E. Schneegans in LGRP 34:121-24, 1913.

— Œuvres complètes de Rabelais. Texte établi et présenté par Jean Plattard. Roches, 1929. 5 v. (TF)   819

I. 61-219 p. II *(Pantagruel)* 219 p. III *(Tiers livre)* 313 p. IV 332 p. V 399 p. *Quart livre* had been offered in version of *édition dite partielle* as a *thèse complémentaire* in 1909, a year before published date of the principal thesis. These texts, of convenient format and moderate price evidently done in answer to Plattard's desire for a smaller edition which has

profited by modern research. For Bks IV-V, not yet in the Lefranc edition, they are of even greater service. Glossaries useful, but notes not especially original, though brought up to date where necessary.

Review : H. Hatzfeld in DLit 50:1187, June 22, 1929.

— Ouvrage publié pour le quatrième centenaire de sa mort, 1553-1953. Geneva, Droz, and Lille, Giard, 1953. 277 p. (THR)   819A

Twenty-three articles, including review of high spots in R. scholarship in recent years. Many of greatest names in the field represented in this list.

Articles, however, variable as to quality, some extremely original, others of the *mise au point* category, good syntheses but no more. Much overlapping as to subject matter, several details appearing in more than one place and with points of view sufficiently different to make their possible correlation exciting. In any event, no scholar in this field can afford to ignore the book.

— Grande et vraye pronostication nouvelle pour l'an 1544. Lucien Schéler, ed. Geneva, Droz, 1947. 22 p., with 8 p. facsimile.   820

Reprint, with introduction, of an almanac type book, now extremely difficult of access. Important in showing an obscure phase of R.'s activity. In this particular case, the little known pseudonym, Séraphino Calbarsy, is given attention.

Françon, Marcel. Le vroye Gargantua, réimprimé d'après l'exemplaire unique de la Bibliothèque nationale. Préface de Henri Peyre. Nizet, 1949. 145 p.   821

Important for chronology of various Chroniques associated with work of R. This topic handled in introduction, which lists principal ones; cf. Porcher. Saulnier's criticism (no. 830) is subject to caution, quotations from Françon being at times out of context.

Marichal, Robert. François Rabelais, le Quart livre. Lille, Giard, and Geneva, Droz, 1947. 413 p. 822

No reference to Plattard's earlier work (1910), whose introduction he does not supersede, especially in study of language and detailed analysis of sources, better in Plattard. On the other hand, Marichal's notes more elaborate and his *index verborum* has real utility.

Plan, Pierre-Paul. Bibliographie rabelaisienne; les éditions de Rabelais de 1532 à 1711. Imprimerie nationale, 1904. 277 p. 823

According to Rackow (829, p. 211), quoting H. Schneegans, to be used with caution. Still offered, however, by *État présent* (p. 9) and Seymour de Ricci as the place to look for editions of R. Plan not superseded by similar research of RER. Cf., for instance, discussion of title pages (p. 66). Number of useful facsimiles. Immense improvement on Brunet, but retains some queer ideas, e.g. that the *Grandes chroniques* are attributable to R.

Reviews : J. Boulenger in Rcr ns 59:307-311, 1905; M.D. in JS 335-37, 1905; M. L. Poulain in RER 3:93-98, 1904.

Present State of Rabelais Studies

Bezzola, Reto Roberto. Rabelais im Lichte der neueren Forschungen. ZFSL 54:257-280, 1930. 824

Most extensive bibliography of R. since 1927, date of Plattard's *État présent*. Devotes much attention to author's *Fortleben*. Excursions into related areas makes for diffuseness. Emphasis on ideas rather than aesthetics.

Lacroix, Paul. Catalogue de la bibliothèque de l'Abbaye de Saint-Victor au seizième siècle, commenté par le bibliophile Jacob [*pseud.*]. Techener, 1862. 406 p. 825

Detailed history of library with special reference to books mentioned by R. (Book 2, Ch. 7). Useful, but many attempts to identify these works are mere guesses. Needs to be supplemented by Léopold Deslisle's *Le cabinet des manuscrits de la Bibliothèque impériale*, 1868-81, v. 2, p. 232.

Lebègue, Raymond. Où en sont nos connaissances sur Rabelais ? IL 1:85-89, 1949-1950. 826

Essential *mise-au-point*, without being original to any great extent, on what is today known concerning R., his life and works. Excellent starting point for one interested in this subject.

Plattard, Jean. État présent des études rabelaisiennes. Société d'édition Les belles lettres, 1927. 91 p. 827

Like others in the series of *état présent* under same auspices, not bibliographies as much as histories of research in the field and attitudes taken in succeeding periods. A magnificent production and altogether indispensable. Chapter on life of R. might appear overweighted (p. 11-57 in a book so small) but at that time, the most significant research had been in that direction. Some bibliographic indications might have been somewhat fuller, e.g. concerning P. P. Plan. Not without inaccuracies; cf. à propos of Boulenger.

Review : P. Villey in RHL 35:445-46, 1928.

Porcher, Jean. Bibliothèque nationale, Paris, Rabelais; exposition organisée à l'occasion du quatrième centenaire de la publication de Pantagruel. Éditions des Bibliothèques nationales de France, 1933. 206 p. 828

I. *Vie de Rabelais.* II. *Les portraits de Rabelais.* III. *La bibliothèque de Rabelais.* IV. *L'œuvre.* In this chapter is the catalogue of the *chroniques* to which Françon refers. A *Deuxième partie* contains two chapters : I. *Rabelais et son temps.* II. *Rabelais et Gargantua depuis le XVIe siècle.*

Much more than the description of an exposition. Rather an indispensable working bibliography, which deals even with sources of R., giving contemporary books on games to match famous chapter of Gargantua. One may well approve his statement in the first page of the introduction that the bibliography of R. is " une des plus touffues qui soient."

Rackow, Paul. Der gegenwärtige Stand der Rabelaisforschung. GRM 18:198-211 and 277-90, 1930. 829

Helpful not merely as supplement to the *État présent* (827) but in stressing German contribution to R. studies, a point on which author is sensitive.

Saulnier, Verdun L. Dix années d'études sur Rabelais. BHren 11:105-28, 1949. 830

More penetrating job than Rackow, even allowing for difference in dates. However, often a means of conveying author's own ideas on a number of topics, which makes it rather less objective than *État présent* (827).

Life and Personality of Rabelais

Nouvelles littéraires, Apr. 9, 1953. (No. 1336).   831

Rabelais anniversary number, *see* 889.

Cerf, Barry. Rabelais : an appreciation. RR 6:113-49, 1915.   832

Last word of title self-explanatory. Unfortunate that this type of article is published in a specialized journal where the one to whom it will be most advantageous, namely the educated non-specialist, is not likely to seek a synthesis of this kind. Despite a few over-generalizations, worth reading even by those acquainted with the man and the period. Latter will find nothing new, but a lot that is old is well organized in relatively small space.

Chappell, Arthur Fred. The enigma of Rabelais; an essay in interpretation. Cambridge University Press, 1924. 196 p.   833

A pupil of Tilley, says Rackow. Takes up several cogent problems, e.g. why character of Frère Jean was not developed, for which, however, *see* R. H. Armitage, in PMLA 59:944-51, 1944. Another question, the religion of R., has since been ably developed by Febvre (862). Obviously to be consulted by anybody on the search for similar problems.

Reviews : H. Jacoubet in BUAT 35:92-98, 1926-27 (review-article); J. Plattard in RHL 32:606, 1925.

Charpentier, John. Rabelais, le génie de la renaissance. 1944. 316 p.   834

Factually nothing new. Old sources, however, enriched with considerable marginal reading that gives his treatment a distinctive flavor. Why, on the other hand, an odd reverence for the opinions of Léon Daudet? Conclusions to be accepted only with caution. Book riddled with misprints.

France, Anatole. Rabelais. Calmann-Lévy, 1928. 246 p.   835

Originally lectures delivered in Argentine, evidence of over-unctuousness not uncommon under these circumstances. Remains worthwhile as the word of a great writer towards another with whom he had sympathy. Available facts gathered from authoritative sources and critically handled to form a solid basis for more subjective

portions, which in this case are of obvious interest. Even as scholarship, chapters on R.'s influence in his own country have not been superseded.

Guerlin de Guer, Charles. Rabelais. *In his:* Le lexique du xvie siècle. Fmod 2:302-04, 1934.   836

Reviews linguistic studies on R., with copious bibliography. Indispensable, especially in view of date.

Jourda, Pierre. François Rabelais. *In:* Joseph Bédier. Littérature française, publiée sous la direction de Joseph Bédier et Paul Hazard. See 95, v. I, p. 201-18.   837

Indispensable *mise-au-point*, completely renewed from older edition.

Lote, Georges. La vie et l'œuvre de François Rabelais. Droz, 1938. 574 p.   838

Has advantage of being a very cautious and critical weighing of judgments on R. by his defamers and apologists, with author endeavoring to decide. Some unusual features, e.g. a chapter on medieval *merveilleux*, 15th century writers' influence on the language of R.

Plattard, Jean. L'œuvre de Rabelais. Champion, 1910. 374 p.   839

In *État présent*, p. 19, n. 1, refers to this work as " ma thèse. " Subtitle *Sources, invention, composition* self-explanatory, but it is the sources, mainly humanistic, that are emphasized. Chap. I, *L'œuvre de Rabelais et la littérature romanesque* is meager on *chroniques;* II, *Les souvenirs de son temps de moinage;* III, *La respublica scholastica dans l'œuvre de Rabelais* (on student milieu); IV, *Le droit;* V, *Les études médiévales* are good chapters, but the prize is VI, a huge and still valuable repertory entitled *L'humanisme;* VII, *L'esprit populaire;* VIII, *Les caractères généraux du style* are in the main superseded.

Reviews : P. A. Becker in DLit 32:1257-59, May 20, 1911; V. L. Bourrilly in RHM 15:68-71, 1910; A. Morf in Archiv 125:260-261, 1910; F. E. Schneegans in LGRP 32:195-99, 1911; H. Schneegans in ZFSL 36²:248-61, 1910; A. Tilley in MLR 5:536-539, 1910; P. Villey in RHL 18:200-03, 1911.

— Vie de François Rabelais. Paris & Brussels, Van Oest, 1928. 246 p.   840

Capital book. Factual, rather than interpretative, though keen on certain points, e.g. Thélème as possibly viewed by

Marguerite de Navarre (p. 139). Some attention to later public opinion. Less occupied with the aesthetic. Indispensable, however, as starting point for any aspect of R.

Reviews : G. Cohen in Rcr ns 96:317-20, 1929; L. Delaruelle in AM 41:186-89, 1929; A. Lefranc in RSS 16:160-66, 1929; P. Villey in RHL 36:458-60, 1929.

— La vie et l'œuvre de Rabelais. Boivin, [c. 1939.] 133 p. 841

In series *Le livre de l'étudiant*, a self-explanatory caption. Serviceable *Guide bibliographique*, p. 129 ff. : *De quel texte se servir pour étudier Rabelais ?*

Review : F. Bérance in NL Mar. 18, 1939, p. 5.

Powys, John Cowper. Rabelais, his life, the story told by him; selections therefrom newly translated, and an interpretation of his genius and his religion. London, Bodley Head, 1948. 424 p. 842

Biography has nothing new. Essays in back of book dithyrambic and subjective; *Rabelais and the wisdom of blasphemy* a typical caption. Political (left) bias. Best feature, decidedly worth reading, is Preface on *Rabelais among the Anglo-Saxons*, also a chapter on art of translation. His own renditions have sparkle and individuality, but not always accurate. He is wrong in blaming Urquhart, as he does constantly. Many misprints.

Reviews : Anon in TLS, Aug. 14, 1948, p. 460; H.B.C. in MGW, July 1, 1948, p. 10; G. Jones in LL 58:244-46, 1948; D. Saurat in Spec 181:84-86, July 16, 1948.

Putnam, Samuel. François Rabelais : man of the renaissance; a spiritual biography. New York, Cape & Smith, 1929. 530 p. 843

Product of considerable reading in authoritative sources. Some data comprehensible only to people who have some knowledge of that same continually deprecated scholarly research or at least an equipment in French letters, this in an *œuvre de vulgarisation*. Much straight Putnam, not always germane, though interesting, even if on " smart " side. To be used with caution.

Stapfer, Paul. Rabelais, sa personne, son génie, son œuvre. Colin, 1889. 507 p. 844

Biographic portion dated, not always trustworthy, e.g. Chinon the birthplace of R. Unfortunately followed here is the

article on R. in *Encyclopedia Brittanica*, a treatment, incidentally, in urgent need of revision. Rest of Stapfer deserves reading today. Many an idea originated by him is put forth as new by more recent critics; see, for instance, treatment on religion of R. Critique is that of a keen mind.

Reviews : A. Lefranc in Rcr ns 29:89-92, 1890; H. Pergamini in RBelgique 64:254-282, 1890.

Willcocks, Mary Patricia. The laughing philosopher, being a life of François Rabelais. London, Allen & Unwin, 1950. 845

Vulgarization, but well documented (even to a firsthand knowledge of Galenus), and handled with taste. Has a decidedly archeological bias. Some acute observations — " All Rabelais' tales are the better for being read aloud." (p. 83) So Lefranc always used to say in his classes.

Critical Studies on Rabelais

Boulenger, Jacques. Rabelais à travers les âges. Le divan, 1925. 247 p. 846

Less attention to 16th century, unfortunately, than to subsequent periods. It is a gap, among others in this book, to be filled in. Mentioned by Plattard, *État présent* (no. 827), p. 10, n. 1, but comment has several errors : The *Examen de ses autographes* should read *Les autographes de Rabelais* and is by S. de Ricci, a detail not provided in the note. An omission is the *Études sur les portraits* by Clouzot. Nor is it fair to call the book a " compilation."

Reviews : J. Plattard in RSS 12:429-31, 1925; RHL 33:632-33, 1926.

— Rabelais. Éditions Colbert. c. 1942. 231 p. 847

Intended to initiate a collection of Great Europeans. Very well documented and has therefore bibliographical value, especially *Guide bibliographique*, which forms Chap. V. Latter gives evaluations of his own and other works. Some circumspection necessary in accepting certain statements; not possible to find a *bibliographie complète du sujet* in RER, RSS or Hren.

Brémond, Félix, ed. Rabelais médecin, notes et commentaires. I Gargantua. Pairault, 1879. 310 p. II Pantagruel. Maloine, 1888. 211 p. III Tiers livre. Maloine, 1901. 205 p. IV Quart livre, Maloine, 1911, 227 p. 848

Less a connected exposition than a series of notes, as title indicates. Sufficient grouping to allow general conclusions. Work has been the subject of much discussion, for which, as for other aspects of R.'s medical importance, *see* rich bibliography *in: United States. Surgeon General's Office. Library. Index-catalogue of the Library of the Surgeon-General's Office, United States Army. Washington, Govt. Prtg. Off.*, 1880-95. 3rd ser., v. 9:14, 1931.

Brown, Huntington. Rabelais in English literature. Cambridge, Harvard University Press, 1933. 254 p.   849

Survey from Holyband and Cotgrave to Tom Brown and others. Some parallels do not seem overly close. Nevertheless a job that needed to be done, Sainéan's *Les interprètes de Rabelais en Angleterre et en Allemagne* not being sufficient. There would seem to be room for somewhat more work on the period preceding 18th century, which begins the more thorough part of book. *See* 2828.

Review : E. A. Baker in MLR 29:458-459, 1934.

Busson, Henri. Rabelais et le miracle. RCC 30¹:385-400, Feb. 15, 1929.   850

What is a " miracle " according to R. How R. fits in with his times as to what is to be accepted. He will, for instance, believe in astrology. Problem of biblical miracle. How these considerations shed light on R.'s text. Excellent piece of scholarship.

Carpenter, Nan Cooke. The authenticity of Rabelais' Fifth book : musical criteria. MLQ 13:299-305, 1952.   851

Shows that not only do R.'s musical allusions or procedures persist in 5th book, but rise to a new climax. Often very convincing, but not always. More detailed than Van den Borren (908) and better integrated as evidence for authorship of Book V.

— Rabelais and the chanson. PMLA 65:1212-32, Dec., 1950.   852

Excellent illustration of a rare type of research, contribution of musicology to comprehension of literary texts. Author proves R.'s familiarity with the genre as practiced in his period, both as to words and their settings. Very useful repertory of songs and their composers known to R.

— Rabelais and musical ideas. RR 41:14-25, 1950.   853

R.'s technical knowledge. Importance of music, not only as one of mediaeval liberal arts, but as element in education of renaissance gentleman. Music and stylistics, i.e. as concerns imagery. Cf. also her article in RR 40:3-17, 1949.

Chappell, Arthur F. Rabelais and the authority of the ancients. MLR 18:29-36, 1923.   854

R.'s evolution in this respect, especially in the *Tiers livre*. " For the first time classical authority is weighed in the balances (of experience) and found wanting." (p. 36). Fine piece of scholarly presentation, earnestly recommended for facts and excellent style.

Clement, Nemours Honoré. The influence of the Arthurian romances on the five books of Rabelais. Berkeley, University of California Press, 1926, p. 147-257. (CPMP, v. 12)   855

Makes a distinction between " Gest " romances and Arthurian type. Especially Grail romances influenced quests of the 4th (and 5th ?) books. He rides his hobby somewhat too hard. Problems posed often outdated, but book still useful. More remains to be done on the *succès de librairie* of prose romances, as of those in verse. *See* 2805.

Reviews : H. C. Lancaster in MLN 42:52-53, 1927; R.V. Merrill in MP 24:361-62, 1926-27; J. Plattard in RSS 13:289-90, 1926.

Clouzot, Henri. Furetière et Rabelais. RSS 3:76-77, 1915.   856

Phase of R.'s influence not included in Boulenger. *See* 846-47.

Cohen, Gustave. Rabelais et le théâtre. RER 9:1-72, 1911.   857

Essential reading for R.'s contacts with medieval survivals in theatre, especially staging, not excluding renaissance spectacles *(Sciomachie)*. Celebrated *premières* and settings. Special place of Patelin, of the monologue. Illustrations valuable.

Coutaud, Albert. La pédagogie de Rabelais. Librairie de la France scolaire, 1899. 278 p.   858

Good synthesis of influences surrounding formation of educational ideas of R. and his time, e.g. gaps (lack of female education) as well as progress made. Not a little of the book's value lies in the eleven page preface of the eminent Compayré.

Reviews : J. Feller in RIPB 43:123-24, 1900; C.E.R. in Rcr 48:453, Dec. 4, 1899.

Dontenville, Henri. La mythologie française. Payot, 1948. 227 p.   859

Deals largely with origins and manifestations of Gargantua and Pantagruel as folk heroes. Loaded with facts and no little evocation. Worth reading but not easy to read. Breadth of scope illustrated by final chapter, *Résistance et survivance de Gargantua* (p. 205-23); " résistance " is that of World War II, and the conclusion is addressed " Aux jeunes qui cherchent leur voie."

Review : M. Françon in FR 23:138-39, 1949-50.

Droz, Eugénie. Rabelais versificateur. Hren 3:202-06, 1936.   860

Repertory and form analysis of verse either quoted by R. or written by him. Useful parallel notes for study of contemporaries.

Dubouchet, A. F. Rabelais à Montpellier, 1530-1538. Montpellier, Coulet, 1887. 124 p.   861

The subtitle : *Etude biographique d'après les documents originaux, avec facsimile en héliogravure*, slightly misleading, since it is, firstly, not one but several *études;* secondly, there are several facsimiles—not merely one — finely reproduced. Still worth knowing, not alone for biography of R. but for *université de médecine* and its milieu.

Febvre, Lucien. Le problème de l'incroyance au seizième siècle; la religion de Rabelais. Michel, 1942. 547 p. *See* 869. 862

Takes cue from Plattard, *Etat présent*, p. 80, n. 1 : " la question serait à reprendre." Elaborate defense of R. against statements that contemporaries accused him of " atheism." Takes each one of those accusations, with attempt to prove that a) terms are not understood then as now; b) evidence is to be reappraised, reference being often to another man. An effort of ten years, ingenious and scholarly, but requiring circumspection. Large, classified bibliography, not without omissions, e.g. N. H. Clement. Nevertheless an essential for this aspect of R.'s thought.

Reviews : M. Bataillon in AHS 5:5-27, 1944; G. Charlier in RBP 23:374-77, 1944; E. Dolleans in Cr 22:236-42, 1948.

Françon, Marcel. Les chroniques gargantuines. FS 2:247-52, 1948.   863

List of the *chroniques* with attempt at dating them. More convenient arrangement than Porcher's but to be checked against it.

— Influence des Chroniques gargantuines sur Ronsard et sur J. Du Bellay. SP 50:144-148, 1953.   864

Continues, from his articles in MLJ 35:622-23, 1951, the theme of " aguillons à soif." Interest of this entry is that Ronsard uses a direct idea from *Croniques* in an epitaph to R. and Du Bellay does same in a satire on Pope Julius III, showing that these predecessors of R. were known to the Pléiade. Would not more research along this line be productive?

— Notes sur les chroniques admirables FR 24:9-12, 1950-51.   865

Emphasis on " popular tradition," and extent thereof. Negative conclusion on datability. Valuable for bibliography in a field not well known.

— Sur la genèse de Pantagruel. PMLA 62:45-61, 1947.   866

Nature of the *chroniques*, which may be " digests " of anterior versions. Complexity of dating problems. His procedure, in this connection, attacked by Saulnier (*see* 830), for making a distinction between approach of " bibliographers " and that of " folklorists."

Gebhart, Emile. Rabelais, la renaissance et la réforme. Hachette, 1877. 300 p. 867

A quite remarkable book in its grasp of both the ideas of R. and of his artistic form. In his day, Gebhart showed originality in things now taken for granted, e.g. R.'s incapacity to grasp certain phases of the renaissance, like the new position of women (though there is *Thélème*!), R.'s position in struggle of philosophies, especially vs. scholasticism. *See* 2888.

Gilson, Etienne. Notes médiévales au Tiers livre. RHFr 2:72-88, 1925.   868

Deals, as one might expect, largely with philosophy, but includes scientific terms from other areas, e.g. commutative. Important for matters of unusual contexts.

— Rabelais franciscain. *In his :* Les idées et les lettres. Vrin, 1932. p. 197-241. 869

Effort to show continuity of medieval thought into renaissance. Years of R.'s " moinage " leave traces, not only in

theology but even in special " sel franciscain," often mistaken merely for " sel gaulois." Shows direct reference to Fra Salimbene and similar " farceurs " of a well defined Franciscan tradition, now difficult for us to grasp, though Wadding, in 17th century, still accepts him as a " Scriptor Ordinis." Gilson adds and corrects many an item in Lefranc edition. Anticipates Febvre on smaller scale in defending R. against accusation of atheism; see 862.
Review : D. Mornet in RHL 41:138-40, 1934.

Girault, François. The tale of Gargantua and King Arthur, ed. by Huntington Brown. Cambridge, Mass., Harvard University Press, 1932. 132 p.   870
Reprint of *Chroniques admirables* and *Grandes chroniques*, with an introduction on influence of the legend of Gargantua in England and its connection with Arthurian legend. Some account taken of Rabelaisian influence and its dating. Rather popular in character.

Guiton, Jean. Le mythe des paroles gelées (Rabelais Quart livre-LV-LVI). RR 31:3-15, 1940.   871
Shows not only sources, but also poetic sensibility of R. to the " cosmic " in linguistic resources.

Heulhard, Arthur. Rabelais, ses voyages en Italie, son exil à Metz. Allison, 1891. 404 p.   872
An old book, but still interesting for numerous detailed sidelights, e.g. on Loire valley, Du Bellay family, Dolet, on several aspects of contemporary history. *See* 2707.

Jourda, Pierre. Le Gargantua de Rabelais. SFELT, 1948. 192 p.   873
Thoroughly competent book by good authority on renaissance. Narrowly misses being very original on several occasions, especially on p. 100, where, à propos of Louis XI and Louis XII he touches on question of mediaeval sources.
Reviews : F. de Dainville in Études, Nov., 1948, p. 280-81.

Keller, Abraham C. Anti-war writing in France, 1500-60. PMLA 67:240-50, Mar., 1952.   874
Partly devoted to R. Notes chiefly his abandonment of " non-aggression " principle once circumstances take him into royal orbit.

Krailsheimer, Alban J. Rabelais and the Pan legend. FS 2:158-61, 1948.   875
Shows R.'s independence of Eusebius and his desire to show, by identification of Christ with Pan, continuation of Classical into Christian world.

Lebègue, Raymond. Rabelais et la parodie. BHren 14:193-204, 1952.   876
Shows not only sources and methods of parody, including stylistic resources, but indicates a number of Rabelaisian texts not previously given as parodistic.

— Rabelais, the last of the Erasmians. JWI 12:91-100, 1949.   877
" If the scholars of the twentieth century, unlike the Romantics, praise Rabelais rather for his narrative and dramatic powers and for his verbal artistry, than as a thinker, this is because most of his ideas are anticipated in the books of the earlier humanists, and above all in those of Erasmus." (p. 99)
Article intended as a start towards a general treatment of Erasmus in France. Essential reading.

Le Double, Anatole Félix. Rabelais anatomiste et physiologiste. Leroux, 1899. 440 p.   878
Introduction deals with history of R.'s medical studies. Difficult to see where physiology comes in, since anatomy takes up virtually the whole book. Exceedingly detailed, important for R.'s lexicography in this domain.

Lefranc, Abel. La pensée secrète de Rabelais. RFrance 2 (pt. 3) : 326-58, May 15, 1922.   879
Aims to show R. actually irreligious, under influence of Lucian. Writing for " grand public " he is more dogmatic than usual, also less convincing. That is also the impression of Febvre (no. 862) and Plattard (*État présent*), both refuting his arguments.

— Les navigations de Pantagruel. Leclerc, 1905. 353 p.   880
Utopia voyage of Pantagruel as preview of Bks. IV-V, these in turn reflecting contemporary voyages of discovery. Cf. the *résumé* in his *État présent*, p. 67, n. 1. Numerous appendices (A to L), mostly on phases of these voyages.
Reviews : (Anon) in LZD 57:1148-49, 1905; (Anon) in Archiv 115:479-80, 1905; (Anon) in RU 14²:414, 1905; J. Boulenger

in RER 3:229-32, 1905; H.D. in JS, 1905, 54-56; G.D.F. in Jdéb, June 17th, 1905.

– Le Platon de Rabelais. BBB 1901:105-14; 169-81.   881

Capital article. After a bibliographic note on Aldine Plato of 1513 and R. autograph, shows influence of Academy on formation of R. Not Plato per se, but Greek incurred displeasure of monks at Fontenay, since Ficino's translation is found in the abbey. Full of odd documentary facts.

– Rabelais et les Estienne; Le procès du Cymbalum de Bonaventure des Périers. RSS 15:356-66, 1928.   882

R. attacked by Estienne, in turn involved with Bonaventure, whose *Cymbalum* was ordered destroyed by Parlement. Important phase of " incroyance " question.

ote, Georges. La politique de Rabelais. RCC 37¹:64-79 ; 464-80, 882-47 ; 1935-1936.   883

I. *Principes et théories*. R. conservative as to monarchic institutions and does not even attack nobility, but wishes for an ideal relation of governor to governed. II. *L'Angleterre, l'Empire*. Patriotic and traditional. Sources of his information on a question of unusual contemporary interest. III. *L'Empire, la Papauté*. Antiimperial stand (Pichrochole identified with Charles V) brings him into conflict with political aspirations of the papacy. Excellent summation, more valuable in being posterior in date to Lefranc's discussion in introduction to Bk. III of his edition.

MacMinn, George Rupert. English and American appreciation of Rabelais. *In:* The Charles Mills Gayley anniversary papers. Berkeley, University of California Press, 137-51, 1922. (CPMP, v. 11)   884

What critics saw—and failed to see. Long, detailed list of quotations from a large variety of authors. Excellent piece of work, result of an obviously considerable amount of research, done with discrimination.

Marichal, Robert. Rabelais et la réforme de la justice. BHren 14:176-90, 1952.   885

François, son of the " robin " Antoine Rabelais, is sufficiently in tune with this group to sympathize with its aims and to know royal politics as to reduction of judiciary, but he sides with monarchy none the less. Baché incident of Bk. IV typi-

fies literary treatment of a familiar situation. In general an excellent analysis whereby the historical illumines the literary.

Morçay, Raoul. Fusion de l'humanisme et de la renaissance, Rabelais. *In his:* La renaissance, Gigord, 1933, 172-242.   886

As a chapter of a volume, in turn part of an *Histoire de la littérature française*, it will be widely read. Interesting and at times original treatment, especially on R.'s shallow characterizations (p. 238); the opinions far from being invariably convincing and the book is to be used with caution.

Mulertt, Werner. Rabelais und die Melusinen-Geschichte. ZFSL 62:325-41, 1938-1939.   887

Essentially a critique of N. H. Clement's overemphasis (at least, so he believes) of medieval influences. Lusignan-Mélusine story was more effective with R. as a Poitevin survival, due to his sojourn in that region, than as a carry-over of Middle Ages.

Nock, Albert Jay. A journey into Rabelais's France. New York, Morrow, 1934. 303 p.   888

Popular, amusing, yet well written and *con amore*, with first hand knowledge of terrain, described *à l'américaine*. Exploding myth of a " plantureuse Touraine," he opines : " The county of Sussex in New Jersey has it beaten hands down." (p. 18). Review : Margaret de Schweinitz in Hren 2:319-20, 1935.

Nouvelles littéraires, Apr. 9, 1953. (No. 1336).   889

Rabelais anniversary number, containing articles of varying originality, among which are :

Bourin, André. *Itinéraires de Rabelais*, p. 1-2.
Cohen, Gustave. *Rabelais éducateur*, p. 5.
Dontenville, Henri. *Le mythe de Gargantua*, p. 5.
Febvre, Lucien. *Humanisme pantagruélique*, p. 1-2.
Lebègue, Raymond. *Rabelais et son temps*, p. 3.
Pincherle, Marc. *La musique dans Rabelais*, p. 10.
Porcher, Jean. *Rabelais à travers les siècles*, p. 4.
Prinet, Jean. *Imagiers et illustrateurs*, p. 3.
Prouteau, Gilbert. *Rabelais et le sport*, p. 6.

Saulnier, Verdun L. *La langue de Rabelais*, p. 4.

Vallery-Radot, Pierre. *Rabelais médecin*, p. 5.

O'Kane, Eleanor. The proverb : Rabelais and Cervantes. CL 2:360-69, 1950.   890

Heavily biased in favor of Cervantes (author is evidently a Hispanist) as a more " popular " handler of the proverb, article suggests a new vista for R.'s mediaeval influences in his treatment of this stylistic device. Worth pursuing.

Plattard, Jean. L'adolescence de Rabelais en Poitou. Les belles lettres, 1923.   209 p.
890A

Follows in detail R.'s sojourn at Ligugé, Maillezais and other places that had a rôle in his formation. Shows results in such chapters as *La culture juridique de Rabelais*, *La matière de bréviaire*. A good deal of that material necessarily incorporated in later works, but this book still has its use because of great detail involved.

Reviews : L. Delaruelle in RER 11:323-325, 1924; J. P[orcher?] in BSHP 73:145-48, Apr.-June, 1924.

— L'écriture sainte et la littérature scripturaire dans l'œuvre de Rabelais. RER 8:257-330, 1910.   891

Analysis of citations, book by book. Restoration to context by completion of quotation, association of ideas, comparison with recurrences elsewhere in R., connection with exegetes past and contemporary. Reveals, besides obvious knowledge of scriptures, " évangélique " tendencies at one time. Suppressions and modifications of 1542 edition reveal also desire to mollify theologians rather than recant possible errors. Irreverence often merely that of typical medieval clerk. Fifth book shows marked differences in technique.

Decidedly worth study as capital picture of R.'s equipment.

— Flaubert lecteur de Rabelais. RER 10:288-90, 1912.   892

Earlier period one of pastiches. Letters to Caroline show admiration strong in 1880, but real content in his imitations definitively gone during Bouvard-Pécuchet.

— Guide illustré au pays de Rabelais. Les belles lettres, 1931.   77 p.   893

Preface of P. Vallat. More full of data than Nock, more serious. Requires greater knowledge of R. to follow than

Nock, less attractive therefore to average American reader. Good especially in architectural detail, e.g. comparison of Bonnivet and Thélème.

Review : P. Jourda in RSS 18:356-57, 1931.

— La procédure au XVIᵉ siècle d'après Rabelais. RSS 1:28-49, 1913.   89

After lexicographic examination of individual terms, finds R. did not, as in some technologies, locate them in some book but drew on family background.

Sainéan, Lazare. L'histoire naturelle et les branches connexes dans l'œuvre de Rabelais. *See* 326.   89

Under *branches connexes* study goes beyond field of natural history to include even items like *tanquart, pot à boire*. Most useful lexicographical study, rather than a synthesis. The Delaunay who wrote review below was in charge of medical notes for *Tiers livre* of Lefranc edition.

Review : P. Delaunay in RSS 10:219-21, 1923. *See* 2112.

— L'influence et la réputation de Rabelais; interprètes, lecteurs et imitateurs; un rabelaisien (Marnix de Saint-Aldégonde). Gamber, 1930.   322 p.   896

Key words of title constitute divisions of work. Fuller than Boulenger in having more facets to treatment, e.g. chapter on editors, not in Boulenger (nos. 846-47) at all, and in greater attention to detail. Division into numerous subheads unnecessarily complicated, making for harder reading than his predecessor. Thought-provoking work, suggesting more study, e.g. on translations of R. *See* 2889.

Reviews : R. R. Bezzola in ZFS 56:252-254, 1932; K. Glaser in LGRP 51:368-69, 1930; J. Plattard in RER 17:176-78, 1930.

— Les interprètes de Rabelais en Angleterre et en Allemagne. RER 7:137-258, 1909.   897

Acceptance of R. outside Protestant countries almost nil. His " interprètes " are, therefore, Cotgrave—an Englishman, Urquhart—a Scot, and Fischart—a German-speaking Alsacian. Sainéan's analysis of first named outstanding, even apart from his rôle as " glossateur de Rabelais." Penetrating, and essential, is his study of the Urquhart translation, considered philologically. Fischart, more remote for Anglo-Saxon reader, also gets an exceedingly able linguistic discussion in the attempt to dress R. in German clothes, which was naturally doomed to failure. A masterly article.

aulnier, Verdun L.   Rabelais et le populaire. LH 8:149-79, 1949.   898
Goes beyond title in discussing matters like Erasmian influence, but mostly concerned with various *Chroniques* and their dates. Extremely detailed, valuable for its information, but apparently due to meet with opposition, hence to be used with some caution.

– Sur la date de naissance de Rabelais. BHren 7:245-46, 1945.   899
Denies validity of objections made by Lefranc to the date 1483, on grounds " adulescens " has been found to apply to men over thirty.

cheler, Lucien.   Une pronostication inconnue de Rabelais. BHren 8:119-28, 1946.   900
Argument in favor of his authorship, partly on typographical grounds, hence its chief interest. Covers an obscure period of his life. Question of these prognostications, almanacs and the like might well be subject of more unified treatment over wider scope.

creech, M. A. R.   De Billon and Erasmus. BHren 13:241-65, 1951.   901
Cornelius Agrippa, rather than De Billon, as primary source. Not Rondibilis but Hippothadée, with biblical ideals, voice of R. Latter an Erasmian, believes in subordinate status of women, but not anti-feminist. Screech is wrong in thinking R. not influenced by Tiraqueau. Notarial inventories attest latter's popularity.

mith, W. F.   Les proverbes de Rabelais. RER 7:371-76, 1909.   902
List of proverbs compared with similar collections of R.'s day, which, by their popularity, may have actually been sources. Scattered commentary.

pitzer, Leo.   Le prétendu réalisme de Rabelais.   MP 37:139-50, 1939-40.   903
R.'s stylistic processes accentuate exaggerated and chaotic, to attain something essentially true. Feels called upon, in treating " l'irréel," to criticize group of Lefranc for their insistence on element of realism. Provocative. Not to be neglected are a series of *Annexes* or additional notes.

Thuasne, Louis.   Études sur Rabelais. Bouillon, 1904.   450 p.   904
Chapters on *Sources monastiques*, Erasmus, Folengo, plus a series of *Mélanges*. Used by Lefranc, but much remains for interested reader that is not in the edition. First chapter, the thinnest, suggests more to be done on late 15th and early 16th century sermons attacking monastic life and institutions.
Reviews : J. Boulenger in RER 3:101-04, 1905; W. Küchler in ZFSL 28²:204-06, 1905.

Tilley, Arthur.   Rabelais and geographical discovery. *In his:* Studies in the French renaissance. Cambridge, University Press, 1922, p. 26-65.   905
Mine of information on renaissance geographers. Shows also, besides probability of their being sources for R., manner in which those sources were handled. Excellent documentation.

— Rabelais and Henri II. *In his:* Studies in the French renaissance. Cambridge, University Press, 1922, p. 66-84.   906
R.'s attempts to win favor of a monarch more orthodox than his father, however Gallican, ended in failure. Defense of Anti-Vatican policy and flattering allusions to historic incidents did not prevent condemnation of *Quart livre*. As one may expect, excellent and well-documented treatment.

— Rabelais and the fifth book. *In his:* Studies in the French renaissance. Cambridge, University Press, 1922. p. 85-122.   907
Minute analysis of texts as transmitted. Conclusions, as stated on p. 120-21, are that whole of *Isle sonante* is R.'s, but not seen through the press by him. Rest of *Fifth book* in the main his, but with interpolations and certainly not in anything like the form R. would have wished to present. R. must have left a very rough draft, later reworked by others.

Borren, Charles van den.   Rabelais et la musique. BCBA 24:78-111, 1942.   908
Mostly a listing of R.'s contacts with contemporary musical genres and their public representations. Not as comprehensive as articles of Carpenter (852-53) but should have been mentioned by her. Studies complement each other.

Villey, Pierre. Les grands écrivains du xviᵉ siècle. Évolutions des œuvres et invention de formes littéraires. v. I, Marot et Rabelais. Champion, 1923. 431 p. (BLR) 909

Two separate divisions on authors concerned. Part dealing with R. extends from p. 151 to p. 431, a comprehensive treatment still much worth reading. Some material old, a good deal that is new has apparently remained unnoticed, e.g. his anticipation of Febvre by stating Voulté's attacks against Lucianism not directed at R. at all. Has no hesitation in contradicting Lefranc.

Review : J. Plattard in RSS 11:105-09, 1924.

Language of Rabelais

Bertoni, Giulio. La lingua di Rabelais. AR 22:429-35, 1938. 910

Does not add greatly to known facts on R. as affording a junction of popular and cultured, except for noteworthy observations concerning his using certain techniques of renaissance buffoons, whom he could have seen at Italian courts.

Huguet, Edmond. Étude sur la syntaxe de Rabelais comparée à celle des autres prosateurs de 1450 à 1550. *See* 595. 911

Bibliography on syntax of R. large and selectivity not easy. Huguet is, according to Plattard (*État présent*, p. 84, n. 1), " le livre capital " on the subject, although its methodology is of its day and nothing much is done on stylistics. Highly useful as repertory of constructions.

Reviews : J. Buche in RPF 9:65-67, 1895; A. Delboulle in Rcr 57:87, 1895; L. Fränkel in ZFSL 17:168-73, 1895; Kn. in LZD 6:194-95, Feb. 9, 1895; W. Meyer-Lübke in LGRP 15:399-401, 1894; H. Schneegans in ZRP 19:118-31, 1895; A. Stimming in Archiv 95:207-16 and KJRP 2:205, 1891-94.

La Juillière, Pierre de. Les images dans Rabelais. Halle, Niemeyer, 1912. 156 p. (Beihefte of ZRP, No. 37) 912

Quite the catalogue type of presentation, but useful, not merely for number of items, but for some well-written generalizations at end of each chapter, e.g. concerning R.'s indifference to animals, their suffering, intelligence, etc. Makes distinction between Examples (with proper names), Comparisons (common nouns), Metaphors and Personifications.

Reviews : P. A. Becker in DLit 34:1705 1706, July 5, 1913; E. Bourciez in Rc ns 76:314-15, 1913; N.S. in LZD 64:1610 1611, 1913; L. Spitzer in ZFS 42:66-67 1914.

Lanson, Gustave. Rabelais. *In his:* L'ar de la prose. Librairie des annales, 2ᵉ éd 1909, 28-38. 91

Many have praised style of R.; few a enthusiastically as this. A masterly treat ment by a master of prose style.

Poirier, Abbé A.-D. La langue de Rabelai dans ses rapports avec le Bas-Poitou. Fmo 12:109-71, 1944. 91

First part general. Conclusion : " Maî tre Alcofribas semble parfois n'écrire qu pour les seuls Poitevins parmi lesquels avait vécu... " Even so, dialect frequentl dressed up for general reader. In secon part chief merit is in glossary, provide with detailed notes, outcome of his desir to do the job of both a local connoisseu and a professional linguist. Despite tha ambition, he lends himself to the criticis of Saulnier, BHren 11:126, 1949.

Sainéan, Lazare. La langue de Rabelai *See* 601. 91

Essential work on subject. Method study is to align words and expression under subjects, e.g., Navigation. Show that R. was well informed about his time While Jal (RER 8:3-56, 1910) had ques tioned R.'s knowledge of nautical term Sainéan in present work vindicates R. technical proficiency. Organization book in places awkward, but indices hel greatly. Introduction of folklore (Go Magos) goes beyond linguistics. Va erudition, which makes of this study som thing of a renaissance encyclopedia. Thu Sainéan points out reforms of Pléiade ha already been put into practice by R.

Reviews : K. Glaser in ZFSL 47:208-1. 1925; M. Roques in Rom 49:318, 192

Saulnier, Verdun L. Rabelais devar l'écolier limousin. MerF 304:269-7. Oct. 1, 1948. 91

" Le procédé de l'Écolier ... est ur machine éternelle de rire, et non ur machine polémique d'époque." Is throwback to mediaeval macaronic trad tion. Article a necessary corrective opinions of wide currency relative to rô of R. as satirist of " écumeurs de latin.

CHAPTER VII. CONTEURS AND NOVELISTS
(Nos. 917-1045)

J. W. HASSELL AND W. L. WILEY

Conteurs

(Nos. 917-1012)

General Studies

DeJongh, William F. J. A bibliography of the novel and short story in French from the beginning of printing till 1600. University of New Mexico Press, 1944. 79 p. (NMBS, v. 1, No. 1) *See* 1017. **917**

Carefully compiled and useful annotated bibliography of first editions of works of novelistic fiction in French which were published during 15th and 16th centuries. Includes French translations of foreign works of prose fiction.

Flake, Otto. Der französische Roman und die Novelle; ihre Geschichte von den Anfängen bis zur Gegenwart. Leipzig, Teubner, 1912. 130 p. **918**

Excellent, very concise summary of development of French novel and short story. Now somewhat out of date.

Gerhardt, Max. Der Aberglaube in der französischen Novelle des 16 Jahrhunderts. Schöneberg bei Berlin, Langenscheidt, 1906. 158 p. (Diss., Rostock) **919**

Interesting but somewhat cursory discussion of superstitions in the *conte*. Deals chiefly with Rabelais. Much illustrative material.

Loviot, Louis. Études de bibliographie littéraire, auteurs et livres anciens (XVIe et XVIIe siècles). Fontemoing, 1917. (Extrait de RLA, 1 and 2.) 206 p. **920**

Reprint of Loviot's articles in *Revue des livres anciens*, 1 (1914) and 2 (1917).

Paris, Gaston. La nouvelle française au XVe et XVIe siècles. JS 3rd ser. 60:289-303 and 342-61, 1895. **921**

Standard piece of criticism on *conte*. Cf. Toldo, *Contributo* (925) cited below.

Redenbacher, Fritz. Die Novellistik der französischen Hochrenaissance. ZFSL 49:1-72, 1926. *Reprinted*: Munich, 1926, 76 p. **922**

Splendid study of French short story as an art form. Includes fairly complete bibliographical information on renaissance *conte*.

Reynier, Gustave. Le roman sentimental avant l'Astrée. Colin, 1908. 406 p. **923**

Supplements well his *Origines* (924); especially relevant are Pt. I, ch. 10, and Pt. II, ch. 1. *See* 1022.

— Les origines du roman réaliste. Hachette, 1912. 340 p. **924**

Good short history of French 16th century *conte* literature, with emphasis upon its relationship to contemporary life. Foreign influences, especially Italian and Spanish, mentioned briefly. *See* 1021.

Toldo, Pietro. Contributo allo studio della novella francese del XV e XVI secolo. Rome, Loescher, 1895. 153 p. **925**

Out of date in many respects, but still valuable. Good general discussion of relationship between Italian literature and French folk tradition, with reference to the *conte*. Chief fault of work is strenuous intent to prove Italian influence.

Anonymous Collections

Frank, Félix, ed. Les comptes du monde adventureux. Lemerre, 1878. 2 v. **926**

Latest, most scholarly edition of *Les comptes*. For further criticism of this collection, *see* general studies on the *conte*, especially Toldo (925) and G. Paris (921), 351 ff.

Les joyeuses adventures. Lyons, 1555. 160 feuillets. **927**

Although similar in content to *Joyeuses aventures* of 1575, 1577, etc., this anonymous collection is generally considered a separate work.

Bolte, Johannes. Les joyeuses adventures, ein französisches Schwankbuch des 16. Jhs. Archiv 150:220-27, 1926.   928
Since Bolte did not know previously published studies of Loviot on same subject matter, his work largely out of date when it appeared. Nevertheless, it complements usefully Loviot's work; of particular interest to those concerned with the origins of :
1. *Les joyeuses adventures et plaisants facetieux deviz.*
Its content is carefully compared with that of the *Cent nouvelles nouvelles*, the *Wendunmuth* of Kirchhof, and the *Recueil des plaisantes et facetieuses nouvelles.* Antwerp, 1555.
2. *Les joyeuses aventures et nouvelles recréations.*
3. La Motte-Roullant, *Les fascetieux devitz des cent nouvelles nouvelles.*
4. *Recueil des plaisantes et facetieuses nouvelles.* Lyons, Barricat, 1555, and Antwerp, Spelman, 1555.
(Bolte refers to the latter as a pirated edition.)
5. The spurious stories added to the tale collection of Des Périers.

Les joyeuses aventures, et nouvelles recreations. Bonfons, 1575. 136 feuillets.   929
First edition of this obscure anonymous tale collection. Most tales taken from *Les fascetieux devitz* of La Motte-Roullant; not, as Brunet states, from Des Périers. Other editions of 1577, 1582, and 1602.

Loviot, Louis. Les joyeuses aventures. 1575, 1577, 1582 & 1602. RLA 1:210-11, 1913-14.   930
Concise description of content of these four editions. Some material on sources.

Les joyeuses narrations advenues de nostre temps. Lyons, Rigaud & Saugrain, 1557. 224 p.   931
Anthology of tales, derived for most part from Poggio and Boccaccio. No original material. Brunet mentions an edition of 1572; Newberry Library in Chicago has a copy. Only two copies of 1557 edition exist. A third edition, of 1596, reproduces the text of that of 1557. 1596 edition, published at Lyons by Rigaud, contains 223 numbered pages.

Loviot, Louis. Les joyeuses narrations. 1557 & 1596. RLA 1:303-04, 1913-14. 932

Gives brief discussion of bibliography and content of *Les joyeuses narrations.* Identifies source of each of the twenty-five tales included in the collection.

Boccaccio, Giovanni. Le parangon des nouvelles honnestes et delectables. Réimprimé d'après l'édition de 1531 et précédé d'une introduction par Émile Mabille. Brussels, Gay, 1865. 170 p.   933
Edition limited to 100 copies. Introduction considers Italian background of *Parangon.* Content same as indicated by Brunet.

Recueil des plaisantes et facétieuses nouvelles recueillies de plusieurs auteurs, reueues et corrigées de nouueau : avec plusieurs autres nouuelles non par cy deuant imprimées. Antwerp, Spelman, 1555.   357 p.   934
Anthology. Five tales in common with *Joyeuses adventures*, Lyons, 1555. Contains 108 stories, of which 95 appear to have been taken from La Motte-Roullant. Another edition of Lyons, Barricat, 1555, contains 109 tales, of which 97 are derived from La Motte Roullant.

Contes, by Author

Jean Bergier, Sieur de Saint-Clément

(No. 935)

Loviot, Louis. Jean Bergier. Discours modernes et facecieux. 1572. RLA 1:304-07, 1913-14.   935
Brief discussion of authorship and content of *Discours modernes.* Indicates five of these tales, of which there are in all thirteen, were incorporated into *Nouveaux recits ou comptes moralisez* of Duroc Sort Manne. Five of *Discours modernes* also added to the Micard, 1582 edition of the *Comptes du monde adventureux.*

François Béroalde de Verville
(pseud. for François Brouard)

(Nos. 936-940)

Béroalde de Verville, François. Le moyen de parvenir. Dernière édition exactement corrigée (précédée d'une Dissertation de La Monnoye) et augmentée d'une table de matières. Nulle part, 1732. 2 v. in 1.   936
Important early scholarly edition. Reprinted at least five times during 18th century.

— Le moyen de parvenir; notice, variantes, glossaire et index des noms par Charles Royer. Lemerre, 1896. 2 v. (BDC) 937
Best scholarly edition to date. Introductory material superseded in part by more recent investigation.

Reiche, Herbert, Le moyen de parvenir von Béroalde de Verville mit besonderer Berücksichtigung der Quellen und Verfasserfrage. Cobourg, 1913. 78 p. 938
Review : J. Plattard in RSS 2:135, 1914.

Sainéan, Lazare. Le moyen de parvenir. *In his:* Problèmes littéraires du seizième siècle. Boccard, 1927. p. 99-250. 939
Discusses literary production of B. Expresses doubt that he is author of *Le moyen de parvenir.*
Review : J. Plattard in RSS 14:403-06, 1927.

Saulnier, Verdun L. Étude sur Béroalde de Verville. BHren 5:209-326, 1944. 940
Meticulously thorough study of life and literary work of B. Extensive bibliography appended. *See* 1357.

Guillaume Bouchet, sieur *de Brocourt*

(Nos. 941-942)

Bouchet, Guillaume. Les serées de G. Bouchet, sieur de Brocourt, avec notice et index par C. E. Roybet. Lemerre, 1873-1882. 6 v. 941
Standard scholarly edition; well annotated from a linguistic point of view. Introduction gives in concise form principal facts relative to B. and his work.

Michaud, G. L. The Spanish sources of certain sixteenth century French writers. MLN 43:157-63, 1928. 942
Discusses Spanish influence on several French authors, among them N. de Cholières and B. Erroneously refers to latter (p. 162) as " Jean Bouchet." *See* 2856.

Gabriel Chappuys

(No. 943)

Chappuys, Gabriel. Les facétieuses journées, contenant cent certaines et agréables nouvelles ... par G.C.D.T. Houzé, 1584. 357 ff. 943
First and only edition.

N. De Cholières (pseud. *for Jean Dagoneau*) (Nos. 944-947)

Cholières, N. de. Œuvres du seigneur de Cholières; édition préparée par Ed. Fricotel, notes, index et glossaire par D. Jouaust. Préface par Paul Lacroix. Jouaust, 1879. 2 v. 944
Standard critical edition of C. Well annotated.

See 942. 945

Loviot, Louis. Le mystérieux seigneur de Cholières. RLA 1:37-49, 1913-14. 946
Identifies N. de Cholières as Jean Dagoneau, " prieur de la chartreuse du Mont-Dieu," who died in 1623.

— Un manuscrit de Dagoneau-Cholières. RLA 2:313, 1914-17. 947
Additional evidence to support Loviot's theory that N. de Cholières was pen name of Jean Dagoneau. Sum total of evidence offered by Loviot seems conclusive.

Bonaventure des Périers

(Nos. 948-957)

Despériers, Bonaventure. The mirrour of mirth and pleasant conceits. Englished by T. D. London, Danter, 1592. 88 p. 948
Relatively faithful translation of thirty-one tales of D. Introduction by translator, who signs himself " T.D. " One copy of this work is held by the Folger Library, Washington, D.C.
Trinity College Library of Cambridge University owns a copy of an earlier edition of *The mirrour of mirth,* dated 1583, which the compilers of this bibliography have not examined.
The Mirrour of mirth is the only known translation into English of any of the stories of D.

— Les contes, ou les nouvelles récréations, nouvelle édition, avec des notes historiques et critiques par de La Monnoye. Amsterdam, Chatelain (Paris, Piget), 1735. 2 v. 949
Important for notes.

— Œuvres françoises de Bonaventure des Périers, revues sur les éditions originales et annotées par Louis Lacour. Jannet, 1856. 2 v. 950
Somewhat old, but possibly still standard edition of D.

— Nouvelles récréations et joyeux devis. Ed. by Louis Lacour. Jouaust, 1874. 2 v.   951
Well annotated, beautifully executed edition. Introduction out of date. Supplements well the 1856 edition without replacing it.

Becker, Ph. Aug. Bonaventure des Périers als Dichter und Erzähler. Vienna, Holder-Pichler-Tempski, 1924. 90 p.   952
Latest and possibly best general study on D.
Reviews : H. Heiss in ZFSL 48:171-77, 1925-26; J. Plattard in RSS 14:406-09, 1927.

Chenevière, Adolphe. Bonaventure des Périers, sa vie, ses poésies. Plon, 1886. 261 p.   953
Classic study on D., though now to a certain extent superseded by work of Becker.

— and Félix Frank. Lexique de la langue de Bonaventure des Périers. Cerf, 1888. 239 p.   954
Excellent dictionary of language of D.; contains all words except those preserved in modern French in same sense as that in which D. used them. Compilers have provided at least one example of D.'s use of each word listed. Modern French for each word given. Editors have erred in some instances, however; see Sainéan, *Les provincialismes...* (956) cited below.

Haubold, Rudolph Hermann. Les nouvelles récréations et joyeux devis des Bonaventure des Périers in litterar-historischer und stilistischer Beziehung. Reudnitz, Hoffmann, 1888. 67 p.   955
Best study on *Nouvelles récréations* alone. Needs expanding, but constitutes excellent foundation for future research.

Sainéan, Lazare. Les provincialismes de Des Périers. RSS 3:28-59, 1915.   956
Study of regionalism in work of D., primarily from linguistic point of view. Concludes by examining question of authorship of *Joyeux devis*, deciding in favor of D.

— Bonaventure des Périers. In his : Problèmes littéraires du seizième siècle. See 939, p. 275-82.   957
Includes study of question of authorship of *Joyeux devis*; concludes that they have been rightly attributed to D.
Review : J. Plattard in RSS 14:403-06, 1927.

Noël Du Fail
(Nos. 958-965)

Du Fail, Noël. Les baliverneries et les contes d'Eutrapel, par Noël du Fail. Texte original et glossaire, avec notice, par E. Courbet. Lemerre, 1894. 2 v.   958
Good, scholarly edition, with variants, glossary, and some notes. Text of *Les baliverneries* based on 1549 edition, while that of *Contes* is based on Rennes 1585 edition.

— Les propos rustiques de Noël du Fail; texte original de 1547, interpolations et variantes de 1548, 1549, 1573; avec introduction, éclaircissements et index par Arthur de La Borderie. Lemerre, 1878. 297 p.   959
Standard edition through latter part of 19th century.

— Propos rustiques de Noël du Fail, suivis des Baliverneries, avec une introduction, des notes, un glossaire et une bibliographie, par L. R. Lefèvre. Garnier, 1928. 196 p.   960
Review : J. Plattard in RSS 16:341-42, 1929.

Dédéyan, Charles. Noël du Fail et la structure des Propos rustiques. FS 4:208-215, 1950.   961
Discusses unity in structure of *Propos rustiques*.

Loviot, Louis. Les éditions parisiennes des Propos rustiques, 1547 & 1548. RLA 2:119-22, 1914-17.   962
Valuable brief discussion of first editions of *Propos rustiques*. Points out existence of previously unnoted edition of Paris, Groulleau, 1547.

— L'imprimeur des Contes d'Eutrapel, 1585. RLA 2:312-13, 1914-17.   963
Proves that first edition of *Contes d'Eutrapel* was actually printed in Paris by Jean Richer; not, as the rubric in the edition states, at Rennes " pour Noël Glamet."

Philipot, Emanuel. La vie et l'œuvre littéraire de Noël du Fail. Champion, 1914. 552 p.   964
The standard study on D.
Review : L. Sainéan in RSS 3:18-27, 1915.

— Essai sur le style et la langue de Noël du Fail (avec un lexique). Champion, 1914. 173 p.   965

Standard study on language and style of D.

Review : L. Sainéan in RSS 3:18-27, 1915.

Duroc Sort-Manne
(pseud. for Romannet Du Cros)
(No. 966)

Duroc Sort-Manne (pseud.). Nouveaux recits ou comptes moralisez. Bonfons, 1573. 178 ff. 966

First edition. Second of Antwerp, Kauffman, 1576. 374 p.

Antoine Du Verdier
(No. 967)

Loviot, Louis. Le compseutique d'Antoine du Verdier. RLA 1:212-14, 1914. 967

In his Bibliothèque françoise, D. lists among his own works : Le compseutique, ou Traits facétieux, imprimé par Jean d'Ogerolles, 1584. Loviot states that this work has been lost and that Compseutique is known today only through some extracts from the original which are appended to the following edition of Escraignes dijonnaises:

Les escraignes dijonnoises, composées par le feu sieur du Buisson.... Plus quelques petits contes facecieus, tirez du Compseutique de A.D.V. Non encores veus par cy devant. Lyons, Sovbron, MDXCII.

Library of Wolfenbüttel possesses a copy of this edition.

Citations from Compseutique begin on p. 115 and consist of 15 anecdotes, one of which is quoted by Loviot.

Henri Estienne
(Nos. 968-970)

Estienne, Henri. Apologie pour Hérodote (satire de la société au XVIe siècle), par Henri Estienne. Nouvelle édition faite sur la première et augmentée de remarques, par P. Ristelhuber. Liseux, 1879. 2 v. 968

Standard edition. Extremely well annotated and indexed. Preface thorough and of considerable value.

Clément, Louis. Henri Estienne et son œuvre française. See 575. 969

Standard work on E.'s literary production in French. See 1971, 2121.

Toldo, Pietro. L'Apologie pour Hérodote von Henri Estienne. ZFSL 31:167-238, 1907. 970

Comprehensive article on varying backgrounds of episodes in Apologie.

Review : Anon in GSLI 50:449, 1907.

Jeanne Flore
(No. 971)

Flore, Jeanne. Comptes amoureux, par Madame Jeanne Flore; réimpression textuelle de l'édition de Lyon, 1574, avec une notice bibliographique par le bibliophile Jacob. Turin, Gay, 1870. 170 p. (RarB) 971

Only critical edition. For additional information on Comptes amoureux and its author, see Reynier, Le roman sentimental avant l'Astrée, (923), Ch. 10; also introduction to edition of the first story of collection published under title : Histoire de la belle Rosemonde et du preux chevalier Andro, par Jeanne Flore. (Publié par Albert de Rochas.) Marchand, 1888, 38 p.

Vérité Habanc
(Nos. 972-973)

Habanc, Vérité. Nouvelles histoires tant tragiques que comiques. Guillemot, 1585. 16 ff. not numbered, 272 ff. 972

Only edition of this rare collection, of which there is a copy in the Arsenal Library. Collection contains eight tales.

Loviot, Louis. Vérité Habanc; Nouvelles histoires tant tragiques que comiques, 1585. RLA 1:308-09, 1913-14. 973

Gives brief general discussion and summarizes content of H.'s work.

La Motte-Roullant
(Nos. 974-975)

La Motte-Roullant. Les fascetieux devitz des cent nouvelles nouvelles, tres recreatives et fort exemplaires, veuz et remis en leur naturel, par le seigneur de La Motte Roullant. Réal, 1549. 128 feuillets. 974

Rare first edition. Reprinted in 1550, 1570 and 1574. Of 109 tales in collection, 86 are versions of stories in the 15th century Cent nouvelles nouvelles. Remaining 23 appear to be original. The Fascetieux devitz are important, because they were basis for several later tale collections and supplied five of spurious tales added to Nouvelles récréations et joyeux devis of Des Périers.

Loviot, Louis. Les Cent nouvelles nouvelles adaptées par La Motte-Roullant (1549). RLA 1:254-63, 1913-14.   975
Brief but valuable general discussion of *Les fascetieux devitz* of L.

Marguerite de Navarre
(Nos. 976-987)

Marguerite de Navarre. Histoire des amans fortunez dédiée à l'illustre princesse, madame Marguerite de Bourbon, duchesse de Nivernois. Robinot, 1558. 184 ff.   976
Original Boaistuau edition; several book-dealers handled it.

— L'Heptaméron des nouvelles de très illustre et très excellent princesse Marguerite de Valois, royne de Navarre, par Claude Gruget. Caveiller, 1559. 212 ff.   977
First Gruget edition. Several book-dealers handled it.

— L'Heptaméron des nouvelles de Marguerite d'Angoulême, reine de Navarre; nouvelle édition publiée sur les manuscrits par la Société des bibliophiles français. Lahure, 1853-54. 3 v.   978
In this edition, three *nouvelles*, XI, XLIV, and XLVI, supplanted in Gruget edition by less salacious stories, are replaced. Also in other *nouvelles* the satiric and strong passages and proper names which had been omitted by Gruget are included. First thoroughly scholarly edition of the *Heptaméron*.

— L'Heptaméron des nouvelles de Marguerite de Navarre, publié sur les manuscrits par les soins et avec les notes de MM. Le Roux de Lincy et Anatole de Montaiglon. Eudes, 1880. 4 v.   979
Edition recommended by Pierre Jourda, scholarly biographer of M.

— L'Heptaméron. Nouvelle édition rev. sur les manuscrits avec une introduction, des notes et un index des noms propres, par Michel François. Garnier, 1943. 516 p. (Reprinted in 1947)   980
Compact edition, with brief introduction, good bibliography, notes and variants. Crowded pages.
Review : M. Rat in MerF 301:715-16, Dec. 1, 1947.

Ely, Gladys. The limits of realism in the Heptaméron of Marguerite de Navarre. RR 43:3-11, 1952.   981

Author concludes : " No realist on the broadly social plane, nevertheless in the realm of personal relations at her own high-born level, Marguerite offers perceptive realism."

Febvre, Lucien. Autour de l'Heptaméron; amour sacré, amour profane. *See* 762   982
Careful study of religion of Marguerite; also of her psychology, especially as reflected in the *Heptaméron*.
See especially M. Bataillon, *Autour de l'Heptaméron, à propos du livre de Lucien Febvre*, in BHren 8:245-53, 1946.
Reviews : W. H. Evans in FS 1:56-58, 1947; Adrienne Haye in Eras 1:151-53, 1947; H. W. Lawton in MLR 42:142, 1947; L. R. Lefevre in NL Feb. 21, 1946, p. 5; Y. R. in RHE 41:189, 1946.

Jourda, Pierre. Marguerite d'Angoulême, duchesse d'Alençon, reine de Navarre (1492-1549); étude biographique et littéraire. *See* 657.   983
Magnificent study of M. as a writer, woman, and queen; standard work on her. Thoroughly indexed, contains excellent bibliography. Many reviews : *see* especially that of J. Plattard in RSS 18:175-78, 1931. *See* 764.

— Récents écrits italiens sur Marguerite de Navarre. RSS 11:273-88, 1924.   984
Criticism of following studies :
1. Pietro Toldo. *Rileggendo il novelliere della Regina di Navarra*. RI 26:380-405, Jul. 15, 1923.
2. Carlo Pellegrini. *La prima opera di Margherita di Navarra e la terza rima in Francia*. Catania, Battiato, 1920. 77 p.

Livingston, Charles H. The Heptaméron des nouvelles of Marguerite de Navarre : a study of nouvelles 28, 34, 52, and 62. RR 14:97-118, 1923.   985
Comparison of *Heptaméron, nouvelles* 62, 28, and 52 with *Cent nouvelles nouvelles* of Philippe de Vigneulles, *nouvelles* 64, 48 and 24 respectively. Cites the *fabliau, Du sot chevalier*, as a parallel of *Heptaméron, nouvelle* 34. Included is the full text of the cited *nouvelles* of Philippe de Vigneulles.

Telle, E. V. L'œuvre de Marguerite d'Angoulême, reine de Navarre, et la Querelle des femmes. *See* 774.   986
Important study on general question of feminism in 16th century.
Reviews : H. W. Lawton in MLR

35:103-04, 1940; R. Marichal in Hren 5:183-87, 1938; E. F. Meylan in MLN 53:608-10, 1938.

— La source de la nouvelle 55 de l'Heptaméron. RR 39:278-81, 1948. 987

Suggests as source of *nouvelle* 55 of *Heptaméron* a passage from *Epistola incitativa ad vitam contemplativam activamque fugiendam*, which Telle dates as of about 1510.

Nicolas de Troyes
(Nos. 988-991)

Nicolas de Troyes. Le grand parangon des nouvelles nouvelles recueillies par Nicolas de Troyes, publié pour la première fois et précédé d'une introduction par Emile Mabille. Brussels, Gay, 1866. 283 p. 988
Incomplete edition.

— Le grand parangon des nouvelles nouvelles, composé par Nicolas de Troyes et publié d'après le manuscrit original par Émile Mabille. Franck, 1869. 299 p. (BE) 989
Edition not complete. *See* Toldo's *Contributo* (925).

Livingston, Charles H. Decameron, VIII, 2 : earliest French imitations. MP 22:35-43, 1924-25. 990
Cites *Decameron* VIII, 2, as source of *nouvelle* 71 of Philippe de Vigneulles' *Cent nouvelles nouvelles* and also of *nouvelle* 148 of *Grand parangon des nouvelles nouvelles* of Nicolas de Troyes. Full text of both tales given. In footnote 2, p. 39, Livingston makes an important observation on content of the two incomplete 19th century editions of *Grand parangon*. *See* 2745.

Urwin, Kenneth, and J. H. Watkins. Notes lexicographiques sur le Parangon des nouvelles nouvelles (1536). Hren 7:229-33, 1940. 991
List of substantives not common to written language before the *Parangon*.

Philippe de Vigneulles
(Nos. 992-996)

Livingston, Charles H. Les cent nouvelles nouvelles de Philippe de Vigneulles, chaussetier messin. RSS 10:159-203, 1923 (*Also*, Champion, 1924.) 992
Concise summary of life of P. followed by a brief outline of earlier studies on him. Careful description given of unique manu-

script of P.'s *Cent nouvelles nouvelles*. Dated as of 1515. Livingston gives full text of *nouvelles* LX, LXXXIV, and LXXXIX, which he compares with Des Périers' *Nouvelles récréations et joyeux devis*, nouvelles XX, XLIX, and LXXVII, respectively.

— Deux historiettes de Philippe de Vigneulles. MélAJ, p. 469-76. 993
The hitherto unpublished text of *nouvelles* LIII and LXXIIII (sic) of *Cent nouvelles nouvelles* of P.

— The fabliau Des deux Anglois et de l'anel. PMLA 40:217-24, June, 1925. 994
Includes full text of *nouvelle* IV of the *Cent nouvelles nouvelles* of P.

— Rabelais et deux contes de Philippe de Vigneulles. MélAL, p. 17-25. 995
Includes full text of P.'s *nouvelle* 78 *(Le pot au lait)* and *nouvelle* 7. Former compared with a passage in *Gargantua*, XXXIII, and with Des Périers' *nouvelle* XII; latter with an incident in *Pantagruel*, I, XVI.

Vigneulles, see 990. 996

Bénigne Poissenot
(Nos. 997-999)

Poissenot, Bénigne. L'esté, contenant trois journées, ou sont déduites plusieurs histoires et propos récréatifs tenus par trois escoliers. Micard, 1583. 8 feuillets non numérotés et 224 feuillets ch. 997
The first and only edition.

— Nouvelles histoires tragiques de Bénigne Poissenot. Bichon, 1586. 12 feuillets (not numbered); 468 p., pagination stopping at p. 467 but text continuing on next page; three feuillets not numbered. 998
The first and only edition.

Loviot, Louis. Le conteur Bénigne Poissenot. RLA 1:285-95, 1913-14. 999
Valuable brief discussion of life, career, and narrative work of P.

Estienne Tabourot, seigneur des Accords
(Nos. 1000-1003)

Tabourot, Estienne. Les Bigarrures du seigneur des Accords avec les apophthegmes du sieur Gaulard et les escraignes dijonnoises. Brussels, Mertens, 1866. 3 v. 1000

Unfortunately, relatively rare edition; only 106 copies printed. Includes text of Colletet's biography of T. Fairly well annotated but lacks adequate indexing. Text of *Escraignes dijonnoises* based on 1588 edition; that of *Apophthegmes* on editions of 1585 and 1588.

— Les Escraignes dijonnaises. Rouen, Du Mesnil, 1640. 79 p. (*Reprinted*, Dijon, Darantière, 1922.)   1001
Only modern publication of any of narrative works of T.

Choptrayanovitch, Georges. Etienne Tabourot des Accords (1549-1590); étude sur sa vie et son œuvre littéraire. Dijon, Belvet, 1935. 227 p.   1002
Standard study on life and works of T. Includes list of editions of his works and lengthy bibliography on him.

Conner, Wayne. The influence of Tabourot des Accords on Balzac's Contes drolatiques. RR 41:195-205, 1950.   1003
Shows that Balzac is heavily indebted, especially in second dixain of the *Contes drolatiques*, to T. for both situation and language.

Jacques Tahureau
(Nos. 1004-1006)

Tahureau, Jacques. Dialogues non moins profitables que facétieux. Ed. by F. Conscience. Lemerre, 1870. 201 p.   1004
Edition includes brief notice on T., table of materials on the *Dialogues*, and index.

Besch, Emile. Un moraliste satirique et rationaliste au XVIᵉ siècle : Jacques Tahureau (1527-1555). RSS 6:1-44, 157-200, 1919.   1005
Most important study of life and works of T. *See* 1396.

Chardon, H. La vie de Tahureau. RHAM 16:297-368, 1884.   1006
Detailed study on family history of T. and on lady of his affections.

Antoine Tyron
(Nos. 1007-1008)

Tyron, Antoine. Recueil de plusieurs plaisantes nouvelles, apophthegmes et recreations diverses, faict français, par Ant. Tyron. Antwerp, Hendricx, 1578. 173 p.   1007

The first edition. The only other edition of which there are extant copies is that of 1596. *See* Loviot, 1008.

Loviot, Louis. Recueil de plusieurs plaisantes nouvelles, 1578 et 1596. RLA 2:372-374, 1914-17.   1008
Brief description of editions mentioned· Seems to be only two known copies of that of 1578; both in private libraries. Each edition contains 156 stories; ten which appear in first edition have been replaced with new tales in that of 1596. Loviot mentions but does not describe editions of 1593 and 1595.

Jacques Yver
(Nos. 1009-1012)

Yver, Jacques. Le printemps d'Yver, contenant plusieurs histoires discourues en cinq journées. Langelier, 1572. 225 p.   1009
Several editions in 16th century. The *Printemps d'Yver* has also been inserted into a volume of *Panthéon littéraire*, 1841, entitled *Les vieux conteurs français.*

Atkinson, Dorothy F. The source of Two gentlemen of Verona. SP 41:223-34, 1944.   1010
Discusses Henry Wotton's 1578 English translation of *Le printemps d'Yver.* Cites last story as a source of Shakespeare's *Two gentlemen of Verona. See* 2826.

Clouzot, Henri. Jacques Yver, lecteur de Rabelais (1520-71). RSS 17:322-24, 1930.   1011
Two pages of parallel passages showing borrowings from Rabelais in Y.'s *Printemps.*

Lohr, Paul. Le printemps d'Yver und die Quelle zu Fair Ém. Berlin, Felber, 1912. 57 p. (LF, no. 49)   1012
Of interest principally for discussion of sources and influence of *Le printemps d'Yver.*

Novelists
(Nos. 1013-1045)

Note : In addition to entries listed below, attention is invited to appropriate sections of *A critical bibliography of French literature*, v. I, especially Ch. XV.   1013
Students of the late renaissance novel will find much of value in studies on Honoré d'Urfé, in histories of 17th century novel such as those of Körting (*Geschichte des französischen Romans im* XVII. *Jahr-*

hundert. Oppeln and Leipzig, Franck, 1891, 2 v.) and Magendie (*Le roman français au* XVII*ᵉ siècle, de l'Astrée au Grand Cyrus.* Droz, 1932. 457 p.), and related studies such as Marsan's *La pastorale dramatique en France à la fin du* XVI*ᵉ et au commencement du* XVII*ᵉ siècle.* Hachette, 1905. 524 p. Since these works belong primarily in 17th century and will doubtless be treated fully in v. III, they have been omitted from v. II. For a comprehensive listing of such studies, *see* bibliographical references given below, and particularly bibliography in Rose Marie Daele's *Nicolas de Montreulx* (1016).

General Studies

Williams, Ralph C. Bibliography of the seventeenth century novel in France. New York, Century, 1931. 355 p.   1014

Not altogether reliable; should be used only after consulting review by Rolfe (below). Nevertheless a useful work, not only for 17th century, but also for novelists of transition between 16th and 17th centuries.

Reviews : N. A. Bennetton in MLJ 17:153-55, 1922-23 ; H. C. Lancaster in MLN 47:55-56, 1932; F. P. Rolfe in PMLA 49:1071-86, Dec., 1934.

Besch, Émile. Les adaptations en prose des chansons de geste au xvᵉ et au xviᵉ siècle. RSS 3:155-81, 1915.   1015

Somewhat out-of-date; not altogether reliable. (*See* Doutrepont, *Les mises en prose* (1019), p. 372-73, 414-15.) Nevertheless, a useful survey of prosifications of the *chansons de geste.*

Daele, Rose Marie. Nicolas de Montreulx (Ollenix du Mont-Sacré) arbiter of European literary vogues of the late renaissance. New York, Moretus Press [1946]. 360 p. (Diss., Columbia)   1016

Chapters I-III of Book Two (p. 99-170), provide valuable discussion of evolution of the novel during last part of 16th and first part of 17th centuries.

Comprehensive bibliography of works of Montreulx and of works pertinent to study of the novel of this period is provided, p. 283-334. *See* 1039, 2385, 2860.

DeJongh, William F. J. A bibliography of the novel and short story in French from the beginning of printing till 1600. *See* 917.   1017

Carefully compiled and very useful annotated bibliography of first editions of works of novelistic fiction in French published during 15th and 16th centuries. Included are French translations of foreign works of prose fiction.

Didot, Ambroise Firmin. Essai de classification méthodique et synoptique des romans de chevalerie inédits et publiés. Didot, 1870. xxiv-15 p. 15 p. and 15 tableaux.   1018

Old but still useful reference work. Shows in a series of tables various forms which individual *chansons de geste* and similar works have assumed through the centuries.

Doutrepont, Georges. Les mises en prose des épopées et des romans chevaleresques du xivᵉ au xviᵉ siècle. Brussels, Palais des Academies, 1939. 732 p. (MARB, 40)   1019

Invaluable study of prosification of *épopées* and *romans antiques et chevaleresques.* Includes individual studies of each of *mises en prose* considered, giving title of prose text, history of the text, manuscripts which preserve it, original or originals from which it is derived, editions which have been made of and studies which have been devoted to it, and any special remarks which may be relevant. Valuable bibliographical references supplied in Introduction, Chapters I and II, and on p. 709-17.

Reviews : F. Desonay in Hren 7:325-26, 1940; G. de Poerck in RBP 21:226-29, 1942; M. Roques in Rom 67:543-45, 1942-43.

Morçay, Raoul. Le roman. *In his :* La renaissance. Gigord, 1933-35. v. II, part 3, p. 225-45. (Histoire de la littérature française pub. sous la direction de J. Calvet. II, 3)   1020

Excellent summary of history of French novel from end of 16th century through first part of 17th. Useful but by no means complete bibliography, p. 262-63.

Reynier, Gustave. Les origines du roman réaliste. *See* 924.   1021

Excellent study of a part of narrative literature of French renaissance. Title a little misleading, since work is concerned more with *conte* than the novel properly speaking. Useful chronological table appended, p. 336-40; unfortunately no general bibliography nor index.

— Le roman sentimental avant l'Astrée. See 923. 1022

Excellent study of development of the novel of sentiment in 16th and early 17th centuries. Valuable bibliographical data appended. Well indexed. Reviews : F. Baldensperger in Rcr 67:133-34, 1909; W. Küchler in ZFSL 35²:202-07, 1910.

Saintsbury, George. History of the French novel (to the close of the nineteenth century). London, Macmillan, 1917-19. 2 v. 1023

Despite occasional inaccuracies, first eight chapters of first volume (p. 1-273) provide a useful survey of origins of French prose fiction up to and including *Astrée*. Valuable for discussion of some of the more obscure authors and works.

Tilley, Arthur. Les romans de chevalerie en prose. RSS 6:45-63, 1919. 1024

Reprinted in *Studies in the French renaissance*, Cambridge, University Press, 1922, p. 12-25. Brief history of printing of prose *romans de chevalerie*. Features table giving titles of the *romans*, date and place of original publication, date of composition, source from which derived. Includes useful bibliographical data on many of *romans* listed. J. J. Parry, listing same work in *Critical bibliography of French literature*, v. I (1952), no. 1234, warns that section three of above mentioned table is to be used with caution.

Individual Authors

Vital d'Audiguier
(No. 1025)

Ardenne de Tizac, Gaspard d'. Étude historique et littéraire sur Vital d'Audiguier, seigneur de La Menor au pays de Rouergue. Villefranche-de-Rouergue, Dufour, 1887. 146 p. 1025

A copy in the BM. Union catalogue does not list.

François Béroalde de Verville
(No. 1026)

Vordemann, Elisabeth. Quellenstudien zu dem Roman Le voyage des princes fortunez von Béroalde de Verville. Göttingen, Schönhütte, 1933. 121 p. (Diss., Göttingen.) 1026

States *Le voyage des princes fortunez* based upon an Italian original, Christoforo Armeno's *Peregrinaggio di tre giovani*, which first appeared in 1557. Included in the study are a detailed analysis of content of B.'s novel, a study of parallels of principal themes used, sections on life and works of author, and a bibliography.

Jacques Corbin
(No. 1027)

Beall, C. B. Deux romans peu connus du XVIIᵉ siècle français. MLN 52:482-85, 1937. 1027

Calls attention to two rare novels : C.'s *Ierusalem regnante*, l'Angelier, 1600; and Sergé's *Jerusalem regnante, ou la suite du Tasse; traduction.* Du Brueil, 1680. Author believes both are based upon an unidentified Italian original.

Helisenne de Crenne
(pseud. *of Marguerite Briet*)
(Nos. 1028-1029)

Lefranc, Abel. A propos d'Helisenne de Crenne : Guenelic et Quezinstra. RLA 2:376-77, 1917. 1028

Identifies Guenelic as an anagram of " Guecelin " (or " Gueslin ") and Quezinstra as an anagram of " Quezinsart."

Loviot, Louis. Helisenne de Crenne. RLA 2:137-45, 1917. 1029

Identifies C. as Marguerite Briet of Picardy, who married Philippe Fournet, *seigneur de Crɛsne*. Gives a few other biographical details. Refutes theory that 1538 edition of *Angoysses* is not the first. Locates copies of that edition, which are quite rare, in libraries of Besançon and in the BN.

Pierre de Deimier
(No. 1030)

Patterson, W. F. Further notes on Pierre de Deimier. SP 36:609-21, 1939. 1030

Survey of literary production of D. Included in discussion is *Histoire des amoureuses destinées de Lysimont et de Clytie*, 1608, a prose novel of chivalry.

Guillaume Des Autels
(Nos. 1031-1035)

Des Autels, Guillaume. Mitistoire barragouyne de Fanfreluche et Gaudichon. Jannet, 1850. 58 p. 1031

Only modern edition. Except for brief remarks on p. 58, no notes or commentary. Editor, identified only by initials A. V., states this edition is based upon text of Lyons, 1574, and Rouen, 1578, editions.

Brunet, G. Notice sur un livre fort peu connu, faisant partie de la famille rabelaisienne. BB 4:363-73, 1847.   1032

Brief introduction precedes main part of the article, a detailed summary of content of *Mitistoire barragouyne de Fanfreluche et Gaudichon.* Discussion based on Rouen, 1578, edition.

Colletet, Guillaume. Guillaume des Autels. Ad. van Bever (ed.). Rren 7:193-218, 1906.   1033

" Cette vie de Guillaume des Autels est extraite d'une copie du manuscrit original, des *Vies de poëtes françois* de Guillaume Colletet, exécutée pour Aimé-Martin (Bibliothèque nationale. Nouv. acq. fr. 3073, ff. 24 et ss.) "

Text commented upon at length by editor.

Hartmann, Hans. Guillaume des Autels (1529-1581 ?), ein französischer Dichter und Humanist. Zürich, " Academia," 1907. 127 p.   1034

Detailed biographical study of D. Study proper preceded by two valuable bibliographies, one on D. himself, and other dealing with his literary production. No index.

Saulnier, Verdun L. Contribution à l'étude de la langue facétieuse au xvie siècle : la Mitistoire barragouyne de Fanfreluche et Gaudichon. Fmod 12:281-95, 1944. 1035

Analysis of content, language, and style of *Mitistoire.* Concludes that " L'imitation de Rabelais est donc fidèle mais sans esclavage " (p. 289).

Sieur Des Escuteaus

(No. 1036)

Bichlmaier, Karl. Die Preziosität der sentimentalen Romane des Sieur des Escuteaux. Wertheim a. M., Bechstein, 1931. 88 p. (Diss., Erlangen)   1036

Chiefly of interest for summaries and analyses of content of *Amours diverses, Les traversez hasards de Clidion et Armirie,* and *Les admirables faits d'armes d'Alcestes servant l'infidèle Lydie.* Also a lengthy discussion of the style of D.

Antoine Du Périer, sieur de La Salargue

(No. 1037)

Chinard, Gilbert. Un romancier bordelais inconnu : Antoine du Périer, sieur de Sarlagues. RHB 5:361-78, 1912.   1037

Analysis of D.'s novel, *Les amours de Pistion.* Chinard dates first edition as of 1601.

Marie le Jars de Gournay

(No. 1038)

See Ch. X on Montaigne for additional bibliography on Marie de Gournay.

Michaud, G. L. Le Proumenoir de Montaigne. RHL 41:397-98, 1934.   1038

Cites a story in *Discours des champs faez* of Claude de Taillemont as source of *Proumenoir.* A comparison of texts, says Michaud, reflects no credit on G.

Nicolas de Montreux

(Nos. 1039-1041)

Daele, Rose Marie. Nicolas de Montreulx (Ollenix du Mont-Sacré), arbiter of European literary vogues of the late renaissance. *See* 1016.   1039

Excellent, thorough study of life and dramatic and novelistic works of M. Author makes a more favorable estimate of his writings than did Mathorez (1040). Useful bibliography included. *See* 2385, 2860.

Review : R. V. Merrill in RR 38:173-74, 1947.

Mathorez, Jules. Le poète Olényx du Mont-Sacré, bibliothécaire du duc de Mercœur (1561-1610). BBB 76:357-71 and 479-95, 1912.   1040

Study of life and works of M. Author's estimate of his work unfavorable.

— Notes complémentaires sur Olényx du Mont-Sacré. RLA 2:124-29, 1917.   1041

Supplement to earlier study by Mathorez published in 1912. Author states, " Je souhaite actuellement rectifier et compléter sur quelques points la bibliographie des œuvres du protégé de Mercœur." (p. 124). Among the three works discussed is *Seizième livre d'Amadis,* which, far from being a translation, is almost entirely an original composition, according to Mathorez.

Antoine de Nervèze
(No. 1042)

Hoefer, J. C. F. Nervèze. *In his :* Nouvelle biographie générale. Didot, 1852-68. 37 : col's. 767-68.   1042

Very brief discussion of life and works of N. Mention made of some source materials. More thorough study of N. should be made.

Pierre Faifeu
(Nos. 1043-1045)

Bourdigné, Charles de. La légende de Pierre Faifeu : publiée par D. Jouaust, avec une préface par le bibliophile Jacob. Librairie des bibliophiles, 1880. 160 p. (CB no. 25)   1043

Only modern scholarly edition. Preface useful but not altogether reliable. Notes. Text that of the Angers, 1532, edition.

— La légende joyeuse ou faitz et dictz joyeulx de Pierre Faifeu, escolier d'Angers ... d'après l'édition de 1532. Willem, 1883. 72 p.   1044

Includes only text and table of contents. Editor not named, but Abel Lefranc identifies him (RER 3:219, 1905) as Anatole de Montaiglon.

Lefranc, Abel. Les plus anciennes mentions du Pantagruel et du Gargantua. RER 3:216-21, 1905.   1045

See p. 218-20. Lefranc establishes convincingly that the Angers, 1532 edition of *La légende de Pierre Faifeu* is first edition.

CHAPTER VIII. THE PLÉIADE
(Nos. 1046-1400)

MORRIS BISHOP, R. J. CLEMENTS, J. C. LYONS, ISIDORE SILVER

Theories, General Studies
(Nos. 1046-1060)

ROBERT J. CLEMENTS

Chamard, Henri. La doctrine et l'œuvre poétique de la Pléiade. Guillon, n.d. 185 p. (CDF) 1046

A *précis* of Chamard's course on the Pléiade given at *Faculté des lettres* of University of Paris. Photo-offset reproduction and paper binding. Work may be considered a preliminary compend of Chamard's *Histoire de la Pléiade* (1047). Clear and simple exposition of the Pléiade movement, told in a precise but personal manner (without footnotes) and concerned primarily with the group's program and accomplishments prior to 1555. Excellent introduction for students approaching subject for first time. Carelessly executed typescript.

— Histoire de la Pléiade. Didier, 1939-40. 4 v. 1047

Veritable storehouse of essential information about the Pléiade. V. I follows closely chapter-divisions of Chamard's earlier *La doctrine et l'œuvre poétique de la Pléiade*, telling story of the Pléiade up to middle 1550's. V. II continues that history until after death of Du Bellay (1560). V. III treats of the end periods of individual poets, leaving for the last tome full discussions of the Pléiade's language and style, metrics and prosody, and basic conception of poetry. Chamard groups within the term Pléiade the Marty-Laveaux roster of members : Dorat, Ronsard, Du Bellay, Baïf, Belleau, Jodelle, and Tyard, adds Peletier for good measure. Analytical bibliography of studies on members of the Pléiade, arranged by centuries, is useful and informative. Emphasis on biographies and intellectual development of poets informs first three volumes. Seasoned throughout with well-chosen excerpts from poetry of the Pléiade.

Clements, Robert J. Pléiade censure of classic mendacity. PMLA 56:633-44, Sept., 1941. 1048

Charges that humanists of the Pléiade not reticent about taxing writers of Greece and Rome with mendacity. Materials later incorporated into (1050).

— Anti-Petrarchism of the Pléiade. MP 39:15-21, 1941-42. 1049

Contends that revolt against Petrarch and Petrarchism, resulting from ethical objections to insincerity of Petrarchism, at length caused members of the Pléiade to react against Petrarchan sonnet. Materials later incorporated into No. 1050. *See* 2723.

— Critical theory and practice of the Pléiade. Cambridge, Harvard University Press, 1942. 288 p. 1050

Presents familiar critical theories contained in the Pléiade's prose treatises, supplementing them with further ideas encountered throughout the Pléiade's poetic works. Lists principal criticisms by these poets on classic and renaissance writers, investigating literary convictions behind these judgments. Classifies theories of the Pléiade into chapters on : ethics, values, communication, function, and inspiration of poetry, and examines briefly classical antecedence of these theories. Analyzes some of the group's conventional poetic imagery and relates it to their poetic theory. Includes not seven but fifteen or more poets under the title of Pléiade. Emphasis placed on aesthetic ideas rather than on prosodic reforms.

Dargan, E. Preston. Trissino, a possible source for the Pléiade. MP 13:685-92, 1915-16. 1051

Suggests that Trissino's *Poetica*, especially parts I-IV, influenced the Pléiade's ideas on diction and rhythm. Shows that Trissino had briefly proposed lexical enrichment through *provignement*. Points out similarity between Trissino's theory of epic and that of Ronsard. Affinity presented as a possible project for investigation; Dargan refrains from setting down definite claims or conclusions. *See* 2795.

Levengood, Sidney L. The use of color in the verse of the Pléiade. Presses universitaires, 1927. 124 p. (Diss., Princeton)   1052

Levengood examines abundant use of color in the Pléiade's descriptions of persons, external nature, and miscellaneous objects. Passages quoted from Ronsard, Belleau, Du Bellay, Baïf, Jodelle, Tyard, and Peletier in turn. Although some of these seem to constitute a mere enumeration, author offers conclusions and several interesting observations. Old French literature furnished the Pléiade with much lexical pigment. Color terms, similes, epithets also derived from Greek, Latin, and Italian sources. The Pléiade did, however, introduce new color terms and types. Glossary lists chief common colors and many terms by which they were designated. (Ronsard replaced *blanc* by *albâtre, argentelet, blafard, blême, chenu, écumeux, ivoirin*, etc.). *See* 1149.

Neri, Ferdinando. Il Chiabrera e la Pléiade francese. Turin, Bocca, 1920. 219 p.   1053

Begins with a general statement on the Pléiade's fortunes in Italy during latter half of the *Cinquecento*. Gabriello Chiabrera adopted metres of Ronsard and Baïf, and attempted in Italian the French alternation of masculine and feminine rimes. Chiabrera's *forme nove*, superseding metric systems of Petrarchists and Bembists, were adaptations of French rhythmics. Italian poet continued Anacreontic tradition of the Pléiade, and was influenced by Belleau's lapidary verses. Chiabrera's classicism reinvigorated Italian literature much as the Pléiade's Hellenism proved a tonic for French poetry.

Kerr, W. A. R. The Pléiade and Platonism. MP 5:407-21, 1907-08.   1054

Platonism here limited in meaning to Platonic love, " that doctrine of spiritual love of a woman " which became a theme of French renaissance poetry. Ronsard's distaste for Petrarchists led him to dislike " Platonic " poets. Du Bellay was more receptive to Platonism although reacting after the *Honneste amour* sonnets. Platonism descended from a doctrine to a fashion. Tyard sympathetic to it; Ronsard, Baïf, Belleau, and Jodelle remained

antipathetic to transcendental love creed of a Castiglione or Héroët. Subsequent investigation in this field by Merrill and others has brought further light and precision on subject.

Patterson, Warner Forrest. Three centuries of French poetic theory : a critical history of the chief arts of poetry in France (1328-1630). *See* 115.   1054A

Certain reviewers criticised work as somewhat lacking in compactness and originality, but it has many interesting observations and contains a wealth of excerpts from texts not generally or readily available outside of France. V. I presents history and summaries of (and quotations from) principal treatises on rhetorical and poetic theory from 14th century to Malherbe and Colletet. Greater part of volume deals adequately with rise and decline of conventional Pléiade reforms and theories. Competent and thorough bibliographies. V. I overreaches with gratuitous bibliographies of Plato, Aristotle, Plotinus, et al., and unnecessary summaries of Horace's and Boileau's *artes poeticae*. V. II includes useful chronological lists of French and Italian treatises, with emphasis on 16th century, and an anthology of thirty-one verse forms (identified as genres). A handbook valuable especially for its *loci critici*. *See* 323.

Pieri, Marius. Le pétrarquisme au XVIe siècle; Pétrarque et Ronsard, ou De l'influence de Pétrarque sur la Pléiade française. Marseille, Laffitte, 1896. 342 p.   1055

Competent general statement of Petrarchism of the Pléiade. Notes Petrarchistic influence in ideas, poetic language and style, metrics and rhythms of French group, and makes careful note of slight dissimilarities between love expressed by the Pléiade and that set down by Petrarch. Conventionalized style and poetic language of 16th century made of Petrarchism an artificial literary vehicle. Pieri recognizes weaknesses and limitations of the Pléiade's Petrarchism, but he does not mention widespread revolt against Petrarchism in which all members of this group participated. *See* 1167.

Rosenbauer, A. Die poetischen Theorien der Pléiade nach Ronsard und Du Bellay. Erlangen, Deichert, 1895. 161 p. (MBP, no. 10)   1056

Competent summary of literary theory and counsel on prosody contained in Ronsard's works, particularly prefaces and prose treatises. Du Bellay relegated to a secondary role. The six chapters treat of : Ronsard as theorist and critic; aesthetics; theory on the genres; ideas on diction and style; remarks on versification; reputation in his lifetime and before posterity. Position of Du Bellay minimized. Numerous correlations established with theories of Peletier, Sebillet, Vauquelin de La Fresnaye, and Julius-Caesar Scaliger. Ronsard viewed as founder of French classicism in its Horatian aspects. Still a useful manual, although its bibliographies superseded. *See* 1175, 1290.

Sainte-Beuve, C. A. Tableau historique et critique de la poésie française et du théâtre français au xvie siècle. Charpentier, 1843. p. 1-171.   1057

Revised version of this early essay marks Sainte-Beuve as pioneer critic of French renaissance verse. Gives evidence of a surprising familiarity with major and minor poets as well as accuracy of perception and appreciation. Criticisms amplified but scarcely modified by later scholarship. Preceded present-day anthologies in choosing quotations throughout these pages. Sainte-Beuve discovered Du Bellay's *Vanneur de blé* long before Walter Pater. As the essay ranges from Villon down to Malherbe and Mlle de Gournay, the Pléiade does not enjoy exclusive *droit de séjour*, but Ronsard receives most attention.

Strowski, Fortunat Joseph. La Pléiade : la doctrine et l'œuvre poétique. Centre de documentation universitaire, 1933. 2 v. in 1.   1058

Although interesting reading, this mimeographed outline in no way covers materials announced in title. Strowski refers his students to compend of Chamard (1047) and states he is supplementing Chamard with some " essais." Uses Ronsard as a point of departure for interpretations of and generalizations on renaissance. No appreciable mention of any member of the Pléiade save Ronsard (and occasionally Du Bellay). Strowski illustrates the " movement " or " inspiration " of 16th century poetry with modern poets, almost never with the Pléiade. Considers Ronsard (and Du Bellay) *Rinascimental* by reason of language, politics, patriotism, Italianism, enthusiasm, lyricism.

Warshaw, J. Recurrent préciosité. MLN 31:129-35, 1916.   1059

The Pléiade espoused preciosity, thus anticipating early 17th century writers.

Strong feminine influence over the Pléiade and their contemporaries, with resultant preciosity. Argument scarcely convincing. Tends to confuse Pléiade's effort to enrich vernacular with new, imported, and inevitably strange words with a conscious attempt to create a *précieux* style and language.

Wyndham, George. Ronsard and la Pléiade. London, Macmillan, 1906. 266 p. *See* 1195.   1060

First sixty pages contain an essay on the Pléiade; remainder of them consist of selections from the Pléiade, including several translations retaining original metres. Essay represents dilettantism in better sense of word. Embodies a spirited defense of the Pléiade against conventional censure of earlier classical critics. Claims that the Pléiade exerted a greater influence upon Elizabethan writers (Spenser, Sydney, Watson, Daniel, Chapman, Herrick) than previously suspected. This is noticeable in both practices and theories of Elizabethans. Suggests that England was launching a campaign in the 1580's which had already been won by the Pléiade in the 1540's.

Ronsard
(Nos. 1061-1195)

MORRIS BISHOP
Bibliographies

Laumonier, Paul. Tableau chronologique des œuvres de Ronsard. Hachette, 1911. 143 p.   1061

Detailed chronological list of all R.'s poems and prose works. Indispensable for study of R.'s poetic development.

Raymond, Marcel. Bibliographie critique de Ronsard en France (1550-1585). Champion, 1927. 150 p. (Thèse complémentaire.)   1062

Bibliography of contemporary references to R., of works influenced by R., and of indications of success of Pléiade. Invaluable for students of period.

Pereire, Alfred. Bibliographie des œuvres de Ronsard. BBB ns 15:494-503, 540-46, 1936; 16:20-26, 68-75, 108-14, 352-60, 447-51, 506-12, 556-60, 1937; 17:16-18, 54-59, 158-61, 268-71, 304-07, 357-62, 488-492, 1938; 18:67-75, 104-110, 204-15, 1939.   1063

Exhaustive descriptions, with facsimiles, of early editions of R., including musical collections. Uncompleted.

Works

Ronsard, Pierre de. Œuvres. Buon, 1560.
4 v.   1064
First collective edition.

— Œuvres. Buon, 1584. 7 parts.   1065
Last edition to appear during R.'s lifetime. Thoroughly revised by R., to be his
monument.

— Œuvres complètes, ed. by Prosper Blanchemain. Jannet, 1855-67. 8 v. (BE)   1066
First collected edition since 1630. Well
printed; good paper; pleasant to read.
A few notes and variants. V. 8 contains
biography by Blanchemain, interesting
collection of poetic 19th century tributes
to R., Du Perron's *Oraison funèbre sur la
mort de Monsieur de Ronsard*, (p. 179-221),
Mathurin Régnier's *Le tombeau de P. de
Ronsard* (p. 235 - 92), poetic offerings by
R.'s contemporaries. Blanchemain takes
as a basic text the edition of 1560, with
earliest texts for later poems. However,
he chooses sometimes capriciously, without
warning, later readings suiting his personal
preferences. Expurgates without textual
indication. Many typographical and other
errors. Edition harshly criticized by Paul
Laumonier in RHL 9:29-87, 1902, for
infidelity to texts, faulty chronology, in-
sufficiency of variants and notes. But
Laumonier blames Blanchemain because,
in 1860, Blanchemain did not make a
critical edition according to standards of
1900. Blanchemain proposed only to
present R. in best light to the general
reader.

— Œuvres complètes, ed. Ch. Marty-
Laveaux. Lemerre, 1887-93. 6 v. (CPI)
                                          1067
De luxe limited edition; rare. Italic
type on tinted paper hard to read. V. I-V
contain works as printed in R.'s own
definitive edition of 1584. V. VI assembles *pièces retranchées* from this and other
editions and all other works attributable
to R. Few variants given, and these
unsystematic. Notes unsystematic, uncritical, mostly reproduced from early
editions. But some useful linguistic and
lexicological notes. Virtues of this edition
preserved in Laumonier's edition, Lemerre,
1914-19, (1069).

— Œuvres complètes, ed. Paul Laumonier.
Hachette, 1914— (STFM)   1068
Monumental edition, the sole essential,
when completed. Text of earliest edition

given, with all succeeding variants listed,
and with ample notes, textual, interpretative, linguistic, bibliographical, historical.
Done with scrupulous care by most eminent
authority, who gave whole scholarly life
to study of R. System permits reader to
follow R.'s change of inspiration, evolution
of method, development of art. Arrangement ideal; each page contains text,
variants, and notes. Last volume now
published (XVI) contains Franciade.
Isidore Silver appointed to finish great
work.

— Œuvres complètes, ed. Paul Laumonier.
Lemerre, 1914-19. 8 v.   1069
Laumonier has taken as base Marty-
Laveaux edition, which reproduces text of
R.'s final complete edition of 1584.
V. I-V follow Marty-Laveaux; v. VI contains works published posthumously, with
pièces retranchées, works attributed to R.,
and works published during R.'s lifetime
outside his own collections, and printed
with his works only after his death or not at
all. V. VII contains prose works, descriptions of lost works, and Notes. Notes
continue in V. VIII, followed by Marty-
Laveaux's biography of R., considerably
revised by Laumonier, *Pièces justificatives*,
Bibliographie, and ample indexes. Notes
of great value, condensing results of
Laumonier's lifetime of research in R.
Few variants given.
Most complete, best documented, most
useful edition. Will no doubt remain so
until Laumonier edition for STFM is
completed.

— Œuvres complètes. Texte de 1578, publié
avec compléments, tables, et glossaire par
Hugues Vaganay. Garnier, 1923-24. 7 v.
                                          1070
1578 edition chosen as base, on assumption (hardly warranted) that 1584 edition
(base of Marty-Laveaux, Laumonier-
Lemerre) suffered from enfeeblement of
R.'s judgment. 1578 more homogeneous,
shows fewer excisions than 1584. (True;
but 1584, final form of poet's thought,
generally preferable until STFM edition is
completed.)
Carefully edited; index and glossary, but
no notes. Good appreciative introduction
by P. de Nolhac. Paper of ordinary edition bad, already brown and crackling,
hence inadvisable for library.

— Œuvres complètes. Texte établi et annoté
par Gustave Cohen. Éditions de la Nouvelle revue française, nd, 2 v. (BibP) 1071

Handsome thin-paper edition; well printed, beautiful type. Text established on 1584 edition. Excellent summary of different collective editions in Introduction. Notes give elucidatory, linguistic information useful to reader, not burdensome to him. Some variants given, evidently only when they give preferable readings. Most satisfactory edition for general reader, indeed only complete edition readily available.

— Un discours inédit de Ronsard. Ed. Roger Gaucheron. MerF 176:604-13, 1924. 1072

Text of *Discours de la joie et de la vie*, otherwise available only in Edouard Frémy : *L'Académie des derniers Valois* (194), where it is attributed to an anonymous physician. Champion accepts it as in R.'s handwriting. (*See his: Ronsard et son temps*, 1098, p. 366.)

— Les amours ... commentées par Marc Antoine de Muret ... d'après le texte de 1578, par Hugues Vaganay. Champion, 1910. 494 p. 1073

Text of 1578, with record of page on which each poem appears in every edition through Marty-Laveaux, all variants through 1587, and Muret's commentary. Supplement of poems not reproduced in 1578, and elaborate analyses of each edition. Preface by Joseph Vianey discusses R.'s corrections, praises Muret's commentary. Beautiful scholarly edition, but unnecessary for those who have Laumonier's STFM edition, no. 1068.

— Discours des misères de ce temps : texte établi et présenté par Jean Baillou. Société Les belles lettres, 1949. 331 p. (TF) 1074

Best readily available edition. Text of 1584, with 55 p. of variants, 54 p. of notes, valuable bibliography. Good historical introduction, discussion of Ronsard's stand in the polemics. Model of care and acumen.

— Poésies choisies. Ed. Pierre de Nolhac. Garnier, 1924. 546 p. 1075

Best selection of poems for general reader. " Il a été composé pour faire mieux comprendre Ronsard, c'est-à-dire le faire mieux aimer." Poems grouped according to theme, e.g., *La nature, La mythologie*. Best texts chosen, regardless of date. Spelling and punctuation modernized. *Lexique* and notes, aiding comprehension and appreciation. These might well have been made more ample.

Though Ronsardisants will miss certain favorites, they will find book a model of learning, judgment, and taste.

— Œuvres choisies, avec notice, notes et commentaires par C. A. Sainte-Beuve. Sautelet, 1828. 350 p. (PFSS, v. 2) 1076

Edition of historic interest, being first in two centuries; restored R.'s fame.

— Textes choisis et commentés par Pierre Villey. Plon-Nourrit, 1914. 313 p. 1077

Good selection of poems (based on 1587 edition) with excellent running comment by eminent *seizièmiste*. Admirable for class use or for general reader.

— Hymne des daimons. Ed. A. M. Schmidt. Michel, 1939. 90 pp. 1078

Valuable critical edition, almost line by line analysis of R.'s *Hymne des daimons*. Running commentary is an erudite and heavy treatment of a curious subject, with numberless references to demonologists of the ages and history of demonology. R. familiar with writings on demonism as well as current superstitions but *Hymne* serves to crystallize his personal ideas. Based on text of 1555. Lists variants and includes bibliography of old books which deal with demonism.

— Sonnets pour Hélène. Édition critique publiée par Jacques Lavaud. Droz, 1947. 135 p. 1079

Meritorious brief critical edition, with variants. In 34-page introduction editor sustains thesis that R. used Hélène as pretext for a series of neo-Petrarchan sonnets to outdo Desportes; and that the liaison was merely a " jeu poétique."

— Ronsard et sa province. Anthologie régionale. Ed. by Paul Laumonier. Presses universitaires, 1924. 268 p. 1080

Charming anthology, glorifying R. and his province. Selections chosen for their beauty as well as for localism. Excellent introduction, biographical and appreciative, by Laumonier, himself Vendômois; he permits himself a pleasant emotional mood banished from his severer works. Useful notes. Many good illustrations, pleasing format. Agreeable but not essential book.

Critical Studies

Addamiano, Natale. Il rinascimento in Francia : Pietro Ronsard (1524-1585). Palermo, Sandron, 1925. 560 p. *See* 2710. 1081

Long, diffuse review of historical background, poetical predecessors, R.'s life and work. Well-informed review of Italian influences. Author works his way through Laumonier's Lemerre edition, judging according to personal taste, condemning liberally. With some condemnations we may agree, as of absurdities of Pindaric odes. But when author calls R. with Trissino, " pessimi versificatori, " speaks of " la vacuità dell'opera sua," says of *Amours de Cassandre :* " come una plumbea palude tutto è eguale," calls *Elégie 23* " stupendamente comicissimo," says we must wait for arrival of Molière and Racine for appearance of true poetry in France, we must dismiss his taste as meaningless to others.

Alliot, Maurice, et Jean Baillou. Ronsard et son quatrième centenaire. Les belles lettres, 1926. 109 p. (EF, 7)   1082

Very valuable critical review of works on R. appearing between about 1914 and 1925, with description of functions marking anniversary. Review of general state of scholarly opinion and new contributions on R.'s literary education, development of his work, contemporaries, themes of inspiration, art, place in French literature, and special points. Critical comments marked by calm judiciousness. Precious bibliography lists 32 editions of works by R. and 216 books and articles about him. Essential.

Banville, T. de. Pierre de Ronsard. *In his :* Petit traité de poésie française. Charpentier, 1894. p. 273-328.   1083

Chapter on R., abounding in praise. Of historical interest.

Bellessort, André. Notre Ronsard. RDM 6th per. 5:530-56, Oct. 1, 1911, and Oct. 15, p. 772-804.   1084

Pleasant retelling of R.'s life and appreciation of his work, based on best authorities.

Binet, Claude. Critical edition of the Discours de la vie de Pierre Ronsard par Claude Binet, ed. by Helene M. Evers. Philadelphia, Winston, 1905. (Diss., Bryn Mawr.)   1085

Laudable thesis, displaced by Laumonier edition (1086).

— La vie de Pierre de Ronsard. Édition critique par Paul Laumonier. Hachette, 1909. 259 p. (Thèse pour le Doctorat ès lettres.)   1086

Model critical edition. Scrupulous reproduction of 1586 text with variants and additions. Masterly introduction on Binet, his sources of information, method, etc. 186 close-packed pages of notes, containing masses of more or less pertinent information, otherwise unavailable, which have provided raw material for a dozen biographers. Necessary book.

Bishop, Morris. Ronsard, prince of poets. New York, Oxford University Press, 1940. 253 p.   1087

" This is a perfect biography for a poet." (Albert Guérard, in HTB, June 23, 1940, p. 4) " As an introduction to Ronsard for the general public, *Ronsard, prince of poets,* fulfills its function admirably." (Justin O'Brien, in TBR, May 12, 1940, p. 2). " ... a biography which is accurate, amply documented, profound and unpretentious, and superbly alive." (Henri Peyre in YR 30:172, 1940-41). " ... un ouvrage bâtard qui n'appartient à aucun genre connu ... une de ces bonnes intentions dont l'Enfer, paraît-il, est pavé." (M. E. Coindreau in RR 32:86, 89, 1941.) " If you are a doctrinaire of any kind, leave this book alone." (Albert Guérard, *ut supra,* p. 4.)

Bonnefon, Paul. Ronsard ecclésiastique. RHL 2:244-48, 1895.   1088

Concludes, contrary to present prevailing opinion, that R. was in fact ordained priest.

Borren, Charles van den. Les musiciens de Ronsard. Rmus 5:45-64, May 1, 1924.   1089

Leans heavily on Tiersot, Expert, etc.

Brunet, Gabriel. Ronsard. MerF 174:599-644, Sept. 15, 1924.   1090

Examines some less well-known works; rehabilitates *Odes pindariques, Franciade.* Racine read *Franciade,* profiting by it for *Andromaque. Hymnes* regarded as forerunners of symbolists. Brunet develops *universalité* of R., his passionate nature, his duality; he is Don Quixote and Sancho. Novel and stimulating.

Brunetière, Ferdinand. Un épisode de la vie de Ronsard. RDM 4th ser. 159:371-89, May 15, 1900. *Reprinted :* Études critiques, 7th ser., Hachette, 1903. p. 1-26.   1091

Brunetière lauds the *Discours des misères de ce temps* unreasonably as a capital work because of its " nationalisme." Sees it as a forerunner of 17th century literature.

— L'œuvre de Pierre de Ronsard. RDM 183 (per. 5, v. 23):751-804, Oct. 15, 1904. 1092

Good over-all treatment, now somewhat dated.

Busson, Henri. Sur la philosophie de Ronsard. RCC 31¹:32-48, 172-85, 1929-1930. 1093

R.'s view of divinity, cosmology, *le monde sublunaire.* His evolution toward materialism, pantheism.

Caisso, R. La vente de la forêt de Gastine à l'époque de Ronsard. Hren 4:274-85, 1937. 1094

New documents.

Cameron, Alice. The influence of Ariosto's epic and lyric poetry on Ronsard and his group. Baltimore, Johns Hopkins Press, 1930. 187 p. (JHSR, v. 15) 1095

Mostly on R. Painstaking, thorough, judicious thesis. R. and his group pillaged Ariosto, and passed from him to his classic sources. *See* 1225.

Chamard, Henri. L'invention de l'ode et le différend de Ronsard et de du Bellay. RHL 6:21-54, 1899. 1096

(1) Sebillet credits Marotic school with invention of Ode. Indeed, Marot, Saint-Gelais, and others used word, fumbled with idea. But R. first to define and popularize form based on Pindar and Horace. (2) Much-bruited quarrel of R. and Du Bellay in fact trifling and quickly past. *See* 1229.

Champion, Pierre. Pierre de Ronsard et Amadis Jamyn; leurs autographes. Champion, 1924. 30 p. 1097

Reproductions of R.'s handwriting and that of his secretary. Champion proves that autographs ascribed to R. were in fact often written by secretary. Book contains also pleasant appreciation of Jamyn's poetry, and statement of R.'s influence.

— Ronsard et son temps. Champion, 1925. 508 p. 1098

Essential biography of R., for scholar as well as general reader. Champion loves R.; "il a agi sur moi comme un philtre." (p. viii) He approaches the man through his poetry. He situates R. in midst of his times; "notre méthode consiste à rattacher l'individu à son temps par mille liens." (p. viii) Book is picture of court and country life of century, with numberless curious and rare details, brilliant

ensemble pictures. Story told with gusto, humor, emotion. 24 excellent full-page plates. Rich, beautiful, amiable volume.

— Ronsard et Villeroy. Champion, 1925. 57 p. 1099

Study of manuscript collection of occasional verse by R. and others, written mostly in hand of Villeroy. Intimacy of royal secretaries and poets revealed. Booklet subtitled : *Contribution à l'histoire de la société polie.* 10 fine reproductions of mss.

Charbonnier, F. Pamphlets protestants contre Ronsard (1560-1577). Champion 1923. 71 p. 1100

Valuable bibliography for researcher. Three unedited attacks on R. reproduced *in extenso,* and one very rare pamphlet. Useful examples of anti-Ronsardian polemics, which we read about without reading.

Charlier, Gustave. Un amour de Ronsard : Astrée. RSS 7:123-44, 1920. *Reprinted, with the title :* L'Astrée de Ronsard, *in his :* De Ronsard à Victor Hugo, Brussels, Revue de l'Université de Bruxelles, 1931. p. 10-36. 1101

Supports Beaunier (RDM 6th per. 90:201-12, Nov., 1920) on identification of Astrée with Mme d'Estrées. Holds that R. was genuinely in love with her.

— Ronsard au XIXᵉ siècle avant Sainte-Beuve. RCC 41¹:369-81, Feb. 29, 1940. 1102

Viollet-le-Duc, father of architect, rediscovered and announced R.'s greatness in 1822. Sainte-Beuve, aware of fact, never admitted it, to secure credit of rediscovery for himself. Convincing.

— Ronsard et la Belgique. Brussels, Palais des Académies, n.d. (c. 1924). 29 p. 1103

Relations with Des Masures and Utenhove, and influences on 16th century Belgian poets.

Cohen, Gustave. Ronsard, sa vie et son œuvre. Boivin, 1924. 288 p. 1104

Important over-all study, with center of interest rather in history and critique of poems than in biography. Cohen's wide knowledge of background and predecessors permits situation of R. in his frame, social and political as well as literary. Valuable references to medieval parallels and contrasts. These Sorbonne lectures intended to rouse sympathetic response among auditors, to stimulate appreciation of poetic beauty. Hence many long quotations from R., which should be properly rendered by Cohen's voice.

Comte, Charles, and Paul Laumonier. Ronsard et les musiciens du XVIᵉ siècle. RHL 7: 341-81, 1900.   1105
Good article, especially on influence of music on R.'s verse form, but largely displaced by later work.

Dédéyan, Charles. Henri II, la Franciade et les Hymnes de 1555-1556. BHren 9:114-28, 1947.   1106
Shrewd setting in order of *Hymnes*, showing their internal relation with *Franciade*, their external relation to favor of Henri II.

De Schweinitz, Margaret. Les épitaphes de Ronsard. Presses universitaires, n.d. (1925). 187 p. (Thèse pour le doctorat de l'université.)   1107
Praiseworthy thesis. Study of genre before R., historical commentary on R.'s 53 *épitaphes*, literary commentary (not important). Useful appendix, listing all variants of *épitaphes*.

Desonay, Fernand. Ronsard, poète de l'amour. I : Cassandre. II : De Marie à Genèvre. Brussels, Palais des académies; Gembloux, Duculot, 1952-54. 281 p. 1108
Solid, well-based, well-annotated, sensitive, readable study. Desonay concerned chiefly with analysis and appraisal of poems; by the way judges previous critical judgments, makes excursions into biography. Would diminish alleged Petrarchan influence; protests scholars' tendency to make Cassandre-poems a purely intellectual exercise; R. neither pedant nor imitator. Valuable study of musical settings. Exhaustive study of R.'s corrections and alterations.
Review : P. Jourda in BHren 15:147-49, 1953.

— Métrique et lyrisme : à propos du Ronsard qui chanta d'amour Marie l'Angevine. LR 3:283-308, 1949.   1109
What is R.'s " style bas, " with which he celebrated Marie? Answer : a disciplined, workmanlike handling of alexandrine, " le vrai rythme de Ronsard," in which love's inspiration had no part. R. loved only poetry.

Dubedout, E. J. Les Discours de Ronsard. MP 1:437-56, 1903-04.   1110
R.'s faith and utterances sincere, not determined by political and other expediency.

Dufay, Pierre. De Cassandre aux Musset. MerF 175:668-76, Nov. 1, 1924.   1111
Genealogical contributions on Cassandre, ancestor of Alfred de Musset.

Etienne, S. Ronsard a-t-il su le grec? MélPL, p. 201-18.   1112
Answer is, " No." Well argued. But argument refuted by Hutton, no. 1135, Silver, 1178-79.

Expert, Henry. La Fleur des musiciens de P. de Ronsard. Cité des livres, 1923. 104 p.   1113
Contemporary musical settings of 32 poems. Original form preserved, but transcribed in modern clefs. Handsome volume.

Faguet, Emile. Education littéraire des hommes de la Pléiade. RCC 25 (Iʳᵉ ser.) : 289:305, 385-403, 1924.   1114
Influences of *Roman de la rose*, Petrarch, Le Maire de Belges, Scève.

— Ronsard. In his : Seizième siècle; études littéraires. Boivin, 1894. p. 199-288. 1115
Lucid, perceptive *vue d'ensemble*. Some individual provocative judgments. Excellent on *Doctrines littéraires de la Pléiade*, in which he treats *Défense et illustration* as more R.'s work than Du Bellay's. Good on *Ronsard imitateur, Ronsard écrivain, la rythmique de Ronsard*. Regards R. as forerunner of classicism. Some views too novel; to be treated with caution.

Les fêtes du 4ᵉ centenaire de Ronsard en Vendômois. BSV, 1924. 102 p.   1116
Interesting as evidence of R.'s continuing fame. Good addresses by Laumonier and Cohen.

Folkierski, W. Ronsard et la Pologne. RLC 4:443-48, 1924.   1117
Mostly on Kochanowski.

Fontainas, André. La poésie lyrique. Œuvre et inspiration de P. de Ronsard. MerF 174:289-310, Sept. 1, 1924.   1118
Ardent tribute by poet. Not much for scholar.

Foulet, Lucien. Dorat et Ronsard. RHL 13:312-16, 1906.   1119
Dorat's influence minimized.

Franchet, Henri. Erasme et Ronsard. RHL 39:321-38, 1932.   1120
In R.'s *Discours des misères de ce temps* he reproduced arguments and turns of phrase

of Erasmus' *Contra quosdam qui se falso jactant evangelicos. See* 2892.

— Le poète et son œuvre d'après Ronsard. Champion, 1923. 356 p. (Thèse pour le doctorat ès lettres.) 1121

Useful, exhaustive book on limited theme, R.'s conception of poet and poetic production. Based essentially on R.'s prose works. Chapters on *La fureur poétique, La vertu, La gloire, Le savoir*, with their applications in R.'s poetry. Typical good thesis, proving laboriously the previously implicit. Good *Notes bibliographiques.*

Françon, Marcel. Un amour de Ronsard. FR 17:83-88, 1943-44. 1122

Sonnets pour Astrée were *pièces de circonstance* on behalf of duc d'Anjou.

Fuchs, L. Comment le XVIIᵉ et XVIIIᵉ siècles ont jugé Ronsard. Rren 8:228-38, 1907; 9:49-72, 1908. 1123

Author claims R. was not put into sudden eclipse at his death nor restored to favor dramatically in 19th century. Argument supported by quotations from Malherbe, Boileau, Sorel, Fontenelle, Marmontel, etc. Valuable, though excessive, critique of accepted opinion.

Gabillot, Cyrille. Les portraits de Ronsard. GBA 49 (3rd per. 37) : 487-501, June 1, 1907. 1124

Summary of existing portraits (including bust), with thorough description and appreciation. Illustrated.

— La tombe de Ronsard. RPar 17:599-612, Oct. 1, 1910. 1125

Useful background documentary material.

Gambier, Henri. Pierre de Ronsard. *In his :* Italie et renaissance poétique en France. Padua, Cedam, 1936. p. 115-211. 1126

Secondary and unimportant. *See* 2669.

Gandar, E. Ronsard considéré comme imitateur d'Homère et de Pindare. Metz, Blanc, 1854. 211 p. 1127

First critical study of R. after Sainte-Beuve. Substance now available elsewhere. *See* 2542A.

Glaser, Kurt. Ronsard Erinnerungen. ZFSL 50:191-203, 1927. 1128

Sympathetic attempt to explain complexity of R., who united in himself Humanism, Catholicism, paganism, Christianity. He was exponent of spirit

of his times, typical man of renaissance. Many good comments, as on R.'s appreciation of nature, on Sainte-Beuve's rediscovery of R., etc.

Guy, Henry. " Mignonne, allons voir si la rose..." Réflexions sur un lieu commun. RPB 5:250-68, 1902. 1129

History of rose-theme, from Psalms and Homer to Malherbe. " Cette image appartient à ce fonds de demi-vérités, d'observations sans critique et d'adages contradictoires qui constituent la sagesse des nations " (p. 266). Guy moralizes agreeably on poet's function to be poet, not philosopher.

— Les sources françaises de Ronsard. RHL 9:217-56, 1902. 1130

Comparison of some of R.'s ideas, characters, and expressions with French predecessors, particularly Marot, *Roman de la rose*, and romances. Proves R.'s indebtedness. *See* 2434.

Harrison, T. P. Spenser, Ronsard and Bion. MLN 49:139-45, 1934. 1131

Credits R. as source of passages in *Shepherd's calendar* and *Astrophel.*

Hauvette, Henri. Note sur Ronsard italianisant. RLC 4:476-80, 1924. *See* 2711. 1132

Metric borrowings from Alamanni.

Hervier, Marcel. La valeur éducative de Ronsard. Nrev 73:139-53, Sept. 15, 1924. 1133

Recommends reading of R. as means of self-education. But article mostly familiar praise of R.

Humiston, Clinton C. A comparative study of the metrical technique of Ronsard and Malherbe. Berkeley and Los Angeles, University of California Press, 1941. 180 p. 1134

R. anticipated Malherbe in his metrical doctrine and practice.

Hutton, James. Ronsard and the Greek anthology. SP 40:103-27, 1943. 1135

" Up to 1559 Ronsard's knowledge of Greek epigrams that of schoolboy." (p. 109). His knowledge of Greek broadened; from 1569 studied and imitated erotic epigrams, using Greek texts without teacher's aid. Demolishes thesis of Etienne (1112). Admirable reconstruction of R.'s work on sources; circumspect and trenchant. Indeed, a model for any worker studying a poet's use of his materials. *See* 2559.

Jones, P. Mansell. The approach to Ronsard. Criterion 12:571-84, 1933.   1136
Review of 19th and 20th century English critical misunderstanding of R. Defends R. against charge of dryness, of burying emotions under learned decoration. R. was classic rather than romantic. Good.

Jusserand, Jules. Ronsard. Hachette, 1913. 215 p. (GEF)   1137
Still excellent introduction to R.'s life and works, though later research invalidates some statements. Good picture of times and assessment of contemporary poetry. Shrewd analysis of character and judicious study of R.'s poetic theories and achievements. Written with charm, lucidity, unobtrusive scholarship. Fine example of *haute vulgarisation*.

— Ronsard and his Vendômois. *In his :* The school for ambassadors and other essays. New York, Putnam, 1925. p. 161-218.   1138
First-person account of visit to Vendômois, done with Ronsardian grace and emotion.

Koehler, Friedrich. Die Alliteration bei Ronsard. Erlangen, Deichert, 1901. 152 p. (MBP, v. 20)   1139
History of alliteration, and compilation of R.'s alliterative lines. Unsatisfactory statement of significance of findings.

Kuhn, Paul. L'influence néo-latine dans les églogues de Ronsard. RHL 21:309-25, 1914.   1140
Borrowings from Navagero in R.'s *Bergerie*.

Lange, Maurice. Quelques sources probables des Discours de Ronsard. RHL 20:789-816, 1913.   1141
Sources sought in Michel de L'Hospital, etc.

Lanson, Gustave. Comment Ronsard invente. RU 15ᵉ année, 1:29-39, 1906.   1142
Explication de texte on *L'ode de l'élection de son sépulcre*. Lanson disentangles 3 themes from antiquity with many *souvenirs de détail*; shows how result is happy, easy blend. Good model for similar scholarly exercises.

Laumonier, Paul. Ronsard et l'Écosse. RLC 4:408-28, 1924.   1143
Effort to ascertain, mostly from British

and Scottish sources, information about R.'s stay in Scotland. Few facts emerge. Also account of R.'s relations with Mary Queen of Scots.

— Ronsard, poète lyrique. Hachette, 1909. 806 p. (Thèse pour le doctorat ès lettres.)   1144
The great work on R.'s poetry. Introduction is history of French ode. Part I, *Genèse et évolution de l'œuvre lyrique de Ronsard*, shows influences upon him, classifies his styles, fixes dates, lists later variants, elucidates separate poems. Tendency is to show R. returning to French tradition, despite his pronouncements. Part II, *Sources et originalité de Ronsard poète lyrique*, shows his methods of imitation, preserving spirit, eschewing translation. Part III, *Rythmique des odes et chansons de Ronsard*, is elaborate study of verse structure, with his indebtednesses and originalities. " L'objet de notre longue étude a été de montrer ce que Ronsard a voulu au fur et à mesure qu'il la (i. e., son œuvre) produisait, les moyens qu'il a employés pour atteindre ses fins, les résultats éternellement durables auxquels il est arrivé." (p. 711). Book is a triumph of understanding, thoroughness, exactness.

— Ronsard poète pétrarquiste avant 1550. MélGL. p. 109-14.   1145
Proves Petrarchan influence before 1550, despite common statement to contrary. *See* 2733.

— Le second livre des Meslanges et la Sinope de Ronsard. RSS 13:205-30, 1926.   1146
Substance reproduced in Laumonier's STFM edition (1068), Introduction.

— Sur la bibliothèque de Ronsard. RSS 14:315-35, 1927.   1147
Some books from R.'s library still extant.

Lee, Sir Sidney. The French renaissance in England. *See* 662.   1148
100 pages of this masterly book deal with R. and Pléiade in England. Sensitive and erudite study of influences on Elizabethan themes, sentiments, metre, vocabulary. Though seldom acknowledged, Ronsardian influences appear in Lyly, Daniel, Lodge, Drayton, Dekker, Spenser, Shakespeare, Chapman. Many devices, such as *vocables composés*, taken over. Illuminating volume, sole in field; should inspire comparatiste to carry study into later times. *See* 1658, 2800.

Levengood, Sidney L. The use of color in the verse of the Pléiade. *See* 1052. 1149 Why?

Lewis, D. B. Wyndham. Ronsard. New York, Coward-McCann and Sheed and Ward, 1944. 340 p. 1150
Good biography, from standard French sources; excellent appreciation of poetry, by fervent admirer; much extraneous information, often recondite, often *tiré par les cheveux*, always curious and interesting. Gay, boisterous style; truculent English Tory Catholic manner; numberless excursions to rap heads and toes, of English Whigs, Queen Victoria, Walter Pater, etc. General reader will enjoy book's gusto, wit, skillful writing, wealth of curious reference. Those who are infuriated by hearty Bellocian Catholicism had better skip it.

Longnon, Henri. Pierre de Ronsard. Les ancêtres — la jeunesse. Champion, 1912. 512 p. 1151
Well informed, well pondered study of R.'s ancestry (80 p.) and youth (through *Amours de Marie*). Much valuable material from archives, including 37 p. of *pièces justificatives*. Author, who first proposed identification of poet's Cassandre with Cassandre Salviati, makes many other suggestions, many of which have now entered canon of R.

— Les déboires de Ronsard à la Cour. BHren 12:60-80, 1950. *See* 723. 1152
Libellous poem of Mellin de Saint-Gelais was aimed at R.; Hélène de Surgères was the heroine of a scabrous adventure reported by Brantôme. Both contentions pretty far-fetched.

— Pierre de Ronsard et la Réforme. Runiv 15:145-62, Oct. 15, 1923. 1153
As loyal adherent of Valois, R. feared unsettling effect of Reformation. As clerk in orders, professing Catholic, he detested Lutheranism, felt need of mysteries in church. As humanist, he rejected Protestant " opinion " or personal interpretation of Scriptures. Good article.

Lucas, F. L. The prince of court-poets. *In his:* Studies French and English. London, Cassell, 1934. p. 76-114. 1154
Delightful re-telling of life and appreciation of work by humane scholar who knows classic and English literature as well as French. Valuable for its estimation of

R. in world-literature and refreshing for its charm of style.

Magne, Emile. Le folâtrissime voyage d'Arcueil. Ill 164:445-48, Nov. 24, 1924. 1155
Delightful reconstruction, with improbable illustrations. Nice to show to class.

Martellière, Jean. Pierre de Ronsard, gentilhomme vendômois. Lemerre, 1924. 286 p. 1156
Collected series of articles by Vendômois *chercheur*, who has unearthed many valuable references to presumable ancestors and relatives of R., to transformations of his name, to Cassandre Salviati, and to local friends. Raises questions as to date of R.'s birth, identification of poet's Cassandre, etc. Some delightful descriptions of places connected with R. His conclusions have been much opposed; book to be used with caution, as well as gratitude.

Maugain, Gabriel. Ronsard en Italie. Les belles lettres, 1926. 343 p. (PFS, 2nd ser., fasc. 2.) 1157
Valuable study of influence of R. in Italy, 1550-1925. Ample background, rendering study a history of Italian thought and taste. Ample (100 page) treatment of influence of R. on Chiabrera. Many novel contributions to field of study little explored. Appendix : list of early editions of R. in Italian public libraries. *See* 2697.

Mellerio, L. Lexique de Ronsard. Préface de Louis Petit de Julleville. (Ed. Elzévirienne.) Plon, 1895. 251 p. 1158
Valuable lexicon of R.'s Graecisms, Latinisms, borrowings from other languages, archaisms, dialectalisms, trade and hunting terms, formations of words and compounds. Introduction alleges relative paucity of such novelties. To be used with caution; claims excessive, listings incomplete.

Nolhac, Pierre de. Pierre de Ronsard. RFrance 3:93-112, Jan.-Feb., 1923. 1159
Authoritative review of R.'s life and works, with shrewd judgments and comments. Charming brief treatment.

— Ronsard et l'humanisme. Champion, 1921. 365 p. 1160
Learned, readable study by eminent humanist. First half deals with R.'s knowledge of classic authors. Much on Dorat and R.'s companions at Coqueret. Part two, R. and humanists of his time.

R. shown as one of leading humanists of Europe. Part 3 on R.'s Latin writings. Curiously little critical judgment of R.'s Latin, though it is characterized as Erasmian "bon gros latin." Part 4, account of R.'s relations with Pierre de Paschal. Book assembles results of wide, recondite reading, but with little generalization. Remains standard work on classic sources and humanist influences.

— La vie amoureuse de Pierre de Ronsard. Flammarion, 1926. 187 p.   1161

Despite alarming title, book is charming retelling of R.'s loves, derived, necessarily, from his own poems. Familiar story told with grace, affection, and (needless to say) ample knowledge of subject and background.

(Nolhac, P. de, and others). Ronsard et son temps. Morancé, 1925. 119 p.   1162

Descriptive catalogue of tercentenary exhibit at Bibliothèque nationale, 1924. Listed are original editions of R., music, works of Pléiade, regional prose and poetry, works on social background, many manuscripts, and medals, drawings, paintings, engravings. Scholarly descriptive and critical comment. Valuable for any explorer of period.

Parducci, Amos. Le imitazioni ariostee nella Franciade del Ronsard. AR 14:361-394, 1930.   1163

Adds more examples to those of Ariostean imitation given by Vianey (no. 1191). See 2758.

Parturier, E. Quelques sources italiennes de Ronsard au XVe siècle. Rren 6:1-21, 1905.   1164

R. was probably helped in translations from ancients by Italian versions of Poliziano and Lorenzo de' Medici.

Perdrizet, Pierre. Ronsard et la Réforme. Fischbacher, 1902. 182 p.   1165

Prize essay by Swiss Protestant theologian. Judicious, well informed, especially on background of theological controversy. R.'s knowledge of Protestant position adjudged slight, effect of his polemics however considerable. Critical bibliography of controversy included, also 30 page appendix of inédits and rarities. Book important only for researcher in special field.

Photiadès, Constantin. Ronsard et son luth. RPar 32:849-71, Feb. 15, and 81-108,

Mar. 1, 1925. Reprinted : Plon, 1925. 109 p.   1166

Review, from standard texts, of R.'s musical education and theories. Useful discussion of music and musicians of renaissance, and of R.'s efforts to wed poetry and music. Effort failed, says Photiadès, because of nature of polyphonic music of time.

Pieri, Marius. Pétrarque et Ronsard. See 1055.   1167

Subtitled : De l'influence de Pétrarque sur la Pléiade française. Historical background of Petrarchism in France and analysis of influences. Excellent study of transmission of Petrarchan ideas, poetic language, style, metrics, and rhythms. Still valuable, despite later work by Laumonier, etc.

Prunières, H. Ronsard et les fêtes de cour. Rmus 5:27-44, May 1, 1924.   1168

R. as impresario of entertainments ; influence of these fêtes on ballet de cour. Some interesting estimates from musician's point of view.

Ranjard, R. La découverte des restes de Ronsard; prieuré de Saint Cosme, 10 mai, 1933. Sauvegarde de l'art français, 1933. 23 p.   1169

Excellent account of discovery of R.'s remains and circumspect methods of identification. 12 photographs.

Raymond, Marcel. L'influence de Ronsard sur la poésie française (1550-1585). Champion, 1927. 2 v.   1170

Magisterial study of R.'s influence on Pléiade, followers, rivals, and enemies, including Desportes, Du Bartas, d'Aubigné and host of minor and provincial writers. As author recognizes, book is history of French poetry in second half of century. R.'s influence found everywhere; its waning due in part to removal of his personal ascendancy, in part to external causes. Book done with taste, sobriety, judgment, and vast knowledge of field. See 1346.

— A propos des Amours de Ronsard. RSS 9:180-209, 1922.   1171

Annihilation of Sorg's theory (1182) that Cassandre, Sinope, Marie, are one.

— Ronsard et du Bellay. RHL 31:573-603, 1924.   1172

Du Bellay, though deeply influenced by R.'s dominant personality and doctrines, does not directly imitate him. Common sources for both poets. The *Défense* " almost a collective work." *See* 1287.

Remigerau, François. Ronsard sur les brisées de Du Fouilloux. RSS 19:47-95, 1932-33. 1173

R.'s hunting lore lifted from Du Fouilloux's *La vénerie*, not, as Laumonier alleged, from classical sources.

Rocher, Edmond. Pierre de Ronsard, prince des poètes. Presses universitaires, 1924. 81 p. 1174

Unimportant appreciative essays, with extensive bibliography (32 p.). Bibliography by no means complete, contains nevertheless many items which would otherwise escape future bibliographer, for whom it is essential.

Rosenbauer, A. Die poetischen Theorien der Plejade. *See* 1056. 1175

Chiefly on R. Displaced by later studies.

Schmidt, Albert Marie. Pierre de Ronsard, poète scientifique. *In his :* La poésie scientifique en France au seizième siècle. *See* 327, p. 71-107. 1176

This section on R. deals with development of his cosmology, conception of the universe, readings of the Stoics, attitude toward demons, destiny, nature, gods, augury, magic, celestial powers. Difficult, exasperating volume. *See* 1347.

Schutz, A. H. Ronsard's Amours XXXII and the tradition of the synthetic lady. RP 1:125-35, 1947. 1177

Other sources than Hesiod for indicated sonnet. Special but sound.

Silver, Isidore. The Pindaric odes of Ronsard. André, 1937. 137 p. (Diss., Columbia) 1178

Useful complement to Laumonier. Thorough analysis of R.'s debt to Pindar, in thought and expression. Conclusion : R. failed to equal Pindaric grandeur, for reasons of temperament, etc.

— Ronsard and du Bellay on their Pindaric collaboration. RR 33:3-25, 1942. 1179

Contends that Du Bellay strove to imitate Pindar, under inspiration of R. Well argued, but argument must rest on inferences and interpretations, sometimes cloudy.

— Ronsard's early philosophy. SP 45:119-133, 1948. 1180

Deals with period of *Odes*. Occasionalism of court life and renaissance eclecticism determined R.'s thought, did not inspire philosophic system. Though R. does not attain intellectual grandeur, he is not paltry or inane. Well informed, well thought, well written.

Simone, Franco. L'avviamento poetico di Pierre de Ronsard. Florence, Istituto nazionale di studi sul rinascimento, 1942. 87 p. 1181

Praiseworthy exercise; but nothing here for the specialist.

Sorg, Roger. Cassandre, ou le secret de Ronsard. Payot, 1925. 263 p. 1182

Retelling, not without grace, of R.'s life, especially love-life. Incorporated is inadmissible theory that Marie, Genèvre, and Sinope were disguises of Cassandre. Hélène is accepted as real. 104 pages of marginalia, necessary for researcher, propound bold theses, e.g., R.'s birth in 1522, Moravian origin of family. Based on documentary research, but conclusions universally disapproved. Assembles studies which had previously appeared, especially in RHL 29:1-16, 1922 and in RFrance 4th yr. 2:515-46, 1924.

Souza, Robert de. Les origines du vers moderne; la rythmique de Ronsard. MerF 175:89-121, Oct. 1, 1924. 1183

Discerning analysis of treacherous subject : poet's methods of obtaining rhythmical effects. Close relation between R., Marot, and *Rhétoriqueurs* suggested. Movement of R.'s verse ascribed to phonetic harmony, asymmetric balance, and composition by metrical feet. Thus a tendency to liberation of " rythmique naturelle" is noted.

Storer, Walter H. Virgil and Ronsard. Champion, 1923. 143 p. (Diss., Illinois) 1184

Laudable and evidently thorough.

Thibault, Geneviève, and Louis Perceau. Bibliographie des poésies de P. de Ronsard mises en musique au XVIe siècle. Droz, 1941. 121 p. 1185

Ample, exact bibliography of R.'s poems set to music and published in vocal collections of century. Also, *table générale des incipit, table des noms cités, table des volumes cités*. Supplement reproduces four settings of *chansons*, unknown or rare. " C'est un instrument de travail; ce n'est pas une étude historique, chronologique ou littéraire; on ne trouvera ici aucun commentaire sur l'union de la musique et de la poésie telle que la concevait Ronsard." Model bibliography, within its set limits.

Tiersot, Julien. Ronsard et la musique de son temps. Leipzig, New York, Breitkoff & Haertel, 1903. 78 p. 1186

32-page introduction, good appreciation and judgment of musical settings of *Amours.* Reproduction in modern notation of these settings, and of requiem sung at R.'s funeral. Valuable.

Tilley, Arthur. Ronsard's poetic growth. MLR 29:32-51, 1934 ; 30:460-71, 1935 ; 31:161-75, 1936. 1187

Well-informed personal judgments. Emphasizes R.'s mastery of poetry of nature. Not essential.

Tonnelat, Ernest. Deux imitateurs allemands de Ronsard : G. R. Weckherlin et Martin Opitz. RLC 4:557-89, 1924. 1188

Useful for specialist.

Vaganay, Hugues. Les odes pindariques après Ronsard. Mâcon, 1923. 14 p. 1189

Brief descriptive notices.

Various. Ronsard et la Pléiade. MuF 3:1-203, Feb. 10, 1924. 1190

Collection of essays and poems honoring fourth centennial anniversary. Some well known scholars contribute, Nolhac, Franchet, Cohen, Laumonier, etc. Contributions brief, unimportant for scholar. Poems by eminent names, Régnier, Ctesse de Noailles, etc., as undistinguished as most such poetic garlands. To be compared with *Tombeau de Ronsard* in Blanchemain edition (1066).

Vianey, Joseph. L'Arioste et la Pléiade. BI 1:295-317, 1901. 1191

Two episodes of *Franciade* evidently imitated from Ariosto. *See* 1332.

— Les grands poètes de la nature en France : Ronsard-La Fontaine. RCC 27:3-19, Dec. 15, 1925. 1192

Good appreciation, acclaiming R. as first great French poet of nature.

— Les odes de Ronsard. Société française d'éditions littéraires et techniques, 1932. 203 p. 1193

Analysis and appreciation of *Odes,* their origins, development, influences in France and Italy. Vianey shows in them a forecast of Malherbian reforms. History of

fame and appreciation of odes until our times. Well informed, based on best recent scholarly studies.

Wolfe, Humbert. Ronsard and French romantic poetry. Oxford, Clarendon Press, 1935. 31 p. (The Zaharoff lecture for 1934.) 1194

R.'s genius was un-French; was characteristic of renaissance. Incisive, shrewd, amusing.

Wyndham, George. Ronsard and la Pléiade. *See* 1060. Introductory essay reproduced in Wyndham, George, Essays in Romantic literature. London, Macmillan, 1919, p. 65-113. 1195

Enthusiastic study, interesting as example of English revival of interest in R. and for discussion of R.'s influence on English poets. Some good verse translations.

Joachim Du Bellay

(Nos. 1196-1341)

ISIDORE SILVER

Van Bever, Ad. Bibliographie de Joachim Du Bellay. Rren 13:176-88, 1912. 1196

Advance publication of a part of bibliography of works of the poet which was to appear the same year in Van Bever's edition of *Divers jeux rustiques,* p. 73-91.

Chamard, Henri. Bibliographie des éditions de Joachim du Bellay. BBB 1949, p. 400-15, 445-63. 1197

Careful listing of 83 titles of works by D., all but one dating from 16th century. All necessary bibliographical information furnished. Supersedes earlier descriptions by J. Ch. Brunet, *Manuel du libraire,* 1860[5], as completed by P. Deschamps and G. Brunet in *Supplément* of 1878; by Camille Ballu in his *Œuvres choisies de Joachim du Bellay,* 1894, p. 251-68; by Ad. van Bever in his edition of *Jeux rustiques,* 1912, p. 73-91; and by Marty-Laveaux in second volume of his edition of D., 1866-1867, p. 545-77.

Works

Du Bellay, Joachim. Œuvres françoises de Ioachim du Bellay, gentil-homme angevin. Edited by Charles Marty-Laveaux. Lemerre, 1866-67. 2 v. (CPF) 1198

Based upon posthumous first collective edition (1568) prepared by friends of the poet, Guillaume Aubert and Jean Morel, and following the arrangement adopted by them, which Chamard has described as "un pur chaos chronologique." (*In his* edition of D., v. I, p. vii.) Contains a *Notice biographique* of the poet and many helpful notes at end of each volume.

— Œuvres complètes de Joachim du Bellay, edited by Léon Séché. Rren 1903-13, 4 v.   1199

In stating that except for the *Deffence*, nothing but fragments of D. had been published since 1597, Séché was obviously unfair to edition of Marty-Laveaux (se above). The *Commentaire historique* limits itself rather arbitrarily to negative task of pointing out errors which had acquired credit until coming of Séché. No critical apparatus, but a promise in *Avertissement* that notes of Reinhold Dezeimeris, prepared in view of a D. anthology, would be employed. Alas! the promise is withdrawn in a note on p. 230 of first volume.

Review : J. Vianey in RHL 10:523-25, 1903.

— Œuvres choisies de Joachim du Bellay. Edited by Léon Séché. Edition du monument, 1894. 270 p.   1200

In Introduction supplied by the editor are treated a number of subjects which he was later to amplify in Rren. Most valuable feature of the edition was the *Notice sur Joachim du Bellay* by Camille Ballu. There are four pages at end in which Jules Bordier has set to music the sonnet *Heureux qui comme Ulysse*; a genealogical table of D. family from 13th to 17th centuries.

— Œuvres poétiques. Edited by Herri Chamard. Cornély, 1908-31. 6 v. (STFM) 1201

Definitive edition superseding all earlier ones. Constructed on rational principles : arrangement of compositions by genres (sonnets, lyrics, epistles, hymns, discours) : and adoption in each genre of a chronological order by date of publication. Edition provided throughout with an excellent *apparatus criticus* and very helpful notes. Regrettably, circumstances have not favored completion of the edition along lines announced in *Avertissement* to v. I. *Société des textes français modernes* is to be congratulated, however, for having decided to publish new (1948) and revised version of Chamard's 1904 edition of the *Deffence*.

Reviews : J. Plattard in RER 8:374-75, 1910 (v. II); in RSS 1:449, 1913 (v. III); in RSS 7:275, 1920 (v. IV). (Comments, not full scale reviews).

— Les Antiquitez de Rome et les Regrets, avec une introduction. Ed. by Eugénie Droz. Droz, 1945. 163 p.   1202

Has an informative introduction, but no critical apparatus; few notes. Partial list of D.'s sources based on notes of critical edition of Chamard, and a useful index of names and places.

— La deffence et illustration de la langue françoyse par Ioachim du Bellay; reproduite conformément au texte de l'édition originale avec une introduction, des notes philologiques et littéraires et un glossaire, suivie du Quintil Horatian (de Charles Fontaine). Edited by Emile Person. Cerf, 1892. 214 p.   1203

Until appearance in 1904 of Chamard's critical edition, this was most accessible and most useful publication of D.'s manifesto. Attribution of *Quintil* to Charles Fontaine has long been recognized as false. *See* article by Chamard, *La date et l'auteur du Quintil Horatian*, RHL 5:54-71, 1898.

— La deffence et illustration de la langue françoyse. Édition critique par Henri Chamard. Fontemoing, 1904. 236 p. 1204

Since its appearance this has remained definitive edition of D.'s declaration of principles. Model edition of a difficult renaissance publication. No pains spared in preparation of abundant commentary which clarifies the text in a multitude of ways : philological, historical, literary. Critical apparatus leaves nothing to be desired, although variants are more often orthographical than substantive, which was usual case with D. *Tables* particularly valuable, especially *Table des choses*, which places at reader's disposal the full thought of D. on a host of interesting subjects. *Quintil Horatian*, Barthélemy Aneau's running comment on "aucuns pointz qui me semblent dignes de correction amiable " (p. 23), has been usefully distributed throughout notes at points of maximum relevance; bibliography gives generous information on old and modern editions of *Deffence*, and on renaissance and modern writings which help to illuminate it.

Reviews : E. Huguet in RHL 12:158-159, 1905; P. Laumonier in Rcr ns 57:241-250, Oct. 10, 1904.

— La deffence et illustration de la langue françoyse. Édition critique par Henri Chamard. Didier, 1948. 206 p. (STFM) 1205

Published by *Société des textes français modernes* as a complement to Chamard's edition of D., volume naturally adopts usual format of STFM publications. Differs in other ways from its predecessors : reduction of critical apparatus, suppression of philological commentary, renovation of historical and literary remarks in light of researches carried out since 1904. Fortunately *Quintil Horatian* is again diffused strategically throughout the notes. Absence of *Tables*, no doubt required by demands of conformity with other STFM editions, will continue to put a premium on the *Deffence* of 1904, which will become even more " introuvable dans le commerce " as the *Deffence* of 1948 is in turn exhausted.

— La deffence et illustration de la langue françoyse. Fac-similé de l'édition originale de 1549. Introduction by Fernand Desonay. Geneva, Droz; Lille, Giard, 1950.   1206

Introduction has 33 pages, but facsimile itself is without pagination. Celebrates the 400th anniversary of appearance of *Deffence*; a facsimile often provides the scholar with information which he cannot obtain in even best critical editions.

Introduction discusses *Deffence* at first " sous les traits d'un personnage humain," (Desonay gives, p. xi-xxi, a brief biographical and literary sketch of D., of his meeting with Ronsard, of his studies with Dorat); and secondly as an " ... événement littéraire aux étonnantes répercussions...," largely on account (p. xxi ff.) of reactions of the Pléiade to theoretical treatise by Sebillet.

Debt to Henri Chamard so considerable throughout Introduction that it is hardly gracious to classify him among " ... ces hommes, qui, pour avoir dénombré tous les arbres, seraient bien empêchés de voir la forêt." (p. vii.) And to consider Emile Roy, who at best wrote several pages on *Deffence*, together with Chamard, as among " ... les spécialistes qui ... ont scruté le dernier mot et la moindre intention du porte-parole de la Brigade..." (p. vii) is a perplexing rapprochement.

— Divers jeux rustiques et autres œuvres poétiques publiés sur l'édition originale de 1558 et augmentés des lettres de l'auteur, avec une Notice de Guillaume Colletet, une Bibliographie et des Notes. Ed. by Adrien Van Bever. Sansot, 1912. 288 p.   1207

Subsequent publications have much diminished value of edition, but it may still be recommended for its reproduction (p. 11-72) of Colletet's life of D., and for useful information contained in *Bibliographie*.

— Divers jeux rustiques. Édition critique par V. L. Saulnier. Lille, Giard; Geneva, Droz, 1947. 220 p.   1208

Excellent edition provided with a full and richly informative introduction, a note giving major variants, well-presented and well-annotated text, *annexe* giving most important sources, and good glossary.

— Les lettres de Joachim du Bellay, publiées pour la première fois d'après les originaux, par Pierre de Nolhac. Charavay, 1883. 102 p.   1209

Publication of ten unedited letters of the poet; precious, rare. First six, addressed to D.'s friend, Jean de Morel, on personal and literary matters; in seventh and eighth he excuses himself to Cardinal du Bellay for publication of *Regrets* which must have caused the prelate some distress in presence of his colleagues; remaining ones deal with ecclesiastical affairs. Appendix contains letters by contemporaries referring to the poet. Cf. below, Nolhac, *Une lettre inédite de Joachim du Bellay*, and *Documents nouveaux sur la Pléiade*.

— Poésies françaises et latines de Joachim du Bellay, avec notice et notes, par Ernest Courbet. Garnier, 1918. 2 v.   1210

Though he admits that edition of Chamard is better organized and clearer than that of Marty-Laveaux, editor states he has adopted latter's arrangement out of gratitude to his teacher in bibliographical science, a principle which does more honor to editor's sense of piety than to his sense of regard for needs of reader. There is a biographical *Notice*; end of v. I reproduces *Brieve exposition*, which Jan Proust wrote for *Recueil de poésies*. Valuable feature of this edition is first modern reproduction of four books of Latin compositions of D.

— Joachim du Bellay : Les Regrets suivi des Antiquitez de Rome. Texte établi, annoté et précédé d'une introduction par Pierre Grimal. Éditions de Cluny, 1948. 296 p.   1211

Well-presented popular edition, containing brief life of poet and Introduction, which help prepare reader to understand mood and intention of the two sonnet sequences. Too much insistence on D.'s worldly ambition—" Du Bellay est pressé " (p. 12); " ... cherche un raccourci à la gloire " (p. 13); " son ambition, le ressort profond de sa vie " (p. 17); " il prend position (in the Deffence) aussi bruyamment que possible " (p. 12). This squares poorly with D.'s modesty, often so touching, and with the editor's own comment on publication of D.'s *Olive*, or, to be more exact, the initial group of fifty sonnets : " Celui-ci est publié prudemment." And after remarks on difficulties of the text for modern reader one expects a somewhat ampler provision of notes. No glossary. Discussion of nature of literary sincerity (p. 29-30) merits attentive consideration.

Critical Works on Du Bellay

Addamiano, Natale. Delle opere poetiche francesi di Joachim du Bellay e delle sue imitazioni italiane. Cagliari, Ledda, 1920, and Paris, Champion, 1921. 260 p.   1212

More than usually loyal to his subject, author states in Preface that he is able to affirm after a careful study of the two poets, that D. is far superior to Ronsard, whose work is largely a nauseating adulation of the powers that be. Ronsard's sins of sycophancy were indeed great, but few men of his time who depended on the court for a living, D. included, were free of this weakness. Apart from this *incartade*, humbly repented in preface to Addamiano's *Il rinascimento in Francia: Pietro Ronsardo* (1524-1585), Rome, Sandron, 1925, book is a normal study of life and work of the poet, following chronological order. Absence in a volume of this size of chapter divisions and of an index is a genuine defect.

Review : J. Plattard in RSS 9:91-92, 1922.

— Quelques sources italiennes de la Deffence de Joachim du Bellay. RLC 3:177-89, 1923.   1213

Intended to complement work of Pierre Villey on Italian sources of *Deffence*, study examines relationship between that work and *Prose* of Bembo, *Cortegiano* of Castiglione, and the dedication by Paulo Manuzio to Diego Hurtado de Mendoza of first part of his edition of philosophical works of Cicero. Demonstration often persuasive, and in case of the address to Mendoza, as compelling as that of Villey. Cf. author's *Delle opere poetiche francesi di Joachim du Bellay*, p. 52-58, for an earlier treatment of similar material.

Adler, Alfred. Du Bellay's Antiquitez XXXI; structure and ideology. BHren 13:191-95, 1951.   1214

Author has invested this relatively simple and unimpressive sonnet with too imposing a scaffolding of analysis. Not easy to

assent to a proposition like the following, which seems to subvert the end of poetry from a presumably aesthetic function to that of providing matter for ideological analysis : " From the point of view of normative criticism, the poem is good inasmuch as its structure becomes the occasion for an ideological analysis " (p. 195).

Aebly, Hedwig. Von der Imitation zur Originalität; Untersuchungen am Werke Joachim du Bellays. Zürich, 1942. 135 p. (Inaug. Diss., Zürich.)   1215

Studies rôle of imitation in *Deffence* and in certain sonnet sequences of D. *(Olive, Antiquitez, Regrets)* with following purposes : " 1. zu beobachten, welche Verwandlung übernommene Stellen und Motiven erfahren; 2. zu verfolgen, wie einzelne, herkömmliche Formen sich bei ihm entwickeln." (p. 5). Author also points out growth of personal element in D.'s poetry : " Was du Bellay in früheren Dichtungen nur in seltenen Momenten war, hier in den ' Regrets ' ist er es ganz " (p. 113). In reality, however, study less evolutional than title implies.

Ambrière, Francis. Joachim du Bellay. Didot, 1930. 202 p.   1216

In spite of author's assertion in *Notes pour le lecteur* that his book is not in the least novelized, one wonders what other adjective would describe it better.

Belloc, Hilaire. Joachim du Bellay. *In his :* April, being essays on the poetry of the French renaissance. London, Sheed & Ward, 1945. p. 69-74.   1217

Composed of three ingredients : pure myth, pure error, and a sediment of truth that somehow has filtered through first two.

Belowski, Eleonore. Du Bellay und Lukrez. *In her :* Lukrez in der französischen Literatur der Renaissance. Berlin, Ebering, 1934. p. 36-45. (RSE, v. 36)   1218

Discusses influence upon the Angevin poet of the Lucretian concept of power of love in cosmos; it describes difficulty in distinguishing, sometimes, between a Virgilian and a Lucretian source; mentions some six or eight passages in which D. appears to have been indebted to Lucretius.

Blanchet, Adrien. Une Faustine à Rome au milieu du XVIᵉ siècle. Aréthuse 2:41-49, Jan., 1925.   1219

Piquant study suggesting that Faustine who bewitched D. in Rome may be identical with the handsome woman whose portrait is seen on a rare Italian medal dating from 16th century. *See* below, Moulié (1271).

Bourdeaut, A. La jeunesse de Joachim du Bellay. MSNA 5th ser. 15:5-225, 1912. *See* 1314. 1220

Thorough investigation of ancestry of the poet on both paternal and maternal sides; of places in Anjou that he celebrated in his compositions (Liré, Drain, Bouzillé, le Marillais, Saint-Florent-le-Vieil, Montjean); of neighboring families, friendly and otherwise; of humanistic influences the poet underwent. Two appendices discuss friends of the poet at Angers, and part played by René du Bellay in death of a certain Boisgency, a bandit in the service of Malestroit family.

— Joachim du Bellay et Olive de Sévigné. MSNA 5th ser. 13:1-54, 1910. 1221

Author asserts against Séché, who identified Olive with Marguerite de France, sister of Henri II, and against Chamard, for whom Olive was without historical reality, that person to whom D. had addressed his first sonnets was poet's cousin, Olive de Sévigné. Hypothesis illuminates many passages in D.'s first sonnet sequence and in other compositions of D. P. 37-54 contain a convincing refutation of position of Séché. *See* Chamard's remarks in his *Histoire de la Pléiade* 1:33 and 232-33.

— Les Malestroit d'Oudon et les Du Bellay de Liré. Oudon et le livre des Regrets. MSNA 5th ser. 14:9-88, 1911. 1222

Shows that an important cause of misfortunes which contributed so much to melancholy tone of *Regrets* was marriage of René du Bellay, Joachim's elder brother, into notorious family of Malestroit, an act which was destined to bring the poet into direct conflict with Connétable de Montmorency.

Bruel, André. Le sentiment de la patrie dans l'œuvre de Joachim du Bellay. MSNA 6th ser. 5:159-71, 1930. 1223

States that D.'s concept of *patrie* went beyond his own province to embrace all of France, and that he was propagator of this concept among his contemporaries.

Brunot, Ferdinand. La première édition lyonnaise du Discours de Du Bellay " sur le faict des quatre estats du Royaume " (1567). RPF 8:89-100, 1894. 1224

Lists various editions of this poem. Greater part of article devoted to an analysis of variants of Lyons edition of 1567, that of Marty-Laveaux being adopted as standard.

Cameron, Alice. Joachim du Bellay. *In* her: The influence of Ariosto's epic and lyric poetry on Ronsard and his group. *See* 1095, p. 94-116. 1225

Second chapter devoted to a chronological discussion of D.'s debt to Ariosto for following periods : 1549-54; Roman period; period following his return to France and until his death. Competent study, though very pedestrian in gait, and somewhat suffocated by choice of a chronological order of exposition, instead of an order determined by subject matter.

Review : P. Jourda in Rcr 97:328-29, 1930.

— A note on Desportes and Du Bellay. MLN 50:378-80, 1935. 1226

Shows debt of Desportes to D. for an image whose ultimate source is in Ariosto's *Orlando furioso*, XXIII, 113.

Chamard, Henri. Un ancien exemplaire de Joachim du Bellay. Rbib 19:154-58, 1909. 1227

Description of a precious *recueil factice* of D. acquired by the Sorbonne in 1909 and containing following four items : 1. *Quatriesme livre de l'Eneide...* together with the *Œuvres de l'invention de l'autheur* (1552); 2. edition of *Deffence*, apparently unique, dating from 1553; 3. *L'Olive augmentée* (2nd ed., 1550) with *Musagnœomachie* and five odes that accompany it; 4. *Anterotique, Vers lyriques* and *Epitaphe de Clement Marot* in a booklet which had originally formed part of a copy of third edition of *Olive* (1554).

— Histoire de la Pléiade. Didier, 1939-40. 4 v. 1228

Crowning publication of a distinguished career devoted to literature of French renaissance and particularly to that of Pléiade and D. Contains substance of Chamard's dissertation on D. modified by results acquired in four decades that had intervened. The *Considérations bibliographiques* (Ch. II), supplemented by generous additional data supplied in notes, of fundamental value in preparation of present article. Like rest of this vast summation of our present knowledge of poetry of French renaissance, sections on D. characterized by gifts rarely found in so harmonious a synthesis : a sovereign sense of balance in literary judgments; a warmth that arises as much from personality of the scholar himself as from meaningfulness of his subject matter; a psychological insight into nature of D. that is at once penetrating and impartial, sympathetic but without sentimentality; and an attitude of equitable magnanimity toward efforts of other students of renaissance, combined with courage required to express a justified negative judgment. At end of v. IV is a valuable *Chronologie de la Pléiade* which begins with year 1469 (birth of Ronsard's father) and ends with years 1629-30 (publications of ninth posthumous edition of works of Ronsard). Followed by *Index analytique des noms et des idées* containing in some eighty pages a remarkably detailed and serviceable guide to contents of the four volumes.

Reviews : R. Lebègue in RHL 52:84-87, 1952; I. Silver in BHren 12:341, 1950. (Brief appreciation.)

— L'invention de l' " ode " et le différend de Ronsard et de Du Bellay. *See* 1096.   1229

Pioneering article that may still be read with great profit. Asserted Ronsard had not invented the French word " ode," but was creator of the ode in France, if by that word we understand poetic form as it was practised in antiquity, and especially by Horace. On the essentials Chamard, in his *Histoire de la Pléiade*, has not modified his views, despite exceptions taken to them by Paul Laumonier in Introduction to his thesis on *Ronsard poète lyrique*, Hachette, 1909[1], 1923[2], 1931[3]. As to alleged quarrel between Ronsard and D. over theft of a sheaf of odes, Chamard had no difficulty in demonstrating unreliability of testimony of Claude Binet, who had initiated the tradition. *Cf.* below, Isidore Silver, *Ronsard and Du Bellay on their Pindaric collaboration* (1322).

— Joachim du Bellay, 1522-1560. Lille, au siège de l'Université, 1900. 545 p.   1230

Great thesis on Angevin poet which inaugurated series of Chamard's works culminating in *Histoire de la Pléiade*. Life of the poet himself naturally suggests two broad divisions of work into periods preceding and following his voyage to Rome in 1553. Author studies simultaneous evolution of the man and poet : difficult childhood, years of retarded education, first literary successes, powerful impression that Rome made upon him,

his life, hopes, and disappointments in the Eternal City, literary productions of this four-year interlude of growing nostalgia, return to France, and last years. Except in matters of detail, which are stated by Chamard himself with perfect candor in his *Histoire* (1:46-47), thesis remains today as robust as it was at beginning of century.

Reviews : P. Laumonier in ALAM 1901, p. 211-17; J. Vianey in RHL 8:151-55, 1901.

— Joachim du Bellay à Poitiers. MélJV. p. 133-38.   1231

Interesting account of an important moment of the life of the poet. Found again in v. I of author's *Histoire de la Pléiade*, p. 91-95.

— Sur une page obscure de la Deffence. RHL 4:239-45, 1897.   1232

Replying to a question by E(mile) R(oy) in RHL 2:468, 1895, Chamard elucidates obscure passage by identifying anonymous poets as C. Marot, Héroët, Bouju, and Scève.

Chambers, Frank M. Lucan and the Antiquitez de Rome. PMLA 60:937-48, Dec., 1945.   1233

Interesting development of article by Vianey, *Les Antiquitez de Rome : leurs sources latines et italiennes* (*see* 1331), demonstrating that D.'s material debt to Lucan greater than had been supposed, and that the Latin poet may even have been primarily responsible for inspiration of this sequence of sonnets.

Clédat, Léon. Le musée de sculptures du Cardinal Du Bellay à Rome.   CDA 3:99-100, 206-07, 1883.   1234

Extract from a document dated May 29, 1556 in the *Archivio di stato* in Rome listing 134 items of sculpture, ancient and modern, sold to Cardinal Du Bellay by Pietro della Stampa for 1000 gold crowns, Interesting both for history of art and for light it sheds on milieu in which the poet lived. *See* Pichon and Vicaire, 80, 1284.

Clément, Louis. Le poète courtisan de Joachim du Bellay. Rren 5:225-65, 1904.   1235

Asserts with much probability against Séché (*La vie de Joachim*, 1318), that object of D.'s raillery in *Le poète courtisan* was Charles Fontaine, not Mellin de Saint-Gelais, and that date of composition was 1559, not 1550.

Derocquigny, J. Quelques notes à la Deffence de Du Bellay. RHL 11:652-53, 1904.   1236
Notes suggested by a reading of the *Deffence* in the first critical edition by Chamard.

Duhem, Jules. Le premier poète de l'aviation; essai sur les éditions de Sannazar, de Tansillo et de Joachim du Bellay. BBB 1946, p. 157-63.   1237
Incorrect attribution to D. of priority in introduction into France in 1560 of poetry of "aviation," i.e. of Icarus legend. Ronsard had employed the theme ten years earlier.

Elcock, W. D. English indifference to Du Bellay's Regrets. MLR 46:175-84, 1951.   1238
Represents very sound reaction against sentimental verbalism of Walter Pater's essay on D. in *The renaissance* (1281). Author wonders, probably with justification, whether Pater had any first-hand acquaintance with *Regrets*; and shows that this lack of recognition had very largely characterized preceding generations of English literature back to Elizabethan period. Article concludes with speculations as to reasons for this neglect.

Espiner-Scott, Janet G. Some notes on Du Bellay. MLR 36:59-67, 1941.   1239
Scattered notes on poet's literary sources and on his social, vocational, and sexual adjustments.

Fletcher, Jefferson B. Areopagus and Pléiade. JEGP 2:429-53, 1898-99.   1240
On the basis of Spenser-Harvey correspondence of 1579-80, asserts existence in England at that time of a coterie of poets, the Areopagus, much influenced by Pléiade, whose poetry they imitated and whose principles they adopted; devotion to Platonic conception of nature of poetry; a linguistic transformation characterized by poetic archaism, a taste for neologisms and a preference for classical allusion; cultivation of genres favored by Pléiade.

Foulché-Delbosc, Raymond. Notes sur le sonnet Superbi colli. Rhisp 11:225-43, 1904.   1241
Besides the sonnet *Sacrez costaux* ... which Morel-Fatio (RHL 1:97-102, 1894) had shown to be indebted to this Italian sonnet by Baldassare Castiglione, author finds genuine reminiscences of it in two

other pieces of D., and then goes on to trace its fortune in England, Spain, and France.

François, Alexis. Les sonnets suisses de Joachim du Bellay expliqués et commentés. Lausanne, Librairie de l'Université, 1946. 123 p.   1242
Interesting discussion of two groups of sonnets by D. inspired by his passage through Switzerland on return from Rome, and by a sonnet, allegedly that of a Calvinist, accusing him of impiety and other offensive qualities. Useful appendix contains a number of contemporary documents. *See* 2885.

Froger, Louis. Les hommes de lettres au XVIe siècle dans le diocèse du Mans : Joachim du Bellay. Rren 4:47-54, 1903.   1243
Study of Archives of department of Sarthe to determine benefices possessed by D. in Le Mans.

Fucilla, Joseph G. A sonnet in Du Bellay's Antiquitez de Rome. MLN 61:260-62, 1946.   1244
Presents evidence demonstrating that both Chamard and Foulché-Delbosc were correct in supposing, respectively, that D. was indebted to Lazzaro Bonamici and to Baldassare Castiglione for his sonnet *Toy qui de Rome....*

— Sources of Du Bellay's Contre les Pétrarquistes. MP 28:1-11, 1930-31.   1245
Asserts that Mellin de Saint-Gelais and Bembo were important sources of this poem, but that D. drew upon his own earlier work and upon that of Ronsard and Petrarch for objects of his satire. *See* 2730.

Hallays, André. Le "petit Lyré" de Joachim du Bellay. Jdéb, May 24, 1912, p. 1.   1246
Sensitive account of a visit to the D. country : "le petit Lyré"—a pleasant village on the Loire near Ancenis; la Turmelière—site of ruins of manorhouse in which poet was born.

Herriot, Edouard. Défence et illustration de la langue française. RevHM 12:1-6, May, 1950.   1247
Erudite statesman sees in the *Deffence*, at commemoration of its fourth centenary, expression of poet's patriotic magnification of his native tongue. Now that effects of the late war have begun to recede, language and literature of France are recovering

their eminent place in world letters, and shade of D. may rejoice.

Hill, Raymond Thompson. The influence of the Noie on the poetry of Joachim du Bellay. EssAF, p. 85-92. 1248

Finds clear evidence, particularly in *Regrets*, of poet's acquaintance, perhaps by way of Italian literature, with the Provençal *Noie* and *Plazer*.

Hulubei, Alice. Virgile en France au xvie siècle : éditions, traductions, imitations RSS 18:1-77, 1931. 1249

Contains a brief but careful study (p. 39-42) of D.'s mediocre translations of Virgil. The *Bibliographie des versions de Virgile en France au XVIe siècle* (p. 74-77) is valuable.

Jacoubet, Henri. Pourquoi Du Bellay s'est-il rajeuni ? MAT 12th ser. 10:25-31, 1932. 1250

Rather feeble hypothesis that D. pretended to be younger than he was out of a sense of shame at being so far behind his coevals in educational achievements.

Jasinski, René. Sur la composition des Regrets. MélAL, p. 339-48. 1251

Valuable and illuminating analysis of " logique profonde " of the order of sonnets in *Regrets*. Study might have gained by taking into account investigation by Bourdeaut (*Les Malestroit d'Oudon*, 1222), on one of the causes of melancholy tone that characterizes this sonnet sequence.

Krappe, Alexander Haggerty. Une source virgilienne de la Défence et Illustration de la langue française de Joachim du Bellay (Liv. II, Chap. 12). RSS 15:342-43, 1928. 1252

Shows last chapter of poet's manifesto owed much to *Georgics* 2:149-70.

Langeard, Paul. Joachim du Bellay à Louis des Masures : un sonnet oublié. BBB ns 10:108-10, 1931. 1253

Reproduces D.'s sonnet *Autant comme l'on peut en un autre langage* from liminary pages of translation of *Aeneid* made in 1560 by Des Masures. Overlooked by editors of D.

Lebègue, Raymond. Dans l'entourage de Du Bellay. BHren 4:171-76, 1944. 1254

Brings to light a hitherto unedited sonnet of D. addressed to Jacques de La Taille. First appeared at end of latter's *Alexandre* published in 1573 by his brother, Jean.

— Horace en France pendant la renaissance. Hren 3:141-64; 289-308 ; 384-419, 1936 1255

Valuable study, rich in materials. *See* especially p. 293-95 for a succinct statement of D.'s debt to Horace. Published separately by E. Droz in 1936 under same title.

Le Bourgo, Léo. De Joach. Bellaii latinis poematis. Cognac, Bérauld, 1903. 64 p. 1256

Discusses life and personality of D. as revealed in his Latin compositions, as well as nature and manners of the Roman society that he frequented, book of *Amores* inspired by Faustine, and why D. wrote in Latin at all after his energetic exhortations to his countrymen to avoid writing in ancient languages. Author puts aside graceful rationalizations of D. and Sainte-Beuve (p. 38), and states what appears to him to be genuine, if very simple, reason : " Nec rursus mirum si, postquam latinos poetas admiratus erat, aemulatione generosa instinctus, iisdem pressis vestigiis, iisdem armis, lingua eadem instructus, eorumdem famam paribus artibus assequi tentaverit " (p. 41-42).

L., C. [Charles Lenient ?] Du Bellay : 1525-1560. *In :* Les poetes français : Recueil des chefs-d'œuvre de la poésie française depuis les origines jusqu'à nos jours une notice littéraire sur chaque poëte ... publié sous la direction de M. Eugène Crépet. Quantin, 1887. v. 2, p. 55-62. 1257

Author shows how much Malherbe and his generation owed to that of D., and writes a brief appreciation of career and work of the poet.

Leonetti, A. Le sonnet du " petit Lyré " : variations sur l' " air marin." RU 57:146-150, 1948. 1258

Believes " air marin " of last line of D.'s famous sonnet, *Heureux qui comme Ulysse ...* identified with spring and summer wind known as the Ponentino. *See* same periodical for 1949, p. 15-16, for an exchange of correspondence between author and Jean Mougeot on value of this identification.

Leroy, André. Une amitié littéraire : Ronsard et Du Bellay. MélPL, p. 219-42. 1259

Sympathetic study of relations of the two poets which brings out differences in character that made a perfect intimacy between them impossible.

Letessier, Fernand. Note sur la première rencontre de Ronsard et Du Bellay. RU 59:85-87, 1950.   1260

Rejects both traditional date of 1549 given by Binet in his *Vie de Ronsard* (p. 14-15 of Laumonier edition) for meeting of the two poets, and date of 1547 suggested by Chamard, in favor of March 5 or 6, 1543, when the young men may have met at obsequies of Guillaume du Bellay. Presence of Joachim is only hypothetical, and even if it were established beyond question, would not of itself be positive proof that he had then met Pierre. A position resting upon two conjectures loses plausibility with geometrical rapidity.

Lüken, Erich. Du Bellays Deffence et illustration de la langue françoyse in ihrem Verhältnis zu Sebillet's Art poétique. Oldenburg i. Gr., Littmann, 1913. 64 p.   1261

Methodical comparison from points of view of theory, genre, style, and versification.

McPeek, James A. S. The major sources of Spenser's Epithalamion. JEGP 35:183-213, 1936.   1262

Earlier analyses " do not consider fully enough the debt of Spenser to other poets of his time, particularly to La Pléiade... " (p. 183-84). Article of careful workmanship; author supplies a number of Spenser's sources, hitherto unnoticed, in D., Ronsard, and Remy Belleau, but majority are from Buttet.

Merrill, Robert V. Considerations on Les amours de I. du Bellay. MP 33:129-38, 1935-36.   1263

Author presents well-reasoned argument for identifying person to whom D. addressed twenty-nine sonnets of this group with Diane de France, duchesse de Montmorency.

— Du Bellay's Olive CXII and the Rime diverse. MLN 60:527-30, Dec. 1945. 1264

Discusses D.'s immediate debt to a sonnet by Veronica Gambara which appeared in both editions of *Rime di diversi*... Giolito di Ferrarii MDXLVII and MDXLVIII, and ultimate debt to Saint Paul's *Epistle to the Romans*, VIII, v, 28 ff., for greater part of sonnet CXII of the *Olive. See* 2699.

— Jean Lemaire, Du Bellay, and the second Georgic. MLN 51:453-55, 1936.   1265

D. indebted to Lemaire, and through him to Virgil, for image of a forest fire in sonnet XIII of his *Amours*.

— Lucian and Du Bellay's Poète courtisan. MP 29:11-20, 1931-32.   1266

Turnèbe's Latin composition addressed to Léger Duchesne : *De nova captandae utilitatis e literis ratione epistola* (1550), a satire directed against Pierre de Paschal, and D.'s *Poète courtisan*, probably of same date, were both based on the *Rhetoron didaskalos* of Lucian, or on some intervening model of Lucianic tone.

— A note on the Italian genealogy of Du Bellay's Olive, sonnet CXIII. MP 24:163-166, 1926-27.   1267

Traces filiation from Petrarch's sonnet *O tempo, o ciel volubil che fuggendo* (*Canzoniere* CCCLV) through Sannazaro and Daniello to famous sonnet CXIII of *Olive : Si nostre vie est moins qu'une journée. See* 2698.

— The Platonism of Joachim du Bellay. *See* 741.   1268

Sound and thoughtful work. First chapter provides some fundamental definitions and distinctions and very useful lists of Greek editions and French translations of Plato's *Dialogues*, and of Italian and French Platonistic works. Having thus forged instruments of his research, author considers in following chapters the Platonistic concepts in works of D. (the cosmos, the nature of beauty and virtue, the soul), and sources, development, and character of his Platonism. Discussion clear and vigorous, rises easily to highest levels of Plato's thought, and evaluates sympathetically and fairly the presence of that thought in poetry of D. Lacks bibliography and index. *See* 2574.

Review : H. Harvitt in MLN 42:138-139, 1927.

Moreau, Pierre. En marge de trois vers latins des Regrets. MélHC, p. 71-79. 1269

Commentary on Latin composition *Ad lectorem* which precedes the *Regrets*. On basis of detailed study of these sonnets author shows how exact was D.'s assertion that his book was composed of spleen, honey, and salt. Admirably complement René Jasinski's study, *Sur la composition des Regrets (see* 1251).

Morel-Fatio, Alfred. Histoire d'un sonnet RHL 1:97-102, 1894.   1270

Proves that a manuscript fragment of Italian sonnet *Superbi colli*, not an unfinished exercise of the poet, but part of an incompletely transcribed sonnet by Baldassare Castiglione. *See* above, article by Foulché-Delbosc (1241) which amplifies greatly the account, lightly sketched by Morel-Fatio, of the fortune of this Italian sonnet.

Moulié, Charles. Joachim du Bellay à Rome : Les amours de Faustine. RCIL 29:470-80, 1920.   1271

Narrates story of D.'s alleged liaison with Roman matron, Faustine. Adds nothing to our knowledge, but in the course of article author correctly observes that French literature of 16th century has a Neo-Latin twin that has been undeservedly forgotten. On Faustine *cf.* above, Blanchet, *Une Faustine à Rome.* (1219)

Nagel, Heinrich. Die Strophenbildung Baïfs im Vergleich mit der Ronsard's, Du Bellay's und Remy Belleau's. Archiv 61:439-462, 1879.   1272

Describes Baïf's use of strophes varying in length from three to fourteen lines. Each strophe studied for rhyme scheme and metrics, comparisons made with practices of Ronsard, D., and Belleau.

Neri, Ferdinando. Nota ai Regrets. Ath 7:185-93, 1919.   1273

Adds observation or two to reinforce position of Vianey in *La part de l'imitation dans les Regrets* (1333), that D.'s originality in the composition of this sequence not as absolute as he would have had reader imagine. But Neri's remarks on nature of personal relationship between Ronsard and D. seem somewhat idealized. This essay included in author's *Letteratura e leggende*, Turin, Chiantore, 1951. p. 225-232.

Nitze, William A. The sources of the ninth sonnet of Les regrets. MLN 39:216-19, 1924.   1274

First line of sonnet in question *(France, mere des arts, des armes & des loix)* traced to a passage in Petrarch's *Hymn to Italy :* " Armorum legumque eadem veneranda sacrarum/Pyeridumque domus." *See* 2734.

Nolhac, Pierre de. Un centenaire oublié : Joachim du Bellay. RDM 92 (7th ser. v. 12) : 71-86, Nov. 1, 1922.   1275

Author moved to write article so that fourth centenary of D.'s birth might not pass quite unobserved. No new contribution to our knowledge of the poet but reader relives some of more famous incidents of his life, and sees him in relation to contemporaries who were closest to him : Ronsard, Magny, Cardinal Du Bellay, and others.

— Documents nouveaux sur la Pléiade : Ronsard, Du Bellay. RHL 6:351-61, 1899. 1276

Of three documents presented, only last relates to D. It is a letter from the poet to Jean de Morel asking him to have printed " une coppie de la transformation de la nymphe Veronis en la fontaine de Veron... " (p. 360), a Latin composition of D.

— Une lettre inédite de Joachim du Bellay. RHL 1:49-51, 1894.   1277

Publication of an additional letter throwing light on difficulties experienced by the poet in carrying out his task of representing Cardinal Du Bellay in administration of diocese of Paris. Will be best understood if read in conjunction with P. de Nolhac's *Lettres de Joachim du Bellay*, 1883.

Noo, Hendrik de. Thomas Sebillet et son Art poétique françoys rapproché de la Deffence et illustration de la langue françoyse de Joachim du Bellay. Utrecht, Beijers, 1927. 162 p. (Diss., Amsterdam.)   1278

Introductory chapter on Marot and the *marotiques*; discussions of various technical aspects and genres of French poetry according to Sebillet; detailed comparisons between his poetic theory and that of D. Studies of Chamard, of Gaiffe, and earlier, almost identical work of Lüken (1261), of whose existence author appears to have been unaware, have left little genuinely new to be said on subject.

Reviews : F. Gaiffe in RHL 38:108-10, 1931; J. Plattard in RSS, 14:409-10, 1927.

Outrey, Amédée. Joachim du Bellay et la fontaine de Véron. RSS 19:246-61, 1932-33.   1279

Describes a document in the form of a letter (September 1, 1558) from Jean Penon to the poet, mentioning forthcoming publication by a printer (Gilles Richeboys) of Sens, of Latin poem by D. entitled *Veronis in fontem sui nominis.* Library of Auxerre possesses a *tirage à part* of this composition. *See* P. de Nolhac, *Documents nouveaux sur la Pléiade* (1276).

— Recherches sur la maison habitée par Joachim du Bellay au cloître Notre-Dame. BSHP 61:76-102, 1934.   1280

Exceedingly careful investigation establishing that from 1557 until his death D. shared with Claude de Bèze, an Angevin and protégé, like himself, of Cardinal Du Bellay, a house called " maison des Trousseaulx " in Cloître Notre-Dame, a slight distance northeast of apse of the cathedral.

Pater, Walter Horatio. Joachim du Bellay. *In his:* The renaissance; studies in art and poetry. *See* 134, p. 162-85.   1281

Essay in *haute vulgarisation* which should be read with caution by those whose acquaintance with D. and the Pléiade is young. Too much quaintness, weirdness, and daintiness in Pater's conception of French renaissance and of its poetry. One learns with surprise of transparency of D.'s prose. Evaluation of Ronsard's work as characterized by " an exquisite faintness, *une fadeur exquise,*" not less astonishing. For sound comments on Pater's study *see:* W. D. Elcock's article, *English indifference to Du Bellay's Regrets* (1238).

Perrotin, Léo. Pour Didon : Sur quatre vers d'Ausone traduits par Joachim du Bellay. MélPL, p. 189-200.   1282

Elaborates a passage in D.'s *Epistre* to Jean de Morel which introduces poet's translation of two books of the *Aeneid* and in which D. states he added a version of an epigram of Ausonius in order that true account of Dido's chastity might counteract false one made current by Virgil.

Pflänzel, Max. Über die Sonette des Joachim Du Bellay, nebst einer Einleitung: Die Einführung des Sonetts in Frankreich. Saalfeld (Saale), 1898. 87 p.   1283

After introduction incorrectly asserting priority of Mellin de Saint-Gelais in the French sonnet, author discusses form, content, and character, of genre as treated by D. Final chapter evaluates D. as a sonneteer.

Pichon, Jérome, et Georges Vicaire. Documents pour servir à l'histoire des libraires de Paris, 1486-1600. BBB, 1894, p. 26-44.   1284

Contains (p. 38-40) inventory dated July 2, 1560 of volumes that had belonged to Cardinal Du Bellay, and so may have an indirect bearing on our knowledge of books accessible to the poet. *See* 80, 1234.

Ploetz, Gustavus Carl. Étude sur Joachim du Bellay et son rôle dans la réforme de Ronsard. Halle, n.d. also Berlin, 1874. (Inaug. diss., Halle.)   1285

Slight work, superannuated, containing errors that might have been avoided by attention. Halle edition partial (32 p.); complete Berlin edition contains 68 p.

Raibaud, Gabriel. Glanes dans les Regrets de J. du Bellay. RU 49:120-27, 1940-1941.   1286

Comments on probable borrowing of Ronsard from D., of Racine from Ronsard, and of all of them from Ovid; on D.'s taste for punning (but is there any real ground for saying that the Regrets reawakened Ronsard's similar taste ? Had it ever been dormant ?); his gift for finding the " côté éternel " in an ordinary metaphor; his impressions of the Asiatic buffalo, common in renaissance Rome.

Raymond, Marcel. Ronsard et Du Bellay. *See* 1172.   1287

Study of influence of Ronsard on works of D., substance of which eventually formed part of author's thesis, *L'influence de Ronsard sur la poésie française (1550-1585)* (1170). Yielding to a natural tendency to find in Ronsard as many sources of D. as he can, author does not sufficiently envisage possibility of reciprocal influences. (*Cf.* below, the article by I. Silver, *Ronsard imitator of Du Bellay,* 1323.)

Renwick, W. L. Mulcaster and Du Bellay. MLR 17:282-87, 1922.   1288

Points out identity between ideas of Spenser's teacher, Mulcaster, in *The first part of the elementarie* (1582) and those of D.'s *Deffence* in respect to nature of language, to classics, and introduction of new words into their respective languages.

Rivière, Jacques. Portrait de Joachim du Bellay. NRF 7²:519-22, Apr. 1, 1912. *Also in his:* Nouvelles études, 9th edition, Gallimard, 1947. p. 29-31.   1289

Somewhat idealized; on the whole, true and delicate appreciation of poet's personality.

Rosenbauer, A. Die poetischen Theorien der Plejade nach Ronsard und Du Bellay; ein Beitrag zur Geschichte der Renaissancepoetik in Frankreich. *See* 1056.   1290

Despite fact that D.'s name figures in title, study almost exclusively devoted to Ronsard's theory of poetry. References to

D., though frequent, are incidental. Useful as a guide to Ronsard's various theoretical statements, book appears to have been put together hastily and contains many erroneous references.

Rouault, Joseph. Découverte d'un important inédit latin de Joachim du Bellay (1559). Eur, Dec., 1933. (No pagination.) 1291

Photographic reproduction, palaeographic transcription, and translation of manuscript poem (v. 736, f. 253 r⁰ of *Fonds Dupuy* of the BN) attributed to D. Page reproduced bears title *Ecclesiae querimonia*, under which appears, in a different and clearer hand, " per Joach. Bellay. 1559." If the attribution is well-founded, this composition of six elegiac distichs makes an interesting addition to D.'s criticism of Church and Papacy in *Regrets*, by revealing his impatience with interminable deliberations of Council of Trent. Commentary supplied by author useful, but we wonder whether he was justified in taking as basis of his translation, not the authentically 16th-century document, but a copy " en écriture moderne." This was the less justifiable because the modern copy (v. 697, f. 371 r⁰, *Fonds Dupuy*) contains a full distich of tendentious character which is not in the earlier version.

— L'humanisme de Joachim du Bellay, Angevin, et l'amour de la nature; Joachim du Bellay au jardin de l'humanisme. Eur, May-June, 1936. (No pagination.) 1292

D. learned to love nature from contemporary writers, but most especially from Cardinal Jean Du Bellay, who was an ardent cultivator. Substance of article is a reproduction of D.'s *Votum rusticum : Iolas.*

— L'humanisme de Joachim du Bellay Angevin et le regret de la patrie. RQH 64:42-62, Jan., 1936. 1293

Points out parallelism between D.'s Latin poem *Patriae desiderium* and many sonnets in the *Regrets;* shows that Alciati, Sannazaro, Flaminio, Dolet, L'Hôpital, Dorat, and Cardinal Du Bellay, not to mention Ovid, preceded D. in writing in Latin on theme of nostalgia.

— Larmes sur les soldats tombés en la bataille de Saint-Quentin : poème latin de Joachim du Bellay. Eur, Aug., 1933. (No pagination.) 1294

Good translation in free verse, preceded by half page of explanatory historical comment, of D.'s moving poem on those who fell in the vain defense of St. Quentin in 1557.

— La philosophie humaniste de Joachim du Bellay : regards sur la mort. Eur, Jan.-Feb., 1934. (No pagination.) 1295

Language excessive in sentimentality; author, on basis of two Latin epitaphs, imposes on D. an elaborate philosophy of Love, Death, and Nature revolving upon a center of pure nonsense.

— La philosophie humaniste de Joachim du Bellay : regards sur la vie. Eur, Sept.-Oct., 1934. (No pagination.) 1296

Good essay, less rhapsodic style than customary with this author; containing little new on subject of D.'s conception of *otium* and on his nostalgia for France during sojourn at Rome. A prose translation of D.'s Latin elegy *In vitae quietoris commendationem.*

— Sous le signe de Coqueret : premiers documents originaux sur le Collège de Coqueret. Eur, Oct., 1933. (No pagination.) 1297

Reproduction, with prose translations, of three Latin poems, two addressed to Robert Dugast, one to Gervais Rétien, principal and regent, respectively, of Collège de Coqueret. Poems the work of Hubert Sussanneau (or Sussannée) and appeared in a volume by him entitled *Ludorum libri* published by Simon de Colines in 1538. A fourth poem, inscribed *Ad auditores pictanicos,* is an exhortation to his Poitevin students to work earnestly in field of humanities. Compositions in honor of his two superiors are expressions of adulation which every student of renaissance has read to satiety. To speak of Sussanneau as " une figure de premier plan de l'humanisme du temps " is to provide Guillaume Budé, Henri Estienne, and Erasmus with an unexpected colleague.

Roy, Emile. Charles Fontaine et ses amis; sur une page obscure de la Deffence. *See* 705. 1298

Accepts conclusions of Henri Chamard, *Sur une page obscure de la Deffence (see* 1232), except that for Bouju he would substitute the name of Charles Fontaine.

— Lettre d'un Bourguignon contemporaine de la Deffence et illustration de la langue françoyse. RHL 2:233-43, 1895. 1299

Coup d'état is rare in the republic of letters. Way had long been prepared for *Deffence,* many of whose ideas were already common property in 1548. As proof, author reproduces a letter written in that year by a certain Jacques de Beaune, in which some general ideas of *Deffence* are found.

Ruutz-Rees, Caroline. Some debts of Samuel Daniel to Du Bellay. MLN 24:134-37, 1909.   1300

Good discussion of some of Daniel's borrowings from D., who was himself indebted to Ariosto, and use of similar material by Ronsard and Desportes.

Sainati, Augusto. Iacopo Sannazaro e Joachim du Bellay. Pisa, Spoerri, 1915. 71 p.   1301

Reminiscent, as to method, of *Parallel lives* of Plutarch. Study attempts to bring out similarities of character : sensitivity, love of nature, desire for a life of quiet contemplation, patriotism; and of literary production : resemblance, for example, between Sannazaro's elegy *Ad ruinas Cumarum* and D.'s *Antiquitez de Rome*, or between invective of former and latter's gift for satire.

Saint-Denis, E. de. Des vers latins de Hildebert aux Antiquités de J. du Bellay. EC 8:352-58, 1939.   1302

Plausible conjecture that D.'s thirteenth sonnet of the *Antiquitez de Rome* is indebted to a passage by Hildebert on ruins of that city (*Patrologie Migne*, v. 171, p. 1409).

Sainte-Beuve, Charles Augustin. Joachim du Bellay. RDM 24:161-90, Oct. 15, 1940. *Also in his :* Tableau historique et critique de la poésie française et du théâtre français au XVIᵉ siècle. See 2289, p. 333-64.   1303

Study of considerable literary wisdom; correctly assesses merits of the poet and usually avoids pitfalls left by a faulty tradition. Sainte-Beuve recounts, after Bayle, who in turn follows Binet, dubious story of a lawsuit brought by Ronsard against D. for recovery of a stolen sheaf of odes, but rejects it as improbable and not in character of poet of Anjou. In attributing D.'s death to the departure of Madame Marguerite for Savoy, we may have the origin of Séché's infatuation with the idea that Marguerite de France was Olive. (*See* above, articles of Séché and Bourdeaut, 1221.)

— Œuvres françoises de Joachim du Bellay, gentilhomme angevin, avec une Notice biographique et des Notes par M. Ch. Marty-Laveaux.   JS 1867, April, p. 205-21; June,

p. 344-59; August, p. 483-503. *Also in his :* Nouveaux lundis, Lévy, 1870, v. 13, p. 266-356.   1304

Study occasioned by publication of first volume of *Collection de la Pléiade* by Marty-Laveaux. Records transformation of French attitude toward generation of Ronsard and D. which had occurred in four decades that had elapsed since appearance of Sainte-Beuve's *Tableau historique* (1828); defends, against Léon Gautier, reputation for patriotism of writers of French renaissance; describes evolution toward classical doctrine accomplished by Pléiade; criticizes weaknesses of *Deffence;* and recognizes what is loftiest in its message. Sainte-Beuve still has much to say to us.

Samaran, Ch. Un document notarié sur Joachim du Bellay (5 décembre 1559). MélAL, p. 349-53.   1305

Text of a document according to whose terms Claude du Bellay, nephew of the poet, grants to his uncle and to his aunt, Catherine du Breuil, sister of Joachim, an annual income of 600 *livres tournois*.

Saulnier, V. L. Les Antiquitez de Rome de Joachim du Bellay. Centre de documentation universitaire, 1950. 93 p.   1306

With great amplitude, author discusses fecundity of D.'s Roman period, analysis of the Roman *milieu* with its attractions and disappointments, date of composition of this sequence of sonnets, intentions of the poet, his understanding and presentation of Roman history, and matters of imagery and style.

— Brantôme et Joachim du Bellay. BBB 1951, p. 107-25.   1306A

On Brantôme's quotations, translations, commentaries, and imitations of D., and on copies, containing numerous unedited variants, of certain of the Angevin's compositions found in manuscript of Brantôme's *Recueil d'aulcunes rymes* (BN, *Nouvelles acquis. franç.*, No. 11688).

— Commentaire sur les Antiquitez de Rome. BHren 12:114-43, 1950.   1307

Author has studied the *Antiquitez* with unusual thoroughness under following headings : I. Mythological, historical, and geographical allusions; II. Zoological references; III. Metaphysical sonnets; IV. Meteorological sonnets; V. Influence of Petrarch and Lucretius; VI. Stylistic difficulties; VII. Significance of the title; VIII. Relationship between the *Antiquitez* and the *Regrets*. Saulnier sheds light on many a difficult passage of these sonnets. Some of this commentary appears also in author's *Les antiquitez de Rome* de Joachim du Bellay (*see* 1306).

— Du Bellay, l'homme et l'œuvre. Boivin, 1951. 167 p. 1308

Useful presentation of life and work of D. One chapter of biography, followed by several which analyze and paraphrase works of the poet chronologically. Description of *Deffence* as a text more influential by its tone than its content is probably exact. One is less willing to accept the assertion that the allegedly synchronous composition of *Antiquitez, Regrets*, and *Jeux rustiques* was result of a " calcul minutieux " (p. 73). Last chapter, *L'art personnel*, seems most rewarding and contains greatest personal contribution of author. Bibliography over-condensed and occasionally confusing.

Reviews : F. Desonay in BHren 13:395-397, 1951; P. Jourda in RHL 53:233-34, 1953.

— Introduction à l'étude de Joachim du Bellay. IL, Jan.-Feb., 1950, p. 1-7. 1309

Describes available scholarly literature on D., notably that furnished by researches of Henri Chamard; proposes diversion of attention from certain problems that had interested earlier students of the poet (identity of Olive, origins of Joachim and his family) to those which deal with his temperament, with a closer study of certain aspects of *Deffence*, with the poet in relation to his time, with his evolution; discusses difficulty, variety, sincerity, novelty, power, and modernity of D.'s work. Interesting discussion which assures us that the study of D., soundly based upon investigations of Henri Chamard, will continue to go forward.

— Sur deux poèmes des Jeux rustiques de Joachim du Bellay. RU 59:265-71, 1950. 1310

Studies of *Contre une vieille* and *Le vœu d'un vanneur de blé* as representative of satirical and graceful aspects, respectively, of *Divers jeux rustiques*. Valuable details on bibliography of first and on the fortune of second.

Séché, Léon. La famille de J. du Bellay. Rren 11:105-06, 1910. 1311

Notes which complete and rectify earlier studies by the author on same subject (*see* 1312).

— Joachim du Bellay. Didier, 1880. 60 p. 1312

Contains early versions of a number of subjects (*Le petit Lyré, Angevins et Bretons de la Loire, Origine et généalogie de la famille du Bellay*, etc.) that author was to develop later in pages of *Rren* which he founded in 1900.

— L'Olive de J. Du Bellay; lettre ouverte à M. l'Abbé Bourdeaut, vicaire à Nozay (Loire-Inférieure). Rren 11:1-21, 1910. 1313

Intemperate reply to article by Abbé Bourdeaut (*Joachim du Bellay et Olive de Sévigné*—1221 above and *cf.* also *JAn* for January, 1910 and *RAn* for August of that year, in which article originally appeared). Séché's letter itself occupies only first six pages. Rest is a reproduction of most important passages from Abbé's article accompanied by Séché's commentary " dont le moins qu'on puisse dire est qu'il manque totalement de sérénité scientifique." (Chamard, *Histoire de la Pléiade* 1:232, note 8).

— Les origines de Joachin (sic) Du Bellay. Rren 1:9-31, 1901. 1314

Interesting for genealogy of the poet and for an appreciation of region in which he grew up, but must be carefully checked by studies of Abbé Bourdeaut, especially his *La jeunesse de Joachim du Bellay*, p. 17, note 2. (*See* 1220.)

— Le pays de Joachim du Bellay. Rren 2:82-93, 169-80, 213-33, 1902. 1315

Descriptions of la Turmelière, of Ancenis, of Lyré; early history of region; qualities of its inhabitants as shown in their proverbs; influence of environment on the poet. Substance of these articles reproduced in author's *Recherches sur la Pléiade : Joachim du Bellay et la Bretagne-Angevine* (n.p., n.d.).

— Sur la dame qui fut Olive. Rren 1:239-241, 1901. 1316

Unconvincing identification of Olive with Marguerite de France. *Cf.* Abbé Bourdeaut's *Joachim du Bellay et Olive de Sévigné* (no. 1221) and J. B. Tielrooy's *De celle qui fut Olive* (no. 1326), two studies written independently of each other, but in agreement against position of Séché. *See* discussion by Chamard in his *Histoire de la Pléiade* 1:231-33.

— Sur la prononciation du mot Joachim. Rren 1:8, 72, 1901. 1317

Abortive attempt to change spelling of poet's name to Joachin in order to stabilize its pronunciation.

— La vie de Joachim du Bellay. Rren 1:73-93, 129-162, 1901.   1318

Did not add materially to body of information available on the poet, coming as it did a year after publication of Chamard's thesis. Disfigured by an unjustified polemical attitude against latter's researches.

Silver, Isidore. Did Du Bellay know Pindar? PMLA 56:1007-19, Dec., 1941.   1319

Strives to prove that D. knew the odes of Pindar independently of Ronsard and that contrary hypothesis, namely, that evidence of Pindar in works of D. results from imitation of Ronsard, leads to inextricable difficulties.

— Du Bellay and Hellenic poetry; a cursory view. PMLA 60:66-80, 356-63, 670-81, 949-58, 1945.   1320

Matter contained in this series sufficiently indicated in names of separate articles : I, *The poet's Hellenizing program and his translations from Homer.* II, *Allusions to, and imitations of, the non-lyric poets of Greece.* III, *The poet's knowledge of the theory and methodology of the Greek ode.* IV, *Imitations of the Greek lyric poets.*

— Pindaric parallelism in Du Bellay : a proof of his independent imitation of Pindar. FR 14:461-72, 1940-41.   1321

In his *Ode sur la naissance du petit duc de Beaumont* and again in his *Ode au prince de Melphe,* D. has employed same motifs borrowed from fifth Pythian ode of Pindar, and ignored by Ronsard.

— Ronsard and Du Bellay on their Pindaric collaboration. RR 33:3-25, 1942.   1322

Attempts to establish by a close examination of early texts of the two poets that in spite of D.'s frequent assertions that lofty Pindaric style was inaccessible to him, he did, in fact, and with encouragement of Ronsard, imitate Pindar both as to form and substance.

— Ronsard imitator of Du Bellay. SP 38:165-87, 1941.   1323

Suggests that there may be too facile a tendency to suppose, in cases of similarity between compositions of Ronsard and D., that latter is borrower. Discussion leads to an investigation of validity of

dates assigned by Paul Laumonier to certain compositions of Ronsard : the *Hymne triumphal sur le trepas de Marguerite de Valois* and the ode *Aux cendres de Marguerite de Valois.*

Steiner, Arpad. Glosses on Du Bellay. MP 24:167-71, 1926-27.   1324

Indicates, sometimes on rather tenuous grounds, obligation of D. to Catullus, Horace, Virgil, and others for parts of the sonnet *Heureux qui comme Ulysse...*; and, on even more tenuous grounds, to Angeriano for his conception of the ideal poet.

Stemplinger, Eduard. Joachim du Bellay und Horaz. Archiv 112:80-93, 1904.   1325

Only article devoted exclusively to study of relationship between D. and Horace. Solidly documented. Table of parallels at end should be especially useful. May be supplemented by Raymond Lebègue's *Horace en France pendant la renaissance,* 1255.

Tielrooy, J. B. De celle qui fut Olive. Néo 1:18-22, 1916.   1326

Argues that contrary to thesis of Séché in *Sur la dame qui fut Olive* (1316), D. could not have intended his first sonnet sequence for princesse Marguerite, sister of François I, since the little volume had been completed before he had made her acquaintance. Strengthens position of Bourdeaut in *Joachim du Bellay et Olive de Sévigné* (no. 1221.)

Turquety, Edouard. Poëtes françois du seizième siècle. BBB ser. 16:1125-59, 1864.   1327

Somewhat rhetorical rather than scholarly in style, containing a number of incorrect assertions, this early study of D. nevertheless interesting for its sincerity and criticism of certain weaknesses in the poet's program.

Vaganay, Hugues. Du nouveau sur Du Bellay. BBB ns 8:268-69, 1929.   1328

Discovery of an earlier form (1551) of *Ode au seigneur des Essars sur le discours de son Amadis* differing materially from that published following year in *Œuvres de l'invention de l'auteur.*

— Joachim du Bellay et les Rime diverse di molti eccellentiss. autori. RHL 8:687, 1901.   1329

Believes that D. probably made use of first editions of two of the anthologies published by Giolito under above and other similar titles. *See* Vianey, *Les sources italiennes de l'Olive*, 1336. *See* 2700.

Van Bever, Ad., ed. La vie de J. du Bellay par Colletet. Rren 13:83-103, 1912. 1330
Advance publication of a part of Colletet's life of the poet which was to appear same year in Van Bever's edition of *Divers jeux rustiques*, 1207, p. 11-72.

Vianey, Joseph. Les Antiquitez de Rome : leurs sources latines et italiennes. BI 1:187-199, 1901. 1331
Antiquitez, transitional between *Olive* and *Regrets*, is closer to former than latter from point of view of imitation of poets, ancient and modern. Among principal sources are Horace, Virgil, Propertius, Ovid, Lucan, Ariosto, Castiglione. Substance of this article is in author's *Le Pétrarquisme en France au XVIᵉ siècle* (784). Les *Antiquitez de Rome de Joachim du Bellay* (1306, p. 5), combats hypothesis of transitional nature of this sequence; for him these sonnets were written at the same time as those of *Regrets*.

— L'Arioste et la Pléiade. *See* 1191. 1332
Though devoted largely to other members of Pléiade, this article, which was absorbed into author's *Le Pétrarquisme en France au XVIᵉ siècle* (784), contains material on D. complementary to that presented in Vianey's article on *Les sources italiennes de l'Olive* (1336).

— La part de l'imitation dans les Regrets. BI 4:30-48, 1904. 1333
In spite of professions of literary independence with which D. begins his *Regrets*, he is indebted to Alisandro Piccolomini's *Cento sonetti* (1549) for idea of keeping a in sonnets and to a number of Petrarchan poets (Sasso, Philoxeno, Chariteo, Burchiello, Berni) for style and substance of a number of these compositions.

— Les Regrets de Joachim du Bellay. Malfère, 1930. 162 p. 1334
Best study of *Regrets*. Author devotes four chapters to education of the poet, his theory of poetry, early writings, and first appearance of elegiac and satiric strains in D.'s work. Separate chapter devoted to each of these two tendencies in *Regrets*, and there are others dealing with the reception and fortune of these sonnets in France.

Review : J. Plattard in RSS 18:187, 1931.

— Le sonnet LXXXIV de l'Olive. RHL 8:323-24, 1901. 1335
Finds source of D.'s sonnet *Seul et pensif ... in Arcadia* of Sannazaro, *Prosa settima.*

— Les sources italiennes de l'Olive. Mâcon, Protat, 1901. 36 p. 1336
One of author's most important articles announcing discovery that D. had found the matter of some eighteen sonnets of the *Olive* in Ariosto, that he had been indebted to almost thirty other Italian sonneteers, samples of whose work had appeared in two anthologies published by Giolito at Ferrara : *Rime diverse ...* 1546 and *Delle rime di diversi ...* 1548.

Viatte, August. Du Bellay et les démoniaques. RHL 51:456-60, 1951. 1337
Analysis of two sonnets of *Regrets* (XCVII and XCVIII) which deal in obviously satirical language with exorcism of young girls possessed by demons. Author shows that they refer, in all probability, to an event that took place in Rome during D.'s residence there. Statement that in the second of these compositions " il me semble voir une ombre de scepticisme " is a tribute to author's sense of scientific prudence. On the other hand, the serious student of the renaissance will agree entirely with the position that we must not neglect " a priori le fait historique de croyances jugées absurdes " (p. 460).

Villey, Pierre. Les sources italiennes de la Deffense et illustration de la langue françoise de Joachim du Bellay. Champion, 1908. 162 p. (BLR, 1st ser., v. 9). 1338
Remarkable study which threw a new light on the manifesto of Pléiade by showing that it was deeply indebted for some of its fundamental ideas to *Dialogo delle lingue* of Sperone Speroni, first published in 1542. Dialogue reproduced in appendix. *See* 2793.

Review : J. Vianey in BI 9:185-87, 1909.

Williams, Ralph C. Metrical form of the epic, as discussed by sixteenth-century critics. MLN 36:449-57, 1921. 1339
Straightforward account of opinions of Italian and French critics and poetic theorists. Mention of D.'s use of term " vers heroiques " for decasyllable. Reference to Ronsard's disappointment at not having been able to use the alexandrine in *Franciade*.

Wilmotte, Maurice. La tradition didactique du moyen âge chez Joachim du Bellay. *In his:* Études critiques sur la tradition littéraire en France. Champion, 1909, p. 179-200.   1340

Valuable for understanding of the fortune of D. in France in early 19th century and of contribution made by Pléiade to establishment of classical doctrine in France. Though one may readily agree that on many points D. continues literary traditions of middle ages, is difficult to accept author's suggestion that *rhétoriqueurs* are scarcely less acquainted with antiquity than D.

Ziemann, Georg. Vers- und Strophenbau bei Joachim du Bellay. Königsberg i. Pr., 1913. 127 p.   1341

Discusses technical practices of D. under following headings : treatment of mute *e*, hiatus, caesura, enjambement, rime, use of different meters, euphony, alliteration, and strophic structure.

Minor Poets
(Nos. 1342-1400)

J. CORIDEN LYONS

Lachèvre, Frédéric. Bibliographie des recueils collectifs de poésies du XVIᵉ siècle. Champion, 1922. 613 p.   1342

Immense collection of poetic *recueils*, an admirable contribution to study of 16th century French poetry. Lachèvre's identification of many items in various collections most helpful, though some identifications have been disputed. Organization somewhat confusing. *See* 1392. Review : J. Plattard in RSS 9:294-95, 1922.

Champion, Pierre. Henri III et les écrivains de son temps. BHren 1:42-172, 1941.   1343

Not a capital article, contains some interesting bits of information on relationships between Henri III and literary figures of his time; many of these were poets, or at least wrote some poetry.

Charbonnier, Abbé F. La poésie française et les guerres de religion (1560-1574). Revue des œuvres nouvelles, 1919. 538 p.   1344

In addition to well-known pieces by Ronsard and Jodelle, study considers some contributions of Denisot, Belleau, Florent Chrestien, Jacques Grévin, and others. Intriguing study of " propaganda poetry " of the religious war period.

Review : J. Lavaud in RSS 11:103-05, 1924.

Hulubei, Mme Alice. L'églogue en France au XVIᵉ siècle, époque des Valois (1515-1589). Droz, 1938. 794 p.   1345

Useful and conscientious study which contains a great deal of scattered miscellaneous information outside the strict range of vernacular and Latin eclogue. Various minor poets considered briefly, on whom information is not readily available elsewhere (*i.e.* François Habert, J. Béreau, Estienne Forcadel, G. Sepin, Claude de Morenne, Pierre de Montchault, etc.). Excellent bibliography pertains to genre rather than individual poets. Work to be supplemented by same author's *Répertoire des églogues en France au XVIᵉ siècle, (époque des Valois, 1515-1589), see* 2562.

Raymond, Marcel. L'influence de Ronsard sur la poésie française, 1550-1585. *See* 1170.   1346

Indispensable item for study of French poetry up to 1585. Contains much information not found elsewhere. Title somewhat misleading; author does not pursue Ronsard's influence beyond lifetime of the poet. Comprehensive bibliography would have been useful. Well organized and indexed, invaluable for study of minor poetic figures in period 1550-1585.

Schmidt, Albert Marie. La poésie scientifique en France au XVIᵉ siècle. *See* 327.   1347

Very lucid and badly-needed analysis of a thorny subject. Schmidt has pulled out threads of scientific erudition which appear constantly in poetry of the 16th century (more prominently in some individuals than in others) and has woven them into a fabric of continuous development. Much information not found elsewhere on such minor figures as La Boderie, Isaac Habert, Du Monin, Bretonnayeau, Du Chesne, Gamon, etc. Six pages of bibliography (363-68) contain some highly useful and rarely mentioned items. *See* 1176.

Théodore Agrippa d'Aubigné
(Nos. 1348-1355)

Aubigné, Théodore Agrippa d'. Le printemps, L'hécatombe à Diane. Ed. by Bernard Gagnebin. Lille, Giard, and Geneva, Droz, 1948. 155 p. (TLF)   1348

Supplies scholarly apparatus lacking in earlier Réaume-Caussade edition of this work (*Œuvres*, Lemerre, 1873-92, 6 v.). Helpful introduction, very useful bibliography. Especially interesting is the confronting of variants from two of A.'s manuscripts, which reveals changes in taste and language between 1580 and 1625.

Review : S. F. Will in RR 40:143, 1949.

— Les tragiques. Ed. by Georges Mongrédien. Garnier, 1931.   1349

Very poor edition which adds little to that done by Charles Read back in 1872. Bears all the marks of hasty work and would seem to have been rushed to completion to take advantage of tercentenary of A.'s death.

Review: J. Plattard in RSS 18:181, 1931.

— Les tragiques; critical edition by J. Plattard and A. Garnier. Droz, 1932. 4 v. (STFM)   1350

Excellent historical introduction, superb critical apparatus explaining bases on which text was established. Variants from 1616 edition and Tronchin manuscript and (where deemed advisable) corrections in basic text itself (a Swiss edition, probably printed in Grenoble under the poet's personal supervision). Elaborate and illuminating notes. The *Lexique grammatical* at the end very useful.

Review : P. Jourda in RSS 19:142-44, 1932-33.

Buffum, Imbrie. Agrippa d'Aubigné's Les tragiques; a study of the baroque style in poetry. New Haven, Yale University Press, 1951.   151 p. (YRS, 2nd ser., v. 1).   1351

Excellent study follows increasingly prevalent tendency to treat French 17th century (and especially first half of century) as a baroque period. Introduction stresses necessary parallelism between literature and graphic arts and states the assumptions which underlie definition of the term " baroque " as it is applied to A. Fine analysis of *Les tragiques* from " baroque approach " presents Protestant poet in an entirely new light, and shows he possessed talents and craftsmanship only slightly appreciated when his works are examined from the " classic approach." Selected bibliography provides an excellent introduction to the study of late 16th and early 17th centuries in France as a baroque period.

Droz, Eugénie. Le premier séjour d'Agrippa d'Aubigné à Genève. *See* 2884.   1352

Garnier, Armand. Agrippa d'Aubigné et le parti protestant; contribution à l'histoire de la réforme en France. Fischbacher, 1928. 3 v.   1353

One of the capital studies on the great French Protestant poet. Also presents a comprehensive picture of 16th century Protestant movement and sheds light on many of A.'s associates. *Appendice bibliographique* in v. III especially valuable.

Plattard, Jean. Une figure de premier plan dans les lettres de la renaissance : Agrippa d'Aubigné. Boivin, 1931. 143 p. (BRCC)   1354

Very terse and condensed treatment of main aspects of life and career of A.; excellent. The *Chronologie de la vie d'Agrippa d'Aubigné* most useful. Copy listed above given clearly of a later publication date than 1931 (although this fact is not mentioned), since the very complete bibliography of works by and about A. added to book by Raymond Lebègue contains items as recent as 1945.

Rocheblave, Samuel. Agrippa d'Aubigné. Hachette, 1910. 202 p. (GEF)   1355

Earliest basic study on A.; displaced by more recent works. Gohin's review more of a supplement than a review; discusses certain aspects of Platonism of A.

Review : F. Gohin in RHL 18:446-5c, 1911.

Albert Babinot
(No. 1356)

Raymond, Marcel. Deux pamphlets inconnus contre Ronsard et la Pléiade. RSS 13:243-64, 1927.   1356

Reference made to B.'s Christian epic, *La christiade*, which appeared at Poitiers in 1559, which has an interesting prose preface by André de Rivaudeau. In this preface Rivaudeau condemns obscurity, immoral reputation, and paganism of Pléiade poets and calls for a poetry of religious and Christian inspiration, of which his friend B. is herewith giving an example.

François Béroalde de Verville
(No. 1357)

Saulnier, Verdun L. Étude sur Béroalde de Verville. *See* 940.   1357

Clear and straightforward article, really a small monograph, gives most adequate study to date on one of the most perplexing figures of late renaissance. The 14-page bibliography makes the citation of earlier studies on B. almost unnecessary.

Jean Bertaut
(Nos. 1358-1359)

Lebègue, Raymond. Deux poèmes de Bertaut. BHren 7:205-43, 1945.   1358
Main purpose of this article is to refute, in part at least, conclusions of Vaganay and Vianey (1359) by showing that B. gave evidence of " Malherbian " tendencies at a time when " he could not possibly have known Malherbe and his work. Therefore B. and his generation were simply following the linguistic and stylistic trend of the times, rather than undergoing personal influence of Malherbe. This is the conclusion to which G. C. S. Adams came in 1934 (1359).

Vaganay, Hugues and Joseph Vianey. Bertaut et la réforme de Malherbe. RHL. 19:161-67, 1912; 22:217-20, 1915.   1359
These articles show that by 1609 the former disciple of Desportes had been converted to the doctrine of Malherbe. Actually, B. was simply following linguistic evolution and trend of taste of his time. Subject has been amplified and expanded by G. C. S. Adams : *Malherbe's principles of grammar and rhyme as applied to the poetry of Jean Bertaut*, a University of North Carolina unpublished M. A. thesis, 1934.

Marc Claude de Buttet
(No. 1360)

Buttet, Marc Claude de. Œuvres poétiques. Ed. by Paul Lacroix. Librairie des bibliophiles, 1880. 2 v.   1360
Only relatively satisfactory edition in modern times of poetic works of B. Although he is not one of the best poets of his time, as Lacroix calls him, he is more deserving of an up-to-date critical edition than some who have been so favored. 40-page introduction gives what was known of B. in 1880, but modern scholarship could make many additions and corrections. Text based on editions of 1561 and 1588. Brief (I, p. 161-66) *Auteur au lecteur* contains some random observations on critical and linguistic principles. V. I made up almost entirely of 128 sonnets to B.'s beloved Amalthée; v. II divided into two *livres*, mostly odes in praise of various contemporaries and friends. Notes leave much to be desired.

Nicolas Denisot (du Mans)
(No. 1361)

Jugé, Clément. Nicolas Denisot du Mans (1515-1589); essai sur sa vie et ses œuvres. Le Mans, Leguicheux; Paris, Lemerre, 1907. 158 p.   1361
This supplementary thesis, done in connection with author's main thesis on Jacques Peletier (1383) is as inadequate as its companion piece. However, it is to date only study of any length on D.

Philippe Desportes
(Nos. 1362-1366)

Desportes, Philippe. Les imitations de l'Arioste, suivies de poésies inédites ou non recueillies. Ed. by Jacques Lavaud. Droz, 1936. 180 p.   1362
Introduction of this by-product of his doctoral dissertation on D., Lavaud defines debt of D. to Ariosto and emphasizes originality of his borrowings. Part I (p. 4-99), reproduces texts of those items taken in whole or in part from Ariosto. Part II (p. 103-67) gives texts of certain unpublished poems of D. Appendix (p. 169-80) lists : 1, *Ecrits en prose de Desportes*; 2, *Œuvres perdues*; and 3, *Œuvres faussement attribuées à Desportes*. This last item is especially useful and interesting.

— Chansons au luth et airs de cours français du xvie siècle. Société de musicologie française, 1934.   1363
Introduction, commentary and music. Contains chansons of Marot, Ronsard and D.

Clements, R. J. Desportes and Petrarch. RR 36:103-12, 1945.   1364
Clements contends that D.'s borrowings from Petrarch were more extensive than indicated by J. Lavaud (1366). Asserts that D. borrowed directly from Petrarch more heavily than he did from neo-Petrarchists. *See* 2724.

Lanson, Gustave. Études sur les rapports de la littérature française et de la littérature espagnole au xviie siècle (1600-1660). RHL 4:61-73, 1897.   1365
In this section of the study Lanson treats D. and Bertaut; demonstrates that D. knew and borrowed heavily from Montemayor in composing his *Diane*. Fact and extent of Bertaut's debt to same Spanish author less clear.

Lavaud, Jacques. Un poète de cour au temps des derniers Valois : Philippe Desportes (1546-1606). Droz, 1936. 576 p. 1366

Excellent study provides for D. the sort of service rendered Ronsard by Paul Laumonier in his *Ronsard, poète lyrique* (1144) which, incidentally, it resembles so strongly as to suggest that Laumonier's work must have served Lavaud as a model. Emphasis is strongly historical, sheds a useful light on the age and the poet's contemporaries. Exhaustive and valuable bibliography. Style somewhat diffuse, analysis of poetic qualities of D. inadequate. Thus, the definitive study on D. remains to be done, but this book is now the capital study on him, and probably will never be entirely displaced.

Reviews : P. Laumonier in Hren 4:340-344, 1937; R. Lebègue in RHL 45:379-382, 1938.

Guillaume de Salluste, seigneur Du Bartas

(Nos. 1367-1368)

Du Bartas, Guillaume de Salluste, seigneur. The works of Guillaume de Salluste, sieur Du Bartas. Ed. by U. T. Holmes, Jr., J. C. Lyons and R. W. Linker. Chapel Hill, University of North Carolina Press, 1935-1940. 3 v. 1367

Only modern critical edition of works of this distinguished apologist of French Protestantism. V. I summarizes all critical appreciations of D. up to 1935, gives history of the publication of his work through various editions, and presents sources and derivations of his ideas. Full critical apparatus. *Appendices* reproduce letters and other documents pertaining to his life. V. II and III present texts of all known extant works, with notes and variants. Appendix to V. III summarizes his influence in England and America. Bibliography at end of v. III makes references to earlier studies unnecessary here.

Taylor, George Coffin. Milton's use of Du Bartas. Cambridge, Harvard University Press, 1934. 129 p. 1368

Study intends to prove that English scholars have been wrong in minimizing influence of D. on Milton. Taylor cites so many and such close parallels between the two poets that he is forced to conclude that Milton leaned heavily on the French Protestant. *See* 2844.

Charles d'Espinay

(No. 1369)

Busson, Henri. Charles d'Espinay, évêque de Dol, et son œuvre poétique. Champion, 1923. 201 p. 1369

Excellent study presents clearly one of the more interesting contemporaries of Ronsard : since E. was primarily a soldier and a political figure, and a poet only by avocation, book lays great emphasis about the period of the civil wars. Prose introduction by E. is interesting, and eight liminary sonnets by Ronsard, Belleau, Grévin, Des Autels, etc. show us who his friends were. 50 sonnets in the collection are second-rate lyric efforts. Useful bibliography.

Jacques Grévin

(Nos. 1370-1371)

Grévin, Jacques. Théâtre complet et poésies choisies; notices et notes by Lucien Pinvert. Garnier, 1922. 365 p. *See* 2373. 1370

Excellent edition of four plays and selected sonnets. Publication of remainder of G.'s sonnets and his other lyric poetry would have been welcome. Notes good, but not numerous enough.

Review : J. Lavaud in RSS 12:173-75, 1925.

Pinvert, Lucien. Jacques Grévin (1538-1570), sa vie, ses écrits, ses amis; étude biographique et littéraire. Fontemoing, 1898. 396 p. (Diss., Nancy) 1371

Includes a bibliography of G.'s works. Still, despite its age, best over-all study on this poet and dramatist. *See* 350, 440, 2375, 2563.

Amadis Jamyn

(No. 1372)

Graur, Theodosia. Un disciple de Ronsard: Amadis Jamyn, 1540?-1593; sa vie, son œuvre, son temps. *See* 218. 1372

Excellent treatment of a hitherto neglected figure of considerable importance. Author does not overemphasize place of J. in literary history. Preliminary bibliography useful to readers who are not specialists in field. Somewhat verbose, but, in general, well done. *See* 2543.

Review : Françoise de Borch in RSS 17:171-73, 1930.

Estienne de La Boétie
(No. 1373)

La Boétie, Estienne de. Œuvres complètes. Ed. by Paul Bonnefon. Bordeaux, Gounouilhou, 1892. 444 p.   1373

Only three sections of this classic edition of L. are concerned with his poetry : his Latin verse (p. 203-44), miscellaneous verse, which includes 25 sonnets (p. 247-284), and 29 sonnets which form the 29th chapter of Book I of Montaigne's essays. Notes well chosen and helpful, edition is excellent. *See* 1404, 2589.

Jean Bastier de La Péruse
(No. 1374)

Banachevich, Nicolas. Jean Bastier de La Péruse (1500-1554); étude biographique et littéraire. Les presses universitaires de France, 1923. 244 p.   1374

Work by a Serbian scholar is an excellent and concise study of the short life of L. Role of his posthumous editor, Scévole de Sainte-Marthe, also considered. *See* 2379.

Review : J. Plattard in RSS 11:109-11, 1924.

Madeleine de Laubespine
(No. 1375)

Lachèvre, Frédéric. Les Chansons de Callianthe sont-elles de Madeleine de Laubespine? BBB ns 6:246-56, 1927.   1375

On the question of whether " Callianthe " poems were written by Madeleine de Laubespine or Héliette de Vivonne, *see* J. Lavaud's volume on Desportes, (1366, p. 503-08), Lavaud concludes that Lachèvre may not be wholly right, but that Roger Sorg's contention in : *Une fille de Ronsard : la bergère Rosette*, RDM 7th per. 13:128-44, Jan. 1, 1923, appears to be entirely wrong.

Gui Lefèvre de La Boderie
(No. 1376)

Lefèvre de La Boderie, Gui. La Galliade, ou de la révolution des arts et des sciences. *See* 321.   1376

Of special interest is section (or " cercle ") V, which deals with poetry and L.'s literary contemporaries in France.

Pierre Le Loyer
(No. 1377)

Le Loyer, Pierre. Pierre Le Loyer's version of the Ars amatoria, ed. by W. L. Wiley. Chapel Hill, 1941. 74 p. (NCSR no. 3)   1377

Some information about *Le bocage de l'art d'aimer*, its 16th-century editions, and about author. Gives text of the poem. Conclusion provides interesting information about L.'s literary techniques and suggests why he ignored third section of Ovid's work. Notes furnish parallels between L. and Ovid and explain how the renaissance poets interpreted Aristotle's doctrine of mimesis.

Jean Macer
(No. 1378)

Macer, Jean. Philippique contre les poëtastres et rimailleurs français de notre temps. Gaillard, 1557. (Only copy is at the Bibliothèque de l'Arsenal).   1378

Prose work is an attack on "new school" of poets, especially against Ronsard. Pléiade group accused of decadence, depravity, and unfounded pretentiousness. Attacks are similar to those contained in *Temple de Ronsard* a few years later.

Olivier de Magny
(No. 1379)

Favre, Jules Eugène. Olivier de Magny, (1529?-1561), étude biographique et littéraire. Garnier, 1885. 451 p. (Diss., Paris)   1379

Chronology of the poet's life and activities has been severely criticized.

Pierre de Paschal
(No. 1380)

Nolhac, Pierre de. Le Cicéronien de la brigade : Ronsard et Pierre de Paschal. *In his:* Ronsard et l'humanisme. *See* 1160, p. 271-338.   1380

Devoted entirely to P., his career, relationships with Ronsard and other literary figures of his time, role in literary controversies of his day, etc.

Jacques Peletier (du Mans)
(Nos. 1381-1384)

Peletier, Jacques. L'amour des amours. Introduction by Adrien Van Bever. Société des médecins bibliophiles, 1926. 159 p. 1381

Facsimile reproduction of the 1555 Lyonese printing by Jean de Tournes. Editors have seen fit, wisely, to include the famous *Avertiçment aux lecteurs* from the 1581 Paris (Coulombel) edition of *Œuvres poétiques* because of the explanation it contains of P.'s theories about spelling reform. Foreword emphasizes P.'s accomplishments in field of medicine, but adds little to what Jugé has already said (1383).

— L'art poétique de Jacques Peletier du Mans. Éd. by André Boulanger. Les belles lettres, 1930. 240 p. (PFS, v. 52) 1382

Interesting edition of a highly important document in the history of development of the Pléiade. Editor managed to have special printing type prepared, and reproduces curious spelling devices of this reformer. Introduction repeats what little is known of the life of P. Notes are judicious and instructive. *See* 2341.

Review : J. Plattard in RSS 18:364-65, 1931.

Jugé, Clément. Jacques Peletier du Mans. Le Mans, Leguicheux, Lemerre, 1907. 447 p. (Diss., Caen) 1383

Very poor study which bears every mark of what it was : an inferior doctoral dissertation. Only full-length study of this very interesting friend of the Pléiade. Jugé's evaluation of P.'s spelling reform theories is especially weak. *See* 2342.

Review : J. Plattard in RHL 18:451-52, 1911.

Saulnier, Verdun L. Une œuvre inédite de Jacques Peletier du Mans : l'oraison funèbre de Henri VIII, 1547. BHren 11:7-27, 1949. 1384

Article deserves more than the casual attention usually given a journal study. Not only does it reproduce a most interesting text of a most interesting author, with appropriate critical apparatus, but the writer gives a splendid analysis of the technique of composing an *oraison funèbre* in mid-16th century. *See*, by same author: *L'oraison funèbre au XVIe siècle*, BHren 10:124-57, 1948.

Guy du Faur, seigneur de Pibrac
(Nos. 1385-1386)

Cabos, Alban. Guy du Faur de Pibrac, un magistrat poète au XVIe siècle (1529-1584). Champion, 1922. 500 p. 1385

Unusually fine doctoral dissertation provides a long-needed scholarly study of one of the most interesting figures of the French 16th century. Sections dealing with P.'s sojourn in Poland with Henri III, and with P.'s role as Chancellor of Marguerite de Navarre especially interesting. Cabos's treatment of *Quatrains* and *Plaisirs de la vie rustique* fills a gap of long standing. Excellent bibliography indispensable for students of this author.

Review : J. Plattard in RSS 10:114-17, 1923.

Vaganay, Hugues. Les Stances de M. de Pibrac. RSS 4:195-202, 1916. 1386

Vaganay recalls the edition of *Quatrains* by Claretie in 1874, which concludes with 30 *Stances* taken from *Fleurs des plus excellens poètes de ce temps* (1599). Vaganay also recalls *Bibliographie des recueils collectifs de poésies* by Frédéric Lachèvre (1342), who states that the same *Stances* had appeared in two other collections during the same year (1599).

Pierre de Laval
(No. 1387)

Pierre de Laval. Les rimes de Pierre de Laval. Ed. by Pierre Barrière. Bordeaux, Delmas, 1937. 174 p. 1387

Short introduction on critical procedure and essential known facts about the poet. Poems taken from ms. 5 of *Bibliothèque municipale de Périgueux*. Sonnets and stances make up most of collection, but inclusion of a number of *épîtres* show this provincial to be an *attardé*, still using this form in 1576. Linguistic and historical notes adequate.

Nicolas Rapin
(No. 1388)

Plattard, Jean. Poèmes inédits de Nicolas Rapin, RSS 9:269-80, 1922. 1388

A certain amount of bibliographical information, together with three hitherto unpublished poems, one Latin, one French, one Greek.

Scévole de Sainte-Marthe
(No. 1389)

Farmer, Albert John. Les œuvres françaises de Scévole de Ste-Marthe, 1536-1623. Toulouse, Privat, 1920. 149 p. 1389
Treatment of S. not very sympathetic; actually, he is a much better poet than Farmer makes him out to be.
Review : J. Plattard in RSS 8:264-65, 1921.

Jean de Sponde
(Nos. 1390-1394)

Boase, Alan M. Du nouveau sur Jean de Sponde. MerF 312:641-47, Aug. 1, 1951. 1390
Brief outline of career of S., who is seen " ... figurer en humaniste, en alchimiste, en administrateur ... d'une ville importante... " (p. 641). Analysis of his work, closing with S.'s *Méditation sur le psaume XLVIII*, which recalls Pascal, and may well be compared with latter's most famous pages, thinks Boase (p. 644).

Droz, Eugénie. Les années d'études de Jean et d'Henry de Sponde. BHren 9:141-50, 1947. 1391
Some interesting information about university years of this young Protestant, and letters exchanged with Théodore de Bèze.

Lachèvre, Frédéric. Bibliographie des recueils collectifs de poésies du XVIe siècle. *See* 1342. 1392
Lachèvre states here that one collection, published by Raphaël du Petit Val at Rouen in 1597 or 1598 was devoted largely (50 out of 67 items) to vernacular poetry of S.

Ruchon, François, and Alan Boase. La vie et l'œuvre de Jean de Sponde. Geneva, Cailler, [c1949]. 150 p. 1393
Good 67-page life of S. by Ruchon, carefully documented, result of five years of research. Study of work of S. by Boase excellent, marked by careful analysis of the poetry of his subject, and rich in comparisons with work of many other poets. No bibliography, no index; volume clearly intended to be a contribution to history of belles-lettres rather than to academic scholarship.

Schoell, Franck Louis. Un humaniste français oublié; Jean de Sponde (Johannes Spondanus). RSS 12:361-400, 1925. 1394

This appreciation confined entirely to S.'s commentaries on *Iliad* and *Odyssey* and says nothing about his French lyric poetry. Article contains some valuable bibliographical information.

Jean Tagaut
(No. 1395)

Raymond, Marcel. Jean Tagaut; poète français et bourgeois de Genève. RSS 12:98-140, 1925. 1395
Sole study on an interesting friend of Ronsard's early years. He later retired to Geneva and became a close friend of Théodore de Bèze. Work contains some *morceaux choisis* from his works.

Jacques Tahureau
(No. 1396)

Besch, Emile. Un moraliste satirique et rationaliste du XVIe siècle : Jacques Tahureau (1527-1555). *See* 1005. 1396
Only p. 10-20 deal with T.'s French poetry; remainder of study devoted to his. *Dialogues.*

Jean Vauquelin de La Fresnaye
(Nos. 1397-1400)

Vauquelin de La Fresnaye, Jean. Œuvres diverses. Ed. by Julien Travers. Caen, Le Blanc-Hardel, 1872. 338 p. 1397
Contains *Foresteries* and other incidental poems which had been omitted from *Diverses poésies* issued three years earlier. Also various prose compositions. As had been promised in the earlier publication, editor includes a more extensive essay on the poet's life. At end of volume is a glossary to cover all three volumes. Introduction has been superseded; glossary both incomplete and faulty.

— Les diverses poésies. Ed. by Julien Travers. Caen, Le Blanc-Hardel, 1869. 872 p. 1398
Short introduction, so vague as to be almost worthless. Editor stays close to 1602 text, even to reproducing italic type so tiring to the eyes. Notes and the *Dictionnaire* of proper names still of some value, but largely outmoded. Inclusion of prose prefaces supplement the poet's critical ideas which appear in *Art poétique.* Work should be used in conjunction with

Œuvres diverses edited by same man three years later. Both are old and out of date by modern critical standards, but still best available.

— L'art poétique de Vauquelin de La Fresnaye. Ed. by George Pellissier. Garnier, 1885. 230 p. *See* 2345. 1399

Best edition of *Art poétique* to date. Excellent introduction traces evolution of French poetic theory during half-century before V.'s time and presents a tableau of French poetry at end of 16th century.

Some corrections must be made in the light of later scholarship, but the introduction is still excellent. Study on the syntactical usage, spelling and metrics of *Art poétique* included. Glossary useful, but could have been more elaborate.

Vanuxem, Paul Félicien. Un Normand volé : Vauquelin de La Fresnaye. Argentan, Éditions du pays d'Argentan, 1932. 1400

Author suggests that a sonnet by V. inspired the famous line of Du Bellay, " Heureux qui comme Ulysse...."

CHAPTER IX. ETIENNE DE LA BOETIE
(Nos. 1401-1487)

Editions

Kurz, Harry. Critical bibliography on La Boétie. RR 37:20-36, 1946. 1401

Really an *état présent des études*, with a full listing of items connected with the dispute on the authorship of *Contr'un*, for which *see* items 1457-87. *See* 1457, 1643.

La Boétie, Estienne. Œuvres. Edition prepared by Michel de Montaigne. Morel, 1571. 2 v. 1402

Contains translations from Xenophon and Plutarch, poems in Latin and French and Montaigne's letter on the death of L., each piece with a dedicatory epistle by Montaigne. Missing are the *Contr'un* and the *Mémoire sur l'édit de 1562*.

— Œuvres complètes, réunies pour la première fois par Léon Feugère. Delalain, 1846. 532 p. 1403

The *Contr'un* appears for the first time separate from Montaigne's *Essais*, text borrowed from the Coste edition of the *Essais*, Geneva, 1727. Beginning of the revival of L. as an author. *See* 1428.

— Œuvres complètes, ed. by Paul Bonnefon. *See* 1373. 1404

Basic text and definitive edition of all of *Œuvres* except *Mémoire sur l'édit de Janvier, 1562*. *See* 1417, 2589.

Discours de la servitude volontaire (le Contr'un) : 1405

a) Anonymous fragment in Latin, Dialogi ab Eusebio Philadelpha, Edimburgi (Bâle ?), 1574, at end of 2nd dialogue.

b) Anonymous, without opening paragraphs, Le réveille-matin des François. Paris, Edimbourg (Lausanne), 1574.

c) Anonymous, complete, Mémoires de l'estat de France sous Charles neufiesme, Goulart, Genève, 1576, and Meidlebourg, 1577 and 1578, III.

d) For the first time appended to Montaigne's Essais, Coste ed., Geneva, 1727, 1729, and 1745; London, Nourse, 1739 and 1745; thereafter, in most editions of Montaigne.

e) Discours de Marius plébéien et consul, traduit en prose et en vers français du latin de Salluste, suivi du discours d'Étienne de La Boétie De la servitude volontaire, traduit du français de son temps en français d'aujourd'hui, par l'Ingénu, soldat dans le régiment de Navarre, 1789 (ed. mentioned by Sainte-Beuve, no. 1446).

f) L'ami de la Révolution ou Philippiques dédiées aux représentants de la nation, aux gardes nationales, et à tous les Français, 1790. 8th Philippic, p. 137-43 has a supplement Discours sur la servitude et la liberté extrait d'Etienne de La Boétie.

g) Separately, Delance, 1802; Chamerad, 1835; Daubrée et Cailleux (Lamennais preface), 1835, 149 p.; Reschatelet (Charles Leste), Brussels and Paris, 1836.

h) All preceding use text of c). Payen gives first ed. of Henri de Mesmes ms., Bibl. Nat. no. 839, Didot, 1853, basis of all subsequent editions, Vermorel, 1863; Jouaust (Bibliophiles), 1872.

i) Œuvres de Montaigne, XI, ed. Armaingaud, Paris, Conard, 1939, prints in italics passages interpolated by Montaigne, according to editor.

See Contr'un, Payen ed., 1441, for bibliography to 1853; Œuvres, Bonnefon ed., c, most complete to 1892; Plattard, État présent des études sur Montaigne, 1482. *See also* 463, 1457-87.

— Discours de la servitude volontaire, suivi du Mémoire touchant l'édit de janvier (inédit) et d'une lettre à m. le conseiller de Montaigne; introduction et notes de Paul Bonnefon. Bossard, 1922. 214 p. 1406

For a review of *Mémoire touchant l'édit de janvier*, (1562) see Patry, 1440.

144

Translations

The Contr'un in English (Coste ed.), Smith, London, 1735; Anti-dictator, Kurz, (de Mesmes ms.) New York, 1942; in Italian, Parabelli, Naples, 1800 and Fanfani, Milan, 1864 (both Coste); in German, Freiwillige Knechtschaft, Boenheim, Berlin, 1924; also in English translation of the 29 sonnets in chapter XXIX of the Essais, Louis How, Boston, 1915.   1407

— Il contr'uno, a translation of the Contr'un by Pietro Fanfani. Milan, Daelli, 1864. 64 p. *Also:* Florence, Le Monnier, 1944. 157 p.   1408

Interesting because of the years of publication, revealing strange destiny of L.'s essay as an inciting political document. 1864 edition is a call to Venice and Rome to join the rest of unified Italy. 1944 edition plays a role in the downfall of the *Duce*.

— Freiwillige Knechtschaft, a translation of the Contr'un by Felix Boenheim. Berlin, Malik, 1924. 45 p. *See 1416.*   1409

Translation is, rather, an adaptation, but date is noteworthy : one year after the abortive Nazi *putsch* against the Weimar Republic.

— Anti-dictator, a translation of the Contr'un, by Harry Kurz. New York, Columbia University Press, 1942. 54 p. *See 1430.* 1410

In this war year, the translator read part of the Contr'un via short wave to France. Reviewed as a *New York Times* editorial *An Anti-Nazi of 1548*, April 5, 1942.

— XXIX sonnets by Estienne de La Boétie. *In :* Montaigne, Michel Eyquem de. Montaigne's Essay on friendship & XXIX sonnets by Estienne de La Boétie. Trans. by Louis How. Boston, Houghton, Mifflin, 1915. 31-63 p.   1411

L.'s sonnets beautifully done by the translator, whose version communicates faithfully their quaint renaissance flavor acquired from Petrarch.

Studies

Aublé, Emile. Esquisse sur la vie et les ouvrages de Étienne de La Boétie. MAV 13:116-28, 1883.   1413

Emphasizes youth and warmth of Contr'un and its importance as first of political pamphlets, though not addressed to a particular tyrant. Appreciates its Latin strength and French vividness. Analysis of L.'s poems. Calls Mon-

taigne's letter on L.'s death the French *De amicitia.* Study is warm, appreciative; source of oft quoted phrases on L.'s true quality.

Barrère, Joseph. Observations sur quelques ouvrages politiques anonymes du XVIᵉ siècle. RHL 21:375-86, 1914.   1414

Important study on *Réveille-matin,* among others, with comparison of Latin and French versions of Contr'un, and decision based on various uses of the term " Franco-gallia " that François Hotman was translator of L., 1405, a, as well as general editor of two volumes containing first French printing of the Contr'un (1405, a, b, c).

Baudrillart, Henri. [Contr'un]. *In his :* Jean Bodin et son temps. *See* 2045, p. 68-73.   1415

Good analysis of Contr'un, and of its use by Protestants. Thinks we are inclined to exaggerate its importance today.

Boenheim, Felix. Über freiwillige Knechtschaft. Berlin, Malik, 1924. p. 1-8. 1416

Valuable for its indications of history of Contr'un in Germany. Refers to its issue (during French Revolution) in *Neuen deutschen Merkur* by Wieland with quotations on democracy from that poet and from Kant.

Bonnefon, Paul. La Boétie. *In :* Œuvres de La Boétie. Ed. by Paul Bonnefon. Rouam, 1892. Introduction, p. 85. *See* 2589.   1417

Most complete and authoritative study available of L.'s life, works, and relation to Montaigne. Appendix (p. 119 ff.) contains textual notes, biographical documents, and bibliography to 1892.

— Montaigne, l'homme et l'œuvre. Rouam, 1893. p. 63-123.   1418

Ch. 3, *Montaigne magistrat,* points out interesting contrasts in careers of L. and Montaigne as judges at Bordeaux.

— La Boétie (1530-1563). *In his :* Montaigne et ses amis. Colin, 1898, v. I, p. 105-224. 1419

Section on L. consists of four chapters, *Vie, Discours de la servitude volontaire, Traducteur et poète, La Boétie et Montaigne.* Much of this material already presented in the Bonnefon edition of *Œuvres,* but this study better organized and brought up to date by the best specialist, and beautifully told. Footnotes report specific recent

146 CRITICAL BIBLIOGRAPHY OF FRENCH LITERATURE

findings (e.g., influence of Cardinal Gaddi, p. 109; identification of Longa, p. 114; additional family papers, career as judge, tax conditions). Asks (p. 156) if Montaigne might have made changes in *Contr'un* but admits that L. at Orléans, under influence of liberal Anne du Bourg, might have done so. L.'s erudition as translator from classics closely analyzed. Last chapter shows that others beside Montaigne felt peculiar personal charm of L.: Lambert Daneau, fellow student, Baïf, Dorat. Remains still best study of life and works of L.

Review : L. Clément in RHL 5:647-50, 1898.

Claretie, Jules. La Boétie. *In his:* La libre parole. Librairie internationale, 1868. p. 147-57.　　　　1420

Keen analysis of 16th century as marking a renascence of human liberty through the growth of a new force, public opinion. This background gives strong credence to L. as writing against the savageries of Montmorency at Bordeaux. In *Contr'un* can be seen emergence of "liberté, égalité, fraternité." Author sees in portrait of tyrant traits of Henri II. Clear adherence to notion that *Contr'un* is a tract for the time of 1548, with added qualities that give it immortality.

Combes, François. Essai sur les idées politiques de Montaigne et La Boétie. Bordeaux, 1882. 57 p.　　　1421

Traces reference to the "mignons," in *Contr'un,* to the court of François II. *See: Dispute,* no. 1457-87. Armaingaud, Bonnefon, Villey.

Demeure, Fernand. Montaigne et La Boétie, by Fernand-Demeure. MerF 245: 206-12, July 1, 1933.　　　1422

Analysis of Montaigne's contradictory statements on date of composition of *Contr'un.* Attributes these to forgetfulness and embarrassment at the subject matter of *Discours,* with an attempt to minimize its contemporary significance. Shows L. a true predecessor of Bodin, Hotman, Languet.

Desgranges, Guy. Montaigne et l'histoire. FR 23:371-77, 1949-50.　　　1423

Continues discussion started by Williamson on the liberalizing of Montaigne. Analyzes attitudes of Montaigne and L. toward history, their preference for biographies, crises of their times leading both toward conservatism, effectually divorcing

their criticism of abuses from action leading to correction. Concerned mainly with Montaigne with implications on L.

Desjardins, Albert. La Boétie. *In his:* Les moralistes français au seizième siècle. Didier, 1870. p. 131-46.　　1424

Keen interpretation of L.'s unique personality and his teaching in *Contr'un* that dignity and moral significance of individual can render an imposed tyranny ineffective.

Dezeimeris, Reinhold. La Boétie. *In his:* De la renaissance des lettres à Bordeaux au 16e siècle. AAB 3rd ser. 25:557-63, 1853.　　　1425

In this enthusiastic essay Dezeimeris recreates the enthusiasm animating him and his group. *Contr'un* not a revolutionary tract, is instead a philippic against indifference of people. Of special interest is a listing of citations from L. and Rousseau, showing similar faith in forces of democracy. Explains that L. did not write mere declamation, language shows he was sincere. Believed what he said, like Descartes and Pascal. Calls *Contr'un* "Provinciale contre l'abandon des droits de tous au profit d'un seul."

— **Ed.,** La Boétie, Etienne. Remarques et corrections ... sur le traité de Plutarque intitulé Eroticus. Bordeaux, 1868. 80 p.　　　1426

Comments on the BN copy of the Ferron translation of Plutarch containing some 101 notes by L. showing extent of his collaboration with Ferron and his excellence as a Hellenist.

Dieu, Marcel. Etienne de La Boétie. Debresse, 1939. 72 p. Author's pseud., Hem Day, at head of title.　　　1427

Preface related *Contr'un* to World War II, tyrant replaced by "servitude collective." Essay itself presents little of value, consists of long quotations from Feugère, Lamennais, Sainte-Beuve, and barely one mention of Bonnefon. Last chapter, *Esprit éternel,* is best, showing that L. teaches that tyranny crumbles by inner revolution in the slave, not by acts of external violence.

Feugère, Léon. Etienne de La Boétie, ami de Montaigne. Labitte, 1845. 309 p. 1428

Significant early study marking revival of interest in L. *Avant-propos* valuable for sketch of neglect of L. in 17th century. Despite title, 75 p. devoted to French literature before L. Study on L. valuable when it deals with his classical background. Two appendices on L. as a Latin poet, and on his prose translations. Accepts Bordeaux revolt as inspiration of *Contr'un*. Leisurely *résumé* of L.'s French poems and of the *Contr'un*. On the whole, discursive but pioneering.

Kurz, Harry. The actuality of Étienne de La Boétie. BA 23:127-28, 1949.   1429

Stresses a tradition of liberal social and political thought set going by *Contr'un*, lists some historic documents and crises that summoned its eloquence to spread ideas of personal liberty and dignity.

— Introduction to Anti-dictator, translation into English of Contr'un. New York, 1942. p. ix-xxii.   1430

Remarks on curious history of the essay, its reappearance at times of crisis, and its political interpretation.

Laborde-Milaà, Auguste. La Boétie et Montaigne. REH 68:362-68, 1902.   1431

Note inversion in title of article. Author shows clearly that L. was stronger, maturer, more positive personality and left permanent mark on Montaigne and his thought. When they first meet, L. is more than two years older, has acquired definite reputation, is married to an elderly widow, has foster children. The friendship lasting six years is then traced with indications of L.'s presumable initiative in the relationship.

Lamennais, Hugues Félicité Robert de. Preface to La Boétie's De la servitude volontaire. Brussels, Hauman, 1836. p. 5-42.   1432

Mainly oratorical praise about the liberty-loving youth who wrote the essay, but is interesting as showing what facts were known about L. before studies on him by Feugère and Payen. Contains excellent *résumé* of *Contr'un*, with well-chosen citations. Lamennais is sure no more dictatorships are possible in Europe.

Lénient, Charles. La Boétie. *In his :* La satire en France ou la littérature militante au 16ᵉ siècle. Hachette, 1877. v. I, p. 287-95.   1433

This section important for two sources on inspiration of *Contr'un :* a) Bordeaux revolt, against taxation in 1548 and cruel Montmorency punishment, quoting Jacques Auguste de Thou's Latin reference to *Spontanea servitute* in his *Historiarum sui*

temporis, liber CXXXVIII, London, 1733, p. 136; b) Agrippa d'Aubigné's anecdote, *Histoire universelle*, Amsterdam, 1726, v. I, p. 670. *See* 1854.

Lugli, Vittorio. Une amitié illustre. Florence, Nuova Italia, 1935. 63 p.   1434

Analysis of Montaigne's letter on L.'s death, then details of Montaigne's dedications of L. mss. to various contemporaries, references to L. in *Essais*. Interprets attitude toward *amitié* in *Contr'un* which accounts for Montaigne's attraction to, L., also 3 Latin poems addressed by L. to Montaigne. Attempts to date I, 28 of *Essais* as of 1573, with indication of role of this friendship in Montaigne's career.

Lyons, J. Coriden. Conceptions of the republic in French literature of the sixteenth century : Etienne de La Boétie and François Hotman. RR 21:296-307, 1930.   1435

Examines political doctrines in *Servitude volontaire* and *Franco-gallia*. Considers L.'s digressions pointless and *Contr'un* as lacking progressive unity. Passing reference to Armaingaud dispute. It is questionable that L. even considers the Republic in his essay. Hotman section of this study is more extensive. *See* 2081.

Maubourguet, Jean. Notes sur La Boétie. BHAP 62:248-55, Jan., 1935.   1436

Report of newly found text in *Archives de Dordogne*. Facts on Boyt family of Sarlat, ancestors of L. Goes back to 1470 and gives family tree of Etienne. Listing of property and dates when acquired. Career of Antoine, father of Etienne. Boyt became Boytia for the estate, then Boytie by 1520. Pronunciation in 16th century of name spelled by Montaigne in *Essais*, La Boitie. Study of Etienne's uncle, curé de Bouilhonac, Etienne's protector when orphaned. Terms of L.'s will leaving all to uncle except library to Montaigne.

Maze-Sencier, Georges. La Boétie. *In his :* Les vies closes. Perrin, 1902. p. 2-84.   1437

Describes moderates in 16th-century sectarian disputes, L'Hospital, Pasquier, Montaigne, shows how they prepare way for accession of Henri IV. Into this background he fits L. Skillful psychological approach to L. as a liberal of his time with excellent *résumé* of political concepts expressed in *Contr'un*. Insists that L. was not a *révolté*, but one whose views led him to admiration of former republics of Sparta and Venice. Charming and sensitive biographical essay.

Mesnard, Pierre. La Boétie, critique de la tyrannie. *In his:* L'essor de la philosophie politique au XVIᵉ siècle. Boivin, 1936. p. 389-406.   1438

Very sensitive analysis of L.'s criticism of tyranny, assigning a probable date for composition of *Contr'un*, interpreting its arguments and ideas on relationship between a prince and his subjects; also on regicide, finally relating it to humanist movement in politics and rejecting clearly Sainte-Beuve's comment on it as schoolboy rhetoric.

Monzie, Eugène de. La Boétie d'après de nouveaux documents. RFrance 24:503-28, Aug., 1877.   1439

Study of his coat of arms, pronunciation of name, family background, relationship with Montaigne, bookplate, *Pax et lex*, cases he tried as judge, his death, Montaigne's choice of a " parrain " for each ms. included in his edition of L.

Patry, H.   Etienne de La Boétie et l'édit du 17 janvier, 1562. BSHP 72:116-21, Apr., 1923.   1440

Brief dependable outline of L.'s concept of causes of religious strife and the solution to be sought in France. Sidelight on L.'s devout Catholicism coupled with understanding of Church weakness; L. liberal enough to abolish statues and relics from church as unessential but insistent on maintenance of one church in state. Article, really a review of Bossard edition of L.'s *mémoire* turned up by Bonnefon (1461), reveals its real significance in religious history of this period. L. is a radical thinker, in true tradition of the spirit of *Contr'un*.

Payen, J. F.   Notice bio-bibliographique sur La Boétie. Didot, 1853.   145 p.   1441

70 p. preface of author's edition of *Contr'un* based on Mesmes ms. Sections on family of L., career, friendship with Montaigne, fate of his mss., death, all so accurately treated that only Bonnefon really adds new elements. Clarifying comments (p. 42) on 29 sonnets in *Essais*, I, 29, and 25 more in Montaigne's edition of *Œuvres*. Ends with list of 33 possible sources of references to L., some of them 17th century, most between 1835 and 1853, useful to mark growing interest from Lamennais to Feugère to Payen.

Plattard, Jean.   Un ami : Estienne de La Boétie. *In his:* Montaigne et son temps. Boivin, [c1933.]   p. 57-79.   1442

Points out extraordinary admiration of Montaigne for L. Explains it partly on basis of L.'s culture. Footnote contains excellent *résumé* of contentions in the dispute on authorship of *Contr'un*. Examines possible influence of L. on Montaigne's political ideals through analysis of *Mémoire sur l'édit de janvier 1562*, promulgated by Catherine de Médicis at the instigation of Michel de l'Hospital. Also comments on 29 sonnets included in the *Essais*.

Review : P. Laumonier in RHL 42:601-604, 1935.

Prévost-Paradol, Lucien Anatole Prévost, called. La Boétie. *In his:* Études sur les moralistes français. Hachette, 1865.   p. 41-78.   1443

Part I begins with analysis of friendship between L. and Montaigne, follows with character and psychology of L., ends with a *résumé* of *Contr'un*. Warm, appreciative study. Part II is a political analysis of *Contr'un* as a relative concept of " obéissance raisonnable " deriving from L.'s fundamental concept of individual's sense of inner dignity. Where there is no humiliation, there is no servitude. Essay has permanent value as a document on relationship of the people and their government. *See* 1713.

Réaume, Eugène.   La Boétie. *In his:* Les prosateurs français du 16ᵉ siècle. Didier, 1869.   p. 181-95.   1444

Charming sensitive essay on friendship with Montaigne. References to other illustrious friendships of 16th century. Eloquent appreciation of vigor of *Contr'un* attributed here to tax reprisals at Bordeaux. Does not accept Montaigne's attempt to minimize its significance. Recognizes anti-Machiavellian tone of L.

Riveline, Maurice.   L'amitié de Montaigne pour La Boétie. *In his :* Montaigne et l'amitié. Alcan, 1939. p. 40-123. *See* 1722.
                                    1445

Thorough treatment, with frequent juxtaposition of quotations from both authors, of their preparation for meeting and subsequent unique relationship, throws psychological light on it from modern point of view including Nietzsche (p. 51), has long analysis of Montaigne's letter on death of L. Then ch. III takes up account of 20 years of Montaigne's life after death of his friend, showing his deprivation as indicated frequently in *Essais*, study of his attitude on women, the publication of L.'s works and dedications, his relations with contemporaries (Charron, Mlle de Gournay, p. 102-10), summation of his attitude on friendship; thorough scholarly presentation by judicious choice of textual testimony.

Review : Anon in BSAM 7:120, Oct., 1939.

Sainte-Beuve, C. A. Etienne de La Boétie. *In his:* Causeries du lundi, 2nd ed. Garnier, v. IX, p. 112-28. (Dated Nov., 1853.) *Also in his:* Galerie de portraits littéraires, Garnier, 1893. p. 1-17.   1446

Discusses Feugère and Payen editions of *Œuvres*. Sketches life of L., compares him to Vauvenargues. Considers *Contr'un* a mere classroom product, admires its vigor. Charming analysis of " amitié-passion." Essay still enchants with its urbanity and adroit flow from literature into life. Contains Sainte-Beuve's own translation of large section of L.'s Latin *épîtres* to his friend.

Schmidt, Hans. Etienne de La Boéties Discours de la servitude volontaire und seine Beziehungen zu der Staatspolitischen Schriften des 16 Jahrhunderts in Frankreich. Marburg, Bauer, 1934. 66 p.   (Diss., Marburg)   1447

Begins with a 3 p. bibliography. Has eight chapters tracing specific political ideas found in *Contr'un* through Calvin, Machiavelli, Hotman, Du Plessis-Mornay, Bodin, with a final flash ahead to Rousseau. Example : " Tyrannenmord " or regicide, how L. shies off (though not according to Armaingaud), how it excites interest in 16th century, disappears in 17th, re-emerges with Rousseau. Clear treatment, for each political writer, of special quality of his doctrine. Comparison of L. and Rousseau stresses their common quality of "pitié pour l'humanité," both of them independent of history, both revolutionaries. Schmidt admires passive resistance, does not attribute a system of government to L. but sees clearly the true strength of *Contr'un*.

Stapfer, Paul. Etienne de La Boétie. *In his:* Montaigne. Hachette, 1895. p. 19-25. (GEF)   1448

This section has curious analysis of Montaigne as a non-sentimentalist with two exceptions in his life, his father and his friend. *See* 1744.

— Etienne de La Boétie. *In his:* La famille et les amis de Montaigne. Hachette, 1896. p. 129-56.   1449

This chapter gives full account of L.'s censorship of plays at *Collège de Guyenne*, his trip to Paris on behalf of Bordeaux tribunal, his efforts to conciliate sectarians at Agen. All this already reported in Bonnefon preface. Stapfer accepts Bordeaux revolt as inspiration for *Contr'un* on ground that while essay is a classical exercise, its anger and fire are stirred by definite provocation. *See* 1743.

Tallemant des Réaux, Gédéon. Contr'un. *In his:* Les historiettes. 3rd ed. Garnier, n.d. 2 v. in l. v. II, p. 203.   1450

Here is told the famous story of Richelieu asking to see a copy of *Contr'un* mentioned in *Essais*, finally procured ingeniously by the book dealer Blaise.

Tiddeman, L. E. The friends of Montaigne. WR 159:29-39, Jan., 1903.   1451

Analysis of relationship between Montaigne and Mlle Marie de Gournay and L. Psychological differences between the men, emphasizing L.'s strength of character and his moral influence on Montaigne.

Tilley, Arthur. Etienne de La Boétie. *In his:* The literature of the French renaissance. *See* 123, v. II, p. 138-40.   1452

Tilley dismisses Bordeaux revolt genesis of *Contr'un* and tries to reconcile Montaigne's divergent accounts. Montaigne would not know when L. wrote the *Discours*, whether at 16 or 18. L. could have revised it, 1550-1552, inserting references to La Pléiade. Explanation coincides with Bonnefon's theory that L. was at the University of Orleans, influenced by Anne du Bourg, his law professor. Revision later would help account for comparative maturity of style.

Review : G. Saintsbury in MLQL 7:164-165, Dec., 1904.

— Réveille-matin. *In his:* Studies in the French renaissance. Cambridge, University Press, 1922. p. 298-302.   1453

Has detailed description of *Réveille-matin des françois* (1574), in which appears long extract of *Contr'un*. Authorship and editorship of 2 v. of *Réveille-matin* examined. Tilley inclined to view L.'s work as a schoolboy declamation, but its use at this time is significant.

Review : J. Plattard in RSS 10:112-14, 1923.

Villey, Pierre. La Boétie. *In his :* Les Essais de Michel de Montaigne. Malfère, 1932. p. 20. (GEL)   1454

Interesting to note that this scholar in tracing evolution of *Essais* disposes of L.'s influence in one page (p. 20), but changes in his next study.

— La Boétie. *In his :* Montaigne. Rieder, 1933. p. 22-28.   1455

Clear analysis of L.'s significance as a writer inspired by classical studies, this forming basis of Montaigne's admiration for him. Much importance attributed to L.'s *Mémoire sur l'édit de janvier, 1562*, as influencing Montaigne's political thinking. Ends with good analysis of background needed to understand attitude of both men towards the problem of the single religious sect.

Review : D. Mornet in RHL 40:594, 1933.

Williamson, Edward. On the liberalizing of Montaigne : a remonstrance. FR 23:92-100, 1949-50.   1456

Points out Montaigne's conservatism, its underlying causes, refutes modern tendency to impute democratic ideals and religious tolerance to his writing. Half of essay devoted to L.'s *Mémoire touchant l'édit de janvier, 1562* and *Contr'un*, emphasizing danger of attributing current ideals to these two humane thinkers of the 16th century.

Dispute of the Authorship of the Contr'un
(Nos. 1457-1487)

NOTE : In this section, Arthur Armaingaud, though not the subject of the section, is represented by the initial A. Items in this section are arranged approximately in chronological order. References to the *Contr'un*, here and in the Index, naturally are understood to include the names of La Boétie and Montaigne.

Kurz, Harry. Critical bibliography on La Boétie. *See* 1401.   1457

Lists in chronological order studies grouped around the dispute on authorship of *Contr'un. See* 1643.

Armaingaud, Arthur. Le Discours sur la servitude volontaire; La Boétie et Montaigne. AMP 64th year, ns 161:640-43, 1904.   1458

First statement in 6 points of author's suspicion of Montaigne's role in appearance of *Contr'un* under Protestant auspices and preliminary conclusion of Montaigne's complicity.

— Montaigne et La Boétie. RPP 47:499-522, Mar., 1906; 322-48, May, 1906.   1459

Full explanation of grounds on which he maintains that Montaigne interpolated and reworded passages in *Contr'un* and handed it over to the Protestants to be used by them in protesting against the Bartholomew massacre. Satire is pointed at Henri III. Historical identifications of references in *Contr'un*. Date of the use of the term " mignon " fixed at 1575, therefore this word slipped into essay for timely propagandist purposes. Montaigne is not always straightforward in *Essais* about his family and friends. Strongly persuasive and scholarly study.

Villey, Pierre Louis Joseph. Le véritable auteur du Discours de la servitude volontaire, Montaigne ou La Boétie? RHL 13:727-36, 1906.   1460

Refutation of A.'s thesis. Detailed comparison of three early versions. *Réveille-matin, Mémoires de l'état de France sous Charles IX*, and Mesmes ms. Slight differences have caused confusion of A. Minimizes application of details on tyrants in essay to Henri III, showing they are conventional concepts. Villey considers *Contr'un* inspired " travail d'école," as Sainte-Beuve put it, " un des mille forfaits classiques qui se commettent au sortir de Tite-Live et de Plutarque." Convincing study. For A.'s reply, *see* 1476, p. 199-216.

Bonnefon, Paul. Post scriptum. RHL 13:737-41, 1906.   1461

This addition to the preceding study shows that in October 1574, *Mémoires sur l'état de France sous Charles IX* are mentioned by the scrupulous Pierre L'Estoile in his *Registre-journal (see* 2220), and this date is too early to apply to Henri III, as maintained by A. Adds that if Montaigne wanted to aid Protestants, the L. *Mémoire sur l'édit de 1562* would have been more apt. Such action, however, not consistent with character of Montaigne. Concludes that several mss. were available of *Contr'un*, one of which was seized by Protestants for their purpose. Very convincing.

— La Boétie, Montaigne et le Contr'un. RPP 51:107-26, Jan., 1907.   1462

Takes up one by one arguments of A., showing different history of *Mémoire sur l'édit de 1562* of which there was only one ms. in Montaigne's possession, and *Contr'un*, an early work, of which several mss. circulated before the two men met. Also shows reasons why Montaigne refused to publish the essay and could not have been guilty of the infamy to his friend's memory suggested by A. Strong scholarly presentation of majority view. For A.'s answer, *see* 1466, p. 91-135.

Strowski, Fortunat. Montaigne et l'action politique. RPB 10:59-72, Feb. 1907. 1463

Close analysis of three earliest versions of *Contr'un* and decision that it is entirely L.'s work. Excellent refutation of A.'s arguments, explaining Montaigne's hesitation about publishing the essay. For A.'s answer, *see* 1476, p. 140-65.

La Valette Monbrun, Amable de. Autour de Montaigne et de La Boétie. BHAP 34:253-66, 421-51, 1907. 1464

All Périgord, insulted at A.'s allegations, rushes to defense of Montaigne's character. Article, however, is solidly done. Answers textual points raised by A., weakens his identification of the tyrant by comparing dates, shows patriotism in essay, not revolutionary doctrine, stresses relation between Montaigne and Henri III, advances explanations for Montaigne's inconsistency in the chapter on friendship. Possible interpolations in *Contr'un* attributed to Protestants who published the essay and Montaigne's brother Beauregard is suggested as the one who furnished the ms. For answer to all these points, see A., *Montaigne pamphlétaire*, 1476, p. 135-39.

Champion, Edme. Montaigne et les Huguenots. RPL 45:366-69, Mar., 1907. *Also in:* A. Armaingaud, Montaigne pamphlétaire (1476, p. 323-33). 1465

After *résumé* of A.'s main points, author accepts evidence favoring identification of tyrant with Henri III, convinced that certain passages in *Contr'un* are directed against him. Since L. could not have written them, Montaigne presumably did so. Author then tries to explain why Montaigne did not change inappropriate sentences in *Essais*, I, 28. Answer, to cover his tracks since he was giving *Contr'un* to be used by Protestants. Interesting study by mere fact it is the only one accepting A.'s thesis.

Armaingaud, A. La Boétie, Montaigne et Le contr'un; réponse à M. Paul Bonnefon. RPP 52:128-50, Apr., 1907. 1466

Answer leveled at Bonnefon, Strowski, and Villey. Stresses that Montaigne's act in giving his friend's essay to be used as a weapon against a murderous tyranny was not a villainy, but what L. himself would have done. Also in consonance with Montaigne's prudence, well-known sympathy with Henri IV, and indignation at the Massacre.

Dezeimeris, Reinhold. Sur l'objectif réel du Discours d'Etienne de la Boétie de la servitude volontaire. AAB 3rd ser. 69:5-28, 1907. 1467

Attack on A.'s thesis by pointing out that he is misled by Protestant use of *Contr'un*. Article weak as direct rebuttal of A.'s points but very important in its advancement of a new thesis to replace A.'s : i.e., that L. had in mind an attack against Charles VI of France. Numerous citations from *Contr'un* set against historical records of Charles VI would make out that L. was reporting what he had read and heard from his own family. Weakness of this thesis : it makes *Contr'un* historical essay and denatures its essence, which is outcry against tyranny. For A.'s reply, *see* 1476, p. 166-98.

Review : L.D. in AM 20:406-08, 1908 (1469).

Delaruelle, Louis. Montaigne et La Boétie; le véritable auteur du discours Sur la servitude volontaire. AM 20:402-06, 1908. 1468

Excellent account of A.'s thesis (1459) together with a refutation based on (a) comparison of stylistic items with Latin translation of 1574, (b) dates affecting Henri III. A strong article, essential in this dispute.

— Sur l'objectif réel du discours d'Etienne de La Boétie, De la servitude volontaire. AM 20:406-08, 1908. 1469

Refutes thesis of Dezeimeris (1467) about identity of the tyrant in *Contr'un*. Lists historians whose works might have been consulted by L. for information on Charles VI, and shows that they all picture his reign as one of anarchy and not of tyranny.

Barrère, Joseph. Etienne de La Boétie contre Nicolas Machiavel. Bordeaux, Mollat, 1908. 98 p. 1470

Il principe, published in Rome, 1532, five years after author's death. Fourteen years later young Frenchman from Sarlat who reads Italian writes his answer to its cynicism. Barrère contrasts passages and themes and tries to show L. combating Machiavelli on friendship, fate of tyrants, morality in politics. Makes most of recurrence (four times) of " maintenir " in *Contr'un*, the term " mantenere " being very common in *Il principe*. Makes out case that " formulaire " in *Contr'un* is reference to *Il principe*. Interprets *Contr'un* as " Contr'un seul livre." Evidence that L. knew Italian is his translation of 400 lines of Ariosto. Other points of contact : " Vénitiens, Hiéron de Syracuse, troupes nationales et troupes mercenaires, peuple d'Israël, le Grand Turc, fêtes au peuple, le manteau de la religion." *See* Barrère, 1479, ch. IX.

Armaingaud, A. Le véritable auteur du Discours de la servitude volontaire, Montaigne ou La Boétie? RHL 16:354-68, Apr., 1909.   1471

Contains : a) *Réponse à M. Villey*, b) *Réponse à M. Bonnefon*. *See also* p. 369-370, a final word by Villey. Important presentation of A.'s arguments directed against points made by his opponents. Invokes further historical identifications of references in the essay with early reign of Henri III. Villey in his final word insists he is not moved from his view that no particular tyrant is indicated in *Contr'un*.

Barckhausen, Henri. A propos du Contr'un. RHB 2:77-81, 1909.   1472

Sharp reproving attack on weaknesses of A.'s thesis. Shows that reference to Ronsard's *Franciade*, published in 1572, is in future tense in *Contr'un* and stresses with strong evidence that several copies of the essay were passing from hand to hand and that therefore Montaigne was not sole possessor of ms. later used by Protestants. Deduces in fact that ms. was not in L.'s library bequeathed to Montaigne and when he finally located a copy, the times were not right for its publication. For A.'s rebuttal, *see* 1476, p. 232-51, or RHB 2:152-64, 1909.

Armaingaud, A. A propos du Contr'un; réponse à M. H. Barckhausen. RHB 2:152-164, May, 1909. *Also in* : 1476, p. 232-251.   1473

Spirited defense of tense " a couru " with reference to time Montaigne wrote the verb and published his *Essais*. Cites two contemporary references to *Contr'un* on its influence as a revolutionary document.

— La Boétie et Machiavel, d'après une publication récente. RPB 11:296-307, 1908; 12:30-42, 1909. *Also in*: 1476, p. 252-85.   1474

Satirical, almost personal, attack on Barrère's idea (1470). Emphasizes that regicide in *Contr'un* is not an answer to Machiavellism. Ridicules use of " mantenere " as a test of Italian influence upon L. Mentions youth of L., 16 to 18, making highly improbable Barrère thesis, as L.'s knowledge of Italian would be weak, and French translation of *Le prince* appeared only in 1553. Article makes Barrère thesis untenable.

Barrère, Joseph. La Boétie et Machiavel—réponse à M. le Dr. Armaingaud. RPB 12:183-88, 1909.   1475

Insists that his thesis finds no favor because A. can see only his own theory. Hints also that A. does not know *Le prince*, and confronts him with a bit of plagiarism, reproducing texts.

Armaingaud, A. Montaigne pamphlétaire; l'énigme du Contr'un. Hachette, 1910. 341 p.   1476

Complete presentation of the thesis that Montaigne interpolated and pointed up passages in *Contr'un* and gave it to Protestants for publication after Saint Bartholomew. A. describes (p. 1-90) how Montaigne's *De l'amitié* first aroused his suspicions, points out radicalism in other chapters of *Essais*, lists allusions by which he identifies the tyrant in *Contr'un* with Henri III. All this is amplification of arguments already stated in RPP and RHL. After p. 90, A. reprints refutations, and various " réponses aux objections " of Bonnefon, Barckhausen, Dezeimeris, Strowski, Villey; adds a new reply (p. 223-231) to Villey's *Un dernier mot*, RHL 16:369-70, 1909, *see* 1471, and a Chapter VI attacking in detail Barrère thesis concerning Machiavelli (1475). *Contr'un* is then reprinted (p. 287-323) with passages touched up by Montaigne in italics. Book ends with the article by E. Champion, 1465, and a further supporting letter. Mainly a source book containing practically all A. has written on subject. (See Conard edition of Montaigne for his latest essay, 1939, 1483, showing his viewpoint unchanged.) *See* 1507.

Delaruelle, L. L'inspiration antique dans le Discours de la servitude volontaire. RHL 17:34-72, 1910.   1477

Refutation of A., Dezeimeris, and Barrère. Insists that L. is devoted humanist by tracing exhaustively his allusions and ideas to their Greek and Latin sources, citing texts and showing parallels. Attempts to date composition of the essay and gives explanation of its contemporary elements, Pléiade, Longa, etc. Strong study.

Morize, André. Problem of the attribution of the Discours de la servitude volontaire. *In his:* Problems and methods of literary history. Boston, Ginn, [c1922] p. 176-189. *See* 1507. 1478

Among sub-divisions of the chapter are : *Statement of the question*; *Theory of Dr. Armaingaud*; *The counterattack.* Report clarifies evidence and arranges in clear perspective contentions of both sides up to 1922. Excellent *résumé* of distinctive contributions of Bonnefon and Villey, to whom Morize gives the decision in the dispute with A.

Barrère, Joseph. L'humanisme et la politique dans le Discours de la servitude volontaire. Champion, 1923. 244 p. 1479

Essential book for setting *Contr'un* into its background. Analysis of L. as humanist not only borrowing from classics thoroughly listed, but from near contemporaries, Erasmus, Machiavelli, Castiglione. In latter aspect, he is not a political pamphleteer like Languet and Hotman, whom he influenced, but speaks for all time to all nations. Barrère then restates fully his case of *Contr'un* as inspired by general anti-Machiavellian reaction in France, L. thus becoming a leader against perfidy and tyranny. Period of composition of *Contr'un* coincides with probable period of dissemination of *Le prince* in France. Last chapter, *Contribution politique des humanistes*, shows *Contr'un* as an " Institution du peuple " compared to the numerous " Institution du prince " following in wake of Machiavelli.

Reviews : P. Courteault in RHB 17:47-48, 1924; A. Renaudet in RHL 32:286-87, 1925.

Plattard, Jean. Le procès du protestantisme. *In his:* La renaissance des lettres en France de Louis XII à Henri IV. *See* 117. p. 194-197. 1480

Touches indirectly L. enigma by discussing Montaigne's Catholicism (p. 194), not as a complete adherence to all dogma, but as a refusal to examine because outside province of human reason or logical certainty. Such a point of view would hardly permit anti-Catholic action argued by A.

Review L. Delaruelle in RSS 13:150-152, 1926.

Lablénie, Edmond. L'énigme de la Servitude volontaire. RSS 17:203-27, 1930. 1481

Excellent *résumé* and bibliography of dispute. Contrasts *Contr'un* and *Essais*, vocabulary different, classical names used by L. in French while Montaigne prefers originals, finally in style L. is hortatory, urgent, while Montaigne is philosophic, reflective, this last neatly contrasted in passages from *Essais* referring to tyrants. Important study based on close, textual scrutiny, destructive of A. thesis. *See* 1647.

Plattard, Jean. Amitié de Montaigne pour La Boétie. *In his:* État présent des études sur Montaigne. Les belles lettres, 1935. p. 14-18. 1482

Analysis of dispute concerning authorship of the *Contr'un*, with current bibliographical mentions.

Armaingaud, Arthur. Étude sur le discours de la servitude volontaire. *In:* Montaigne, Michel Eyquem de. Œuvres complètes de Michel de Montaigne. Conard, 1924-1939. v. XI, p. 9-84. 1483

Final re-statement of A.'s contention that Montaigne added passages and placed *Contr'un* in hands of the Protestants after the Bartholomew massacre. Elaborated from previous articles by the author with added arguments aimed at Bonnefon, especially that Montaigne possessed the sole manuscript available, and that it could not have resulted in its present form from L.'s academic background. Closely-knit argument, continuing the impasse. *See* 1405, i.

Aymonier, Camille. Quel est l'auteur du Discours sur la servitude volontaire ? RHB 32:145-58, 1939. 1484

Analyzes what moved Montaigne to publish L.'s " reliques," his deep respect for his friend's thought. Quotes last words of L. as reported in Montaigne's letter on L.'s death and shows how justified by them is Montaigne's suppression of *Contr'un*. Shows A.'s weak point, that Montaigne was altering a work already known and circulated. Study of date of composition from internal evidence, such as reference to Pléiade. Compares style of both men, L. with " large période," Montaigne as " causeur sec et nerveux." Takes passage not selected by A. as interpolated and shows its resemblance with others attributed to Montaigne. Total impression destructive of A.'s thesis.

Salles, A. Montaigne a-t-il remanié le Contr'un? BSAM 6:54-56, 1939; 7:96-99, 1939.   1485

Historical sketches of the mss. of L. in possession of Montaigne : his publication of all except two; appearance of *Contr'un* under Protestant auspices. Mentions Bonnefon explanation of later revisions by L. and likelihood that copies were made of the original ms. at Bordeaux. Part II furnishes incomplete bibliography of the dispute, lists main points of argument by A., expresses doubts, ends with a list of arguments made by E. Lablénie (*see* 1481) and decides " L'énigme du *Contr'un* se résume, en somme, en une simple hypothèse."

Kurz, Harry. Did Montaigne alter La Boétie's Contr'un? SP 43:619-27, 1946.
                                            1486

Review of A.'s analysis of problem of L.'s age when he wrote his essay, history of the manuscript, Montaigne's suppression of it from his *Essais*, and a listing of arguments to date for and against the idea that Montaigne had a part in the Protestant publication. Weight of evidence against A. *See* 1644.

— Montaigne and La Boétie in the chapter on friendship. PMLA 65:483-530, June, 1950.   1487

Studies chapter 28, *Essais* I, and problem of the missing *Contr'un*. Analyzes Montaigne's hesitations about publishing it as promised, throws light on his dilemma by discussing presumable date of its composition, controversial aspects, adoption by the Protestants as a weapon of propaganda, poignancy of the " unpleasant season " 1560-80, attitude of L. and Montaigne toward monarchy and their role in Catholic Counter-Reformation, citing available historical and documentary evidence to demonstrate Montaigne's unique relation to his friend and sensitivity to his reputation, all leading to his final unhappy decision. *See* 1645.

CHAPTER X. MICHEL EYQUEM DE MONTAIGNE

(Nos. 1488-1806)

RICHARD R. STRAWN AND SAMUEL FREDERIC WILL

Montaigne, Michel de. Œuvres complètes de Michel de Montaigne. Texte du manuscrit de Bordeaux. Étude, commentaires et notes par le dr. A. Armaingaud. Conard, 1924-41. 12 v.   **1488**

> V. 1-6, *Essais*; v. 7-8, *Journal de voyage*; v. 9, *La théologie naturelle de Raymond Sebon*, I, preface by Armaingaud; v. 10, *La théologie naturelle*, part II, followed by *La théologie naturelle et les théories de la traduction au XVIe siècle*, by Jean Porcher; v. 11, *Discours de la servitude volontaire, Lettres, Ephémérides, Notes marginales. Observations et étude du Dr. Payen*; v. 12, *Annotations sur les Annales de Nicole Gilles, Annotations sur le Quinte-Curce de Froben, Inscriptions de la Librairie, Notes par le Dr. A. Armaingaud. Étude et commentaires de R. Dezeimeris. Textes établis par Mlle Jeanne Duportal.* I, 1-257, consists of ten studies on different phases of M.'s work, most of which were previously published in divers periodicals. Differs from all other editions in that it includes *Discours de la servitude volontaire* among M.'s works. Commentary somewhat biased.

— Liste chronologique des éditions des Essais depuis l'édition originale (1580) jusqu'au 31 décembre 1912. BSAM 1re sér. 2:63-72, 1913.   **1489**

— Les essais de Messire Michel, seigneur de Montaigne, chevalier de l'Ordre du Roi et gentilhomme de sa chambre. Livres I et II. Bordeaux, Millanges, 1580. 2 v.   **1490**

> First edition of first two books.

— Les essais... Cinquième édition, augmentée d'un troisième livre et de six cents additions aux deux premiers. L'Angelier, 1588. 992 p.   **1491**

> Last edition published during M.'s lifetime. (Despite title page, apparently only fourth.) On a copy of it M. added changes in wording, order, spelling. Upon his death that copy was given by his wife to Order of Feuillants in Bordeaux; at the time of the Revolution it passed to Bordeaux library. In binding, edges were trimmed and pieces of M.'s changes in the printed text lopped off. (Parts lost in binding are customarily supplied from text of 1595 edition.) Known as *Exemplaire de Bordeaux*, has served as Vulgate for all important editions since *Edition municipale* (no. 1494).

— Les essais... Édition nouvelle trouvée après le décès de l'auteur; revue et augmentée par lui d'un tiers plus qu'aux précédentes impressions. L'Angelier, 1595. 1010 p.   **1492**

> Edition supervised and slightly edited by Marie de Gournay; made from Pierre de Brach's copy of M.'s ms. changes in 1588 text. Mlle de Gournay's dithyrambic preface in praise of *Essais* was withdrawn from 1598 edition; reinstated somewhat amended in later editions, plus a dedication to Cardinal Richelieu. Basis of almost all later editions until 20th century (principal of which are edited by Coste [1724], Dezeimeris and Barckhausen [1870-73], Courbet and Royer [1872-1900]; edition of Motheau and Jouaust, 1873-75, reproduces 1588 text plus 1595 variants). Chapter 14, Book I, of 1588 version printed as Ch. 14, Book I, of 1588 version printed as Ch. 14, shoving original chapters 15 through 40 back one number. Mlle de Gournay's changes limited to punctuation and arrangement to make text conform to usage of her day; she in no way changed M.'s fundamental meaning (cf. Zeitlin translation, 1498, v. 1, Appendix).

— Les essais de Montaigne, reproduction typographique de l'exemplaire annoté par l'auteur et conservé à la Bibliothèque de Bordeaux. Imprimerie nationale. v. 1, avec un avertissement et une notice par Ernest Courbet, 1906 on title page, but actually 1913; cf. v. 3, p. vi; v. 2, avec une étude sur Michel de Montaigne, sa vie, ses actes et ses écrits, par M. le Dr. A. Armaingaud, 1927; v. 3, avec notices par M. le Dr. A. Armaingaud, tome publié en collaboration avec Mlle Jeanne DuPortal, 1931.   1493

On verso, 1588 text; on facing recto, M.'s ms. changes. More easily decipherable than photographic edition but less revealing of stops and starts in successive changes. Monumental, but with municipal and photographic editions available, unnecessary.

— Les essais de Michel de Montaigne publiés d'après l'exemplaire de Bordeaux, avec les variantes manuscrites & les leçons des plus anciennes impressions, des notes, des notices et un lexique. Par Fortunat Strowski (& François Gebelin, in v. 3). Bordeaux, Pech, v. 1, 1906; v. 2, 1909; v. 3, 1919; v. 4, Les sources des Essais, annotations et éclaircissements, par Pierre Villey, 1920; v. 5, Lexique de la langue des Essais et Index des noms propres, par Pierre Villey avec la collaboration de Miss Grace Norton, 1933.   1494

First edition to reproduce Bordeaux copy exactly; gives all 1580 and 1582 readings and most of 1595 readings (on supposition that where 1595 edition and Bordeaux copy do not coincide an editor cannot presume either is more or less authentically M.'s final version). Distinguishes texts of 1580, 1588 and ms. changes. Called Edition municipale, is basis for all important 20th-century editions. V. 4 leaves only a few passages of obvious borrowing unattributed to a source; handy compendium of information published in scattered places. Lexique very incomplete, needs revising with aid of Huguet's Dictionnaire de la langue française du 16e siècle (no. 613), but accurately done and shows sensitive reading of Essais.

— Les essais de Michel de Montaigne; nouvelle édition conforme au texte de l'exemplaire de Bordeaux, avec les additions de l'édition posthume, l'explication des termes vieillis et la traduction des citations, une chronologie de la vie et de l'œuvre de Montaigne, des notices et un index par Pierre Villey. Alcan, 1922-23. 3 v. 1495

First readily available 20th-century edition; distinguishes texts of 1580, 1588, and ms. changes by symbols. Introduction to each chapter discusses main ideas and date of composition. Edition reprinted in 1930-31 with substantially same commentary; catalogue of M.'s books and a list of inscriptions in his library added. Best modern, in-octavo edition

with commentary, unfortunately out of print.

Reviews: G. A. Jekel in LGRP 56:115-120, 1935 (of 1930-31 reprint); D. Mornet in RHL 31:324-25, 1924; J. Plattard in RSS 9:210-11, 1922.

— Essais. Texte établi et présenté par Jean Plattard. Roches, 1931-32. 6 v. Reprinted 1946-48. (TF)   1496

Critical apparatus much the same as Villey editions; no commentary other than brief introduction on M.'s life, history of editions of Essais, preparation of this edition.

Reviews : F. Desonay in RBP 12:189-190, 1933; É. Magne in MerF 242:127-132, Feb. 15, 1933.

— Essais, texte établi et annoté par Albert Thibaudet. Argenteuil, Coulouma, 1933. 1089 p. Nouvelle revue française, 1937, 1950. (BP)   1497

Contains Avertissement, chronology, short bibliography of editions and important works on M. Reproduces Bordeaux copy as completed by 1595 edition. 1595 variants of Bordeaux copy (but only those of some length or significance) and glosses of certain archaic words given in notes. M.'s ms. " repentirs " given whenever interesting enough. Best single-volume, no-commentary edition to appear.

— The Essays of Michel de Montaigne. Jacob Zeitlin, tr. and ed. New York, Knopf, 1934-36. 3 v.   1498

Based on Bordeaux copy. Includes introduction (Life and Essays); notes (on sources, references, dating, largely following Villey's findings, and discussions of ideas of each essay); appendix in v. 1 on relation of 1595 text to Bordeaux copy (Mlle de Gournay made no fundamental changes in meaning of M.'s text, according to Zeitlin's well-reasoned and documented discussion, but rearranged it here and there to make it conform to usage of her day); appendix in v. 3 (supplementary notes on some ms. changes in Bordeaux copy important for illustrating M.'s train of thought); index of names and subjects; index of sources, quotations, and allusions. Translation much more accurate than Florio's, less staid than Cotton-Hazlitt, but inclined to sound either awkward or unemotional at times. Indexes most thorough of any available. Discussion in introduction neat summation of work done on M. up to time of publication and praiseworthy clarification of many points at issue (cf. section on *Apologie de Raimond Sebond*). Far outstrips the "fig-leaf" version of George Ives (Harvard University Press, 1925, commentary by Grace Norton); almost equal in quality of translation to that of E. J. Trechmann (Oxford University Press, 1927).

Reviews : Anon in TLS 34:377, May 15, 1937; J. Boorsch in SRL 11:489, Feb. 16, 1935; M. Lowenthal in NNY 143:453, Oct. 17, 1936; C. Wright in YR 24:862-864, 1934-35.

— The Essayes or morall, politike & millitarie discourses of Lo : Michaell de Montaigne. First written by him in French. And now done in English. In three parts, each with special title page. (John Florio, tr.). London, V. Sims for E. Blount, 1603.   1499

First English translation (of 1595 edition) of note; most popular one during most of 17th century. In 18th century yielded to Cotton's version; in 19th was rivalled by W. C. Hazlitt's edition of Cotton translation. Remarkable performance of substituting Elizabethan English rhythm and flourish for M.'s more nervous and economical prose. Although extremely unfaithful to M.'s text by modern standards of translation, is still best rendering of *Essais* into another idiom and remains a masterpiece in its own right. Available in Modern Library reprint.

— Journal du voyage de Michel de Montaigne en Italie, par la Suisse et l'Allemagne en 1580 et 1581, avec des notes par M. de Querlon. Le Jay, 1774. (One, two and three volume editions published at same time.)   1500

Original edition of a manuscript not discovered until 18th century. Edited with notes on archaisms, history and geography of places mentioned, quotations from other authors about same events and places. Contains *Discours préliminaire* explaining discovery of ms. and translation (by a certain M. Bartoli, p. vii.) of a section written by M. in Italian. Ms. of *Journal* has been lost; Querlon's edition only source for later editions (A. d'Ancona, 1889; L. Lautrey, 1906, with modernized spelling and vocabulary normalized to correct what looked to Lautrey like bad editing by Querlon; A. Armaingaud, v. 7 & 8 of his *Œuvres complètes de Michel de Montaigne*, 1928-29; Pierre d'Espezel, 1931; Edmond Pilon, 1932; Maurice Rat, 1942; Charles Dédéyan, for series *Les textes français*, 1946). Later editions have gener-

ally only added to Querlon's original notes and reproduced his text integrally.

— Lettres de Montaigne. *In :* Les Essais de Montaigne. Ed. by Ernest Courbet and Charles Royer. Lemerre, 1872-1900. v. 4, p. 287-365.   1501

Thirty letters, 1568-1590. Revised and corrected text of these letters, most of which had already been published by Feuillet de Conches (1611), and others.

— Le livre de raison de Montaigne sur l'Ephemeris historica de Beuther; reproduction en fac-similé avec introduction et notes publiée pour la Société des amis de Montaigne par Jean Marchand. Préface d'Abel Lefranc. Compagnie française des arts graphiques, 1948. 362 p.   1502

Exhaustive presentation of everything having to do with this famous volume and its contribution to M.'s biography.

Review : Anon in TLS, Dec. 2, 1949, p. 794.

— Reproduction en phototypie de l'exemplaire avec notes manuscrites marginales des Essais de Montaigne appartenant à la ville de Bordeaux, publiée avec une introduction par M. Fortunat Strowski. Hachette, 1912. 3 v. *See* 1544.   1503

Three volumes of facsimile reprints. Not as essential as *Édition municipale* as a working tool for textual study.

Review : Anon in ICC 67:79-80, Jan. 20, 1913.

Alexander, W. H. Montaigne's classical bookshelf. UTQ 11:78-86, 1941-42.   1504

Review of M.'s reading in Greek and Latin writers; his aptitude for concise ethical judgments may have been stimulated by his acquaintance with the ancients.

— The sieur de Montaigne and Cicero. UTQ 9:222-30, 1939-40.   1505

As Muretus was one of first scholars to deplore emptiness of Ciceronianism, so M., as layman, came to same *avant-garde* judgment, independently : Cicero's eloquence is unparalleled; Cicero's imitators are vapid.

Armaingaud, Arthur. Montaigne était-il ondoyant et divers? Montaigne était-il inconstant? RSS 10:35-56, 1923.   1506

Reproduced in his edition of M.'s works, I, 83-106. "Nous croyons en avoir assez dit pour pouvoir conclure que, contrairement à l'opinion commune, universelle même, Montaigne n'a jamais été un homme ondoyant et divers, ni un esprit sans suite, sans conséquence et sans unité, mais qu'il a au contraire montré un esprit très résolu, très un et très constant " (p. 56).

— Montaigne pamphlétaire : l'énigme du Contr'un. *See* 1476.   1507
Brings together numerous articles previously published in periodicals. Tries to show that M. is the author of many passages in *Contr'un* which attack Henri III and not tyranny in general. Part II, p. 91-295 replies to criticism of his ideas by Bonnefon, Strowski, Dezeimeris, Villey, Barckhausen, and Barrière. Reprints text of *Discours de la servitude volontaire*, with passages attributed to M. in italics; reproduces an article of Edme Champion (1465), which supports his claim.

Controversy over authorship of *Contr'un* discussed as a model of method by André Morize in *Problems and methods of literary history* (1478, p. 176-89).

Reviews : J. Frank in Archiv 127:438-448, 1911; (of controversy with Villey and Strowski) J. de La Rouxière in Rren 8:197-99, 1907; H. Schoen in ZFSL 37:20-28, 1910; L. Séché in Rren 11:107-112, 1910.

— Montaigne, Socrate et Épicure. Nrev sér. 4, 42:97-104, Jul. 15, 1919; 215-24, Aug. 1, 1919; 309-18, Aug. 15, 1919.   1508
M. never Stoic, always Epicurean, Villey and Strowski to the contrary.

— Y a-t-il une évolution dans les Essais? BSAM 1re sér. no. 2:117-60, 1913; no. 3:254-265, 1914.   1509
Denies evidences of evolution found by Villey and Strowski, insists that M. was always an Epicurean.

Audra, Émile. Montaigne. *In his :* L'influence française dans l'œuvre de Pope. Champion, 1931.   p. 466-80. (BRLC, v. 72.)   1510
Excellent evaluation of Pope's debt to M.

Auerbach, Erich. L'humaine condition. *In his :* Mimesis, dargestellte Wirklichkeit in der abendländischen Literatur. Bern, Francke, 1946.   p. 271-97.   1511
Sensitive, expertly developed analysis of first paragraphs of III, 2 *(Du repentir)*. M.'s frank, ironic, lively, sometimes almost lyrical " dialogue " used as example of M.'s undertaking : description of the whole of any one life. With M., for first time, man's life seen as problematic; his irony,

refusal of pretense, deep and calm self-satisfaction keep him from reaching beyond the problematic to expression of the tragic—a sense of which is latent in M.'s text but not there overtly. One of most revealing chapters on M. yet written.

— Der Schriftsteller Montaigne. GRM 20: 39-53, 1932.   1512
A non-specialist in an era of specialists, M. is first layman to exist intellectually as creator of a book *(Schriftsteller)*. His method unscientific; his purpose self-description. Relished himself not from sentiment but because his self was the irreducible, inescapable minimum of the human condition.

Aymonier, Camille. Montaigne à table. RPB 37:179-91, 1934.   1513
Detailed study of M.'s remarks concerning food, drink, table service, and table manners; with conclusion that they probably reveal both his curiosity and his *gourmandise*.

— Montaigne et la médecine en Aquitaine. RHB 26:49-61, 1933; 97-107, 1933.   1514
Excellent study of practices of empirical medicine in M.'s day, and of defense of doctors in Laurent Joubert's *Erreurs populaires et propos vulgaires touchant la médecine et le régime de la santé* (Bordeaux, Millanges, 1578). Finds that M. saw need of experimental method, but was more interested in observing errors than in starting the search for positive truth, as did Bacon.

— Montaigne et la sorcellerie. RPB 37:78-94, 1934.   1515
M.'s ideas on sorcery violently criticized by the Jesuit Del Rio and by Pierre de Lancre in his *Tableau de l'inconstance des mauvais anges et démons* (1612). Excellent analysis of Lancre's book, which resulted from investigation of sorcery in Bordeaux region in 1609, and led to eighty burnings.

— Montaigne et les femmes. RPB 36:52-74, 1933.   1516
Traces M.'s remarks on women through *Essais* and *Journal de voyage*, reaches no definite conclusion except that his attitude toward them is *ondoyant et divers* and that he is not a feminist.

— Montaigne incrédule? RHEF 96:289-316, Jul.-Sept. 1936.   1517
Review of remarks about M.'s religiosity. Clear vote of confidence in Strowski,

Villey, Busson, and especially H. Janssen; clear hatred of interpretations of Gide and Armaingaud. Conclusion : M. lived and died sincere Catholic. Little indication of importance of religious question for interpreting *Essais*.

Bailly, Auguste. L'écrivain en voyage. Les essais et Mademoiselle de Gournay. *In his* : La vie littéraire sous la renaissance. Tallandier, 1952. p. 271-99. 1518

Sees M. as " le premier de nos grands reporters," whose *Journal de voyage* " nous révèle certains modes de pensée et d'observation, certaines formes de curiosité, qui sont caractéristiques de toute une époque " (p. 272). Good popular discussion of *Journal*, paying little attention to *Essais*.

— Montaigne. Fayard, 1942. 353 p. 1519

Contains no new facts or ideas concerning M.'s life and works, but presents an " exposé solide et aimable qui, à défaut de nouveauté, apporte au lecteur qui n'a pas le loisir de relire d'une traite les *Essais*, une peinture assez finement nuancée de cet homme ondoyant et divers." (Henri Hauser in Rhist 194:325-26, 1944).

Baldensperger, Fernand. L'humour dans Montaigne. RCC 21:118-35, 1912-13. 1520

After observing, rightly, that M. has a humorist's love of anecdotes and penchant for describing the irrational, author denies, still rightly, that M. had a humorous intent; but errs in also denying any humorous twist to M.'s style.

Ballaguy, Paul. La sincérité de Montaigne. MerF 245:547-75, Aug. 1, 1933. 1521

Attacks M.'s sincerity on many points : chastity during travels in Italy, pretentions to nobility and to military distinction. Claims M. sought appointment as mayor of Bordeaux.

Barrière, Pierre. Montaigne. *In his* : La vie intellectuelle en Périgord, 1550-1800. Bordeaux, Delmas, 1937. p. 69-143. 1522

Studies M. as representative of the province which produced, among other men of letters, Fénelon, Maine de Biran, Brantôme, La Calprenède. Good discussion of his intellectual background, life, works, and influence.

Review : P. Laumonier in RHL 44:567-569, 1937.

— Montaigne, gentilhomme français. (2nd, revised ed.) Bordeaux, Delmas, 1948. 205 p. 1523

Semi-popularization of M.'s life, followed by rather superficial survey of *Essais*, which are characterized as *mémoires*, closer to a *livre de raison* than to a philosophical inquiry. Mixture of keen insights and twisted understanding of M.'s text.

Review : J. Sartenaer in LR 5:355-56, 1951.

Beck, Christian. Le voyage de Montaigne et l'évolution du sentiment du paysage, essai de psychologie sociale. MerF 98:298-317, Jul. 16, 1912. 1524

Feeling for landscape did not exist in M.'s day. His description of Alps shows esthetic pleasure unique in literature of period.

Belleli, Maria Luisa. Modernità di Montaigne. Rome, Formiggini, 1933. 196 p. 1525

Studies influence of M. on Renan, Anatole France, Barrès, Gide, Valéry, and Proust.

Bennett, Roger E. Sir William Cornwallis's use of Montaigne. PMLA 48:1080-89, Dec., 1933. 1526

Cornwallis influenced by M. more than any other English essayist before Cowley. But, author shows, " Montaigne was an extreme individualist, and true imitation of him consists in being an equally frank and courageous individualist."

Bernard, Paul. A l'école de Montaigne. Comment devenir un homme cultivé. Nathan, 1938. 250 p. 1527

Guide to use of *Essais* as a textbook for self-education. Intended for " ceux qui, en toute modestie et discrétion, veulent consacrer à leur culture intellectuelle les loisirs que leur laisse leur profession ou, comme on le dit, leur ' besogne salariée ' " (p. 5).

Bertoni, Giulio. De Pétrarque à Montaigne. REI 1:156-65, 1936. 1528

Petrarch, the mystic, loses faith in knowledge but not in religion. M.'s only faith is in knowledge. They express humanism of two different periods, but both primarily interested in same eternal problem, man and his place in the universe.

Bespaloff, Rachel. L'instant et la liberté chez Montaigne. Deucalion 3:65-107. (Etre et penser, trentième cahier, Neuchâtel, La Baconnière, 1950.) 1529

A rather lucid examination of M.'s philosophy, from the point of view of Existentialist doctrine.

Blasberg, Hans. Die Wortstellung bei Montaigne. Bochum-Langendreer, Pöppinghaus, 1937. 68 p. (Diss., Westfälischen Wilhelms-Universität, Münster, 1935.)   1530

Considerations of affective construction, rhythm, and logic—in that descending order—condition M.'s word order. Study worth consulting for stylistic classifications, if not for interpretations, which are beside the point when they are not mistaken.

Blinkenberg, Andreas. Quel sens Montaigne a-t-il voulu donner au mot Essais dans le titre de son œuvre? MélMR, p. 3-14. 1531

Thorough semantic study of 16th-century meanings of word *essai*. Conclusion : " Montaigne a choisi pour titre de son œuvre un mot qui avait un sens assez large, assez peu précis, si peu en effet que plusieurs fois, en se corrigeant, il l'a écarté de son texte pour le remplacer par des synonymes prêtant moins à la confusion.

" Mais dans le titre même il ne l'a pas précisé, donc probablement il n'a pas voulu préciser. Le mot y reste volontairement sans détermination aucune; il garde toute la largeur, toute la valeur latente d'un mot isolé, sans contexte " (p. 12).

Boas, George. The happy beast in French thought of the seventeenth century. Baltimore, Johns Hopkins Press, 1933. 159 p.   1532

Authoritative treatment of origins and influences of M.'s theriophily (" the beasts—like savages—are more ' natural ' than man, and hence man's superior.") (p. 1). M. influenced by Plutarch and *Paradoxes* of Landi, Giraldi, and Boaystuau. Excellent account of 17th-century attack on M. and his disciples, Pasquier and Charron, by Père Garasse, Dupleix, Chanet, Descartes, Bossuet, etc. Philosophical defense of theriophily by Cureau de La Chambre and Gassendi, and satirical defense by Cyrano de Bergerac and Mme Deshoulières.

Reviews : Anon in TLS 32:514, Jul. 27, 1933; C. A. Kofoid in Isis 22:240-41, 1934-35.

Boase, Alan M. The fortunes of Montaigne : a history of the Essays in France, 1580-1669. London, Methuen, 1935. 462 p.   1533

Important study. Covers some material treated in Villey's *Montaigne devant la postérité* (no. 1788). Discusses both influence of M. and criticism and appreciation of *Essays*. Authors considered include Charron, Camus, Descartes, Gassendi, La Mothe Le Vayer, Chapelain, Balzac, La Rochefoucauld, St. Évremond, Pascal, Molière, La Fontaine, etc. Excellent bibliography of 16th and 17th-century authors quoted.

Reviews : Anon in TLS 34:511, Aug. 15, 1935; G. Boas in MLN 51:256-58, 1936; J. Hayward in NSN, ns 10:198-99, Aug. 10, 1935; R. Pintard in RHL 43:434-36, 1936; H. Robinson in AHR 1935-36; H. F. Stewart in MLR 31:584-586, 1936; A. J. Symons in FortR, ns 138: 499-500, Oct., 1935.

— Michel de Montaigne et la sorcellerie. Hren 2:402-21, 1935.   1534

Tries to show there were no witchcraft cases in Bordeaux courts before 1594, that " Des boyteux " represents protests against increasing judicial severity following death of Lagebâton in 1583, and that M. expresses attitude towards witchcraft of more tolerant early part of his century.

— Montaigne annoté par Florimond de Raemond. RSS 15:237-78, 1928.   1535

Raemond's annotations, which identify friends of M. mentioned but not named in *Essays*, are reproduced, with commentary and biographical details concerning M.'s friends.

Bonnefon, Paul. La bibliothèque de Montaigne. RHL 2:313-71, 1895.   1536

Reproduces corrected version of inscriptions in M.'s library first published by Galy and Lapeyre (no. 1618). Gives detailed description of 76 volumes known to have belonged to M.

— Montaigne, l'homme et l'œuvre. Bordeaux, Gounouilhou; Rouam, 1893. 502 p. (*Also* Picard, 1943, 502 p.)   1537

Still standard biographical work. Utilizes and coordinates research of Dr. Payen, Malvezin, and their contemporaries, on biographical details. Republished without illustrations as *Montaigne et ses amis* (Colin, 1898, 2 v., 413 p.) with added chapters on La Boétie, Charron and Mⁱˡᵉ de Gournay.

Reviews : W. Baldensperger in ZFSL 15:202-05, 1893; L. Clément in RHL 5:647-50, 1898.

— Les moralistes : Montaigne, La Boétie, Charron, Du Vair. *In* : Petit de Julleville, Louis, ed. Histoire de la langue et de la littérature françaises des origines à 1900. *See* 116. V. III, p. 406-71, bibl. p. 483-485. 1538

Excellent general view of M.'s life and works, although written prior to the epoch-making studies of Villey and Strowski.

Borel, Pierre. Autour de Montaigne : études littéraires. Neuchâtel and Paris, Delachaux et Niestlé, 1945, 139 p. 1539

La position de Montaigne and *Montaigne vu à travers les Essais* (p. 13-68) treat M. as representative of all civilizations : disciple and emulator of the ancients, devout Christian and Catholic, and precursor of modern thought " dans ce qu'elle a de critique, de sensualiste et de négateur," as represented by Voltaire, Rousseau, the Encyclopedists, Renan, Anatole France, Gide, and Proust.

Bouillier, Victor. La fortune de Montaigne en Italie et en Espagne. Champion, 1922. 72 p. 1540

Italian admiration of M. has developed chiefly since beginning of 19th century. Read and admired by Giuseppe Giusti, Francesco de Sanctis, Benedetto Croce. Literary historians like F. Neri have devoted worth-while studies to him.

In Spain, Francisco de Quevedo admired him. Almost totally ignored in 17th and 18th centuries. Present generation interested in him : Menéndez y Pelayo, Azorín.

Reviews : Anon in RLC 3:331-32, 1923; J. Plattard in RSS 10:119-20, 1923.

— Montaigne en allemand : Christoph Bode, son grand traducteur. RLC 13:5-13, 1933. 1541

High praise of fidelity of Bode's translation (1793-99) to both spirit and letter of M.'s original.

— Montaigne et Goethe. RLC 5:572-93, 1925. 1542

Careful analysis of Goethe's references to M., and of their similarities and differences, without any effort to show definite influence of M.

— La renommée de Montaigne en Allemagne. Champion, 1921. 64 p. 1543

M. had little influence but many admirers in Germany, including Bodmer, Lessing, Herder, Goethe, Kant, Schopenhauer, and especially Nietzsche. Includes good evaluation of studies on M. by German scholars. *See* 2886.

Review : Anon in RLC 2:155-56, 1922.

Brunetière, Ferdinand. Publications récentes sur Montaigne. RDM 5th ser. 35:192-227, Sept. 1, 1906. *Reprinted :* Études critiques sur l'histoire de la littérature française, 8e sér. Hachette, 1907. p. 1-55. 1544

Supposedly a discussion of the evolution of *Essais* as revealed in first volume of Strowski's Municipal edition (no. 1503) and in his Montaigne (no. 1747) and of volumes by Zangroniz (no. 1805), Dowden (no. 1599), and Edme Champion (no. 1557). Some good discussion of first three, none of Dowden, and little of Champion. Considerable development of author's ideas on M. as a *curieux*, of his laying foundations of classicism by his interest in " observation psychologique et morale," and explanation of apparent incoherence of M.'s philosophy as due to the fact that it is a philosophy of life.

Brunschvicg, Léon. Descartes et Pascal lecteurs de Montaigne. New York and Paris, Brentano's, 1944. 239 p. (Neuchâtel, La Baconnière, 1945. 210 p.) 1545

Study of turning point from renaissance-reformation to modern philosophy. Both Descartes and Pascal, agreeing partially but not fundamentally, handle their problems, and particularly that of validity of subjective evidence, in terms bequeathed them by M. Brunschvicg presents those terms largely as they occur in *Apologie de Raymond Sebond*, and since he is a better reader of Descartes and Pascal than of M. his argument becomes slightly twisted. Most attention paid to metaphysical concerns, far from the heart of *Essais*. Pithy book, forbiddingly yet humbly written and somehow unimposing despite its obvious fairness and good sense, but at least the next-to-last word on the subject.

Reviews : Anon in RPFE 135:273-74, 1945; A. M. Boase in FS 2:360-61, 1948; L. Febvre in AESC 6:115-17, 1951; A. Guérard in BA 19:160-61, 1945; R. Mehl in RHPR 26:315-18, 1946; A. Roche in MLJ 28:693-94, 1944; G. Weill in Ren 1:445-62, 1943.

— Le moment historique de Montaigne. *In his :* Le progrès de la conscience dans la philosophie occidentale. Alcan, 1927. p. 118-35. 1546

" En fin de compte, Montaigne sera le moraliste de la conscience pure, de celle qui se décrit, se scrute, s'approfondit, avec la seule ambition d'être en soi et de se développer pour soi, sans aucun souci de rejaillir et de peser sur autrui " (p. 131).

Bruwaene, Léon van den. Les idées philosophiques de Montaigne. RNS 35:339-78, Aug., 1933; 489-515, Nov., 1933.   1547

Concise, penetrating review of M.'s ideas on nature, reason, artfulness, judgment; conclusion that they make a philosophy whose chief concern is not what questions to ask, but how to ask them. Less than a metaphysician, M. is rather an individual, for whom the psychological aspect of a problem has first importance.

Buck, Philo M., Jr. Que sçais-je ?— Montaigne. *In his:* The golden thread. New York, Macmillan, 1931. p. 336-368.   1548

Sound and readable treatment of M. and his place in world literature. Sees M. as more than a sceptic; his moderation lies somewhere between idealism of Dante and materialism of Sancho Panza.

Buffum, Imbrie. L'influence du voyage de Montaigne sur les Essais. Princeton University Press, 1946. 153 p. (Diss., Princeton.)   1549

Studies changes in M.'s thought after 1580; concludes that travels influenced ideas on experience, diversion as a means of combatting pain and melancholy, solitude, custom, and diversity of mankind. Introduction points out traits of M. revealed in *Journal* but not in *Essays.* Useful complement to Villey's studies on sources and evolution of *Essays.* Bibliography.

Reviews : H. C. Lancaster in MLN 62:345-48, May, 1947; S. F. Will in Symp 1:124-26, Nov., 1947.

BSAM, 1ʳᵉ série. Ed. by A. Armaingaud. Durel, 1913-1921, Fasc. 1-2, 1913; 3, 1914; 4, 1921.   1550

Contents of first series summarized in second series, no. 2, p. 92-93.

— 2ᵉ série. Conard, 1937-1949.   1551

Fourteen numbers published at irregular intervals, edited by A. Salles (1937-41) and G. Guichard (1941-49). Articles usually brief, frequently taken from other periodicals. Contents of numbers 3-14 summarized in SP annual bibliography as follows : nos. 3-4, 36:344-45, 1939; nos. 5-7, 37:372-73, 1940; no. 8, 38:347, 1941; no. 9, 40:316-17, 1943; nos. 10-14, 47:345-346, 1950.

Busson, Henri. De Montaigne à Charron. *In his:* Les sources et le développement du rationalisme dans la littérature française de la

renaissance (1533-1601). *See* 188, p. 434-459.   1552

Sees M. as product of Pomponazzi and Paduan school. " Montaigne du reste n'est pas un ' libertin,' c'est un padouan, par l'étendue et la nature de son scepticisme.... Mais à le considérer au point de vue métaphysique Montaigne ne paraît pas un esprit avancé pour son époque. Son attitude religieuse et philosophique est celle que cinq ans de pénétration italienne ont modelée dans l'élite des intelligences françaises de la seconde moitié du xviᵉ siècle " (p. 449). *See* 2051, 2666.

— L'influence de Montaigne et de Charron. *In his:* La pensée religieuse française de Charron à Pascal. *See* 1836, p. 177-224.   1553

Good summary of M.'s influence in 17th century. For more thorough treatment *see* Boase, no. 1533.

Canac, Albert. La philosophie théorique de Montaigne. Sansot, 1908. 80 p.   1554

Finds M.'s philosophy " une philosophie optimiste et consolante. Au sens où l'entend Montaigne, la vertu est un plaisir, puisqu'elle résulte d'une satisfaction harmonieuse de nos tendances, et de tous les plaisirs que nous connaissons, la poursuite même en est plaisante " (p. 79-80).

Cancalon, A. Auguste. L'esprit positif et scientifique dans Montaigne. Éditions d'art Édouard Pelletan, 1911. 42 p.   1555

Considers M.'s discussion of intelligence of animals the central theme of *Apologie,* " celui pour lequel tout le reste a été écrit." Makes this the scientific basis of M.'s philosophy of Nature, conceived as a Providence and substituted for God. Hails M. as a founder of comparative psychology of men and animals.

Chambers, Frank M. Pascal's Montaigne. PMLA 65:790-804, Sept., 1950.   1556

Detailed discussion of Pascal's expressed opinions of M.; conclusion that M. served Pascal as Virgil served Dante. Guide through human realm, leaving Pascal to deal alone with man's relation to God.

Champion, Edme. Introduction aux Essais de Montaigne. Colin, 1900. 313 p.   1557

Presents M. primarily as man of action, writing essays to serve others by criticizing their faults as he sees them in himself, indifferent to religion and increasingly anti-Christian. One of first to note evolution of M.'s thought. Important study in its day; now outdated.

Review : É. Faguet in RPL 37:397-400, Sept. 29, 1900.

Charpentier, John. Montaigne ou l'humaniste véritable. MerF 242:257-78, Mar. 1, 1933.   **1558**

Intelligent appreciation of *Essais*, intended for general reader.

Chasles, Philarète. Shakespeare traducteur de Montaigne. *In his*: L'Angleterre au seizième siècle. Charpentier, 1879. p. 115-139.   **1559**

Exaggerated estimate of M.'s influence on Shakespeare. Claims that M. transformed the poet into a thinker and philosopher, and put him on the track of the great tragedies written after 1603.

Chinard, Gilbert. Un défenseur des Indiens : Montaigne. *In his*: L'exotisme américain dans la littérature française au XVIᵉ siècle. Hachette, 1911. p. 193-218.   **1560**

Des cannibales (1578-79) shows mere curiosity about inhabitants of New World. *Des coches* (1586-87) reveals indignation at Spanish atrocities against conquered peoples, shows M. as humanitarian.

Citoleux, Marc. Le vrai Montaigne, théologien et soldat. Lethielleux, 1937. 313 p.   **1561**

Well-documented presentation of a new and rather extreme point of view. M. believes in superiority of ancients, but has no leaning toward paganism. Sebond and M. are neither rationalists nor fideists but, like all good Christians, both at the same time, with full confidence in reason supported by faith. His pyrrhonism solely for purposes of argumentation. Moderation of M. achieved only after long and concerted effort, sustained by faith and striving for *entière réformation*. M. an outright theologian in his translation of Sebond, in the chapter *Des prières*, and *Apologie*.

Reviews : E. Jourdan in Poly 194:117-118, 1937; J. Plattard in RHL 45:97-99, 1938; M. Raymond in Hren 4:345-50, 1937.

Clément, Louis. Antoine de Guevara, ses lecteurs et ses imitateurs français au XVIᵉ siècle. RHL 7:590-602, 1900; 8:214-33, 1901.   **1562**

M. may have borrowed from him and his

followers ideas on women and marriage, old age, doctors. *See* 2867.

Collins, J. C. Shakespeare and Montaigne. *In his*: Studies in Shakespeare. New York, Dutton, 1904. p. 277-96.   **1563**

" The true nature of Shakespeare's indebtedness to Montaigne may be fairly estimated if we say what, we believe, may be said with truth, that had the *Essays* never appeared there is nothing to warrant the assumption that what he has in common with Montaigne would not have been equally conspicuous" (p. 296).

Compayré, Gabriel. Montaigne. *In his*: Histoire des doctrines de l'éducation en France depuis le seizième siècle. 6ᵉ éd. Hachette, 1898. v. 1, p. 88-115.   **1564**

One of the most competent 19th-century analyses of M.'s ideas on education.

— Montaigne et l'éducation du jugement. Delaplane, 1905. 122 p. (English translation, New York, Crowell, 1908. 139 p.)   **1565**

Presents M.'s ideas on education primarily from point of view of their application today. Sees M. as ancestor of educational ideas of Port Royal, Fénelon, Locke, and Rousseau. Copious quotations from *Essays* reveal M. as a dilettante rather than a dogmatic theorist.

Cons, Louis. Montaigne et l'idée de justice. MélPL, p. 347-54.   **1566**

Uncertainties of justice observed during his experience in the courts may furnish a partial explanation of M.'s pyrrhonism, conservatism, and respect for custom.

— Montaigne et Julien l'Apostat. Hren 4:411-20, 1937.   **1567**

Julian and M. both conservatives. M. admires Julian as defender of established paganism and as enemy of " nouveleté " of Christianity (" De la liberté de conscience ").

Coppin, Joseph. Étude sur la grammaire et le vocabulaire de Montaigne d'après les variantes des Essais. Lille, Morel, 1925. 112 p. (MFCL, fasc. 29.)   **1568**

As classified by Coppin, variants follow no pattern; but faulty classification made on superficial data and according to no clear notion of stylistic method. Conclusion (that variants reveal artistic rather than grammatical concerns on M.'s part) is true but elementary.

— Montaigne. *In:* Dictionnaire des lettres françaises, le seizième siècle. Fayard, 1951. p. 517-25.   1569

Excellent brief presentation of M., followed by very useful bibliography marred only by an excess of typographical errors.

— Montaigne traducteur de Raymond de Sebond. Lille, Morel, 1925. 269 p. 1570

Finds Sebond and *Liber creaturarum*, which had been neglected by Villey and Strowski, to be an important source of *Apologie.* Considers M. a faithful translator who knew Sebond well and did not betray him.

Reviews : J. Plattard in RSS 13:286-89, 1926; P. Villey in RHL 34:589-91, 1927.

— La morale de Montaigne est-elle purement naturelle? MFCL, fasc. 32, 1927, p. 105-120.   1571

Presents M. as a weak Christian, sometimes contradicting Christian morality, but gradually reconciling opinions and practi . Holds it impossible to conclude that 1 .ason rather than Christian faith is the source of his *morale.*

— Quelques procédés de stile *(sic)* de Montaigne. RPF 40:190-201, 1928.   1572

Study of *De l'art de conférer.* Isolates five devices used by M. : noun of action in place of verb; abstract noun instead of adjective; adjective instead of analytical phrase; assonance and alliteration; appositive phrases for effect of rapidity and curtness.

Courteault, Paul. La mère de Montaigne. RHB 27:5-14, 1934; 49-60, 1934. *Reprinted in* MélPL, p. 305-27.   1573

Significant additions to biographical details published by Malvezin (no. 1667). Establishes that M.'s mother was daughter of Pierre Lopez and descended from a family of Jewish business people in Saragossa, which settled in Toulouse at end of 15th century and was ennobled. She died in 1601. Reproduces her will, which shows her to be " une femme de tête, une ménagère très stricte et, semble-t-il, âpre au gain " (p. 323).

— Le IVe centenaire de Montaigne à Bordeaux. RPB 36:75-93, 1933.   1574

Excellent account of exhibits pertaining to M.'s life, iconography of M., his *librairie,* and Bordeaux in his day. Especially useful for study of portraits of M. and account of research leading to identification of his residence in Bordeaux.

Cresson, André, *éd.* Montaigne, sa vie, son œuvre. Avec un exposé de sa philosophie. Presses universitaires, 1947. 144 p. (Cph)   1575

An essay on M.'s philosophy, agreeable but not profound, followed by 70 pages of extracts from the *Essais* and the *Journal de voyage.*

Croll, Morris W. Attic prose in the seventeenth century. SP 18:79-128, 1921. 1576

Part concerning M. shows him chiefly representative of *genus humile* or *lene,* something of a rhetorician in spite of himself, and, like a sage, expressing himself with a style whose intricacies have been wrought to reveal a mind's solitary struggle with unfamiliar truth.

— Attic prose : Lipsius, Montaigne, Bacon. *In:* Schelling anniversary papers. New York, Century, 1923. p. 117-50.   1577

M.'s search for greatest possible naturalness in style equates with quest for the natural man in himself and forms particular tendency within Anti-Ciceronianism : " libertine " prose. Equal facility in Latin and in vernacular gives M. a style " which renders the process of thought and portrays the picturesque actuality of life with equal effect and constantly relates the one to the other...."

Article antedates Croll's piece on baroque style; not invalidated by it, except perhaps slightly in terminology.

— The baroque style in prose. *In:* Studies in English philology : a miscellany in honor of Frederick Klaeber (Kemp Malone and Martin B. Ruud, eds.). University of Minnesota Press, 1929. p. 427-56. 1578

Baroque style, with M. " after he has found himself " as one example of it, is *coupé* (" curt ") and Senecan; has four marks : " studied brevity of numbers," " the hovering, imaginative order," " asymmetry," " the omission of the ordinary syntactic ligatures," and is characterized by a spiral movement that views the same point from different levels. The " loose " period typical of M. " is not made; it becomes. It completes itself and takes on form in the course of the motion of mind which it expresses."

— Juste Lipse et le mouvement anticicéronien à la fin du XVIe et au début du XVIIe siècle. RSS 2:200-42, 1914.   1579

Lipsius and M. shared a scorn for the classical period. Their brevity and directness rhetorical elements of evolution of renaissance thought out of ancient world into modern.

Cruchet, René. Montaigne et les médecins. Montaigne chez lui. *In his:* France et Louisiane. Médecine et littérature. Montaigne et Montesquieu at home. University, La., Louisiana State University Press, 1939. p. 113-39; 249-71.   1580

M.'s ideas on medecine so similar to those of doctors that one may wonder whether he might not have studied medicine in his youth. In spite of quips against medicine, he entertained constant hope of an eventual cure. Classifies M. as neuro-arthritic rather than as a hypochondriac.

Second study presents a lively and sound description of M.'s life in his château.

Daudet, Léon. Montaigne et l'ambiance du savoir. *In his:* Flambeaux. Grasset, 1929. p. 77-149.   1581

Brilliant but very subjective treatment of M., drawing too heavily on Daudet's own medical experiences. Considers M. " le plus grand de nos conciliateurs," in contrast with Rabelais, " le plus grand de nos polémistes." " Voilà, selon moi, la clé de Montaigne; il est arrivé à ce point extrême de criticisme intérieur où celui qui doute doute de son doute; et c'est par ce chemin, comme l'a très bien vu Pascal, au cours de l'entretien avec M. de Sacy, qu'il est arrivé, ou plutôt qu'il est revenu, à la croyance " (p. 111-12).

Dawson, J. C. A suggestion as to the source of Montaigne's title : Essais. MLN 51:223-26, 1936.   1582

At Floral Games in Toulouse during M.'s time, tie contests were broken by writing " essays " : poems written on a verse used as subject. M. uses " essai " in precisely that same sense; his early essays follow similar pattern : commentary on anecdote or quotation from ancients.

Dédéyan, Charles. Deux aspects de Montaigne. BHren 6:302-27, 1945.   1583

M.'s service as mayor of Bordeaux helped him achieve " la connaissance définitive de soi. C'est elle (la cité) qui en l'obligeant à défendre Montaigne contre le Maire, l'essayiste contre le magistrat municipal, le moi contre l'envahissement des fonctions publiques, lui permettra de circonscrire son être, d'en savoir l'étendue et la puissance, de mesurer sa volonté " (p. 312).

M.'s concept of " honnête homme " distinguished by " la mesure, la modération." " Il y a aussi la modestie, l'effacement devant la compétence, et surtout le refus d'être un professionel " (p. 323-24). M. the true father of 17th century " honnête homme."

— Essai sur le Journal de voyage de Montaigne. Boivin, 1946. 218 p.   (ELEC) 1584

" Its only real weakness in my opinion is that it fails to fulfill the early promise of the author to try to make *Journal* contribute ' à préciser la personnalité et la pensée de l'auteur des Essais '." (Frame, review below, p. 261). Like Buffum (no. 1549) he does not try to make *Journal* a literary masterpiece. " That the trip furnished him with certain illustrations no one can deny, that it may have strengthened his ideas about the unity of mankind is highly probable, but to the question whether or not it had the fundamental importance attributed to it by Buffum and Dédéyan, Montaigne himself would probably have answered ' Que sais-je ? ' " (Lancaster, review below). *See* 2705.

Reviews : G. Charlier in RBP 26:181-84, 1948; D. M. Frame in RR 38:258-62, 1947; H. C. Lancaster in MLN 62:345-348, 1947; P. Moreau in RHL 48:90-95, 1948; B. Munteano in RLC 22:584-89, 1948; J. Sartenaer in LR 2:342-44, 1948; A. M. Schmidt in Cr 1:419-22, Oct. 1946.

— L'humanisme et le classicisme de Montaigne. IL 1:127-33, 1949.   1585

Good statement of elements in M. which characterize humanism of the renaissance and of the principles of 17th-century classicism embodied in *Essais*.

— Montaigne chez ses amis anglo-saxons. Boivin, 1946. 2 v.   1586

V. I studies M.'s influence on English and American letters between 1760 and 1900. V. II made up of excerpts from various authors on M., and an extensive bibliography. " The book as a whole is thorough, judicious, unbiased and eminently readable." (Frame, review below.) But Frame, Lancaster and other reviewers point out many minor inaccuracies and questionable conclusions.

Reviews : G. J. A. in RPar 53:161-62, Nov. 1946; Anon in TLS, Aug. 30, 1947, p. 433-44; J. M. Carré in RLC 21:306-09, 1947; G. Charlier in RBP 26:181-84, 1948; D. M. Frame in RR 38:258-62, 1947; H. C. Lancaster in MLN 62:345-48,

1947; P. Moreau in RHL 48:90-95, 1948; A. M. Schmidt in Cr 1:419-22, Oct. 1946.

Dedieu, Joseph. Montaigne et le cardinal Sadolet. BLE 1:8-22, Jan. 1909.   1587
Treats influence of Sadolet, " le grand apologiste de la douceur " (p. 13), on M.'s educational ideas. " Tous deux, Montaigne et Sadolet, préparent l'homme de salon, superficiel, mais infiniment souple et séduisant " (p. 22). See 1787.

Delacroix, Raymond. Montaigne malade et médecin. Lyon, Rey, 1907. 111 p.   1588
Interesting study, in spite of its one-sided approach. Tries to show that " la connaissance intime de Montaigne ne peut être réelle si l'on n'étudie auparavant en médecin sa vie et son œuvre " (p. 10). Traces character and temperament to Jewish origin of mother and to father's death of " lithiase vésicale." Considers him defender of empiricism rather than precursor of experimental method.

Delboulle, A. Charron plagiaire de Montaigne. RHL 7:284-96, 1900.   1589
Eleven pages of parallel passages, leading author to conclusion that Charron is servile imitator of M.

Desgranges, Guy. Montaigne historien de sa vie publique. MLQ 12:86-92, 1951. 1590
Concludes, without convincing proof, that M.'s public life was a failure. " Prudence et nécessité politiques, préjugé nobiliaire et conscience d'une certaine infériorité sociale, volunté (sic) de cohérence dans l'image du sage sous laquelle il veut apparaître à son lecteur, coquetterie morale, telles sont donc les causes des transformations que Montaigne fait subir à la réalité de ses origines sociales, de sa vie professionnelle, de ses ambitions et de son expérience politiques " (p. 92).

Dezeimeris, Reinhold. Annotations inédites de Michel de Montaigne sur les Annales et chroniques de France de Nicole Gilles. RHL 16:213-58, 734-73, 1909; 19:126-49, 1912; 20:133-57, 1913; 21:101-41, 1914.   1591
Careful analysis of M.'s notes, and discussion of their relation to Essais, but lacks an over-all evaluation of the significance of M.'s debt to Gilles.

— Annotations inédites de Michel de Montaigne sur le De rebus gestis Alexandri Magni de Quinte-Curce. RHL 23:399-440, 1916; 24:605-36, 1917; 25:595-622, 1918; 26:577-600, 1920; 28:528-48, 1921. 1592

M.'s Quinte-Curce, printed by Froben in 1545, preserved in library of château de la Brède, formerly owned by Montesquieu. Detailed analysis of annotations and their relation to Essais. Last installment announces a final one which did not appear.

— De la renaissance des lettres à Bordeaux au xvie siècle. Bordeaux, Gounouilhou, 1864. 66 p.   1593
Excellent discussion of intellectual milieu in which M. spent his early years. Well documented.

— Plan d'exécution d'une édition critique des Essais de Montaigne. Bordeaux, Cadoret, 1903. 24 p.   1594
Outlines method of indicating date of each passage in Essais, thus showing evolution of M.'s thought. His method followed by most modern editors.

— Recherches sur l'auteur des Épitaphes de Montaigne. Lettres à M. le Dr. J. F. Payen. Bordeaux, Gounouilhou, 1861. 82 p.   1595
Attributes them to Saint-Martin. His discussion of other possible authors illuminates intellectual milieu of Bordeaux at end of 16th century.

Doumic, René. La famille de Montaigne. RDM 4th per. 132:433-44, Nov. 15, 1895. Reprinted as L'égoïsme de Montaigne in his Études sur la littérature française, 1re sér. Perrin, 1896. p. 53-77.   1597
Excellent article occasioned by Stapfer's La famille et les amis de Montaigne (no. 1743) and its argument that charge of egotism leveled at M. is unjust. Desiring to describe the human condition, M. inevitably found himself as worthy a representative as any man. Opposite of Rousseau, in Confessions, who considered his case inimitable.

Dow, Neal. The concept and term " nature " in Montaigne's Essays. Philadelphia, 1940. 68 p. (Diss., Pennsylvania.)   1598
" We are not going to draw any far-reaching conclusions. The purpose of this thesis has been avowedly negative. We have endeavored to demonstrate simply the danger in interpreting the ideas in Montaigne's Essays, by the use of a single generalizing term Nature " (p. 64). Would avoid use of words nature and natural in interpreting M., since the essayist uses these words in such a wide variety of meanings.

Dowden, Edward. Michel de Montaigne. Philadelphia & London, Lippincott, 1905. 383 p. (FMLS)   1599

Excellent general treatment of M. in its day, based upon knowledge of *Essais* and of M. scholarship just before publications of Strowski and Villey. Very interesting bibliography of books on M. in the author's possession, showing the three phases of 19th-century publications to which he refers : laudatory period, period of documentary discoveries by Malvezin and Dr. Payen, and period of coordination as represented by Bonnefon.

Dréano, Maturin. La pensée religieuse de Montaigne. Beauchesne, 1936. 501 p.   1600

Sound and thorough study of M.'s religion, and an examination of *Essais* from point of view of M.'s thought and actions. Shows M. a firm Catholic, recognized by his contemporaries as a practicing Christian. " Pour lui le pyrrhonien est même le plus docile des croyants." For M. the real danger lay in private judgment on religious and civil affairs, leading to civil war and anarchy.

Reviews : M. Citoleux in Poly 194:38-39, 1937; W. G. Moore in MLR 34:608-10, 1939; M. Raymond in Hren 4:345-50, 1937.

— La renommée de Montaigne en France au XVIIIe siècle, 1677-1802. Angers, Éditions de l'Ouest, 1952.   589 p.   1601

Very important and excellent work, bridging most of the gap between studies of Boase (no. 1533) and Frame (no. 1614). Bibliography of works cited, p. 555-71. Index.

Review : Anon in FL, May 10, 1952, p. 8.

Duviard, Ferdinand. La révision du Cas Montaigne. La Délivrance méconnue des critiques. Montaigne chrétien. Neo 34:1-9, 129-41, 1950.   1603

Extracts from as yet unpublished *Présence de Montaigne*. M. wrote *Essais* more as a way of venting his emotions and playing with them as accurate record of his experience. Argues strongly that he was a Christian.

Ellerbroek, G. G. Notes sur la fortune de Montaigne en Hollande. Neo 32:49-54, Apr. 1, 1948.   1604

Definite proof that M. was much read in Holland, and strong indications that he exerted considerable influence on Dutch letters.

Emerson, Ralph W. Montaigne; or, the skeptic. *In his*: Representative men. Boston and New York, Houghton, Mifflin, 1903, p. 149-86.   1605

For Emerson, M. is a stage that one passes through; beyond M.'s scepticism lies awareness of an Eternal Cause. M., as Emerson was able to know him, served him as a lure more than as a satisfaction. Despite the fact that Emerson wrote about M. before era of editions of *Essais* distinguishing 1580, 1588, and post-1588 passages, his appreciation is remarkably penetrating. Of more interest, however, for understanding Emerson than for judging M. See 1804.

Faguet, Emile. Montaigne. *In his*: Seizième siècle : études littéraires. See 101, p. 365-421.   1606

Interesting and stimulating essay, although many modern scholars would question some of his conclusions, such as : " Le fond de la morale de Montaigne, c'est un stoïcisme déridé et souriant " (p. 392). " Par tournure d'esprit il serait républicain " (p. 400-01). Describes M. as " Un philosophe ancien, éclectique, avec une teinture assez légère du christianisme " (p. 385). Tries to show that M. wrote exclusively on human nature and that his scepticism is an invention of Pascal.

Faure, Elie. Montaigne. GR 110:353-62, Jan. 1923; 110:562-75, Feb. 1923; 111:32-42, Mar. 1923; 111:277-86, Apr. 1923.   1607

Portrays M. as " le premier homme libre qui ait paru en Occident. Le premier être autonome, si l'on veut—et peut-être même le seul.... En lui toutes les croyances peuvent prendre racine. Par lui, toutes les croyances se peuvent déraciner. Depuis lui, tout dogmatisme, en naissant, est frappé à mort " (p. 362).

— Montaigne et ses trois premiers-nés. Crès, 1926. 230 p. (Also Prolibro, 1948. 230 p.)   1608

M. as spiritual father of Shakespeare, Cervantes, and Pascal, a family united by lyrical impulse and posing modern Europe's fundamental question : what are the uses of intelligence ? Faure's explanation of how each one answers the question often exasperating in vocabulary but never quite wrong, and, except for a strong disposition toward racism, usually to the point. Makes M. out a doubting stoic, centrally concerned with man, with man's conscience as touchstone of morality, and with man's intelligence as illumination and even control of his human fate. *See* 2872.

Feis, Jacob. Shakspere and Montaigne : an endeavour to explain the tendency of Hamlet from allusions in contemporary works. London, Paul Trench, 1884. 210 p. 1609

His thesis : " We believe we can successfully show that the tendency of Hamlet is of a controversial nature. In closely examining the innovations by which the augmented second quarto edition (1604) distinguishes itself from the first quarto, published the year before (1603), we find that almost every one of these innovations is directed against the principles of a new philosophical work—*The essays of Michel Montaigne*—which had appeared at that time in England, and which was brought out under the high auspices of the foremost noblemen and protectors of literature in this country " (p. 4-5). Makes M. center of controversy involving Ben Jonson, Dekker, Chapman, and Marston. Few scholars would accept his ideas today. *See* 2831, 2833, 2839, 2845.

Feuillâtre, Emile. Les emprunts de Montaigne à Hérodote dans l'Apologie de Raymond Sebond. MélPC, p. 246-58. 1610

More ample discussion of M.'s borrowings from the Saliat translation of Herodotus than that given by Zangroniz (*see* 1805), whom Feuillâtre does not even mention.

Feuillet de Conches, F. S. Lettres inédites de Michel de Montaigne. Plon, 1863. 318 p. (Reproduced in Causeries d'un curieux, Plon, 1862-68, v. III, 231-360.) 1611

Chiefly from collection of Prince of Monaco, descendant of Maréchal de Matignon, to whom 11 of the 15 letters are addressed. Includes also studies on reception of *Essais* in the 17th and 18th centuries, and on historical events of M.'s day. Rather diffuse study.

Forest, A. Montaigne humaniste et théologien. RSPT 18:59-73, 1929. 1612

Adduces new evidence of M.'s Christian sincerity from the *Apologie*.

Review : J. Plattard in RSS 16:345-46, 1929.

Frame, Donald M. Did Montaigne betray Sebond? RR 38:297-329, 1947. 1613

One of most solid studies on M. and religion. Shows that Sainte-Beuve's brilliant portrait of M. in Port-Royal is inaccurate, and that the critic presents a very different M. in his later writings. M. entirely aware of his differences from Sebond, considered his arguments weak but useful. May have used Sebond as a pretext for his attack on human knowledge and presumption.

— Montaigne in France, 1812-1852. Columbia University Press, 1940. 308 p. (Diss., Columbia.) 1614

Well-documented analysis of attitude of French writers toward M.'s personality, ideas, and style. Excellent bibliography of Montaigne in France, 1812-1852 (p. 243-291). Model for studies of this type.

Reviews : W. G. Moore in MLR 37:391-92, 1942; H. Peyre in RR 32:302-306, 1941.

Friedrich, Hugo. Montaigne. Bern, Francke, 1949. 512 p. 1615

Best single book about M. Thoroughly but unobtrusively documented, an eminently human interpretation of the man and work. Introductory description of *Essais*, chapters on their background and structure, on Man belittled, on Man affirmed, on self-affirmation, M. and death (published earlier as *Montaigne und der Tod* in RFor 61:32-88, 1947), M.'s wisdom, on his literary awareness and the form of *Essais*. Theme : M. saw Man and Nature as seldom but possibly in harmony, present moment as the important one to live through as harmoniously as possible; Man is lower than the angels and can be comfortable down there.

Reviews : E. Auerbach in MLN 66:562-564, 1951; M. Ruch in BHR 12:301-11, 1950; T. Spoerri in Eras 4, no. 1-2; 23-24, 1951.

— Montaigne über Glauben und Wissen. DV 10:412-35, 1932. 1616

For M., true knowledge of a subject is impossible, but we act nevertheless, supported by religious faith. Bent upon questioning everything, we should finally love the world as it is. Nature of that world most obvious in oneself.

Fusil, C. A. Montaigne et Lucrèce. RSS 13:265-81, 1926. 1617

M. cites Lucretius more frequently than any authors except Plutarch and Seneca. Charmed by Lucretius' literary beauty and his morality, little influenced by his philosophy and physics. Excellent analysis of M.'s borrowings from Lucretius.

Galy, E., and L. Lapeyre. Montaigne chez lui, visite de deux amis à son château. Lettre à M. le Dr. J. F. Payen. Périgueux, J. Bonnet, 1861. 69 p. *See* 1536, 1708. **1618**

Gives an account of M.'s château (burned in 1885) and of his tower (still standing), including library and study. Furnishes transcription of Greek and Latin sentences painted on beams of library. Valuable contribution.

Gauthiez, Pierre. Michel de Montaigne. *In his:* Études sur le seizième siècle. Lecène, Oudin, 1893. p. 191-303. **1619**

Attitude of author relatively unfavorable to M. Considers him " un épicurien infiniment subtil, un sceptique de rare esprit, de caractère droit; le plus ambigu, le plus complexe des philosophes du second ordre, et, ... l'un de nos plus grands écrivains dans le premier siècle qu'ait vu la prose française " (p. 302). Concludes further that : " Intéressant, comme tout autre théoricien de génie, Montaigne offre, comme tout autre, une étude, un enseignement : il ne saurait plus exercer nul effet direct sur les âmes " (p. 302).

Gide, André. Essai sur Montaigne. Schiffrin, Éditions de la Pléiade, 1929. 143 p. **1620**

Consists of two parts : *Essai sur Montaigne* and *Suivant Montaigne*. Part I, differing from Schiffrin edition only by a change in one quotation and by a retraction of a judgment on Goethe, first appeared in Comm 18:5-48, Winter, 1928. Part II first appeared in NRF 32:745-66, June 1, 1929. Both parts also published in Gide's *Œuvres complètes*, NRF, v. 15 (1939) : 1-31, 33-68. English translation by S. H. Guest and T. E. Blewitt, titled *Montaigne: An essay in two parts*, London, Blackmore Press; New York, Liveright, 1929. Translation, made under Gide's supervision, by Dorothy Bussy-Strachey, printed in YR ns 28:572-93, Spring, 1939, and again as introduction to *The living thoughts of Montaigne*, New York, Toronto, Longmans, Green, 1939. Bussy translation follows a text somewhat emended from that of original texts and has an introductory essay added.

Culling of quotations—mostly about individuality, inconstancy, religion, freedom of expression—that, by Gide's admitted intent, show us the Gide in M. and the M. in Gide. Gide's comments reveal him, expectedly, as a latter-day M., but with emphasis on disparateness, originality, independence that to some

degree warps M.'s text. More revelatory, in short, of Gide than of M.

Reviews : F. Aitken in BL 77:376, Mar. 1930; C. H. H. in MGW 22:93, Jan. 31, 1930; H. Hazlitt in NNY 130:365-66, Mar. 26, 1930.

Giraud, Victor. Les époques de la pensée de Montaigne. *In his:* Maîtres d'autrefois et d'aujourd'hui. Hachette, 1912. p. 1-54. **1621**

Extensive discussion of evolution of M.'s thought as revealed in Villey's *Sources et évolution des Essais de Montaigne* (1794) and his *Livres d'histoire moderne utilisés par Montaigne* (1783). Also discusses M. as an artist; his religion, concluding that " ... il n'est guère chrétien, et il est fort peu croyant " (p. 30); his " morale," with conclusion that " Son plus grave défaut est de n'avoir d'une morale que le nom; elle ne résout pas les questions, elle les élude; elle ne définit pas le devoir, elle le supprime " (p. 48); and M. as " honnête homme."

Gohin, Ferdinand. La Fontaine et Montaigne. Mfran 13:28-45, 1934. **1622**

Comparison of ideas of the two writers concerning knowledge of future, man's superiority over animals, and illusions of the senses, to show that La Fontaine imitates M. and at same time refutes him. M. examples taken from *Apologie*. Extremely tenuous, except last comparison, where La Fontaine, in *Un animal dans la lune*, takes opposition to M. in what may well be an intentional manner.

Goutchkoff, Théodore. Les vues esthétiques de Montaigne. Sansot, 1907. 71 p. *Also in:* Occ 11:20-27, Jan. 1907; 76-88, Feb. 1907. **1623**

M.'s esthetic preoccupation is to keep art rooted in the natural. His particular esthetic nature essentially visual, and very close to Impressionism; whence his enmity toward bombast, effort to reconcile two facts : independence of spirit, and adherence to custom. Acute, sensible interpretation of M.'s mental situation.

Groethuysen, Bernhard. Montaignes Weltanschauung. FestEW, p. 219-28. (BBRP, no. 1.) **1624**

Like typical renaissance man, M. lives in world of infinite variety and possibilities, half-way between faith and certain knowledge. God, in this world, is great Unknowable. Oneself is inescapably touchstone of oneself and of oneself as part of world.

M. does not ask why he lives, only what it is like to live.

Grün, Alphonse. La vie publique de Michel Montaigne. Amyot, 1855. 414 p. 1625

Useful early attempt to study M.'s rôle in affairs of his day, in spite of many errors pointed out by Dr. Payen in his *Recherches sur Montaigne, documents inédits,* No. 4 (no. 1701).

Guaglianone, Manon V. La personalidad de Miguel de Montaigne en la historia de las ideas educacionales. Buenos Aires, Guillermo Kraft, 1939. 230 p. (Diss., Buenos Aires.) 1626

Contains no new ideas, but furnishes good illustration of South American interest in M. Bibliography, p. 225-27, full of typographical errors.

Guiton, Jean. Où en est le débat sur la religion de Montaigne? RR 35:98-115, 1944. 1627

Excellent evaluation of the ideas of Pascal, Voltaire, Sainte-Beuve, Brunschvicg, Armaingaud, Villey, Lanson, Strowski, Gide, Cons, Zeitlin, Thibaudet, Plattard, Forest, Coppin, Janssen, Busson, Dréano, and Citoleux. Concludes that " Montaigne fut toujours, humblement, naturellement, et par l'exercice d'une raison toujours soumise à la vérité révélée, un bon chrétien " (p. 114-15).

Guizot, Maurice Guillaume. Montaigne, études et fragments. Hachette, 1899. 269 p. 1628

Brilliant but incomplete results of twenty-five years' study of M. by a Protestant who admired but did not approve of him. Egotism and lack of will power M.'s chief faults. Considers him a sceptic, not a Christian, but concedes that he thought himself to be one. Not a new interpretation, but a forceful attack on M.'s character and opinions by one who is completely seduced by the essayist's charms. Excellent 41-page preface by Émile Faguet.

Review : A. Sorel in *Études de littérature et d'histoire* (Plon, 1901), p. 1-13.

Harmon, Alice. How great was Shakespeare's debt to Montaigne? PMLA 57:988-1008, 1942. 1629

Study of what M. and Shakespeare could have got from commonplace books of the renaissance, with the conclusion that we cannot even prove that M. served Shakes-

peare as a storehouse of material. *See* 2832.

Hauchecorne, F. Une intervention ignorée de Montaigne au Parlement de Bordeaux. BHren 9:164-68, 1947. 1630

While planning to receive visit of Charles IX in January, 1565, M. urged Parlement to insist that King visit his domains frequently, pointed out that disorders of justice result from " l'infini nombre d'officiers qu'on y met," from poor selection of officers, and from their venality.

Henderson, W. B. D. Montaigne's Apologie of Raymond Sebond, and King Lear. BSA 14:209-25, Oct. 1939; 15:40-54, Jan. 1940. 1631

Resemblance in vocabulary, theme, and particularly in concept of the ruler shows that Shakespeare *may* have been inspired by M.

Hill Hay, Camilla. Montaigne, lecteur et imitateur de Sénèque. Poitiers, Société française d'imprimerie et de librairie, 1938. 202 p. (Diss., Poitiers.) 1632

Excellent demonstration of similarities of M.'s style and ideas to those of Seneca, and a good argument for Senecan influence. Includes (p. 3-74) treatment of the Senecan tradition before and during the renaissance.

Reviews : J. Lavaud in Hren 5:505-06, 1938; A. Salles in BSAM ns, no. 4:33-34, Nov. 1938.

Hooker, Elizabeth R. The relation of Shakespeare to Montaigne. PMLA 17:312-366, 1902. 1633

Sober examination of many parallel passages, and conclusion that Shakespeare was not a disciple of M. but used *Essais* as a storehouse of material. *See* 2833.

Isola, Maria dell'. Études sur Montaigne. Pavia, Mattei, 1913. 149 p. 1634

Seven studies on various phases of *Essais :* M.'s intention in writing, thoughts on religion and death, his pedagogy, etc. Finds that *Apologie* represents only one side of M.'s philosophy; that most important lesson of the *Essais* is " jouir de son être "; that " Montaigne est un philosophe qui a marché admirablement dans les chemins de la terre, mais sans jamais apercevoir la route qui amène à l'idéal " (p. 149). Interesting primarily as an example of M.'s appeal to modern Italian readers.

Jansen, Frederik Julius Billeskov. Sources vives de la pensée de Montaigne : étude sur les fondements psychologiques et biographiques des Essais. Copenhagen, Levin & Munksgaard; Alcan, 1935. 95 p.   1635

Assuming that unity of *Essais* is to be explained by studying personality of their author, and wishing to explain as well as to define M.'s philosophy, Jansen tries to show M. as a " penseur vivant." Studies his skepticism, humanité, stoicism, and naturisme from three angles : " La réalité intérieure, l'âme du penseur; la réalité extérieure vivante, les rencontres et les actes de sa vie; la réalité extérieure inanimée, les livres qui lui ont valu des inspirations et des idées " (p. 9).

One of best-reasoned and documented studies of M. as seen through the *Essais* up to Friedrich's time (*see* 1615-16).

Review : M. Raymond in Hren 4:344-345, 1937.

Janssen, Herman. Montaigne fidéiste. Nijmegen and Utrecht, Dekker, Van de Wegt and Van Leeuwen, 1930.   167 p.   1636

Important examination of M.'s religious ideas, from point of view of a Catholic theologian. Holds that M. did not renounce his Christian faith, but became increasingly fideistic in *Apologie* and in later works.

Reviews : J. Coppin in RSS 17:314-21, 1930; P. Villey in RHL 39:460-63, 1932.

Jasinski, René. Sur la composition chez Montaigne. MélHC, p. 257-67.   1637

Disorderly composition of *Essais* only superficial. Earliest essays follow traditional rhetorical order; in Book II order more rigid and plain. Book III shows loose linear order but logical development in overlapping circles of argument. Lack of explicit transitions is the beclouding element.

Jeanson, Francis. Montaigne et l'expérience de soi. Esprit 19:321-42, Sept. 1951.   1638

" Les plus éminentes qualités humaines de Montaigne sont négatives : sa tolérance, son respect des opinions d'autrui, c'est une indifférence à peu près totale à l'égard de ces opinions.... Cet ' humaniste ' n'aime pas les hommes : il s'aime à travers eux, il a besoin d'eux pour se rencontrer.... Non pas exactement négative, mais plutôt défensive : telle est bien la morale qui se dégage des *Essais* " (p. 340).

— Montaigne par lui-même; images et textes présentées par Francis Jeanson. Éditions du seuil, 1951.   191 p.   (CET)   1639

Patchwork of quotations and commentaries, copiously illustrated. For general reader. " La longue préface de Francis Jeanson comptera parmi les études qui auront renouvelé la connaissance d'un Montaigne si lu toujours, et si mal interprété encore." (S. in MerF 315:734, Aug. 1952.)

Jones, P. Mansell. French introspectives from Montaigne to André Gide. Cambridge University Press, 1937.   115 p.   1640

Contains two excellent chapters on nature of M.'s introspection (p. 22-41), concluding that : " In contradistinction to other explorers of the ego, Montaigne was one who, as we have tried to show, thought and wrote with a social implication, even when concentrating upon himself."

Jullian, Camille. Bordeaux au temps de la mairie de Michel de Montaigne. RHB 26:5-18, Jan.-Feb., 1933.   1641

Finds nothing in 16th-century Bordeaux to arouse in M. the enthusiasm he felt for Paris and Rome. " C'était une ville toute du moyen âge, gothique et turbulente, où la renaissance n'avait encore effleuré que l'esprit de quelques intelligences d'élite et la façade de quelques rares monuments " (p. 7).

King, Paul C. Montaigne as a source of La Fontaine's fable La mort et le mourant. PMLA 52:1101-13, Dec., 1937.   1642

Convincing demonstration that La Fontaine's ideas on death follow closely M.'s *Que philosopher c'est apprendre à mourir*.

Kurz, Harry. Critical bibliography on La Boétie. *See* 1401.   1643

Thorough and competent evaluation of studies touching on La Boétie and M. Especially valuable for summaries of arguments on authorship of *Contr'un*. *See* 1457.

— Did Montaigne alter La Boétie's Contr'un ? *See* 1486.   1644

Objective review of the controversy between Armaingaud and his critics, concluding that " the *Contr'un* is the unadulterated work of a very gifted young man whose name was Étienne de La Boétie."

— Montaigne and La Boétie in the chapter on friendship. *See* 1487.   1645

Important article. Excellent analysis of M.'s relations with La Boétie, of their similar political opinions, and of the controversy over authorship of *Contr'un* arising from M.'s carelessness and inconsistencies in his references to his friend. Concludes that arguments of Armaingaud are untenable.

Labande, L. H. Correspondance de Montaigne avec le Maréchal de Matignon (1582-1588), nouvelles lettres inédites. RSS 4:1-15, 1916. 1646

Three letters not included with those published by Feuillet de Conches (no. 1611). Republished with slight corrections by Paul Courteault in RHB 9:309-315, Nov., 1916.

Lablénie, Edmond. L'énigme de la Servitude volontaire. *See* 1481. 1647

Examines language and style of *Contr'un*, is convinced that M. had nothing to do with it.

Lamandé, André. La religion de Montaigne. Corr 330:481-97, Feb. 25, 1933; 703-13, Mar. 10, 1933. 1648

Good popular defense of M.'s Christianity, based on evidence given in *Essais*. " L'amour du prochain, l'amour de la justice, l'amour de la vérité, l'humilité de l'esprit,—et, par surcroît, la pratique religieuse de chaque jour,—n'est-ce pas là un faisceau de vertus capables de faire, non certes un martyr ou un saint, mais un chrétien fort suffisant, comme dit Faguet, et même un peu plus? " (p. 713).

— La vie gaillarde et sage de Montaigne. Plon, 1927. 301 p. (RGE) Translated into English as Montaigne grave and gay. New York, Holt, 1928. 303 p. 1649

Interesting and sprightly biographical novel, must be read as such.

Reviews : Anon in TLS 27:143, Mar. 1, 1928; L. Maury in RPL 66:20-22, Jan. 7, 1928.

Lange, Maurice. Le pragmatisme de Montaigne. Rmois 19:455-91, Apr. 10, 1915. 1650

M. a pragmatist before the event : with Wm. James, M. sees world as fluidity, truth as relative to a man's condition. Additional remarks on M. as Stoic (he was one at first, and more than superficially) and M. as Christian (he was one in name only).

Langlais, Jacques. L'éducation avant Montaigne et le chapitre De l'institution des enfants. Croville-Morant, 1907. 83 p. (First published as L'éducation en France avant le seizième siècle. Rren 6:33-40, 91-103, 149-68, 1905; and La pédagogie de Rabelais et de Montaigne, Rren 6:185-208, 259-68, 1905.) 1651

Good exposition of educational practices in France during Middle Ages, and of reforms proposed by Rabelais and M. Good bibliography.

Lanson, Gustave. L'art de Montaigne : l'art de " se dire." *In his:* L'art de la prose. Librairie des Annales, 1911. p. 39-54. 1652

M.'s prose seen as a model of his imagination and turn of mind; elements consciously (artistically) chosen or accepted.

— Les Essais de Montaigne: étude et analyse. Mellottée, 1930. 384 p. (CLE) 1653

Orderly *exposé* of M.'s thought, intended as introduction to *Essais*. First chapters on M.'s family, life, the milieu and the moment of *Essais*, their composition; then chapters on M.'s stoicism, scepticism, definitive philosophy, with sections on M.'s idea of man, morality, politics, religion, and, especially noteworthy, his search for a method of organizing experience. Final chapters on M.'s conclusion about life, on his art and influence. Short bibliography. Lanson prone to rate history, and man's rational control of its forces, above psychology and man's feelings about his place in the historical world; within that bias this book a masterly job of interpreting M.

Reviews : W. A. Nitze in MP 28:501-02, 1930-31; L. P. G. Peckham in MLN 46:260-62, 1931; P. Villey in RHL 39:300-03, 1932.

— La vie morale selon les Essais de Montaigne. RDM 19, 7e sér. : 603-25, Feb. 1, 1924; 836-58, Feb. 15, 1924. 1654

Excellent article. Tries to show that M. had no theoretical system of morality, but " ... propose une forme de vie raisonnable, sans fondement ni épanouissement mystiques, désirable à la fois et réalisable pour l'homme cultivé des temps modernes " (p. 850).

Lanusse, Maxime. Montaigne. *In his:* De l'influence du dialecte gascon sur la langue française de la fin du xve siècle à la seconde moitié du xviie. Grenoble, Allier, 1893. p. 157-447. (Diss., Paris.) 1655

M. treated as half French, half Gascon, and stronger literarily for the mixture. Valuable only for lists of Gascon locutions in *Essais:* vocabulary (p. 277-368) and syntax (p. 369-447).

Laumonier, Paul. Madame de Montaigne, d'après les Essais. MélAL, p. 393-407. 1656

Cites evidence from *Essais* to contradict Bonnefon's conclusion that M. was happily married. " Il souffrait à la fois de l'entêtement, de l'humeur acariâtre, de la jalousie, de la sottise et même de la négligence domestique de sa femme " (p. 406).

— Montaigne précurseur du xviiᵉ siècle. RHL 3:204-17, 1896. 1657

His cult of antiquity, " bon sens," artistic and humanistic tastes, psychological curiosity, and philosophical conclusions, make him practically a contemporary rather than a precursor of classicism.

Lee, Sidney. Montaigne. *In his:* The French renaissance in England. *See* 662, p. 165-79. *See* 1148. 1658

Sane but summary evaluation of M.'s influence on Bacon, Ben Jonson, Sir William Cornwallis, and Shakespeare. " From Montaigne came pointed fluency and a cheerful habit of reflecting detachedly on life " (p. 179).

Le Géard, Jean. Contribution à l'étude de l'histoire de la médecine : Montaigne hydrologue. Legrand, 1930. 60 p. 1659

Medical importance of *Journal de voyage* twofold : provides physical and psychological details of M.'s illness, and information on watering places of Eastern France, Switzerland, Germany, and Italy in 16th century.

Leveaux, Alphonse. Étude sur les Essais de Montaigne. Plon, 1870. 473 p. 1660

Not in any sense a study on *Essais,* but citations and brief commentary on each essay, written to " inspirer au lecteur ... le désir de lire le livre entier." Interesting revelation of state of M. scholarship in 1870.

Lévis-Mirepoix, Antoine, *duc de.* Montaigne et le secret de Coutras. RLH, Oct. 1, 1950, p. 461-72. 1661

Henry of Navarre visited M. three days after Coutras, sent him to Paris to try to effect compromise with Henry III. Author tries to show importance of M. as man of political action.

— Montaigne et l'individualisme. Runiv ns 58:721-34, May 25, 1943. 1662

M., resisting all formulas, neither entirely individualistic nor altogether sociable but a combination of " quant à soi " and " sociabilité," a libertine privately and an ultra-conservative in public matters, including religion, and sincere in both regards.

Lowndes, Mary E. Michel de Montaigne : a biographical study. Cambridge, University Press, 1898. 286 p. 1663

Presents M. as representative of a type which " is wanting in the inner springs of action, and ... is content to accept the world fragmentarily, as it is presented in experience, and seeks neither to remould it in actuality to an ideal nor to reduce it to unity in thought " (p. 227).

Review : Anon in Acad 54:3-4, Jul 2, 1898.

Lucas, F. L. The master-essayist. *In his:* Studies French and English. London, Cassell, 1934. p. 115-37. 1664

Excellent general appreciation of M. and his significance to modern world.

Lugli, Vittorio. Montaigne. Milan, Carabba, 1935. 169 p. 1665

Well-informed general study of M.'s life and works.

Machabey, Armand. Montaigne et la musique. Rmus 9:260-71, Jul. 1928; 342-50, Aug. 1928; 465-74, Oct. 1928; 10:37-45, Nov. 1928. 1666

M. was for popular " simple " music; especially struck by music's physiological effect.

Malvezin, Théophile. Michel de Montaigne, son origine, sa famille. Bordeaux, Lefebvre, 1875. 346 p. *See* 1573. 1667

Ranks with publications of Dr. Payen as authoritative on questions of family origins. Reproduces many documents found in archives of Gironde and in church records.

— Notes sur la maison d'habitation de Michel de Montaigne à Bordeaux. Bordeaux, Féret, 1889. 63 p. 1668

Important historical research, augmented somewhat by Paul Courteault's findings in no. 1574. In the PSAB, v. 13, 1888, p. xxxiii-iv, this study was mentioned and summarized.

Marchand, Ernest. Montaigne and the cult of ignorance. RR 36:275-82, 1945.
1669

" Three things in Montaigne's sketch—non-academic training, physical culture, and useful studies—are the seeds of ' outside activities,' athletics, and a narrow vocationalism, which together have made something of a farce of learning among us, whatever they may have done for ' education ' " (p. 282).

Masson, André. Notes sur la bibliothèque de Montaigne. Hren 6:475-93, 1939. 1670

Describes volumes by Saint Justin, Diogenes Laertius, Horace, and Philibert Delorme which belonged to M. Discusses dispersal of M.'s books and recovery of 26 volumes now in Bordeaux library.

Matthiessen, F. O. Florio's Montaigne (1603). In his : Translation, an Elizabethan art. Cambridge, Harvard University Press, 1931. p. 103-68. 1671

Excellent analysis of literary merits and defects of Florio's translation, and a summary evaluation of M.'s popularity and influence in 17th-century England.

Mauzey, Jesse V. Montaigne's philosophy of human nature. Annandale-on Hudson, N. Y., St. Stephen's College, 1933. 98 p. (Diss., Columbia.) 1672

Finds M.'s importance in his " exaltation of self-expression from a literary device to philosophic method " (p. 93). From Essais draws paradoxical conclusion that : " All men possess a common humanity, which reveals itself in diversity, and an equality which is established by differences " (p. 95).

May, Marcel. Une influence possible de Montaigne sur Shakespeare dans Henry V, Acte IV, Scène I. RAA 9:109-26, 1931-1932. 1673

Substantial evidence, handled cautiously and expertly, to show that Shakespeare borrowed directly from Florio's rendition (while it was still in ms.) of Book I, Ch. 42, De l'inégalité qui est entre nous.

Mayer, Gilbert. Les images dans Montaigne d'après le chapitre De l'institution des enfants. MélEH, p. 110-18. 1674

M. used many extremely concrete images, " ... moins dans le dessein de persuader que par un besoin naturel de son tempérament... " (p. 110).

Meauldre de Lapouyade, Maurice, and Comte de Saint-Saud. Les Makanam. Les Ayquem de Montaigne. Recherches historiques. Bordeaux, Féret, 1943. 187 p. 1675

Part II, p. 119-87, devoted to genealogy of the Bussaguet and du Taillan branches of Ayquem de Montaigne family, from 16th to 19th century.

Menut, Albert D. Montaigne and the Nicomachean ethics. MP 31:225-42, 1933-1934. 1676

" In their final form ... it can be fairly maintained that Essais contain all the essential principles of the ethical doctrine propounded by Aristotle " (p. 226-27).

Merlant, Joachim. Les rencontres de Montaigne, and La doctrine intérieure de Montaigne. In his : De Montaigne à Vauvenargues, essais sur la vie intérieure et la culture du moi. Société française d'imprimerie et de librairie, 1914. p. 31-56, 57-87. 1677

Excellent study of M.'s ideas on " vie intérieure " and " culture du moi." Considers M. " un admirable exemple de la vie intérieure de l'intelligence," but finds that " Il a manqué à Montaigne d'avoir souffert et d'avoir été je ne dis pas ému, mais troublé par la douleur des autres" (p. 86-87).

Merleau-Ponty, Maurice. Lecture de Montaigne. Tmod 3:1044-60, Dec., 1947. 1678

" La conscience de soi est sa constante, la mesure pour lui de toutes les doctrines. On pourrait dire qu'il n'est jamais sorti d'un certain étonnement devant soi qui fait toute la substance de son œuvre et de sa sagesse. Il ne s'est jamais lassé d'éprouver le paradoxe d'un être conscient " (p. 1045).

Micha, Alexandre. Montaigne et le drame de l'intellect. MerF 303:453-62, Jul., 1948. 1679

M.'s goal constant throughout his life, " savoir être à soi." Drama comes from fact that his head is both " trop pleine " and " trop bien faite," serving as a solvent rather than enabling him to grasp essence of things. Comparison to Valéry's Monsieur Teste.

Michaud, Régis. Une alliance intellectuelle, Emerson et Montaigne. In his : Mystiques et réalistes anglo-saxons d'Emerson à Bernard Shaw. Colin, 1918. p. 1-50. 1680

Excellent analysis of M.'s contribution to Emerson's thought, and differences between the two essayists.

— Emerson et Montaigne. RG 10:417-42, 1914. 1681

With intimate knowledge of *Essais*, Emerson enlarged upon certain of M.'s ideas (especially concerning friendship, teaching, books, history and heroes, scepticism), setting them on base of transcendentalism—whose principles were present in *Essais* but not with importance they have for Emerson. M. represents transition in Emerson's thought from world of appearance to world of transcendent reality.

Michel-Côte, P. Le mobilisme de Montaigne. MerF 252:225-41, June 1, 1934. 1682

Argues against Thibaudet's presentation of M. as precursor of modern philosophy.

Montagnon, F. Trois portraits de Montaigne. Toulouse, Guitard, 1928. 153 p. 1683

Three essays on 1580 edition, 1588 edition, and Bordeaux copy. Intended for general reader.

Moore, W. G. Montaigne's notion of experience. StGR, p. 34-52. 1684

M. probably uses " expérience " to refer to something felt or perceived in contrast to that apprehended by the mind. Author interprets " De l'expérience " as protest against " an intellectualism divorced from life." " His essay is not a disquisition, it is a subtle mixture of argument, intuition, and example " (p. 50). Its plan is that of an artist rather than of a logician.

Morçay, Raoul. Montaigne. *In his:* La renaissance. Gigord, 1933-1935. v. 2, p. 156-89. (Histoire de la littérature française, pub. sous la direction de J. Calvet ... II, 3). 1685

One of best brief discussions of M.'s life and works. " Montaigne est le premier humaniste de notre langue.... Montaigne est vraiment le premier de notre langue qui nous ait appris à nous pencher sur nous-mêmes, à ne point tirer notre valeur d'un savoir étranger, à connaître notre être pour le développer harmonieusement." (p. 188-189)

Moreau, Pierre. Montaigne, l'homme et l'œuvre. Boivin, 1939, 165 p. (LE) 1686

Excellent introduction to M. For stu-

dents and general readers, like all the volumes in this series.

Murry, John Middleton. Montaigne : the birth of an individual. *In his:* Heroes of thought. New York, Messner, 1938. p. 49-62. 1687

Sees M. as striving to realize himself through understanding of his own experience. *Essais* are faithful and unpruned record of that experience. M. heroic chiefly because he " rediscovers—in a new world of freedom and responsibility— ' the misery and grandeur of man ' " (p. 62). An appreciation, full of feeling and accurate; best interpretation before Hugo Friedrich's *Montaigne* (no. 1615).

Naves, Raymond. Montaigne, rien que l'homme. Montaigne, tout l'homme. *In his:* L'aventure de Prométhée. Toulouse, Privat; Paris, Didier, 1943. p. 20-49. 1688

Takes M. as point of departure in study of critical spirit which animates French literature. " L'âge classique a ses moralistes, le xviiie siècle ses ' philosophes,' le romantisme ses désenchantés. Tous procèdent de Montaigne, que nous pourrions appeler notre Homère " (p. 18). M.'s " vivre à propos " leads to measure and wisdom, the expression of the complete man.

Neri, Ferdinando. Sulla fortuna degli Essais. RivI 19:275-90, Feb., 1916. 1689

Refutation of G. Setti's argument (no. 1739) that Tasso was familiar with *Essais*. Lists 16th, 17th, and 18th century Italian translations of *Essais*.

Neyrac, Joseph. Montaigne. Bergerac, Castanet, 1904. 338 p. 1690

Four studies important for details of local history, written by the Curé of Saint-Michel-Montaigne. 1. Le château de Montaigne, p. 1-35, gives a history of M.'s château, of its ownership before the Eyquems, and of the Eyquem family. 2. Montaigne intime, p. 37-165, treats M.'s relations with his family, drawn from *Essais*, *Journal de voyage*, and *Ephémérides* of Beuther. 3. Pierre Magne (1806-1879), p. 167-271. A biographical sketch of the minister of finance who bought the château in 1860. 4. Monographie de Saint-Michel-Montaigne, p. 273-327. History and description of 12th-century church named for M.

Norton, Grace. The early writings of Montaigne and other papers. New York, Macmillan, 1904. 218 p. 1691

Interesting and useful essays on M.'s translation of Sebond and letters, on his family, M. as a traveller, men of letters at Bordeaux in the 16th century, etc.

— The influence of Montaigne. New York and Boston, Houghton, Mifflin, 1908. 205 p.   1692

Not a study of M.'s influence, but a compilation from French and English writers of comments on M., allusions to M., and plagiarisms from M. Still an interesting and useful volume.

— Le Plutarque de Montaigne. Boston and New York, Houghton, Mifflin, 1906. 192 p. 1693

Not a study, like that of Zangroniz (no. 1805), but selections from Amyot's translation of Plutarch arranged to illustrate Montaigne's Essais, as indicated in subtitle. See 2533.

— ed. The spirit of Montaigne : some thoughts and expressions similar to those in his Essays. Boston and New York, Houghton, Mifflin, 1908. 233 p.   1694

Claims no direct influence, but shows through her selections similarities of M.'s thoughts with those of later writers. Special emphasis on Bacon, Locke, and Rousseau. An interesting compilation.

— Studies in Montaigne. New York, Macmillan, 1904. 290 p.   1695

Tries to show that Apologie consists of two parts written at different times, and that De la vanité is made up of two different essays, De la vanité and Des voyages, which M. blended into one. Important contribution in its day, although her conclusions have been somewhat modified by later research. Also includes interesting chapters on The inscriptions in Montaigne's library, and on Montaigne as a reader and student of style.

Review : P. Villey in RHL 12:517-22, 1905.

Owen, John. Montaigne. In his: The skeptics of the French renaissance. London, Sonnenschein. See 196. p. 423-490.   1696

An intelligent and well-informed discussion of M.'s philosophy, seeing him primarily as a skeptic but not closing the door to other interpretations.

Pattison, Mark. Life of Montaigne. In: Essays by the late Mark Pattison. Oxford, Clarendon Press, 1889. v.2, p.323-349. 1697

A sound attack on over-emphasis which Grün (no. 1625) assigns to M.'s rôle in public affairs.

Payen, J. F. Appel aux érudits. Citations, faits historiques, allégations, etc., qui se trouvent dans les Œuvres de Montaigne et dont la source n'a point été indiquée par les éditeurs. Guiraudet et Jouaust, 1857. 24 p. Also in : BSAM 1st ser. 1:177-91, 1913. 1698

Important stimulus to research on sources, calling attention to many problems which needed to be solved.

— Documents inédits ou peu connus sur Montaigne. (Techener, 1847. 44 p. Also in : BSAM sér. 1, 2:165-203, 1913; 3:279-312, 1914.) Nouveaux documents inédits ou peu connus sur Montaigne. (Jannet, 1850. 66 p.) Documents inédits sur Montaigne, no. 3. (Jannet, 1855. 40 p.) Recherches sur Montaigne, documents inédits, no. 4 (Techener, 1856. 68 p.) 1699

Extremely important for biographical details. Letters by and to M., list of books owned by him and annotated by him, etc. No. 3 contains M.'s manuscript notes in Ephémérides of Beuther. No. 4 devoted largely (p. 3-66) to criticism of Grün's La vie publique de Montaigne.

Review : (of no. 3) E.I.B. Rathery in BBB, Apr., 1855, p. 185-89.

— Notice bibliographique sur Montaigne. In : Buchon's Œuvres de Montaigne. Desrez, 1837. p. xiii-xlviii. Published also with Premier supplément à la notice bibliographique. Duverger, 1837. 76 p.   1700

A pioneer effort, important in its day.

— Recherches sur Michel Montaigne; correspondance relative à sa mort. BBB, 1862. p. 1291-1311.   1701

Pierre de Brach to Juste Lipse, M. de Cessac to Mme de Montaigne, 3 letters from Marie de Gournay to Juste Lipse, 2 letters from Juste Lipse to Marie de Gournay.

Peyre, Albert. Du prestige de la pensée. Debresse, 1936. 259 p.   1702

Devotes p. 9-231 to study of different aspects of M.'s thought. " Ce livre a pour objet de faire l'inventaire des richesses contenues dans les Essais de Montaigne et d'initier ses lecteurs à l'activité d'une pensée dont la substance et la couleur sont dues principalement à une connaissance approfondie de l'antiquité Gréco-Romaine " (p. 23).

Pilon, Edmond. Le voyage de Montaigne. Runiv 47:412-36, Nov. 15, 1931. 1703

Good general discussion of *Journal*, taken from introduction to his edition of this work (*Œuvres représentatives*, 1932).

Plattard, Jean. L'Amérique dans l'œuvre de Montaigne. RCC 35, sér. 1:12-21, Dec. 15, 1933. 1704

New world furnishes arguments to support his idea that happiness depends upon obedience to law of nature. Criticizes colonists' interest in gold and their brutality to the natives.

— État présent des études sur Montaigne. Belles lettres, 1936. 92 p. 1705

A survey of our knowledge of M., and an indication of its lacunae, rather than an evaluation of individual studies on M.

Reviews : G. in Neo 22:228-29, 1936-1937; P. Jourda in Rcr 69:164-65, 1935.

— Montaigne. *In his:* La renaissance des lettres en France de Louis XII à Henri IV. *See* 117, p. 178-206. 1706

Good introduction to M., intended for students and general readers.

— Montaigne et son temps. Boivin, 1933. 297 p. 1707

Written for the fourth centenary of M.'s birth. Fully availing himself of all previous research, Plattard here presents a volume which is intended to facilitate the reading of *Essais* and to show M.'s relations with important events and currents of ideas of 16th century. Very useful for both the scholar and general reader.

Reviews : G. Hess in Dlit 56:59-62, Jan. 13, 1935; F. C. Johnson in MLR 29:470-72, 1934; P. Jourda in Rcr 68:322-324, 1934; W. Kalthoff in LGRP 57:47-48, 1936; P. Laumonier in RHL 42:601-04, 1935; P. Sakmann in Archiv 166:277-78, 1935.

— Les sentences inscrites au plafond de la bibliothèque de Montaigne. RCC sér. 1, 36:19-31, 1934-35. 1708

Interesting description of M.'s tower, photographs of his library and of inscriptions on wall beams, and commentary on inscriptions first published by Galy and Lapeyre (no. 1618) and here reproduced.

Porteau, Paul. Montaigne et la vie pédagogique de son temps. Droz, 1935. 330 p. 1709

M.'s ideas on education not entirely result of experience and observation; based partly upon his reading, borrowed partly from antiquity. He was sincere, however, in urging an educational plan which would meet needs of the non-specialist and especially of nobility. Includes useful bibliography of 16th century works on education.

Review : M. Raymond in Hren 5:507-510, 1938.

— Sur un paradoxe de Montaigne. MélPL, p. 329-46. 1710

His frequent discussions of dangers and disadvantages of learning, a frequent renaissance theme, intended to stimulate thought of readers rather than to instruct them.

Poulet, Georges. Montaigne. *In his:* Études sur le temps humain. Plon, 1950. p. 1-15. 1711

Studies *Essais* as first modern expression of the idea of continuous creation. "A force de peindre le passage, voici que Montaigne obtient communication à l'être; car l'être véritable n'est point une entité métaphysique, mais l'action continue d'une pensée sur les choses et sur la durée" (p. 15).

Prévost, Jean. La vie de Michel de Montaigne. Gallimard, 1926. 227 p. (VHI) 1712

Not a scholarly work. Written in a sprightly manner, and quite interesting for those who desire a superficial acquaintance with M.

Review : Anon in TLS, Dec. 9, 1926, p. 914.

Prévost-Paradol, L. A. P. Montaigne. *In his:* Études sur les moralistes français. *See* 1443. p. 3-40. 1713

A brilliant and sound appreciation of *Essais*, stressing especially M.'s temperance, moderation, and sincerity. Concerns himself chiefly with skepticism in *L'apologie*.

IVe centenaire de la naissance de Montaigne, 1533-1933. Conférences organisées par la ville de Bordeaux et catalogue des éditions françaises des Essais. Bordeaux, Delmas, 1933. 388 p. 1714

Lamandé, André. *Montaigne et l'esprit gascon.* p. 27-69.

Courteault, Paul. *Montaigne, maire de Bordeaux.* p. 71-162.

Laumonier, Paul. *La pensée de Montaigne.* p. 163-81.

Creyx, Dr. Maurice. *Montaigne malade, médecin, hydrologue.* p. 183-211.

Bonnafous, Max. *Montaigne et l'éducation.* p. 213-37.

Hubrecht, Georges. *Montaigne juriste.* p. 239-97.

Guillaumie, Gaston. *Montaigne, périgourdin.* p. 299-331.

Galland, René. *Montaigne et Shakespeare.* p. 333-71.

Liste des éditions françaises des Essais de 1580 à nos jours. p. 373-88.

Important volume. Articles prepared as public lectures and hence represent a sort of *mise au point* rather than original research. Most important is Courteault's article, which presents some new material on M. as mayor of Bordeaux. List of editions prepared by partisan of Dr. Armaingaud, credits M. with authorship of *Discours de la servitude volontaire.*

Raymond, Marcel. Entre le fidéisme et le naturalisme : à propos de l'attitude religieuse de Montaigne. *In:* FestET, p. 237-47. *Reprinted as* L'attitude religieuse de Montaigne *in his* Génies de France. Neuchâtel, La Baconnière, 1942. p. 50-67.   1715

" Qui saura jamais si la croyance religieuse et l'attachement aux dogmes, en ce Montaigne de 1588, était plus qu'une habitude, et le fidéisme autre chose qu'une postulation de l'esprit...? Ce qui apparaît évident, en revanche, c'est que si le chrétien sommeille, le naturaliste n'est pas près de se passer de Dieu " (p. 66).

Renart, François. Zigzags dans les parterres de Montaigne. Renée Lacoste, 1951. 251 p.   1716

Not a scholarly work, but six personal and thought-provoking essays written " pendant quelques semaines d'un congé forcé que la guerre me fit subir loin des bibliothèques et des livres." Chapters on : *Le fervent du pyrrhonisme, Le bréviaire des honnêtes gens, L'amitié de Montaigne, L'éducation humaniste, Montaigne et Pascal, L'humaniste et le chrétien.* Concludes with *Post scriptum* measuring his thoughts by standards established by Villey and Strowski.

Renault, Jules. Les idées pédagogiques de Montaigne. Lethielleux, 1921. 53 p. (IP)   1717

Not a critical study, like those of Compayré (no. 1564-65) and Porteau (no. 1709-

1710), but a gleaning of " les conseils les plus opportuns et les plus adéquats à l'époque actuelle " (p. 3).

Revol, General Joseph Fortuné. Montaigne et l'art militaire. Chapelot, 1911. 32 p.   1718

Interesting analysis of M.'s statements on military subjects. His opinions on war similar to those of Tolstoi. Writes frequently on military tactics, " ruses de guerre," and on military psychology, especially in regard to fear of death.

Richou, Gabriel, ed. Inventaire de la collection des ouvrages et documents réunis par J. F. Payen et J. B. Bastide sur Michel de Montaigne, rédigé et précédé d'une notice par Gabriel Richou, suivi de lettres inédites de Françoise de Lachassagne. Téchener, 1878. 396 p.   1719

Invaluable guide to the Payen collection of the BN.

Ritter, Raymond. Au pays de Montaigne : 1533-1933. Ill 184:233-36, Feb. 25, 1933.   1720

Description of M.'s château, including excellent photographs of his tomb, tower, bedroom, library, etc.

— Cette Grande Corisande. Michel, 1936. 411 p.   1721

Excellent biography of Diane d'Andouins, mistress of Henri IV and friend of the essayist. Her friendship with M. discussed especially in *Rencontre avec un sage,* p. 71-92 and *Le conseil de Montaigne,* p. 187-206.

Riveline, Maurice. Montaigne et l'amitié. Alcan, 1939. 268 p.   1722

Detailed and well-documented study of role of friendship in M.'s life, of his conception of friendship, and of the influence of friendship upon *Essais.* Presents no new material, but provides an interesting development of one side of M. The reader must not forget the author's warning that : " il ne peut être question ... de déterminer quel fut le Montaigne réel, mais de montrer l'un des Montaigne possibles." (p. 3). *See* 1445.

Reviews : Anon in BSAM 2nd ser. 7:120, Oct., 1939; M. Raymond in Hren 7:246-48, 1940.

Robertson, John M. Montaigne and Shakespeare, and other essays on cognate questions. London, Adam and Charles Black, 1909. 358 p. (1st ed., 1897.)   1723

Tries to show, p. 3-231, that the greatness of Shakespeare, both in thought and in style, was largely due to influence of M. *See* 2839.

Reviews : A. B. in DSGJ 35:313-14, 1899; R.W. Bond in MLR 5:361-70, 1910.

Roth, Cecil. L'ascendance juive de Michel de Montaigne. RCC ser. 1, 39:176-87, 1937-38. 1724

Research in Archives of Saragossa reveal that " ... Montaigne était à la septième génération un descendant direct de Mayer Paçagon, juif de Calatayud, converti au christianisme vers le début du xve siècle, sous le nom de Juan Lopez de Villa-Nueva " (p. 182).

Rouillard, Clarence D. Montaigne et les Turcs. RLC 18:235-51, 1938. 1725

Few allusions to Turks in 1580 and 1588, approximately 50 in 1595, drawn largely from Chalcondyle and Postel. M. interested in military, moral, and religious qualities of Turks.

Routh, H. V. The origins of the essay compared in French and English literatures. MLR 15:28-40, 143-51, 1920. 1726

A good treatment of M.'s contribution to the development of the essay.

Ruel, Édouard. Du sentiment artistique dans la morale de Montaigne. Hachette, 1901. 432 p. 1727

A novel approach which makes M. primarily an artist, both in his ideas and in the form of *Essais*. Tries to show artistry in M.'s faculty of observation, his love of truth, sense of personality, sympathy for misery and human weakness, feeling for life, sense of moderation, and idealism. Considers the form of *Essais* a direct imitation of Nature. Accepts M. as a Christian, while admitting that his morality is not Christian. Treatment of M.'s philosophy, interrupted by author's death, limited to fragments. Laudatory 64-page preface by Émile Faguet.

Review : Anon in Rren 2:64-65, 1902.

Sabrié, J. B. De l'humanisme au rationalisme. Pierre Charron (1541-1603). Alcan, 1913. 552 p. 1728

The most authoritative study on M.'s friend and disciple. Refers constantly to influence of M. and *Essais*.

Sacy, Sylvestre de. Les Essais de Montaigne et ses lettres inédites publiées par

M. Feuillet de Conches. BBB 1865, ser. 16, p. 281-95. 1729

Appreciation of Prévost-Paradol's preface to Garnier edition (reprint of 1826 Leclerc ed.) of *Essais:* Prévost-Paradol makes M. too anticlerical; criticism of Feuillet de Conches for printing letters of no importance; a warning against being seduced by M.'s morality.

— Montaigne essaie ses facultés naturelles. MerF 315:285-306, Jun. 1, 1952. 1730

Good development of idea that the man and his book are identical. " On ne voit guère d'autre exemple d'une aussi étonnante correspondance entre une vie et une œuvre " (p. 303).

Sáenz Hayes, Ricardo. Miguel de Montaigne. Buenos Aires, Espasa-Calpe, 1939. 428 p. 1731

The first book written on M. in Spanish. An excellent general study of M. and the *Essais*, followed by a summary treatment of the literary fortunes of the *Essais* in France, England, Germany, Italy, Spain, and North and South America. Good *Bibliografía somera* and index of persons cited.

Reviews : M. Carayon in BH 42:29-38, 1940; P. Descaves in NL, p. 6 ; Feb. 11, 1939; P.Hazard in RLC 19:477-82, 1939.

St. John, Bayle. Montaigne the essayist, a biography. London, Chapman and Hall, 1858. 2 v. 1732

" The first English book on Montaigne, and the first extended life of Montaigne in any language." (Tilley, *Montaigne's interpreters*, No. 1769, p. 273). Avoids dogmatism in his interpretation of *Essais.*

Salles, A. Les principales éditions de Montaigne. BSAM, 2e série, no. 4, Nov. 1938, p. 27-32; no. 5, Feb. 1939, p. 24-27; no. 6, Jun. 1939, p. 60-61; no. 7, Oct. 1939, p. 101-102; no. 8, Mar. 1940, p. 16. 1733

Miscellaneous notes concerning various editions.

— Un peu de nouveau sur Montaigne. BBB ns 14:198-205, 1935. 1734

Four minor points of textual criticism, plus an unpublished letter from the duc d'Aumale to Dr. Payen concerning M.

Schiff, Mario Lodovico. La fille d'alliance de Montaigne, Marie de Gournay. Champion, 1910. 146 p. 1734A

An authoritative and well-documented study of her life and relations with M. (p. 1-

53), followed by annotated editions of her *L'égalité des hommes et des femmes* and *Grief des dames.*

Reviews : J. Frank in ZFSL 37:28-31, 1911; H. C. Lancaster in MLN 26:125-127, 1911.

Sclafert, Clément. L'âme religieuse de Montaigne. Nouvelles éditions latines, 1951. 315 p.   1735

Justly remarks that every other critic of M. " le tire à son système " (p. 8) and then proceeds to do the same thing. Divides study into two parts : *La foi religieuse de Montaigne* and *La morale chrétienne de Montaigne.* His conclusions : " Il nous est apparu peu à peu que la religion tient dans ce livre une place centrale et que la théologie la plus orthodoxe s'y trouve répétée, que sans la religion et sans la théologie, ce livre ne saurait se comprendre; que jamais peut-être aucun laïque n'a si bien exposé dans sa complexité, ni si bien résolu le problème religieux; que ce ' docte profane ' est le meilleur apologiste par la profondeur de ses vues sur l'âme et que Pascal n'a fait que le copier; que Mademoiselle de Gournay qui l'appelait un pilier de l'Église n'était pas une sotte et que Montaigne n'était pas un sot ni un fourbe quand il assurait que cette ' fille ' était celle qui l'avait le mieux compris " (p. 7-8).

Seillière, Ernest. La doctrine de la bonté naturelle de Montaigne à Delisle de Sales. AMP 1er sem. 1925, p. 369-410.   1736

From a questionable interpretation of what *Essais* say, Seillière tries to show that M. is naive in his examples of how Nature dictates morality, chiefly because he fell victim to misinformation about the natural world.

— Le naturisme de Montaigne et autres essais. Éditions de la Nouvelle revue critique, 1938. p. 9-85.   1737

Tries to show that Villey's studies on M. and *Essays* reveal a much stronger current of naturisme than Villey admitted, and that this naturisme is especially noticeable in 17th and 18th century authors influenced by *Essays.*

Selby, F. G. Bacon and Montaigne. Criterion 3:258-77, Jan. 1925.   1738

Extensive examination of similarities and dissimilarities of thought in numerous parallel passages, reaching no definite conclusions as to influence of M. on Bacon. Sees M. as pagan and is shocked by " the gross and wanton indecencies and obscen-

ities in which unhappily the little man delights " (p. 277).

Setti, G. Tassoni e Montaigne. *In :* Miscellanea tassoniana di studi storici e letterari. Modena, Formiggini, 1908. p. 227-42.
                    1739

Tries to show that Tasso was familiar with *Essais.* See Neri, no. 1689.

Sichel, Edith. Michel de Montaigne. London, Constable, 1911. 271 p.   1740

Good introduction to *Essais,* well-written and sound, intended for general reader. Bibliography (p. 259-63) now out of date.

Smith, William F. Vives and Montaigne as educators. Hisp 29:483-93, 1946.   1741

Shows similarities and differences of M.'s ideas on education and those of Vives; concludes that M. borrowed either directly or indirectly from Vives.

Solmi, Sergio. La salute di Montaigne. Cult 12:281-99, 1933.   1742

Writing because he must, to express himself and consequently realize himself, creating a book which is consubstantial with its author and which is centered on man, M. comes to accept his condition as he learns to know it. His whole aim is to " reintegrare insensibilmente nella vita, per minacciata e manchevole que essa sia, ogni valore umano.... Insomma, il processo della saggezza di Montaigne consiste in una progressiva corrosione di tutti gli ideali e gli scopi che rendono difficile la vita, per proporre l'ideale più elementare e semplice possibile : quello di uno sciolto, esatto aderire dell'individua al naturale movimento e ritmo della vita stessa. Un ideale che potrebbe chiamarsi, con parola intesa in senso lato, la salute."

One of the best articles yet published on M. and certainly the soundest compressed appreciation of *Essais.*

Stapfer, Paul. La famille et les amis de Montaigne. Hachette, 1896. 360 p. 1743

Interesting collection of " causeries " based on his lectures at University of Bordeaux in 1893-1894. Contains no new material on M., but draws heavily on *Essais* and shows familiarity with previous research. Contains chapters on M.'s ancestors, on members of his family, and on La Boétie, Mlle de Gournay, Pierre de Brach, Charron, and *Raimond de Sebonde et le christianisme de Montaigne.* Tries to destroy legend of M.'s egotism. See 1449.

— Montaigne. Hachette, 1895. 200 p. (GEF) 1744

Probably the best general presentation of what M. meant to the generation which preceded the studies of Villey and Strowski. Like other volumes in this excellent series, well written and readable. *See* 1448.

Reviews : Anon in AnP 6:310-11, 1895; J. Frank in ZFSL 17:235-41, 1895.

Strowski, Fortunat. Les apprentissages de Michel de Montaigne. L'homme dans les Essais. *In his:* La sagesse française. Plon, 1925. p. 53-106. 1744A

Not a detailed study, but an excellent discussion of M.'s thought and evolution of his morale. From lectures given at Columbia University on *Les moralistes français.*

— A propos de Montaigne. RPB 10:49-72, Feb., 1907. 1745

A thorough and favorable study of Lautrey's edition of *Journal de voyage* (no. 1500) and of Zangroniz's *Montaigne, Amyot et Saliat* (no. 1805); and a refutation of Armaingaud's arguments attributing *Discours de la servitude volontaire* to Montaigne (no. 1507).

— La jeunesse de Montaigne. RCC 39 : 1ʳᵉ sér. 577-85, 681-91; 2ᵉ sér. 129-36, 1938. 1746

Four sections of article : *La tribu Eyquem. La tribu Lopez de Villanueva. Naissance et éducation de Michel de Montaigne. Montaigne à vingt ans.*

A good synthesis of what we know of M.'s early years, drawn from *Essais* and from research of many other scholars.

— Montaigne. Alcan, 1906. 356 p. 2nd ed. revised, 1931. (GP) *See* 1544. 1747

Marks beginning of a new era in study of M. and *Essais.* First study of M. from point of view of evolution of his philosophy, written while Villey was preparing his *Sources et évolution* (no. 1794),. each scholar being unaware of the other's work. Not so broad in scope as Villey, but reaches many of same conclusions. Traces M.'s evolution from Stoicism, to scepticism, to " l'équilibre du bon sens," to man of action, to dilettantism. His whole life a quest for liberty, which he achieved through strong will power, a religious soul, a keen and detached mind, and a gentle human heart.

Reviews : Anon in TLS, Sept. 17, 1931, p. 701; J. Frank in ZFSL 33:194-201,

1908; J. Hanse in RBP 11:189-93, 1932; P. Jourda in Rcr 65:258-62, 1931; B. Kubler in RHph 5:422-24, 1931.

— Montaigne. *In his:* Histoire du sentiment religieux en France au xviiᵉ siècle; Pascal et son temps. Plon, 1907-08. v. 1, p. 28-58. *See* 2282. 1748

Presents M. primarily as a creator of Neo-Stoicism, " ... un stoïcisme francisé, humanisé, vivant et aimable " (p. 30).

— Montaigne lu à Bordeaux : étude sur l'édition des Essais de 1580. RPB 5:193-218, 1902. 1749

Shows that 1580 edition is much more concerned with people and events of Bordeaux region than later editions. Its unity contrasts with disorder of 1588 and 1595. " Autre surprise : pas de grossièretés, pas d'indécences.... Enfin, le style proprement dit a plus de tenue " (p. 217). This is the edition admired by Charron and the only one read by Saint François de Sales.

— Montaigne, sa vie publique et privée. Nouvelle revue critique, 1938. 284 p. 1750

Biography plus commentary. Illustrations, appendixes on château, and portraits of M. Information exact and tidy, presented with warmth and judiciousness.

Reviews : M. Richard in RFrance 18:541-543, Oct. 15, 1938; A. Salles in BSAM 4:59, Nov., 1938.

— Une source italienne des Essais de Montaigne. L'Examen vanitatis doctrinae gentium de François Pic de la Mirandole. BI 5:309-13, 1905. 1751

Contributed to the skepticism of the *Apologie.*

— La vocation de Montaigne. Corr 251:934-947, June 10, 1913. 1752

M. was a born man of letters, even though he tried many other things. " Le vrai Montaigne, c'est ce petit homme chauve, qui est dans sa tour.... Tantôt il rêve et tantôt il ' registre et dicte ' en se promenant. Puis il s'assied; il polit sa phrase; il est heureux, il est tranquille, il est satisfait, les rois ne l'auront pas; les doctes muses le retiennent. Il est définitivement installé dans sa vocation " (p. 947).

Taffe, Valentine. Bacon et Montaigne essayistes. RAA 1:505-16, Aug. 1924. 1753

Good analysis of differences between the

two essayists. Sees Bacon as cold and calculating scientist, M. as a charmer.

Tannenbaum, Samuel A. Michel Eyquem de Montaigne (a concise bibliography). New York, Samuel A. Tannenbaum, 1942. 137 p. (EB, no. 24)   1754

Lists 2973 items. Indispensable volume, despite minor defects : incomplete references, numerous errors, inconsistency of styling, and the annoying habit of using abbreviation " MM " often when the name in the title is only Montaigne. Relatively complete, but includes many items of questionable value.

Tauro, Giacomo. Montaigne. Rome, Albrighi-Segati, 1928. 340 p. (BPI)   1755

Five well-written and well-informed chapters on : *Montaigne e il suo tempo, La dipintura di se stesso, Il problema educativo, Della filosofia di Montaigne,* and *L'eredità di Montaigne.* A good study for the Italian general reader.

Tavera, François. Le problème humain : l'idée d'humanité dans Montaigne. Champion, 1932. 332 p.   1756

His thesis : " L'idée humaine, ... c'est l'idée du moi qui se suffit, qui peut et doit se suffire pour accomplir sa destinée " (p. 9). Holds to Stoic interpretation throughout, and ignores evolution of M.'s thought, dates of different essays, and additions which reveal changed points of view. Considers M. an unbeliever, interested only in the complete emancipation of human conscience.

Reviews : P. Jourda in Rcr 66:345-48, 1932; É. Magne in MerF 242:127-38, Feb. 15, 1933; W. G. Moore in MLR 30:98-99, 1935; J. Plattard in RSS 19:302-304, 1933; B. M. Woodbridge in RR 25:161-64, 1934; G. Vanwelkenhuyzen in RBP 14:119-21, Jan.-Mar., 1935.

Taylor, George C. Montaigne-Shakespeare and the deadly parallel. PQ 22:330-37, 1943.   1758

Impassioned defense of the type of literary evidence used in his *Shakespere's debt to Montaigne* (no. 1759), and an attempt to refute the conclusions of Miss Alice Harmon in *How great was Shakespeare's debt to Montaigne?* (no. 1629).

— Shakespere's debt to Montaigne. Harvard University Press, 1925. 66 p.   1759

Studies parallel passages in Shakespeare and Florio's M.; concludes that Shakespeare, although not a disciple of M.,

" was most profoundly and extensively affected by the Florio Montaigne in every way immediately after he had first had the opportunity to become familiar with the work in its entirety, and that, as time passed, the Montaigne influence became less and less apparent although Shakespere bore Montaigne's marks upon him to the grave " (p. 33). *See* 2845.

Reviews : Anon in TLS, Dec. 24, 1925, p. 895; C. R. Baskervill in MP 23:499-500, 1925-26; É. Legouis in RLC 6:538-39, 1926; J. W. Tupper in MLN 41:209-10, 1926.

Taylor, Henry Osborn. Montaigne. *In his :* Thought and expression in the sixteenth century. New York, Macmillan, 1920. p. 1:359-75.   1760

Accomplishes well the author's purpose : " to distinguish his [M.'s] place in the intellectual development of sixteenth century France " (p. 374).

Taylor, James S. Montaigne and medicine. New York, Hoeber, 1921. 244 p.   1761

Good example of M.'s appeal to medical profession. " In analyzing human thought and conduct he was a model for the physician who studies pathology and symptoms, and many are the analogies between his situation, his mode of thought, his character and temperament and those of the profession " (p. vii). Uses many quotations from *Essais,* with commentary on pertinence of M.'s experiences to those of modern medical practitioners.

Teulié, Henri. Projet d'une prétendue traduction des Essais de Montaigne au xviiie siècle. MélPL, p. 415-34.   1762

L'Abbé Trublet's curious project of translating, modernizing, correcting, moralizing and completing the *Essais* (1733), fortunately prevented by the criticisms of Paul Desforges-Maillard.

Texte, Joseph. La descendance de Montaigne, Sir Thomas Browne. *In his :* Études de littérature européenne. Colin, 1898. p. 51-63.   1763

Excellent study of M.'s influence on Browne. " Browne était né à la fois épicurien et mystique, sceptique et croyant. L'épicurien s'est fait une joie d'imiter l'auteur des *Essais,* s'est amusé de ses doutes et de sa belle humeur, s'est complu dans ce que sa philosophie a d'aimable et de nonchalant; il lui a emprunté tout un art dans la guerre qu'il a fait à la raison, a joui de ses victoires et ri de la déconvenue de ses ennemis " (p. 92).

Thibaudet, Albert. Le quadricentenaire d'un philosophe. RPar 40:755-76, Feb. 15, 1933. 1764

M. introduced three important thoughts which helped shape modern philosophy : " la pensée de l'homme qui s'appelle Calias " (individualism); " la pensée du mouvement " (Bergson's *mobilisme*); and " la pensée de la nature " (modern naturalism).

— Le roman de Montaigne : de Mauriac à Montaigne. Runiv 60:655-77, Mar. 15, 1935. 1765

M.'s chief interest, " la condition humaine," is the theme of Mauriac and many other modern novelists. " Du roman de l'humaine condition, qui n'était pas viable au temps de Montaigne, les *Essais* peuvent passer pour la maquette " (p. 677).

Thomas, Jean. Sur la composition d'un essai de Montaigne. Hren 5:297-306, 1938. 1766

Refutation of Grace Norton's thesis (1695), which was partly supported by Villey, that III, 9, *De la vanité*, is composed of two separate essays, one on traveling and the other on vanity, later amalgamated and perhaps intended as preface to Book III.

Tilley, Arthur. Follow nature. *In his:* Studies in the French renaissance. *See* 1024, p. 233-58. 1767

Rabelais' concept of nature, p. 233-47. Defines M.'s idea of following nature (p. 247-58) as follows : " Man is a law to himself; let him follow his constitution or nature—not his mere animal instincts—or the dictates of passion, humour, or willfulness, but his higher nature as purified and developed by reflection and conscience " (p. 256).

— Montaigne. *In his:* The literature of the French renaissance. No. 123, v. II, p. 136-79. 1768

Excellent general discussion. Bibliography, p. 176-79, now out of date.

— Montaigne's interpreters. *In his:* Studies in the French renaissance. *See* 1024, p. 259-93. 1769

Excellent survey of interpretations of M. from 17th through 19th century, followed by a penetrating analysis of interpretations of modern scholars : Guizot,

Ruel, Edme Champion, Strowski, and Villey.

Toffanin, Giuseppe. Montaigne e l'idea classica. (2nd revised ed.) Bologna, Zanichelli, 1942. 98 p. 1770

A not unsubtle argument to prove that M. is representative of Italian humanism, the *idea classica*, where *sapienza* is a religious value and which means a resurgence of Platonic spiritualism against Aristotelian naturalism. But Toffanin's reading of *Essais* has given him the idea that M. is never a psychologist, always a moralist, rather close to Sebond despite obvious differences, and actually the antagonist of the " stendhaliani " and the " proustiani " who try to adopt him. The argument, calling itself unprejudiced, as it is on some scores, but actually vitiated by a thorough-going bias, is of a kind that seems to be native to discussions of M., and needs to be guarded against.

Toldo, Pietro. L'homme sage de Montaigne. MélGL, p. 132-53. 1771

Studies *Essais* as autobiography, finds that M. gave too favorable a picture of himself and of his " sagesse " as judged by known facts concerning his life. M. forgot that he too was " ondoyant et divers."

Trueblood, Ralph W. Montaigne the average man. PMLA 21:215-25, 1906. 1772

" Whatever other contributing influences may exist, the one thing above all else which must consciously or unconsciously appeal to us, is that everywhere he consistently represents and personifies the viewpoint of that great ' middle region ' of mankind to which the majority of his readers belong " (p. 218). An interesting point of view, but its importance might easily be exaggerated.

Türck, Suzanne. Shakespeare und Montaigne, ein Beitrag zur Hamlet Frage. Berlin, Junker und Dunnhaupt, 1930. 160 p. (Diss., Göttingen.) 1773

Examines parallel passages and finds what she considers to be unquestionable evidence of influence of *Essais* on Hamlet. *See* 2847.

Reviews : T. Brooke in JEGP 30:605-06, 1931; W. Franz in NSp 40:106-08, 1932; H. de Groot in Est 14:220-24, 1932; H. Jantzen in Beibl 42:124-26, 1931; W. Keller in DSGJ 67:85-86, 1931; E. A. Philippson in LGRP 54:17-19, 1933; H. Schoeffler in DLit 53:931-36, May 15,

1932; Max J. Wolff in ES 66:425-26, 1931-32.

Turner, Albert M. Charles Reade and Montaigne. MP 30:297-308, 1932-33. 1774
Borrowed extensively from *Journal de voyage* in *Cloister and the Hearth.*

Upham, A. H. The French influence in English literature from the accession of Elizabeth to the Restoration. Columbia University Press, 1911. 560 p. 1775
Montaigne, p. 265-307. Not a detailed study, but a moderate and sane judgment of M.'s influence on Sir William Cornwallis, Bacon, Shakespeare, Ben Jonson, Marston, Sir Walter Raleigh, William Drummond of Hawthornden, Burton, John Taylor the Water Poet, and Sir Thomas Browne. Appendix C (p. 524-53) cites parallel passages from M. and Bacon, M. and Shakespeare, M. and Jonson, M. and Raleigh, M. and Drummond, M. and Burton.

Ustick, W. L. Emerson's debt to Montaigne. WUS 9:245-62, 1922. (Heller memorial volume.) 1776
Emerson's style differs from that of M., although both wrote by " skirmishes " rather than " pitched battles." Similarity of their intellectual life is more striking.

Vallery-Radot, Pierre. La médecine et les médecins dans l'œuvre de Montaigne. Le François, 1942. 24 p. 1777
Finds M.'s skepticism on doctors and medicine justifiable, and considers him useful even today in combating presumption and over-confidence in medical profession.

Vianey, Joseph. Montaigne conteur. MélEH, p. 200-10. 1778
M.'s way of telling an anecdote, paring it to the bone, portends the classical manner : going straight to the mark, " ... amener l'action à l'issue exigée par le jeu naturel des sentiments ... démontrer la vérité que l'action doit illustrer " (p. 200).

Villey, Pierre. Les Essais de Michel de Montaigne. Sfelt, 1932, 1946. 179 p. (GEL) 1779
One of the best short volumes on *Essais*, recommended for both students and specialists.
Reviews : E. Magne in MerF 242:127-138, 1933; E. Seillière in *Sur la psychologie du romantisme français.* Éditions de la NRC (1933), p. 22-28.

— Les idées nouvelles au seizième siècle et leur diffusion. *In his :* Les sources d'idées; textes choisis et commentés. Plon, [c1912]. p. 1-17. 1780
Good but brief discussion of diffusion of new ideas in 16th century, followed by discussion and examples of translations from poets of antiquity and Petrarch; Greek, Latin, Italian and Spanish prose writers; and French travel accounts. Important but not exhaustive work. Not specifically a study of M.'s sources, but demonstration of source materials available to him.

— L'influence de Montaigne sur Charles Blount et les déistes anglais. RSS 1:190-219, 392-443, 1913. 1781
Like Voltaire and the Encyclopedists, Blount, Sir William Temple, George Savile and Bolingbroke considered M. primarily a Pyrrhonist, drew heavily on him for their ideas. A sound and well-documented study, showing M.'s popularity in England at a time when the French considered him dangerous.

— L'influence de Montaigne sur les idées pédagogiques de Locke et de Rousseau. Hachette, 1911. 270 p. 1782
A model of moderation among studies on literary influences. Shows how Locke accepts all of M.'s ideas and adds much to them; how Rousseau accepts their ideas on integral education but adds education of the senses and other elements which sprang from his philosophy and from changes in the times. All three have same essential doctrine : the education of the complete individual and his adaptation to the social milieu.
Reviews : A. François in AJJR 8:341-342, 1912; J. de La Rouxière in Rren 12:119-20, 1911; A. Messer in ZFSL 40:211-12, 1913; D. Mornet in RHL 19:220, 1912; J. Plattard in RER 9:333-35, 1911.

— Les livres d'histoire moderne utilisés par Montaigne. Hachette, 1908. 262 p. (Diss., Paris.) 1783
A further study of M.'s sources. Lists the historians read by him and points out the traces which they left in *Essais.* An important appendix treats ancient historians read by M. in French translation. *See* 1794.
Reviews : G. Lanson in RHL 15:755-58, 1908; J. Plattard in RER 7:506-08, 1909.

— Montaigne. Rieder, 1933. 104 p. 60 planches hors texte en héliogravure. (MDL) 1784
" Elle résume avec aisance et agrément ce que les autres travaux savants de l'auteur nous ont révélé " (Mornet, review below).
Review : D. Mornet in RHL 40:594, 1933.

— Montaigne. In : Bédier, Joseph. Histoire de la littérature française illustrée, publiée sous la direction de MM. Joseph Bédier ... et Paul Hazard. See 94, v. I, p. 202-13. Revised ed., 1948. v. I, p. 277-91. 1785
One of the best treatments of M. and importance of Essais in French literature.

— Montaigne a-t-il eu quelque influence sur François Bacon? Rren 12:121-58, 185-203, 1911;13:21-46, 61-82, 1912. 1786
Thorough and detailed study. Concludes that M.'s influence on Bacon the essayist is of little importance, but that " il se pourrait que Montaigne, lu de bonne heure de Bacon, eût éveillé et aiguisé son esprit critique, que lui montrant la pauvreté des méthodes en usage et la faiblesse de la raison humaine abandonnée à ses seules forces, il l'eût incité à construire sa méthode " (p. 82).

— Montaigne a-t-il lu le Traité de l'éducation de Jacques Sadolet? BBB 1909, p. 265-278. 1787
Refutation of thesis, supported by Joseph Dedieu in the BLE, Jan., 1909 (no. 1587), that M. had read Sadolet's treatise and had borrowed heavily from it in writing De l'institution des enfants.

— Montaigne devant la postérité. Boivin, 1935. 376 p. See 1533. 1788
Undertaken as a general study of Montaigne's influence in France, England, Germany, and Italy, this work was interrupted by Villey's death and prepared for publication by Jean Plattard. These fragments provide a study of the fortunes of Essais in France from 1580 to 1610, plus two chapters on the success of Essais in 18th century and on the idea of the " honnête homme " in M. and during the classical period.
Reviews : Anon in TLS, Aug. 15, 1935, p. 511; P. A. Becker in ZFSL 60:109-13, 1937; G. in Neo 24:300-01, 1938-39; P. Jourda in Rcr 69:165-66, 1935; B. Matulka in RR 27:39-42, 1936; F. Ed. Schneegans in BLS 14:290-93, 1935-36; H. F. Stewart in MLR 31:584-86, 1936.

— Montaigne en Angleterre. RDM 17:115-150, Sept. 1, 1913. 1789
Excellent general treatment of M.'s influence in England, written for non-specialist.

— Montaigne et les poètes dramatiques anglais du temps de Shakespeare. RHL 24:357-93, 1917. 1790
Amazing success of Florio translation (1603). Examines nature and extent of its influence on Marston and Webster, studied in many parallel passages. Takes moderate attitude on Shakespeare's debt to M., points out ridiculousness of exaggerated claims by Robertson (see 1723) and others. See 2848.

— Note sur la bibliothèque de Montaigne. RHL 17:335-53, 1910. 1791
Adds ten titles of books owned by M. to the list given in Les sources et l'évolution des Essais, 1908 (1794).

— La place de Montaigne dans le mouvement philosophique. RPFE 101:338-59, 1926. 1792
M., usually accorded little space by historians of philosophy, deserves to be considered an important link between philosophy of Middle Ages and modern philosophy, because of the goal he set for himself in Essais and because of the method he followed.

— Une source inconnue d'un essai de Montaigne. RHL 19:802-17, 1912. 1793
De la force de l'imagination heavily indebted to Cornelius Agrippa's De occulta philosophia.

— Les sources et l'évolution des Essais de Montaigne. Hachette, 1908. 2 v. 1794
Among most important works ever published on M. Indispensable tool for any serious study of Essais, based upon a comparative study of the 1580, 1588, and 1595 editions. Treats three main themes : Les lectures de Montaigne et leur chronologie, Chronologie des Essais, and L'évolution des Essais.
His method of establishing the chronology of Essais discussed as a model of method by André Morize in Problems and methods of literary history, no. 1478, p. 149-156.
Reviews : G. Deschamps in Rren 9:170-179, 1908; J. Frank in ZFSL 35:70-81, 1910; G. Lanson in RHL 15:755-58, 1908; H. Monod in BBB 1908, p. 369-75;

J. Plattard in RER 7:506-08, 1909; A. Tilley in MLR 4:401-07, 1908-09.

Vinet, Alexandre. Michel de Montaigne. *In his:* Moralistes des seizième et dixseptième siècles. 2nd ed., Fischbacher, 1904. p. 53-123.   1795
Excellent presentation of the attitude of a Protestant professor and theologian who greatly influenced Sainte-Beuve. Appreciates M.'s portrayal of " l'incohérence de l'homme," and his " morale descriptive," but finds his " morale du précepte " weakened by his lacking a concept of the relations of man to the infinite, especially as regards God and death. Accuses him of substituting conscience for moral law, and condemns his attitude towards " volupté."

Voizard, Eugène. Étude sur la langue de Montaigne. *See* 607.   1796
Earliest study of any consequence of M.'s writing (spelling, grammar, syntax, vocabulary, style) but now considered superficial and *passé*.

Wadsworth, Charlotte R. Molière's debt to Montaigne. MLQ 8:290-301, Sept., 1947.   1797
Discusses common themes : satire of doctors and medicine, hypocrisy, pedants, *préciosité*, avarice, etc., and concludes that Molière is indebted to M. " for much of the philosophical expression which distinguishes his comedies " (p. 301).

Weigand, Wilhelm. Michel de Montaigne. Muenchen, 1910. 280 p.   1798
Competent general study of life and works. Reproduces inscriptions on beams of M.'s study, p. 261-71. Bibliography, p. 272-80.

Weiler, Maurice. La pensée de Montaigne. Bordas, 1948. 187 p.   1799
Treatment of M.'s religion follows Armaingaud, presents M. as an enigma. Later chapters much more original, and provide good exposition of M.'s thought. Reviews : D. M. Frame in RR 40:203-207, 1949; P. Jourda in RHL 50:437-38, 1950; N. Sabord in NL, Nov. 18, 1948, p. 3.

Willis, Irene Cooper. Montaigne. New York, Knopf, 1927. 135 p.   1800
A well-written little book, done by an amateur with the avowed purpose of advertising M. Not a scholarly study, but interesting for the general reader.

Review : Anon in TLS, Mar. 1, 1928, p. 143.

Woodbridge, Homer E. Montaigne, the friend. SoR 1:106-19, Sept., 1915-16.   1801
Tries to draw a positive portrait of M., in opposition to the negative implications of interpreting him as a sceptic. Stresses friendship, love of truth, courage, generosity. Sound and well-written article.

Woolf, Virginia. Montaigne. *In her :* The common reader. New York, Harcourt, Brace, 1948. p. 87-100.   1802
A delightful examination of *Essais* as " an attempt to communicate a soul."

Yates, Frances A. The translation of Montaigne. *In her :* John Florio, the life of an Italian in Shakespeare's England. Cambridge University Press, 1934. p. 213-245.   1803
Interesting study of the literary qualities of Florio's translation, and of the difference between his style and that of M.

Young, Charles L. Emerson's Montaigne. New York, Macmillan, 1941. 236 p.   1804
" No book before or since was ever so much to me as that," wrote Emerson of Cotton's translation of M. An excellent study of Emerson's acquaintance with M., and of likeness and dissimilarity of the two writers. Shows that Emerson took from M. those ideas which he liked and ignored those with which he disagreed. His concept of M. more like himself than like the original M. Good bibliography and index. *See* 1605.
Reviews : C. Gohdes in SAQ 41:224, 1942; R. L. Rusk in MLN 58:238-39, 1943; R. E. Watters in MLQ 3:490-91, 1942; S. E. Whicher in NEQ 14:769-71, 1941.

Zangroniz, Joseph de. Montaigne, Amyot and Saliat, étude sur les sources des Essais. Champion, 1906. 196 p. (BLR, v. 7). 1805
Excellent study of M.'s borrowing (or copying) from Amyot, translator of Plutarch and Diodorus Siculus, and from Saliat, translator of Herodotus. Shows how the prose of Amyot and Saliat blends into that of M. in such a way that M.'s copying becomes apparent only when he is compared to 16th-century translations. Also, even when M. copies, he gives an original turn to the things he copies. *See* 1544, 2539.

Reviews : Anon in Rren 7:120, 1906; W. Martini in ZFSL 31:42-43, 1907; J. Plattard in RER 4:281-82, 1906.

Zeitlin, Jacob. The development of Bacon's essays—with special reference to the question of Montaigne's influence upon them. JEGP 27:496-519, 1928. 1806

Careful analysis of similarities and dissimilarities of style and thought in Bacon and M., and conclusion that M.'s influence on Bacon has been exaggerated by Villey and other scholars. See 2850.

CHAPTER XI. WRITERS ON RELIGION
(Nos. 1807-2040)

HELMUT A. HATZFELD AND GEORGE B. WATTS

The Catholic Controversialists
(Nos. 1807-1847)

HELMUT A. HATZFELD

Bibliographies and Special References

Hurter, Hugo. Nomenclator literarius theologiae catholicae (1564-1663). V. I of first ed. : Œniponte, Wagner, 1892. 630 p. (1109-1563). V. II of second ed. : Œniponte, Wagner, 1906. 1590 p.   1807

Offers quick orientation about writers on theological matters, helped by chronological tables with arrangement according to countries. Particularly important with regard to Frenchmen writing in Latin on controversial problems such as Robert Gaguin, Claude Seyssel, Christophe de Longueil, etc.

Reviews : A. B. in RHE 5:158, 1904; J. Lebon in RHE 7:716-17, 1906.

Dictionnaire des lettres françaises, Le seizième siècle. See 99.   1808

Indispensable up-to-date reference work with bio-bibliographical articles on authors and trends. Particularly rich in religious material. First class collaborators. See 127, 315.

Reviews : H. Harvitt in FR 26:61, 1952; R. Lebègue in RHL 52:379-80, 1952.

Dagens, Jean. Bibliographie chronologique de la littérature de spiritualité et de ses sources (1501-1610). Desclee de Brouwer, 1952. 208 p.   1809

This Bibliography responds to one of the most urgent desiderata. It is a rather complete catalogue of the French books on asceticism, mysticism and any form of spiritual life connected with religious reform movements of 16th century, practically promoted by and sketched first in Henri Bremond's monumental Histoire littéraire du sentiment religieux en France (no. 156).

Quilliet, H. Controverse. DTC 3^2 : col. 1694-1748.   1810

16th century is treated in chapter V. En France. Colloques entre Catholiques et Réformés, col. 1721-27 describes the Colloque de Poissy, 1561 (Montluc and Théodore de Bèze) and Conférence de Fontainebleau, 1600 (Du Perron and Du Plessis-Mornay).

Controversy in Colloques and Sacred Eloquence

Radouant, René. L'éloquence dans les assemblées du clergé au XVIe siècle. RHL 21:556-91, 1914.   1811

Highly interesting and important attempt at defining a natural ecclesiastical eloquence in the making by excerpts and analyses of speeches made in clerical assemblies by Cardinal Charles de Lorraine; Langelier, bishop of Saint-Brieuc, Arnaud Sorbin, bishop of Nevers; Renaud de Beaune, archbishop of Bourges and others.

Saulnier, Verdun L. L'oraison funèbre au XVIe siècle. BHren 10:124-57, 1948.   1812

History, themes, style and representatives (Pierre Doré, Arnaud Sorbin, Pierre Fenouillet) of the funeral oration in the making, followed by an important bibliography. Remarkable study.

Labitte, Charles. Les prédicateurs de la Ligue. Fournier, 1841. 402 p.   1813

A long historical and critical introduction based on formal, ideological and political considerations (p. I-LXXV) is followed by four descriptive chapters which deal with impact of the predication on the great political events : I(1-77) De Saint Barthélemy à la mort de Henri III; II (78-130) Depuis l'assassinat de Henri III jusqu'à la levée du siège de Paris; III (131-190) Depuis la levée du siège de Paris jusqu'à l'abjuration de Henri IV; IV (191-286) Depuis l'abjuration de Henri IV jusqu'à son entrée à Paris. Appreciations of the different sermon styles are not lacking.

Lezat, Adrien. De la prédication sous Henri IV. Thorin, 1872. 269 p. (Diss., Paris.) 1814

This study tries to trace evolution of the art of the sermon from political pamphleteer to pure religious oratorical style at end of 16th century. It extends to 17th, and comprises names such as Jean Dubois, Valadier, Charron, Du Perron, Coeffeteau, Bertaut, Saint François de Sales.

Grente, G. Jean Bertaut, abbé d'Aunay, premier aumônier de la reine, évêque de Séez (1552-1611). Lecoffre, 1903. 438 p., 1815

Stresses qualities of the preacher Bertaut, known generally only as court poet of Henri III and Henri IV.

Reviews : B. Heurtebize in RHE 5:881-883, 1904; J. Vianey in RHL 11:156-63, 1904.

Evennett, H. O., ed. Claude d'Espence et son Discours du Colloque de Poissy; étude et texte. Rhist 164:40-78, May-June, 1930. 1816

Biography of this Jesuit and Rector of Sorbonne (1511-71), Catholic defender of tolerance (p. 40-59), is followed by his report on the Colloquium of Poissy, 1561 (p. 60-78), different from Protestant sources and published from MS Dupuy BN v. 309, fol. 7-17.

Sainctes, Claude de. Confession de la foy catholique contenant en brief la réformation de celle que les ministres de Calvin présentèrent au Roy en l'assemblée de Poissy; adressée au peuple de France. Fremy, 1561. 81 p. 1817

This condensation of truths of Catholic faith is given as though it were an amendment to the two harangues made in this matter by Protestant Théodore de Bèze (which are bound together with de Sainctes' work) before the King (Charles IX) and Queen Mother, Catherine de Médicis, respectively. (Copy at NYPL)

Du Perron, Jacques Davy. Les diverses œuvres de l'illustrissime Cardinal du Perron, archevesque de Sens, Primat des Gaules et de Germanie et Grand Aumosnier de France. Seconde édition. Estienne, 1629. 1221 p. 1818

Volume followed by tables without pagination may be roughly subdivided into 1. Réplique à quelques ministres (1-502); 2. Discours (503-648); 3. Oraison funèbre sur la mort de Ronsard (649-76); 4. Sermons, lettres, traductions (677-893); Examen du livre du sieur du Plessis contre la messe (894-1104); 6. Poésies (1105-1221).

— Oraison funèbre de Monsieur de Ronsard (1586). Pierre de Lacretelle (ed.). Éditions du Genêt, 1948. 93 p. 1819

Splendid modern edition of this rhetorically manneristic funeral oration (" Conjoignez vos plaintes avec celles des Muses," p. 79), preceded by three short essays on Ronsard's death (p. 9-17), the funeral ceremony (p. 18-20), and the orator (p. 21-32).

Hippeau, Célestin. Le cardinal Du Perron. In his : Les écrivains normands au XVIIᵉ siècle. Caen, Buhour, 1858. 1-62 p. 1820

With regard to small amount of extant information, still a valid biographical sketch, mentioning also the conversion, through the Cardinal, of (the newly discovered baroque poet) Jean de Sponde (p. 35).

Feret, Pierre. Le cardinal Du Perron, orateur, controversiste, écrivain; étude historique et critique. Didier, 1877. 452 p. 1821

Still the most extensive and informative study on Du Perron dealing in four books with his qualities as poet, orator, conférencier and prose writer. An appendix considers Du Perron épistolographe (p. 372-94), and adds interesting notes (p. 395-447).

Grente, Georgius. Quae fuerit in cardinali Davy Du Perron vis oratoria. Lecoffre, 1903. 100 p. (Diss., Paris.) 1822

Explains in five chapters Du Perron's achievements in the art of academic, civic and ecclesiastical oratory, despite his humanistic mannerisms. The Appendix (p. 87-94) analyzes five orations of different types.

Review : B. Heurtebize in RHE 5:883-884, 1904.

Sorbin, Arnaud. Histoire contenant un abbrégé de la vie, mœurs et vertus du roy très chrestien et debonnaire Charles IX, vrayement piteux, propugnateur de la foy catholique et amateur des bons esprits. Par A. Sorbin, dit De saincte foy, son predicateur, Doc. theologal de Thoulouse. Seconde édition. Lyons, Rigaud, 1574. 108 p. 1823

The famous preacher uses " le règne des merveilles " of Charles IX for a collection of superstitions and sanctimonious stories with the tendency to blame any evil imaginable and even the death of the King on the Huguenots. " Croyez donc, Lecteurs, que les hérétiques François ... ont esté les meurtriers de sa vie, plus que l'altération de ses poulmons " (p. 73).

Doctrinal and Moral Treatises Based on Controversy

Bosquier, Philippe. Tragoedie nouvelle, dicte Le petit razoir des ornemens mondains, en laquelle toutes les misères de nostre temps sont attribuées tant aux héresies qu'aux ornemens superflus du corps, composée par F. Philippes Bosquier, Montois, religieux en l'ordre de Sainct François. Mons, Michel, 1589. Réimpression Brussels, Mertens, 1863.   114 p.   1824

Bibliophile rarity of only 106 *copies de réimpression*. Sermon-drama dealing with appointment of Duke of Parma, Alexander Farnese, as governor of the Low Countries, contains in Act IV, scene 2, p. 76-89 the friar's sermon as announced in title.

— Le fouet de l'Academie des pecheurs. Arras, La Rivière, 1597.   354 p.   1825

Picturesque late renaissance treatise on penance, full of Latin and Greek quotations from ecclesiastical and secular sources with a dedication to archbishop of Cambrai, Jean Sarrazin.

Berson, Jacques. La saincte et très chrestienne résolution de Monseigneur, l'illustrissime et révérendissime cardinal de Bourbon pour maintenir la religion catholique et l'église romaine. Julien, 1586. Reprinted in Archives curieuses de l'histoire de France, 1ʳᵉ série, tome 11ᵉ. Beauvais, 1836. p. 63-87.   1826

Description of interior struggle of Cardinal between his pastoral love and apostolic zeal in reconverting Protestants of his diocese, with reproduction of his allocution.

Boulaese, Jehan. Le manuel de l'admirable victoire du corps de Dieu sur l'esprit maling Beelzebub obtenue à Laon 1566 au salut de tous. Du Val, 1575.   319 p.   1827

Extensive story of Nicole Obry Pierret, sixteen-year-old wife of Loys Pierret, healed from an alleged diabolic possession and—it is implied—from the danger " d'estre tuée par les Heretiques Huguenotz." The original short report on cure is added in form of an illustrated chart between pages 8 and 9 of main text as well as in an appendix of 16 sheets numbered only on the *recto* (Belot, 1573). Official documents, starting with two pontifical admonitions in the matter, fill the first 62 unnumbered pages. (Copy at Harvard)

Cathalan, Antoine. Passevent parisien respondant à Pasquin romain; de la vie de ceux qui sont allez demourer à Genève, et se disent vivre selon la réformation de l'évangile; faict en forme de dialogue. Réimprimé sur la troisième édition (1556). Liseux, 1875. 118 p.   1828

This dialogue, sometimes erroneously attributed to Artus Désiré, with an introduction of 16 pages called *Epistre au lecteur chrestien* is an answer to Th. de Bèze's *Epistola passavanti* and represents a kind of novelistic though biased *Chronique scandaleuse* concerning some leading Calvinists such as Pierre Viret, Bèze, Cordier, Malingre, etc.

Coyssard, Michel. Petit sommaire de la doctrine chrestienne, mis en vers français. Lyon, Pillehotte, 6ᵉ éd. 1608.   142 p.   1829

Practically a rhymed Catechism of 94 pages followed by a hymnal of 48 pages, written by well-known Jesuit lexicographer (1547-1623). Hymns followed by author's own *Odes spirituelles*, once famous due to their music by composer Giovanni Ursucci.

Glen, Jean Baptiste de. Histoire pontificale ou plustost demonstration de la vraye Eglise, fondée par Jesus-Christ et ses Apostres, contenante sommairement les faicts plus signalez advenus en icelle et les plus preignantes marques de la vraye Eglise. Liége, Coersuvarem, 1600.   889 p.   1830

Preface on non-paginated sheets and indices of 40 pages; main part of the book (889 p.) contains life sketches of the popes in which their dogmatic decisions and liturgical innovations are included. (Copy at NYPL)

Désiré, Artus. Les batailles et victoires du chevalier celeste contre le chevalier terrestre, l'un tirant à la maison de Dieu, et l'autre à la maison du prince du monde, chef de l'église maligne. Ruelle, 1564.   175 p.   1831

Rhymed *exposé* on dogmatic differences between Catholic and Calvinistic teaching, illustrated by woodcuts.

Doré, Pierre. Instructoire des Chrestiens en la foy, esperance, et amour en dieu. Brouill, 1545.   145 p.   1832

Elegantly written catechism which stresses, calmly, controversial points such as *De l'oraison qu'on faict aux sainctz et sainctes* (p. 110 ff.). The author has been mentioned by Rabelais as Doribus.

Fontaine, Simon. Histoire catholique de nostre temps touchant l'estat de la religion chrestienne contre l'histoire de Jean Sleydan. Antwerp, Streelsius, 1558. 245 p. **1833**

Enraged by certain vilifications by Protestants and particularly Jean Sleydan (" pourceaux Thomistes " p. 63), author presents, with no more restraint, evolution of Reformation from his viewpoint, in seventeen chapters, with sheet, not page numbers. Model opponents of Reformation are considered English controversialist-martyrs Thomas Morus and bishop John Fisher (p. 124). (Copy at NYPL)

Richeome, Louis. Trois discours pour la religion catholique : des miracles, des saints et des images. Rouen, Osmont, 1604. 646 p. **1834**

Moderate in tone, these three *discours,* dedicated to Henri IV, deal with main controversial points between Catholics and Protestants. " Mon intention est d'aider tous ceux qui pourront prendre fruit de ce mien labeur : les Catholiques en les confirmant en leur foy : les autres en monstrant leur erreur en la personne des ministres, lesquels je refute " (Preface). Richeome quotes many authorities, Greek and Latin, but all translated into French, a novelty. " Je les fais parler françois afin d'aider particulierement la France nostre commune Mère."

Saconay, Gabriel de. Genealogie et la fin des huguenaux, et descouverte du calvinisme : où est sommairement descrite l'histoire des troubles excitez en France par les dits huguenaux, jusqu'à present. Lyons, Rigaud, 1573. 157 p. **1835**

Passionate diatribe against Huguenots, who are interpreted by a fantastic etymology as " les guenaux de Hus," i.e., apelike imitators of earlier reformer, and invited to return to Mother Church.

Busson, Henri. La pensée religieuse française de Charron à Pascal. Vrin, 1933. 665 p. **1836**

Fundamental study showing haziness of Charron's (like Montaigne's) Christianity coming close to a " sceptique chrétienne " (p. 204), origin of which is looked for in Agrippa von Nettesheim, *De incertitudine scientiarum* (1527). Busson's exaggerations have been mitigated by recent studies of L. Febvre and Raymond Lebègue. See 1553.

Review : P. Groult in RHE 30:168-73, 1934.

Conciliatory Devout Humanism

Charron, Pierre. Les trois veritez contre tous athées, idolatres, juifs, mahumetans, heretiques, et schismatiques, le tout traicté en trois livres. Reveu, corrigé et augmenté de nouveau. Fouet, 1595. 621 p. **1837**

This complete edition, replacing first (Bordeaux, Millanges, 1593, 551 p.), represents one of the strongest apologies for the truth invested exclusively in Catholic Church : " Il est question de trouver une règle certaine pour nous conduire seurement en la Religion et des marques pour cognoistre la vraye Eglise " (p. 5 of non-paginated introduction). The three books are called : *Vérité première, seconde* et *troisième.*

— La replique de Maistre Jean le Charron *(sic!)* sur la responce faite à sa troisième vérité cy devant imprimée à la Rochelle. Vallet, 1595. 459 p. **1838**

Answer to Duplessis-Mornay's *Traité de l'église.* Charron feigns not to know the author and stresses point that problem of finding Christ outside and inside Catholic Church is a matter of degree and fullness, regrets his own bitter words, invites adversary to a public disputation and blames his " longues invectives, qui ne font qu'infecter le papier."

— De la sagesse, trois livres par Pierre Charron. Leiden, Elsevier, 1626. 770 p. **1839**

Marginal subtitles help the understanding of the three books as an optimistic, in so far anti-reformatory, approach to life with the device : " La vraye pieté, premier office de sagesse " (p. 323). Introduction stresses work as a moral aid " à bien vivre et bien mourir ", as Charron's earlier work *Les trois vérités* (1593) was a doctrinal aid " à bien croire."

— Discours chrestiens de la divinité, création, rédemption et octaves du saint sacrement. Bertault. 1604. 827 p. **1840**

These strictly theological *exposés* are made on a very high level, so that " ils heurtent plusieurs opinions receuës communement par les superstitieux et faux religieux " (*Epistre* to the posthumous edition by Gabriel Michel de Rochemaillet). They deal with Divine providence (p. 1-268), Natural creation (with dedication to Philippe Desportes and new pagination, p. 1-187), Redemption and eucharist (1-356, with erroneously continued pagination 190 and 191 instead of 2 and 3).

Wessel, Ludwig. Die Ethik Charrons. Erlangen, Vollrath, 1904. 42 p. (Diss., Erlangen.)   1841

Correct appraisal of separation of natural ethics from Christian morals in Charron who despite his almost " deistic " tolerance rejects any community with Protestantism (p. 33).

Wendt, Karl. Pierre Charron als Pädagoge. Neubrandenburg, Dörnbrack, 1903. 88 p. (Diss., Rostock.)   1842

This study tries to differentiate Charron's ideas on education from those of Montaigne. His stronger dogmatic leanings give the pupil less liberty in his " self-realization."

Du Vair, Guillaume. Les œuvres de Messire Guillaume Du Vair evesque et comte de Lizieux, garde des seaux de France. Dernière edition, revue, corrigée et augmentée. Cramoisy, 1641. 1183 p.   1843

Volume contains besides well known treatises : *Le manuel d'Epictète*, p. 289-302; *De l'éloquence françoise et des raisons pourquoy elle est demeurée si basse*, p. 387-410, and on non-paginated sheets : *Traittez de piété et saintes meditations. See* 2256.

— Actions et traictez oratoires. René Radouant (ed.). Cornély, 1911. 319 p. (STFM)   1844

This critical edition with introduction and glossary is based on three editions of *Recueil des harangues et traictez du Sr. Du Vair* as well as on an edition of *Discours*, ten of which are printed, among them : *Oraison funèbre de Marie Stuart* (p. 1-32), and *Response d'un bourgeois de Paris à la lettre de Mgr. le Légat* (p. 145-88). Radouant made earlier a critical edition of Du Vair's *De l'éloquence française* (1907). *See* 2257, 2259.

— Traité de la constance et consolation ès calamitez publiques, écrit par Guillaume Du Vair pendant le siège de Paris de 1590. Jacques Flach et F. Funck-Brentano (ed.). Tenin, 1915. 255 p.   1845

Modernization of text as found in 1606 edition of Du Vair's *Traictez philosophiques*. Introduction (1-48) stresses religious character of a political attitude distinguishing between Catholic and Spanish as befitting a *Ligueur* faithful to French cause, worthy of the Bishop of Lisieux. *See* 2265.

Radouant, René. Guillaume du Vair; l'homme et l'orateur; jusqu'à la fin des troubles de la Ligue (1556-1596). Lecène, Oudin, 1908. 464 p. (Diss., Paris.)   1846

Very extensive and reliable work, dealing with biography of Du Vair and analyzing his main treatises, among which *L'oraison funèbre de Marie Stuart* (Ch. VII, p. 105-129), *Le traité de la constance* (Ch. XII, p. 310-42). *See* 2278.

Mesnard, Pierre. Du Vair et le néostoicisme. RHph 2:142-66, 1928.   1847

Proof that philosophical writings of Du Vair are no less Christian than his theological ones. His neostoicism is fundamentally Christian, as based on hope, providence, and immortality. *See* 2275, 2580.

The Protestant Writers

(Nos. 1848-2040)

George B. Watts

The compiler, invited late in 1952 to attempt this section, with the understanding that it must be completed within a very few months, was forced, by the pressure of a full teaching load and other responsibilities, to rely on flying trips to near and distant libraries, inter-library loans, and to call for aid from outstanding Reformation scholars. He is heavily indebted to Professors Paul T. Fuhrmann of Gammon Theological Seminary, Roland H. Bainton of Yale Divinity School, and especially John T. McNeill of Union Theological Seminary, material from whose letters, published writings, and conversations he has used extensively—with and without quotation marks. Without their generous advice and aid it would have been impossible to prepare the following entries, many of which are less extensive and complete than they would have been if more time had been allotted. Several obvious sources such as Moréri, the *Encyclopédie*, and the catalogues of the *Bibliothèque nationale* and the *British Museum* have been consulted, are important, but are not included among the entries. Inasmuch as it is possible that theologians, as well as students of French literature, may find this section useful, a rather extended, and perhaps disproportionate list of Calvin studies, especially the more recent, has been examined.

General Sources

Allier, Raoul, ed. Anthologie protestante française. xviᵉ et xviiᵉ siècles. 3rd ed., Crès, 1918. 323 p. Geneva (Éditions Atar), 1917. 2 v.   1848

Useful work " destined not for professional scholars but for the general public." Deals with principal French Protestant writers of 16th and 17th centuries, giving extracts and concise preliminary statements (with selective bibliographies) of following 16th century writers: Farel, Marot, Olivétan, Calvin, Palissy, Castellion, Paré, Languet, Bèze, Anne du Bourg, François Hotman, François de Serres, du Bartas, du Plessis-Mornay, d'Aubigné, Sully, Odet de La Noue. He also treats Lefèvre d'Étaples and Marguerite de Navarre, neither of whom broke with the Catholic Church.

Bayle, Pierre. Dictionnaire historique et critique. 5th ed., Amsterdam, Brunel, etc., 1734. 5 v.   1849

Although later scholarship has antiquated the data found here, the then bold articles are still of interest. Consult following : Bèze, v. I, p. 796-810; Calvin, v. II, p. 240-54 ; Hotman, v. III, p. 410-16 ; Languet, v. III, p. 611-13; Viret, v. V, p. 475-78.

Bonnefon, Paul. Les écrivains scientifiques. Bernard Palissy, Ambroise Paré, Olivier de Serres. *In:* Petit de Julleville, Histoire de la langue et de la littérature française. Colin, 1896-99, v. III, p. 488-529.   1850

Good analyses of their works and influence. Useful bibliography, p. 528-529.

Encyclopédie des sciences religieuses; publiée sous la direction de F. Lichtenberger. Sandoz et Fischbacher, 1877-1882. 13 v.   1851

Valuable source for brief, well written, informative articles on Protestant writers. Among useful articles are those on Beza (II, 258-73 by A. Viguié), Calvin (II, 529-557 by A. Jundt), Castellio (II, 672-77 by H. Lutteroth), Estienne, R. and H. (IV, 560-67 by A. Bernus), Farel (IV, 676-81 by H. Heyer), Hotman (VI, 374-382 by F. de Schickler), Lambert d'Avignon (VII, 681-91 by Ch. Dardier), Languet (VII, 730-33 by A. Viguié), La Noue, François and Odet (VII, 734-35 by Ed. Sayous), Marnix de Sainte-Aldegonde (VIII, 403-04 by G. Leser), Mornay (IX,

426-41 by M. J. Gaufrès), Palissy (X, 147-153 by O. Douen), Paré (X, 193-99 by O. Douen), Serres (XI, by C. Dardier), and Viret (XII, 402-08, by J. Gaberel).

Haag, Eugène. La France protestante, ou vie des protestants qui se sont fait un nom dans l'histoire depuis les premiers temps de la réformation jusqu'à la reconnaissance du principe de la liberté des cultes par l'Assemblée nationale; ouvrage précédé d'une notice historique sur le protestantisme en France, et suivi de pièces justificatives par MM. Eug. et Em. Haag. Paris and Geneva, Cherbuliez, 1846-59. 10 v. 2nd ed. by Henri Bordier. Sandoz and Fischbacher, 1877-1888. 6 v.   1852

Biographical dictionary of French Protestantism. Essential work. Gives life history and bibliography, usually with history of editions and characterization of works. Good treatment of Beza (II, 259-284), Calvin (III, 109-62), Estienne, H. and R. (V, 1-39), Farel (V, 59-72), Hotman (V, 525-40), Languet (VI, 264-78), Mornay (VII, 512-42), La Noue, F. and Odet (VI, 280-303), Olivétan (VIII, 44-45), Palissy (VIII, 69-97), Paré (VIII, 124-43), Serres (IX, 256-63) and Viret (IX, 513-21).

Herminjard, Aimé Louis. Correspondance des réformateurs dans les pays de langue française, recueillie et publiée avec d'autres lettres relatives à la réforme et des notes historiques et biographiques. Geneva, Georg, and Paris, Lévy, 1866-97. 9 v. 1853

Indispensable source, containing letters of Calvin, Farel, Viret and many other Reformers. Goes only to 1544. Carefully annotated. Supplements the correspondence in the *Opera*.

Lenient, Charles Félix. La satire en France, ou La littérature militante au xviᵉ siècle. *See* 1433.   1854

Essential work. Considers many Protestant writers, their polemics, and Catholic satires against them. Important chapters on Beza (1:184-93), Calvin (1:170-83), Duplessis-Mornay (1:258-62), Hotman (2:18-26), Languet (2:26-30). (The *Vindiciae* is ascribed to him), Marnix de Ste. Aldegonde (1:262-66), and Viret (1:194-203).

Petit de Julleville, L. Théologiens et prédicateurs : Calvin, Farel, Viret, Th. de Bèze, Duplessis-Mornay. *In his:* Histoire de la langue et de la littérature française. *See* 116, v. III, p. 319-54.   1855

14

Excellent, well documented, concise statements. Useful notes. Good bibliography, p. 403-04.

Sayous, Pierre André. Études littéraires sur les écrivains français de la réformation. Fischbacher, 1881. 2 v.   1856

Useful, authoritative study of many French Reformation authors. V. I considers Farel, Calvin, Viret and Beza; v. II Hotman, Robert and Henri Estienne, François de La Noue, Duplessis-Mornay, and d'Aubigné. Conclusion (v. II, p. 313-98) discusses such matters as influence of French writers of reformation on contemporary thinking and literature, French language, and direct and indirect influences on the following century. No bibliography, but footnotes give much helpful information. *See* 1942, 1974, 2039.

Théodore de Bèze
(Nos. 1857-1868)

Bèze, Théodore de. La Bible, qui est toute la saincte Escriture : asçavoir, le vieil et nouveau testament : avec argumens sur chacun livre, annotations augmentées, et nouvelles sur les Apocryphra. Quant au nouveau testament a este reveu et corrigé sur le Grec par les ministres de Genève, comme on verra en leur Epistre qui est à la fin de l'Apocalypse. Geneva, Barbier & Courteau, 1561.   1857

Revision of Olivétan's translation. Many later editions, of which one, that of Geneva of 1567, uses the term *La vieille et nouvelle alliance.* This edition has in v. IV *Les Pseaumes mis en rime françoise par Clément Marot et Théodore de Bèze.* Later editions put out in La Rochelle, Amsterdam, Basel, and London.

— Discours de M. Theodore de Besze, contenant en bref l'histoire de la vie et mort de Maistre Jean Calvin avec le testament et derniere volonté dudit Calvin et le catalogue des livres par luy composez. Geneva, Perrin, 1564. 63 p.   1858

Written August 19, 1564, shortly after Calvin's death, it was first printed as preface to an edition of Calvin's *Commentaires ... sur le livre de Josué,* Geneva, Perrin, 1564, 12 folio pages. Many later editions and translations, among which are two American, the most recent by Henry Beveridge, Philadelphia, Westminster Press, 1909, 115 p. Reprinted in v. XXI of the edition of Calvin's works in the *Corpus reformatorum,* Brunswick, Schwetschke, 1879, p. 20-50.

— Histoire ecclésiastique des églises réformées au Royaume de France. Antwerp, Rémy, 1580. 3 v.   1859

The first third by B., the remainder compiled by Jean des Gallards. A collection of documents of great value. J. G. Baum and E. Cunitz put out a scholarly critical edition with Fischbacher, 1883-89, 3 v.

Aubert, Fernand. Correspondance de Théodore de Bèze, 1539-1564. Inventaire par Fernand Aubert et Henri Meylan. Geneva, Musée historique de la réformation, 1950. 38 p.   1860

Mimeographed edition. Covers B.'s correspondence from the time of his law practice in Paris to the death of Calvin.

Baird, Henry M. Theodore Beza, the counsellor of the French reformation. New York & London, Putman's, 1899. 376 p. (Half-title : Heroes of the reformation, v. 4.)   1861

Good solid narration, without any particular flair.

Baum, Jean Guillaume. Theodor Beza, nach handschriftlichen Quellen dargestellt. Leipzig, Weidmann, 1843. 2 v.   1862

Before sickness intervened, Baum completed the first two volumes of a biography of B. based on a serious study of the sources. Narrative goes only to that point in B.'s life where he was on the verge of taking Calvin's place.

Bernus, Auguste. Théodore de Bèze à Lausanne. Lausanne, Bridel, 1900. 112 p.   1863

Excellent brochure covering Lausanne period of B.'s career.

Borgeaud, Charles. L'Académie de Calvin. V. I of his Histoire de l'Université de Genève. Geneva, Georg, 1900. 662 p.   1864

Gives an excellent and full account of B.'s services as first Rector of the Academy of Geneva.

Choisy, Eugène. L'état chrétien calviniste à Genève au temps de Théodore de Bèze. Geneva, Eggiman; Paris, Fischbacher, 1902. 620 p.   1865

Authoritative thesis on relations between church and state in Geneva in B.'s time.

Douen, Orentin. Les Psaumes de Bèze and Bèze traducteur. *In his :* Clément Marot et le psautier huguenot, étude historique, littéraire et bibliographique. Imprimerie nationale, 1878-79. v. 1, p. 547-99. 1866

In this essential work Douen traces meticulously the history of B.'s translations of *Psalms*. He lists the first edition, *Trente-quatre pseaumes de David, nouvellement mis en rime françoise au plus près de l'hébreu par Th. de Besze de Vezeley en Bourgogne*, published by Crespin in Geneva in 1551. In the following year these translations by B. were joined with forty-nine of Marot's in an edition of *Octantetrois pseaumes* and printed by Berjon of Geneva. In 1554 a new edition was put out by Crespin of Geneva, augmented by six new B. translations. Douen mentions (p. 552-62) at least 72 editions by 1565 and says : " aucun livre sans doute, même les romans les plus goûtés, n'a jamais eu fortune si prodigieuse " (p. 562). For a useful study of Marot's translations *see* P. Villey, *Tableau chronologique des publications de Marot*, no. 620, especially p. 86 and 92. There were almost numberless editions of the psalter which has been said to have become the food of Huguenot piety for centuries. The Harvard Houghton Library has an excellent copy of *Les Psaumes de David mis en rime françoise par Clement Marot et Theodore de Bèze*, containing 150 translations of psalms with music, a church calendar, prayers, church forms, confession, etc., published in La Rochelle by Villepoux in 1590, pages unnumbered.

Geisendorf, Paul F. Théodore de Bèze. Geneva, Labor et fides, 1949. 456 p. 1867

Based on thorough and conscientious research in French and Swiss archives and study of B.'s manuscript correspondence, this definitive work, for first time in French or other languages, gives complete story of life and works of Calvin's successor. Good estimates of earlier studies on B. Excellent bibliography, p. 431-38.

Review : J. D. Benoît in RHPR 31:466-467, 1951.

Heppe, Heinrich Ludwig Julius. Theodor Beza. Leben und ausgewählte Schriften. Elberfeld, Friderichs, 1861. 384 p. 1868

Heppe, professor at Marburg, specialist in history of Protestantism in second half of 16th century, wrote this excellent but incomplete work, lacking original Genevan and French sources. Work supplements with a few chapters the copious but unfinished biography of Baum (no. 1862).

Jean Calvin
(Nos. 1869-1954)

Bibliography

Bainton, Roland H. Bibliography of the continental reformation : materials available in English. Chicago, American society of church history, 1935. 54 p. (MCH no. 1) 1869

Indispensable list (for C., see p. 36-44), with bibliography, sources in translation, general works on C. and Calvinism, literature of the C. Commemoration of 1909, miscellaneous bibliographical points, C.'s opponents, thought, doctrines, ethics, political theory, and associates.

Barth, Peter. Fünfundzwanzig Jahre Calvinforschung 1909-1934. TR 6:161-75, 246-67, 1934. 1870

Well chosen selection of French and German studies on C.

Calvin. [Classified index of Calvin items for the years 1921-45.] RHPR 25:144, 1945. 1871

Erichson, Alfred. Bibliographia Calviniana, Berlin, Schwetschke, 1900. 161 p. 1872

Reprinted, with additions and revisions, from v. LIX of *Calvini opera*. First 68 p. contain chronological list of C.'s works in many languages to 1899. P. 69-149 have alphabetical list of books and articles (880 entries) on C. in several languages to 1900, followed by an index. Authoritative essential work which should be supplemented by later bibliographies.

Haag, Eugène. La France protestante, by Eugène and Émile Haag. *See* 1852. 1873

Useful bibliography on C. up to 1852 is found in 3:143-62.

Lang, August. Recent German books on Calvin. EQ 6:64-81, 1934. 1874

Reviews notable German books of early thirties.

McNeill, John T. Thirty years of Calvin study. CH 17:207-40, 1948, and Addendum. CH 18:241, 1949. 1875

Essential tool for recent studies. Recognized reformation authority analyzes bibliographies, editions, and works on C. under such headings as general works, doctrinal studies, economic, social and political ethics. These illuminating articles are of first importance, and have been used extensively (with the author's permission) in preparation of this section.

Parker, T. H. L. A bibliography and survey of the British study of Calvin, 1900-1940. EQ 18:123-31, 1946.   1876
Valuable for English contributions to C. literature.

Schottenloher, Karl. Bibliographie zur deutschen Geschichte im Zeitalter der Glaubensspaltung 1517-1585. Leipzig, Hiersemann, 1933-40. 6 v.   1877
In v. I and II *(Personen)* and v. V *(Nachträge)* there is a reasonably comprehensive listing of C. materials up to 1940.

Editions of Calvin's Works

Calvin, Jean. Ioannis Calvini opera quae supersunt omnia. Ed. by J. W. Baum, E. Cunitz, E. Reuss, P. Lobstein, and A. Erichson. Brunswick, Schwetschke, 1863-1900. 59 v.   1878
The standard edition of C.'s works. Forms v. XXIX-LXXXVII of *Corpus reformatorum.* Brunswick, 1834-1900.

— Opera selecta. Ed. by Peter Barth and Wilhelm Niesel. Munich, Kaiser, 1926-1936, 5 v.   1879
Critical edition, well edited. Full text of *Institutes* of 1559 included. Work has been criticized for weaknesses and errors by Hans Rückert and others. Rückert felt that the task should have been done by a group of scholars in collaboration.

— Calvin translations. Edinburgh, Calvin translation society, 1843-55. 48 v.   1880
Contains large amount of C.'s writings : sermons, commentaries, tracts, *Institutes.* Another important undertaking in English is contemporary C. translations being published in Grand Rapids by Eerdmans. 75 v. of commentaries, 3 v. of sermons, 1 v. of tracts, and the *Institutes.*

— Christianae religionis Institutio. Basle, 1536.   1881
Later editions in Strasbourg in 1539, 1543, and 1545; in Geneva in 1550, 1553, 1554, 1559, and 1561; and in Strasbourg (9th edition) in 1561. After C.'s death nineteen editions appeared up to 1637, of which fifteen were printed in Geneva. Three were printed in Lausanne and one in London. This London printing of 1576 is the only Latin edition to be printed on English-speaking soil. In 1654 the splendid Elzevir edition was published. It was reprinted in v. IX of the Amsterdam

edition (1667). In 1834 Tholuck printed his useful hand edition, reprinted in 1846. In 1863-64 the great critical edition of Baum, Cunitz, and Reuss was published in Brunswick, it being the first two volumes of their edition of C.'s *Opera*. It was reprinted as a separate issue in 1869.

— Institution de la religion chrétienne en laquelle est comprinse une somme de piété. Composée en latin par J. Calvin et translatée en françoys par luy mesme. Geneva, 1541.   1882
Translation of second Latin edition of 1539. Twenty-one French editions appeared up to 1566. Final French edition is noteworthy; former editions had repeated, with revisions, original translation of 1541 but after definitive Latin edition of 1559 C. undertook a new French translation. 17th century saw but two French versions, one in 1609 and one by a French pastor of Bremen, Charles Icard, from 1696 to 1713. It was reprinted in Geneva in 1818. French *Institution* appeared in the Brunswick edition of C.'s *Opera* in 1865. Three hand editions were put out in 19th century, one in Paris by Meyrueis in 1859 (published partly by aid of an appropriation voted by Presbyterian Committee of Philadelphia), another in 1888 in Geneva, " revised and corrected from the edition of 1560, by Frank Baumgartner," in two volumes; the third, a one volume edition of Baumgartner's version. In the present century two French editions have been published, one in 1911 by A. Lefranc, H. Chatelain, and J. Pannier, the last in 1936-39, by Les belles lettres. Last French edition has excellent historical and textual notes. Introduction emphasizes C.'s effort to turn his Latin into completely intelligible French. Last volume has important glossary and name index.
Review of Pannier ed. : R. Centlèvre, in RTP 28:363, 1940.

— Institutes of the Christian religion.   1883
The *Institutes* have been translated three times into English. Thomas Norton's translation was published in London in 1561 and often thereafter until 1634; in 1762 reprinted in Glasgow. John Allen's first translation appeared in London in 1813; republished in London in 1838, and again in 1844. The first American edition was printed in Philadelphia in 1816. Later editions have appeared in New York in 1819, and in Philadelphia in 1841, 1843, 1844, 1886, 1887-96, 1909, 1932,

1935, and 1936. Henry Beveridge's translation was published in Edinburgh in 1845-46, and again in 1863.

— A compend of the Institutes of the Christian religion by John Calvin. Ed. by Hugh Thomson Kerr. Philadelphia, Presbyterian board of Christian education, 1939. 228 p. First ed., same place and publisher, 1935.
1884

Well selected extracts from *Institutes*, making up about one-tenth of Allen's translation. Called by Quirinus Breen a " stream-lined edition of Calvin's *Institutes* " (review, below, p. 91).

Review : Q. Breen in CH 9:91-92, 1940.

Nixon, Leroy. Complete indexes to the Institutes of the Christian religion. Grand Rapids, Eerdmans, 1950. 1885

Useful index of scriptural references, authors quoted, tables of Hebrew and Greek words explained, and comprehensive exhaustive index.

Calvin, Jean. Instruction et confession de foy, dont on use en leglise de Genève. Geneva, 1537. 1886

A Latin translation of this catechism was published by C. in 1538. Reprinting in 1878 by Rilliet et Dufour. Another catechism published in French in 1545, 1549, 1552, and 1553. Latin translations in 1545, 1550, and 1551.

— Instruction in faith. Translated with a historical foreword and critical and explanatory notes by Paul T. Fuhrmann. London, Butterworth, and Philadelphia, Westminster Press, 1949. 96 p. 1887

Written in 1537 with intention of inspiring a simple faith in people of Geneva, this is C.'s own popular compendium of his earlier *Institutes*. This statement of faith soon disappeared from circulation and became buried in the mass of C.'s later productions. H. Bordier discovered an original copy in Paris in 1877. Republished in Geneva in 1878 by A. Rilliet and Th. Dufour, in Germany in 1880 and 1926, in Italy in 1935, and now in America. A painstaking and scholarly translation from French and Latin editions of original of this hitherto neglected treatise of great theological and historical importance. Valuable historical foreword and notes.

Reviews : H. T. Kerr in TT 7:270-71, July, 1950; E. Lewis in CH 18:247-48, 1949.

— Textes choisis par Charles Gagnebin, préface de Karl Barth. Egloff, 1948. 322 p.
1888

Attractive volume of extracts taken chiefly from C.'s sermons and *Institutes*. Editor has chosen subjects which make up web of daily life : work, use of property, married love, behavior toward fellow men, politics. Editor's wish was to acquaint French people with C., who, in general, do not know him or who see him in caricature. Main theme of extracts is God's sovereignty and man's dependence.

Review : J. D. Benoît in RHPR 30:246-248, 1950.

General Biography and Criticism

Audin, J. M. V. Histoire de la vie, des ouvrages et des doctrines de Calvin. New ed., Maison, 1843. 2 v. 1889

A partisan and polemic work by a Roman Catholic. English translation by John McGill, London, 1843. German translation, 1843. Author boasts of having consulted more than one thousand volumes on C. Work disowned and virtually refuted by such fair-minded Catholics as Kampschulte of Bonn and Funk of Tübingen.

Bainton, Roland H. The Reformation in the sixteenth century. Boston, Beacon Press, 1952. 276 p. 1890

Perhaps best brief introduction to reformation movement of 16th century. Ch. VI, *The reformed church of Geneva: Calvinism*, is an excellent and succinct treatment of " activism " of C., *Institutes*, and his rigoristic regime in Geneva. Ch. IX, *The fight for recognition of the Calvinist faith*, gives a useful history of Calvinism in France during 16th and 17th centuries. A work which shows author's scholarship and ripe judgment. Illustrated.

Reviews : N. V. Hope in PSB 46:50, 1952, and in TT 9:552-53, 1953.

— The travail of religious liberty. Philadelphia, Westminster Press, 1951. 272 p.
1891

Ch. III, *The victim of Protestant persecution, Michael Servetus*, is an objective and authoritative treatment of clash between C. and Servetus. Ch. IV, *The remonstrator Sebastien Castellio*, is a good account of C.'s relationships with Castellio. In his introduction to this important new book, Bainton has an understanding analysis of the theory of persecution, similarities and differences of 16th century Protestant and Catholic views on persecution, and of C.'s acceptance of feudal conception of sin. For additional data on Servetus see same author's *The present status of Servetus studies* in JMH 4:72-92, 1932, and also *The two treatises of Servetus on the Trinity*. Cambridge, Harvard University Press. Trans. by Earl Moore Wilbur. 1932. 264 p. (*Added to t. p.*: Harvard theological studies ... 16.)

Review : W. Hubben in TT 9:263-64, 1952.

Barth, Karl. Nein! Antwort an Emil Brunner. Munich, Kaiser, 1934. 63 p. (TEH, no. 14)   1892

Barth flatly denies a natural theology in C. The divergent views on C. of Barth and Brunner gave rise to numerous studies from scholars, of whom some, like Pierre Maury in *La théologie naturelle d'après Calvin*, BSHP 84:267-79, 1935, and Peter Barth in *Das Problem der natürlichen Theologie bei Calvin*, Munich, Kaiser, 1935, 60 p. (TEH, no. 18) deny any trace of natural theology in C. Others, like Günther Gloede in *Theologie naturalis bei Calvin*, Stuttgart, Kohlhammer, 1934, 355 p., and Auguste Lecerf in RTP 15:319, 1927, support Brunner's position.

Benoît, Jean Daniel. Calvin, directeur d'âmes; contribution à l'histoire de la piété réformée. Strasbourg, Oberlin, 1947. 281 p.   1893

Sympathetic attempt to make one feel C.'s soul live and palpitate, and to reveal him as a great spiritual director, not, as so often seen, merely as a theologian, a man of doctrine, or a heresy hunter. An important chapter deals with C.'s correspondents, kings and queens, great lords and ladies, prisoners and martyrs. A sequel to the author's *Direction spirituelle du protestantisme*, Alcan, 1940. 320 p.

Review : J. D. Benoît in RHPR 26:322-323, 1946.

— John Calvin : la vie, l'homme, la pensée. 2nd ed., Carrières-sous-Poissy, La cause, 1948. 312 p.   1894

Author says his work is " the quintessence of the seven big volumes of my old master, Dean Émile Doumergue." Work is mainly an excellent condensation of Doumergue, but Benoît reveals also a personal knowledge of the sources.

Bèze, Théodore de. Discours de Théodore de Bèze, contenant en bref l'histoire de la vie

et mort de Maître Jean Calvin. *In:* Œuvres françaises de J. Calvin. Gosselin, 1842. v. 21, p. 1-24. *See* 1858.   1895

Bohatec, Josef. Budé und Calvin; Studien zur Gedankenwelt des französischen Frühhumanismus. Graz, Böhlaus, 1950. 491 p.   1896

First part (p. 3-117) deals with renaissance and Budé's theology and philosophy; second is *Calvin und der Humanismus*. With an authority gained from a meticulous study of all available sources, this recognized C. scholar treats exhaustively Reformer's attitude toward humanism. Definitive work on a specialized subject.

•Reviews : M. Ruch in BHren 13:96-112, 1951; F. Wendel in RHPR 31:456-463, 1951.

Borgeaud, Charles. Calvin fondateur de l'Académie de Genève. Colin, 1897. 53 p.   1897

Valuable study of C. as an educator, published as first chapter of author's *Histoire de l'Université de Genève*. *See* 1864.

Bossert, Adolphe. Calvin. Hachette, 1906. 222 p.   1898

Interesting for analysis of C.'s language ability. Discusses the barbarous Latin and unpolished French spoken in schools of the time. C. was equally facile in Latin and French, but kept the two languages rigorously apart. Much more than Rabelais, and more than Montaigne, he approaches prose of 17th century. In development of French language, C. has a place immediately before Pascal.

Breen, Quirinus. John Calvin : a study of French humanism. Grand Rapids, Eerdmans, 1931. 174 p. (Diss., Chicago.) 1899

Careful, specialized study of C.'s youth, early classical studies, and influence of humanism on his mature mind. Stimulating.

Review : W. Pauck in CH 1:169-70, 1932.

Brunetière, Ferdinand. L'œuvre littéraire de Calvin, RDM 70:898-923, Oct. 15, 1900. English trans. in PRR 12:393-414, July, 1901.   1900

Brunetière considers *Institutes* one of great French prose works, whose proportions, arrangement and construction are monumental. He calls it first classic of the French. Says it attains its position by virtue of greatness of its conception, dignity of its plan, unity of its treatment, close concentration of its thought, its rhetorical grace, sustained gravity of its style, and purity of its language.

Brunner, Emil. Natur und Gnade. Tübingen, Mohr, 1934. 44 p.   1901

Brunner affirms a natural theology in C.—man's knowledge of God by his own reasoning, apart from Divine revelation, a mark of God left in man's intellect and in indications in the natural universe of a creative intelligence. One should, says Brunner, restore natural theology and grapple with problems it raises, such as Christianity and culture, reason and revelation.

Review : A. Jundt in RHPR 14:455-57, 1934.

Bungener, Laurence Louis Félix. Calvin, sa vie, son œuvre et ses écrits. Cherbuliez, 1862. 515 p.   1902

Well-written, but added little to then existing knowledge of the subject. Republished the following year and also translated immediately into English (Edinburgh, 1863). Point of view is apologetic without suppressing any facts.

Calvinistic Action Committee. God-centered living; or, Calvinism in action; a symposium. Grand Rapids, Baker, 1951. 270 p.   1903

Designed to help " those who desire to know what the will of God is for the practical guidance of their lives." Not a " scholarly book with extensive research." Notable for its bibliography, p. 257-70, which lists other important bibliographies and a long list of works on C., including many Dutch titles, which are not covered sufficiently in other bibliographical studies.

Castrén, Olavi. Die Bibeldeutung Calvins. Helsinki, Suomalaien, Tiedeakatemia, 1946. 159 p. (AASF, series B, v. 56, part 3.) 1904

Scholarly study on such subjects as God and creation, soteriology, intellectualism, and appropriation of salvation. Has important bibliography of recent works.

Chenevière, Marc Edouard. La pensée politique de Calvin. Éditions " je sers, " 1937. 383 p.   1905

Important monograph by one trained in law and theology. Author examines C.'s treatment of law, the state, forms of government, people, and magistrate, find-ng him to be far from spirit of modern

democracy. Gives interpretation of C.'s view of natural law, associating it with conscience rather than reason.

Damagnez, Albert. Influence de Calvin sur l'instruction. Montauban, Granié, 1886. 52 p. (Diss., Montauban.) 1906

Meritorious example of many important theses published at Montauban which cover practically whole field of C.'s thought and activity.

Davies, Sir Alfred T. John Calvin and the influence of Protestantism on national life and character. London, Walter, 1946. 46 p.   1907

Essay awarded Samuel Cocker prize on 400th anniversary of C.'s birth. Written to make " acknowledgement of the immense indebtedness to that remarkable Frenchman." Republished, with revisions and additions, as : *John Calvin, many-sided genius.* New York, American tract society, 1947. 92 p.

Doumergue, Émile. Jean Calvin, les hommes et les choses de son temps. Lausanne, Bridel, 1899-1927. 7 v.   1908

A work of great value. Leaves little to be desired in elaborateness of discussion and fullness of treatment. An industrious researcher, Doumergue makes his reader familiar not only with C., but also with findings and opinions of many writers in whole history of C. interpretation. Despite fact that Doumergue is occasionally led into exaggeration by his enthusiasm for C., and that his critical judgment is sometimes impaired by his desire to show Reformer in most favorable light, his work has great significance. It is and should remain an indispensable tool for student of C. In v. IV he lists several hundred of the appreciations, critiques, treatises, and sermons composed for quatercentenary of C.

Dowey, Edward A., Jr. The knowledge of God in Calvin's theology. New York, Columbia University Press, 1952. 261 p. (Diss., Zürich.)   1909

One of the best recent C. studies. Well documented, skillfully organized interpretation of C.'s doctrine of the knowledge of God, the " duplex cognitio Domini "—the knowledge of God the Creator and God the Redeemer. Valuable bibliography, especially for latest works on C.

Review : J. F. Jansen in TT 9:285-86, 1952.

Dyer, Thomas, H.   The life of John Calvin. New York, Harper, 1850.   458 p.   1910

Careful, but too sympathetic an account, based largely on a study of C.'s correspondence, containing a brief discussion of his origin and early history, and a thorough treatment of Genevan controversies.

Etudes sur Calvin et le calvinisme présentées à Paris pendant une exposition à la Bibliothèque nationale à l'occasion du IVe centenaire de l'Institution chrétienne. Fischbacher, 1935.   p. 63-292.   1911

An extract from the BSHP, 84th year, April to June, 1935.

Fairbairn, Andrew M.   Calvin and the Reformed Church. *In :* Cambridge modern history, London and New York, Macmillan, 1903-1910.   v. 2, p. 342-76.   1912

Brief summary of C.'s work marked by deep insight into its ruling purposes and spiritual significance.   Useful bibliography, listing works on C. under such headings as life, thought, theology, C. educator and statesman, and C. and French literature.

Foster, Herbert D.   Calvin. *In his :* Collected papers of Herbert Foster. Hanover, N. H., Privately printed, 1929.   p. 1-178.   1913

Considers aspects of C.'s ethics, church discipline, political ideas and influence. Among the studies are *Calvin's programme for a Puritan state in Geneva*, and *Geneva before Calvin*.

Freschi, Renato.   Giovanni Calvino. Milan, Corticelli, 1934.   2 v.   1914

First volume *La vita* gives good treatment of C.'s life and labors.   Second volume *Il pensiero* especially important and revealing.   An independent piece of work, but shows evidence of author's knowledge of many special studies.   Among important and most complete of modern general works on C.   Given history award by Italian Academy.

Fuhrmann, Paul Traugott.   God-centered religion. Grand Rapids, Zondervan publishing house, 1942.   237 p.   1915

Important study on C.'s life and doctrine.   In introduction author specifies the two currents of contemporary awakening of Calvinism as " the Barthian and the classical."   Leader of the first is Karl Barth, " the modern Swiss prophet who dared "; the second current, anterior to

Barth, is represented by Dean Doumergue, Pastor Jacques Pannier and Professor Lecerf.   In his Bibliography (p. 223-27) Fuhrmann emphasizes mass of modern C. material, suggests that one consult independent historians, Autin, Bossert, Freschi, and Imbart de La Tour, and " approach Calvin by reading Calvin himself."

Gourmaz, Louis.   Timothée, ou le ministère évangélique d'après Calvin, etc.   Préface de Jean Daniel Benoît.   Lausanne, Concorde, 1948.   173 p.   1916

Author, Doctor of Theology, treats, not C.'s theology, but his " pastoral soul, beset, like St. Paul's, by concern for all the Churches."   From *Commentaries* especially he " borrows the tones with which he paints Timothy (Calvin), the ideal pastor."

Harkness, Georgia E.   John Calvin : The man and his ethics.   New York, 1931. 266 p.   1917

Mature and unprejudiced estimate of C.'s person and ethics.   First part is general biography, based largely on secondary sources.   Second part is from direct reading of C. and is better on that account than the first.   Third part, *The Calvinistic conscience and man's duty to man*, contains a discussion of C.'s views on such matters as domestic relations and middle class virtues, and gives what has been called " the first detailed objective exposition of the social teachings of Calvin."

Reviews : Q. Breen in CH 1:125-26, 1932; J. T. McNeill in JR 12:124-25, 1932.

Hauser, Henri.   L'économie calvinienne. BSHP 84:227-42, Apr.-June, 1935.   1918

An authoritative historian, Hauser has made several important studies on C. and his relation to economic life, of which this is one example.   He discusses C.'s sanction of interest in 1545, ascribes to him two main principles of social and economic life—the laicization of holiness and social relativism—and is unsympathetic with Weber's oft debated thesis.   *See* 1952.

Henry, Paul.   Das Leben Johann Calvins des grossen Reformators.   Hamburg, Parthes, 1835-44.   3 v.   1919

Good early biography.   Highly eulogistic.   Well documented.   Now largely superseded by later publications, but epoch-marking for its times.   Important notes and appendices.   English translation by Henry Stebbing. New York, Carter, 1851-52. 2 v.

Hunt, Robert N. C. Calvin. London, The Centenary Press, 1935. 385 p.   1920

Reveals significant events and personality of C., with many fine insights. Moderately acquainted with recent literature, author omits references to much recent C. discussion. Some inaccuracies in sections dealing with Servetus, but as a detached biography of C., among best modern works.

Hunter, A. Mitchell. The teaching of Calvin, a modern interpretation. Glasgow, Maclehose, Jackson, 1920. 304 p.   1921

Solid piece of work, not too illuminating, but shows careful workmanship. Good discussion of distinctive features of C.'s doctrinal, ecclesiastical, and legislative system, based largely on *Institutes*, but also on his commentaries, treatises and correspondence. Hunter is appreciative of his subject, but tempers his work with gentle criticism.

Hyma, Albert. The life of John Calvin. Grand Rapids, Eerdmans, 1943. 118 p. 1922

If C. should return to this earth, says Albert Hyma, Professor of History at the University of Michigan, he would be indignant at great ignorance of experts who have made pronouncements on his political, economic, and sociological opinions without ever having read his own writings. To understand what C. is and was, we must return to a study of original sources. C.'s political and economic theories are outlined further in author's *Christianity, capitalism, and communism* (Ann Arbor, Wahr, 1937. 303 p.), *Christianity and politics* (Philadelphia, Lippincott, 1938. 331 p.), and *Calvinism and capitalism in the Netherlands, 1555-1700*, JMH 10:321-43, 1938.

Imbart de La Tour, Pierre. Jean Calvin et l'Institution chrétienne. Didot, 1935. 506 p.   1923

Forms v. V of author's *Les origines de la réforme*, Hachette, 1905-08. Imbart died before volume was completed and unfinished manuscript was edited by J. Chevalier. A Roman Catholic layman, author in this fundamental work finds C.'s personality and mind fascinating but lacking tenderness. Acknowledges C.'s realization that if a new faith was to replace the old it would have to be a new type of Catholicism based solely on God's word,

and embodying the Catholic concepts of universality and authority.

Review : A. Lang in *Drei neue Calvin Biographien* (Hunt, Imbart, and Mackinnon) in TSK 107:448-63, 1936.

Kampschulte, F. W. Johann Calvin, seine Kirche und sein Staat in Genf. Leipzig, Dunker & Humblot, 1869, 1899. 2 v. 1924

Very able, critical, remarkably fair and liberal work, drawn in part from unpublished sources by a Roman Catholic professor of history at Bonn.

Lecerf, Auguste. Études calvinistes, recueillies et introduites par André Schlemmer. Neufchâtel, Delachaux et Niestlé, 1949. 148 p.   1925

Fourteen studies, printed during Lecerf's lifetime, dealing mostly with aspects of C.'s thought and influence. Among them are *Calvinisme et capitalisme, De l'autorité dans le Calvinisme*, and *La souveraineté de Dieu d'après le Calvinisme*.

Reviews : G. S. Hendry in TT 8:273-75, July, 1951; L. J. Trinterud in JR 30:283-84, 1950.

Lefranc, Abel Jules Maurice. La jeunesse de Calvin. Fischbacher, 1888. 228 p. 1926

A study of C.'s youth of much significance.

Mackinnon, James. Calvin and the reformation. London and New York, Longmans, Green, 1936. 302 p.   1927

Sober, important estimate of C.'s labors and influence, gathered from both primary and secondary sources. Attempts to show C. as an international, not merely local or national figure, who had his finger on pulse of Reformation in many lands. Finds C. not so original a religious thinker as Luther, but superior to him as organizer and ecclesiastical statesman. There is a good brief account of C.'s monumental work as a Protestant theologian. Forty pages are devoted to Servetus affair. Book has been generally coolly reviewed.

Reviews : C. H. Moehlman in Chris 2:333, 1937; W. Pauck in CH 6:388-89, 1937.

McNeill, John T. John Calvin : Institutes of the Christian religion. *In his:* Books of faith and power. New York, Harper, 1947. p. 29-57.   1928

Useful chapter by specialist in period of Reformation. Author states essential facts about C. and hi mes, summarizes contents of the book, and gives own evaluation of its worth.

Review : E. T. Thompson in TT 5:443-444, Oct., 1948.

Merle d'Aubigné, Jean Henri. Histoire de la réformation en Europe au temps de Calvin. Lévy, 1863-78. 8 v. English trans. London, 1863-78, and New York, Carter, 1870-79. 5 v.   1929

Widely read in English speaking countries. Based on documentary sources, but is partisan and often over-dramatic. Still useful and important for its citations from sources.

Mesnard, Pierre. Calvin. *In his:* L'essor de la philosophie politique au xvi⁰ siècle. *See* 1438, p. 269-308.   1930

Intelligent analysis of C.'s ideas. Finds that his aim was not to conquer the state but rather to " galvanize it by the formidable electricity " of his spirit, and C. had a high concept of secular government, rights of the people, and personality—all subordinate to God's word.

Moore, W. G. La réforme allemande et la littérature française : recherches sur la notoriété de Luther en France. *See* 164.   1931

Important study, especially for early Protestantism in France. Asserts that C. had come in contact with Luther's writings in Paris, Orleans, and Bourges. *See* 772.

Morçay, Raoul. Le protestantisme et les lettres françaises. *In his:* La renaissance. Histoire de la littérature française, publ. sous la direction de J. Calvet. v. II, part 3, p. 1-72.   1932

A history of ideas as well as of literary forms. Treats C. and the French Protestant poets with admiration.

Nürnberger, Richard. Die Politisierung des französischen Protestantismus. *See* 173.   1933

Has as subtitle *Calvin und die Anfänge des protestantischen Radikalismus.* A political history of French Protestantism. Considers the beginnings with C. and Farel, political maneuvers under Henri II, and crisis of French Protestantism to Edict of January, 1562.

Omodeo, Adolfo. Giovanni Calvino e la riforma in Genevra. Opera postuma a cura di B. Croce. Bari, Laterza, 1947. 153 p.   1934

Sympathetic and reverent course of lectures by the late scholar, who was not a Calvinist. Gives history of Reformation in several lands, C.'s life, theology, faith, church, theories of the sacraments, powers as a preacher. Last chapter is succinct, clear *exposé* of connection between Calvinism and moral and political concept of liberty.

Pannier, Jacques. Calvin écrivain, sa place et son rôle dans l'histoire de la langue et de la littérature françaises. Fischbacher, 1930. 32 p. (PSCF, no. 3.)   1935

One of several important recent studies on C.'s style and historic position as one of chief founders of modern French prose. For other examples, see Abel Lefranc, *Calvin et l'éloquence française* in BSHP 83:173-93, 1934; Jean Plattard, *Le beau style de Calvin* in BAGB 62:22-29, Jan., 1939, and *Calvin et l'éloquence française* in RPL 73:206-10, Mar. 16, 1935. Stresses C.'s use of simple images, his " tristesse," and brevity.

Parker, T. H. L. The oracles of God—an introduction to the preaching of John Calvin. London, Lutterworth, 1947. 175 p.   1936

Studies in C.'s aims and methods as a preacher, and circulation of his sermons in Tudor and Stuart England. Author suggests that C.'s sermons affected norms of English prose style, as well as English preaching. Useful appendix, giving list of sermons, and bibliography of works on C. as a preacher. Written, says author, a curate in Kent, to be useful to those " ... who are faced with the task of preparing and preaching two sermons a week " (p. 9).

Pfister, Oskar. Calvins Eingreifen in die Hexer- und Hexenprozesse von Peney 1545 nach seiner Bedeutung für Geschichte und Gegenwart : ein kritischer Beitrag zur Charakteristik Calvins und zur gegenwärtigen Calvin-Renaissance. Zurich, Artemis, 1947. 209 p.   1937

Author, a Protestant minister, assails C.'s unchristianlike behavior in the trials for witchcraft of Peney. Also questions desirability of present day " theological-religious Calvin renaissance " and deplores absence in C.'s teachings of love of Christ. This investigator of psychological, religious, and moral problems attempts to present " the true picture of the disputed Reformer : his greatness and his mistakes." Matter is further treated in author's article *Calvin im*

Lichte der Hexenprozesse von Peney, ein Epilog in TZ 4:411-34, 1948. Many will hold that his polemic against neo-Calvinists is unjustified and unenlightened.

Review : F. Büsser in TZ 4:310-13, 1948.

Plattard, Jean. L'éloquence : Calvin. *In his:* La renaissance des lettres en France. Colin, 1925. p. 70-78.   1938

Stresses importance of C.'s writings for French prose and states that his clearness and order anticipated Descartes.

Reyburn, Hugh Y. John Calvin; his life, letters and work. London & New York, Hodder & Stoughton, 1914. 376 p.   1939

An objective, vivid, complete and careful treatment of C.'s life and work.

Roget, Amédée. Histoire du peuple de Genève depuis la réforme jusqu'à l'escalade. Geneva, Jullien, 1870-83. 7 v.   1940

Covers period from 1536 to 1567. Impartial and objective. Especially important for its citations from archives of Geneva, which author, a Professor at the University of Geneva, knew well.

Ruff, Hedwig. Die französischen Briefe Calvins; Versuch einer stilistischen Analyse. Glarus, 1937. 129 p. (Diss., Zürich.)   1941

Examines C.'s letters to important personages : Francis I, Somerset, Coligny and others. Points out C.'s canons of style; demand for order, clarity, brevity, sincerity; and vitality of his writing. Gives examples of his irony, variant moods of his exhortation, use of figures of speech, and his habit of writing words in pairs.

Sayous, Pierre André. Jean Calvin. *In his:* Études littéraires sur les écrivains français de la réformation. *See* 1856. v. I, p. 67-180.   1942

Good treatment of C.'s contribution to French style by former Professor at the Academy of Geneva.

Schaff, Philip. The reformation in French Switzerland, or the Calvinistic movement. *In his:* History of the Christian church. New York, Scribner, 1882-92. v. 7, p. 223-875.   1943

Careful sketch of C.'s career and significance, marked by his well-known merits and limitations. Bibliography now somewhat out of date, but useful because of brief critical estimates of works listed.

Schulting, Cornelis. Bibliothequae catholicae et orthodoxae contra summam totius theologiae calvinianae, etc. Cologne, Hemmerden, 1602. 2 v.   1944

Jesuit Schulting, while attacking C. and his system and using extravagant language, finds methods of *Institutes* so fine and artistic that it is to be compared with Justinian's *Institutes*, " the most methodical of books."

Société de l'histoire du protestantisme français, Paris. Calvin et la réforme française; exposition organisée à l'occasion du quatrième centenaire de la publication de l'Institution de la religion chrétienne. Bibliothèque nationale, 1935. 120 p.   1945

Lists the 482 items of the exhibit. Illustrated. Important preface by Abel Lefranc, who protests " ... contre l'erreur trop répandue qui représente le style de Calvin comme empreint de tristesse " (p. iv), and lauds the brevity, clarity, order and method of C.'s writing.

Stickelberger, Emanuel. Calvin : eine Darstellung. Gotha, Ott, 1931. 179 p. Stuttgart, 1943.   1946

Ardent admirer of C., author gives a lively, well-documented portrait, marked by use of striking quotations and vivid comments. He is intent on defending C. against antagonistic biographers " who did not grasp Calvin and did not like him."

Strohl, Henri. La pensée de la réforme. Neuchâtel, Delechaux et Niestlé, 1951. 264 p.   1947

Dean Strohl of University of Strasbourg, author of many authoritative studies on figures of Reformation, gives a particularly vivid, concise, and clear view of spiritual foundation of movement, taken mostly from earlier works of Reformers themselves. Valuable compend of origins and general principles of Protestant Church, especially for non-specialist.

Reviews : P. T. Furhmann in JR 32:282-283, 1952; A. P. in BSHP 6th ser. 29:125-128, Apr.-June, 1952.

Stuermann, Walter E. A critical study of Calvin's concept of faith. Tulsa, 1952. 397 p.   1948

A lithoprinted Chicago thesis. Exhaustive study of nature of faith and its effects as conceived by C. Author finds that for C., a former humanist who turned Protestant, whole substance of Gospel is comprised in two points : repentance and remission of sins. Discusses brief treatments of this subject in journals and monographs and more extensive works such as that of Simon P. Dee, *Het geloofsbegrip van Calvijn*, Kampen, Kok, 1918. 215 p.

Review : F. V. Filson in JR 21:119, Apr., 1953.

Tholuck, A. Die Verdienste Calvins als Ausleger der Heiligen Schrift. Vermischte Schriften, Hamburg, 1839. v. II, p. 330-360. 1949

Tholuck mentions as most prominent qualities of C.'s commentaries the following : doctrinal impartiality, exegetical tact, various learning, and deep Christian piety. English translation by W. Pringle, London, 1845.

Walker, Williston. John Calvin. New York, Putnam, 1906. 456 p. 1950

Authoritative, well-written account of C.'s life, traits, and theology. It is accurate, well-balanced, and fair. Probably the best succinct statement. Has valuable bibliographical notes and illustrations. A French edition, Jean Calvin, translated by E. and N. Weiss, was published in Geneva in 1909.

Warfield, Benjamin B. The literary history of the Institutes. *In :* Calvin, Jean. Institutes of the Christian religion. Philadelphia, Presbyterian board of publication, 1909. v. I, p. i-xlvi. 1951

Important account of the several Latin, French, German and other versions of *Institutes* and *Instruction in faith.* First printed in memorial edition of 1909 of American *Institutes,* reprinted in the 1936 edition.

Weber, Max. Die protestantische Ethik, und der Geist des Kapitalismus. Tübingen, Mohr, 1904. 206 p. Trans. by Talcott Parsons : The Protestant ethic and the spirit of capitalism. London, Allen & Unwin, 1930. 292 p. (Trans. from ed. of 1920) 1952

Vigorous statement that modern capitalism was nurtured if not generated by C.'s teachings. Weber drew his illustrations largely from Puritanism, and seems never to have studied thoroughly C.'s own teachings. This essay had been the cause of much recent research, both from the side of economic history and of C. scholarship. Many studies of economic conditions in Calvinistic and non-Calvinistic areas in Europe have given evidence of pre-Protestant capitalism, and have exposed the vulnerability of Weber's thesis. Work was

republished (Tübingen, 1922), summarized and developed, with some modifications, by Ernst D. Troeltsch in his *Die Sozialleheren der christlichen Kirchen und Gruppen,* Tübingen, Mohr, 1919, 994 p., and was translated into English as : *The social teaching of the Christian churches,* by Olive Wyon, New York, Macmillan, 1931. 2 v.

Wencelius, Léon. L'esthétique de Calvin. Les belles lettres, 1937. 428 p. (Diss., Paris.) 1953

In this Paris doctoral dissertation author studies C.'s aesthetics and finds in him a love of the beautiful in works of God and man that has hitherto often been denied or overlooked. The only source of his study is, says Wencelius, the fifty-eight volumes of *Opera omnia.* Gives a valuable list of studies dealing with various aspects of C.'s aesthetics, such as Jacques Pannier, *Calvin écrivain, sa place et son rôle dans la formation de la langue française,* Fischbacher, 1909, 16 p. with second edition, *Calvin écrivain, sa place et son rôle dans l'histoire de la langue et de la littérature françaises* (no. 1935), and Émile Doumergue, *L'art et le sentiment dans l'œuvre de Calvin,* Geneva, Société genevoise d'édition, 87 p.

Wendel, François. Calvin, sources et évolution de sa pensée religieuse. Presses universitaires, 1950. 296 p. (Diss. Strasbourg) 1954

Objectively and with reliance on historical method Wendel gives here a precise and succinct estimate of main points of C.'s religious thinking, with emphasis on aspects which determined originality of Calvinism. Significant as first work in French which gives, in easily accessible form, a complete treatment of the subject. Noteworthy work, conceived with no apologetic preoccupations.

Reviews : E. Cailliet in JR 31:138-39, 1951; F. Wendel in RHPR 30:270-72, 1950.

Sébastien Châteillon
(Nos. 1955-1969)

Châteillon, Sébastien. Biblia sacra latina. Basel, 1551. 2 parts in 1 v. 1955

A French translation in 1555; *La Bible avec des annotations sur les passages difficiles,* in 2 folio volumes. Preface to King Edward VI of England, in which C. expressed his indignation at persecution in name of religion.

— De haereticis. Magdeburg, Rausch, 1554. 173 p. 1956

Two Latin editions were printed ostensibly in Magdeburg in 1554. French version in same year, ostensibly in Rouen. A new French version, *Traité des hérétiques, à savoir, si on les doit persécuter, et comment on se doit conduire avec eux, selon l'avis, opinion, et sentence de plusieurs auteurs, tant anciens, que modernes, par Sébastien Castellion*, published by A. Olivet, with a preface by E. Choisy, in Geneva, 1913. Charles Bost in *Sébastien Castellion et l'opposition protestante contre Calvin* in RTP ns 2:301-21, July, 1914, calls attention to several misprints in this edition.

— Dialogorum sacrorum libri quatuor. Basel, Oporinum, 1551. 277 p.   1957

Popular work for children on Bible history. Many editions printed at Basel, London, Edinburgh, and in Germany.

— Castellio concerning heretics. New York, Columbia University Press, 1935. 342 p.
1958

Accurate translation of *De haereticis* and excerpts from C.'s other works, with critical introduction and scholarly essay on the attitude of the Church toward heretics by R. H. Bainton. Fully documented. Excellent bibliography, well-chosen illustrations.

Reviews : C. H. Moehlman in Chris 2:332-35, 1937; W. Pauck in CH 5:100-102, 1936.

Bainton, Roland H. Castellioniana; quatre études sur Sébastien Castellion et l'idée de la tolérance. Leiden, Brill, 1951. 111 p. 1959

Published by Dutch committee of commemoration of Servetus and C., Van der Woude, pastor of Amsterdam, contributes *Gestaltung der Toleranz;* Bainton of Yale, *Sebastian Castellio, champion of religious liberty;* Valkhoff, University of Witwaterstrand, *Sébastien Castellion et l'idée de la tolérance au XVIe siècle;* and Bruno Becker, University of Amsterdam, *Un manuscrit inédit de Castellion.*

Review : R. H. Bainton, in CH 9:270-272, 1940, reviews Becker's edition of the C. manuscript.

— Sebastian Castellio and the toleration controversy of the sixteenth century. *In:* Persecution and liberty. New York, 1931. p. 183-209.   1960

Important.

Bonnet, Jules. Sébastien Castalion, ou la tolérance au XVIe siècle. BSHP 16:465-480, 529-45, 1867; 17:2-15, 49-64, 1868.   1961

Well-written, interesting study. Published also in author's *Nouveaux récits du seizième siècle.* Grassart, 1870. p. 53-169.

Buisson, Ferdinand Édouard. Sébastien Castellion : sa vie et son œuvre, 1515-1563. Hachette, 1892. 2 v. (Diss., Paris.)   1962

Authoritative and complete two-volume work of pure documentation. Crowned by *Académie française*, it was for years standard biography of C. Bibliography of C.'s works, all editions, in 2:339-80, followed by unpublished correspondence.

Review : R. C. Christie in Spect. 69:264-65, Aug. 20, 1892.

Cantimori, Delio. Per la storia degli eretici italiani del secolo XVI in Europa. Delio Cantimori and Elisabeth Feist, editors. Rome, Reale accademia d'Italia, 1937. 432 p. (RAI, no. 7.)   1963

Publishes for first time C.'s *De arti dubitandi et confidendi et sciendi*, one of the most significant of his works.

Christie, Richard Copley. The first preacher of religious liberty. Spect. 69: 264-265, Aug. 20, 1892. *Reprinted in his:* Selected essays and papers. London, Longmans, Green, 1902. p. 350-55.   1964

Essay, in form of a book review of Buisson's *Sébastien Castellion* (no. 1962), which gives extracts, portraits, and plates.

Giran, Étienne. Sébastien Castellion et la réforme calviniste; les deux réformes, avec une préface de Ferdinand Buisson. Hachette, 1914. 576 p.   1966

Authoritative work. Author warns " ... personnes pieuses qui tiennent Calvin pour un saint homme de Dieu... " not to read his book (p. xi-xii) for their idol might lose some of his luster. Follows Buisson, who in preface admires the book's " attrait." Giran includes new data, and analyzes the place and importance of the man Buisson calls " ... l'humble professeur au Collège de Genève et de l'Université de Bâle ... le défenseur des hérétiques, et premier protagoniste de la liberté de conscience religieuse... " (p. vi).

Jones, Rufus M. Sebastian Castellio : a forgotten prophet. *In his:* Spiritual reformers in the sixteenth and seventeenth centuries. London, Macmillan, 1914. p. 88-103.   1967

Good treatment of life and works of C. and others.

Maehly, Jakob. Sebastian Castellio, ein biographischer Versuch nach den Quellen. Basel, Bahnmaier, 1862. 151 p.   1968
Excellent and substantial study by a Professor at University of Basel.

Zweig, Stefan. Castellio gegen Calvin; oder ein Gewissen gegen die Gewalt. Vienna, Reichner, 1936. 333 p. English version : The right to heresy ; Castellio against Calvin. New York, Viking Press, 1936. 238 p.   1969
In a journalistic manner, with few source references, Zweig assails Calvin's despotism and extolls C., " the lonely idealist, who, in the name of freedom of thought, had renounced allegiance to Calvin's as to every other spiritual tyranny." Vivid narration of " murder of Servetus," and C.'s defense. Much information on subject and some errors of statement. Useful bibliographical note on C., and *Items of sixteenth century chronology*, p. 233-38. Illustrated.
Review : C. H. Moehlman in Chris 2:332-35, 1937.

Robert et Henri Estienne
(Nos. 1970-1974)

Estienne, Robert. Ad censuras theologorum parisiensium. n.p., Etienne, 1552. 255 p.   1970
Publication of his folio edition of New Testament in 1550 aroused antagonism of faculty of theology and caused him to take refuge in Geneva. This answer to his accusers was published in French the same year under the title : *Les censures des théologiens de Paris par lesquelles ils avoyent faulsement condamné les Bibles imprimées par Robert Estienne, avec la response d'iceluy.* 156 ff. In 1553 he printed Calvin's edition of Olivétan's Bible.

Clément, Louis. Henri Estienne et son œuvre française. *See* 575.   1971
Henri Estienne, printer, editor, publisher of eighteen first editions of Greek authors and one Latin, and original author, unlike many earlier French scholars, did not despise or neglect his own language. This authoritative thesis by a *lycée* professor, gives much useful information on his French writings and his influence. *See* 969, 2121.

Feugère, Léon. Essai sur la vie et les ouvrages de Henri Estienne, etc. Delalain, 1853. 371 p.   1972
Detailed story of E.'s life, varied activities, troubles, and works. His French, Latin, and Greek works are analyzed. Appendix has several letters and critical bibliography. Same volume contains essay on Scévole de Sainte-Marthe.

Greswell, Edward. A view of the early Parisian Greek press : including the lives of the Stephani : notices of other contemporary Greek printers of Paris : and various particulars on the literary and ecclesiastical history of their times. Oxford, Collingwood, 1883. 2 v.   1973
Lengthy work; treats several subjects : early Greek and Latin press of Paris, life and contributions of Henri and Robert Estienne, Calvinism, matter of carrying of Royal Types to Geneva.

Sayous, Pierre André. Robert et Henri Estienne. *In his*: Études littéraires sur les écrivains français de la réformation. *See* 1856, v. II, p. 59-138.   1974
Especially useful study. Gives life and analyses of writings of father and son. Points out that Henri Estienne's important part in Reformation is not evidenced so much in his satire against Catholic Church clergy in his *Apologie pour Hérodote*, but rather in his disdain for routines, the independence of his literary criticism, his crusades against superstition.

Guillaume Farel
(Nos. 1975-1979)

Farel, Guillaume. Sommaire : c'est une briefve declaration d'aucuns lieux fort nécessaires à un chacun chrestien pour mettre sa confiance en Dieu et à ayder son prochain. " Turin, " i.e. Basel, 1525. Reprinted from an original in the British Museum by Arthur Piaget in 1935, Droz. 206 p. Second ed., 1534. Reprinted by J. G. Baum, Geneva, 1867. Third ed. Geneva, 1552.   1975
Very important as early statement of Reformed Christianity. Paul T. Fuhrmann has an English manuscript translation. For additional data *see* notes (p. 80) and introduction to Paul Traugott Fuhrmann's *Instruction in faith.* Trans. by Paul T. Fuhrmann, Philadelphia, Westminster Press, 1949. 96 p. and notes to Fuhrmann's *Calvin, the expositor of scripture.* Inter 6:188-209, 1952.

Comité Farel. Guillaume Farel 1489-1565; biographie nouvelle écrite d'après les documents originaux par un groupe d'historiens, professeurs et pasteurs de Suisse, de France et d'Italie. Neufchâtel and Paris, Delachaux et Niestlé, 1930. 780 p.   1976

Work of twenty collaborators, including Louis Albert, Jean Jalla, and N. Weiss. Monumental work, richly illustrated. Treats F.'s life and activities, and gives history of Protestantism in Switzerland and Waldensian Valleys. Important introduction gives estimate of F.'s historical role, present value of his work, character, style, thought and doctrine. Complete chronological bibliography of editions of F.'s writings, with useful description of all known works, and very complete general bibliography from 16th century to present.

Delattre, S. Guillaume Farel, réformateur de la Suisse romande du pays de Montbéliard et de Gap. Privas (Ardèche), Delattre, éd., 1931. 264 p.   1977

Running account of F.'s life, travels, and labors. Has borrowed from other writers, especially from *Nouvelle biographie*, Merle d'Aubigné, and F. Puaux, *Histoire de la réformation française*. Grassart, 1857. No footnotes or references. Admits that F. was "violent," but says this violence "gushed from a heart overflowing with love."

Kirchoffer, M. Das Leben W. Farels. Zurich, 1831-33. 2 v.   1978

Important earlier study. Author clears up several biographical and bibliographical points here and in his article on F. in TSK:4, p. 283.

Schmidt, C. Wilhelm Farel und Peter Viret, nach handschriftlichen und gleichzeitigen Quellen. Elberfeld, Friderichs, 1860. 71 p. (LAS, v. 9.)   1979

Important treatment of lives and works —printed and manuscript—of F. (p. 1-38) (ten works listed), and Viret (p. 39-71) (thirty-eight works listed). *See* 2040.

François Hotman

(Nos. 1980-1985)

Blocaille, Étienne. Étude sur François Hotman; La Franco-Gallia. Dijon, Jobard, 1902. 270 p.   1980

Useful work, containing life of H., analysis of *Franco-Gallia*, and bibliography of H.'s works.

Dareste de La Chavanne, Rodolphe. Essai sur François Hotman. Durand, 1850. 94 p.   1981

Good concise treatment of H.'s life and works, based primarily on 16th century sources. Dareste says that all biographies of H., posterior to that of P. Nevelet, printed at beginning of collection of H.'s works, Geneva, Vignon & Stoer, 1599-1600, 3 v., copy it without adding anything new.

— Étude sur François Hotman. RLJ 38:257-288, May-Aug., 1850.   1982

Careful student of H. admires his thought and style. Calls his language clear, rapid, vigorous and elegant. Same author has several useful specialized studies in other journals : *François Hotman et la conjuration d'Amboise*, BEC 3ᵉ sér. 5:360-375, 1854; *François Hotman, sa vie et sa correspondance*, Rhist 1²:1-59, 367-435, 1876, and *Hotman d'après de nouvelles lettres des années 1561-1563*, Rhist 97:297-315, Jan.-Apr., 1908, which supplements preceding article by publishing twenty-five important letters written to H. by Philip, Landgrave of Hesse during the first war of religion.

Foster, Herbert Darling. Political theories of Calvinists before the Puritan exodus to America. AHR 21:481-503, 1915-16.   1983

Good modern estimate of H.'s *Franco-Gallia*, which, he says, "follows Calvin's *Institutes* in picturing the easy lapse from royalty to tyranny," and its influence on Beza and Milton. Same article is important for political theories of Beza, Mornay, and Marnix St. Aldegonde. *See* 2011.

Reynolds, Beatrice. Proponents of limited monarchy in sixteenth century France : Francis Hotman and Jean Bodin. New York, Columbia University Press, 1931. 211 p. (Diss., Columbia.)   1984

Good treatment of H. and his ideas of representative government and an elective monarchy. *See* 2074.

Smith, David Baird. Francis Hotman. SHR 13:328-65, 1915-16.   1985

Clear concise account of H.'s life, travels, material misfortunes, and works. *See* 2083.

François Lambert d'Avignon

(Nos. 1986-1988)

Lambert d'Avignon, François. Somme chrestienne. Marburg, 1529.   1986
One of earliest Protestant treatises. Recently discovered. " Only one copy of it exists and is in the Library of French Protestantism " (Paul Traugott Fuhrmann in *Instruction in faith*, p. 93-94). As Fuhrmann points out, Calvin's first *Institutio* " stated clearly the faith already set forth in print somewhat confusedly by Farel in 1525 and by Lambert d'Avignon in 1529 " (*Instruction in faith*, p. 79).

Baum, J. W. Franz Lambert von Avignon. Strasbourg, Treuttel & Würtz, 1840. 236 p.   1987
Important monograph by distinguished Protestant scholar. Gives story of life and labors of L. and a catalogue of his writings.

Ruffet, Louis. Biographie de François Lambert d'Avignon. Bonhoure, 1873.   189 p.
1988
Useful French biography of this Protestant reformer, disputer of Zwingli, preacher of Strasbourg, and professor at University of Marburg. Dardier has good article on him in *Encyclopédie des sciences religieuses*, v. VII, p. 681-91. Haag covers him adequately in *La France protestante* (1852) and lists his works.

Hubert Languet

(Nos. 1989-1992)

Languet, Hubert. De la puissance légitime du prince sur le peuple et du peuple sur le prince. Geneva, 1581.   229 p.   1989
Translation by François Estienne of *Vindiciae contra tyrannos* which appeared in 1579 under the pseudonym of Junius Brutus. Was called " one of the most dangerous works of its kind ever written."

— A defence of liberty against tyrants; a translation of the Vindiciae contra tyrannos, by Junius Brutus, *pseud.* with historical introduction by Harold Joseph Laski. London, Bell, 1924.   229 p.   1990
Reprinting of English translation of 1689. Introduction gives useful background for understanding text. Discusses views of many authors, including Bayle, as to real authorship of this famous polemic and concludes that it probably was

work of Philippe Du Plessis-Mornay, and not of L. No bibliography, but many good footnotes.
Review : H. D. Foster in AHR 30:852-53, 1924-25.

Chevreul, Henri. Hubert Languet. Potier, 1852.   239 p.   1991
Readable treatment of L.'s life, career, travels and works. Examination of *Vindiciae contra tyrannos* and a comparison with other political works of the day. Catalogue of L.'s works, 209-12.

Sidney, Sir Philip. Correspondence of Philip Sidney and Hubert Languet. Ed. by William A. Bradley. Boston, Merrymount Press, 1912.   230 p.   1992
Important correspondence between Sidney and his close friend and travelling companion, L. Correspondence first translated from Latin and published with a memoir in 1845 by S. A. Pears, London, Pickering, 1845.   240 p. Useful bibliographical note, p. 229-30.

François de La Noue

(Nos. 1993-1997)

La Noue, François de. Discours politiques et militaires. Basel, Forest, 1587.   711 p.
1993
Twenty-six discourses written when L. was prisoner of Duke of Alva in Limburg. Saw war " as a human drama." Other writings were his notes on Plutarch's *Lives* and *Déclaration sur la prise d'armes pour la juste défense de Sedan et Jametz*. Verdun, Marchant, 1588.   21 p. His correspondence was published in 1854.

Cougny, Edme. Le capitaine François de La Noue, *dit* Bras-de-Fer. Durand et Pedone-Lauriel, 1872.   1994
Pamphlet dealing with L.'s many military campaigns and posts.

Hauser, Henri. François de La Noue, 1531-1591. Hachette, 1892.   336 p.   1995
Good study of L. and his times. Hauser is somewhat of an apologist for his subject and stresses his modesty, good nature, firm and upright good sense, indulgence, valor, ardent patriotism, and tolerant fervor (p. 289). Says that " l'exemple de La Noue...prouve qu'il y avait alors, chez les protestants, un parti modéré, disposé à une transaction, à tout le moins respectueux de la liberté individuelle " (p. 287). Complete bibliography of L.'s works and

studies on him, p. i-viii. One may also consult a more popular book by a facile writer, Cécile Vincens, *François de La Noue dit Bras-de-Fer*, Société des Écoles de dimanche, 1875, 295 p., in *Les héros de la réforme* series. Harvard has a copy of *Discours politiques et militaires du sieur de La Noue, recueillis et mis en lumière par le sieur de Fresnes*, dernière édition, Lyons, Bellou, 1595, 1017 p.

Petitot, Claude Bernard. Mémoires du sieur François de La Noue. *In his:* Collection complète des mémoires relatifs à l'histoire de France. Foucault, 1819-29. 1st series, v. 34, p. 83-296.   1996

Good biographical sketch, p. 85-120; *Mémoires de François de La Noue*, p. 121-296.

Séguer, C. La Noue, notice sur sa vie et ses écrits. Colmar, Decker, 1854. 40 p. (Diss., Strasbourg.)   1997

Useful thesis on L., his *Discours politiques et militaires* and other writings, submitted to faculty of Protestant theology of Strasbourg.

Odet de La Noue

(No. 1998)

Pourtalès, Guy de, *comte.* Odet de La Noue. BSHP 77:81-111, 280-305, 1918.   1998

Good account of life, labors, and writings of this minor Protestant poet, soldier, and politician. Many extracts from his correspondence. Important bibliography. Among works listed are *Paradoxe* (1587), *Poésies chrestiennes* (150 sonnets, 1594), *Le grand dictionnaire des rimes françaises* (1624), and *Éditeur de l'Uranie, ou nouveau recueil de chansons spirituelles et chrestiennes* (1591). Pourtalès wrote this study as part of a projected work : *Les petits poètes huguenots de la IIᵉ moitié du XVIᵉ siècle et du commencement du XVIIᵉ, leurs vies et leurs œuvres françaises avec un essai de bibliographie.*

Philippe de Marnix, *seigneur* de Sainte-Aldegonde

(Nos. 1999-2003)

Marnix, Philippe de, *seigneur* de Sainte-Aldegonde. Œuvres. Brussels, 1857-60. 8 v.   1999

Works deal largely with political matters. Two well-known pieces, however, are religious polemics : *La ruche de la sainte Église*, published originally in Dutch in 1569, had some twenty editions and translations in French, English, and German; and *Tableau des differens de la religion*, 1599. Both are violent satires against Roman church; latter has been called " Une des plus belles œuvres qui aient été écrites en prose française au XVIᵉ siècle " (E. Hubert in *La grande encyclopédie*, v. 23, p. 242).

Govaert, Marcel. Le Tableau des differens de la religion et le Biëncorf de Marnix de Sainte-Aldegonde. RLC 26:15-23, 1952.   2000

Govaert admires M. as one of the most characteristic writers of the renaissance. He characterizes him as an admirable writer, a perfect bi-linguist, and one who desired the salvation of his religion more than that of his country. He states that in the *Biëncorf* M. created Flemish literary prose, while the Rabelaisian *Tableau*, etc. is one of the masterpieces of French pamphlet literature. Discusses century-old question, which of the two writings is original; gives new evidence of priority of French text. Footnotes give useful bibliography.

Oosterhof, Gosselinus. La vie littéraire de Marnix de Sainte-Aldegonde et son Tableau des differens de la religion. Kampen, Zalsman, 1909. 167 p. (Diss., Lille.)   2001

Important study of writings of this distinguished statesman, burgomaster of Antwerp, and privy councilor to Prince of Orange. Believes that *Tableau*, etc. was written prior to *Biëncorf*.

Quinet, Edgar. Marnix de Sainte-Aldegonde. Delahays, 1854. 264 p. *Also in:* Œuvres complètes, Pagnerre, 1857-58. 5:7-171.   2002

Although there were several good Dutch biographies of M. in 19th century, there were few French studies. Examines author's writings and believes *Tableau des differens* was translation of Flemish text.

Wittemans, Frans. Marnix de Sainte-Aldegonde, ministre de Guillaume d'Orange. Brussels, Office de publicité, 1935. 96 p.   2003

Useful especially for political life of author. Wittemans examines his writings and believes that French text of *Tableau des differens* was the original.

Philippe de Mornay,
seigneur **du Plessis-Marly**

(Nos. 2004-2014)

Mornay, Philippe de. De la vérité de la religion chrestienne contre les athées, épicuriens, payens, Juifs, Mahumedistes et autres infidèles. Antwerp, Plantin, 1581. 854 p. Latin edition same year, same publisher.
2004

Other French editions of Antwerp, Paris, Leyden, Saumur, and Lyons from 1582 to 1597. M. claims that Christian religion is the only true faith. He uses some arguments of Scholastics, but, more originally, he attempts to show essential harmony between Gospel and needs of human heart.

— De l'institution, usage et doctrine du saint sacrement de l'eucharistie en l'église ancienne. La Rochelle, Haultin, 1598. 956 p.
2005

One of his many apologies of Protestantism. Contains some 5,000 citations from scriptures, fathers, and schoolmen. Cause of public disputation in 1600, with unfavorable verdict.

— Excellent discours de la vie et de la mort. n.p., 1576. 117 p.
2006

Written as a bridal present for Charlotte Arbaleste whom he married at Sedan, author of his life and memoirs.

— Mémoires de messire Philippes de Mornay, *seigneur* du Plessis-Marli, ... contenant divers discours ... depuis l'an 1573 jusqu'en l'an 1599. La Forest, 1624-25. 2 v. *Also:* Mémoires de messire Philippe de Mornay depuis l'an 1600 jusques à l'an 1623. Amsterdam, Elzévir, 1652. 2 v.
2007

Another edition by Treuttel & Würtz was published, 1824-26 in 12 v. Best is : Mornay, Charlotte Arbaleste de. *Mémoires de Madame de Mornay*, ed. by Madame de Witt. Renouard, 1868-69. 2 v. (SHF). This edition contains several hitherto unpublished letters.

Mornay, Charlotte Arbaleste de. A Huguenot family in the XVI century : the memoirs of Philippe de Mornay, *sieur* du Plessis Marly, written by his wife. Trans. by Lucy Crump. London, Routledge, New York, Dutton, 1926. 300 p.
2008

Good English translation, with a useful introduction.

Ambert, Joachim.   Duplessy - Mornay, 1549-1623. 2nd ed., Comon, 1848. 560 p.
2009

Useful extensive study of " Huguenot Pope "—adviser of Henry of Navarre—and political events of second half of 16th century.

Elkan, Albert. Die Publizistik der Bartholomäusnacht und Mornays Vindiciae contra tyrannos. Heidelberg, Winter, 1905. 178 p.
2010

Important for summaries of M.'s correspondence and memoirs, *Vindiciae contra tyrannos*, and his views on European, especially Dutch, politics. Believed that M. was real author of *Vindiciae*, etc.

Foster, H. D. Mornay. *In his:* Political theories of Calvinists before the Puritan exodus to America. AHR 21:494-97, 1915-1916.
2011

Good treatment of M.'s works and influence. Establishes M.'s authorship of *Vindiciae contra tyrannos* (often ascribed to Languet) by reference to recent studies and Grotius's assertion in 1645. *See* 1983.

Patry, Raoul. Philippe du Plessis-Mornay; un huguenot homme d'état, 1549-1623. Fischbacher, 1933. 670 p.
2012

Definitive, sympathetic, orderly treatment of M.'s life and works, with good accounts of formative years, service of King, struggles against League, governorship of Saumur, relations with Protestant churches, disgrace, and death, based on a careful study of the sources. Biography of M., written by his wife for education of his son, utilized fully. Bibliography of manuscripts, printed works, and studies dealing with M., p. 633-47. Ch. VI has helpful discussion of his several political and religious writings. *See* 2239.

Review : J. T. McNeill in JR 13:338-39, 1933.

Schaeffer, Adolphe. Du Plessis-Mornay considéré comme théologien et principalement comme apologiste. Strasbourg, Berger-Levrault, 1848. 74 p. (Diss., Strasbourg.)
2013

Thesis submitted to Protestant Faculty of Strasbourg. As title indicates, Schaeffer studies M.'s theological views, based on Calvin's reasoning.

Van Ysselsteyn, G. T. L'auteur de l'ouvrage Vindiciae contra tyrannos. Rhist 167:46-59, May, 1931.
2014

Van Ysselsteyn believes that Languet first wrote central section which became part III of finished work, and that M. wrote around Languet's essay the sections which became Parts I, II, and IV of *Vindiciae*, fusing the two works into one.

Pierre Robert Olivétan
(Nos. 2015-2021)

Olivétan, Pierre Robert. La Bible, qui est toute la saincte escripture, en laquelle sont contenues le vieil Testament et le nouveau translatez en françoys. Le vieil de Lebrieu; et le nouveau du grec. Neufchâtel, Wingle, 1535. 2015

First Protestant version of Bible. Translated at request and expense of Waldensian Church of Italy. Some 2,000 folio pages of text, plus *épitres* by Calvin and O., a dedication by "l'humble et petit translateur," table, glossary, and index. Haag states that O. knew Greek less well than Beza affirms, was not especially well versed in Latin, and could not have accomplished, the task save for aid given by French version by Lefèvre d'Étaples, printed in Paris and Antwerp in 1523-28. Another folio edition, corrected chiefly as to language by Calvin, appeared in 1553. Another, corrected by Beza, was put out in Geneva, 1588. It has since undergone several alterations and revisions.

Comba, Ernesto. Storia dei Valdesi. 3rd ed. Torre Pellice, Libreria Claudiana, 1935. 370 p. 2016

Good material (p. 110-12) on visit of Farel, Saunier, and O. to Waldensian Synod of Cianforan, raising of funds by Waldenses for printing of a Protestant Bible, and O.'s translation and publication of first Protestant version.

Delarue, Henri. Olivétan et Pierre de Vingle à Genève, 1532-1533. BHren 8:105-18, 1946. 2017

Questions Herminjard, whose authority was so great that later scholars have erred in following his interpretations. Establishes dates of O.'s movements in Waldensian Valleys, in Neufchâtel, and Geneva. Treats Protestant printers of the day, Vingle and Martin Gonin, who was, perhaps, printer of O.'s *Instruction des enfans*.

Fuhrmann, Paul Traugott. Calvin, the expositor of scripture. Inter 2:188-209, Apr., 1952. 2018

Good material on significance of O.'s translation of Bible.

Künze, Horst. Die Bibelübersetzungen von Lefèvre d'Étaples und von P. R. Olivétan, verglichen in ihrem Wortschatz. Leipzig, 1935. 236 p. (Diss., Leipzig.) 2019

Mainly a vocabulary comparison. Includes data on career of O. of whom little is known. Calls O.'s accomplishment astonishing and noteworthy because of limited resources. Bibliography and index.

Négrier, Charles Abel. Pierre Robert dit Olivétan. Montauban, Granié, 1891. 63 p. 2020

A doctoral thesis submitted to Faculty of Protestant Theology of Montauban. Useful.

Petavel-Olliff, Emmanuel. La Bible en France, ou Les traductions françaises des Saintes Écritures; étude historique et littéraire. Librairie française et étrangère, 1864. 299 p. 2021

Useful study of French versions of Bible. Good treatment of that of O. (Ch. III), and those of Beza, Calvin, and Castellio (Ch. VIII).

Bernard Palissy
(Nos. 2022-2027)

Palissy, Bernard. Les œuvres de Bernard Palissy, publiées d'après les textes originaux, avec une notice historique et bibliographique et une table analytique par Anatole France. *See* 487. 2022

Introduction has good treatment of earlier editions (1777, 1844) of works of this famous Protestant geologist, chemist, agronomist, and potter. 1777 edition dedicated to Benjamin Franklin; best edition said to be that of P. A. Cap, Dubochet, 1844. 437 p.

— Les œuvres de maistre Bernard Palissy. Nouvelle édition revue sur les textes originaux par B. Fillon. Niort, Clouzot, 1888. 2 v. 2023

In two octavo volumes. Has good study of life and works of P. by Louis Audiat.

Audiat, Louis. Bernard Palissy. Didier, 1868. 480 p. 2024

Good treatment by authoritative author of several studies of P. *See* 2156.

Delange, Henri and C. Borneman. Monographie de l'œuvre de Bernard Palissy. 1862. 38 p.   2025

Folio publication with one hundred colored lithographs and text by Alexandre Sauzay.

Lasteyrie du Saillant, Ferdinand Charles Léon, *comte* **de.** Bernard Palissy, étude sur la vie et sur ses œuvres. Pillet, 1865. 20 p.   2026

Readable brief sketch by authoritative writer on the fine arts, especially archaeology.

Rossignol, Ferdinand. Bernard Palissy. *In his:* Portraits-biographies. Les protestants illustrés. Meyrueis, 1862. v. I, p. 117-28.   2027

Study of life and works of P. from a Protestant viewpoint.

Ambroise Paré
(Nos. 2028-2031)

Paré, Ambroise. Œuvres complètes d'Ambroise Paré : revues et collationnées sur toutes les éditions. Ed. by J. F. Malgaigne. Baillière, 1840-41. 3 v.   2028

Most useful edition of P.'s works, of which there were three folio editions during his life (1575, 1579, 1585), frequent posthumous editions, and several translations in Latin, English, Dutch, and German. Dr. Malgaigne, eminent surgeon, includes a lengthy critical and historical introduction, in which he expressed his belief that P. was a Catholic. *See* 452, 2086.

Le Paulmier, Claude Stephen. Ambroise Paré d'après de nouveaux documents découverts aux Archives nationales et des papiers de famille. Charavay, 1884. 420 p. 2029

Dr. Le Paulmier believes that his exhaustive researches provide sufficient proof that P., who remained aloof from the religious divisions of his day, was indeed a Protestant.

Packard, Francis R. Life and times of Ambroise Paré, 1519-1590, with a translation of his Apology and an account of his journeys in divers places. New York, Hoeber, 1921. 297 p.   2030

In addition to translations there are some 126 pages devoted to the life and times of P., 22 illustrations, 27 full page plates, and two folded maps of Paris in the 16th and 17th centuries. *See* 452.

Paget, Stephen. Ambroise Paré and his times, 1510-1590. New York, Putnam, 1897. 309 p.   2031

Based on works of Malgaigne, Le Paulmier, and Louis Jacques Bégin, this illustrated study offers little new. Paget admired P. and held that his life was so filled with good works, adventures, and romance that it should be better known and honored abroad.

Olivier de Serres, *seigneur* du Pradel
(Nos. 2032-2036)

Serres, Olivier de, *seigneur* du Pradel. Le théâtre d'agriculture et mesnage des champs; nouvelle édition conforme au texte, augmentée des notes et d'un vocabulaire; publiée par la Société d'agriculture du département de la Seine. Huzard, 1804-05. 2 v. *See* 339.   2032

First edition of this " rural encyclopedia " appeared in-folio in 1600. There were 19 editions up to 1675. This most recent edition, the twenty-first, two volumes with portraits and figures, includes eulogy of S. by Count François de Neufchâteau, Minister of Interior under Directory, historical essay on European agriculture in 16th century, and a bibliography of editions by J. B. Huzard of Institute.

Baudrillart, Henri. Olivier de Serres. *In his:* Gentilhommes ruraux de la France. Didot, 1893. p. 109-45.   2033

Good study of S. Baudrillart discusses S.'s part in wars of religion in RDM 60:889-907, Oct. 15, 1890. *See* 2185.

Combes, Anacharsis. Olivier de Serres et le Théâtre d'agriculture, Jacques Vanière et le Praedium rusticum, 1590-1720, étude agronomique. Castres, Grillon, 1867. 96 p.   2034

Satisfactory treatment of de S.'s chief work and his importance to French agriculture.

Lavondès, Mlle A. Olivier de Serres, *seigneur* du Pradel. Carrières-sous-Poissy, La cause, 1936. 317 p.   2035

Author gives sympathetic and authoritative treatment of life and principal work, *Le théâtre d'agriculture* of her noble forbear. She shows how he preached and practiced on his domain full use and improvement of soil and diversification of crops. Good analysis of this early " rural encyclopedia." Study of the many editions. Good bibliography (p. 306-11) of biographies, editions, and works on agriculture. *See* 2191.

Vaschalde, Henry. Olivier de Serres, *seigneur* du Pradel; sa vie et ses travaux, documents inédits. Plon-Nourrit, 1886. 232 p. 2036

Important work by capable Ardèche collector and bibliographer, organizer of a centenary celebration in 1882 on occasion of a visit by Pasteur to Vivarais region. Author had access to previously unpublished family documents at Pradel. Illustrated. Lavondès complains that despite this and other studies on her noble ancestor he still remained " unappreciated." *See* 2193.

Pierre Viret

(Nos. 2037-2040)

Viret, Pierre. Pierre Viret d'après lui-même; pages extraites des œuvres du réformateur à l'occasion du quatrième centenaire de sa naissance. Publiées sous les auspices de la Société vaudoise de théologie, par Charles Schnetzler, Henri Vuilleumier et Alfred Schroeder, avec la collaboration d'Eugène Choisy et de Philippe Godet. Lausanne, Bridel, 1911. 341 p. 2037

V.'s pamphlets are today very rare. The Society has chosen extracts under several headings : autobiographical, correspondence, the pastor, preacher, polemist, satirist, theologian, and moralist.

Barnaud, Jean. Pierre Viret, sa vie et son œuvre. Saint-Amans (Tarn), Caryol, 1911. 703 p. (Diss., Paris.) 2038

Barnaud, pastor at Clairac, and author, with Charles Schnetzler, of most complete bibliography of V., and of a collection of manuscript letters by V., published this important study of eloquent preacher and theological teacher on occasion of fourth centenary of V.'s birth.

Sayous, Pierre André. Pierre Viret. *In his :* Études littéraires sur les écrivains français de la réformation. *See* 1856, v. I, p. 181-240. 2039

Good account of V.'s life and labors in many centers : Geneva, Nîmes, Montpellier, Paris, and Orthez.

Schmidt, Charles. Wilhelm Farel und Peter Viret, nach handschriftlichen und gleichzeitigen Quellen. *See* 1979. 2040

P. 39 - 71 treat life and works of V. 38 writings in Latin and French are listed.

CHAPTER XII. POLITICAL WRITERS
(Nos. 2041-2084)

NORMAN B. SPECTOR

Jean Bodin
(Nos. 2041-2078)

Bodin, Jean. La méthode de l'histoire. Pierre Mesnard, ed. Algiers, 1941. (PFLA, IIᵉ série, tome XIV.) 2041

Translation into French of *Methodus*. Does not identify in notes various authors mentioned by B. in his text (cf. translation of *Methodus* into English by Beatrice Reynolds, *see* 2042), but has a useful *index nominum* and *table analytique* of subject treated. Bibliography.

— Method for the easy comprehension of history. Trans. by Beatrice Reynolds. New York, Columbia University Press, 1945. (RCSS v. 37). 402 p. 2042

Translation into English of *Methodus*. Has very helpful notes on identity of authors referred to by B. Bibliography.

Reviews : W. J. Schlaerth in FR 19:324-325, 1945-46; M. H. Shepherd, Jr. in ATR 28:49, 1946; TLS 44:478, Oct. 6, 1945.

Allen, John William. Jean Bodin. *In his :* A history of political thought in the sixteenth century. London, 1928. p. 394-446. 2043

Thorough analysis of B.'s works and good treatment of idea of sovereignty as presented in *Republic*.

Baldwin, Summerfield. Jean Bodin and the League. CHR 23:160-84, July, 1937. 2044

Discusses B.'s relations to the League; concludes that his adherence to it was not only genuine and whole-hearted, but had also a religious basis.

Baudrillart, Henri Joseph Léon. Jean Bodin et son temps; tableau des théories politiques et des idées économiques au seizième siècle. Guillaumin, 1853. 219 p. 2045

Old, but still useful study of B.'s relations to political and economic currents of 16th century. Part I summarizes

political and economic writings in 16th century France up to time of B. Treats Thomas More, Luther, Calvin, Hotman. Part II studies life and works of B. Third and longest section is limited to a detailed analysis of *Republic*. *See* 1415.

Benz, Ernst. Der Toleranz-Gedanke in der Religionswissenschaft. (Über den Heptaplomeres des Jean Bodin) DV 12:540-71, 1934. 2046

Analysis of *Heptaplomeres*, tracing current of free thought in the work as predecessor to rationalism of such thinkers as Bayle, Voltaire, Leibnitz, Lessing.

Bezold, Friedrich von. Jean Bodins Colloquium Heptaplomeres und das Atheismus des 16. Jahrhunderts. HZ ser. III, 17:260-315, 1914. 2047

Solid study of background of *Heptaplomeres* in B.'s works, showing its place in the current of rationalism and free thought in renaissance.

Bredvold, Louis Ignatius. Milton and Bodin's Heptaplomeres. SP 21:399-402, 1924. 2048

Discusses brief possession by Milton of a copy of the manuscript, then extremely rare and sought after, of *Colloquium heptaplomeres*. Indicated as " ... additional evidence of Milton's interest in radical or ' libertine ' thought and his intimate connection with people of advanced views " (p. 401).

Brown, John Lackey. Bodin et Ben Jonson. RLC 20:66-81, 1940. 2049

Studies B.'s influence on English writers of first part of 17th century, in particular Jonson's mistaken idea that B. was an atheist and a professed disciple of Machiavelli.

— The Methodus ad facilem historiarum cognitionem of Jean Bodin; a critical study. Washington, The Catholic University of America Press, 1939. 212 p. (Diss., Catholic University of America.) 2050

Excellent study of *Methodus* showing relation to other *artes historicae* of renaissance and evolution of B.'s political and economic thought towards *Republic.* Full bibliographical references to other aspects of B.'s life and works. Indispensable for study of B.

Review : G. Toffanin in Rin 3:295-300, Apr., 1940.

Busson, Henri. Un "Achriste" : Jean Bodin. *In his:* Les sources et le développement du rationalisme dans la littérature française de la renaissance (1533-1610). *See* 188, p. 539-65. 2051

Analyzes *Republic* and shows B.'s rationalism. "Sous une forme diffuse et savante, le livre est la somme de la théologie libertine de la renaissance " (p. 565).

Cardascia, G. Machiavel et Jean Bodin. BHren 3:129-67, 1943. 2052

Excellent analysis of Machiavelli's influence on B. Latter was an "antimachiavelliste sincère," but his opposition remained purely in realm of intention, "... un antimachiavellisme tardif, inspiré à Bodin par les protestants " (p. 166). *See* 2655, 2761.

Chauviré, Roger, tr. Colloque de Jean Bodin des secrets cachez des choses sublimes entre sept sçauans qui sont de differens sentimens. Champion, 1914. 212 p. 2053

Chauviré's *thèse complémentaire*, which presents a translation of extracts of *Heptaplomeres*, along with critical notes.

— Jean Bodin, auteur de la République. Champion, 1914. 543 p. 2054

Basic *œuvre d'ensemble.* Chauviré's thesis represents point of departure of all subsequent studies on B. Studies B.'s life, intellectual growth, religion, sources of *Republic,* B.'s politics. Full bibliography of B.'s works.

Review : V. L. Bourrilly in RSS 6:127-131. 1919.

Chevallier, Jean-Jacques. Les Six livres de la République de Jehan Bodin (1576). *In his:* Les grandes œuvres politiques de Machiavel à nos jours. 2nd ed. Colin, 1950. p. 38-51. 2055

Contrasts *Republic* with *Il principe* and gives brief analysis of theory of sovereignty contained in B.'s work.

Church, William Farr. Jean Bodin and his contemporaries. *In his:* Constitutional thought in sixteenth-century France : a

study in the evolution of ideas. Cambridge, Harvard University Press; London, Milford, Oxford University Press, 1941. p. 194-271. 2056

Excellent analysis of *Republic.* Considers also background and contemporaries of B. in 16th-century France as setting for his ideas. Bibliography, p. 339-50.

Cook, Thomas I. Bodin : kingly sovereignty and the new middle class. *In his:* History of political philosophy from Plato to Burke. New York, Prentice-Hall, 1936. p. 365-396. 2057

Appreciation of B.'s sociological approach; his theory of history as an aid to practical activity; his economics (as basis for national prosperity); his concept of political authority; his views on form of the state and bases of successful statecraft. Conclusion deals with B.'s significance and influence, contrasting him with such thinkers as Dubois, Montesquieu, and Hobbes. "... In terms of intellectual influence, Bodin is an interesting link between Aristotle and Montesquieu on the one hand and the Roman Imperialists and Hobbes on the other. More fundamentally, whatever the narrowing of his vision and the adaptation by him of principle to particular interests, he stands in that great line of thinkers who proclaim that the moral purpose of the state is the welfare of the people " (p. 395).

Dean, Leonard F. Bodin's Methodus in England before 1625. SP 39:160-66, 1942. 2058

Points out influence of *Methodus* on such writers as Sidney, Harvey, Thomas Rogers, Nash, Spenser, Bolton, Hobbes, Thomas Heywood, and Degory Wheare. "Bodin almost certainly contributed to the development of the kind of rationalistic, political history-writing of which Bacon was the chief Tudor exponent " (p. 166).

Droz, Eugénie. Le Carme Jean Bodin, hérétique. BHren 10:77-94, 1948. 2059

Supports Naef's argument that B. was converted to Protestantism. *See* 2072.

Ebenstein, William. Bodin. *In his:* Introduction to political philosophy. New York, Rinehart, 1952. p. 117-21. 2060

Brief consideration of B.'s preference of monarchy to aristocracy and democracy. Contrasts B.'s state with that of Machiavelli. The former's "... is strong but not aggressive; monarchical but not tyrannical. It became the model for the new national state in which the interests of the monarchy were allied with those of the rising merchant and middle classes against church and aristocracy " (p. 121). Useful bibliographical notes (p. 289-90).

Fournol, E. Bodin, prédécesseur de Montesquieu; étude sur quelques théories politiques de La république et de l'Esprit des lois. Rousseau, 1896. 176 p. 2061

Analysis of *Republic* and the idea of sovereignty. Studies theory of influence of climate on forms of government as contained in B.'s work and its reappearance in Montesquieu's *Esprit des lois*.

Gianturco, Elio. Bodin et Vico. RLC 22:272-90, 1948. 2062

Interesting study of B.'s influence on development of Vico's system of law. " Bodin perhaps was instrumental in directing Vico's glance on the closely knit, compactly structural organism of the early Roman family. Whoever realizes the importance that Vico's conception of the early Roman *testamentum* had in the elaboration of his view of early Roman history will see at once the fertility of the parallelism suggested to Vico by the reading of Bodin " (p. 290). *See* 2689.

Ho, Yung-Chi. Bodin in England. *In his:* The origin of parliamentary sovereignty or " mixed " monarchy; being a study of the political implications of Calvinism and Bodinism, from the mid-sixteenth to the mid-seventeenth century, chiefly in France and England. Shanghai, The Commercial Press, 1935. p. 244-304. 2063

Discusses influence of *Republic* on such English political thinkers as Hooke, Sir John Eliot, Dudley Digges, Thomas Hobbes, Robert Filmer.

— Bodin on sovereignty. *In his:* The origin of parliamentary sovereignty or " mixed " monarchy; being a study of the political implications of Calvinism and Bodinism, from the mid-sixteenth to the mid-seventeenth century, chiefly in France and England. *See* 2063, p. 178-243. 2064

Analysis of concept of sovereignty in *Republic*.

Levron, Jacques. Jean Bodin, sieur de Saint-Amand ou Jean Bodin, originaire de Saint-Amand. BHren 10:69-76, 1948. 2065

Contests Naef's claim that B. ever went to Geneva or was converted to Protestantism (*see* 2072).

Mantz, Harold Elmer. Bodin and the sorcerers. RR 15:153-78, 1924. 2066

Penetrating analysis of *Démonomanie* and B.'s attitude towards witchcraft. Concludes that although he had " formidable erudition..., his eclecticism often amounts to mere prejudice when he cites an author with respect in one place, only to discard him without criticism in another, whenever his own argumentation seems to require it " (p. 178).

Mesnard, Pierre. Jean Bodin à Toulouse. BHren 12:31-59, 1950. 2067

Studies B.'s life at Toulouse, his relationship with the University, and his literary activity there.

Review : Beatrice Reynolds in RenN 3:70, 1950.

— La République de Jean Bodin. *In his:* L'essor de la philosophie politique au xvie siècle. Boivin, 1936. p. 473-546. 2068

Detailed analysis of *Republic*, together with an interpretation of B.'s " sociologie." Concludes that B. merits " le titre de créateur de la méthode comparative et de fondateur de la politique expérimentale " (p. 541). Bibliographical notes.

Moreau-Reibel, Jean. Bodin et la Ligue d'après des lettres inédites. Hren 2:422-440, 1935. 2069

B.'s adherence to the League, in 1589, was the reasonable course of a man who knew it was the only way to " ... éviter à ses concitoyens—et sans doute du même coup à sa famille et à lui-même—les horreurs des massacres urbains cent fois pires que la guerre en règle, et à sa bonne ville de Laon, la ruine intérieure cent fois pire qu'un siège " (p. 438).

— Jean Bodin et le droit public comparé dans ses rapports avec la philosophie de l'histoire. Vrin, 1933. 278 p. 2070

Studies B.'s development as a humanist and jurist. Analyzes *Republic* and B.'s theory of sovereignty. Treats specifically nature of sovereignty in England, Poland, and Scandinavian countries. Bibliography.

Reviews : C. Curcio in RIFD 15:441-42, 1935; J. Dumas in BSHP 83:341-43, 1934; L. Febvre in Rsyn 7:165-68, 1934; A. Gardot in TVR 13:232-47, 1933; G. de Lagarde in RHEF 20:635-38, 1934; L. Rigaud in Rph ns 5:270-74, 1935.

Murray, Robert H. Sovereignty, national and international. *In his:* History of political science from Plato to the present. 2nd ed. New York, Appleton, 1930. p. 172-186. **2071**

General consideration of B.'s place in history of development of concept of sovereignty. Brief analysis of *Methodus, Heptaplomeres,* and *Republic.* Contrasts Bodin with Plato and Hotman.

Naef, Henri. La jeunesse de Jean Bodin ou les conversions oubliées. BHren 8:137-155, 1946. **2072**

Additional information on B.'s biography, including data on his two marriages and consideration of his disputed voyage to Geneva and conversion to Protestantism. Maintains that both voyage and conversion took place.

Ponthieux, A. Quelques documents inédits sur Jean Bodin. RSS 15:56-99, 1938. **2073**

Collection of letters and notarial documents giving details on B.'s life not contained in Chauviré's biography. *See* 2054.

Reynolds, Beatrice. Proponents of limited monarchy in sixteenth century France : Francis Hotman and Jean Bodin. *See* 1984. **2074**

Penetrating analysis of fundamental disagreement of Hotman and B. on concept of sovereignty : B.'s belief in " semi-divinity " of royalty, his theory of power flowing from the summit down," and Hotman's theory that the king was the " material instrument of the people. Authority came to him from below, as a rising vapor." Useful bibliography.

Reviews : Anon in HLR 44:1021-23, 1930-31; S. Baldwin in HTM 22:233-34, 1931; N. B. Nash in ATR 13:462, 1931.

Sabine, George H. Jean Bodin. *In his:* A history of political theory. New York, Holt, 1937. p. 399-414. **2075**

Treats B.'s views on religious tolerance, the state and family, sovereignty (theory and limitation), and well-ordered state.

Sée, Henri Eugène. La philosophie de l'histoire de Jean Bodin. Rhist 175:497-505, May-June, 1935. **2076**

Points out B.'s claim that history can be explained largely by the constitution of states and their transformations *(rerum publicarum statu et conversionibus).* Shows that B. attempted, in his *Methodus* and *Republic,* to arrive at an understanding of universal history of governments and that he realized that only the comparative method would suffice.

Shackleton, Robert Milner. Botero, Bodin and Robert Johnson. MLR 43:405-09, 1948. **2077**

Robert Johnson, an English translator of end of 16th and beginning of 17th century, made use of B.'s *Methodus* in a supposed translation of Giovanni Botero's *Relationi universali.* Johnson credits B. with 2 sentences (of 19 pages actually taken from *Methodus*), but acknowledges his source in no other way. Shackleton concludes that B.'s reputation in early 17th century England was " ... high enough for occasional mention of his name to be valuable, but the fame of *Methodus* was not so great as to make its arguments and phraseology ... likely to be detected by the general public.... It is curious that the advocate of toleration, Bodin, should be introduced into Protestant England under the aegis or disguise of an Italian Jesuit " (p. 409).

Wagner, Robert Léon. Le vocabulaire magique de Jean Bodin dans la Démono-manie des sorciers. BHren 10:95-123, 1948. **2078**

Analyzes B.'s use of the vocabulary of magic in *Démonomanie. See* 344.

François Hotman, *sieur* de Villiers Saint Paul

(Nos. 2079-2084)

Allen, John William. Hotman and the Réveille-matin. *In his:* A history of political thought in the sixteenth century. London, 1928. p. 305-12. **2079**

Brief analysis of *Franco-Gallia,* which is overrated as a document of influence, according to Allen.

Kocher, Paul H. François Hotman and Marlowe's The massacre at Paris. PMLA 56:349-68, June, 1941. **2080**

Establishes an English translation of H.'s *De furoribus Gallicis* as the main source for the first six scenes and part of the eighth scene of Marlowe's *The massacre at Paris.*

Lyons, J. Coriden. Conceptions of the republic in French literature of the sixteenth century : Etienne de La Boétie and François Hotman. *See* 1435. **2081**

Comparison of La Boétie's *De la servitude volontaire* and H.'s *Franco-Gallia* as anti-monarchical treatises. The former is classified as an idealistic, speculative work, while *Franco-Gallia* is a deliberately partisan Huguenot pamphlet.

Mesnard, Pierre. Hotman. *In his:* L'essor de la philosophie politique au XVI⁰ siècle. Boivin, 1936.   p. 327-36.   2082

Brief treatment of H. and *Franco-Gallia.*

Smith, David B. François Hotman. *See* 1985.   2083

Studies H.'s life and works together with their repercussions on political and religious struggles in 16th century France.

Wagner, Friederich. Franz Hotman und das fränkisch-germanische Staatsbewustsein in Frankreich. VW 7:8-16, 1939.   2084

With *Franco-Gallia* H. for first time brings Huguenot anti-monarchical feeling from realm of purely abstract out into the open one of real, human controversy.

CHAPTER XIII. TECHNICAL WRITERS

(Nos. 2085-2193)

DAVID C. CABEEN AND NANCY OSBORNE

Ambroise Paré

(Nos. 2085-2106)

NANCY OSBORNE

Doe, Janet. A bibliography of the works of Ambroise Paré. Chicago. University of Chicago Press, 1937. 266 p.　2085

Combination biography and bibliography, with full reference to sources. Complete index. Conscientious, scholarly study. "A beautiful illustration of careful workmanship," SL 29:125, Apr., 1938.

Reviews : P. Brooks in TBR, Sept. 18, 1938, p. 28; W. Rachlin in MT 66:270-71, May, 1938; LC. Wroth in HTB, Jan. 16, 1938, p. 13; Anon in NEJM 218:323, Feb. 17, 1938; in JAMA 110:1062, Mar. 26, 1938; in Lancet 1:1200, May 21, 1938.

Paré, Ambroise. Œuvres complètes. Ed. by J. F. Malgaigne. *See* 452, 2028.　2086

Most complete edition. Comprehensive, authoritative survey of surgery. Scholarly, sympathetic biobibliographical study of the great surgeon as the representative of an entire epoch. Critical, running commentary of his works, book by book, with source of his ideas traced, as well as their development. Excellent index.

Anello, Vicente J. Lo pediátrico en la obra de Ambrosio Paré. AAP 18¹:66-80, 1947.　2087

Scholarly and careful account of P.'s contribution to history of pediatrics.

Blaessinger, Edmond. Ambroise Paré. *In his :* Quelques grandes figures de la chirurgie et de la médecine militaires. Baillière 1947, p. 33-51.　2088

Good brief sketch of P.'s rise to fame, his experience in the army, his love of humanity. Bibliography.

Campos, Carlos Angel. Los conocimientos dietéticos en la obra de Ambrosio Paré. PCHM 10:67-84, 1946.　2089

Informative summary of references in works of P. to model diet of the healthy as well as of sick, with special emphasis on diet of sufferers from diabetes and gout. Carefully documented.

Chaussade, M. A. Ambroise Paré. BCHM 2nd ser. 43:290-316, 1927; 44:117-38, 1928.　2090

Brief, accurate account of P.'s life and contributions to surgery. Good picture of the state of surgery of P.'s period. Valuable for references to works on P. Full references to sources.

Delaunay, Paul. Ambroise Paré. BCHM 2nd ser. 44:309-31, 1928.　2091

Brief sketch of P.'s life and personality, with a good study of his medical and surgical works and an excellent, complete bibliography of works upon him.

Dellapiane, Luis. Los conocimientos anatómicos de Ambroise Paré. RAHM 3:25-35, 1944.　2092

Very general, brief account of P.'s knowledge of anatomy based on quotations from his works.

Ferron, M. Ambroise Paré et ses protecteurs. Pméd 74:407-11, Sept. 24, 1946.　2093

Brief description of the most powerful protectors of P., with an account of their influence on him. Excellent bibliography of contemporary sources.

Fitzwilliams, Duncan C. L. Ambroise Paré. MW 71:582-86, Dec. 23, 1949.　2094

Brief, pleasant account of P.'s rise to fame. No new data.

Fox, Ruth. Paré. *In her :* Great men of medicine. New York, Random House, 1947. p. 31-59.　2095

Popular presentation of notable events of P.'s life. Very general, no references.

219

Galliot, A. Ambroise Paré, syphiligraphe. Bméd 26:154-55, Feb. 10, 1946.   2096

Brief recognition of P.'s contribution to treatment of syphilis.

Maltz, Maxwell. Ambroise Paré. *In his:* Evolution of plastic surgery. New York, Froben, 1946. p. 174-85.   2097

Brief account of P.'s role in evolution of plastic surgery. Most of the chapter deals with his treatment of gunshot wounds and of sutures.

Mirabaud, Robert. Une grande âme, Ambroise Paré. Fischbacher, 1928.   130 p.   2098

Revealing study of personality of P., with special emphasis on sincere and intense nature of his Christianity. Number of quotations from his works to show his contributions to surgery.

Oliaro, T. L'influenza dei chirurghi italiani su Ambrogio Paré. MC 1:69-74, Apr., 1946.   2099

Scholarly, interesting account of influence of Italian surgery on P. Influence of Alessio Piemontese especially stressed.

Peel, John H. Milestones in midwifery. PGMJ 23:523-29, Nov., 1947.   2100

Interesting account of P.'s contributions to obstetric practice.

Pollitzer, R. M. Excursions into medical history; Ambroise Paré, renaissance surgeon. JSCMA 43:99-100, Apr., 1947.   2101

Very brief account of P.'s reply to an attack made on him by the Dean of Faculty of Medicine in Paris.

Prinz, Hermann. Paré. *In his:* Dental chronology; a record of the more important historic events in the evolution of dentistry. Philadelphia, Lee and Febiger, 1945.   p. 38, 168, 173.   2102

Brief references to P.'s contribution to dental history.

Ricci, James V. Paré. *In his:* One hundred years of gynaecology : 1800-1900. Philadelphia, Blakiston, 1945.   p. 222, 361, 387, 549.   2103

Brief references to P.'s contributions in history of gynecology.

Ruiz Moreno, Anibal. Las afecciones reumáticas en la obra de Ambrosio Paré. BLCR 7:7-29, Jan.-Mar., 1944.   2104

Interesting short sketch of P.'s treatment

of arthritis. Well documented, valuable for those interested in medical history.

Sigerist, Henry E. Ambroise Paré's onion treatment of burns. BHM 15:143-49, Feb., 1944.   2105

New significance given to P.'s experience with the action of onions on burns. Well documented treatise.

Stone, Mario M. Ambroise Paré, padre de la cirugia moderna. Mlat 7:161-63, 1948.   2106

Brief summary of P.'s contribution to field of surgery. Very general; no new data.

Other Technical Writers :

Belon, Dumoulin, Henri Estienne, Fauchet, Montchrétien, Nostredame, Palissy, Pasquier, O. de Serres

(Nos. 2107-2193)

DAVID C. CABEEN

Pierre Belon

(Nos. 2107-2113)

Delaunay, Paul. L'aventureuse existence de Pierre Belon du Mans. RSS 9:251-68, 1922; 10:1-34, 125-47, 1923; 11:30-48, 222-232, 1924; 12:78-97, 256-82, 1925. *Reprinted:* Champion, 1926.   177 p.   2107

Indispensable for a study of B.; detailed analysis of his life and works, with good bibliography, arranged chronologically. Author considers B., with Paré, as " ... parmi les créateurs de la prose scientifique française... " (RSS, v. 12, p. 266). *See* 367.

Gudger, E. W. Pierre Belon. *In his:* The five great naturalists of the sixteenth century : Belon, Rondelet, Salviani, Gesner and Aldrovandi; a chapter in the history of ichthyology. Isis 22:21-40, 1934-35. Belon, p. 26-28.   2108

Points out that B.'s first published work (1551) was on fishes, and was, in fact, first printed book on them with the name on title page. Describes B.'s claim to be called founder of ichthyology.

Hauréau, Barthélemy. Belon (Pierre). *In his:* Histoire littéraire du Maine. Le Mans, Lanier, 1843-52.   v. 3, p. 252-66.   2109

Good biography, with analysis of B.'s works; conclusions sometimes debatable. Closes with a defense of B. against charge of plagiarism.

Legré, Ludovic. La botanique en Provence au xvi⁰ siècle : Pierre Belon. MAM, 1901-1903, p. 85-114. *Reprinted:* Marseilles, Aubertin and Rolle, 1901. 2110

Ascribes high value to B. as a naturalist. Bulk of study devoted to listing trees and bushes of Provence which could be acclimated in the forests of France.

Potez, Henri. Belon. *In his:* Deux années de la renaissance d'après une correspondance inédite. RHL 13:658-92, 1906. 2111

Prints a long letter from Denys Lambin (p. 687-90) which criticizes B. for not knowing Latin. Potez defends B., and observes that he inaugurated a rigorous and exact method of scientific observation (p. 691).

Sainéan, Lazar. L'histoire naturelle dans l'œuvre de Rabelais. *See* 326. 2112

Scholarly work, with many scattered citations from B.'s books. Shows that B. not only liked to read Rabelais, but even took latter's list of names of fish as a point of departure for his own studies on ocean fish (RSS, v. 5, p. 34-36). *See* 895.

Vaganay, Hugues. Notes sur la langue du xvi⁰ siècle : Pierre Belon (1518-1564) et le vocabulaire français actuel. RPF 43:173-206, 1931. 2113

Adds about 100 words to the 30 which *Dictionnaire général* (Adolphe Hatzfeld and Arsène Darmesteter, *Dictionnaire général de la langue française*, etc. 8th ed., Delagrave, 1926, 2 v.) cites as being used by B. B.'s use of these words is shown by sentences taken from *Observations* and *Nature des oyseaux.*

Charles Dumoulin
(Nos. 2114-2118)

Aubepin, F. A. H. De l'influence de Doumoulin sur la législation française. RCLJ 3:603-25, 778-806, 1853; 4:27-44, 261-300, 1854; 5:32-62, 305-32, 1854. 2114

" Dumoulin, comme légiste, avait en présence deux ennemis, la féodalité et l'église " (v. 3, p. 608). Sound study of this and related problems.

— Doctrine de Doumoulin sur les promesses de vente, etc. *In his:* Origines et progrès en France du droit coutumier, féodal et privé, sur la nature des ventes, échanges et promesses de vente, jusqu'au temps de Pothier. RCLJ 14:412-23, 1859. 2115

Excellent summary, by a specialist, of D.'s comments on these subjects.

Brodeau, Julien. La vie de maistre Charles Du Moulin. Guignard, 1654. 214 p. 2116

Frequently quoted study; most detailed biography of D. available, with a considerable amount of useful material on his works.

Haag, Eugène. Charles Dumoulin. *In his:* La France protestante, by Eugène and Emile Haag. Cherbuliez, 1846-49. 10 v. v. 4 (1853), p. 411-19. 2117

Excellent biography; factual, but by no means impersonal. Extensive bibliography, with careful analytical annotations of more important items.

Le Goff, Marcel. Du Moulin et le prêt à intérêt; le légiste, son influence. Bordeaux, Cadoret, 1905. 250 p. (Diss., law, Poitiers.) 2118

Careful, detailed study of this specialized subject, important both in canon and civil law of the century, a century in which the problem was cleared of many of the previous misconceptions upon it. Le Goff considers D. most influential writer of his time on the matter : " Il aura traité le sujet avec l'audace d'un protestant, corrigé par la circonspection d'un légiste " (p. 245).

Henri Estienne
(Nos. 2119-2121)

Estienne, Henri. La précellence de la langue française. Ed. by Edmond Huguet. *See* 562. 2119

A 26-page *Préface* by Petit de Julleville gives an excellent brief summary of E.'s work. Useful edition, with 27 pages of *Observations grammaticales* and a 46-page *Lexique-Index.*

Brunetière, Ferdinand. Henri Estienne. *In his:* Trois artisans de l'idéal classique au xvi⁰ siècle : Henri Estienne, Jacques Amyot, Jean Bodin. RDM 5th per. 38:7-18, Mar. 1, 1907. 2120

The critic believes that if it were not for E.'s *Apologie pour Hérodote* " ... on aurait le droit de ne voir en lui qu'un érudit... " (p. 7-8). But Brunetière does not regard this work highly, and considers it " banal " and " vulgaire " (p. 9).

Clément, Louis. Henri Estienne et son œuvre française. *See* 575. 2121

Indispensable study; careful, analytical bibliography; index of words, etc., used by E. Places its greatest emphasis upon E.

as a grammarian. Gives a somewhat exaggerated estimate of importance of E. in his century. *See* 969, 1971.
Reviews : M. J. Minckwitz in ZFSL 22:155-69, 1900; E. Roy in RHL 7:144-48, 1900; A. Tobler in Archiv (54th year) v. 104:238-40, 1900.

Claude Fauchet
(Nos. 2122-2131)

Fauchet, Claude. Recueil de l'origine de la langue et poésie françoise, rymes et romans. Livre Iᵉʳ. Ed. by Janet G. Espiner-Scott. Droz, 1938. 150 p. (Thèse complémentaire, Paris.)   2122
Indispensable. Editor took as her text the first edition (1581); she notes the variants in the three later ones. Full bibliography; notes give intellectual background, Italian influence, F.'s own marginal notes, list of quotations, index of names and places.
Review : R. Marichal in Hren 6:103-04, 1939.

Bisson, S. W. Claude Fauchet's manuscripts. MLR 30:311-23, 1935.   2123
Lists some 59 manuscripts which were certainly known to F. which he owned or borrowed, and a number of others which Bisson believes he may have known from hearsay. Bisson considers F. as France's first literary historian in point of time.

Espiner, Mrs. Janet Girvan (Scott). Claude Fauchet, sa vie, son œuvre. Droz, 1938. 450 p. (Diss., Paris, Docteur-ès-lettres.)   2124
Indispensable work, of a broad and exact scholarship, with a well-documented biography of F. and excellent treatment of him as a literary historian and translator. Has an appendix on etymologies, an alphabetical index and a fairly complete bibliography. She hails F. as " ... un des plus grands médiévistes... " (p. ix).
Reviews : R. Marichal in Hren 6:104-110, 1939; W. G. Moore in MLR 36:413-414, 1941; W. F. Patterson in RR 31:74-75, 1940.

— Claude Fauchet et Etienne Pasquier. Hren 6:352-60, 1939.   2125
Notes parallelism in careers and subject-matter of the two writers. Differences between them are marked : Pasquier was more creative and more interested in the life of the time, F. the more scholarly.

F.'s learning impressed several of his contemporaries, who seem not to have known of Pasquier.

— Claude Fauchet et l'Italie. Hren 6:546-555, 1939.   2126
F., though he belonged to the third generation of his family who had traveled in Italy, showed slight signs of Italian influence. Study concludes that this was due to his " ... personalité trop fortement trempée et un esprit trop critique... " (p. 555). The subject deserves further examination.

— Claude Fauchet and Romance study. MLR 35:173-84, 1940.   2127
Discussion of role played by conversation between groups of young renaissance scholars, poets and men of law in F.'s *Recueil*. Supplements her critical edition of Book I of F.'s *Recueil*. Perhaps best section of article is last (4th) in which she shows how many of F.'s ideas agree with best findings of modern scholarship.

— Correspondence. MLR 37:236, 1942.   2128
A letter to the Editor giving data about her main thesis (*see* 2124), and the subsidiary one (*see* 2129). The very moderate prices of these books were set by publisher without reference to cost of printing, but with reference to what *érudits* " ... were likely to pay without difficulty.... "

— Documents concernant la vie et les œuvres de Claude Fauchet. Droz, 1938. 291 p. (Thèse complémentaire.)   2129
Important study. F.'s scholarship was the most like that of the present day of any man of his century, though he underestimated the value of literature of Middle Ages. The study lists more than 150 documents of F.'s extensive library.
Review : R. Marichal in Hren 6:104-10, 1939.

Holmes, Urban T. and Maurice L. Radoff. Claude Fauchet and his library. PMLA 44:229-42, Mar., 1929.   2130
Agrees with Gröber that F. founded study of mediaeval French literature. This study attempts a list of manuscripts owned or borrowed by F. Believes that F. " ... exercised little discrimination in his use of mediaeval materials...." (p. 242).

Langlois, Ernest. Quelques dissertations inédites de Claude Fauchet. EtGP, p. 97-112.   2131

Publication of five dissertations of F. which are of interest for light they throw on his character and biography. They show him as a " ... vieillard aimable, instruit, pas du tout pédant... " (p. 97).

Antoine de Montchrétien
(Nos. 2132-2141)

Montchrétien, Antoine de. Traicté de l'œconomie politique, avec introduction et notes. Ed. by Th. Funck-Brentano. Plon, 1889. 398 p. 2132

Indispensable edition. Editor is rather partisan at times; text has been cut some. Introduction of 117 p. needs checking in places. Adequate bibliography, excellent analytical index.

Cf. : W. J. Ashley in EHR 6:779-81, 1891; H. Baudrillart : *Gentilhommes ruraux de la France*, Didot, n.d., 149-60; J. Bodin : *La vie chère au XVe siècle*, Colin, 1932, p. LXXIV-V; G. H. Bousquet : *Essai sur l'évolution de la pensée économique*, Giard, 1927, p. 11-12; A. Shadwell, QR 245:347-348, 351-52, 1925.

Calkins, Gladys Ethel. Antoine de Montchrestien. Les lacènes; a critical edition. Philadelphia, 1943. 162 p. (PPRL, Ext. ser. No. 8.) (Diss., Pennsylvania.) 2133

Study shows that M. took subject of *Les lacènes* from Plutarch's *Life of Agis and Cleomenes* and has " ... followed closely the expression of Amyot's translation " (p. 57). A careful, painstaking piece of editing.

Cole, Charles W. The system of Montchrétien. *In his :* French mercantilist doctrines before Colbert. *See* 376, p. 113-161. 2134

Considers M.'s ideas on economics excellent for his time, and inspired by an eagerness to see France rich and prosperous.

Reviews : J. U. Nef in JPE 41:270-71, 1933; H. Reynard in EJ 42:115-16, 1932.

Duval, Jules. Mémoire sur Antoine de Montchrétien, *sieur* de Vateville. Guillaumin, 1868. 197 p. 2135

Believes that M., while merely an intelligent interpreter of his time as a writer, was one of the greatest economists of the period, in any country.

Haag, Eugène and Émile. Antoine de Montchrestien. *In their :* La France protestante. (1852) v. 7 (1857), p. 462-468. 2136

Brief but adequate biography. Good analysis of *Traicté*, with brief mention of M.'s other work.

Harsin, Paul. Montchrétien. *In his :* Les doctrines monétaires et financières en France du XVIe au XVIIIe siècle. Alcan, 1928. p. 75-77. 2137

Credits M. with creation of expression *économie politique* (p. 75-76). Considers him to have been, for most part, an imitator of Bodin.

Joly, Aristide. Antoine de Montchrétien, poète et économiste normand. MAC, 1865, p. 328-446. *Reprinted :* Caen, Le Gost-Clérisse, 1865. 135 p. 2138

Bulk of study devoted to a discussion of M.'s tragedies, works of his youth, in which " ... on voit naïvement exprimées les faiblesses et les insuffisances de la tragédie française... " (p. 329). M.'s mature work, *Traité*, receives careful and respectful analysis.

Lanson, Gustave. La littérature française sous Henri IV : Antoine de Montchrétien. RDM 3rd per. 107:369-87, Sept. 15, 1891. *Reprinted in his :* Hommes et livres, Lecène, Oudin, 1895. p. 57-86. 2139

Outstanding contribution; best brief study available for an understanding of M. and his work, with high praise for both.

Shadwell, A. The father of political economy. QR 245:346-60, Oct., 1925. 2140

Brief but adequate biography of M., based largely on work of Funck-Brentano in his 1889 edition of *Traicté* (*see* 2132), with summary and analysis of M.'s main ideas. Useful work.

Vène, André. Montchrétien et le nationalisme économique. Recueil Sirey, 1923. 110 p. 2141

Stresses careful study made by M. of England's commercial policies. Comparison of his conceptions with those of Adam Smith. Praises highly soundness of M.'s economic views, even by modern standards, and his enlightened patriotism.

Jehan de Nostredame
(Nos. 2142-2149)

Nostredame, Jehan de. Les vies des plus célèbres et anciens poètes provençaux. Nouvelle édition préparée par Camille Chabaneau et Joseph Anglade. Champion, 1913. 2 v. in 1, 176 and 407 p. 2142

When Chabaneau died in 1908 he had been working for twenty years on a re-edition of N.'s book; Anglade, using his predecessor's notes, completed a scholarly 160-page introduction. This is a definitive edition with numerous footnotes which, however, Mario Roques (*infra*, p. 315) believes should have indicated more fully " ... les sources où Nostredame a puisé les éléments de ses audacieuses inventions." Reviews : E. Langlois in BEC 75:115-116, 1914; M. J. Minckwitz in LGRP 36:94-97, 1915; M(ario) R(oques) in Rom 43:314-15, 1914; O. Schultz-Gora in ZFSL 43:141-47, 1915; G. M. Wenderoth in RFor 19:54-56, 1905-06 (of the edition of 1575).

Anglade, Joseph. Nostradamica; encore Le moine des Isles d'Or. Rom 41:321-30, 1912. 2143
Essential for study of N.'s *Vies*. Lists Provençal poets given by Soliers and quoted by Chabaneau. *See* 2146.

Aruch, Aldo. Le Biografie provenzali di Jehan de Nostredame e la loro prima traduzione italiana. SM 4:193-212, 1913. 2144
Studies of Alberto Malaspine, Cibo, Jules Raymond Soliers and their relationship with *Vies*. Well documented with bibliographical and literary notes.

Bartsch, Karl. Die Quellen von Jehan de Nostredame. JREL 13:1-65, 121-49, 1874. 2145
Studies sources of N.'s *Vies*, shows what of his narration is true and what is invented. This study is criticized by Meyer (*infra*) for ignoring some 15 of the *Vies*. Review : P. Meyer in Rom 2:142, 1873.

Chabaneau, Camille. Le moine des Isles d'or. AM 19:364-72, 1907. *Reprinted :* Toulouse, Privat, 1907. 13 p. 2146
Chabaneau considers *Moine* to be an invention of N. " Le Monge des Isles d'Or, en tant qu'historien des troubadours, n'est donc ... que Nostredame lui-même, dissimulant sa personnalité sous le nom et sous l'anagramme du nom de deux de ses amis, Cibo et Soliers " (p. 371).

Crescini, Vicenzo. Un autografo di Jehan de Nostredame. RMP 10:49-56, 1907. *Reprinted*, Padua, Società cooperativa tipografia, 1907. 16 p. 2147
Description and reprinting of N.'s letter to Cibo dated at Aix, January 25, 1510. Important letter, with explanatory and bibliographical notes.

Meyer, Paul. Les derniers troubadours de la Provence. BEC 30:245-69, 461-531, 649-87, 1869; 31:412-62, 1870. 2148
Discussions of the troubadours are valuable in themselves; relevant to this section as showing how unreliable is much of information in N.'s *Vies*. Meyer believes that, to names of the troubadours and to other information conveyed by manuscripts which he saw, N. " ... a ajouté toutes les inventions qui lui ont paru propres à glorifier son pays " (v. 30, p. 258).

Varenne, Marc. Jehan de Nostredame et les troubadours. Rren 14:150-56, 1913. 2149
Study of *Vies*, including influences, inaccuracies, sources and other points as suggested by Chabaneau-Anglade edition. " Le procédé de fabrication de Nostredame apparaît dans sa magnifique impudence lorsqu'il s'agit de parler des troubadours. Alors, rien ne l'arrête " (p. 152-153).

Bernard Palissy

(Nos. 2150-2171)

Palissy, Bernard. Œuvres de Bernard Palissy, revues sur les exemplaires de la Bibliothèque du Roi, avec des notes par MM. Faujas de Saint-Fond et Gobet. Ruault, 1777. 734 p. 2150
First complete edition; contains much detailed information, now, naturally, outdated on many points.

— Œuvres complètes ... avec des notes et une notice historique par Paul-Antoine Cap. Dubochet, 1844. 437 p. 2151
Notice historique has 35 pages; only occasionally cited, but still worth reading. No footnotes or other scholarly material; meager name and subject index.

— Les œuvres ... nouvelle édition revue sur les textes originaux par B. Fillon. Notice historique, bibliographique et iconographique par Louis Audiat. Niort, Clouzot, 1888. 2 v. 2152
Most widely available edition; critical bibliography and useful list of words calling for a definition or explanation.

— Monographie de l'œuvre de Bernard Palissy, suivie d'un choix de ses continuateurs ou imitateurs, dessinée par MM. Carle Delange et C. Borneman, et accompagnée d'un texte par M. Sauzay et de M. Henri Delange. Martinet, 1862. 10-38 p. 215:

Has 14 pages on P.'s life and 12 on his work, followed by 100 remarkable colored plates which present an admirable picture of his genius. Object of volume is to emphasize artistic rather than industrial influence of P.'s work in field of ceramics.

Allbutt, Sir Thomas C. Palissy, Bacon and the revival of natural science. PBA 6:233-247, 1913-14. 2154

Contains many interesting comments, among them : that P.'s numerous books have few ideas on pottery because : " ... the artist may ... have deliberately chosen to keep his trade secrets to himself " (p. 236). Ascribes considerable influence to P.'s lectures in Paris on scientific subjects. Devotes last three pages to intellectual relationship between P. and Francis Bacon; latter was in Paris from 1576-79 and must have heard P.'s " notorious lectures " (p. 245).

Aubigné, Théodore Agrippa d'. Bernard Palissy. *In his :* Histoire universelle. Laurens, 1886-1909, v. 8, p. 151-52. (SHF, v. 275.) 2155

Interview between P. and Henri III, giving brave and noble reply of former to the King. Important incident, often quoted.

Audiat, Louis. Bernard Palissy : étude sur sa vie et ses travaux. *See* 2024. 2156

Detailed, careful, colorfully written biography of P., which examines all phases of his work. Author considers him " ... le père de la géologie et des sciences naturelles " (p. v).

Borlé, Edouard Th. Observations sur l'emploi des conjonctions de subordination dans la langue du XVIe siècle, étudié spécialement dans les deux ouvrages de Bernard Palissy. *See* 590. 2157

Useful in a limited way as reference book. Tables of conjunctions, well classified and arranged. Shows extent to which P. was ahead of his times in his style and especially in his use of certain conjunctions.

Brogniart, Alexandre. Bernard Palissy. *In his :* Traité des arts céramiques ou des poteries. Bechet, 1844. v. 2, p. 61-69. 2158

Author, director of the Sèvres porcelain factory, has the highest regard for P. as a man. Criticizes P.'s only work on pottery and enamel ware because it imparts nothing of value. Believes that P.'s work

is remarkably individualized, with no real painting, but " ... reliefs coloriés " (p. 65).

Burty, Philippe. Bernard Palissy. Rouam, 1886. 56 p. 2159

Begins with comment on the " resurrection " of P. by 18th century : he was read by Fontenelle, Jussieu, Buffon, and by German scientists. Superseded for factual information; is still of interest for several of its opinions.

Dupuy, Ernest. Bernard Palissy, l'homme, l'artiste, le savant, l'écrivain. New edition. Société française d'imprimerie et de librairie, 1902, 342 p. 2160

Indispensable, and best-known biography, with much material not generally presented. Vocabulary of words used by P. which require an explanation; brief bibliography. Conveniently divided into four parts to conform to the sub-title.

Fillon, Benjamin. Palissy. *In his :* L'art de terre chez les Poitevins. Niort, Clouzot, 1864. p. 114-28. 2161

Scattered references to P. under other headings; one chapter is specifically devoted to him and another to *Elèves et continuateurs de Palissy* (p. 129-44). Refuses to grant to P. originality of inspiration; thinks that " Son rôle consista donc à exploiter, d'une façon originale, l'idée d'autrui " (p. 123).

Haag, Eugène and Emile. Bernard Palissy. *In their :* La France protestante. (1852) v. 8 (1858), p. 69-97. 2162

Highly eulogistic article, well-known, but with several debatable statements. Describes P.'s work in ceramics; gives some analysis of his literary work and indicates his place as a forerunner in field of sciences. Account of his persecution and tragic death.

Lamartine, Alphonse Marie Louis de. Bernard de Palissy. *In his :* Vies des grands hommes. Aux bureaux du Constitutionnel, 1853-56. v. 2, p. 393-443. 2163

Describes P.'s writings in prisons as : " ... véritables trésors de sagesse humaine, de piété divine, de génie éminent, de naïveté, de force et de couleur de style " (p. 338). Here, as elsewhere, Lamartine shows himself as a more capable critic of spiritual and aesthetic values than of intellectual ones.

Leroux, Désiré. La vie de Bernard Palissy. Champion, 1927. 128 p. 2164

Readable book, though it adds little to our knowledge of P. Good study of its subject in his many-sided role as an artist and as a scientist.

Review : C. Beaulieux in RSS 17:167-69, 1930.

L'Estoile, Pierre de. Bernard Palissy. *In :* Registre journal de Pierre de l'Estoile (1574-1589); notice et extraits inédits d'un nouveau manuscrit conservé à la Bibliothèque nationale, publiés par H. Omont. MSHP 27:1-38, 1900. *See* 2220.   2165

Describes well-known interview between Captain Bussy-Leclerc and P. in which latter, though threatened with burning at stake, refused to recant. *Also in :* N. Weiss, BSHP 50:545-48, 1901; E. Dupuy (2160), p. 65-67. *See also :* E. Chevreul, JS 1849, p. 730.

Montaiglon, A. de. Bernard Palissy : payement de la grotte de terre émaillée des Tuileries, etc. AAF 9:14-29, 1857-58.   2166

Montaiglon defines *grotte* as used in 16th century; describes the drawing which he believes to have been the " grotte de terre émaillée " mentioned in the two documents which are printed in the article.

Morley, Henry. Palissy the potter; the life of Bernard Palissy of Saintes. Petter and Gapin, 1878. 320 p.   2167

First published in 1852. Methodical, scholarly work, divided into periods, thus : *Early years and background; The field of labour; The potter; The reformer; The naturalist.* Useful name and subject index. Lively, personalized biography, with a study of P.'s work which, however, should be checked against other sources.

Patry, H. Un mandat d'arrêt du Parlement de Guyenne contre Bernard Palissy et les premiers fidèles des églises de Saintes et de Saint Jean d'Angely. BSHP 51:74-81, 1902.   2168

Stresses important role played by P. in establishment of the church at Saintes; article is especially interesting because P. himself does not mention the *arrêt*.

Read, Charles. Bernard Palissy considéré comme évangéliste ou prédicateur de la réforme et comme écrivain. BSHP 1:23-34, 83-94, 1853.   2169

Believes that P. had " la foi active et vivante " and was " un poëte du premier ordre." Thinks that good judges have sometimes rated his style and his diction " au-dessus de ceux de Montaigne "

(p. 24). Study is of interest chiefly as showing a revival of awareness of P. in 19th century.

Weiss, N. Bernard Palissy devant le Parlement de Paris; arrêt inédit du 12 janvier 1587. BSHP 52:31-40, 1903.   2170

Document containing P.'s first condemnation, with useful critical material.

— L'origine et les derniers jours de Bernard Palissy, d'après deux textes inédits. BSHP 61:389-407, 1912.   2171

Valuable article giving photographs of *registre d'écrou* of Conciergerie which Weiss found and which contains the condemnations of P., in the first of which he is listed as a " natif d'Agen." Useful material on P.'s biography.

Etienne Pasquier

(Nos. 2172-2184)

Pasquier, Etienne. Œuvres choisies d'Étienne Pasquier, accompagnées de notes et d'une étude sur sa vie et sur ses ouvrages par Léon Feugère. Didot, 1849. 2 v.   2172

An essential edition; editor's work contains much critical and bibliographical material of high value.

Review : C. A. Sainte-Beuve *in his : Causeries du lundi,* v. 3 : 249-50 : " ... un travail biographique, littéraire et même grammatical très soigné...."

— L'interprétation des Institutes de Justinien avec une introduction et des notes de Ch. Giraud. Videcoq, 1847. 809 p.   2173

A *Notice* of 108 p. precedes text; no bibliography, but numerous footnotes furnish indispensable references.

Review : C. A. Sainte-Beuve *in his : Causeries du lundi,* 3rd ed., v. 3:249 : " Un très beau travail biographique et historique."

Baudrillart, Henri. Estienne Pasquier, écrivain politique. AMP 65 (4th ser. 15) : 449-86, 1863.   2174

Well-reasoned article on royal power, Parlement, Church and State as observed by an able public servant of 16th century. Has high praise for P. based on *Pourparler du prince, Pourparler de la loi, Recherches de la France* and *Lettres.* Defines P.'s ideal : " Un pouvoir monarchique se tempérant lui-même par une assemblée purement consultative... " (p. 483).

Bouteiller, P. Un historien du XVIe siècle : Etienne Pasquier. BHren 6:357-92, 1945.
2175

Careful enumeration and analysis of many and varied sources P. consulted for his *Recherches de la France*. Author believes that P.'s principal value and originality to have been that he was "... un des premiers à comprendre que l'organisation intérieure d'un pays était un sujet aussi digne de l'histoire que les grands événements politiques et militaires " (p. 384).

Chamberland, Albert. Estienne Pasquier et l'intolérance religieuse au XVIe siècle. RHM 1:38-49, 1899. 2176

Questions theory of Feugère that P. favored tolerance for Protestants but believes, rather, that P. would have liked to accord them an absolute minimum of concessions. Carefully documented study of a highly controversial matter.

Glaser, Kurt. Note sur le texte de La congratulation de la paix d'Estienne Pasquier. Rren 8:136-40, 1907. 2177

The *Congratulation* was addressed to Charles IX on occasion of *Edit de pacification* addressed by the King to his subjects. Variants in the above text between 1570 edition and *édition classique* of Amsterdam, 1723, are given. Introductory remarks; no commentary.

Glaser, Th. Deux discours manuscrits d'Estienne Pasquier. Rren 8:1-28, 1907.
2178

The *discours* were delivered on June 25, 1586 and Sept. 30, 1587 at *Chambre des comptes de Paris*. Glaser gives circumstances under which *discours* were pronounced; the first, addressed to the King, Henri III, throws an interesting light on P.'s character, since he had the courage to point out unsoundness of royal policies on finance. Article repays reading.

Moore, Margaret J. Estienne Pasquier, historien de la poésie et de la langue française. Poitiers, Société française d'imprimerie et de librairie, 1934. 158 p. (Diss., Poitiers.)
2179

Careful work, showing P. as a forerunner of the modern French literary historian and philologian, based on a detailed study of Books VII and VIII of *Recherches*. Subject matter rather too narrowly selected, and other sources are not enough utilized. Selective bibliography; no proper-name index.

Review : J. G. Espiner-Scott in Hren 6:354 (n. 1), 1939.

Nolhac, Pierre de. Un ami de Ronsard : Etienne Pasquier. Rheb 32:435-45, July, 1923. 2180

Analysis of *Recherches de la France* and of *Lettres* brings out P.'s love of French letters and his pride in their great history. Points out P.'s admiration for Ronsard. Able and intelligent evocation of P. against background of his century.

Sainte-Beuve, Charles Augustin. Etienne Pasquier. *In his:* Causeries du lundi, 3rd ed., Garnier, 1852. v. 3, p. 249-269. 2181

P. is presented as a typical *avocat* and magistrate of 16th century. Penetrating analysis of his character, literary opinions and political theories. " ... Pasquier suit ce grand chemin de raison qui ne donne dans aucun extrême " (p. 268).

Solve, Mrs. Norma Dobie. Chapman's play and its French source. *In her:* Stuart politics in Chapman's Tragedy of Chabot. Ann Arbor, University of Michigan, 1928. p. 63-83. (MPLL IV) (Diss., Michigan.)
2182

Examines *Tragedy of Chabot* in relation to the 9th chapter, book 16 of P.'s *Recherches de la France*. Concludes that the " body " of Chapman's play was drawn from French history, but that its " soul " comes from the State trials of England of the time.

Reviews : W. N. in AHR 35:160, Oct., 1929 ; T. M. Parrott in JEGP 29:300-04, 1930.

Voigt, Kurt. Estienne Pasquier's Stellung zur Pleiade. Leipzig, Pöschel, 1902. 50 p. (Diss., Leipzig.) 2183

Believes that P. was at first an enthusiastic admirer of Pléiade, but that he later became critical of it. A study of uneven value, but of considerable merit. Brief bibliography.

Reviews : K. Glaser in ZFSL 29:23-25, 1906; G. H. Wenderoth in RFor 19:75, n. 1, 1905-06.

Wenderoth, Georg Hermann. Estienne Pasquiers poetische Theorien und seine Tätigkeit als Literarhistoriker. Marburg, Junge, 1903. 38 p. (Diss., Marburg.) Enlarged, RFor 19:1-75, 1905-06. 2184

Careful study and analysis of the subject matter in *Recherches*, well worth examination. Literary criticism is not as good as research method. No bibliography or proper-name index. Review : K. Glaser in ZFSL 29:23-25, 1906.

Olivier de Serres
(Nos. 2185-2193)

Baudrillart, Henri. Olivier de Serres; son rôle dans les guerres de religion. RDM 3rd per. 101:889-907, Oct. 15, 1890.   2185

Examines the controversies on subject of S.'s participation in these wars, as found in works of Vaschalde (*see* 2193), Chenivesse (*see* 2188), Mollier and Vidal. Has high praise for S. as a man, a scientist and a literary artist. *See* 2033.

Review : N. W(eiss) in BSHP 39:614-16, 1890.

Bonnaud, Paul. Un agronome français au XVIᵉ siècle. JE 6th ser. 8:161-77, 1905.
2186

Interesting study; discusses ideas of S. in his *Theatre d'agriculture* (no. 339) on main products of his region from a scientific standpoint. Shows also how sound his ideas were on subject of human relations and conduct in farm life.

Bost, Charles. Notes sur Olivier de Serres. BSHP 88:27-44, 134-58, 287-311, 1939.
2187

Soundly documented biography; useful as such. Interesting, also, as giving a picture of troubled times of the wars of religion and persecution of Protestants.

Chenivesse, Jean Baptiste. Olivier de Serres et les massacres du 2 mars 1573 à Villeneuve-de-Berg. BDV 9:143-54, 169-186, 1888-89. *Reprinted*, Valence, Céas, 1889, 29 p.   2188

Important study of this controversial question; undertakes to refute Vaschalde's defense of S. (*see* 2193). Concludes that S. instigated the siege and the massacres, even if he did not kill anyone himself.

Esil, Claude. Le quatrième centenaire d'Olivier de Serres, père de l'agriculture française. RFrance 19:22-33, July 1, 1939.
2189

Tells how Arthur Young, in 1789, made a pilgrimage to Pradel and saluted memory of S. as " Père de l'agriculture française." Pleasantly written, competent summary, for general reader, of value and place of S., not only in agriculture, but as a writer. Believes that " Pour qui aime la vie rustique, la lecture du *Theatre d'agriculture* vaut le plus passionnant des romans " (p. 32).

Haag, Emile and Eugène. Serres ou Serre, branche du Pradel. In their : La France protestante (1852). v. 9 (1859), p. 253-263.   2190

Still of interest and value, though superseded in many respects. Good account of S.'s work and influence, with annotated list of his works.

Lavondès, A. Olivier de Serres, *seigneur du Pradel*. *See* 2035.   2191

Interesting description of Vivarais, the *pays* of S., with a well documented study of his life and of his activities as a farmer, both practical and theoretical. Good bibliography. Work of uneven merit, but well deserving of study.

Reviews : E. D. in Hren 5:193-94, 1938; A. Jundt in BSHP 86:74-75, 1937.

Scheifley, William H. The father of French agriculture. SR 29:467-71, 1921.
2192

Best brief summary of life of S., and of his contribution to French agriculture. Affirms that " many a breeder of our time would do well to read his discussion of the care of horses, cattle, sheep, hogs and poultry..." (p. 469).

Vaschalde, Henry. Olivier de Serres, *seigneur du Pradel, sa vie et ses travaux, documents inédits. *See* 2036.   2193

First serious, scholarly study made of S. Later works have supplemented this book, but not made it out of date. Biography is incomplete, but book is particularly valuable for its study of S. as an agriculturalist.

Review : N. W(eiss) in BSHP 36:671-73, 1887.

CHAPTER XIV. HISTORIOGRAPHERS AND WRITERS OF MEMOIRS
(Nos. 2194-2255)

OLIVER TOWLES

General

Bates, Blanchard Wesley. Literary portraiture in the historical narrative of the French renaissance. New York, Stechert, 1945. 168 p. (Diss., Princeton.)　2194

A very brief history of the portrait in the work of historians and memoir writers with special reference to Paolo Emilio, Matthieu, de Thou, d'Aubigné and Masson. Attention is focused on Brantôme, " the social columnist " (p. 45-72), Montaigne (p. 73-98) and travel literature (p. 99-119).

Reviews : F. Acomb in JMH 19:355, 1947; H. Baron in AHR 52:499-501, 1946-1947; D. M. Frame in RR 37:276-79, 1946; H. W. Lawton in MLR 42:143, 1947.

Bourrilly, V. L., ed. Le journal d'un bourgeois de Paris sous le règne de François Ier (1515-36). Picard, 1910. 480 p. (CTEH, n. 43.)　2195

A text that has been welcomed because of exactitude of reproduction of the sole manuscript and excellent arrangement of notes and commentary.

Reviews : H. Hauser in Rhist 105:373, 1910; L. G. Pélissier in RQH 91:621-22, 1912; J. Plattard in RER 8:222-24, 1910.

Buchon, Jean Alexandre. Choix de chroniques et mémoires sur l'histoire de France. Desrez, 1836. 818 p.　2196

Referred to in this section as " Buchon."

Michaud, Joseph François. Nouvelle collection des mémoires pour servir à l'histoire de France, by J. F. Michaud and Jean Joseph Poujoulat. Lyons, Guyot, 1851. 32 v. 1st and 2nd series.　2197

Referred to in this section as " Michaud."

Radouant, René. L'éloquence militaire au XVIe siècle. RHL 18:503-52, 1911.　2198

Influence of this stylistic trait in works of Du Bellay, Montluc, Tavannes, La

Popelinière, Cayet, Belleforest, Brantôme, etc. Examples of its survival in 17th century.

Thierry, Augustin. Notes sur quatorze historiens antérieurs à Mézerai. *In his:* Dix ans d'études historiques. v. 6 of Œuvres complètes d'Augustin Thierry, Furne, 1846. p. 298-354.　2199

Includes a brief discussion of following : Paul-Emile, p. 304-09; Girard du Haillan, p. 311-19; Papyre Masson, p. 319-22; Du Tillet, p. 327-30; Pasquier, p. 330-39; Belleforest, p. 339-43; Jean de Serres, p. 343-45.

Thompson, James Westfall. A history of historical writing. New York, Macmillan, 1942. 2 v. *See* 2245.　2200

Referred to in this section as " Thompson."

Jean Bouchet
(Nos. 2201-2202)

Bouchet, Jean. Les Annales Dacquitaine. Faictz & Gestes en sommaire des Roys de France & Dangleterre & pays de Naples & de Milan. Poitiers, Bouchet, 1535. 221 p.　2201

Many editions in 16th century. An edition at Poitiers appeared : Mounin, 1644, 666 p.

Hamon, Auguste. Un grand rhétoriqueur poitevin : Jean Bouchet, 1476-1577? Oudin, 1901. 430 p. (Diss., Paris.)　2202

P. 170-207 are devoted to B. as an annaliste, and particularly to his most important historical work, Les annales d'Aquitaine. B. merits praise for his energy in utilizing previous historical work, documents and local traditions. His trustworthiness is diminished by strong patriotism and favoritism for local families.

229

Pierre de Bourdeille,
seigneur **de Brantôme**

(Nos. 2203-2208)

Brantôme, Pierre de Bourdeille, *seigneur* **de.** Recueil des dames, publ. par Roger Gaucheron. Payot, n.d. (1926).   2203

A number of *Vies des dames* (*see: Vie des dames galantes*, Garnier, 1841. 390 p.), and unedited *contes* based on mss in the gift of Baroness de Rothschild to BN.

Review : J. Plattard in RSS 13:298-99, 1926.

Crucy, François, Brantôme. Rieder, 1934. 113 p.   2204

For general public. Without notes or references. Profusely illustrated.

Reviews : H. Hauser in Rhist 175:605, May-June, 1935; P. Jourda in Rcr 68:326, 1934.

Lalanne, Ludovic. Brantôme, sa vie et ses écrits. Renouard, 1896. 384 p. (SHF, no. 284.)   2205

A reputed autobiography of B. was lost in the 18th century. One must depend largely for details of his life upon passing references that B. has scattered through his writings. Lalanne emphasizes importance of B.'s extensive travels, and by abundant and judicious quotations brings out many interesting facts about B.'s life and character.

Review : P. Bonnefon in RHL 4:141-42, 1897.

Loss, H. Brantôme, prosateur et poète. RSS 19:159-92, 1933.   2206

Title is misleading. By parallel passages, Loss shows frequent borrowings from *Floresta española, de apotegmas, ó sentencias* by Melchior de Santa Cruz de Dueñas, Toledo, 1574.

Omont, Henri. Notice sur les manuscrits originaux et autographes des œuvres de Brantôme conservés à la Bibliothèque nationale. BEC 65:5-54, 687-88, 1904. *Reprinted:* Nogent-le-Rotrou, Danpeley-Gouverneur, 1904. 54 p.   2207

Material not used by Lalanne in his edition for the SHF.

Pingaud, Léonce. Brantôme historien. RQH 10 (37e livraison) : 186-224, 1876.   2208

Study bears as a sort of sub-title an announcement of Lalanne's edition of works of B. (Renouard, 1864-82, 11 v.), for which opening pages serve as a review Then comes a rapid survey of B.'s life (p. 188-99). Pingaud finds many weaknesses in B. as a historian but, nevertheless classes him in this role with Talleman de Réaux and Bussy in his *Histoire amoureuse des Gaules* (Crès, 1928, 250 p.).

Vincent de Carloix

(No. 2209)

Bondois, Paul Martin. Vincent de Carloys secrétaire du maréchal de Vieilleville. RSS 15:165-67, 1928.   2209

Approves conclusion of abbé Ch Marchand that *Mémoires of François de Scépeaux, maréchal de Vieilleville* are no work of C., but of some unknown secretary of Scépeaux family. A few biographical details of C.'s life are given.

Guillaume du Bellay, *sieur* **de Langey**

(Nos. 2210-2211)

Du Bellay, Guillaume. Fragments de la première Ogdoade, publiés avec une introduction et des notes par V. L. Bourrilly Bellais, 1904. 175 p. (Diss., Paris.)   2210

Other portions of *Ogdoades* have been reproduced by Martin Du Bellay : *Prologue des Ogdoades de messire Guillaume du Bellay, de la perte desquelles ne reste que les trois livres qui ensuyvent. In:* Petitot Claude B., *Collection complète des mémoires. relatifs à l'histoire de France, see* 1996, ser. 1 v. 17, p. 197-224.

Bourrilly, V. L. Guillaume du Bellay seigneur de Langey, 1491-1543. Société nouvelle de librairie et d'édition. 1905 449 p.   2211

Military and diplomatic career. Missions to England in connection with divorce of Henry VIII. Constant associations with contemporary humanist scholars and poets. D.'s conception o history is somewhat that of Comines. His interest is chiefly political. He addresses himself primarily to the ruler; he justifies the lot of men by moral considerations His style is imitated from that of Livy and Paul-Émile.

Review : J. Boulenger in RER 3:222-24 1905.

Bernard de Girard, *seigneur* **du Haillan**
(Nos. 2212-2216)

Girard, Bernard de, *seigneur* **du Haillan.** De l'estat et succez des affaires de France. L'Huillier, 1580. 321 p. 2212
Sub-title says that book covers time from reign of Pharamond to that of Louis XI, with a summary of histories of the heads of the House of Anjou.

— Promesse et dessein de l'histoire de France. L'Huillier, 1571. 25 ff. 2213
See note in RSS 17:179-80, 1930, calling attention to publication in 1570 of a *Promesse et dessein* somewhat different in form.

Bondois, P. M. Henri III et l'historiographe du Haillan. RHL 30:507-09, 1923. 2214
Documents supplementary to those used by Bonnefon in his article in the RHL 22:453-92, 1915 (no. 2216).

Bonnefon, Paul. L'historien du Haillan. RHL 15:642-96, 1908. 2215
Brief biography. Association with François de Noailles, whom D. accompanies to Italy (1557-91?). Secretary to duc d'Anjou (Henri III) whom, however, he does not accompany to Poland. Translations of Eutropius and Nepos.

— L'historien du Haillan. RHL 22:453-92, 1915. 2216
Conception and composition of D.'s historical work. Reprints an interesting *Promesse et dessein de l'histoire de France* (L'Huillier, 1571). D. replaces chronicle-history of his precursors with classical conception of history as it was written in Italy. Bonnefon cites with approval tribute of Thierry : " Du Haillan est le père de l'histoire de France telle que nous l'avons lue et apprise. C'est lui qui a produit Mézeray, l'abbé Daniel, l'abbé Velly et Anquetil " (p. 490).

Robert III de La Marck,
seigneur **de Fleuranges**
(No. 2217)

Fleuranges, Robert III de La Marck, *seigneur* **de.** Mémoires du maréchal de Floranges, dit le Jeune Aventureux. Ed. by Robert Goubaux and Paul André Lemoisne. Renouard, 1913-24. 2 v. (SHF, v. 363, 406) 2217

Second volume (no. 406) contains a 25-page *Notice* on Fleurange, his life, with historical background, an estimate of value of *Mémoires*, and a description of the manuscripts. Cf. : Fleuranges, etc., *Histoire des choses mémorables advenues du règne de Louis XII et François I. In :* Petitot, Claude B., ed., *Collection complète des mémoires relatifs à l'histoire de France.* v. 16 (ser. 2), p. 139-382.
Review : H. Hauser in Rhist 50th year, tome 150:197-99, Nov.-Dec., 1925.

Pierre de L'Estoile
(Nos. 2218-2221)

L'Estoile, Pierre de. Journal pour le règne de Henri III (1574-89) présenté et annoté par Louis Raymond Lefèvre. Gallimard [1943]. 777 p. 2218

— Journal pour le règne de Henri IV. Texte intégral présenté et annoté par Louis Raymond Lefèvre. Gallimard, 1948. 740 p. 2219
Both of these volumes have excellent scholarly apparatus : notes, indices, etc.

— Mémoires-journaux. Best edition is that of G. Brunet, 1875-96. 12 v. 2220
However, see *Registre-journal de Pierre de L'Etoile, 1574-89, notice et extraits d'un manuscrit inédit de la Bibliothèque nationale, publié par H. Omont.* Nogent-le-Rotrou, Daupeley-Gouverneur, 1900. 38 p. *See* 2165.

Bondois, P. M. Pierre de l'Estoile, audiencier de la Chancellerie de Paris. RSS 14:379-80, 1927. 2221
Establishes date of appointment of L. as *audiencier* as 1566.

Jacques de Mailles
(No. 2222)

Mailles, Jacques de. La très joyeuse, plaisante et récréative hystoire composée par le Loyal Serviteur des faiz, gestes, triomphes & prouesses du bon chevalier sans peur et sans reproche, le gentil seigneur de Bayart. 1527. Later edition : Roman, 1878. 512 p. (SHF, no. 180). 2222
Almost certain identification of " Loyal Serviteur " with one of Bayard's companions in arms, and a secretary, Jacques de Mailles, made by Gaston Letonnelier *in his : Étude critique sur le Loyal Serviteur et son Histoire de Bayart.* Grenoble, Saint

Bruno, 1926.   43 p.   (*Reprinted* from the ADB 5th ser. 15:97-139, 1924).   *See* H. Hauser in Rhist 53rd year, v. 159:121, 1928; *also* : Petitot, v. XV, p. 131-398, and v. XVI, p. 1-138; Roucher, v. XIV, p. 301-414, and v. XV, p. 1-477.

Marguerite de Valois,
queen consort of Henry IV, king of France
(Nos. 2223-2231)

Marguerite de Valois.   Mémoires de la reine Marguerite, publiés par Mauléon de Granier.   Chapelain, 1628.   362 p.   **2223**
Many editions, best by Paul Bonnefon, Bossard, 1920.   267 p.   (COI).
Of these *Mémoires*, Sainte-Beuve says (no. 2229, p. 148) that they have "... ouvert dans notre littérature cette série gracieuse des mémoires de femmes qui désormais ne cessera, et que continueront plus tard, en se jouant, les LaFayette et les Caylus." At the conclusion of his essay (p. 162), Sainte-Beuve describes her life as a kind of *fabliau*. He admires " ... son esprit et son talent de bien dire," and continues, " C'est par là, c'est par quelques pages exquises qui sont une date de la langue, qu'elle est entrée à son tour dans l'histoire littéraire... " (*see* 2274).

— La ruelle mal assortie.   Introduction et notes de Jean H. Mariéjol.   La sirène, 1922.   95 p.   **2224**
Mariéjol has introduced this brief, clever debate on the contrasting pleasures of Platonic and physical love with an interesting study (p. 5-45) of temperament and art of M.   At conclusion of debate between her lover and M., senses are shown to triumph over soul.   This is indicated frankly but with delicacy.

Coppin, Joseph.   Marguerite de Valois et le Livre des créatures de Raymond Sebond.   RSS 10:57-66, 1923.   **2225**
Montaigne may have dedicated his *Apologie de Raimond Sebond* to M.   There are indications that she was reading Raymundus de Sebonde in 1576.

Mariéjol, Jean H.   La vie de Marguerite de Valois, reine de Navarre et de France (1553-1615).   Hachette, 1928.   384 p.   **2226**
Supersedes previous studies of M.   Rejects some of sentimental adventures attributed to her.   Her salon during the last ten years of her life establishes a preliminary model for the Hôtel de Rambouillet.

Reviews : L. Febvre in Rcr 63:398-99, Sept., 1929; W. D. Green in EHR 45:309-311, 1930; H. Hauser in Rhist 53rd year, tome 159:166-67, Sept.-Oct., 1928 (a volume indispensable for a proper study of this age); A. LeDuc in RR 20:379-80, 1929.

Merki, Charles.   La reine Margot et la fin des Valois (1553-1615).   Plon, 1905.   448 p.   **2227**
Smoothly written life of M., defending her against all her critics, past and present.
Reviews : E. Armstrong in EHR 21:164-166, 1906; V. L. Bourilly in RHM 6:400-403, 1904-05; H. Hauser in Rhist 88:120-121, 1905.

Ratel, Simonne.   La cour de la reine Marguerite.   RSS 11:1-29, 193-207, 1924; 12:1-43, 1925.   **2228**
Study considers the life of M. during her last years in Paris.   She was popular at the royal court because of her wit and grace.   Her salon was frequented by most of the scholars and poets of the day.   Her life was a " ... mélange de passion, de piété, d'études et de plaisirs..." (v. 11, p. 29).   M. owned a large library, and was particularly interested in neo-Platonic literature.   The author, while undecided about authenticity of *La ruelle mal assortie* (no. 2224), uses it constantly in presenting the conflicting impulses of the Queen.

Sainte-Beuve, C. A.   La reine Marguerite; ses mémoires et ses lettres.   Causeries du lundi, 2nd ed.   Garnier, 1852-62.   v. VI, p. 148-62.   **2229**
" Il y eut au XVIe siècle les trois Marguerite : l'une sœur de François Ier et reine de Navarre, célèbre par son esprit et ses *Contes* dans le genre de Boccace ... l'autre Marguerite ... qui devint duchesse de Savoie ... la troisième Marguerite enfin, fille de Henri II, première femme de Henri IV..." (p. 148).   Latter is subject of present study.   Lauds M.'s delicacy and discretion.   *See* 2223.

Vaissière, Pierre de.   Le divorce satyrique ou les amours de la reine.   RQH 64:131-38, Mar., 1936.   **2230**
Author believes that *Divorce satyrique* was an expression of a personal vengeance; thinks that it was probably written by Charles de Valois, *comte* d'Auvergne.

- La jeunesse de la reine Margot. Hren 7:7-44, 190-212, 1940.   2231

Contrasts adventurous life of M. and her other qualities which have led to her being called " une grande intellectuelle " and " une femme de la renaissance." Explanation is to be sought in her early experiences and influences at Court rather than in her Italian descent. Her contacts with humanists of her time; relations with her mother, Catherine de Médicis, Guise, later Henri III, her brothers, etc.

Jean Papire Masson

(No. 2232)

Ronzy, Pierre. Un humaniste italianisant, Papire Masson (1544-1611). Champion, 1924. 690 p.   2232

Exhaustive and convincing study of life and varied historical and biographical work of M. M. replaced the style in history writing popularized by Paolo Emilio, which in imitation of Livy gave an elegant but false picture of the past, with a restrained, well-authenticated recital that aims at exactitude. He opened a new path to historians by calling attention to neglected sources that should be used, such as manuscripts, archives, letters, etc. M.'s life of Calvin (composed in 1583) was the first impartial one. Of M.'s life of Charles IX Ronzy says : " Aujourd'hui encore cette œuvre, une des vies les plus réussies, se lit avec intérêt " (p. 219). *See* 2704.

Reviews : A. Caraccio in RHL 32:312-314, 1925; J. Plattard in RSS 13:152-54, 1926.

Blaise de Lasseran-Massencome, *seigneur* de Montluc

(Nos. 2233-2238)

Montluc, Blaise de. Commentaires de messire Blaise de Montluc, maréchal de France. Bordeaux, Millanges, 1592. 284 ff.   2233

The Baron de Ruble in his edition of *Commentaires et lettres* of M. (Renouard, 1864-72, 5 v., SHF) based his text on two MSS discovered in the BN. Best edition of *Commentaires* is that of Paul Courteault (Picard, 1911-25, 3 v.) which may well be the definitive one.

Reviews : V. L. Bourilly in RHM 17:29-30, 1912; A. Lefranc in RER 6:80-81, 1908; M. Prinet in RQH 92:273-74, 1912.

Broqua, J. J. *comte* **de.** Le maréchal de Montluc, sa famille et son temps. Champion, 1924. 312 p.   2234

Author is primarily interested in military history of M., which he gives in detail. M. is here presented favorably on all occasions. Book written in pleasing style; handsomely illustrated.

Courteault, Paul. Blaise de Montluc, historien. Picard, 1908. 688 p. (Diss., Paris.)   2235

Exhaustive and, for the present, a definitive study. M.'s recital is checked by all available contemporary documents. Essential honesty and value of M.'s work in spite of chronological and topographical errors due to failure of memory. One of the fine Paris dissertations appearing in first years of 20th century (Laumonier, Villey, Plattard, *et al.*), which established modern study of the renaissance.

Reviews : A. Biovès in Rcr 42 (ns 66) : 33, July 16, 1908; P. Bonnefon in RHL 15:553-555, 1908; A. Lefranc in RER 6:80-81, 1908.

— Un cadet de Gascogne au XVIᵉ siècle : Blaise de Montluc. Picard, 1909. 308 p.   2236

Reliable life of M., based on same author's *Blaise de Montluc, historien* (2235), and *Commentaires* (2233). While recognizing a number of errors of topography and dating in *Commentaires*, Courteault insists upon essential honesty of M.'s work.

Review (brief comment) : Anon in RHL 16:207, 1909.

Le Gras, Joseph. Blaise de Montluc, héros malchanceux et grand écrivain; portraits et documents inédits. Albin-Michel, 1926. 288 p.   2237

Despite announcement of " documents inédits," nothing of importance has been added to work of P. Courteault (nos. 2235-2236) on M. A brief, pleasantly written biography. Moral portrait of M. seems at times flattered. Author does not always recognize M.'s responsibility for his ill luck.

Reviews : J. Balteau in RQH 106:487-489, 1927; P. Courteault in Rhist 52nd year, tome 156:160-61, Sept.-Dec., 1927.

Sainte-Beuve, C. A. Montluc. *In his:* Causeries du lundi. Garnier, 1852-62. v. XI, p. 49-88. 2238

Moving, eloquent portrait, in Sainte-Beuve's best manner.

Philippe de Mornay, *seigneur* **du Plessis-Marly, called du Plessis-Mornay** (No. 2239)

Patry, Raoul. Philippe du Plessis-Mornay, un huguenot homme d'état (1545-1623). *See* 2012. 2239

Book based on a seemingly exhaustive study of sources. Importance of M. seems somewhat exaggerated at expense of that of Henry IV. Criticism of the Guises appears not always justified.

Reviews : E. Barker in EHR 50:144-45, 1935; A. J. Grant in Hist 19:163-64, 1934-35; P.Mesnard in RSS 19:306-08, 1932-33; A. Paul in RQH 62:515-16, Jan., 1934.

Pierre de Paschal

(Nos. 2240-2241)

Bondois, P. M. Henri II et ses historiographes. BPH, 1925, p. 135-49. 2240

P. 135 : " ... l'historiographe royal, chargé dès la fin du XVe siècle, de donner, en un but de propagande, le récit officiel des annales de chaque règne." Bondois lists attempts to establish history of this office, and names of title-holders. Three historiographes under Henri II are noted, of whom third, Pierre de Paschal, is by far the most important, and upon whom quite a little has been written, in divergent tones. For opinion of Ronsard *see :* Pierre de Nolhac, *L'invective contre Pierre de Paschal, in his : Ronsard et l'humanisme,* 1160, p. 257-339. One of Paschal's works has been published : *Journal de ce qui s'est passé en France durant l'année 1562, principalement dans Paris et à la cour.* Rrét 1st ser. 5:81-116, 168-212, 1834. Bondois believes Paschal worthy of credence as historian.

Nolhac, Pierre de. Un humaniste ami de Ronsard : Pierre de Paschal, historiographe de France. RHL 25:33-59, 243-61, 362-87, 1918. 2241

Early training of P. General enthusiasm over his announced plan to write eulogies of contemporaries. Named historiographer of France. Fails to complete any of the promised works.

Etienne Pasquier

(No. 2242)

Bouteillier, P. Un historien du seizième siècle : Etienne Pasquier. BHren 6:357-392, 1945. 2242

Believes that P. seeks moral and religious lessons. His political theories are those of *Parlementaires.* Gives P.'s historical sources.

Paul-Emile

(No. 2243)

Paulus Aemilius, Veronensis. De rebus gestis francorum. n.d. (1517?). 124 ff. Trans. by Jean Regnart. L'histoire des faicts, gestes, etc., des roys, princes, seigneurs et peuple de France ... avec la suyte de ladicte histoire tiree du Latin de feu Mr. Arnold Le Ferron. Morel, 1581. 687 p. 2243

According to Bates (2194, p. 13), art of history was established in France by Paolo Emilio of Verona.

Family of Saulx-Tavannes

(No. 2244)

Pingaud, Léonce. Les Saulx-Tavannes; études sur l'ancienne société française, lettres et documents inédits. Didot, 1876. 373 p. 2244

P. 1-153 recount the life of Maréchal Gaspard de Tavannes (1509-73) whose so-called *Mémoires* were composed by his son, Jean de Saulx-Tavannes (1555-1629), between 1616 and 1621. They were printed under the eyes of author, who distributed copies secretly. Story of father's life is interrupted by son's personal experiences and opinions. Narrative partial to Catholic side; has little literary merit. Pingaud has added a genealogy of Saulx-Tavannes family. Bibliography is incomplete and not well presented.

Review : G. Baguenault de Puchesse in RQH 11 (39e livraison) : 669-70, 1876.

Jean de Serres

(Nos. 2245-2247)

Serres, Jean de. Commentarium de statu religionis et reipublicae in regno Galliae I partis libri III regibus Henrico secundo ad illius quidem regni finem, Francisco secundo et Carolo nono. n.p., n.d., 1572-80. 2245

This first publication contains three parts. Fourth part appeared in 1574; fifth in 1580, and it alone contains place of publication : J. Jucundus, Leyden. *See:* Thompson, 2200, v. I, p. 561-62.

— Inventaire général de l'histoire de France. Saugrain & Des Rues, 1597. 1203 p. 2246

Narrative ends in 1422. Many later editions have continued the history. Last, in 1660, published by J. Cailloüe (J. Viret) in Rouen, comes down to 1660. Thierry calls this a work of " ... la dernière médiocrité..." (2199, p. 343).

Dardier, Charles. Jean de Serres, historiographe du roi; sa vie et ses écrits d'après des documents inédits (1540-1598). Rhist 8th year, 22:291-328, May to Aug., 1883, and 23:28-78, Sept.-Dec., 1883. 2247

Reputation of S. obscured by that of his more famous brother, Olivier. Use of Latin in his best work, *Commentaires,* and project of reconciliation between Catholics and Huguenots, which pleased neither side, are chief causes of neglect. S. was *Principal de collège* at Lausanne and Nîmes; honest patriot, man of great learning. Noteworthy is his translation of some of Buchanan's poetry into Greek verse. Second half of Dardier's article devoted to an analysis of S.'s *Projet d'accord* and his efforts to advance it.

Arnaud Sorbin, *bishop* of Nevers

(No. 2248)

Forestié, Emerand. Biographie de Arnaud Sorbin, dit de Sainte-Foy, prédicateur de Charles IX, Henri III, et Henri IV, évêque de Nevers. Montauban, Forestié, 1885. 64 p. 2248

Sorbin was the author and translator of numerous religious polemics. Greatly admired for his sermons and *oraisons funèbres,* that of Charles IX in particular. This biography is composed from a strictly clerical point of view.

Jacques Auguste de Thou

(Nos. 2249-2252)

Brugmans, H. Deux historiens du XVIe siècle : de Thou et Emmius. Rhist 145:55-61, 1924. 2249

Portrait of T., estimate of his reputation among his contemporaries. Brief account of his correspondence with his Dutch contemporary Emmius, author of a *Historia nostri temporis; opus posthumum,* 1732.

Collinson, John. The life of Thuanus. London, Longman, 1807. 467 p. 2250

Delightful biography of greatest French historian of 16th century. Summary of critical judgments of De Thou. Story of publication of his *History* usefully supplemented by his *Memoirs,* as published in : Petitot, Claude B., ed., *Collection complète des mémoires relatifs à l'histoire de France.* v. 37 (ser. 1), (1823), p. 187-530. *Also in:* Michaud, Joseph François, and Jean Joseph François Poujoulat. *Nouvelle collection des mémoires pour servir à l'histoire de France.* Lyons, Guyot, 1851. v. 9 (ser. 1), p. 271-374.

Duentzer, Heinrich. Jacques Auguste de Thou's Leben, Schriften und historische Kunst verglichen mit der Alten. Darmstadt, Leske, 1837. 124 p. 2251

Life of T. as a student (under Cujas), scholar and public official is rapidly outlined. Admirable impartiality of T.'s judgments emphasized. Rather unconvincing comparison drawn between historical art of T. and Thucydides, Polybius, Sallust, Tacitus and others.

Harisse, Henry. Le président de Thou et ses descendants, leur célèbre bibliothèque, leurs armoiries et les traductions françaises de J.-A. Thuani Historiarum sui temporis. Leclerc, 1905. 274 p. 2252

History of T. library from its origin in 1573 till its final dispersion in 1789. Family struggles over possession. Financial failure of J.-A. de Thou II. Partial catalogues of collection. Translations of *Historia* into French. Genealogical details on family.

François de Scépeaux, *maréchal* de Vieilleville

(Nos. 2253-2255)

Vieilleville, François de Scépeaux, maréchal de. Mémoires. Ed. by P. Griffet, 1757. 5 v. 2253

Also in Michaud, 1st series, v. IX., p. 3-405.

Coignet, Clarisse (Gauthier). Fin de la vieille France. Un gentilhomme des temps passés, François de Scépeaux, sire de Vieilleville (1509-1571). Plon-Nourrit, 1886. 438 p. *Translation:* A gentleman of the olden time, François de Scépeaux. v. 1. London, Bentley, 1887. 2254

Author announces in introduction that she cannot pretend to any academic or scholarly preparation. Not many documentary or printed sources are cited. Narrative is largely from so-called *Memoirs*, which are accepted as work of Carloix (no. 2209) as they were presented in first edition. Liberties are taken with text in the interest of drama and sentiment. Style is flowing.

Marchand, Chanoine Charles. Le maré chal François de Scépeaux de Vieilleville e ses mémoires. Picard, 1893. 370 p. 225.

Shows that attribution of *Mémoires* t Carloix (Carloix, Vincent, *Mémoires d François de Scépeaux*, etc. *In: Collection universelle des mémoires particuliers relatif à l'histoire de France.* London, Paris v. 28, p. 91, to v. 33, p. 92. First ed. 1757) by Griffet is probably false, and tha they were untrustworthy.

CHAPTER XV. GUILLAUME DU VAIR

(Nos. 2256-2283)

DONALD M. FRAME

Du Vair, Guillaume. Les œuvres de Messire Guillaume Du Vair ... reveues ... et augmentées. *See* 1843. 2256

In 5 parts : 1. *Actions et traictez oratoires*, 2. *De l'eloquence françoise*, 3. *Arrests sur quelques questions notables prononcez en robbe rouge*, 4. *Traictez philosophiques*, 5. *Traictez de pieté et sainctes meditations*. Best edition of complete works, which have not been published since 1641. Political orations in particular, however, are often revised and toned down here, and should be studied in earlier general or individual editions too numerous to list here.

— Actions et traictez oratoires, édition critique publiée par René Radouant. *See* 1844. 2257

Text based on earliest versions of individual speeches, with corrections and variants from the 1606 *Recueil des harangues et traictez* and 1625 and 1641 complete works. Useful bibliographical introduction. No explanatory footnotes, but valuable fifty-page Lexique with page and line references. No merely orthographical variants. Very good critical edition by leading D. scholar.

— De la sainte philosophie. Philosophie morale des Stoïques. Édition annotée par G. Michaut. Vrin, 1945. 122 p. (BTP) 2258

Texts of both works are based on 1625 edition, prefaces on those of 1600 and 1599-1603 respectively, variants of 1600 and 1599-1603. Careful edition in modernized spelling with notes on language and variants, not on sources. In a good bibliographical note on these works (p. 115-122), editor seems to establish that *Manuel d'Epictete* precedes in publication date *La saincte philosophie*, which in turn (against Radouant) dates from before 1585.

— De l'eloquence françoise, édition critique, précédée d'une étude sur le traité de Du Vair, par René Radouant. Société fran-

çaise d'imprimerie et de librairie [1907]. 192 p. (Diss., Paris.) *See* 1844. 2259

Based on 1595 edition, with corrections and variants based on editions of 1606, 1625, and 1641. Useful edition and bibliography of the work, and valuable study (p. 3-123) of French oratory (1550-1600) and D.'s place in it. Good appendix on sources of oratorical erudition at the time.

Review : L. Delaruelle in RHL 16:617-621, 1909.

— Guillaume Du Vair en Normandie. DH 2:184-92, 1911. 2260

Not an article as title suggests, but 12 unpublished letters and fragments by D. (1617-20) concerning bishopric of Lisieux.

— Lettres de Guillaume Du Vair (1599-1620). DH 4:21-52, 1913. 2261

Sequel to preceding item, offering 45 letters " inédites ou peu connues," most of them already published by Radouant in RHL (no. 2279) or by Tamizey de Larroque (no. 2262). These go only up to 1608; promise of sequel is not fulfilled later.

— Lettres inédites de Guillaume du Vair. Ed. by Ph. Tamizey de Larroque. Aubry, 1873. 73 p. RM 18:458-67, 524-43, 561-580, 1872; 19:6-29, 1873. 2262

Good review of earlier D. scholarship and good edition of about 27 letters (1596-1613) mostly to Président de Thou and Henri IV. Excellent notes.

— Testament de Monsieur du Vair. ACHF ser. 1, 15:355-62, 1837. 2263

No critical apparatus. Also available in Sapey (no. 2281).

— The moral philosophie of the stoicks. Englished by Thomas James. Ed. with introduction and notes by Rudolf Kirk. New Brunswick, N. J., Rutgers University Press, 1951. 134 p. (RUSE no. 8) 2264

237

Good edition of first English translation (1598), with useful introductory material (p. 3-37) on D., his neostoicism, his translator, and his influence in England.

— Traité de la constance et consolation és calamitez publiques. Ed. by Jacques Flach and F. Funck-Brentano. *See* 1845.   2265
Also includes *Exhortation à la vie civile* (p. 241-52). Very good edition of text of 1606 with variants mainly of 1618 and 1641. Old spelling except where inconsistent. Good critical bibliography of earlier editions (p. 41-48), very good introduction by Flach (p. 1-39).

Epictetus. Le manuel d'Epictète, suivi des réponses à l'empereur Hadrien et translaté en langue française, par Guillaume Du Vair. Société littéraire de France, 1921.   51 p.
                                    2266
Attractive text, not modernized; no critical material.

— Le manuel d'Epictète, traduit en français par le sieur Guillaume Du Vair. Haumont, 1944. 43 p. (BCA, v. 1)   2267
Good, handsome text of the presumably first edition (Langelier, 1591), including *Au lecteur.* No critical material.

Brunot, Ferdinand. [Du Vair's influence on Malherbe.] *In his:* La doctrine de Malherbe d'après son Commentaire sur Desportes. *See* 574, 59-72. (AUL, No. 1)
                                    2268
Brunot considers D.'s influence on Malherbe very great, especially from 1599 to 1605. Parallel passages are not all very convincing, but there is a good argument for general resemblances : oratorical quality, clarity, etc.

Cougny, Edme. Guillaume du Vair; étude d'histoire littéraire, avec des documents nouveaux tirés des manuscrits de la Bibliothèque impériale. Durand, 1857. 282 p. (Diss., Paris).   2269
Mainly superseded; but good general study of D.'s life, philosophy, eloquence, style and language.

Giraud, Victor. Sur Guillaume du Vair; notes bibliographiques. RHL 13:317-21, 1906.   2270
An *addendum* to Radouant's earlier RHL articles (no. 2279) showing existence of an edition (1591) of *Manuel d'Epictete* alone, probability of separate and joint editions unknown to Radouant. *See* 2580.

Glaesener, Henri. Juste Lipse et Guillaume du Vair. RBP 17:27-42, 1939.   2271
From similarities in treatment and D.'s stay in Leiden in 1581 when the older, famous Lipsius was there, argues influence of Lipsius' *De constantia* on D.'s *Traité de la constance et consolation.* Plausible but not too strong; rather long.

Lebègue, Raymond. Une lettre inédite de Guillaume Du Vair. RHL 48:336-42, 1948.   2272
Offers, with full explanation of circumstances and stylistic notes, an interesting letter of 1617 from D. as *Garde des Sceaux* on a problem of compensating Béarnais Protestant ministers after annexation of Béarn by France.

— Nouvelles études malherbiennes. BHren 5:153-208, 1944.   2273
Excellent study. Second part (p. 174-184) deals with *Les relations de Du Vair et de Malherbe.* Distinguishes three periods : 1600-05 in Aix; 1606-16—for which the correspondence is regrettably lost—when D. was in Aix, Malherbe in Paris; 1616-21 in Paris. Doubts that D.'s literary influence on Malherbe is as strong as Brunot (no. 2268) suggests.

Marguerite de Valois. Mémoires de Marguerite de Valois suivis des Anecdotes inédites de l'histoire de France pendant les xviᵉ et xviiᵉ siècles tirées de la bouche de M. le Garde des Sceaux Du Vair et autres, publiés avec notes par Ludovic Lalanne. Jannet, 1858. 352 p. *See* 2223.   2274
As text shows (p. 221, 227, 230, etc.) these anecdotes (p. 191-336) are not written by D., and some have nothing to do with him. Editor suggests (p. xxvii) that they are mainly by Peiresc.

Mesnard, Pierre. Du Vair et le néostoïcisme. *See* 1847.   2275
Excellent analysis of psychology and operation of morality in D.'s thought, and of key ideas (notions of the Good and of Nature) and their applications. Shows how D.'s Nature is stoical only up to point where it needs Christian God in control; and beyond that point, Christian. *See* 2580.

Michault, J. B. (de Dijon). Guillaume du Vair. *In:* Nicéron, R. P. Jean-Pierre : Mémoires pour servir à l'histoire des hommes illustres dans la république des lettres. Briasson, 1728-45. v. 43, p. 114-64. 2276

Solid biographical and bibliographical study; now outdated, but has been basic to all later work on D.

Naves, Raymond. Un citoyen et un laïque : Du Vair et Charron. *In his :* L'aventure de Prométhée. La patience. Didier; Toulouse, Privat, 1943. p. 50-67. 2277

Excellent sympathetic study which locates D. in the French moralistic tradition of accepting " la condition humaine." Brings out his special flavor, the sense of civic duty as against monastic withdrawal from an evil world *(Exhortation à la vie civile)*. D. discussed p. 50-59, 66-67, 211-12.

Radouant, René. Guillaume Du Vair : l'homme et l'orateur jusqu'à la fin des troubles de la Ligue (1556-1596). *See* 1846. 2278

The most important work on D. Thorough, judicious, impressively documented study of formative, productive, and most active years of D.'s life. Full treatment of D. as orator. Packed, sometimes too much, with details on political events of the time. Good assessment of D.'s difficult political position between the kings, Parlement and *Ligue* before and during 1589-94 siege of Paris.

Review : L. Delaruelle in RHL 16:617-621, 1909.

— Recherches bibliographiques sur Guillaume Du Vair et correspondance inédite. RHL 6:72-102, 253-66, 408-23, 1899; 7:603-623, 1900. 2279

These articles begin modern D. scholarship by seeking a bibliographical foundation for solid research on D. They need correction on many points by Giraud and more recent editors. Radouant describes and locates 160 unpublished letters of D., and publishes a large number of the best.

Reynaud, Georges. Guillaume du Vair, premier président du parlement de Provence. Aix, Remondet-Aubin, 1873. 64 p. 2280

Speech to *Cour d'appel* of Aix, giving many interesting details on D.'s problems and activities during his years as president of Parlement.

Sapey, Charles A. Études biographiques pour servir à l'histoire de l'ancienne magistrature française; Guillaume Du Vair, Antoine Le Maistre. Amyot, 1858. 496 p. *See* 2263. 2281

Treats D.'s life (p. 1-126) and works (p. 127-84), and prints many unpublished letters and other items, including will *(Appendice,* p. 333-488). Profits from constructive criticism of his earlier *Etude sur Du Vair* (1847) by Feugère (NRE 3:583-95, 1847) and others. Impartial in intent, but often almost panegyrical. Main value is in treatment of entire life and works, and in previously unpublished material, much of which is not readily available elsewhere.

Strowski, Fortunat. De Montaigne à Pascal. *In his :* Histoire du sentiment religieux en France au xviie siècle. Plon, 1907-1908. v. 1, p. 70-104. *See* 1748. 2282

Shows Montaigne as modernizer of stoicism, Justus Lipsius as its learned professor, D. as its exponent in high public office. Sees D.'s stoicism as increasing with time, from *La sainte philosophie* (1588) to *Traité de la constance* and then to *Manuel d'Epictète* and *Philosophie morale des stoïques*, which last two he dates at 1594 or later. More recent bibliographical findings (Giraud, 2270, Michaut, 2258) make this unlikely. Location of D. in thought of his time remains valuable.

Review : H. Potez in RHL 14:361-64, 1907.

Zanta, Léontine. Guillaume du Vair, sa vie, l'évolution de son stoïcisme. *In her :* La renaissance du stoïcisme au xvie siècle. *See* 198. 2283

Author finds D.'s stoicism typically eclectic and Christian. Considers that life made D. a stoic, and that he adapted his attitude to public service. Good contribution to location of D.'s stoicism *in his* own life and in thought of his time.

Reviews : P. de Bouchaud in RCC 22²:819-21, 1914 ; V. Giraud in his *Ecrivains et soldats*, Hachette, 1921. p. 5-12; J. Plattard in RSS 6:131-33, 1919; L. Roustan in Rcr ns 80:217-19, 1915; G. Truc in RHL 22:611-14, 1915.

CHAPTER XVI. THEATER
(Nos. 2284-2464)

LANCASTER E. DABNEY, GEORGE OTTO SEIVER AND NORMAN B. SPECTOR

Theater (general)
(Nos. 2284-2414)

LANCASTER E. DABNEY

General Works on the Theater in the 16th Century

Bapst, Germain, Essais sur l'histoire du théâtre, la mise en scène, le décor, le costume, l'architecture, l'éclairage, l'hygiène. Lahure, 1893. 693 p. 2284
General treatment of stage decoration in France with comparisons to foreign theaters. Part II (p. 135-211) gives valuable side-lights on renaissance stage settings for comedy, tragedy, ballet, etc. Conclusions, influenced by Rigal (no. 2288), not in agreement with later critics such as G. Lanson, nos. 2316-17. Abundant illustrations from 16th century Latin and French plays.

Dabney, Lancaster E. French dramatic literature in the reign of Henri IV (1589-1610). Austin, The University Cooperative Society, 1952. 470 p. 2285
Complete coverage of all dramatic writing in this period from standpoint of content and source rather than from that of genre. Extensive quotations from prefaces, dedications and from the plays themselves. Complete index including lists of characters for each play.
Reviews : Elizabeth Armstrong in FS 7:352-53, Oct., 1953; H. C. Lancaster in MLN 68:427-28, 1953; J. C. Lapp in MLQ 14:324-25, 1953.

Lancaster, Henry Carrington. General characteristics of dramatic literature in the reign of Henri IV (1589-1610). *In his:* A history of French dramatic literature in the seventeenth century. V. I, p. 13-22. Baltimore, The Johns Hopkins Press, 1929-1942. 5 v. in 9. 2286
Brief but informative. Value for 16th century is accurate evaluation of source

material. Practically only work dealing with reign of Henri IV.
Review : L. Cons in MLN 45:172-83, 1930.

Rigal, Eugène Pierre Marie. Hôtel de Bourgogne et Marais; esquisse d'une histoire des théâtres de Paris de 1548 à 1635 Dupret, 1887. 116 p. 2287
Brief account of various troupes occupying theaters at Paris. Information accurate and authentic, but needs to be supplemented by later work of Lanson, Lancaster, and others.
Review : H. Koerting in ZFSL 10²:109-110, 1888.

— Le théâtre français avant la période classique. Hachette, 1901. 363 p. 2288
General part of work on Hardy combined with material of his *Esquisse*, etc (no. 2287). Masterly summary of research up to its publication, but puts too much faith in dates of representation as given by Frères Parfait [François and C. Parfait *Dictionnaire des théâtres de Paris.* Rozet 1767, 7 v. Exaggerates importance of Hardy.
Reviews : H. Morf in Archiv 107:443-44, 1901; L. Séché in Rren 1:212, 1901.

Sainte-Beuve, Charles Augustin. Tableau historique et critique de la poésie française et du théâtre français au xvıᵉ siècle. Charpentier, 1828, 1843, 1875. 508 p. 2289
Valuable for sure taste of author. Suffers from inaccuracy of facts taken from Mouhy and from incompleteness of treatment.

General Collections of Plays

Fournier, Edouard. Le théâtre français avant la renaissance (1430-1550); mystères, moralités et farces, précédé d'une introduction et accompagné de notes pour l'intelligence du texte. Laplace, Sanchez, s.d. 1872. 462 p. 2290

Better, more modern collection than Viollet-Le-Duc (no. 2291). Usually available in all libraries. Attacked for lax collating of texts by E. Philipot in *Trois farces du Recueil de Londres*, see 2295, p. 4-6.

Viollet-Le-Duc, Emmanuel Louis Nicolas. Ancien théâtre françois ou collection des ouvrages dramatiques les plus remarquables depuis les mystères jusqu'à Corneille. Jannet, 1854-57. 10 v.   2291
Reprint of collection of British Museum acquired in Germany, 1845. Sixty-four plays in volumes 1 to 3 (moralities, farces, *sotties, sermons joyeux,* one mystery) printed separately in gothic, middle of 16th century at Paris, Lyons, Rouen. This reprint gives no indication of original editions.

Farces

Aebischer, Paul. Trois farces françaises inédites trouvées à Fribourg. RSS 11:128-192, 1924.   2292
Found in cover of document. *Jehan qui de tout se mesle; Farce à cinq personnages; Dialogue de Gautier et Martin.* Published here with notes and introduction.

Farce plaisante et récréative sur un trait qu'a joué un porteur d'eau le jour de ses noces dans Paris. S. C., 1632.   2293
H. C. Lancaster in his *History of French dramatic literature in the seventeenth century* (no. 2286), part I, v. II, p. 666, analyzes briefly; agrees with Petit de Julleville (*Histoire du théâtre en France,* Partie 4, *Répertoire du théâtre comique en France au moyen-âge,* Cerf, 1886, p. 218) that date of composition was much earlier. *See* P. Toldo in SFR 9:238, 1901.

Philipot, Emmanuel. Notes sur quelques farces de la renaissance. RER 9:364-421, 1911.   2294
Editions, variants, sources of seven farces, some not in usual collections : 1. *Femme muette,* 2. *Maistre Mimin le goutteux,* 3. *Robinet badin et la femme veuve,* 4. *Maistre Mimin estudiant,* 5. *Gaudisseur qui se vante de ses faicts,* 6. *Médecin qui guarist de toutes sortes de maladies,* 7. *Ung ramonneur de cheminée.* All these plays are studied with respect to their relation to Rabelais, but are valuable for the history and understanding of plays dealt with.

— Recherches sur l'ancien théâtre français. Trois farces du Recueil de Londres : Le

cousturier et Esopet; Le cuvier; Maistre Mimin estudiant. Textes publiés avec notices et commentaires. Rennes, Plihon, 1931. 171 p.   2295
Although these farces are available elsewhere, this edition is convenient, accurate; introduction gives all historical, bibliographical details needed.
Review : J. Plattard in RSS 18:366-67, 1931.

Picot, Emile and Christophe Nyrop, ed. Nouveau recueil de farces françaises des xve et xvie siècles, publié d'après un volume unique appartenant à la bibliothèque royale de Copenhague. Morgand et Fatout, 1880. 244 p.   2296
Reprint with extensive bibliography and notes of a volume of 173 p. containing nine plays, four not previously known, published at Lyons, 1609. Very useful glossary of unusual words and expressions.
Review : G. Paris in Rom 10:281-85, 1881, makes several corrections, gives other editions of the plays in collection, which he finds inferior to Rousset collection, Paris, 1612.

Monologue Dramatique

Picot, Emile. Le monologue dramatique dans l'ancien théâtre français. Rom 15:358-422, 1886; 16:438-542, 1887; 17:207-62, 1888.   2297
Complete treatment with scholarly bibliography of texts (editions, reprints). Analyzes each of ninety-five monologues; quotes significant passages, usually beginning and end; history of composition, if known; relationship to other monologues, farces, etc. Information concerning author if significant.
Review : A. Tobler in ZRP 12:438-52, 1886.

Moralities and Polemic Comedies

Holl, Fritz. Das politische und religiöse Tendänzdrama des 16. Jahrhunderts in Frankreich. Erlangen, Deichert, 1903. 219 p. (MBP, v. 26)   2298
Continues, completes Picot's *Moralités polémiques* (2299). Extensive bibliography, but information about editions often vague. Enormous number of plays has forced author to be so brief that text is often list of plays with cursory comments. Little attempt, except by distribution into categories, to organize material so as to

show movement as a whole. Supplement with Lebègue.

Review : H. Patry in BSHP 53:82, 1904.

Picot, Emile. Les moralités polémiques ou la controverse religieuse dans l'ancien théâtre français. BSHP 36:169-90; 225-45; 337-364, 1887; 41:561-82, 617-33, 1892; 55:254-262, 1906.   2299

Repertory with comments, summaries (when text is available), bibliographical data. Practically only work on subject; done in Picot's usual scholarly style, but not quite complete.

Shaw, Helen A. Conrad Badius and the Comédie du pape malade. Philadelphia, 1934. 168 p. (Diss., Pennsylvania.) 2300

A reprint of the 1561 edition with introduction and notes. Shows (p. 64) that Thrasibule Phenice is Greek and Latin equivalent for Conrad Badius. Play a mixture of farce, morality and comedy.

Bretog, Jean. Tragédie françoise à huict personnages traictant de l'amour d'un serviteur envers sa maistresse, et de tout ce qui en advint. Composée par M. Jean Bretog de S. Sauveur de Dyve. Lyons, Grandon, 1571. 24 ff. Reprint, "soins de M. Grattet-Duplessis," Chartres, Garnier, 1831. 42 sheets in facsimile.   2301

Really a morality. *See :* Rigal, no. 2288, p. 96; J. B. Suard, *Coup d'œil sur l'histoire de l'ancien théâtre français, in : Mélanges de littérature,* Dentu, 1803-04, v. IV, p. 78.

Coignac, Joachim de. La desconfiture de Goliath, tragédie. Geneva, Riverez, 1551, 71 p.   2302

Polemic imitation of *mystères,* dedicated to Edward VI of England.

Des Autels, Guillaume. Repos de plus grand travail et soulagement d'esprit. Lyons, Tournes and Gazeau, 1550. 141 p.   2303

Contains also *Dialogue moral, sur la devise de Monsieur le reverendissime Cardinal de Tournon,* p. 97-141, which was played " dimenche de my Caresme " in 1549. *See* Jacques Madeleine, *Guillaume des Autels et les Jeux de Romans,* RHL 18:801-809, 1911. Another edition, Paris, Bonfons, n.d., seems lost. *See also* Hans Hartmann, *Guillaume des Autels, ein französischer Dichter und Humanist.* Zurich, Academia, 1907. 127 p. Madeleine's original article is important as setting forth clearly current of opposition to new style of plays introduced by Pléiade.

Geliot, Louvan (Dijonnois). Psyché; fable morale. Agen, Pomaret, 1599. 59 p. 2304

Five acts, *alexandrins,* but really a morality.

Mage de Fiefmelin, André. Alcide, jeu comique et moral en trois pauses. Œuvres, Poitiers, Marnef, 1601. 1250 p.   2305

Imitation of moralities and *sotties.*

Malingre, Mathieu. Moralité de la maladie de la Chrestienté à xiij personnages. Pierre de Vignolle, 1533. 48 ff.   2306

Paris, Pierre de Vignolle, is fictitious for Neufchâtel, Pierre de Vingle, according to E. Picot in BSHP 36:337-42, 1887.

Anon. Moralité nouvelle, récreative et profitable; à quatre personnages, cestasavoir Pyrame, Tisbé, le Bergier, la Bergière. n.p., n.d. 1535.   2307

Edition is : " D'après un exemplaire de la Bibliothèque royale de Dresde," by E. Picot, Leclerc, 1901, with a 15 p. Introduction and 24 p. of text. *Also,* with title *Moralité nouvelle de Pyramus et Tisbée* in BBB, Jan. 15, 1901, p. 1-35. Picot thinks date of composition was " vers 1535 " and author, Jean Crespin or Jean Daniel.

Mysteries

Brooks, Neil C. Notes on performances of French mystery plays. MLN 39:276-81, 1924.   2308

Corrections of details in performance of mysteries as reported by Petit de Julleville, *Histoire du théâtre en France. Les mystères.* Hachette, 1880-86. Partie I, 2:135, 136, 141.

Lebègue, Raymond. Le mystère des Actes des apôtres, contribution à l'étude de l'humanisme et du protestantisme français au XVIe siècle. Champion, 1929. 262 p. 2309

Thèse complémentaire accompanying author's *Tragédie religieuse en France* (no. 2318). Study of editions of the 60,000 verses of the mystery and the representations as a means of showing theatrical tendencies of second quarter of century.

Review : L. Cons in MLN 45:410-11, 1930.

Le Coq, Thomas. Tragédie représentant de l'odieux et sanglant meurtre commis par le maudit Caïn à l'encontre de son frère Abel. Bonfons, 1580. Edition in BN : Paris, s.d. ni nom. Tragédie de Thomas Le Coq.

L'odieux et sanglant meurtre commis par le maudit Caïn, réproduction de l'édition de 1580, précédée d'une introduction par Prosper Blanchemain. Rouen, Boissel, 1879. 40 p.   2310

No acts or scenes. Really a mystery, plagiarized from *Mistère du Viel testament*.

Sotties

Picot, Emile. Recueil général des sotties. Didot, I, 1902. xxi, 270 p. ; II, 1904. 372 p.; III, 1912. 425 p. (SATF)   2311

Introduction adds to article in Rom (no. 2312). Thirty-one *sotties* or fragments, each preceded by discussion and bibliography. Lacks general bibliography. Some of *sotties* published for first time from manuscripts. Combined *table-glossaire* facilitates reading and reference.

— La sottie en France. Rom 7:236-326, 1878.   2312

After showing origin, lack of influence of *sottie* in French and other theaters, Picot lists extant *sotties* chronologically, collects historical references, places with dates of performances. Excellent bibliography including collections of Caron, Fournier, Leroux de Lincy et Michel, Montaiglon, Rothschild, Viollet-Le-Duc.

Review : O. Ulbrich in ZRP 2:497-98, 1878 : " New light on the subject."

Theater of the Renaissance — Origins

Cunliffe, John W. Early French tragedy in the light of recent scholarship. JCL 1:301-323, 1903.   2313

Traces triple influence in French renaissance tragedy of Greek tragedy, authority of Aristotle, Horace, imitation of Seneca, using works of Böhm, Démogeot, Flamini, Baschet, A. Cahuet, Bernardin, Brunetière, Morf, Faguet, Spingarn, Rigal, Breitinger, Du Méril. Concludes that imitation of Seneca became rule of art for early French tragedy; shows lyrical character of tragedy and later disappearance of chorus because of opposition of public.

Kohler, Erwin. Entwicklung des Biblischen Dramas des XVI Jahrhunderts in Frankreich unter dem Einfluss der literarischen Renaissancebewegung. Leipzig, Deichert, 1911. 69 p. (MBP, v. 52)   2314

Review of French biblical plays in 16th century, scarcely more than catalogue with running commentary based only too often

on La Croix du Maine, Faguet, Mouhy; tries to show how developed under influence of " literarischen Renaissancebewegung." This is contribution; chapters on chorus, style, versification, representation, of little value.

Lancaster, H. C. The rule of three actors in French sixteenth century tragedy. MLN 23:173-77, 1908.   2315

Points out mistake of O. Mysing in *Robert Garnier und die antike Tragödie* (2369) by showing that Garnier followed Seneca rather than Greeks. Says there are only three speakers on stage, though a fourth and silent actor may be present.

Lanson, Gustave. Études sur les origines de la tragédie classique en France. Comment s'est opéré la substitution de la tragédie aux mystères et moralités. RHL 10:177-231, 413-36, 1903.   2316

With its sequel (*L'idée de la tragédie en France avant Jodelle*, no. 2317) most important single contribution in field. Shows how Jodelle began substitution of " drame antique aux genres du moyenâge," how Hardy " et ses comédiens achevèrent ce qui était commencé depuis un demi-siècle." Traces spread of change from Paris, Bordeaux, Poitiers, Bourges, Lausanne, as centers. Corrects impression left by Rigal that plays other than Hardy's were not played by giving list of representations (from 1540 on) for which there is documentary proof. Main conclusion of article is still sound, but additions have been made to list of representations.

— L'idée de la tragédie en France avant Jodelle. RHL 11:541-85, 1904.   2317

Lanson, in this article of capital importance, assembles " quelques traces des idées qu'on se faisait de la tragédie entre 1500 et 1550." Shows influence of Latin translators of Greek tragedy, Latin plays composed in France (Buchanan, Stoa, Muret, *et al*), Italians, theorists (translations from Greek, Latin, Italian, Sebillet, Du Bellay), mysteries, moralities, farces.

Lebègue, Raymond. La tragédie religieuse en France; les débuts (1514-1573). Champion, 555 p. (BLR, ns. v. 17)   2318

Has, as he says, read texts of mysteries and other plays, relied very little on secondhand accounts, but tends to incoherence and confusion at times since source of statements often omitted. In spite of this, essential book, especially useful for Buchanan, Rivaudeau, Jean de La Taille, Bèze.

Reviews : G. Cohen in RHL 38:320-22, 1931, approves, but corrects errors, finds history separated from tragedy by isolation of plays with religious subjects; L. Cons in MLN 45:410-11, 1930; A. Götze in Archiv 162:258-59, 1932-33; J. Plattard in RSS 18:189-91, 1931; other errors.

Loukovitch, Kosta. L'évolution de la tragédie religieuse classique en France. Droz, 1933. 468 p.   2319

Only first 137 pages deal with 16th century. Excellent material on Buchanan, Bèze, Grotius, but other authors passed over very sketchily because of author's preoccupation with thesis, which is to show how change from mysteries to humanistic religious treatment and then to classical religious tragedy was accomplished.

Review : H. C. Lancaster in MLN 49:539-41, 1934, points out considerable number of errors.

Greek and Latin Influence

IMITATIONS AND TRANSLATIONS OF GREEK AND LATIN AUTHORS

Böhm, Karl. Beiträge zur Kentniss des Einflusses Seneca's auf die in der Zeit von 1552 bis 1562 erschienenen französischen Tragödien. Erlangen and Leipzig, Deichert, 1902. 163 p. (MBP, 24.)   2320

Comprehensive, though not very important bibliography, with correct evaluation, but takes Parfaict and Mouhy seriously for dates of representations. Lacks other conclusion than table of analogies, comparison of selected parts of Toutain's *Thieste* with Seneca's, and Le Duchat's *Agamemnon* with the original. *See* 2445.

Review : A. L. Stiefel in LGRP 27:237 238, 1906.

Delcourt, Marie. Étude sur les traductions des tragiques grecs et latins en France depuis la renaissance. Brussels, Hayez, 1925. 282 p. (MARB, v. 19)   2320A

About one third deals with 16th century. Because of size of field, not covered with sufficient fullness. Author, good Hellenist, refutes idea that 16th century translations were good and 17th century ones bad. *See* 2416, 2420, 2438, 2552.

Review : R. Lebègue in RSS 13:147-50, 1926, points out omission of Latin translations, unpublished French translations, adaptations.

Lawton, H. W. Contribution à l'histoire de l'humanisme en France; Terence en France au seizième siècle; éditions et traductions. Jouve, 1926. 570 p. (Diss., Paris)   2321

Careful, complete study of over 461 Latin and 176 French editions. *See* 2464.

Review : P. Jourda in RSS 14:180-82, 1927.

Sturel, René. Essais sur les traducteurs du théâtre grec en français avant 1550. RHL 20:269-96, 637-66, 1913.   2322

Discussion by competent scholar of translations into French (printed or manuscript) of Greek dramatists, with comparison of French version with original Greek or Latin or other intermediary version if translation was not made directly. Useful work for study of classical sources of French plays. *See* 2357, 2427, 2553.

PLAYS COMPOSED IN LATIN IN FRANCE IN 16TH CENTURY

Bolte, Johannes. Die Lateinischen Dramen Frankreichs aus dem 16. Jahrhundert. FestJV, p. 591-613.   2323

Bibliography of plays composed in Latin in France in 16th century, printed and manuscript, with editions, reprints, present location of extant copies. Most complete to date, but not definitive.

Fries, Carl. Quellenstudien zu George Buchanan. NJGL 6:177-92, 241-61, 1900; 8:176 (note), 1901.   2324

Seeks sources in Euripides, Seneca, Bible for each play. Important information as to manner of composition of these early Latin language tragedies.

Dejob, Charles. Marc Antoine Muret; un professeur français en Italie dans la seconde moitié du seizième siècle. Thorin, 1881. 96 p.   2325

A fair book but somewhat amateurish, incomplete. Omissions and errors pointed out in review.

Review : P. de Nolhac in Rcr 16 (ns 13) : 483-88, June 19, 1882.

Vodoz, D. Le théâtre latin de Ravisius Textor (1470-1524). Winterthur, Ziegler, 1899. 174 p.   2326

Fuller and more accurate account of theater than that of Louis Massebieau (*De Ravisii Textoris, comoediis*. Bonhoure, 1878, 86 p.) and more generally available.

Review : W. Creizenach in ZFSL 21²:188-90, 1899.

Jesuit and Other School Theaters

Boysse, Ernest. La comédie au collège. Rcon 2nd ser. 72:656-82, 1869.   2327

Brief, intelligent generalization, with some examples, but by no means complete. P. 656-71 devoted to period before 17th century.

Gofflot, L. V. Le théâtre au collège du moyen âge à nos jours, avec bibliographie et appendices. Champion, 1907. 336 p.   2328

Probably best work on subject, although bibliography and list of representations are incomplete. Attempt to gather into one volume the information found in numerous histories of local theaters.

Review : H. Clouzot in RER 5:220-21, 1907, points out lack of reference tables.

Huart, Martin d'. Le théâtre des Jésuites. Luxembourg, 1892. 62 p.   2329

This first part (introduction) serves as an excellent summary of dramatic representations in schools in middle ages and 16th century.

Review : R. Mahrenholtz in ZFSL 14²:184-86, 1892.

Italian Sources

Neri, Ferdinando. La tragedia italiana del cinquecento, Florence, Galletti & Cocci, 1904. 193 p.   2330

Necessary guide for study of Italian tragedy and its influence on French.

Roth, Th. Der Einfluss von Ariost's Orlando furioso auf das französische Theater. Leipzig, Deichert, 1905. 263 p. (MBP, v. 34)   2331

Excellent beginning for Orlando influence on French theater. Introduction gives, with examples, general influence of Italian literature on French. Chapter 4 (dealing with 16th century) : special influence of Ariosto; keen analysis of secondary sources (Parfaict, Léris, Mouhy). Fails to point out, among other things, influence of Angélique's ring in *Les infidelles fidelles. See* 2603.

Reviews : G. Carel in Archiv 116:469-471, 1906, where other publications on same subject are evaluated; A. Stiefel in ZFSL 29²:190-98, 1906.

Toldo, Pietro. Quelques notes pour servir à l'histoire de l'influence du Furioso dans la littérature française. BI 4:49-61, 103-18, 190-201, 281-93, 1904.   2332

Analyzes and compares with source the French plays inspired by *Orlando furioso: La belle Genièvre (see* article J. Madeleine, Rren 1903, p. 30-40), *Bradamante* of R. Garnier, *Isabelle* of N. de Montreux, *Rhodomontade* and *Mort de Roger* of Charles Bauter, another *Mort de Roger*, and *Mort de Bradamante.* Does not mention *Isabelle* of Jehan Thomas. *See* 2605.

Theater of the Renaissance — Tragedy

Faguet, Emile. La tragédie française au xvi⁰ siècle (1550-1600). Hachette, 1883. 389 p. Leipzig, Welter, 1897. 391 p. 2333

Interesting and instructive literary judgments, but inaccurate facts from Mouhy, whose authority he recognizes as " très douteuse." Good account of theories of tragedy.

Review : A. Stiefel in LGRP, 6th year : 377-80, 1885, points out many mistakes, carelessness with dates, but concludes : " eine durch Selbständigkeit fleissiges Studium."

Lanson, Gustave. Esquisse d'une histoire de la tragédie. New York, Columbia University Press, 1920. 155 p. Champion, 1927. 194 p.   2334

Only first ten lessons of this outline (often too elliptical to be of use to any but specialists) deal with 16th century. To be recommended for clear idea of difference between Greek idea of tragedy and that of France in 16th century.

Review : H. C. Lancaster in MLN 36:98-103, 1921. Corrects some errors of printing, dates, etc. Clears up other obscure statements. Review of 1927 edition by Kurt Glaser in Archiv 153:275-76, 1928.

Lebègue, Raymond. La tragédie française de la renaissance. Brussels, Office de publicité, 1944. 93 p.   2335

Valuable summary of 16th century tragedy, but suffers from attempt to cover too much in too little space, so that work is often a succession of names and titles with almost no precise bibliographical information. However, since author has read plays he discusses and has extensive knowledge of the field, evidenced in other publications, he has given clear idea of movements and nature of the plays discussed.

Sixteenth Century Dramatic Theories

MODERN ACCOUNTS

Breitinger, Heinrich. Les unités d'Aristote avant le Cid de Corneille, étude de littérature comparée. Geneva, Georg, 1879. 74 p. Idem, 1895. 79 p.   2336
Shows development of the three unities as separate ideas. Refers also to his article in Rcr ns 8:470-80, 1879. Mistakes are corrected by Arnaud (Charles) in his *Théories dramatiques au XVIIᵉ siècle.* Picard, 1888.
Review : C. T. Lion in ZFSL 1:472, 1879; in Rcr 13 (ns 8) : 462-63, 1879.

Faguet, Emile. Les manifestes dramatiques avant Corneille. RCC 9 (Iʳᵉ série, no. 6) : 240-50, 1900.   2337
Explains how Aristotle's ideas, modified from Plato's were understood in 16th century and in 17th before Corneille.

THEORETICAL WORKS ON TRAGEDY PUBLISHED IN THE SIXTEENTH CENTURY

La Taille, Jean de. L'art de la tragédie. Edition by Frederick West. Manchester, University of Manchester, 1939. 37 p.   2338
Another good edition. Facsimile reproduction of title page of edition of 1572. Bibliography.

— Saül le furieux, suivi de L'art de la tragédie. Morel, 1572. 80 ff. Reprint by A. Werner with discussion and introduction. Leipzig, 1908. 69 p. (MBP, v. 40)   2339
Readily accessible edition with well documented, accurate introduction.

Laudun d'Aigaliers, Pierre de. L'art poétique français divisé en 5 livres. Du Breuil, 1598. 296 p. L'art poétique français; édition critique, essai sur la poésie dans le Languedoc, de Ronsard à Malherbe, thèse pour le doctorat ès lettres, présentée à la Faculté de Bordeaux par Joseph Dedieu. Toulouse, au siège des Facultés libres, 1909. 175 p.   2340
Only available edition of this important art of poetry. Contains accurate life of author, who is also a dramatist, sources of ideas in work. Much of material in *L'art poétique* deals with dramatic theory and practice.

Peletier, Jacques. L'art poétique de Jacques Peletier du Mans (1555); publié d'après l'édition unique avec introduction et com-

mentaire by André Boulanger, 1930. 240 p. (PFS, v. 52) *See* 1382.   2341
Excellent edition, containing all necessary information.
Reviews : R. Lebègue in RHL 40:595-596, 1933; J. Plattard in RSS 18:364-65, 1931.

Jugé, Abbé Clément. Jacques Peletier du Mans (1517-1582); essai sur sa vie, son œuvre et son influence. *See* 1383.   2342
Value of this study lies in its complete bibliography of Peletier, with description and present location of each item. Relationship of Peletier's *Art poétique* to *Deffense et illustration* well shown, but remainder of the work has too many conjectures. Author not sufficiently documented in theory and literary history of 16th century. Unfortunately there is nothing better. Supplement with P. Laumonnier's article *L'art poétique de Jacques Peletier du Mans* in Rren 1:248-76, 1901.
Review : J. Plattard in RHL 18:451, 1911.

Lintilhac, Eugène. Un coup d'état dans la république des lettres : Jules-César Scaliger fondateur du classicisme cent ans avant Boileau. Nrev 64:333-46, 528-47, 1890.   2343
Lintilhac says Scaliger, " père du néo-classicisme," established rules and form over content, preached imitation of certain antique models, invented literary dictatorship of Aristotle, including unities and cult for Virgil based on scorn for Homer. Essential article for understanding Scaliger.

Sebillet, Thomas. L'art poétique françois pour l'instruction des jeunes studieus et encore peu avancez en la poésie françoise. Corrozet (ou Arnould l'Angelier), 1548. 77 p. Avec le quintil horatian sur la Deffence et illustration de la langue françoise. Lyons, Temporal, 1551. 252 p. Edition critique by Félix Gaiffe. Cornély, 1910. 226 p. *See* 684.   2344
Gaiffe's edition contains all bibliographical and other information needed; full discussion of such publications before Sebillet.

Vauquelin de La Fresnaye, Jean. L'art poétique, ou l'on peut remarquer la perfection et le défaut des anciennes et modernes poésies. Caen, Macé, 1605. Reprints by Gentry, Poulet-Malassis, 1862; by Julien Travers, Caen, Leblanc-Hardel, 1869; by G. Pellissier (text of edition of 1605). Garnier, 1885. 230 p. *See* 1399.   2345

Among other matters, work deals with dramatic theories and practices of author's contemporaries. Pellissier's edition is best and most readily obtainable. Introduction shows relations to other *Arts poétiques;* studies syntax, orthography. Glossary.

Diverses tragédies de plusieurs autheurs de ce temps. Rouen, Du Petit Val, 1599. v. I : Ésaü (69 p.), Polyxène (107 p.) by Jean Behourt; Saint Cloud (67 p.), Pyrrhe (71 p.) by Jean Heudon; Médée (48 p.) by La Peruse. v. II : La Machabée of Jean de Virey; Adonis (47 p.) by G. Le Breton; Sophonisbé (107 p.) of Montreux. 2346

Evidently artificial collection of editions already printed. Contains text of plays only with no editorial introductions or notes.

Le théâtre des tragédies nouvellement mis en lumière. Rouen, Du Petit Val, 1620. 2347

Collection of late 16th and early 17th century tragedies by printer who published a large proportion of those printed during latter part of 16th century.

Individual Authors of Tragedies

Anon. La double tragédie du duc et cardinal de Guise jouée à Blois le 23 et 24 dec., 1588. Fleurant Monceaux, 1589. 2348

Not same as Le Guysien. Holl, *Das politische und religiöse tendenzdrama des 16 Jahrhundert in Frankreich* (no. 2298, p. 55), calls it dialogued " Klagegesang."

— Tragédie de Jeanne d'Arques, dite la Pucelle d'Orléans, native du village d'Emprenne, près Vaucouleurs en Lorraine. Rouen, Du Petit Val, 1600, 1603, 1606 (Emprenne changed to Epernay), 1611; Troyes, Oudot, 1628. 48 p. 2349

Tivier, *Histoire de la littérature dramatique en France*, Thorin, 1873, p. 350, mistakenly on too slight evidence attributes this play to Jean de Virey. Editions at BN, BM and Arsenal do not have name of author.

— Tragédie de Saint Estienne, premier roy chrestien de Hongrie, estoc paternel de la très-noble et ancienne maison de Croy. Représentée par les estudians des jésuites de Mons en Hénault, Dec. 20, 1605. Mons, Michel, 1605. 11 ff. 2350

Merely a program, not a full text. See H. C. Lancaster, *French tragi-comedy*, Baltimore, Furst, 1907. p. 170.

Baïf, Jean Antoine de. Antigone, tragédie de Sophocle. *In :* Les jeux, les passetemps, œuvres en rime et les amours de Ian Antoine de Baïf. Breyer, 1572-73. 2 v. Les œuvres en rime avec une notice biographique et des notes par Ch. Marty-Laveaux, Lemerre, 1881-90. 5 v. 2351

Antigone in 3:115-81. Notice, published separately (Lemerre, 1886. lxiii p.), contains good biography based on information furnished by Baïf in his works. *See* 2449.

Baïf, Lazare de. Tragédie de Sophocles intitulée Electra, traduicte du grec, en rythme françoise ligne pour ligne et vers pour vers. Roffet, 1537. 44 p. 2352

A ms. in library of Saint Mark at Venice contains a prologue addressed to the King. *See* 2450.

Pinvert, Lucien. Lazare de Baïf (1496-1547). Fontemoing, 1900. 130 p. 2353

Usable biography, though spoiled by deplorable tendency of author to impertinent digressions. Excellent bibliography and documentation. *See* 2550.

Review : L. Séché in Rren 1:60, 1901.

Keegstra, Pieter. Abraham sacrifiant de Théodore de Bèze et le théâtre calviniste de 1550-66. The Hague, Van Haeringen, 1928. 129 p. (Diss., Groningen) 2354

Purpose is " ... d'étudier plus en détail la pièce de Th. de Bèze, le premier en date, et d'examiner à quel point il est le modèle de ceux qui se sont engagés dans la même voie " (p. 3). Abundantly documented, clear account; contains in appendix a list of 16th-century moralists satirizing the Catholic Church, and a bibliography of secondary articles.

Billard, Claude. Guaston de Foix, tragédie republished with an introduction by E. H. Polinger. New York, Institute of French Studies, 1931. 70 p. 2355

On the whole a good edition.

Review : L. E. Dabney in MLN 47:61, 1932. Points out misprints and corrects some errors.

Dabney, Lancaster E. Claude Billard, minor French dramatist of the early seventeenth century. Baltimore, The Johns Hopkins Press, 1931. 130 p. 2356

Biography based on all sources, prefaces to plays; analyses of all plays, sources, language. *See also :* L. E. Dabney, *More about Claude Billard.* MLN 48:316-17, 1933.

Reviews : J. Plattard in RSS 18:193-94, 1931; E. H. Polinger in MLN 47:59-61, 1932.

Bochetel, Guillaume. La tragédie nommée Hecuba traduicte en rhythme françoise. Estienne, 1550.   2357

Translation of *Hecuba* of Euripides by means of Latin translation of Erasmus. This edition is attributed by catalogue of the BN and by M. Augé-Chiquet in *La vie, les idées et l'œuvre de Jean Antoine de Baïf*, Hachette, 1909, p. 169, to L. de Baïf. *See* René Sturel in RHL 20:280-96, 1913. *See* 2322. Gaiffe in his edition of Sebillet's *Art poétique*, no. 2344, ix, note 2, shows reason for the above attribution. *See* 2442.

Bounyn, Gabriel. La soltane, tragédie (5 a., v., ch.). Morel, 1561. xvi, 74 p. La soltane, Trauerspiel von Gabriel Bounin, 1561. Neudruck besorgt von E. Stengel und J. Venema mit einer literarischen Einleitung von J. Venema. Marburg, Elwert, 1888.   64 p.   (AA, v. 81)   2358

Excellent introduction (1-28); text (29-64) notes paging of 1561 edition.

Review : R. Mahrenholtz in ZFSL 11²:145-47, 1889.

Desmasures, Louis. Tragédies sainctes : David combattant, David, triomphant, David fugitif. Geneva, Perrin, 1563, 1566. 272 p. Critical edition of Ch. Comte. Cornély, 1907. 277 p. (STFM)   2359

Although there were many 16th century reprints, Comte's edition is most satisfactory and readily available.

Du Hamel, Jacques. Acoubar, tragédie tirée des Amours de Pistion et Fortunée en leur voyage de Canada. Rouen, Du Petit Val, 1603 (BM), 1611 (BN).   2360

The earliest French play about America : *Acoubar; ou, La loyauté trahie*, with an introduction by Margaret Adams White. New York, Institute of French studies, [1931], 76 p. This is reprint of 1603 edition at the BM. Information about author collected in introduction, and play is compared with its source, *Les amours de Pistion*, by Antoine du Périer, 1602. Notes are often trivial and in error.

Review : H. C. Lancaster in MLN 48:135, 1933.

Dabney, Lancaster. A sixteenth century play based on the Chastelaine de Vergi. MLN 48:437-43, 1933.   2361

Points out that Du Souhait's tragedy, *Radegonde, duchesse de Bourgogne*, is based on *Chastelaine de Vergi*.

Galaut, Jean. Phalante. *In:* Recueil de divers poèmes et chans royaux avec le commencement de la traduction de l'Aeneid. Toulouse, Calomiez, 1611. p. 73-147. 2362

H. C. Lancaster has shown (MLN 42:71-77, 1927) *Phalante* to have Sidney's *Arcadia* for source, first example of English influence in France. Author died 1605.

Robert Garnier
(Nos. 2363-2372)

Garnier, Robert. Les tragédies. Patisson, 1585.   12 and 332 ff.   2363

First and best complete collective edition. Used as copy for editions of Foerster and Pinvert.

— Les tragédies; treuer Abdruck der ersten Gesammtausgabe (Paris 1585) mit den Varianten aller vorhergehenden Ausgaben einer Einleitung und einem Glossar, by Wendelin Foerster. Heilbronn, Henninger, 1883.   680 p.   2364

Faithful representation of 1585 edition with variants, but bibliography is confused and inexact.

Review : P. de Nolhac in Rcr 18 (ns 17) : 55-57, Jan. 14, 1884.

— Œuvres complètes (théâtre et poésies) publiées avec notice et des notes par Lucien Pinvert. Garnier, 1923.   2 v.   2365

Good popular edition, less suited to use of scholars than Foerster's, except for improved bibliography. Spelling modernized somewhat. Notes meager.

Review : R. Lebègue in RHL 31:129-30, 1924. Corrects errors.

Chardon, Henri. Robert Garnier, sa vie, ses poésies inédites. RHAM 55:70-94, 161-184, 392-408, 1904. 56:86-110, 187-213, 257-87, 1904. 57:41-75, 176-201, 281-98, 1905. *Also printed separately*, Champion, 1905. 279 p.   2366

Good biography, though rambling and *bavard*. All information used by Pinvert in introduction to his edition of G.

Lebègue, Raymond. La tragédie française au XVIe siècle. Robert Garnier. I. RCC 32 (2e série) : 31-47, 1931; II. 33:460-80; III. 33:548-62; IV. 33:526-45; V. 33:648-72, 1932.   2367

Best recent study of G.; uses all previous material of importance. Contributes ideas of G.'s observance of *bienséances*; moral teaching; search for pathetic; chronological progress in technique. Sections on influence, though superficial, indicate the research to be done in field.

— L'unité de lieu dans l'Antigone de R. Garnier. RSS 11:238-51, 1924.   2368

Concludes, contrary to Rigal, that G.'s stage direction at end of argument : " La représentation en est hors les portes de la ville de Thèbes," was an effort to establish unity of place.

Mysing, Oscar. Robert Garnier und die Antike Tragödie. Leipzig, Schmidt, 1891. 56 p. (Diss., Leipzig)   2369

Essentially sound work. Correction of question of three actors supplied by H. C. Lancaster. *See* 2315.

Review : R. Mahrenholtz in ZFSL 14²:7-9, 1892.

Newton, Winifred. Le thème de Phèdre et d'Hippolyte dans la littérature française. Droz, 1939.   167 p.   (Diss., Paris)   2370

Includes a good study of G.'s Hippolyte. Review : H. C. Lancaster in MLN 55:76, 1940.

Rolland, Joachim. La tragédie française au XVIᵉ siècle : Les Juives [de Robert Garnier], 1580. Sansot, 1911.   131 p.
2370A

Really only first volume, devoted to source and other questions concerning G.'s *Juives*.

Review : M. Du Bos in RER 10:146-47. 1912.

Searles, Colbert. The stageability of Garnier's tragedies. MLN 22:225-29, 1907, 2371

Concludes : " To greater or lesser extent are all the tragedies of Garnier playable, or were playable, with probable exception of *Hippolyte* and *Cornélie*." Good study of solutions to 16th century staging problems.

Witherspoon, Alexander Maclaren. The influence of Robert Garnier on Elizabethan drama. New Haven, Yale University Press, 1924.   197 p. (Diss., Yale) 2372

Excellent biography of G. from secondary sources. Defends G. against accusation that he was a slavish imitator of Seneca. Study of Kyd's adaptation of *Cornélie* and Lady Pembroke's translation of *Marc-Antoine*. Review of other plays in English of G. type. *See* 2849.

Other Tragedies

Grévin, Jacques. Théâtre complet et poésies choisies de Jacques Grévin avec notice et notes par Lucien Pinvert. *See* 1370. 2373

With exception of reprint of *César* by Collischonn, the only available edition; very usable one in spite of faults and errors listed in review.

Review : R. Lebègue in RHL 31:128-29, 1924.

Collischonn, G. A. O. Jacques Grévin's Tragödie Caesar in ihrem Verhältnis zu Muret, Voltaire und Shakespeare. Marburg, Elwert, 1886.   86 p.   (AA, v. 52)
2374

P. 1-48 devoted to comparisons of texts for verbal resemblances. P. 49-74, reprint of Grévin's *César*, and 75-86, reprint of Muret's *Julius César, tragoedia*.

Review : C. Barrelet in ZFSL 9²:62-63, 1887.

Pinvert, Lucien. Jacques Grévin, étude biographique et littéraire. *See* 1371. 2375

Best study on Grévin to date. Has some faults and errors, corrected for most part in review below. *See* 350, 440, 2563.

Review : L. Séché in Rren 1:60-61, 1901.

Guérin d'Aronnière, Claude. Panthée ou l'amour conjugal, tragédie. Angers, Hernault, 1608.   87 p.   2376

Manuscript copy of this edition at the BN. Frères Parfaict (no. 2288, v. IV, p. 118) mistakenly refer to this author as Guerin de La Dorouvière.

Jodelle, Estienne. Cléopâtre captive; a critical edition by Lowell Bryce Ellis. Philadelphia, 1946.   128 p.   (PPRL, extra series no. 9)   2377

Has a 59-page introduction. Thorough, workmanlike synthesis of material available on Jodelle and a good study of play's style, composition, sources, language and versification. Concurs with generally accepted opinion of mediocrity of the play, but makes a case for its influence on current of French tragedy.

Review : S. F. Will in FR 20:405-06, 1946-47.

Neri, Ferdinando. La prima tragedia di Estienne Jodelle. GSLI 74:50-63, 1919.
2378

Sees Italian source for *Cléopâtre* in work of Cesare De Cesari, Venice, 1552. Resolves negatively question of Du Bellay's intention to write *Cléopâtre* before Jodelle. *See* 2776.

Review : H. Potez in 29:368-69, 1922. Corrects one error.

Banachévitch, Nicolas. Jean Bastier de La Péruse (1509-1554); étude biographique et littéraire. *See* 1374. 2379

Médée, conceived at Paris between 1551 and 1553, was finished after La Péruse's death by Jean Boiceau de La Borderie and edited by Scévole de Sainte-Marthe. Review : J. Plattard in RSS 11:109-11, 1924.

La Taille, Jacques de. Daire, tragédie (5a., v., 35 ff.) and Alexandre, tragédie (5a., v., 31 ff.). Morel, 1573, 1598. 2380

Composed before 1562, date of author's death. Published posthumously by Jean de La Taille, author's brother.

Baguenault de Puchesse, Gustave, *comte.* Jean et Jacques de La Taille, étude biographique et littéraire sur deux poètes du xvie siècle. Orléans, Herluison, 1889. 66 p. 2381

Compilation of all information previously published, supplemented by manuscript *Vies des poètes français* of Colletet, by study of works of authors, published and manuscript. No analysis or discussion of plays, except for indication of editions. Some errors in dates, etc.

Le Breton, Guillaume, *sieur de La Fon.* Adonis, tragédie, autres vers de luy mesme. L'Angelier, 1579. 54 ff.; Rouen, Du Petit Val, 1597, 1611. 47 p. 2382

Published by F. d'Amboise. Edition of 1579 is earliest known, but a sonnet of F. d'Amboise, dated 1574, may indicate an earlier edition.

Grandmotet (or Grandmotté), Professeur du Collège de Nevers. Étude sur la tragédie d'Adonis de Guillaume Le Breton, seigneur de La Fon. BSNL 1:211-31, 1854. 2383

Accepts Guillaume as given by La Croix du Maine instead of Gabriel as in Du Verdier and title of play published by François d'Amboise. Detailed *résumé* with abundant quotations of Le Breton's tragedy *Adonis*, represented before Charles IX in 1569. Shows classical source of plot and of many passages.

Trissino, Giovanni Giorgio. La tragédie de Sophonisbé. Trans. by Claude Mermet. Lyons, Odet, 1584. 2384

Ludwig Fries in *Montchrétien's Sophonisbé,* Marburg, 1886, p. 9-11, compares translation with original; concludes that translation is a close one.

Daele, Rose Marie. Nicolas de Montreulx (Ollenix du Mont-Sacré) arbiter of European literary vogues of the late renaissance. *See* 1016. 2385

Assembles all available biographical material on Montreux plus something from personal researches in family archives. Valuable because only available work on this prolific dramatist. Useful bibliography would be more valuable if complete titles of plays were given and index revealed pages where they are discussed. *See* 1039, 2860.

Review : Robert V. Merrill in RR 38: 173-74, 1947.

Percheron, Luc. Pyrrhe, tragédie. Crapelet, 1845. 80 p. 2386

An edition of 16 copies of a manuscript in library of Le Mans dedicated to Mlles de Beaumanoir, Apr. 2, 1592.

Charmasse, Anatole de. François Perrin, poète français du xvie siècle, et sa vie par Guillaume Colletet, publiée d'après le manuscrit aujourd'hui détruite de la bibliothèque du Louvre. Autun, Dejussien, 1887. 251 p. *See* 2414. 2387

Very satisfactory biography, using material no longer available.

Review : A. Delboulle in Rcr 21 (ns 24) : 369-71, Nov. 14, 1887.

Molinier, Henri Joseph. Mellin de Saint-Gelais (1490-1558); étude sur sa vie et ses œuvres. *See* 724. 2388

Collects documents, but full of lacunae and errors due to bad printing. No attempt to clear up chronology of manuscripts and editions.

Review : J. Plattard in RHL 18:694-96, 1911.

Schelandre, Jean de. Tyr et Sidon ou Les funestes amours de Belcar et Meliane, tragédie. Edition critique by Jules Haraszti. Cornély, 1908. 168 p. (STFM) 2389

Excellent, accurate introduction with all information available. Important as one of publications opposing Rigal's thesis that only Hardy's plays were represented. Bibliography of Schelandre before this edition carefully listed and summarized.

Literary Studies Based on Tragedies

Andrae, August. Sophonisbé in der französischen Tragödie mit Berücksichtrigung der Sophonisbearbeitungen in anderen Litteraturen. Leipzig, Franck, 1891. 114 p. (ZFSL, sup. VI)　　　　　2390
Lists with bibliographical details tragedies on subject : those of Saint-Gelais and Mermet from Trissino's Italian, Jacques Mondot's as reported by Beauchamps, Montchrétien's. Analyzes with great detail *Sophonisbé* of Nicolas de Montreux. *See Sophonisbearbeitungen* in ZFSL 16:113-16, 1894. Adds list of plays on *Sophonisbé* in other languages.

Haraszti, Jules. La littérature dramatique au temps de la renaissance considérée dans ses rapports avec la scène contemporaine. RHL 11:680-86, 1904.　　　　　2391
Summary by author of his 62-page study, published at Budapest. Refutes Rigal's assertions that (1) 16th century tragedies were neither staged nor intended to be, that (2) tragedy gave way after *Bradamante* to tragi-comedy, that (3) authors of new school gave up idea of staging their plays. Excellent short outline of development of French theater.

Klein, Friedrich. Der Chor in der Wichtigsten Tragödien der französischen Renaissance. Leipzig, Deichert, 1897. 144 p. (MBP, v. 12)　　　　　2392
Long bibliography lacks accurate information concerning editions of texts. Value in clear development of literary theories of 16th century as influenced by Aristotle, Latins, Italians, and application to some ten plays, beginning with Jodelle's *Cléopâtre*.
Review : A. Stiefel in ZFSL 22²:26-27, 1900. Thinks *chœur* less influenced by theorists than by Seneca and Italians as examples.

Moeller, Georg H. Die Auffassung der Kleopatra in der Tragödienliteratur der romanischen und germanischen Nationen. Ulm, Kerler, 1888. 94 p.　　　　　2394
Discusses and analyzes plays of Jodelle, Montreux (he spells Montreuil) from 16th century.
Review : M. Koch in ZVL ns 2:388, 1889.

Puymaigre, Joseph Boudet, comte de. Jeanne d'Arc au théâtre 1439-1890. Savine, 1890. 115 p.　　　　　2395

Plays of Fronton du Duc and Jean de Virey fall in 16th century.
Review : T. de L. in Rcr 24 (ns 30) : 33-34, July 14, 1890.

Ricci, Charles. Sophonisbé dans la tragédie classique italienne et française. Grenoble, Allier, 1904. 223 p.　　　　　2396
Conscientious, meticulous analysis of sources of story and plots of plays by Galeotto del Caretto (1500), Trissino (1515), Saint-Gelais, Mermet, Montchrétien, Montreux, Mairet, Corneille, Pansuti, Alfieri. *Cf.* Andrae (no. 2390).
Review : E. Bouvy in BI 4:267-69, 1904, complains that Ricci does not show historical significance of difference in treatment of material at different times.

Thiel, Maria A. La figure de Saül et sa représentation dans la littérature dramatique française. Amsterdam, H. J. Paris, 1926. 138 p.　　　　　2397
Rather brief analyses of plays in which Saul appears : Jean de La Taille, Des Masures, Claude Billard for 16th century. Interesting, well written study, but not important.
Reviews : H. C. Lancaster in MLN 43:285, 1928; R. Lebègue in RHL 35:118-119, 1928; Anon in Archiv 151:311, 1926-27.

Theater of the Renaissance — Comedy

General Works

Baschet, Armand. Les comédiens italiens à la cour de France sous Charles IX, Henri III, Henri IV et Louis XIII d'après les lettres royales, la correspondance originale des comédiens, les régistres de la trésorerie de l'épargne et autres documents. Plon, 1882, xv, 367 p.　　　　　2398
Considerable authentic information diluted in frank conjectures and garrulous gossip about important people of time. Good index. *See* 2664.
Reviews : T. de L. in Rcr 16 (ns 14):384-387, Nov. 13, 1882; A. L. Stiefel in LGRP 1:27, 1886.

Chasles, Emile. La comédie en France au seizième siècle. Didier, 1862. 214 p. 2399
Best early work. Tried to present a complete picture. Material used by Toldo, no. 2405. To supplement with this and Lintilhac, no. 2402, for general treatment. Hard to find.

Fest, Otto. Der Miles gloriosus in der französischen Komödie von Beginn der Renaissance bis zu Molière. Leipzig, Deichert, 1897. 123 p. (MBP, v. 13)   2400

Much more careful, thorough study than that of Rigal (no. 2404). Traces origin, influence of Plautus, Terence, Spanish, *Commedia dell'arte*, and in twelve comedies of 16th century. Essential for understanding of history of this and other conventional characters.

Review : A. L. Stiefel in Archiv 103:195-201, 1899.

Haraszti, Jules. La comédie de la renaissance et la scène. RHL 16:285-301, 1909.
          2401

Sustains (with Lanson against Rigal and Lintilhac) thesis that comedies were played in provinces. *Résumé* of a publication made at Budapest.

Lintilhac, Eugène François. La comédie régulière de Jodelle à Larivey. *In his :* Histoire générale du théâtre en France. v. II, La comédie : moyen-âge et renaissance. Flammarion, 1905. p. 299-417.   2402

Excellent for first exploration of 16th century comedy from Jodelle through Larivey to Corneille. For popular or student use; not a research study; not complete. Skimpy bibliography and documentation. *See* 2399, 2405.

Mignon, Maurice. Études sur le théâtre français & italien de la renaissance. Champion, 1923. 86 p.   2403

Helpful for understanding Italian influence in such matters as Ariosto's comedies, *La Cassaria, Suppositi*, Italian theater at Lyons. *See* 2674.

Review : W. Smith in MLN 41:401-402, 1926.

Rigal, Eugène. Les personnages conventionnels de la comédie au XVIe siècle. RHL 4:161-79, 1897.   2404

Types : *vieillard amoureux, femme d'intrigue*, valet, parasite, *pédant, soldat fanfaron*. Good general idea of what these types were. No attempt to be complete, to seek origins of types except for valet and braggart soldier. Does for 16th century what Victor Fournel's chapter, *Les types de la vieille comédie* (*in :* Le théâtre au XVIIe siècle*, Lecène, Oudin, 1892, p. 79-121), does for 17th century. *See* 2400.

Toldo, Pietro. La comédie française de la renaissance. RHL 4:336-92, 1897; 5:220-264, 554-603, 1898; 6:571-608, 1899; 7:263-283, 1900.   2405

Best and most complete work on subject. Replaces Chasles (no. 2399); more thorough than Lintilhac (no. 2402). Author uses knowledge of Italian literature to show Italian elements in French comedy. Includes careful collection of all comedies and translations. *See* 2431, 2682.

— Études sur le théâtre comique du moyen âge et sur le rôle de la nouvelle dans les farces et dans les comédies. SFR 9:181-369, 1901.   2406

Finds that comedies, especially farces, largely drew plots from *nouvelles* and *fabliaux* during 15th and 16th centuries.

Review : In Rom 32:175-76, 1908, finds that Toldo does not prove point but has much other good material.

Collections of Comedies

RECUEILS

Fournier, Edouard. Le théâtre français au XVIe et au XVIIe siècle; ou choix des comédies les plus remarquables antérieures à Molière, avec une introduction et une notice sur chaque auteur. La Place, s.d. (1871). 582 p.; Garnier [192—].   2407

Eugène of Jodelle, *La reconnue* of Belleau, *Esprits* of Larivey, *Contents* of Turnèbe, *Néapolitaines* of Fr. d'Amboise, *Les escolliers* of Fr. Perrin from 16th century. clearly printed, well annotated, illustrated collection possessed by most libraries. Essential for 16th century comedy. *See* 2414.

TEXTS OF COMEDIES AND CRITICAL WORKS
ON COMEDIES AND AUTHORS

Nagel, Heinrich. Die Werke Jean Antoine de Baïfs. Archiv 61:53-124, 1879.   2408

Plays (*Antigone, Eunuque, Brave*) in section of *Œuvres* called *Jeux* discussed (p. 108-20) with long quotations from each.

Review : G. Koerting in ZFSL 1:120-122, 1879.

Chappuys, Gabriel. L'avare cornu. Lyons, Honorati, 1580.   2409

Translated from *Avaro cornuto* of A. F. Doni. For details and summary of the play, with extracts, *see* E. Roy in RHL 1:38-48, 1894, *L'avare de Doni et L'avare de Molière*, and P. Toldo in RHL 6:571 (note 2), 1899.

Wenzel, Guido. Pierre de Lariveys Komödien und ihr Einfluss auf Molière. Archiv 82:63-80, 1889. 2410

General discussion, few comparisons of details. No quotations for verbal similarities.

Doumic, René. Les Esprits de Pierre Larivey. RCC I (2ᵉ série, no. 23) : 183-91, 1893. 2411

Delivered as an introduction to first representation of *Esprits* at Odéon in 1893. Concludes that Larivey gave comedies French setting, at least embryonic characters ; influenced Molière and others after.

MacGillivray, John. Life and works of Pierre Larivey. Leipzig, Frankenstein and Wagner, 1889. 55 p. (Diss., Leipzig) 2412

Not very much, but there is little to take its place.

Süss, Wilhelm. Die Nephélococugie des Pierre Le Loyer. ZFSL 36:254-73, 1910. 2412A

Shows resemblance to *Birds* of Aristophanes by analysis and quotations.

Lemaître, Jules. Les contents d'Odet de Turnèbe. RCC I (2ᵉ sér., no. 22) : 150-58, 1893. 2413

Apropos of *première* representation in 1893 at Odéon. Asserts best comedy on Latin model before Molière. Collection of all available material on Turnèbe, summary of plot sources.

Perrin, François. Les escoliers. Chaudière, 1586. Les escoliers, comédie en cinq actes et en vers, réimprimée textuellement sur l'édition de Paris, Chaudière, 1585, par Paul Lacroix, Brussels, Mertens, 1866. 108 p. *Also in* : E. Fournier, compiler. Le théâtre français au XVIᵉ et au XVIIᵉ siècle. *See* 2407, Garnier ed., p. 429-97. 2414

Printed after *Sichem ravisseur*, Chaudière, 1589. For *Les escoliers*, Lacroix used the ms. copy of the 1586 edition, he says, but the ms. has the date 1589, and corresponds in all details to edition of 1589. *See* Charmasse, on Perrin, (no. 2387).

Theater
Translations from the Classics
(Nos. 2415-2464)

GEORGE O. SEIVER AND NORMAN B. SPECTOR

General

Baudrier, Henri. Bibliographie lyonnaise; recherches sur les imprimeurs, libraires, relieurs et fondeurs de lettres à Lyon au XVIᵉ siècle par le Président Baudrier, publiées et continuées par J. Baudrier. *See* 40. 2415

Contains descriptions of 16th century translation of Greek and Latin drama published in Lyons as well as information on printers who published them.

Brisset, Roland. Le premier livre du théâtre tragique de Roland Brisset, gentilhomme tourangeau. Tours, Montroeil and Richer, 1590. 312 p. 2416

This volume contains translations of Seneca's *Hercules furens*, *Thyestes*, *Agamemnon*, and *Octavia*. *Baptiste* of Buchanan is also printed. *See* Marie Delcourt, *Etude sur les traductions des tragiques* (no. 2320A), p. 95-107. For description of the edition *see* Brunet (no. 2417) I, 1262.

Brunet, Jacques Charles. Manuel du libraire et de l'amateur de livres. 6 v. 5th ed. Firmin-Didot, 1860-65 and Supplément (ed. P. Deschamps and G. Brunet). 3 v. Firmin-Didot, 1870-80. *See* 9. 2417

Descriptions of various 16th-century translations of classical dramas.

Bunker, Ruth. A bibliographical study of the Greek works and translations published in France during the renaissance : the decade 1540-1550. New York, Columbia University, 1939. 250 p. (Diss., Columbia) 2418

Miss Bunker's thesis contains chapters on teaching of Greek in 16th century, translations and translators of Greek, and printing and printers of Greek books. *See* particularly Ch. II. *Translations and translators of Greek books*, p. 38-77. Translations of drama listed in the period 1540-1550 are the 1544 *Hecuba* and the 1549 *Iphigenia* (of Sebillet). Miss Bunker notes the dual attribution of *Hecuba* to Lazare de Baïf and to Guillaume Bochetel, but expresses no personal preference for either. Her bibliographical listing, however, reproduces edition as being work of Baïf. *See* 2516.

Chamard, Henri. Deux œuvres collectives. Pontus de Tyard-Antoine de Baïf. 1573. *In his :* Histoire de la Pléiade. *See* 1047, v. III, p. 162-87.   2419

Contains analyses of Baïf's *Le brave, Antigone,* and *L'eunuque.*

Delcourt, Marie. Étude sur les traductions des tragiques grecs et latins en France depuis la renaissance. *See* 2320A.   2420

Analyzes French translations of Greek and Latin classical tragedies from 16th to 19th centuries. First of three chapters devoted to translations " avant le classicisme." Confirms Sturel's contention in his *Essai sur les traductions du théâtre grec en français avant 1500* (2427) that there were both free and literal translations during renaissance as well as in 18th century. Considers literary value of the translations primarily. *See* 2553.

Reviews : E. R. Curtius in NS 34:563-564, 1926; V. Daniel in RBP 5:987-90, 1926; A. Freté in RPLH 50:258-59, 1926; R. Lebègue in RSS 13:147-50, 1926; L. Mench in Poly 2nd ser. 103:276-77, 1926.

— La traduction des comiques anciens en France avant Molière. Liège and Paris, Droz, 1934. 95 p. (BFL Fasc. LIX.)   2421

Studies nature of influence of Plautus, Terence, and Aristophanes on French theater and society from 16th century on. Concludes that Terence's influence was largely a moralistic one during renaissance, in view of the inordinately large number of school editions, translations, and collections of his " sentences " available to the reading public. The influence of Plautus, translated later and less frequently, is seen especially in development of comic drama itself. Aristophanes' role in 16th century French comedy is negligible, a fragment of *Plutus* translated into French (attributed by Claude Binet to Ronsard) and a free rendering of *Birds* (Pierre Le Loyer's *La néphélococugie*) being the only surviving translations. *See* 2554.

Reviews : P. Faider in RBP 15:161-63, 1936; A. Freté in REL 13:185-87, 1935; H. C. Lancaster in MLN 51:64-65, 1936; R. Lebègue in Hren 5:177-78, 1938; R. Marichal in Hren 3:109, 1936; W. Mönch in ZFSL 59:490-92, 1935; D. Mornet in RHL 42:455, 1935.

Graesse, Jean George Théodore. Trésor de livres rares et précieux; ou nouveau dictionnaire bibliographique. Dresden, Kuntze, 1859-69. 7 v.   2422

Description of various 16th century translations of classical dramas. Not as detailed as Brunet.

Hennebert, Frédéric. Histoire des traductions françaises d'auteurs grecs et latins pendant le XVIe et le XVIIe siècles. Brussels, Lesigne, 1861. 261 p. (AUB, 2nd ser., v. I)   2423

Out of date and containing errors of fact with respect to translations of Greek and Latin drama in 16th century; of little more than historical interest. Part I, on 16th century, contains chapters on prose and verse translations from Greek and Latin, a chapter on Amyot, and a chapter on Pléiade. *See* 2519.

Lebègue, Raymond. Tableau chronologique. *In his :* La tragédie religieuse en France; les débuts (1514-1573). *See* 2318, p. 113-16.   2424

Brief chronological table of dates of composition, performance and publication of French renaissance tragedies. Corrections and emendations made in Lebègue's extension of the table to 1610; see 2426.

— Tableau de la comédie française de la renaissance. BHren 8:278-344, 1946.   2425

Table and detailed notes on composition, performance, and publication, giving dates, of all 16th century French comedies. Lists also French translations of classical Greek and Latin comedies. Valuable reference for all study of French renaissance comedy.

— Tableau de la tragédie française de 1573 à 1610. BHren 5:373-93, 1944.   2426

Correction and extension of data contained in chronological table of French tragedies (date of composition, performance, and publication) in Lebègue's *Tragédie religieuse,* no. 2318 (p. 113-16). Corrects attribution of the 1544 translation of *Hecuba* from Amyot to Bochetel.

Sturel, René. Essai sur les traductions du théâtre grec en français avant 1550. *See* 2322.   2427

Detailed and solid study of following translations : (1) Published. Sophocles' *Electra* by Lazare de Baïf (1537); Euripides' *Hecuba* by Guillaume Bochetel (1544); Euripides' *Iphigenia in Aulis* by Thomas Sebillet (1549). (2) Manuscript. Sophocles' *Antigone* by Calvy de La Fontaine (1542); Euripides' *Iphigenia in Aulis* (1545-47) and *Trojan women* (1542-47) by Amyot. Complete description of editions and manuscripts. Indispensable for study of translations. *See* 2553.

Tchemerzine, Avenir. Bibliographie d'éditions originales et rares d'auteurs français des XVe, XVIe, XVIIe, et XVIIIe siècles. *See* 32. 2428

Reproduces title pages of several 16th century translations of Greek and Latin dramas including Lazare de Baïf's *Electra*, Bochetel's *Hecuba* (attributed to Lazare de Baïf), Toutain's *Agememnon*, and the 1555 *Andria*.

Jacques Amyot, bishop of Auxerre
(Nos. 2429-2430)

Amyot, Jacques. Iphigénie à Aulis. (BN ms. fr. 22505) 2429

This manuscript bears no author's name and contains no preface or dedication indicating identity of the author. Sturel, *Essai sur les traductions du théâtre grec*, no. 2427, establishes it to be in the hand of Adam Charles, A.'s copyist and thus concludes it to be by A. Translation was done between 1545 and 1547. A.'s rendering indulges in far less liberty and originality than do those of Thomas Sebillet and Calvy de La Fontaine. He nevertheless expands the sixteen hundred verses of the original to three thousand, one hundred in French.

— Les Troades. (Musée Condé ms. no. 1688). 2430

This anonymous manuscript, in the hand of Adam Charles, A.'s copyist, has been attributed by Sturel to A., who used, for his translation, Latin version of the play by Dorotheus Camillus (1542). " D'une façon générale, Amyot a rendu avec exactitude sinon tous les détails..., du moins toutes les idées du texte grec. Ce serait plutôt, ici, encore, l'excès du développement qu'on pourrait lui reprocher; cette habitude d'allonger le texte pour ne laisser aucune idée obscure, pour unir les phrases entre elles et en souligner la liaison logique, nous la retrouvons dans cette traduction comme nous l'avions notée dans celle d'Iphigénie." (*Essai sur les traductions du théâtre grec*, no. 2322, p. 663-64.)

Aristophanes
(Nos. 2431-2437)

Toldo, Pierre. La comédie française de la renaissance. *See* 2405 2431

See p. 574-79 for an analysis of *La néphélococugie*, Le Loyer's version of *Birds* of A.

Anon. Fragment de la comédie de Plutus. 2432

This fragment consists of a translation of first act plus 47 lines of second act of A.'s comedy. Its attribution to Ronsard by Claude Binet has been contested by Paul Laumonier (critical edition of Binet's *Vie de Ronsard*, p. 102-04) and supported by Marie Delcourt (no. 2421, p. 75-77). Raymond Lebègue (*Tableau de la comédie*, no. 2425, p. 301), basing his hypothesis on a passage in Du Verdier, suggests that translation was a work of collaboration between Jean-Antoine de Baïf and Ronsard while both were studying with Dorat. In any event, the play was performed at Collège de Coqueret in 1548 or 1549. The fragment was published for the first time in the thirteenth collected edition of Ronsard's works (6 v. Buon and Macé, 1617). It has been reprinted in Marty-Laveaux edition of Ronsard (v. VI, p. 290 ff.) and in Blanchemain edition (v. VII, p. 281-305).

Egger, Emile. La comédie en France avant et pendant la renaissance de l'hellénisme. *In his*: L'hellénisme en France. Didier, 1869. II, 1-19. 2433

Contains an analysis of Le Loyer's *Néphélococugie*, the 1578 French version of *Birds* of A.

Guy, Henri. Les sources françaises de Ronsard. *See* 1130. 2434

Shows the archaisms in the fragment of A.'s *Plutus* attributed by Binet to Ronsard (p. 220).

Laumonier, Paul. Commentaire historique et critique. *In his*: La vie de P. de Ronsard de Claude Binet (1586). Édition critique avec introduction et commentaire historique et critique. Hachette, 1910. p. 102-04. 2435

This note to line 7, p. 13 in Laumonier's edition of Binet's biography discusses attribution of a fragment of A.'s *Plutus*, translated into French, to Ronsard. Laumonier concludes that it is not the work of Ronsard in view of the fact that it appeared for the first time only in the 1617 edition of Ronsard's works and that Ronsard himself never made any allusion to it.

Le Loyer, Pierre. Œuvres et Mélanges poétiques, ensemble la comédie Nephelococugie, ou la nuée des cocus, non moins docte que facétieuse. Poupy, 1579. 256 p. 2436

This version of *Birds* of A. was written in
1578. A copy of this edition is located in
Bibliothèque nationale (Réserve p Y e 146).
For description *see* Brunet 3:959.

Süss, Wilhelm. Frankreich im 16., 17. und
18. Jahrhundert. *In his:* Aristophanes und
die Nachwelt. Leipzig, Dieterich, 1911.
p. 55-101. 2437

Study of A.'s influence on French literature of 16th, 17th, and 18th centuries.
See p. 55-76 for brief consideration of
fragment of *Plutus* attributed by Binet to
Ronsard and a detailed analysis of *La
néphélococugie*, Pierre Le Loyer's version of
Birds. Extensive extracts of the French
play are given.

Jean Antoine de Baïf
(Nos. 2438-2439)

Baïf, Jean Antoine de. Le brave, comédie
de Jean-Antoine de Baïf, jouée devant le roy
en l'hostel de Guise à Paris le 28 de janvier
1567. Estienne, 1567. 2438

B.'s translation of *Miles gloriosus* was
later inserted, with no changes, in *Ieux*,
published as part of *Euvres en rime* in
1573. (" Le roy " is Charles IX.) For
description *see* Graesse V, 334; Tchemerzine I, 249.

Augé-Chiquet, Mathieu. L'auteur dramatique. *In his:* La vie, les idées et l'œuvre de
Jean-Antoine de Baïf. Hachette and Toulouse, Privat, 1909. p. 168-202. (Diss.,
Paris.) 2439

Analyzes B.'s translations of Sophocles'
Antigone, Terence's *Eunuchus*, and Plautus'
Miles gloriosus. Contains also brief consideration of the translations lost (Sophocles' *Trachiniae*, A.'s *Plutus*, Terence's
Heautontimorumenos) or incomplete (Euripides' *Helen*, of which only the prologue
was translated). *See* 2450, 2547.

Euripides
(Nos. 2441-2444)

Anon. Les suppliantes d'Euripide. 1536-
1547. 2441

A French translation of E.'s drama
existing only in manuscript. It is mentioned by Lebègue (2441, p. 381) as being
listed in " catalogue de vente de la bibliothèque F.-D., 4 novembre 1938, n° 51,
avec un fac-similé de la reliure du manuscrit aux armes du dauphin Henri."
(The latter became Henri II.)

Bochetel, Guillaume. La tragédie d'Euripide nommée Hecuba, traduite de grec en
rythme françoise, dédiée au roi. *See* 2357.
2442

Despite Sturel's exhaustive proof to the
contrary (no. 2427) this translation is still
erroneously attributed to Lazare de Baïf
in more recent studies. These are evidently following the original attribution to Baïf
of Peletier du Mans in his *Art poétique*,
(no. 1382), La Croix du Maine, and the
erroneous listings in such catalogues as
Brunet, Graesse and Tchemerzine. *See*
Marie Delcourt (no. 2320A), p. 34-36 for
support of Sturel's attribution to Guillaume
Bochetel of this translation (no. 2552).
Edition was reprinted in 1550. *See*
Brunet II, 1104; Graesse II, 523; Tchemerzine I, 343 for descriptions attributing it to
Baïf.

Kuntz, C. Untersuchungen über La tragoedie des Troades d'Euripide anonyme Übersetzung in französischen Versen aus dem
16. Jahrhundert. Greifswald, 1909. 88 p.
See 2548. 2443

Although not attempting to establish
authorship of this manuscript version
[Condé ms.1688, identified by Sturel as the
work of Amyot. *See* 2427.], Kuntz studies
the method, sources, and versification of
the translation; dates it as having been
written between 1550 and 1555. Sturel
places it ca. 1542.

Sebillet, Thomas. L'Iphigène d'Euripide,
... tournée de grec en françois par l'auteur de
l'Art poétique (Th. Sibilet). Corrozet,
1549. 75 ff. 2444

Sebillet, although knowing some Greek,
was not an outstanding scholar of the
language. His translation made use largely of the Latin rendering of *Iphigenia* by
Erasmus, a free translation, the 1650 verses
of the original being expanded to 3300 by
Sebillet. " Encore une fois on a l'impression que c'est surtout un exercice de versification française qu'a tenté Sebillet..."
(Sturel, no. 2427, p. 643). *See* Brunet II,
1105, Graesse II, 524.

Seneca
(Nos. 2445-2448)

Böhm, Karl. Beiträge zur Kenntnis des
Einflusses Seneca's auf die in der Zeit von
1552 bis 1562 erschienenen französischen
Tragödien. *See* 2320. 2445

Studies influence of S. on tragedies of
Jodelle, La Péruse, Des Mazures, Grévin,

Rivaudeau, Jacques de La Taille. Contains chapters listing editions and translations of S. and of classical Greek writers of tragedy.

Reviews : A. Andrae in NPR 21:349-50, 1903; P. A. Becker in DLit 24:1597-99, June 27, 1903; A. Counson in RIPB 46:339-41, 1903; R. Mahrenholtz in ZFSL 26²:16-18, 1903.

Grosnet, Pierre. Les tragédies de Seneque, desquelles sont extraicts plusieurs enseignements, authorités et sentences tant en latin comme en françoys, et en la fin est adjoustée la vie et trespassement du dit Seneque.   2446
Earliest French translation of S. Edition appeared in 1534. *See* Brunet V, 287 and Suppl. 631; Graesse VI, 360 for description.

Le Duchat, François. Agamemnon, tragédie retirée de Sénèque par François Le Duchat, Troyen, dédiée à l'illustre et vertueux prince Antoine Caracciolo de Melfe, évêque de Troies. Breton, 1561.   2447
Le Duchat does not appear to have known *Agamemnon* of Toutain, nor to have made use of it for his translation. *See* Marie Delcourt, no. 2320A, p. 90-95. For description of the edition *see* Graesse 6: 361.

Toutain, Charles. La tragédie d'Agamemnon avec deus livres de chants de philosophie et d'amour, par Charles Toutain. Martin, à l'enseigne S. Christophle, deuant le college de Cambrai, rue S. Ian de Latran. 1557.   2448
Toutain is really first French translator of S. *See* Marie Delcourt, no. 2320A, p. 75-90. Brunet gives place and date of publication of this edition as Martin, 1556. *See* Brunet V. 904: Graesse 6:361; Tchemerzine V, 19.

Sophocles
(Nos. 2449-2451)

Baïf, Jean Antoine de. Antigone tragédie de Sophocle. Par Ian Antoine de Baif. *In :* Les ieux de Ian antoine de Baif. *See* 2351.   2449
Baïf's *Antigone* was perhaps composed considerably earlier than 1573. His intention, according to Marie Delcourt, was to have the play performed, and his translation reflects that purpose. *See her* no. 2320A, p. 71-81. For description of this edition *see* Tchemerzine I, 274, and for text *see Euvres en rime*, ed. Marty-Laveaux *(Pléiade françoise)* III, 115-81.

Baïf, Lazare de. La tragédie de Sophocles intitulée Electra contenant la vengeance de l'inhumaine et très piteuse mort d'Agamemnon roy de Mycène la grant faicte par sa femme Clytemnestra et son adultère Egistus : la dicte tragédie traduicte du grec dudit Sophocles, en rythme françoyse, ligne pour ligne et vers pour vers, en faveur et commodité des amateurs de l'une et l'autre langue. *See* 2352.   2450
The library at St. Mark's in Venice possesses a manuscript redaction of this translation, according to Sturel, who suggests that it was done by Baïf, in France, before his departure for Italy (1529). Brunet, Suppl. 670, lists the title as : *Tragédie de Sophocles intitulée Electra, contenant la vengeance de l'inhumaine et très piteuse mort d'Agamemnon ... Ladicte tragédie trad. du grec dudict Sophocles en rythme françoise, ligne pour ligne, et vers pour vers (par Lazare de Baïf).* Imprimé à Paris pour Roffet, 1537.
For further description *see* Brunet V, 452; Tchemerzine I, 344.

Calvy de La Fontaine. Antigone. (Bibl. de Soissons, ms. 189B)   2451
An " anonymous " translation in manuscript of S.'s play. Sturel (2427) has established its author as Calvy de La Fontaine. The date is 1542. Whether translation was done from a Greek text or from a later rendering cannot be determined. The 1350 verses of original have been expanded to 2200.

Terence (Publius Terentius Afer)
(Nos. 2452-2464)

Anon. Therence en françois, prose et rime, avecques le latin with a colophon : Icy fine Therence en françoys. Verard, ca. 1500. 385 p.   2452
First French translation of T. Lawton refutes attribution of the verse translation to Octovien de Geiais. He suggests that prose translation was done by Guillaume Rippe; verse by Gilles Cybille. *See Térence en France*, no. 2464, p. 350-367. He establishes date of publication as 1500-03. For further description *see* Brunet V, 720- and Supplement 738; Graesse 6², 65.

Anon. Le grant therence en françoys tant en rime que en prose nouuellement imprimé à Paris. Marc Therence Varro liure tresplaisant et joyeulx contenant diverses sentences des facessies et ieux que iadis estoient iouez a Romme quon appelloit les Comedies ... Bossozel, 1539. 389 p.   2453

This edition was put out by two publishers, Guillaume de Bossozel, who printed it, and Guillaume La Bret. It is, textually, a reproduction of 1500-03 Vérard *Therence en françois* (2452). Brunet also lists it as being published by Thielman Kerver (*see* his Supplement, 738). For fuller description *see* Lawton, *Térence en France*, no. 2464, p. 422-25; Brunet V, 720; Graesse 6², 65-66.

Anon. Premiere comedie de Terence appellee L'Andrie : Nouuellement traduite, & mise en ryme françoyse; plus un traité des quatre vertus cardinales, selon Senecque. Lyons, Payan, 1555. 218 p.   2454

La Croix du Maine, Goujet, Brunet, Graesse, Tchemerzine have attributed or accepted attribution of this translation to Bonaventure des Périers. Harold Lawton and Adolphe Chenevière (no. 953) refute this attribution (*see* Lawton, *Térence en France*, no. 2464, p. 459-69). A plausible argument for authorship of Etienne Dolet is presented by Marie Delcourt, *see* 2459A. For description of the edition *see* Brunet V, 722; Graesse 6²: 66; Tchemerzine IV, 360; Baudrier IV, 266.

Anon. P. Terentii Andria Latinogallica. Grandini, 1558.   2455

A school version of *Andria*. *See* Lawton, *Térence en France*, no. 2464, p. 483-88.

Anon. La courtisane romaine, par I. D. B. A. La pornegraphie terentiane, et la complainte de la belle Heaumiere, en elegantes contremises de ieune beauté, et vieille laidure : iadis composée et interpretée. Lyons, Edouard, 1558. Auec priuilege.   2456

Translated extracts from *Eunuchus*, *Heautontimorumenos*, and *Hecyra*, printed with poem of Du Bellay and Villon, portraying the ruses and intrigues of courtesans. *See* Lawton, *Térence en France*, 2464, p. 488-99; Henri Chamard, ed., Joachim Du Bellay, *Œuvres poétiques*, no. 1201, V, p. v-lx for description of this *plaquette*, which is located in *Bibliothèque de l'Arsenal* (B. I. 6488, in-8). *See* Baudrier, no. 40, v. IV, p. 108.

Anon. Terentius in quem triplex edita est P. Antesignansis Rapistagensis commentatio. Primum exemplar. Commentariolum est ex omni interpretationum genere : Secundum exemplar, commentarios expositiones

annotationesque. Tertium exemplar, compendiosam expositionem omneque primi exemplaris argumentum, gallicam praeterea translationem, in tres priores comoedias, tum etiam huius authoris peculiares annotationes plenioresque interpretationes. Editio tertii exemp. Lyons, Bonhomme, 1560.   2457

So-called "triplex" edition of T. Translations are of *Andria*, *Eunuchus*, and *Heautontimorumenos*, by an unknown translator, probably Pierre Davantès. *See* Lawton, *Térence en France*, no. 2464, p. 500-10. They were for school use. *Andria* occupies p. 3-118 of the third volume; *Eunuchus* p. 119-237; *Heautontimorumenos* p. 238-360. *See also* Brunet V, 715 for description.

Baïf, Jean Antoine de. L'Evnuque, comédie de Térence. Par Ian Antoine de Baif. *In :* Les ieux de Ian Antoine de Baif. Breyer, 1572. IV, 232 p.   2458

Bibliothèque nationale has a manuscript copy of the play (Anc. f. fr. 867; anc. Codex Colbert 1296, Regius 7229). It is not in Baïf's hand. This manuscript redaction was " achevée lendemain de Noël davant jour 1565." For description of this edition *see* Tchemerzine I, 265, and for text *see* Baït's *Evvres en rime*, ed. Marty-Laveaux (*Pléiade françoyse*) III, 115-181.

Bourlier, Jean. Les sis comedies de Terence, tres-excellent poete comique, mises en Françoys, en faueur des bons esprits, studieus des antiques recreations. Waesbergh.   2459

This translation, first appearing in 1566, enjoyed great popularity. Editions followed in 1572 (pour Michel Clopieu), 1574 (Micard), 1578 (Micard), 1583 (Brumen, Corbon, Jean de Bordeaux, Robert le Fizelier, Colombel). *See* Lawton, *Térence en France*, no. 2464, p. 526-50. Brunet, Suppl. 738, lists a 1567 edition in Paris by Fleury Preuost for Michel Clopieu. Reinhardstoettner (*Spätere Bearbeitungen plautinische Lustspiele*, p. 20) lists a 1567 edition by Doart which is probably also a re-edition of Bourlier's translation. Lawton indicates that Bourlier copied textually Charles Estienne's 1542 translation of *Andria* and *Triplex* translations of *Eunuchus* and *Heautontimorumenos*. *Phormio*, *Adelphoe*, and *Hecyra* are Bourlier's own translations. Successive editions of Bourlier's translation show various corrections and emendations to the first edition. *See* *Térence en France*, no. 2464, p. 542-50.

Delcourt, Marie. L'Andrie de 1555. Hren 2:276-85, 1935.   2459A

Suggests that Etienne Dolet was author of a 1537 translation of *Andria*, now lost, but of which a reprint, dated 1555, survives. Attribution of this translation to Bonaventure des Périers was previously refuted by Adolphe Chenevière, no. 953, p. 153-54, and Harold Lawton (no. 2321, p. 459-69). For description of the edition see Brunet V, 722 ; Graesse 6: 66 ; Tchemerzine IV, 360.

Ericius, Johannes. Pub. Terentii Heautontimorumenos. Lyons, Payan, 1559.   2460

The second of Ericius's school translations. As in *Eunuchus*, each scene is followed by a syntaxis, containing the French translation, and by *scolia*. *See* Lawton, *Térence en France*, no. 2464, p. 450-58; Baudrier, no. 40, v. IV, p. 279.

— Pub. Terentii Eunuchus, Latine & Gallice in studiosorum adolescentum gratiam enarrata, cum scholiis. Lyons, Payan, 1552.
                                           2461

A school translation. Each scene is followed by a syntaxis, corresponding to the *constructio* in the Estienne translation of *Andria* in 1541 (no. 2462), and by *scholia*. This edition, a posthumous one, was reproduced in 1553 (Lyons, Payan), 1554 (Lyons, Payan or Temporal), 1561 (Lyons, Payan). *See* Lawton, *Térence en France*, no. 2464, p. 450-58; Baudrier no. 40, 4:255, 257, 261, 285, 382.

Estienne, Charles. Premiere comedie de Terence, intitulée l'Andrie, nouuellement traduicte de Latin en François, en faueur des bons esprits, studieux des antiques recreations. Roffet, 1542.   2462

An only edition. Its preface (essentially same as that appearing later at the head of Estienne's *Les abusez*) gives Estienne's views on definition and construction of comedy and tragedy. *See* Lawton, *Térence en France*, no. 2464, p. 426-49. Brunet

5:722, gives title of the edition as follows : *L'Andrie, traduicte en prose par Ch. Estienne, avec un brief recueil de toutes les sortes de jeux qu'avaient les anciens Grecs et Romains, et comme ils usaient d'iceux.* Corrozet, 1542. Another instance of an edition being shared by two publishers. *See also* Graesse 6²: 66.

— P. Terentij Afri Comici Andria : in adolescentulorum gratiam facilior effecta. Addita est constructionis ratio, tum vulgaris, tum etiam Latina : Item scholia, cum Ciceronis & bonorum authorum sermone, corruptam ac vitiatam loquendi consuetudinem emendent. Colinaeum & Stephanum, 1541.   2463

A *version scolaire* in which Latin text is accompanied by a *constructio*, giving Latin commentaries and French translations of the Latin word or phrase, and *scholia*, containing extensive notes and explanations. This edition, very popular during 16th century, was reproduced in 1546 (Robert Estienne), twice in 1547 (François Estienne and Lyons, Thibaud Payan), in 1548 (Robert Estienne,) 1549 (Louvain, Birckmann, with a Spanish translation substituted for the French), and 1561 (Lyons, Payan). *See* Lawton, *Térence en France*, no. 2464, p. 426-39; Baudrier, no. 40, 4:283.

Lawton, Harold W. Contribution à l'histoire de l'humanisme en France; Térence en France au xvie siècle; éditions et traductions. *See* 2321.   2464

Exhaustive bibliographical study of the editions and translations of T.'s works in France during the renaissance. Complete description of over five hundred editions and more than thirty editions of French translations of T. Brief chapter on T.'s influence during the Middle Ages.

Reviews : J. D. Craig in CIR 41:204, 1927; P. Jourda in RSS 14:180-82, 1927; AUP 1:444-45, 1926; TLS Mar. 3, 1927, p. 144.

CHAPTER XVII. TRANSLATORS

(Nos. 2465-2660)

DON CAMERON ALLEN, WILLIS H. BOWEN, JAMES HUTTON, OLIN H. MOORE

Latin
(Nos. 2465-2513)

DON CAMERON ALLEN

Alciati, Andrea. Livret des emblemes. Trans. by Jehan Lefevre, 1536. 124 p. Trans. by Barthélemy Aneau, Lyons, Roville 1549. 267 p. Trans. by Claude Mignault, 1583. *See* 510. 2465

Two hundred woodcuts with maxims and verse explanations. Often quoted and copied. Mignault's annotations and preface on symbolism are very important.

— Emblematum fontes quatuor. Ed. Henry Green. Manchester, Brothers, 1870. 119 p. *See* 510. 2466

A comparative study of editions; suggests a useful method.

— Emblematum flumen abundans. Ed., Henry Green, Manchester, Brothers, 1871. 226 p. *See* 510. 2467

A study of the evolution of *Emblemata*; highly important, but could be improved.

Bianchi, Dante. L'opera letteraria et storica di Andrea Alciati. ASL 40:5-130, 1913. 2468

Excellent account of the writings.

— Vita di Andrea Alciato. BSPS 12:133-205, 1912. 2469

Best short life; an exemplar of biographical scholarship.

Giardini, Ottavio. Nuove indagini sulla vita e le condotte di Andrea Alciato. ASL 19:294-346, 1903. 2470

Important discoveries about the life.

Viard, P. E. André Alciat, 1492-1550. Bordeaux, Société anonyme du Recueil Sirey, 1926. 391 p. 2471

Full-dress life; no great advance on Bianchi (no. 2468).

Beroaldo, Filippo. De la felicité humaine. Trans. Calvy de La Fontaine, Jannot, 1543. 56 p. 2472

On theories of pleasure; a syntagma.

— Trois declamations. Trad. G. Damalis, Lyons, Roy and Pesnot, 1558. 2473

Discussions of whether medicine is better than philosophy or oratory; whether drunkenness is worse than gaming or adultery, etc.

Paquier, Abbé Jules. De Philippi Beroaldi junioris vita et scriptis. Leroux, 1900. 122 p. 2474

Sorbonne dissertation but still standard. Short, well documented biography; good bibliographical account; weak on literary estimates.

Buchanan, George. Le cordelier, ou le sainct François. Trans. by Florent Chrestien. Geneva, L'Estang, 1567. 78 p. 2475

Highly important verse satire on Franciscans by the great Scotch Latin poet greatly prized by Gui Patin and his circle.

— Jephté. Trans. Florent Chrestien. Orléans, Rabier, 1567. 88 p. 2476

A drama on the famous Bible story important for study of the sacred play.

MacMillan, Donald. George Buchanan; a biography. Edinburgh, Morton, 1906. 292 p. 2477

Currently the best biography but essentially amateurish. Little knowledge of biographical or bibliographical problems; no documentation.

Millar, D. A. George Buchanan : a memorial 1506-1906. St. Andrews, Henderson 1907. 490 p. 2478

Series of studies on various aspects of the poet and historian; useful for a future biographer.

Camerarius, Philipp. Les méditations historiques. Trans. Simon Goulard. Geslin, 1608. 2 v. 2479
Collection of learned essays on all manner of subjects; valuable for source-hunting.

Cardano, Girolamo. Les livres, intitulés De la subtilité et subtiles inventions. Trans. R. Le Blanc. Micard, 1556. 36 p. 2480
Compendium of scientific lore beginning with the elements and running through plants, animals, metals, etc. Widely used and quoted.

Rivari, E. La mente di Girolamo Cardano. Bologna, Zanichelli, 1906. 222 p. 2481
Almost an anthology of quotations from Cardano. Author fancies himself as a psychoanalyst.

Carion, Johannes. Chronique. Trans. Jean Le Blond, 1553; S. Goulart, Geneva, Stoer, 1611. 2 v. with additions of Melanchthon and Peucer. 2482
Protestant history of world to 1547; used by literary men as a source.

Ziegler, Hildegard. Chronicon Carionis : ein Beitrag zur Geschichtschreibung des 16. Jahrhunderts. Halle, Niemeyer, 1898. 62 p. (Diss., Halle) 2483
Quite good on Carion's historical method and sources.

Cato disticha. Les mots dorés. Trans. P. Grosnet, 1492, 1530; Mathurin Cordier, 1536; François Habert, 1530; Macé, Lyons, 1533; Philibert Papillon, Lyons, 1546; E. Du Tronchet, 1554. 2484
Best known of school texts; used in the earliest years. Four books of moral sayings; one didacticism per line.

Dürer, Albert. Les quatre livres ... de la proportion des parties et pourtraicts des corps humains. Trans. Louis Meigret, Périer, 1557. 124 p. 2485
Source of most renaissance allusions to relation between color and proportion.

Erasmus, Desiderius. La civilité morale des enfans. Trans. Claude Hardy. Sara, 1613. 124 p. 2486
An essay on education of upperclass children.

Ficino, Marsilio. Trois livres de la vie. Trans. Gui Le Fèvre de La Boderie. L'Angelier, 1581. 200 ff. 2487

General work on protection and prolongation of life; useful for information about astrology, amulets, etc.

Saitta, Giuseppe. La filosofia di Marsilio Ficino. Messina, Principato, 1923. 285 p. 2488
Only substantial full-length account; strong on exposition, less valuable for interpretations.

Giovio, P. Les eloges et vies ... des hommes de guerre. Trans. B. d'Everon. Du Pré, 1559. 70 ff. 2489
Biographies of Charlemagne, Charles VIII, Louis XII, Francis I, Gaston de Foix, etc. by journalist-historian. Highly untrustworthy but interesting.

Ronelli, L. L'opera storica ed artistica di Paolo Giovio. Como, Paolino, 1929. 2490
An apology; takes little account of more recent investigations of Giovio.

Lemnius, Levinus. Les occultes merveilles et secrets de nature. Trans. Jacques Gohory. Du Pré, 1567. 402 p. 2491
A vast physiological storehouse; widely read and translated.

Lipsius, Justus. Les politiques. Trans. Simon Goulart. Geneva, Chouet, 1613. 634 p. 2492
Political aphorisms of best known neostoic of renaissance; useful for any study involving political theory.

Amiel, Emile. Un publiciste du XVIe siècle; Juste-Lipse. Lemerre, 1885. 330 p. 2493
Only attempt at a serious study. Material drawn entirely from Lipsius's writings; no background; no synthesis.

Nisard, Charles. Juste Lipse. In his: Le triumvirat littéraire au XVIe siècle; Juste Lipse, Joseph Scaliger et Isaac Casaubon. Amyot [1852]. p. 1-148. 2494
A lively study of Lipsius.

Steuer, Albert. Die Philosophie des Justus Lipsius. Münster, Aschendorff, 1901. 48 p. 2495
Vague and uncritical, but valuable because it is the only treatment of the subject.

Maffei, G. P. L'histoire des Indes. Trans. Emond Auger. Lyons, 1571; trans. François Arnault de La Borie. Lyons, Pillehotte, 1603. 953 p. 2496

Early account of Portuguese exploration and colonization of Indies and Africa, 1410-1556. Careers of Vasco da Gama, Magellan, etc. Important source.

Baptista, Mantuanus. Les bucoliques. Trans. M. d'Amboise, 1530; trans. Laurent de La Gravière, Lyons, Temporal, 1554. 140 p. 2497

A famous collection of pastoral eclogues used for two centuries as a school text; important for study of vernacular pastoral.

— La Parthenice Mariane. Trans. Jacques de Mortières, Lyons, Nourry and Besson, 1523. 86 p. 2498

Deals with life of Virgin and contains only the first part of original seven-part series of poems.

Fanucchi, P. L. G. Della vita del B. P. Battista Spagnoli detto il Mantovano. Lucca, 1887. 226 p. 2499

Ecclesiastical; no documentation; useful in spite of these faults.

More, Sir Thomas. La description de l'isle d'Utopie. Trans. Jean Le Blond. L'Angelier, 1550. 185 p. 2500

Famous socialist treatise of English Chancellor; important for all studies of government and for its great popularity and literary influence.

Peucer, Kaspar. Les devins. Trans. Simon Goulart. Antwerp, Connix, 1584. 653 p. 2501

An encyclopedia of all forms of divination and forecasting known to man.

Piccolomini, Enea Silvio. L'ystoire de Eurialus et Lucresse. Trans. into French by Octovien de Saint-Gelais. 1493. 93 p. L'histoire délectable et récréative de deux parfaits amans. Trans. by Jean Millet (?), 1537. 2502

Story of tragic love affair between the wife of a citizen of Siena and a young courtier. Discourses on chastity, nobility, etc. Uses an epistolary method.

Raymundus de Sabunde. La theologie naturelle. Trans. Jean Martin, 1551. 2503

One of the greatest works on natural theology before 17th century. Important for Montaigne students.

Coppin, Joseph. Montaigne, traducteur de Raymond Sebon. Lille, Morel, 1925. 269 p. 2504

Biographical account of Sabund in Introduction as well as excellent bibliographical notice. Ch. I contains essay on Raymundus de Sebonde's reputation in France. See 2870.

Sambucus, Johannes, and Hadrianus Junius. Les emblesmes. Trans. Jacques Grévin. See 521. 2505

Originally published separately; follows the method of Alciati; important commentary in Junius' collection.

Scheltema, P. Diatribe in Hadrianii Junii vitam, ingenium, familiam, merita literaria. Amsterdam, 1836. 2506

Only full length study; obsolescent.

Simmler, Josias. La république des Suisses. Trans. Innocent Gentillet. Jacques du Puys. 1579. 467 p. 2507

A first-hand account of how the republic functioned. Principles of the federation; asides on geography, economics, antiquities customs, education, war, peace, etc.

Sleidanus, Johannes. Histoire de l'estat de la religion et republique sous l'Empereur Charles cinquiesme. Trans. Robert Le Prévost. Geneva, Crispin, 1557. 474 p. 2508

A year-by-year account of Europe (1517-66); Protestant bias; useful for social history.

— Trois livres des quatre empires souverains. Trans. Robert Le Prévost. Geneva, Crispin, 1557. 165 p. 2509

The fourth empire begins in 1519. Germany has always resisted the empire-builders as she now resists the Pope (Leo X). Brief; chronological.

Vergilius, Polydorus. Les memoires et histoires de l'origine, invention et autheurs des choses. Trans. François de Belleforest. 1576. 2510

Vergil was one of the first systematic historians; this book was one of the popular reference works of renaissance.

Vida, Marco Girolamo. Hymnes. Trans. Antoine Le Fèvre de La Boderie. 2511

Thirty-seven hymns on saints and martyrs; useful for study of Christian poetry.

— Le jeu des eschecs. Trans. Louis Des Masures. Lyons, 1557; Vasquin Philieul, 1559. 2512

Mock-heroic poem of 600 lines; celestial origin of chess; various gambits; begetter of similar poems.

Wier, Johann. Cinq livres de l'imposture et tromperie des diables, des enchantements et sorcelleries. Trans. Jacques Grévin, 1567.   2513

The chief German contribution to the war against witches; to be compared with Bodin. *See* 344, 2078.

Translators, Greek
(Nos. 2514-2594G)

JAMES HUTTON

Supplemental and explanatory lists of translators will be found in Appendix, p. 305-09.

General Works

Baillet, Adrien. Jugemens des principaux traducteurs. *In his:* Jugemens des savans sur les principaux ouvrages des auteurs. Moette, etc., 1722-30. v. III, p. 1-204.
                                                  2514

This catalogue of translators, extracted from La Croix du Maine and Du Verdier, must still be consulted.

Bellanger, Justin. Histoire de la traduction en France (auteurs grecs et latins). Thorin, 1892. 90 p.   2515

Rapid sketch distinguishing the several periods of translation, with brief criticisms of individual translators; somewhat popular in character and not well documented.

Bunker, Ruth. A bibliographical study of the Greek works and translations published in France during the renaissance : the decade 1540-1550. *See* 2418.   2516

Valuable though somewhat imperfect study of an important decade. Bibliography is preceded by chapters on : *The teaching of Greek, Translations and translators of Greek books, The printing and the printers of Greek books;* Bibliography itself is marred by repetitions, errors and omissions, and is so intricately arranged, with no index, that it is painful to consult.

Egger, Emile. L'hellénisme en France. Didier, 1869. 2 v.   2517

This standard work is less useful for 16th century translations than might be expected. *Leçon* 11 (v. 1), *Les traductions françaises au seizième siècle,* is general in character and only incidentally touches upon individual translators.

Goujet, Claude Pierre. Des traductions des poètes grecs. *In his:* Bibliothèque françoise. Mariette & Guerin, 1741-56. v. 4.   2518

Contains a bibliography. Still to be consulted on translations of the Greek poets.

Hennebert, Frédéric. Histoire des traductions françaises d'auteurs grecs et latins. Ghent, 1858. 261 p. *See* 2423.   2519

Survey of translations in all periods; very uneven, but with an abundance of exact information; though old, not superseded.

Tilley, Arthur Augustus. Translations from the Greek and Latin. *In his:* The literature of the French renaissance. *See:* 123, v. I, p. 35-40.   2519A

A very brief sketch, partly superseded, but includes some first-hand information that should not be overlooked.

Bruneau, Charles. La phrase des traducteurs au XVIe siècle. MélHC, p. 275-284.   2520

Influence, through the translators, of the Greek or Latin sentence upon 16th century style. Suggestive, though frankly tentative in extent of its claims.

Amyot
(Nos. 2521-2539)

Blignières, Auguste de. Essai sur Amyot et les traducteurs français au XVIe siècle. Durand, 1851. 466 p.   2521

Though somewhat antiquated in method and on individual points replaced by more recent studies, this book remains indispensable as only complete review of all A.'s translations; important details on other 16th century translators. *See* 2586.

Review : L. Feugère in *Caractères et portraits littéraires du XVIe siècle.* Didier, 1859. 1:487-506.

Cioranescu, Alexandre. Vie de Jacques Amyot, d'après des documents inédits avec un avant-propos de Pierre Champion. Droz, 1941. 227 p.   2522

A critical biography, carried out with sound judgment and method, and taking account of all recent work on A. Chapters on A.'s literary work, though modest in aim, are important as viewing this activity as part of " moral portrait " of translator. Useful bibliography.

Plutarchus. (Vitae Fr. Amyot) Les vies des hommes illustres grecs et romains; Pericles et Fabius Maximus. Édition critique publiée par Louis Clément. Droz, 1934. 115 p. (STFM) 2523

First published in 1906; gives text of 1567 with variant readings of 1559, 1565, and 1619. Brief *Avertissement* represents the first modern critical work on A.'s text; its principles still stand, though some points concerning value of editions of 1565 and 1619 have been modified by work of Sturel (2535).

Emard, Paul. Jacques Amyot, grand aumônier de France, supérieur des Quinze-Vingts Pauvres Aveugles du Roi (1560-1593). RSS 14:77-115, 281-314, 1927; 15:1-42, 1928. 2524

A.'s activity as supervisor of *Quinze-Vingts*; relates to social life, not to literature.

Grésy, Eugène. Vie de Jacques Amyot, tirée des mémoires concernant l'histoire civile et ecclésiastique d'Auxerre, par l'abbé (Jean) Lebeuf. Michelin, 1848. 95 p. 2525

Lebeuf's *Vie* remains indispensable for light it throws upon A.'s last years (cf. Cioranescu, no. 2522, p. 10), while more than half of the small work (p. 43-95) presents invaluable documents on the same period, when A. was Bishop of Auxerre.

Huguet, Edmond. Les procédés d'adaptation chez Amyot. RSS 12:44-77, 1925. 2526

Examines A.'s method, particularly in his choice of a vocabulary at once true to the facts of ancient life and intelligible to his readers. Valuable article, supplementing Sturel's remarks on same subject. *See* 2535.

Jaeger, Friedrich. Zur Kritik von Amyots Uebersetzung der Moralia Plutarchs. Aktiengesellschaft Konkordia, 1899. 109 p. (Diss., Heidelberg). 2527

Critical study of A.'s translation of *Moralia* in the successive editions; based on a copy of Greek text with A.'s manuscript notes. To a considerable extent anticipates results of Sturel's work on *Lives*. One of the indispensable works on A.

Jung, Friedrich. Syntax des Pronomens bei Amyot. Jena, Neuenhahn, 1887. 53 p. (Diss., Jena). 2528

A.'s pronouns in light of 16th century usage; valuable, but does not take account of A.'s revisions.

Keuntje, Hermann. Der syntaktische Gebrauch des Verbums bei Amyot, dargestelt auf Grund seiner Uebersetzung der Vitae des Plutarch. Ein Beitrag zur französischen Syntax. Bremen, Schunemann, 1894. 67 p. (Diss., Leipzig). 2529

Classifies A.'s uses of the verb, with examples; finds that his syntax is somewhat influenced by Greek original, and hence not so purely French as his vocabulary.

Marchand, Jean. Notes autographes d'Amyot sur un exemplaire de Justin et de Diodore. BBB Aug.-Sept., 1948. p. 371-382. 2530

Description of A.'s copies of Justin and Diodorus in Marchand's possession; brief notes by A.

Nolhac, Pierre de. Jacques Amyot et le Décret de Gratien. BEFR 5:284-94, 1885. 2531

On assistance rendered by A. in Roman edition of *Decretum* (1582); with unpublished letters.

Normand, Jean. Ed. Plutarque, Jacques Amyot. Les vies des hommes illustres grecs et romains; Démosthène et Cicéron. Hachette, 1929. 136 p. (STFM) 2532

Follows and corroborates Clément's principles in regard to the text (no. 2523), but sees more interest in corrections of 1565, and gives better account of variant readings of 1619; had the use of Sturel's notes after latter's death.

Norton, Grace. Le Plutarque de Montaigne. Selections from Amyot's translation of Plutarch arranged to illustrate Montaigne's Essays. *See* 1693. 2533

The work of Zangroniz (2539) appeared while Miss Norton's book was in press; but since Zangroniz only deals with passages in which Montaigne reproduces the words of A., while Miss Norton very properly also considers those which Montaigne has rewritten, her work, while not pretending to be a critical study, should still be consulted.

Sainte-Beuve, Charles Augustin. Essai sur Amyot, par M. A. de Blignières. *In his:* Causeries de lundi, 4th ed., Garnier, 4:450-470. 2534

Still worth reading, though partly antiquated; e.g., A.'s "naïveté" is rather effect of time than the impression he made on his contemporaries. Sainte-Beuve is not entirely free of influence of Bachet de Mézierac's *Discours sur la traduction:* cf.

Paul Bonnefon, *Notes de lecture de Sainte-Beuve sur Agrippa d'Aubigné et sur Amyot*, RU 17:37-41, 128-32, 1908.

Sturel, René. Jacques Amyot, traducteur des Vies parallèles de Plutarque. Champion, 1908. 646 p. (BLR, v. 8)   2535

On the basis of a complete control of the MSS. and editions Sturel renders an exact account of A.'s entire activity with Plutarch's *Lives*, and throws new light on his career; unsurpassed as a study of a renaissance text; demonstrates value of such studies for sound literary criticism; doubtless Sturel gives his proofs in excessive detail. *See* 2587.

Review : P. Villey in RHL 17:190-94, 1910.

— Une traduction manuscrite de sept Vies de Plutarque par Amyot, antérieure de quinze ans à l'édition originale (1559). RHL 14:301-29, 1907.   2536

Substance of Sturel's remarks later incorporated in his book (no. 2535); here, p. 308-29, he prints text of *Vie de Theseus* from Bibl. Nat. MS. Fr. 1396.

Villey, Pierre. Amyot et Montaigne. RHL 14:713-27, 1907.   2537

Corrections of Zangroniz (no. 2539), with important additions.

Weinberg, Bernhard. A false first edition of Amyot's Plutarch. MLN 61:454-58, 1946.   2538

On a supposed first edition in Princeton University Library, with light on other 16th century editions of A. in several American libraries.

Zangroniz, Joseph de. Montaigne, Amyot et Saliat : étude sur les sources des Essais. *See* 1805.   2539

Shows by parallel citations the use made by Montaigne of A. and Saliat, with remarks on his debt to the ancients in general; differences in this regard are found in successive editions of the *Essais*. Despite errors and omissions, an indispensable work; yet limited in scope, and hardly touches the formative influence of Plutarch upon Montaigne.

The Greek Poets

(Nos. 2540-2563)

Becker, Ph. Aug. Hugues Salel. ZFSL 55:475-512, 1932; Neues über Hugues Salel. ZFSL 59:385-90, 1935.   2540

First article sketches Homer in renaissance before Salel, and gives important details on MSS. of Salel's translation. Second article, assuming that Salel mainly depended on the Latin *ad verbum* of Andreas Divus, cites parallels to show that he also used the version of L. Valla; also gives data on editions from an unprinted Würzburg dissertation by Valentin Burger (1926).

Droz, E. Salomon Certon et ses amis. Hren 6:179-97, 1939; Salomon Certon et ses amis, sa correspondance, BHren 2:186-95, 1942.   2541

Several of Certon's letters relate to his translation of Homer.

Egger, Emile. Revue des traductions françaises d'Homère. NRE 1:518-34, Aug., 1846. *Also in his :* Mémoires de littérature ancienne. Durand, 1862. p. 164-86.   2542

Citations with critical remarks; rather superficial; prefers Jamyn to Salel.

Gandar, Eugène. Ronsard considéré comme imitateur d'Homère et de Pindare. *See* 1127.   2542A

Brief description of Samxon's *Iliad;* dates Book I, 1519, Books II-VII, 1523, correcting Brunet.

Graur, Theodosia. Le traducteur d'Homère. *In her :* Un disciple de Ronsard : Amadis Jamyn. *See* 218, p. 205-26.   2543

Careful study demonstrating Jamyn's superiority over Salel; bibliography of Jamyn's translations. " Il avait fallu trois ouvriers et trois quarts de siècle pour que les deux poèmes homériques se vissent vêtus à la française " (p. 225). The " trois ouvriers " were Salel, Jamyn and Certon. *See* 1372.

Marichal, Robert. La première édition de la traduction de l'Iliade par Hugues Salel. Hren 1:156-60, 1934.   2544

Accurate, suggestive article; Marichal believes that a comparison of editions of 1542 and 1545 with existing MSS. would establish whether Salel worked from the Greek or from a Latin translation.

Mazon, Paul. Madame Dacier et les traductions d'Homère en France. Oxford, Clarendon Press, 1936. 27 p. (The Zaharoff lecture for 1935).   2545

The " Budé " translator of Homer on the qualities of the Homeric poems and of their French representatives. Little on

16th century versions, but prefers Salel to Jamyn : " Plus de nerf chez Hugues Salel.... La traduction de Salel est assez vigoureuse et, dans l'ensemble, exacte " (p. 7).

Vaganay, Hugues. Amadis Jamyn a-t-il récrit en alexandrins l'Iliade de Salel? BBB ns 7:551-56, 1928.   2546
    Refutes an idle suggestion that Jamyn did this.

Augé-Chiquet, Mathieu. La vie, les idées et l'œuvre de Jean-Antoine de Baïf. *See* 2439.   2547
    The remarks on Baïf's version of *Antigone* (p. 174-84) are good but brief; they have been developed by Marie Delcourt (2552); similar remarks on Baïf's other translations *passim*, especially on Hesiod and Phocylides (p. 368-73); Appendix I gives a translation of Theocritus omitted from editions of Baïf. A special study of Baïf as translator remains, however, a *desideratum*.

Kuntz, Carl. Untersuchungen über La Tragédie des Troades d'Euripide, anonyme Übersetzung in französischen Versen aus dem 16. Jahrhundert (Handschrift Nr. 1688 des Musée Condé in Chantilly). Greifswald, Adler, 1909. 89 p. (Diss., Greifswald). *See* 2443.   2548
    Careful study, thorough within its limits. By comparing 16th century Latin translations Kuntz proves that translation was made directly from the Greek text (Aldine ed. pr., 1503-04, or Basel reprint, 1537), and by a good scholar; by examining metre and language, he dates it ca. 1550. Sturel has gone further, but this study should not be neglected.

Nolhac, Pierre de. Le premier travail français sur Euripide, la traduction de François Tissard. MélHW, p. 299-307.   2549
    On Tissard's Latin translations of *Medea, Hippolytus,* and *Alcestis,* made in 1507 (MS. Paris. Latin. 7884); gives extracts.

Pinvert, Lucien. Lazare de Baïf (1496?-1547). *See* 2353.   2550
    What Pinvert says of Baïf's translations of Plutarch and Sophocles and his supposed translation of Euripides' *Hecuba*—little in any case—has been superseded by the work of Sturel. Yet the book as a whole remains useful as the only comprehensive study of L. de Baïf.

Sturel, René. A propos d'un manuscrit du Musée Condé. MélEC, p. 575-83.   2551
    Masterly article; shows that *Hécube* of 1544, attributed to L. de Baïf by Peletier and La Croix du Maine, is almost certainly work of Guillaume Bochetel; conjectures that *Troades* of MS. 1688 of the Musée Condé may be his work, with help of Amyot (but *see* no. 2553).

Delcourt, Marie. Étude sur les traductions des tragiques grecs et latins en France depuis la renaissance. *See* 2320A.   2552
    Necessarily dependent on Sturel (no. 2553) for 16th century translations of Euripides and Sophocles, but completes his observations on various points. *See* 2420.
    Review : R. Lebègue in RSS 13:147, 1926, while generally favorable, thinks the work should have been limited to 16th century, and there have encompassed Latin translations, unpublished translations, and free imitations. Yet there is advantage in surveying different modes of translation in successive periods as applied to a single literary type. Work is in no sense superficial.

Sturel, René. Essai sur les traductions du théâtre grec en français avant 1550. *See* 2322.   2553
    Studies L. de Baïf's *Electre*; Bochetel's *Hécube*; Sebillet's *Iphigénie*; Calvy de La Fontaine's MS. *Antigone*; and MS. *Iphigénie* and *Troades*, both of which last he now ascribes to Amyot, *Iphigénie* with certainty. He dates *Troades* MS. ca. 1545-1546 and the translation itself ca. 1542. By comparing 16th century Latin and Italian versions he shows the French translators' methods. *See* 2427.

Delcourt, Marie. La tradition des comiques anciens en France avant Molière. *See* 2421.   2554
    Brief Ch. III on Aristophanes discusses fragments of *Plutus* ascribed to Ronsard, and Pierre Le Loyer's *Néphélococugie* (an adaptation of *Birds*). Against Laumonier (ed. of Binet's *Vie de Ronsard,* no. 1086, p. 102 ff.), Prof. Delcourt sees no good reason to doubt Ronsard's authorship of these fragments; her position seems to be the sensible one.

Delboulle, Achille, ed. Anacréon et les poèmes anacréontiques, texte grec, avec les traductions et imitations des poètes du XVIᵉ siècle. Le Havre, Lemale, 1891. 182 p.   2555

Not a work of scholarly intention; translations selected mainly from Ronsard, Remy Belleau, and Richard Renvoisy; valuable in presenting specimens of Renvoisy's versions, which are otherwise very difficult to find.

Eckhardt, Alexandre. Remy Belleau, sa vie—sa Bergerie; étude historique et critique. Budapest, Németh, 1917. 238 p. 2556

Comments on Belleau's *Anacréon* (p. 33-35, 164-68) are well-informed and helpful as far as they go; those on translation of *Aratus* (p. 35-37) are insignificant.

Sainte-Beuve, Charles Augustin. Anacréon au seizième siècle. *See* 2289, p. 440-456. 2557

Slight sketch, still suggestive; partly antiquated, e.g., assumes that Ronsard's versions were later than Belleau's, whereas they were earlier and influenced Belleau.

Des Guerrois, Charles. Étude sur l'anthologie grecque. MSA 59:159-201, 1895. *Reprinted:* Troyes, Nouel, 1896. 46 p. 2558

A brief, but interesting and well-informed essay.

Hutton, James. Ronsard and the Greek anthology. *See* 1135. 2559

Discusses Ronsard's translations and imitations in relation to Latin versions and Ronsard's probable methods of procedure; repeated in no. 2560.

— The Greek anthology in France and in the Latin writers of the Netherlands to the year 1800. Ithaca, Cornell University Press, 1946. 822 p. (CSCP, v. 28) 2560

Aims to record so far as possible all published translations and imitations of the Anthology, and to establish their interdependence; contains a *Register* (p. 589-806) digesting these echoes under the divisions of the Palatine anthology.

— Cupid and the bee. PMLA 56:1036-58, 1941; cf. J. G. Fucilla's Cupid and the bee addenda. PMLA 58:575-79, 1943. 2561

On Theocritus 19 *(Honey-stealer)* and Anacreontic 35 (40); translations and imitations and their interdependence.

Hulubei, Alice. Répertoire des églogues en France au XVIᵉ siècle (époque des Valois 1515-1589). Droz, 1939. 114 p. 2562

The half-dozen translations from Theocritus' *Idylls* made in French in 16th century are listed in bibliographical

references. Mme Hulubei justifiably says in her *L'églogue en France* (1345), p. 55, of the direct impact of Theocritus : "... le champ d'action de Théocrite est insignifiant."

Pinvert, Lucien. Jacques Grévin (1538-1570). *See* 1371. 2563

Though in general a useful work, remarks (p. 101-11) on Grévin's translations of Nicander are of little value; indicates without proof that translation depends on Latin of Jean de Gorris. *See* 350, 440, 2375.

The Greek Prose Writers

(Nos. 2564-2594G)

Delisle, Léopold. Traductions d'auteurs grecs et latins offertes à François Iᵉʳ et à Anne de Montmorency par Etienne Le Blanc et Antoine Macault. JS Sept : 520-534, 1900. 2564

Deals with MS. of Macault's Diodorus presented to Francis I probably in 1534 (Musée Condé MS. 1672); notes that Macault translated from Poggio's Latin version; sketches his life, discusses his other works; two unpublished letters. Best general account of Macault.

Dufayard, Charles. De Claudii Seisselii vita et operibus. Hachette, 1892. 107 p. (Diss., Paris) 2565

Good dissertation; more on Seyssel as historian, political thinker, and diplomat than as translator. On translations, p. 92-98; Seyssel, ignorant of Greek, used Latin versions—Rufinus for Eusebius, Pier Candido for Appian, L. Valla for Thucydides; had personal help of Janus Lascaris for Diodorus, Xenophon, and Appian (cf. Börje Knös, *Janus Lascaris*, Les belles lettres, 1945, p. 97-98). Seyssel's translations had a practical aim, should be regarded as a phase of his political activity. Bibliography of Seyssel's works and of works on him.

Picot, Emile. Les Français italianisants au XVIᵉ siècle. Champion, 1906-07. 2 v. 2566

Contains informative articles on Claude de Seyssel, Jean de Maumont (translator of Zonaras), Hierosme d'Avost (translator of Eustathius' novel), and Lancelot de Carle (translator of Heliodorus), with full references to earlier studies.

Legrand, Emile Louis Jean. Bibliographie hellénique. Leroux, 1885-1906. 4 v. 2567

Lists works of Jacques de Vintimille, translator of Herodian and of Xenophon's *Cyropaedia* in reliable bibliographical form.

Vauzelles, Ludovic de. Vie de Jacques, comte de Vintimille, conseiller au parlement de Bourgogne, littérateur et savant du seizième siècle, d'après des documents inédits. Orléans, Herluison, 1865. 107 p. 2568
Indispensable as based partly on MS. sources, but does not meet modern critical standards; fails to study Vintimille's translations as such; lists his works, published and unpublished.

Lefranc, Abel. Le Platonisme et la littérature en France à l'époque de la renaissance (1500-1550). RHL 3:1-44, 1896. *Also in his:* Grands écrivains français de la renaissance. *See* 132A, p. 63-137. 2569
Still the capital work on this subject; important remarks on the several translations before 1550. *See* 714, 737, 738.

Delcourt, Marie. Une traduction inédite de Criton antérieure à 1540. RSS 14:49-60, 1927. 2570
Regards this anonymous version as oldest French translation from Plato; MS. to be dated between 1525 and 1535. Prof. Delcourt proves that it was made from Ficino, but not without recourse to Greek text; she remarks on style, but cannot identify the translator.

Christie, Richard Copley. Etienne Dolet, the martyr of the renaissance, 1508-1546. New ed., Macmillan, 1899. 570 p. 2571
On Dolet's translations of *Axiochus* and *Hipparchus*, p. 452-62. Thinks *Axiochus* made from Agricola's Latin version, though Dolet may also have consulted Greek text. Lefranc (no. 2569, p. 108) believes that Dolet probably used Ficino for *Axiochus* and certainly for *Hipparchus*. The question will perhaps bear further study. *See* 2593.

Becker, A. Henri. Un humaniste au XVIᵉ siècle : Loys Le Roy (Ludovicus Regius) de Coutances. Lecène, Oudin, 1896. 409 p. 2572
Becker expands upon style of Le Roy's translations, upon external conditions of their production, and upon what interests him in Le Roy's commentaries; but fails to study the translations against background of 16th century learning. Only of translation of *Phaedo* he remarks that, while influenced by Ficino's Latin, it was made

from the Basel text of 1534; even here he gives no proof. Yet he has studied Le Roy's works at first hand, and book is in general of considerable value; useful bibliography.
Review : Louis Delaruelle in RHL 4:614-19, 1897; rather an independent article than a review, supplying important new details.

Rivaud, Albert. La première traduction française du Timée de Platon. RSS 9:286-289, 1922. 2573
On Le Roy's *Timaeus*, which Rivaud finds to have been made directly from the Greek and to be superior to other 16th century translations and even to some more recent, though he offers no proof of this superiority.

Merrill, Robert Valentine. The Platonism of Joachim du Bellay. *See* 741. 2574
Contains list of translations from Plato to year 1559, with valuable annotations. *See* 1268.

Wasik, Wiktor. L'Aristotélisme populaire comme fragment de la renaissance. RHph ns 3:33-66, Jan. 15, 1935. 2575
Interesting remarks on works of Aristotle and pseudo-Aristotle that were popular in renaissance, with a list of translations into modern languages between 1475 and 1650; list full of errors.

Egger, Emile. Les Oeconomica d'Aristote et de Théophraste : note additionnelle sur la traduction des Économiques d'Aristote attribuée à La Boétie. MAI 30:459-61, 1881. 2576
Points out that this translation printed in Feugère's edition of La Boétie is the same as that published in 1554 over initials G. B. (i.e., according to La Croix du Maine, Gabriel Bounin).

Cartier, Alfred and Adolphe Chenevrière. Antoine du Moulin, valet de chambre de la reine de Navarre. *See* 701. 2577
Fundamental article; bio-bibliographical; includes Du Moulin's translations of *Life of Aesop*, of Epictetus, and of an essay from Plutarch's *Moralia*.

Cougny, E. Du Vair traducteur. *In his:* Guillaume du Vair. Durand, 1857. p. 171-200. 2578
Too general on Du Vair's translation of Epictetus; compares his method with that of other 16th century translators, but does not enter into details.

Giraud, Victor. Sur Guillaume du Vair, notes bibliographiques. *See* 2270.　2579

Supplements Radouant, 2581.

Mesnard, Pierre. Du Vair et le néostoïcisme. *See* 1847.　2580

Not on Du Vair's translation of Epictetus, but a good study of his ideas, emphasizing his effort to combine Stoicism with Christian doctrine. *See* 2275.

Radouant, René Charles. Recherches bibliographiques sur Guillaume du Vair et correspondance inédites. *See* 2279.　2581

Important bibliographical study.

Zanta, Léontine. La traduction française du Manuel d'Épictète d'André de Rivaudeau au XVIᵉ siècle. Champion, 1914.　174 p.
　　　　2582

An edition of Rivaudeau's translation, complementary to Mˡˡᵉ Zanta's *La renaissance du stoïcisme au XVIᵉ siècle*, 198. Introduction (87 p.) discusses 16th century Latin translations, and French versions by Du Moulin, Rivaudeau, and Du Vair. Franck L. Schoell (*Etudes sur l'humanisme continental en Angleterre* (BRLC, v. 29), 1926, p. 108) justly finds the discussion of the Latin translations insufficient; he rehandles this subject. Remarks on French translations are good, demonstrating independence of Rivaudeau.

Reviews : Jean Plattard in RSS 6:131-133, 1919. Favorable, but doubts if material warrants speaking of a "renaissance" of Stoicism in 16th century; L. R. in Rcr ns 80:215-19, Oct. 2, 1915.

Labadie, Ernest. Bibliographie historique d'Élie Vinet. Bordeaux, Cadoret, 1909. 100 p.　2583

Careful bibliographical study, with important historical annotations on each work and a sketch of Vinet's life. Vinet translated *Sphaera* of Proclus.

Mégret, Jacques. Une traduction inconnue de Pontus de Thyard. BBB ns 10:156-59, 1931.　2584

Interesting notice of a copy of Tyard's translation of Agapetus, Rouen, 1604; conjectures that there may have been an earlier Lyons edition. 1604 volume also contains a translation of *Epistle* of Aristeas by an unidentified E. B. L. G.

Jourda, Pierre. Une traduction inédite d'Isocrate. RSS 16:283-300, 1929.　2585

Examines a translation of *Ad Nicoclem* dated 1542, in MS. 2152 of the Bibl. Trivulziana in Milan; agrees with G. Porro that translator may well be Marguerite d'Angoulême; finds translation exact, but does not decide whether it was made from Greek or from a Latin version.

Blignières, Auguste de. Essai sur Amyot, etc. (2521)　2586

Discusses translations of Plutarch by others besides Amyot; useful list of unpublished translations, p. 177.

Sturel, René. Jacques Amyot. (2535)　2587

Discusses translations of Plutarch by others besides Amyot, particularly (p. 7 ff.) unpublished translations of several *Lives* by Simon Bourgouyn and Arnauld Chandon.

Raffin, Léonce. Saint-Julien de Balleure, historien bourguignon (1519?-1593). Champion, 1926.　132 p.　(BLR, ns v. 13)　2588

Brief remarks (p. 53-55, 96) on Saint-Julien's translations of Plutarch, which are from Latin of Erasmus.

La Boëtie, Etienne de. Œuvres complètes d'Estienne de La Boétie, publiées avec notice biographique, variantes, notes et index, par Paul Bonnefon. Bordeaux, *See* 1373.　2589

Introduction III contains a good study of La Boëtie translations from Plutarch and Xenophon. Appendix VI gives La Boëtie's notes on Plutarch's *Eroticus*. Appendix VII reinforces Egger's proof (2576), that translation of Aristotle's *Economics* published as La Boëtie's in 1600 is really the translation published by G. Bounin in 1554; and this translation is reproduced in full. *See* 1404.

Bernard, Auguste Joseph. Geoffroy Tory, painter and engraver, tr. by George B. Ives. Boston and New York, Houghton, Mifflin, 1909.　332 p.　2590

Translated with minor corrections from 2nd edition of Bernard's *Geofroy Tory, peintre et graveur*, see 42. Standard bibliographical work on Tory, with Biography; includes notices of his translations of Cebes, Lucian, Plutarch, and Xenophon.

Bouchard, Ernest. Notice bibliographique sur Blaise de Vigenère. BSB 8:196-212, 1868; repeated in part in 11:349-57, 1870.　2591

Adds little to biographical dictionaries; but gives portrait and useful list of Vigenère's works; no examination of his translations of Philostratus and Callistratus.

Métral, Denyse. Blaise de Vigenère, archéologue et critique d'art (1523-1596). Droz, 1939.   324 p.   2592

A careful examination of Vigenère's writings so far as they touch upon the arts; does not deal with his translations as such; bibliography.

Review : R. Lebègue in RHL 47:276, 1947, who refers to a thesis in preparation dealing with Vigenère's translations.

Christie, Richard Copley. Etienne Dolet. *See* 2571.   2593

Remarks *passim* on translations of Galen by Tolet and others printed by Dolet in 1540-42.

Mitchell, W. S. An apparently unrecorded French translation of Galen. Libr 2:170-171, 1947.   2594

On Bauhin's translation, of which there is a fragment in library of Aberdeen University; Mitchell thinks it may not have been regularly published. *See* his letter in TLS 2349:79, Feb. 8, 1947.

Gerig, John L. Le Collège de la Trinité à Lyon avant 1540. Rren 9:73-94, 1908.
                                        2594A

The only study to this date of Jean Canape; *see also* Baudrier, no. 40, v. 5, p. 292-94.

Chauvelot, R. Un Oresme méconnu du xvie siècle : Jehan Canappe. Fmod 18:267-271, 1950; 19:20, 200, 1951.   2594B

Shows that many medical terms, thought to have been first used in French by Ambroise Paré, had appeared earlier in translations of Canape.

Buget, F. Études sur Nostradamus. BBB, 1860, p. 1699-1721; 1861, p. 68-94, 241-68, 383-412, 657-91; 1862, p. 761-85; 1863, p. 449-73, 513-30, 577-88.   2594C

In the volume of 1861 (p. 395 ff.) are remarks on Nostradamus's translation of Galen (from Latin of Erasmus), with copious extracts.

Aristaenetus. Les Epistres amoureuses d'Aristenet tournées du grec en françois par Cyre Foucault, sieur de La Coudrière, avec l'Image du vray amant, discours tiré de Platon. Notice par A. P. Malassis. Liseux, 1876.   228 p.   2594D

Malassis' brief *Notice* states that Foucault used Josias Mercier's edition of Aristaenetus (2nd ed., Paris, 1595), but does not depend upon Mercier's Latin version; French translation is reasonably faithful. Malassis could learn nothing concerning Foucault's life. (*Image du vray amant* is " Platonic " but not from Plato.)

Bonnefon, Paul. Le premier livre des Aethiopiques d'Héliodore translaté de grec en français par Lancelot de Carle, évêque de Riez, et publié pour la première fois avec une introduction. Bordeaux, 1883. (Reprinted from l'Annuaire de l'Association pour l'Encouragement des études grecques en France, xviie année, p. 327, 1883).   2594E

Lancelot de Carle's translation preceded Amyot's, and was presented to Francis I; it is B. N. MS. fr. 2143. *See also* Émile Picot, *Les Français italianisants* (no. 2566) 1:237-38, and Guillaume Colletet, *Vies des poètes bordelais et périgourdins*, ed. by Philippe Tamizey de Larroque, 1873, p. 13, n. 4.

Hulubei, Alice. Henri Estienne et le roman de Longus Daphnis et Chloé. RSS 18:324-340, 1931.   2594F

The complete text of Longus has only been known since 1810; but Mme Hulubei finds that Estienne's Latin eclogues of 1555 imply a knowledge of the whole romance.

Aesopus. Trois cent soixante et six apologues, tr. Guillaume Haudent, ed. Charles Lormier. Rouen, 1877. (SBN, no. 29)
                                        2594G

Well-informed Introduction by Lormier, who establishes (what indeed Haudent does not conceal) that book is mainly a translation of *Aesopi Phrygis vita et fabulae a viris doctis in latinam linguam conversae*, several times printed, e.g., by R. Estienne, 1537.

Italian (Except Machiavelli)
(Nos. 2595-2639)

OLIN H. MOORE

General Works

Chamard, Henri. La traduction. *In:* Dictionnaire des lettres françaises; le seizième siècle. (ed. by mgr. Georges Grente). *See* 99, p. 669-73.   2595

Satisfactory outline of history of translations in France during 16th century. In spite of limitations of space, author succeeds in making a clear exposition of rival theories of art of translating.

Larwill, Paul Herbert. La théorie de la traduction au début de la renaissance (d'après les traductions imprimées en France entre 1477 et 1527). Munich, Wolf, 1934. 64 p. (Diss., Munich) 2596

Deals particularly with translations of Latin works, but has a useful discussion of translations from Italian, especially *L'histoire de Morgant le géant*, a prose redaction of Pulci's *Morgante*. Emphasizes innate clarity of French translations. Good bibliography.

Lodovico Ariosto

(Nos. 2597-2605)

Ariosto, Lodovico. Roland furieux. Prose trans. falsely attributed to Jehan des Gouttes. Lyons, Thellusson, 1543. 244 p. Trans. by Jehan Martin, Lyons, Thellusson, 1554. 2597

Only complete French translation of *Orlando furioso* in 16th century. *See* 2600, v. I, p. 76-86.

— Roland furieux. Prose trans. by Gabriel Chappuys. Lyons, Honorat, 1576. 802 p. Same, Michel, 1582. 2598

Very casual revision of Lyons, 1543, translation. *See* 2606, v. I, p. 87-89.

— Orlando furioso. Verse translations : Cantos I-XV, Jean Fournier, 1555. 2599

See 2600, v. I, p. 98-99; Canto XXVIII, Rapin, 1572, *see* 2600, v. I, p. 138-39; Cantos I-XII, Jean de Boyssières, Lyons, 1580, reprinted, Lyons, 1608, signed I. D. B. *See* 2600, v. I, p. 99-102.

Cioranescu, Alexandre. L'Arioste en France des origines à la fin du XVIIIe siècle. Les presses modernes, 1939. 2 v. (PERF) 2600

Ch. II (1:76-103) deals with first French translations of A. in France; III (1:104-70) with the formerly so-called " imitations " of *Orlando furioso*. In v. II, p. 225-55, there is a valuable bibliography of translations of A.

Writer generally tries to present impartially every possible view of a question, and thus often gives impression of having discovered little really new. However, book is a mine of bibliographical information and the analyses of translations and imitations are indispensable for the investigator of A.'s influence in France. *See* 2605, 2755.

Fucilla, Joseph G. European translations and imitations of Ariosto. RR 25:45-51, 1934. 2601

Review of *Annali delle edizioni ariostee,* by Giuseppe Agnelli and Giuseppe Ravegnani, Bologna, 1933, 2 v. Of general interest.

Pescatore, Giambattista. La morte di Ruggiero continuata alla materia dell'-Ariosto; Venice, 1549; *reprinted* 1551, 1557. Trans. Gabriel Chappuys, La suite de Roland furieux. Lyons, 1583. 2602

See 2600, 1:93-94.

Roth, Th. Der Einfluss von Ariost's Orlando furioso auf das französische Theater. *See* 2331. 2603

Good bibliography for its time, but numerous errors and gaps. On p. 256-263 are listed 97 French translations of A.

Reviews : A. L. Stiefel in ZFSL 29:190-198, 1906; P. Toldo in GSLI 48:426-429, 1906.

Taillemont, Claude de. Le conte de l'Infante Genièvre; trans. of L. Ariosto's Orlando furioso, Canto V. Lyons, 1556, p. 115-52. 2604

Taken from same author's *La tricarite, plus quelques chants en faveur de plusieurs damoezêlles. See* 2600, v. I, p. 93-94.

Toldo, Pietro. Quelques notes pour servir à l'histoire de l'influence du Furioso dans la littérature française. *See* 2332. 2605

The basic study of the influence of *Orlando furioso* on French tragedy and comedy. It supplements Vianey, no. 1191, on *L'Ariosto et la Pléiade*. The *Orlando furioso* was an even more important inspiration to French dramatists than Tasso's *Gerusalemme liberata*. It was natural that Charlemagne's knights, glorified by A., should be repatriated in France.

Matteo Bandello

(Nos. 2606-2607)

Pruvost, René. Les deux premiers tomes de la version française de Bandello. RLC 12:387-90, 1932. 2606

The British Museum possesses first edition of v. I. of B.'s *Histoires tragiques* translated, in 1559 by Pierre Boaistuau, whose work was continued immediately by François de Belleforest. It possesses also first edition of v. II, by François de Belleforest, published in 1565, and not found elsewhere, nor even listed by Brunet.

Sturel, René. Bandello en France au XVIᵉ siècle. BI 13:210-27, 331-47, 1913; 14:29-53, 211-35, 300-25, 1914; 15:2-17, 56-73, 1915; 16:71-83, 1916; 17:89-95, 1917; 18:1-27, 1918. *Reprinted:* Bordeaux, Feret, 1918. 187 p.   2607

Sturel died in battle August, 1915. Beginning in 1916, his notes were edited by the staff of BI, but his original plan to study the borrowings from Boaistuau's and Belleforest's *Histoires tragiques* in French tragedies could never be carried out. Cf. BI 15:73, 1915.

Two of Sturel's articles, 16:77-83, 1916, and 17:89-95, 1917, concern an unedited poem by Desportes in *Les amours infortunées de Didaco et de Violante*, based on 42nd tale of Book I of B., translated by Boaistuau in 1559. This poem, copied by Sturel from the Ms. Fr. 842 of the BN, appeared in BI 18:1-27, 1918, revised slightly by H. Hauvette.

The series discusses thoroughly 1) *Histoires tragiques extraictes des œuvres italiennes de Bandel, et mises en nostre langue françoise par Pierre Boaistuau, surnommé Launay*, 1559, consisting of six tales by B.; 2) *Continuation des histoires tragiques extraites de l'italien de Belleforest commingeois*, 1559, consisting of 12 tales by B.; with further translations in 1565, 1568, and 1570.

Boaistuau aimed to please, and pretended that all his stories had a solid histoical foundation. He made changes of details, altered events, abridged, sometimes drew on his imagination. Unlike many other 16th century translators, he had no moral preoccupation. On the other hand, Belleforest left out all *contes grivois*, especially those referring to monks, attenuated the faults of heroines; was a preacher, not a satirist. Dominant ideas : Divine providence, and inconstancy of fortune. Belleforest believed man naturally bad. He had two preoccupations, nearly absent in B.; 1) *la morale*; 2) psychological analysis. His modifications of B. were mostly original.

See also: Olin H. Moore, *Le rôle de Boaistuau dans le développement de la légende de Roméo et Juliette*, 2611. *See also* 2773.

François de Belleforest
(No. 2609)

Picot, Emile. François de Belleforest. *In his:* Les français italianisants au XVIᵉ siècle. *See* 2566, v. II, p. 89-93.   2609
Mostly biographical, with some emphasis on acquaintance with Spanish.

Pierre Boaistuau
(Nos. 2610-2611)

Moore, Olin H. Pierre Boaistuau. *In his:* The legend of Romeo and Juliet. Columbus, Ohio State University Press, 1950. p. 87-94.   2610
Maintains that B.'s contribution to development of the legend has been overrated.
Reviews : G. I. Duthie in SQ 3:54-55, Jan., 1952; P. H. Elmen in Ital 29:266-67, 1952; J. D. M. Ford in Spec 26:731-32, 1951; C. T. Prouty in MLN 68:274, 1953; E. H. Wilkins in GSR 4:11-12, 1951.

— Le rôle de Boaistuau dans le développement de la légende de Roméo et Juliette. RLC 9:637-43, 1929.   2611
René Sturel has underestimated B.'s indebtedness to Luigi da Porto, especially for characterization of the corrupt priest.

Giovanni Boccaccio
(Nos. 2612-2620)

Boccaccio, Giovanni. De casibus virorum illustrium. Trans. by Laurent de Premier Fait as : Des cas et ruyne des nobles hommes et femmes reversez par fortune, Jean du Pré, 1483.   2612
See Henri Hauvette, *De Laurentio de Primofacto*, no. 2626.

— De casibus virorum illustrium. Trans. Claude Witart, Eve, 1578. 696 p.   2613
See H. Hauvette, no. 2619.

Hauvette, Henri. Les plus anciennes traductions françaises de Boccace. BI 7:281-313, 1907.   2614
P. 282-92 concern *Treize elegantes demandes d'amour*, extracted from B.'s *Filocolo*, Book IV. This anonymous translation, 1531, was reprinted in Paris, 1541. There are some omissions. Generally Italian text is followed too literally. Translator seems to have been an Italian with an inadequate knowledge of both French and Italian.

P. 290-98 are devoted to A. Sevin's translation of B.'s *Philocopo*, 1542; three reprints in 1555; several in 1575. This is a readable translation, not too literal, but overshadowed by fine contemporary work of Antoine Le Maçon. *See* 2620.

P. 298-313 concern Louis de Beauvau's translation of *Filostrato* (ca. 1440-1450). Beauvau, who knew Italian, was first French translator of B. to translate directly from Italian. Some errors, but exact and clear usually. The name of B. does not appear in the translation, partly accounting for fact that *Filostrato* had much less influence in France than in England.

— Les plus anciennes traductions françaises de Boccace. BI 8:1-17, 1908.   2615

P. 1-7 concern *Complainte tres piteuse de Flamette à son amy Pamphile*, an anonymous translation of B.'s *Fiammetta*, 1532; reprinted Lyons, 1532; 1541. Translation omits last three chapters of *Fiammetta*, and is full of absurdities.

P. 7-11 concern Gabriel Chappuys' excellent translation of *Fiammetta*, with the Italian text on each *verso*, 1585; reprinted, 1609 and 1622. Also, brief but unique account of Chappuys' extensive work as a translator.

P. 11-17 concern Antoine Guercin's *Le nymphal Flossolan*, a rendering of B.'s *Il ninfale Fiesolano*, Lyons, 1556. Guercin knew Italian, but his version was often incorrect and colorless. He made omissions; changed order; embroidered; falsified thought of B.; tried to moralize. Mediocre.

— Les plus anciennes traductions françaises de Boccace. BI 8:189-211, 1908.   2616

P. 189-99 concern a 15th century unedited literal translation ot B.'s *Teseide*. Weak vocabulary, but faithful and clear.

P. 199-204 concern Anne de Graville's *Le roman des deux amans Palamon et Arcita et de la belle et saige Emilia*, a verse translation of part of *Teseide*, 1521. Poem probably based on an anonymous French translation made c. 1460. The *Teseide* becomes a *roman*, with coquettish details, and often jests, added.

P. 204-06 concern *La teseyde*, Lucca, 1597. Reprinted in *Bibliothèque universelle des romans*, July 1779. It is based on N. Granucci's moralized summary of B.'s *Teseide*. Added are a dialogue frame-

work; historical, mythological and moral commentary and a detailed summary of Statius' *Thebaid*.

P. 206-11 concern *Urbain le mescongneu*, an anonymous translation of the *Urbano* falsely attributed to B., Lyons, 1530. Reprinted with liberal changes in *Bibliothèque universelle des romans*, Feb. 1784. Literal and clear rendering; probably based on a bad Italian edition of a mediocre story.

— (with J. Crouzet). Les plus anciennes traductions françaises de Boccace. BI 8:285-311, 1908.   2617

Discussion of Antoine Le Maçon's famous translation of *Decameron*, 1545; reprinted 20 times through 1614.

Scrupulous fidelity in translation. An effortless and ingenious reaction against the too literal translations of 15th century. Le Maçon probably translated, however, from a bad text—some omissions, and some errors in rendering particles and adverbial phrases. Some additions for clarity, and some *délayage*. Le Maçon translates ballads into French verse, attempting to keep Italian strophes, and thus helping to import Italian metres.

— Les plus anciennes traductions françaises de Boccace. BI 9:1-26, 1909.   2618

P. 2-9 concern an ancient version of the Griselda story (*Decameron*, X, 10), with particular reference to Petrarch's Latin version.

P. 9-10 concern Jehan Fleury's *Des deux amans*, a mediocre decasyllabic Latin-to-French version, in octaves, of B.'s story of Ghismonda and Guiscardo, *Decameron*, IV, 1, 1493.

P. 10-14 concern François Habert's inexact French verse dilution of Filippo Beroaldo's prose Latin adaptation of story of Titus and Gisippus (*Decameron*, X, 8), 1551; also Richard Le Blanc's French verse rendering of Beroaldo's version of affair of Ghismonda and Guiscardo (*Decameron*, IV, 1), 1553. The prolix Beroaldo had made alterations, especially in the character of the heroine. He changed Guiscardo to a servant. His extensive omissions made the conduct of Tancredi and Ghismonda incomprehensible.

P. 14-18 concern *Les comptes amoureux de Madame Jeanne Flore*, or translations of 7 tales from *Decameron* before 1540. *Comptes* II-V were reprinted in Lyons, 1540, and Paris, 1541, with altered *dénoue-*

ments. A complete edition was reprinted in Paris, 1543 and 1555; in Lyons, 1574. Translation in the spirit of *Decameron*, but with deviations, especially in *dénouements.*

— Les plus anciennes traductions françaises de Boccace. BI 9:193-211, 1909.   2619

P. 193-96 deal with mediocre anonymous translation of B.'s *De claris mulieribus*, published by Vérard, 1493.

P. 196-200 concern translation of *De claris mulieribus* by L. A. Ridolfi, a publisher of Lyons, of Florentine origin. Verbose, but clear. On the whole, one of the best 16th century translations. However, Ridolfi omits, interprets and modifies at will, though warning reader of changes made.

P. 200-01 are about the too literal anonymous translation of B.'s *De genealogiis deorum gentilium*, published by Vérard, 1499; reprinted, 1531. 13 books translated; last two omitted. Leaves out preamble, with genealogical trees. Keeps only information relative to pagan divinities.

P. 201-03 deal with Claude Witart's *Des mésaventures des personnages signalées*, a translation of B.'s *De casibus virorum illustrium*, 1578. Exact. Moralizing. Language readable, if not elegant or rigorous. Unlike Laurent de Premierfait, does not make disproportionate additions.

P. 203-04 deal with translation by Marguerite de Cambis, a naturalized French citizen of Italian birth, of *Epistre consolatoire d'exil* sent by B. to Pino de Rossi. Lyons, 1556.

P. 206-10 are a valuable table of French translations of B. in 14th, 15th and 16th centuries.

— Une variante française de la légende de Roméo et Juliette. RLC 1:329-37, 1921.   2620

Deals with Adrien Sevin's translation of *Philocope* of "messire Jean Boccace," 1542, which is prefaced among other things by an adaptation of Luigi da Porto's novella *Giulietta e Romeo.* (Reprinted 1555 and 1575. Cf. H. Hauvette in BI 7:293-97, 1907.) Although Sevin knew Italian well, he altered names found in Luigi da Porto's novella, the lovers, for instance, becoming "Halquadrich" and "Burglipha," and the scene being shifted from Verona to "Morée," at "Coron." Sevin introduces motive of *pundonor*, and episode of the apothecary.

Baldassare Castiglione
(No. 2621)

Toldo, Pietro. Le courtisan dans la littérature française et ses rapports avec l'œuvre du Castiglione. Archiv 104:75-121, 313-30, 105:60-85, 1900.   2621

Thorough treatment of the ideal of the courtier, as influenced by Castiglione and nearly contemporary writers, particularly in 16th and 17th century France. Some Italian bias. Represented a sort of chivalrous ideal; the French courtier an ideal more practical and often corrupt. See 2765.

Dante Alighieri
(Nos. 2622-2623)

Dante Alighieri. La comédie de Dante, de l'Enfer, du Purgatoire et du Paradis, mise en rime françoise par Balthasar Grangier. Drobet, 1596-97. 3 v.   2622

A translation whose badness partly accounts for the lack of interest in D. in France during 16th and 17th centuries. *See* Arturo Farinelli, *Dante e la Francia.* Milan, Hoepli, 1908, 1:549-60.

— Les plus anciennes traductions françaises de la Divine comédie. Ed. by Camille Morel. Librairie universitaire, 1897. 623 p.   2623

Contains a 15th century translation of *Inferno*, MS. L. III. 17 of the library of the University of Turin; also a complete translation of *Divine comedy* (second half of the 16th century), partly in alexandrines and partly in ten-syllable couplets, MS 10201 of the former Imperial Library of Vienna, later known as National-bibliothek. Morel reproduces also Bergaigne's too literal and often nonsensical translation of Cantos I, XI, XV, and XVII of *Paradiso.* Little critical apparatus, although on p. 605-23 there are annotations for the first two translations mentioned. *See* Arturo Farinelli, *Dante e la Francia,* Milan, Hoepli, 1908, 1:274-80.

Agnolo Firenzuola
(No. 2624)

Firenzuola, Agnolo. Discours de la beauté des dames, prins de l'italien du seigneur Ange Firenzuole par I. Pallet. First ed., L'Angelier, 1578.   2624

This fairly literal translation consists of two *Dialogues*, printed on 51 double pages, prefaced by an *Epistre* (5 double pages), and 4 pages of verse.

Giovanni Battista Giraldi Cintio
(No. 2625)

Giraldi Cintio, G. B. Les Cent excellentes nouvelles; trans. by Gabriel Chappuys, 1583 and 1584. 2 v. 2625

A translation of *Hecatommithi* without the philosophical dialogues.

For a general discussion of Chappuys' work, *see* H. Hauvette, BI 8:7, 1908.

Laurent de Premierfait
(No. 2626)

Hauvette, Henri. De Laurentio de Primofacto. Hachette, 1903. 109 p. (Diss., Paris) 2626

L. died in 1414, but Hauvette was obliged to deduce all other information about him from his writings. A splendid study, showing how L. was able to compensate in part for a scanty knowledge of Italian.

Review : Anon in GSLI 42:261-62, 1903.

Francesco Petrarca
(Nos. 2627-2632)

Petrarca, Francesco. De remediis utriusque fortunae; trans. Jean Daudin, 1378. 2627

Daudin's translation was printed in Paris, 1523, under the name of Nicole Oresme, " plus célèbre," says H. Hauvette, *Les poésies lyriques de Pétrarque*, 1931, p. 140, implying Oresme had nothing to do with the work, which was an important one.

— Le Pétrarque en rime françoise aveq ses commentaires, tradvit per Philippe de Maldeghem, *seigneur* de Leyschot. 1st ed., Brussels, 1600. 2nd ed., Douai, Fabry, 1606. 547 p. 2628

A fairly literal verse translation of both *Canzoniere* and of *Trionfi*, imitating P.'s rhyme-scheme, but substituting 12-syllable lines for Petrarch's usual hendecasyllables. Analyses in French appear at end of each sonnet and canzone.

Second edition is generally identical with the first, even to the peculiar numbering of the pages. There are minor exceptions, such as the addition of a few woodcuts, slight changes of type on p. 12, etc.

— Les triumphes. Trans. George de La Forge. First ed., 1514; subsequent editions, 1520, 1531, 1554. 2629

Importance of this translation discussed by Bertoni, no. 2631. It appears that the printed editions vary considerably from two of the MSS, BN fr. 1119 and Bibliothèque de l'Arsenal 3086. The subject is clearly worth further investigation.

Bertoni, Giulio. Per la fortuna dei Trionfi del Petrarca in Francia. Modena, 1904. 62 p. 2631

Excellent, especially for discussion of MSS.

Harvitt, Hélène. Les Triomphes de Pétrarque; traduction en vers français par Simon Bougouyn, valet de chambre de Louis XII. *See* 728. 2632

States that this translation (BN MS fr. 2500-01 and MS fr. 12423), previously listed as anonymous, was actually by Simon Bougouyn.

The same claim had been made eighteen years previously. *See* G. Bertoni, *Per la fortuna dei Trionfi del Petrarca in Francia* (2631), p. 31-36; 47-48; 49-50; 56, the translator's name being spelled Simon Bougoyn. In addition to the two MSS cited by Miss Harvitt, a third MS, no. 6480 of the Bibliothèque de l'Arsenal was mentioned. *See* 2731.

Innocenzio Ringhieri
(No. 2633)

Ringhieri, Innocenzio. Cinqvante ieus divers d'honnete entretien, industrieusement inuentés par Messer Innocent Rhinghier, gentilhomme Boloignoys, et fais françoys par Hubert Philippe de Villiers. Lyons, Pesnot, 1555. 308 p. 2633

La fable d'Aristée et de Protée begins (in verse) on p. 286, being printed in italics. Page numbering then skips to p. 292.

Jacopo Sannazaro
(No. 2634)

Sannazaro, Jacopo. L'Arcadie de messire Iaques Sannazar. Trans. Jehan Martin. Vascosan & Corrozet, 1544. 135 ff. 2634

Fairly good free translation. The *terzine* are rendered by rhyming couplets. On p. 115a-33b the glossary is found, with frequent references to such authorities as Dioscorides, Pliny and Ovid. On p. 134a-135b is a verse translation of Horace *Épode* II.

Giovanni Francesco Straparola

(No. 2635)

Straparola, Giovanni Francesco. Les facétieuses nuits; I, trans. Jean Louveau; II, trans. Pierre de Larivey. Lyons, 1560 and 1572, six other ed. through 1585. Revised by Larivey; Lyons, 1595, 2 v., six other ed. through 1726. Original text of Louveau (1585) reprinted in the Bibliothèque Elzévirienne, 1857, 2 v. with introduction by P. Jannet. 2635

Louveau's translation was at once too literal and too inaccurate. Larivey, who knew Italian well, often took great liberties with his text.

Torquato Tasso

(Nos. 2636-2639)

Tasso, Torquato. La Hierusalem du Sʳ Torquato Tasso rendue françoise par B. D. V. P. (Blaise de Vigenère), 1595. Reprinted, 1599; 1610, and 1617. 2636

See Chandler B. Beall, *La fortune du Tasse en France*, no. 2767, p. 28.

— La delivrance de Hierusalem, mise en vers françois, par Jean du Vignau. 1595. 2637

Lacks notes and commentary.

See Chandler B. Beall, *La fortune du Tasse en France*, no. 2767, p. 28 and note 10; Arturo Farinelli, *Dante e la Francia*, Milan, 1908, I, 549, and note 2.

— Four cantos of the Gerusalemme liberata (XVI, IV, XII, II), trans. Pierre de Brach. 1596. 2638

See Chandler B. Beall. *La fortune du Tasse en France*, no. 2767, p. 15-16.

— La croisade, poëme héroique du seigneur Torquato Tasso, traduit stance par stance par Hiérosme d'Avost. Lyons, 1586 (?). 2639

Contains only third canto of *Gerusalemme liberata*. Complete manuscript was delivered to publisher, Barthélemy Honorat, at Lyons, who never printed it. Finally Canto II was included in Du Verdier's *Bibliothèque* (1584). *See* C. B. Beall, *The first French imitation of Tasso's Invocation to the Muse*, MLN 53:531-32, 1938; *also his La fortune du Tasse en France*, no. 2767, p. 17-18, and E. Picot, 2567, 2:215.

Machiavelli

(Nos. 2640-2660)

WILLIS H. BOWEN

Bibliography

Bowen, Willis H. Sixteenth century French translations of Machiavelli. Ital 27:313-20, 1950. 2640

Shows how first French translators presented M. to the public. Mentions some items not found in Gerber. *See* 2760.

Gerber, Adolph. Niccolò Machiavelli. Die Handschriften, Ausgaben und Übersetzungen seiner Werke im 16. und 17. Jahrhundert. Eine kritisch-bibliographische Untersuchung. Gotha, Perthes, 1912. 3 v. in 1. 2641

Indispensable work for study of early history of M.'s writings. Careful information about 16th century French translations and their success. Many facsimiles of titles.

Reviews : M. Roques in Rom 42:155, 1913; J. E. S. in MLN 27:200, 1912.

Harris, Paul H. Progress in Machiavelli studies. Ital 18:1-11, 1941. 2642

Discusses recent work on M. with especial attention to studies on influence in England.

Translation of Arte Della Guerra

L'art de la guerre, composé par Nicolas Machiavelli. L'estat aussi et charge d'un lieutenant général d'armée par Onosander. Le tout traduict en vulgaire françois, par Jehan Charrier. Barbé, 1546. 130 ff. 2643

BN R. 526. Only 16th century translation of this work. Frequently reprinted with *Discours* and *Prince* until 1664. Gerber, 3:27-31.

Translations of the Discorsi sopra la prima deca di Tito Livio

Le premier livre des discours de l'estat de paix et de guerre de messire Nicolas Macchiavegli secretaire et citoyen florentin sur la premiere decade de Tite Live. Traduict d'italien en françoys. Janot, 1544. 65 ff. 2644

BN Rés. E. 41. Translator is Jacques Gohory. First translation of M. in any language. First book only. Brunet, *Manuel*, 3:1279; *Supplément*, I, 916; Gerber, 3:21-22.

Le premier-troisieme livre des discours de l'estat de paix et de guerre, de messire Nicolas Macchiavelli. Sur la premiere decade de Tite-Live, traduict d'italien en françoys. Groulleau et Longnis, 1548. 3 parts in 1 v. 188 ff. 2645

BN E. 125. Translator, Jacques Gohory. Liminary poem by Jean-Pierre de Mesmes says M. better known in France than in Italy. Each part separately titled and paged. Most important French version of *Discorsi*, reprinted about 20 times before 1664. Gerber, 3:22-24 : Rothschild, Nathan James Edouard. *Catalogue des livres composant la bibliothèque de feu m. le baron James de Rothschild.* Morgand, 1884-1920. 5:171-72.

Les discours de l'estat de paix et de guerre de messire Nicolas Macchiavelli sur la premiere decade de Tite-Live, traduict d'italien en françoys, plus un livre du mesme aucteur intitulé : le Prince. Marnef et Cavellat, 1571. 2 parts in 1 v. 784 p. 2646

BN E. 2836 and E. 2851. This was a " pirated " edition, since the translator of *Principe*, Gaspard D'Auvergne, appeared to be responsible for the whole volume, although *Discorsi* were translated by Gohory. The two works continued to be printed together, and were usually known in this form in 16th and 17th centuries. Sometimes *Art de la guerre* was included in the same volume. Gerber, 3:30-33; 39-40.

Les discours de Nic. Macchiavel sur la premiere decade de Tite-Live, dez l'edification de la ville, traduictz d'italien en françois, et de nouveau reveuz et augmentez par Jacques Gohory Parisien. Le Mangnier, 1571. 178 ff. 2647

BN Rés. E. 628. NYPL Reserve. Revision of 1548 edition, published with Gohory's translation of *Principe*. The most careful version of *Discorsi*, but not best known, for it was not reprinted. Gerber, 3:24-27.

Translation of Istorie fiorentine

Histoire de Florence, de Nicolas Machiavel. Nouvellement traduicte d'italien en françois, par le seigneur Yves de Brinon. Borel, 1577. 294 ff. 2648

BN K. 15901. Another copy, La Noue, 1577, BN K. 8574. This remained the standard translation until 1694, being published three times before then. Gerber, 3:36-38.

Translations of Il Principe

Le Prince, de Nicolas Machiavelle. Traduit d'italien en françois, par Guillaume Cappel. Estienne, 1553. 148 p. 2649

BN E. 913. First published translation of *Principe*. Not reprinted. Gerber, 3:33-34; Bowen, p. 315-16.

Le Prince, de Nicolas Macchiavelli. Traduit d'italien en françois par Gaspard d'Auvergne. Poitiers, Marnef, 1553. 96 ff. 2650

BN E. 914. Reprinted about 20 times before 1684, usually with Gohory's *Discours*. Most important 16th century translation of *Principe*. Was source of Dutch and possibly English versions. Gerber, 3:30-32; Bowen, p. 316-17.

Le Prince de Nicolas Macchiavelli secretaire et citoyen de Florence, traduit d'italien en françois. Marnef et Cavellat, 1571. 159 p. 2651

BN E. 2836 and E. 2851. In same volume as " pirated " edition of Gohory's *Discours*. This edition many times reprinted; brought fame to M. in France. It remained the standard version until at least 1684. Gerber, 3:30-39; 40-47.

Le Prince, de Nicolas Machiavel. Traduit d'italien en françois, avec la vie de l'auteur mesme par Jaq. Gohory Parisien. Le Mangnier, 1571. 64 ff. 2652

BN Rés. E. 628. NYPL Reserve. Text of Gohory's translation largely borrowed from Cappel. Life of M. interesting as first of its kind, though sketchy. This edition was not reprinted in 16th century, but there are two modern editions based on it : *Le prince, préface de Benito Mussolini.* Helleu et Sergent, 1929; *Le prince, traduction corrigée et remanié par Yves Lévy.* Éditions de Cluny, 1938. Gerber, 3:43-45; Bowen, 317-22.

Influence During the Sixteenth Century

Allen, John W. The influence of Machiavelli. *In his :* A history of political thought in the sixteenth century. London, Methuen, 1928. p. 488-94. 2653

One must make a careful distinction between influence of M.'s ideas and influence of Machiavellianism, which is a misinterpretation of the man and his works. The latter rose in second third of the century, and after 1570 proved to be the more important. Allen gives a careful, brief account of both influences.

Barrère, Joseph. Etienne de La Boétie contre Nicolas Machiavel. *See* 1470. 2654

" Barrère contrasts passages and themes; tries to show La Boétie combatting Machiavelli on friendship, the fate of tyrants, morality in politics." H. Kurz, no. 1643, p. 33. *See* this Bibliography (no. 1643) for other items concerning M. and La Boétie.

Cardascia, G. Machiavel et Jean Bodin. *See* 2052, 2761. 2655

Writer believes M.'s reputation grew slowly in France. Bodin approved of M. in *Methodus* but in *République* attacks his theories, while adopting many of them. Footnotes on p. 129-31 name most important earliest references to M. in France. These include : La Perrière, Bodin, Loys Le Roy, Gentillet, Belleforest.

Cherel, Albert. La pensée de Machiavel en France. L'artisan du livre, 1935. 350 p. 2656

General work on the intellectual influence of M. " Methodical but poorly equilibrated " (Harris). " Well-documented but uneven " (Luciani). *See* 2762.

Reviews : P. H. Harris in Ital 18:4-5, 1941; V. Luciani in Ital 15:86-88, 1938; R. Pintard in RLC 17:420-22, 1938.

Dreyer, Kenneth. Commynes and Machiavelli; a study in parallelism. Symp 5:38-61, 1951. 2657

M. owed much to Commynes. Parallels traced in lives, interests. Similarities and differences hitherto neglected.

Gentillet, Innocent. Discours d'état sur les moyens de bien gouverner et maintenir en bonne paix un royaume, contre Nicolas Machiavel. *See* 462. 2658

BN E. 2668. Important work for its part in establishing the legend about M. Attacks morality of M. from Huguenot point of view.

Pintard, René. Une adaptation de Machiavel au XVIe siècle; Le prince nécessaire de Jean de La Taille. RLC 13:385-402, 1933. 2659

Though La Taille's poem was not published in 16th century, it shows him a close imitator and possibly the most thorough student of M. in 16th century France. Poem imitates French translation; La Taille probably did not read Italian original. Pintard presents concisely the position of M. in France. *See* 2763.

Villey, Pierre. Le Machiavélisme au temps de Montaigne. *In his:* Les sources et l'évolution des essais de Montaigne. *See* 1794, v. 2:357-62. 2660

Montaigne's attitude toward ideas of M. Montaigne did not take part in the violent attacks indulged in by Protestants and *Ligueurs*. Was willing, like M., to separate politics from ethics, but is repelled by some of the implications in M.'s theories.

CHAPTER XVIII. THE RELATIONS OF THE FRENCH RENAISSANCE WITH FOREIGN LITERATURES
(Nos. 2661-2897)

Edited by W. P. FRIEDERICH

PHILIP MACON CHEEK, WOLFGANG BERNARD FLEISCHMANN, L. N. GOULD, J. CORIDEN LYONS, JAMES S. PATTY, STERLING A. STOUDEMIRE

General Bibliography

(No. 2661)

Baldensperger, Fernand and Werner P. Friederich. Bibliography of comparative literature. *See 2.* 2661

The basic bibliography in this field, augmented by two supplements in *Yearbook of comparative and general literature I and II* (Chapel Hill, N. C., 1952 and 1953 respectively). For French renaissance literature *see* especially *Intermediaries* (p. 32 ff.); *Individual notices* (p. 78 ff.); *Literary genres* (p. 179); *The influence of classical antiquity* (p. 233 ff.); *Hebraism and Christianity* (p. 307 ff.); *Humanism and renaissance* (p. 341 ff.); *Collective and reciprocal influences* (p. 360 ff.); *Italian contributions* (p. 394 ff.), *Spanish contributions* (p. 449 ff.); *French contributions* (p. 482 ff.), *English contributions* (p. 551 ff.) and *German contributions* (p. 620 ff.).

Reviewed by J. Hankiss in Eras 3:744-746, 1950; B. Munteano in RLC 26:273-286, 1952; P. Rosenberg in Grev 26:165-166, 1951; R. Wellek in CL 3:90-92, 1951.

Italo-French Relations

(Nos. 2662-2795)

J. CORIDEN LYONS and JAMES S. PATTY

General Italian Influences upon French Literature
(Nos. 2662-2684)

Attinger, Gustave. L'esprit de la commedia dell'arte dans le théâtre français. Librairie théâtrale, 1950. 489 p. (Diss., Neuchâtel) 2662

Little material on 16th century French comedy, as Italian influence in this period came from " erudite " Italian comedy. Passages on Italian troupes in France summarize Baschet and Lebègue. General conclusions are that " ces troupes furent de véritables troupes de l'art et jouèrent généralement le même répertoire qu'en Italie " and that " les types italiens eurent une diffusion très grande en France dans le dernier tiers du xvie siècle."

Review : A. D. Crow in FS 6:68-70, 1952; H. C. Lancaster in MLN 66:341-43, 1951.

Baillou, Jean. L'influence de la pensée philosophique de la renaissance italienne sur la pensée française : état présent des travaux relatifs au xvie siècle. *See 187.* 2663

In this bibliographical article, author treats the subject under following headings : personal contacts (Claude de Seyssel in Pavia and Turin; De Thou in Rome, Naples, Venice, etc.; Gribaldi in Toulouse; Alciati in Bourges), the study of Platonism (in Ficino, Pico, Bembo, Castiglione, Leone Ebreo), Rationalism (Pomponazzi, etc.), political theory (Machiavelli). Only problems already treated in scholarly monographs are considered.

Baschet, A. Les comédiens italiens à la cour de France sous Charles IX, Henri III, Henri IV, et Louis XIII. *See 2398.* 2664

Although outmoded in many respects because of extensive additional research done in this field since its date of publication, this excellent study still makes a fine starting point for a student not familiar with the subject. In the text, footnotes and appendices there are many interesting documents and items of information not readily available elsewhere. Alphabetical index and detailed chapter analyses add greatly to book's usefulness.

Bourciez, E. E. J.   Les mœurs polies et la littérature de cour sous Henri II.   Hachette, 1886.   437 p.   2665

Chapter on Italianism gives an exceptionally nationalistic and puristic analysis of Italian influences brought to bear on court life in mid-sixteenth century.   Discusses Italian artists, scholars, and courtiers who frequented the court; influence of Catherine de Médicis; vogue of *Cortegiano* (which is condemned as excessively materialistic : " le complément du livre du *Prince* "); Italianization of French language (no allowance is made for comic or polemic exaggeration in parodies of Italianized speech by Henri Estienne and Jacques Grévin).   Later reaction against Italianism is revenge of " le vieux bon sens français "; period of Italian influence is a " crise périlleuse."

Busson, Henri.   Les sources et le développement du rationalisme dans la littérature française de la renaissance (1533-1601).   *See* 188.   2666

Extensive treatment of Italian background of French rationalism (the Paduan Averroists, Pomponazzi, Vicomercato, etc.) and of Franco-Italian intellectual exchanges during renaissance : chapters on French in Italy, Italians in France, Italian sources (of rationalism).   This information is less detailed than in Picot's studies (from which it is taken); largely confined to authors and works outside field of imaginative literature.

Charbonnel, J. R.   La pensée italienne au XVIᵉ siècle et le courant libertin.   *See* 193.   2667

Well known standard work revealing all possible sources of *libre pensée* in Italian renaissance scepticism : Padovan School with Pomponazzi and Cremonini, popularizers Cardano and Vanini, political amoralism of Machiavelli, immanentism of Telesio and Giordano Bruno, experimentalism of Galileo, and harmonization of Campanella.

Flamini, Francesco.   Le lettere italiane alla corte di Francesco I, re di Francia.   *In his :* Studi di storia letteraria italiana e straniera.   Leghorn, Giusti, 1895.   p. 199-337.   2668

Fourth essay in a collection of ten, this study considers the first transmitters of Italian civilization in France : Gregorio da Tiferna, Fausto Andrelini, Alciati, Alamanni, and less known writers like Amomo (whose Petrarchistic poems are discussed), Martelli, Simeoni; also scholars outside the

strictly humanistic field, like the doctor-theologian Paolo Belmissero.

Gambier, Henri.   Italie et renaissance poétique en France.   Padua, Cedam, 1936.   237 p.   2669

Title somewhat misleading, since question of Italian influence on French renaissance poetry is treated only superficially and summarily.   Gambier gives one of the best short and succinct statements of evolution of French poetry from beginning of century through Ronsard.   Book is most useful to graduate students being introduced to study of French renaissance.   *See* 1126.

Gosche, Richard.   Idyll und Dorfgeschichte im Alterthum und Mittelalter.   ALG 1:169-227, 1870.   2670

Demonstrates that stories of *vilain* and *dörper* around 1500 were not able to hold their own against refinement of Italian and Spanish influence in France and Germany.

Lebègue, Raymond.   La comédie italienne en France au XVIᵉ siècle.   RLC 24:5-24, 1950.   2671

A valuable *mise au point* of present knowledge on French contact with Italian comedy in 16th century.   Lists translations, known performances, actors, troupes, French editions of Italian comedies, Italian comedies in *Bibliothèque royale*.   Iconography of 16th and early 17th century representations of scenes and characters from *commedia dell'arte*.

Mathorez, J.   Les Italiens et l'opinion française à la fin du XVIᵉ siècle.   BBB 1914: p. 96-105, 143-58.   2672

Du Verdier, La Noue, Noël du Fail, Henri Estienne and others pamphleteered against Italian influence in France : the Italians are " manieurs d'argent," French resent being " gouvernés par un Italien, morigénés par un évêque florentin, jugés par un conseiller qui parfois ignorait la langue française," and detest Catherine de Médicis as " l'Italienne."

Maugain, G.   L'humanisme italien en France avant 1515.   REI 1:166-74, 1936.   2673

Prospectus for a study of influence of the papal *milieu* in Avignon, prehumanists around Charles VI, Italians involved in teaching of Greek and Latin, effect of printing-press on humanistic French-Italian relations, and importance of personal contacts in these relations.

Mignon, Maurice. Le théâtre italien à Lyon pendant la renaissance. *In his:* Études sur le théâtre français et italien de la renaissance. *See* 2403, p. 62-86. 2674

Rather disorganized sketch centered around three subjects : Giovan Giorgio Alione, possible founder of Italian theatre at Lyons ; performance of Bibbiena's *Calandria* at Lyons in 1548; death of Isabella Andreini in 1604.

Nolhac, Pierre de, and Angelo Solerti. Il viaggio in Italia di Enrico III re di Francia e le feste a Venezia, Ferrara, Mantova e Torino. Turin, Roux, 1890. 343 p. 2675

A reconstruction from eye-witness accounts, ambassadorial reports, letters and orations of Henri III's trip through northern Italy in 1574. Much space is given to describing lavish receptions given him in various cities—dramatic performances, balls, fireworks, and the like. Some interesting unpublished material is reproduced in appendix.

Review : G. B. C. in GSLI, 17:136-39, 1891, rebuttal 17: 446-49, 1891.

Pellegrini, Carlo. Relazioni tra la letteratura italiana e la letteratura francese. *In:* A. Momigliano, ed., Letterature comparate. Milan, Marzorati, 1948. 382 p. 2676

Treats five phases of the subject : *Trecentisti, Cinquecentisti,* theatre from Molière to Goldoni, 18th century, and period from Mme de Staël to d'Annunzio. Neatly avoids nationalistic preconceptions.

Review : W. P. Friederich in CL 3:83-85, 1951.

Picot, Emile. Les Français italianisants au XVIe siècle. *See* 2566. 2677

This item was to be sixth of an elaborate seven-point program which the author announces in introduction, but most of which he never managed to compose. *Les Italiens en France au XVIe siècle* did appear in article form in the BI (2678). The 60 chapters deal with various forms of Italian influence on individual authors of the period. While some of the instances of " Italian influence " are debatable, the work is an invaluable tool for study of this subject.

— Les Italiens en France au XVIe siècle. BI 1:92-137, 269-94, 1901; 2:23-53, 108-47, 1902; 3:7-36, 118-42, 219-34, 1903; 4:123-142, 294-315, 1904; 17:61-75, 160-84, 1917; 18:28-36, 1918. 2678

Work is subdivided as follows (the six articles being distributed over six volumes of BI) : 1. *Les Italiens en France au XVIe siècle* (noble families, military men); 2. *Les diplomates italiens au service de la France;* 3. *Les banquiers italiens en France;* 4. *Influence des Italiens à la cour de France;* 5. *Les artistes italiens en France;* 6. *Les Italiens dans les universités françaises. Les Français dans les universités italiennes.*

— Pour et contre l'influence italienne en France au XVIe siècle. EI 2:17-32, Jan., 1920. 2679

This posthumous article shows turning of tide against Italianism in France, partly because of exhaustion due to plagiaristic imitation (Vauquelin, Passerat, Bertaut, Desportes), partly because of nationalism (Henri Estienne, Noël du Fail, Estienne Pasquier).

Romier, Lucien. Lyon et le cosmopolitisme au début de la renaissance française. BHren 11:28-42, 1949. 2680

Rapid survey of geographical, historical, commercial and cultural factors tending to make Lyons a center of cosmopolitan intellectual and literary activity and particularly of humanism.

Texte, Joseph. L'influence italienne dans la renaissance française. *In his:* Études de littérature européenne. *See* 1763, p. 25-50. 2681

Vague and rhetorical, after manner of most of criticism of that day, Texte's offers pleasant reading but adds little to scholarly baggage of a present-day student of renaissance.

Toldo, Pietro. La comédie française de la renaissance. *See* 2405. 2682

Traces the Italian influence from Larivey up to 17th century. Stresses classical and Italian influences (sees former rather than latter in Jodelle's *Eugène*). A chronological list of translations of Italian comedies from 1573 to 1609 (5:238-39, 1898). A summary of the standardized comic elements in Italian comedy (5:239-264, 1898). Grévin's *Les esbahis* called first original French play to show heavy Italian influence. New sources found for La Taille's *Les corrivaux* and Turnèbe's *Les contens.* Detailed analysis of Larivey's use of his Italian sources (5:588-603, 1898). French renaissance comedy viewed as furnishing indispensable raw material of comedy which became art of permanent worth in hands of Molière and others. *See* 2431.

Vianey, Joseph. L'influence italienne chez les précurseurs de la Pléiade. *See* 800. 2683

Evidence to show that Italian influence on Mellin de Saint-Gelais, Marot, and Scève came from the *Quattrocentisti* (Cariteo, Tebaldeo, Serafino, etc.), whereas the Pléiade proper was to be under influence of Ariosto and Venetian Petrarchists.

Williams, Ralph C. Two studies in epic theory. MP 22:133-51, 1924-25. 2684

Traces critical discussion of verisimilitude, decorum, the marvelous through 16th century Italian criticism into 16th and 17th century French criticism. No questions of influence raised.

Some French Influences upon Italy

(Nos. 2685-2697)

Castets, Ferdinand. Recherches sur les rapports des chansons de geste et de l'épopée chevaleresque italienne. RLR 27:5-42, 1885; 29:5-16, 105-32, 1886; 30:61-237, 1886. *Reprinted:* Maisonneuve, 1887. 259 p. 2685

Texts of poems in Montpellier ms. H. 247 (*Quatre fils Aymon* and its sequels) which represent intermediate stage in elaboration of subject matter treated in *Rinaldo da Montalbano, Spagna,* and *Reali di Francia.* Commentary compares various treatments of the themes.

Gaspary, Adolf. La poesia cavalleresca. *In:* Storia della letteratura italiana. V. I, Turin, 1887-1901. 2nd ed., 1900. 2 v. 2686

Introduction to chapter on Pulci and Boiardo as prolongers of the French mediaeval epic and Arthurian romances.

Toldo, Pietro. Il poema della creazione del du Bartas e quello di T. Tasso. *In his:* Due articoli letterari. Rome, Loescher, 1894. p. 31-51. 2687

Tasso classicized Du Bartas. Baroque mannerism in France should not be attributed to Italian influence (Marino was eleven years old when *La sepmaine* appeared) but to Spanish or even French sources.

Vaganay, Hugues. Un " français italianisant " peu connu : Du Peyrat, Ferrante Guisone, Du Bartas et ... Jacques VI. RSS 16:133-40, 1929. 2688

Text of Du Peyrat's twenty-six *Stances sur la Semaine de G. Saluste Du Bartas:*

*Au S*ʳ *Ferrant Mantoüan* (i.e., Guisone, who translated six days of *Première semaine* into Italian), with bibliographical data on the poem, which is a eulogy of Du Bartas, James VI of Scotland, and Guisone.

Gianturco, Elio. Bodin and Vico. *See* 2062. 2689

Similarities and divergences à propos of sovereignty, Roman law, origin of political power, evolution of state-forms, Roman constitutional history, and feudalism.

Soldati, Paolo. Uomini e cose di Francia nei giudizi di Jacopo Corbinelli. GSLI 110:120-31, 1937. 2690

Corbinelli's reactions to political and religious strife of late 16th century (in general, he was a monarchist politically but not religiously sympathetic to the Huguenot cause).

Dorez, Léon and Louis Thuasne. Pic de La Mirandole en France. Leroux, 1897. 218 p. 2691

Studies and documents relative to Pico's sojourns in France (1485-86, 1487-88) and his difficulties with the Papacy during this period.

Review : R. in GSLI 31:127-31, 1898.

Neri, F. La dubbia fortuna del Rabelais in Italia. RLC 12:577-87, 1932. 2692

Rabelais' influence in Italy before latter 19th century reduced to the vanishing point.

Rajna, Pio. Il Rabelais giudicato da un Italiano del secolo XVI. RER 1:157-65, 1903. 2693

A letter by Corbinelli (which Rajna dates 1568 or 1569) praises Rabelais and compares him to Pulci and Aristophanes. Corbinelli's judgment is called " il più antico che di un italiano sia a noi pervenuto."

Maugain, Gabriel. Les prétendues relations du Tasse et de Ronsard. RLC 4:429-442, 1924. 2694

Concludes against likelihood of any close relations. Serassi's *Vita di Torquato Tasso* (1785) original source of this legend.

Olschki, L. La lettre du Tasse sur la France et les Français. RR 33:336-55, 1942. 2695

Tasso was first great modern writer to give a systematic description of a country based on personal experience, but his prejudices and limited sympathies are in sharp contrast to Montaigne's openminded curiosity. Letter reveals more of Tasso than of France.

Solerti, Angelo. Le voyage du Tasse en France. RLR 36:573-85, 1892. 2696
Recounts voyage in some detail. Analysis of Tasso's letter on France. Remarks on Italianism in France ca. 1570. " Corbinelli ... présenta sans doute à Ronsard son compatriote..." (p. 584).

Maugain, Gabriel. Ronsard en Italie. *See* 1157. 2697
After pointing out difficulty of getting any French author known to and appreciated by Italian public of second half of 16th century, Maugain lists the people, analyzes means by which Ronsard overcame these obstacles. Stresses influence of Muret and other friends of Ronsard who were in Italy. Maugain also stresses role played by Chiabrera's enthusiasm about Ronsard in expanding influence of the French poet in Italian peninsula. Notes that, from 1630 until Romantic era, name of Ronsard is mentioned with scorn when it is mentioned at all. Conclusion gives some very brief statements of fate in Italy of Du Bellay, Belleau, Du Bartas, De Thou, Montaigne, Rabelais, Marot. Good bibliography (p. 313-28) is very useful for study of Franco-Italian literary relations in late 16th and 17th centuries.
Review : G. Cohen in RLC 9:610-12, 1929.

French authors indebted to Italy
(Nos. 2698-2714)

Merrill, Robert Valentine. A note on the Italian genealogy of Du Bellay's Olive sonnet CXIII. *See* 1267. 2698
Petrarch, *Canzoniere*, CCCLV, and Sannazaro, *Arcadia*, eighth *versus*, influenced the Daniello sonnet imitated by Du Bellay.

— Du Bellay's Olive CXII and the Rime diverse. *See* 1264. 2699
His source is Veronica Gambara's sonnet (*Rime* II) : " Scelse da tutta la futura gente...."

Vaganay, Hugues. Joachim du Bellay et les Rime diverse di molti eccellentissimi autori. *See* 1329. 2700
Original publication dates of Giolito's anthology (v. I, 1545; v. II, 1547).

Kastner, L. E. The sources of Olivier de Magny's sonnets. MP 7:27-48, 1909-10. 2701
Petrarch, Sannazaro, Ariosto, Tebaldeo, Sasso, *et al.*

Pellegrini, Carlo. Riflessi di cultura italiana in Margherita di Navarra. *In his :* Tradizione italiana e cultura europea. Messina, Anna, 1947. p. 19-37. 2702
Probably knowing the Blois MS. of *Trionfi*, Marguerite seems to have felt the influence of Petrarch as well as of Dante in her religious poetry and her poetry on death.

Bertoni, Giulio. Clément Marot à Ferrare. REI 1:188-93, 1936. 2703
Reproductions of some newly discovered documents concerning Marot's sojourn in Ferrara.

Ronzy, Pierre. Un humaniste italianisant : Papire Masson (1544-1611). *See* 2232. 2704
A massive study of this Italianizer who wrote a history of the Papacy, lives of Dante, Petrarch, Boccacio, Lorenzo, and other Italians, and whose biographical, historical, and geographical works reflect his profound study of Italian authors. Contains valuable sections on Italian influence in the Forez and literature written in that region, on Franco-Gallia—Italo-Gallia controversy; scattered throughout, abundant indications as to Masson's Italian sources.
Review : J. Plattard in RSS 13:152-54, 1926.

Dédéyan, Charles. Essai sur le Journal de voyage de Montaigne. *See* 1584. 2705
Chapter on *Montaigne et l'Italie* studies Italian influences exerted on Montaigne before his voyage and his reactions to Italy during voyage (including his lack of sensitivity to Italian art). Chapter on *La langue et le style du Journal de voyage* contains remarks on Montaigne's Italian style (many errors, small vocabulary, short sentences, fanciful verb forms). Bibliography lists a large number of works covering Franco-Italian interchanges of all sorts but especially those resulting from travels by Frenchmen in Italy and Italians in France. Many items on Rabelais' Italian journeys, as well as on Montaigne's.
Review : P. Moreau in RHL 48:94-95, 1948.

Françon, Marcel. Les Itinéraires d'Italie et Gargantua. Ital 26:141-45, 1949.   2706
Geographical elements in Rabelais should not be linked with pilgrimage routes. Amusement, not anti-clerical propaganda was Rabelais' purpose (limited scope of evidence hardly justifies the sweeping conclusion).

Heulhard, Arthur. Rabelais, ses voyages en Italie, son exil à Metz. *See* 872.   2707
Rabelais' journeys fully recounted; his relations with Du Bellays'; reception at Papal court; activities in Rome. No special attention given to influence of Italian literature on him. Sumptuous illustrations of persons and places encountered by Rabelais on his trips.

Romier, Lucien. Notes critiques et documents sur le dernier voyage de Rabelais en Italie. RER 10:113-42, 1912.   2708
Itinerary, dates of departure and return; publication of *Sciomachie;* composition of *Quart livre.*

Toldo, Pietro. L'arte italiana nell'opera di Francesco Rabelais. Archiv 100:103-48, 1898.   2709
Lists numerous presumed borrowings from Pulci, Folengo, Poggio, Castiglione, Colonna, and others. These are piled up rather uncritically, but list is useful, suggestive.

Addamiano, Natale. Il rinascimento in Francia : Pietro Ronsard (1524-1585). *See* 1081.   2710
Excellent, valuable summation of poetic atmosphere of the day, as well as of poetry of Ronsard. Especially interesting is table (p. 517-21) in which Addamiano records incidence of imitation of various sources used by Ronsard in various sections of his work. From a mechanical standpoint, there are two regrettable omissions; there are no table of contents and no bibliography. Also, bibliographical indications in notes are rare and scanty.

Hauvette, Henri. Note sur Ronsard italianisant. *See* 1132.   2711
Italian influence (probably through Alamanni) on metrical form of Ronsard's Pindaric odes. Ronsard and Poliziano's *Stanze.*

Nolhac, Pierre de. Ronsard et ses contemporains italiens. EI 3:15-26, 1921. 2712
Endeavors to uncover Ronsard's relations, either personal or literary, with

Torquato Tasso, Lodovico Castelvetro, Traiano Boccalini, Sperone Speroni, Pigafetta, Pietro Barga, etc.

Williams, R. C. Italian influence on Ronsard's theory of the epic. MLN 35:161-65, 1920.   2713
Certain ideas of Ronsard should be attributed to Scaliger, Minturno, Daniello, and Cinthio (epic action limited to one year, distinction between history and poetry, and others).

Saulnier, Verdun L. Maurice Scève et ses parents siennois. RLC 22:398-408, 1948.   2714
Scève's Italian contacts through Tolomei family (his sister Sibylle married Girolamo di Lattanzio Tolomei).

Major Trecentisti
(Nos. 2715-2747)

Clements, Robert J. Marguerite de Navarre and Dante. *See* 761.   2715
Marguerite's borrowings from Dante few in number and confined to *Inferno* I-V. Their differences in theology (Lutheran vs. Catholic), religious feeling, and style very great.

Eckhardt, Alexandre. Marot et Dante : l'Enfer et l'Inferno. *See* 646.   2716
Parallelism of *Inferno* III, 22-35 and *Enfer:* " Mais ains que fusse entré au gouffre noir," et seq. The author claims that " la conception et le titre allégorique " were suggested to Marot by Dante.

Friederich, W. P. Dante's fame abroad, 1350-1850; the influence of Dante Alighieri upon the poets and scholars of Spain, France, England, Germany, Switzerland and the United States. Rome, Edizione di storia e letteratura, 1950. 582 p.   2717
Invaluable summary of knowledge on the subject; devotes some twenty-five pages (paragraphs 27-41) to French 16th century, discussing translations of Dante, introduction of *terza rima* (by J. Lemaire de Belges), François Ier's dislike of Dante (because of *Purg.* XX, 54), Marguerite de Navarre's affinities with Dante, Dante's meager influence on other writers of 16th century, reasons for Dante's unpopularity in 16th century, his role in religious controversies during Wars of Religion.
Two pages of bibliography on Dante in France.

Reviews : T. G. Bergin in Ital 29:139-140, June, 1952; H. Hatzfeld in CL3:372-374, 1951; A. Vallone in GSLI 128:340-347, 1951.

Hauvette, Henri. Dante dans la poésie française de la renaissance. In his: Études sur la Divine comédie. Champion, 1922. p. 144-87.   2718

Section dealing with Dante's influence on French poetry of renaissance is in p. 144-88 of this volume. Unlike most of the work of this distinguished scholar, it is rather vague and poorly documented. One part which is extremely well done, and which should not escape attention of any renaissance scholar, is the demonstration of indebtedness of Marguerite de Navarre to *Divine comedy* in composition of *Le navire* and *Les prisons*.

Kastner, L. E. History of the terza rima in France. ZFSL 26:241-53, 1904.   2719

Sketchy, unanalytical treatment. Lemaire de Belges credited with introduction of *terza rima* into France, but his model is not identified (one early translation of Dante is mentioned, but nothing is said of Petrarch's *Trionfi* and their possible influence).

Morel, Camille. Les plus anciennes traductions françaises de la Divine comédie. Librairie universitaire, 1897. 623 p.   2720

Texts of Vienna ms. (complete *Divina commedia*), Turin ms. *(Inferno)*, and Bergaigne's version of *Paradiso*, with an introductory study and a portfolio of miniature illustrations from mss.

Bullock, Walter L. The first French sonnets. See 639.   2721

Readjustment, in light of Petrarch's work, in dating Saint-Gelais' first sonnet (not before 1538). Remarks on rime schemes in sestet.

Clement, N. H. The first French sonneteer. See 641.   2722

Assigns honor to Marot (1528-31).

Clements, Robert J. Anti-Petrarchism of the Pléiade. See 1049.   2723

Reaction against Petrarchistic artificiality and insincerity appears as early as 1542 (Héroët's *Parfaite amie*) and becomes widespread after 1555.

— Desportes and Petrarch. See 1364.   2724

Adds twelve rapprochements to nine already listed by Lavaud (1366). Des-

portes imitated Petrarch himself more often than he did any of neo-Petrarchists.

Flamini, F. Du rôle de Pontus de Tyard dans le pétrarquisme français. See 781.   2725

Erreurs amoureuses imitate " ce que Pétrarque a de plus étrange, et de plus fade."

Françon, Marcel. Sur l'influence de Pétrarque en France aux xve et xvie siècles. Ital 19:105-10, 1942.   2726

Robertet, Marot, and Ronsard as representative of different phases in evolution of French attitude toward adapting and translating Petrarch.

— Une imitation du sonnet de Pétrarque : Pace non trovo. Ital 20:127-31, 1943. 2727

Dizain de Pétrarque in *Petit œuvre d'amour et gaige d'amitié* (1538) is called " le premier poème français qui soit imité directement d'un sonnet de Pétrarque " (p. 131).

— Vasquin Philieul traducteur de Pétrarque. FS 4:216-26, 1950.   2728

Philieul made first complete translation of Petrarch's Italian works (Book I, 1548; Books II-IV, 1555). Analysis of rime patterns in his tercets.

— Notes sur l'histoire du sonnet en France. Ital 29:121-28, June, 1952.   2729

Rise of French Petrarchism associated with pro-Papal policies of François Ier and Henri II, which prevailed ca. 1533-53. Says Saint-Gelais is author of first sonnet in French (ca. 1533). Lyonnaise influence on early history of French sonnet diminished.

Fucilla, Joseph G. Sources of Du Bellay's Contre les Pétrarquistes. See 1245.   2730

Mellin de Saint-Gelais' *A une malcontente (Œuvres*, ed. Blanchemain, no. 718, I, 196 ff.) the primary source; slight influence of Bembo's *Asolani*. Du Bellay satirized his own Petrarchism.

Harvitt, Hélène. Les Triomphes de Pétrarque; traduction en vers français par Simon Bougouyn, valet de chambre de Louis XII. See 728.   2731

Identity of BN MS. f. fr. 2500-2501 and BN ms. fr. 12423. Both by Symon Bourgouyn. Details on Bourgouyn. His translation should be dated not later than 1530. See 2632.

Kastner, L. E. A propos d'une prétendue traduction française des Triomphes de Pétrarque. ZRP 30:574-77, 1906.   2732

Jean Robertet's so-called translation (BN MS. f. 1717) really only " une succession de quelques huitains " with some extraneous Latin verses. Bourgouyn was probably first to translate *Trionfi* into French.

Laumonier, Paul. Ronsard pétrarquiste avant 1550. *See* 1145.   2733

Ronsard was relatively exempt from influence of Petrarch up to 1550, preferring more sensual and less elevated sources of inspiration. It was only after Cassandra's marriage that he turned somewhat more to Petrarch for ideas and expressions.

Nitze, Wm. A. The sources of the ninth sonnet of Les regrets. *See* 1274.   2734

Opening line (" France, mère des arts, des armes & des loiz ") a reminiscence, perhaps a deliberate reference, to Petrarch's *Hymn to Italy* (" Armorum legumque ... domus ").

Pellegrini, Carlo. Il Petrarca nella cultura francese. RLM 1:75-84, 1946.   2735

Rapid survey of whole subject. Passages on 16th century emphasize influence of *Trionfi*.

— Il Petrarca nella cultura francese. *In his:* Tradizione italiana e cultura europea. Messina, Anna, 1947. p. 3-18.   2736

Petrarch's earliest influence in France exerted by his *Trionfi*; *Canzoniere* prevailed only in 16th century. These conclusions presented in *causerie* fashion.

Piéri, Marius. Le pétrarquisme au XVIe siècle; Pétrarque et Ronsard; ou, de l'influence de Pétrarque sur la Pléiade française. *See* 1055.   2737

Despite its age, this is still a priceless study. The analysis of Petrarch's work given in Introduction, plus story of evolution of Petrarchism in Italy and its penetration into Spain and England are particularly valuable items. This work should be used in conjunction with J. Vianey's later work on same general subject (2740); they complement one another beautifully. As is so often the case with scholarly works of this period, there is no bibliography.

Review : R. in GSLI 28:445-48, 1896.

Saulnier, Verdun L. Maurice Scève et Pontus de Tyard : deux notes sur le Pétrar-

quisme de Pontus. RLC 22:267-72, 1948.   2738

I. Pontus' copy of *Il canzoniere* indicates his unfamiliarity with Italian; his Petrarchism comes secondhand from Scève. II. Pontus' literary début may be dated ca. 1543 rather than 1545.

Simone, Franco. Note sulla fortuna del Petrarca in Francia nella prima metà del cinquecento. GSLI 127:1-59, 1950; 128:1-40, 145-75, 1951.   2739

On the fame and influence of the Latin works and particularly of *Trionfi*. Wide knowledge of and direct contact with Petrarch shown to exist before rise of Petrarchism proper (i. e., influence of *Canzoniere*).

Vianey, J. Le pétrarquisme en France au XVIe siècle. Montpellier, Coulet, 1909. 399 p.   2740

While this study is now outmoded in some respects, due to the more extended research of the last four decades, it still remains a key work in this field. Concise analysis of the work and influence of Chariteo, Tebaldeo and Serafino dall'-Aquila (Ch. I) is invaluable, as is that of resurgence of *Quattrocento* preciosity in Italy and its subsequent passage into France (Ch. III). The two appendices are useful; Appendix I gives in chronological order the principal petrarchistic collections in French in 16th century; Appendix II lists the principal Italian anthologies which the French Petrarchists utilized, with a brief analysis of each. It is to be regretted that Vianey did not include a bibliography.

Reviews : P. Laumonier in RHL 17:859-863, 1910; Ruth S. Phelps in RR 1:215-16, 1910; P. Toldo in GSLI 55:406-11, 1910.

Villey, Pierre. Marot et le premier sonnet français. *See* 694.   2741

The earliest French sonnet claimed for Marot (1536), as is the earliest French sonnet printed in France (1538).

Weber, H. Transformation des thèmes pétrarquistes dans le Printemps d'Agrippa d'Aubigné. MélHC, p. 175-87.   2742

Evidences of directness and originality in d'Aubigné's use of stock themes of renaissance love poetry.

Wilkins, Ernest H. A general survey of renaissance Petrarchism. CL 2:327-42, 1950.   2743

Defining Petrarchism as the influence of *Canzoniere*, author gives an excellent sketch of the whole movement whose general scope does not preclude precision. Italian Petrarchists are neatly grouped into schools (Chariteans, Bembists, Neapolitans, etc.). In the section on French Petrarchism, Wilkins sees influence of Chariteans, especially Serafino, as predominant until near the end of 16th century. Good selective bibliography.

Laserstein, Käte. Der Griseldisstoff in der Weltliteratur. Weimar, Duneker, 1926. 208 p. (Diss., Munich) 2744
16th century in France is practically ignored, as the author does not find the motif occurring between Olivier de La Marche (d. 1502) and Perrault.

Livingston, Charles H. Decameron, VIII, 2 : earliest French imitations. *See* 990. 2745
Philippe de Vigneulles (ca. 1505-10); *La légende de Maistre Pierre Faifeu*, chapter xxxi (1526); Nicolas de Troyes, *nouvelle 148* (ca. 1536).

Saulnier, V. L. Boccace et la nouvelle française de la renaissance. RLC 21:404-13, 1947. 2746
Claudine de Vauzelles (Maurice Scève's sister) identified as translator of pseudo-Boccaccian *Urbano*. Date is ca. 1533. Details on Claudine de Vauzelles.

Sorieri, Louis. Boccaccio's story of Tito e Gisippo in European literature. New York, Institute of French studies, 1937. 269 p. (Diss., Columbia) 2747
This study of the rival-friends motif has a chapter on adventures of Boccaccio story in France (p. 89-143), subdivided into translations and adaptations, and treating imitations in entirety and incorporations of the story in larger compositions, such as pastoral novels. Free adaptations in 16th century are rare, but include *Cinthye et Dellio* in Nicolas de Montreux's *Les bergeries de Juliette*.

Major Cinquecentisti
(Nos. 2748-2768)

Françon, Marcel. Rabelais et Folengo. Ital 28:251-53, Dec., 1951. 2748
Some details which might help determine which edition of *Le maccheronee* Rabelais used.

— Sur une source possible de Rabelais. MLN 66:466-69, 1951. 2749
Folengo, *Maccheronee*, XIX, 448-50, 498, and *Pantagruel*, XXIX (with references to Ariosto and Hugo).

Luzio, Alessandro. Studi folenghiani : imitazioni folenghiane del Rabelais. Florence, Sansoni, 1899. 156 p. 2750
Chapter on Rabelais' imitations of Folengo (p. 11-52) attributes them to his use of marginal notes of Toscolano edition of *Baldus*, which he must have known.

Sainéan, L. Les sources modernes du roman de Rabelais. RER 10:375-420, 1912. 2751
Denies all Italian influence except for slight amounts exerted by Folengo and Colonna's *Dream of Polyphile*. Detailed analysis of Folengo-Rabelais situation reduces latter's debt to " une demi-douzaine de souvenirs ou de suggestions."

Bottasso, Enzo. Le commedie di Lodovico Ariosto nel teatro francese del Cinquecento. GSLI 128:41-80, 1951. 2752
I suppositi exerted some influence, but in general Ariosto's influence on French comedy in 16th century not deep, continuous, or artistically productive.

Cameron, Alice Virginia. The influence of Ariosto's epic and lyric poetry on the work of Amadis Jamyn. Baltimore, Johns Hopkins Press, 1933. 63 p. (JHSR, Extra vol. viii) 2753
Conventional source study which reveals that Jamyn adapted or imitated a number of passages from *Furioso* already popularized by Pléiade (Bradamante's letter, description of Alcina, etc.) and outright translated some of *Opere minori*.

— Desportes and Ariosto; additional sources in the Orlando and the Liriche. MLN 50:174-78, 1935. 2754
Three adaptations and other rapprochements not hitherto noted.

Cioranescu, Alexandre. L'Arioste en France des origines à la fin du XVIIIe siècle. *See* 2600. 2755
Thorough, conscientious treatment of the subject which should remain standard. V. I covers 16th century, answering nearly every need for information on subject. Good illustrations of Ariostean themes in French art.
Review : C. B. Beall in MLN 57:234-235, 1942.

Fucilla, Joseph G. Four notes on Italian influences. RR 26:325-29, 1935.   2756
I. Ariosto, O. F., XI, 70, 1-4, and Ronsard; II. Ariosto, " Chiuso era il sol..." and Scève, Du Bellay, and Ronsard; IV. Accolti's *Verginia* and Mesdames des Roches.

Keyser, Sijbrand. Contribution à l'étude de la fortune littéraire de l'Arioste en France. Leyden, Dubbeldeman, 1933. 225 p. (Diss., Leyden)   2757
Except for Ariosto's influence on the theatre (especially Garnier), there is little material on 16th century. Bibliography, p. 208-16.

Parducci, Amos. Le imitazioni ariostee nella Franciade del Ronsard. *See* 1163.   2758
Classical allusions and reminiscences of *Orlando furioso* often inextricably blended in Ronsard, not always with happy results.

Vianey, Joseph. L'Arioste et les Discours de Ronsard. RU 12^1:473-75, 1903.   2759
Five passages in *Discours* and *Exhortation pour la paix* influenced by *Furioso*.

Bowen, W. H. Sixteenth century French translations of Machiavelli. *See* 2640.   2760
Editions and translations available to Frenchmen before 1572 (i.e., before the rise of anti-Machiavellianism). In general his early reputation in France was good.

Cardascia, G. Machiavel et Jean Bodin. *See* 2052.   2761
Anti-Machiavellianism did not become widespread in France until ca. 1572. Bodin in his *Methodus* (1566) shows wide knowledge of and respect for Machiavelli, but in *République* (1576) Machiavelli infrequently cited and then unfavorably. Bodin theoretically opposed to Machiavelli, but temperamentally and pragmatically " est un machiavéliste qui s'ignore." *See* 2655.

Cherel, A. La pensée de Machiavel en France. *See* 2656.   2762
Excellent summary of influence of Machiavelli in France down to 20th century. Since subject is much too vast to be treated exhaustively in a work of this length, treatment is necessarily selective. One of the best features is critical bibliography (p. 313-38).
Review : R. Pintard in RLC 17:420-22, 1937.

Pintard, René. Une adaptation de Machiavel au XVIe siècle : Le prince nécessaire de Jean de La Taille. *See* 2659.   2763
La Taille's poem one of few works in 16th century showing direct influence of *Il principe*. But author shows basic divergences from Machiavelli on matters of principle.

Ribner, Irving. The significance of Gentillet's Contre-Machiavel. MLQ 10:153-157, 1949.   2764
Denies any special influence of Gentillet's attack in evolution of English anti-Machiavellianism.

Toldo, Pietro. Le courtisan dans la littérature française et ses rapports avec l'œuvre du Castiglione. *See* 2621.   2765
Little treatment of 16th century manifestations of *Cortegiano's* influence. Parallel passages cited, but no relationships established.

Zino, M. Castiglione e Montaigne; relazioni tra Essais e Cortegiano. Con 10:56-60, 1938.   2766
Follows P. Toldo in holding that the doubtful parallels may be due to common classical sources. A certain number of borrowings remain (e.g., nonchalance = *sprezzatura*). Montaigne certainly knew *Cortegiano*.

Beall, Chandler B. La fortune du Tasse en France. Eugene, University of Oregon, 1942. 308 p. (OSLP No. 4)   2767
First three chapters cover period up to 1607. Finds first traces of Tasso's influence appearing ca. 1580 (Desportes). During Tasso's lifetime *Aminta* was his most influential work in France, but soon after his death *Gerusalemme liberata* began furnishing plots for drama and novel. Little direct influence on French epic until later. In general Tasso's influence remained fragmentary and episodic, but there were some lyrics, novels, tragedies, and paintings based entirely on his works. Beall's work is thorough and judicious, with a very large bibliography.
Reviews : A. T. MacAllister in MLQ 3:467-69, 1942; E. Malakis, MLN 58:157-158, 1943; L. Olschki in RR 34:86-89, 1943.

Benedetto, Luigi Foscolo. Il Montaigne a Sant'Anna GSLI 73:213-34, 1919.   2768
Advances arguments for Montaigne's personal contact with Tasso.

Other Italians
(Nos. 2769-2795)

Hauvette, H.   Un exilé florentin à la cour de France au xvie siècle : Luigi Alamanni. Hachette, 1903.   593 p.   2769
This masterly, definitive study on one of the more important secondary figures in Italian literature of first half of 16th century is divided into two parts. Part I is shorter (147 pages); deals with facts of the life and career of the poet. Those sections dealing with his two sojourns in France and his associations with prominent Frenchmen of the day are especially interesting.   Part II consists of an elaborate and methodical analysis of the works of Alamanni; those portions which place him in proper perspective in the literary currents of his time and those which indicate his influence on prominent Frenchmen of his own and a slightly later time are among the most valuable. Appendix IV gives a bibliography of the editions of Alamanni's works through the centuries. This would be most valuable to anyone making an exhaustive study of Alamanni.
Review : P. Laumonier in Rren 4:258-274, 1903.

Vianey, Joseph.   Le modèle de Ronsard dans l'ode pindarique.   RLR 43:433-36, 1900.   2771
Alamanni's *Inni*.

Lyons, J. Coriden.   Notes on Mathurin Régnier's Macette.   SP 28:833-37, 1931.   2772
Probable influence of Aretino's *Ragionamenti* (II, i, and II, 3) in conjunction with Bourdigné's *Légende de Maistre Pierre Faifeu*.

Sturel, René.   Bandello en France au xvie siècle.   See 2607.   2773
Incomplete study confined to *Histoires tragiques* of Boaistuau and Belleforest and a poem (BN ms. fr. 842) ascribed to Desportes : *Les amours infortunées de Didaco et de Violante et leur mort*. Text of this 800-line poem published for the first time in Chapter III. Author painstakingly analyses and evaluates modifications made by Bandello's translators. Some material on publication history of *Histoires tragiques*.
Review : L. Auvray in RHL 29:105-11, 1922.

Bandello, Matteo.   The French Bandello : a selection : the original text of four of

Belleforest's Histoires tragiques. Ed. with an intro. by Frank S. Hook. Columbia, Univ. of Missouri, 1948.   185 p.   (UMS, v. 22, no. 1)   2774
French text of Bandello III, 17; I, 27; I, 4; I, 49 (Belleforest XIII, XVIII, XX, XXI), based on *XVIII Histoires tragiques* (Lyons, 1596) and *Le second tome* (Paris, 1571). Introduction deals primarily with influence of these stories in England. Bibliographical data on complicated publication history of *Histoires tragiques* supplements Sturel, no. 2773.

Ruutz-Rees, Caroline.   A note on Saint-Gelais and Bembo.   See 725.   2775
Saint-Gelais' *Huitain XCI* (*Œuvres*, Bibliothèque Elzévirienne, III, 84) is adapted from Bembo's sonnet XXII.

Neri, Ferdinando.   La prima tragedia di Étienne Jodelle.   See 2378.   2776
Doubtful parallels with Cesare de Cesari's *Cleopatra* (1552).

Sainéan, L.   Le songe de Poliphile.   In his : Problèmes littéraires du seizième siècle. *See* 939, p. 251-60.   2777
Rabelais' use of Colonna's *Poliphili hypnerotomachia*. Reprints passages used by Rabelais in *Le cinquième livre*. Rabelais used original text rather than Jean Martin translation of 1546.

Söltoft-Jensen, H. K.   Le cinquième livre de Rabelais et Le songe de Poliphile.   RHL 3:608-12, 1896.   2778
Direct borrowings from *Gargantua et Pantagruel*, V, xxxvii, xli, xlii, xliv. Possibly of significance in determining authenticity of *Cinquième livre*.

Kastner, L. E.   Desportes et Angelo di Costanzo.   RHL 15:113-18, 1908.   2779
Adds six complete sonnets and six other adaptations from Costanzo's sonnets to attributions made by Flamini. (Vianey, 2780, had already made six of these rapprochements; Flamini himself had noted two; one, according to Vianey, 2781, is erroneous.)

Vianey, Joseph.   Une rencontre des Muses de France et d'Italie demeurée inédite. RHL 13:92-100, 1906.   2780
Nine hitherto unnoticed rapprochements with Costanzo, Tebaldeo, *et al.*, taken from anonymous ms. annotations on 1593 Lyons edition of Desportes. A list of thirty miscellaneous borrowings. General remarks on Desportes' use of Italian

sources. (Slight adjustments in these attributions made by Kastner, RHL 17:127-28, 1910, and Clements, see 1364.)

— Desportes et Angelo di Costanzo. RHL 15:330-31, 1908.   2781

Publication facts on Costanzo's sonnets. Desportes' knowledge and use of his works.

Couderc, Camille. Les poésies d'un Florentin à la cour de France au XVIᵉ siècle. GSLI 17:1-45, 1891.   2782

Biographical sketch of hitherto unidentified author of ms. 7, Bibliothèque du Mans. Analytical index of the 97 poems. Text of seven of the poems and of two letters from Delbene to Catherine de Médicis.

Festugière, A. M. J. La philosophie de l'amour de Marsile Ficin et son influence sur la littérature française au XVIᵉ siècle. See 733.   2783

Interesting and worthwhile addition to the literature on Ficinian platonism and its penetration into France. Festugière fails to give a very clear picture of Ficino's own contribution to renaissance " love doctrine " as distinguished from contributions of others. His assumptions of influence of Ficino on French authors of 16th century are sometimes exaggerated if not entirely gratuitous. Bibliography is useful as far as it goes, but it is certainly far from exhaustive.

Delaruelle, L. Le séjour à Paris d'Agostino Giustiniani. RSS 12:322-37, 1925.   2784

Giustiniani and his Hebraic instruction and scholarship in Paris ca. 1518-22. Remarks on rise of Hebraic studies in Europe.

Kastner, L. E. Desportes et Guarini. RHL 17:124-31, 1910.   2785

Four sonnets borrowed from Guarini via Rime de gli illustrissimi sig. Academici Eterei (1567). Other borrowings (Tasso et al.) from this anthology indicated. Italian sources for other poems of Desportes. Marino's claim that Desportes plagiarized him refuted.

Luciani, Vincent. Francesco Guicciardini and his European reputation. New York, Otto, 1936. 437 p. (Diss., Columbia) 2786

Rich bibliography (p. 407-24). The important chapter is that on French criticism of Storia d'Italia and French replies to Guicciardini's slanderous attacks.

The main opponents in 16th century are Claude du Verdier, Lancelot Voisin de La Popelinière, Brantôme, Du Perron, and Scipion Dupleix.

Lancaster, H. Carrington. Baïf and Pontano. PMLA 48:943, Sept., 1933.   2787

Contradicts L. V. Simpson (PMLA 47:1012-27, Dec., 1932) as to Pontano's influence on J. A. de Baïf, which she had minimized.

Bart, B. F. Aspects of the comic in Pulci and Rabelais. MLQ 11:156-63, 1950. 2788

Rabelais and Pulci separated by temperament and by the literary exigencies of their respective genres. " ... Panurge apart, the debt is unimportant or irrelevant."

Berdan, John M. The migrations of a sonnet. MLN 23:33-36, 1908.   2789

Unconvincing effort to show that Saint-Gelais translated Sannazaro through Wyatt rather than directly.

Ruutz-Rees, Caroline. Charles Fontaine's Fontaine d'Amour and Sannazaro. See 706.   2790

Four " unavowed translations " from Sannazaro not noticed by Torraca. They precede the general vogue of Sannazaro in France and may reflect Fontaine's youthful travels in Italy.

Vaganay, Hugues, et Joseph Vianey. Un modèle de Desportes non signalé encore : Pamphilo Sasso. RHL 10:277-82, 1903. 2791

Twelve instances of borrowing from Sasso. Two from Serafino dall'Aquila.

Françon, Marcel. Note sur Jean Lemaire de Belges et Seraphino dall'Aquila. Ital 28:19-22, Mar., 1951.   2792

Le conte de Cupido et de Atropos an amplification of Serafino's Rime, xi and xii (Bologna, 1894). Dates La concorde des deux langages ca. 1503-04. Lemaire de Belges' use of terza rima an imitation of Boninsegni's eclogues.

Villey, P. Les sources italiennes de la Deffence et illustration de la langue françoyse de Joachim du Bellay. See 1338.   2793

This masterly little study gave new orientation to the whole question of Italian influence on French literature of renaissance. By placing passages from Speroni's dialogue and corresponding passages from Deffence in parallel columns,

Villey shows how servile was Du Bellay's imitation; annihilated Chamard's earlier efforts to find the sources in preceding French literature. Introduction gives an excellent summary of evolution of quarrel over vernacular in Italy. For further enlightenment, Villey presents in Appendix I the entire text of Speroni's *Dialogo* in the original Italian. *See* 1338.

Reviews : R. Sturel in RHL 17:863-66, 1910; P. Toldo in GSLI 53:415-16, 1909.

Jourda, Pierre. Un humaniste italien en France : Theocrenus (1480-1536). RSS 16:40-57, 1929.   2794

Sketch of the life, influence, and fame of Benedetto Tagliacarno, Greek instructor to the sons of François Ier and author of a few Latin verses.

Dargan, E. Preston. Trissino, a possible source for the Pléiade. *See* 1051.   2795

Very brief and tentative suggestions of Trissino's influence on Pléiade critical theory.

Anglo-French Relations

(Nos. 2797-2850)

PHILIP MACON CHEEK

General French Influence upon English Literature

(Nos. 2797-2803)

Kastner, L. E. The Scottish sonneteers and the French poets. MLR 3:1-15, 1907. 2797

Earliest among a series of articles dealing with influence of 16th century French poets on Scottish and English poets of late 16th and 17th centuries. Concerned chiefly with influence of Philippe Desportes on William Drummond of Hawthornden.

— The Elizabethan sonneteers and the French poets. MLR 3:268-77, 1907-08.
                  2798

One in a series of articles tracing indebtedness of Elizabethan sonneteers to their French contemporaries; deals specifically with Samuel Daniel's borrowings from Du Bellay.

Lambley, Kathleen Rebillon. The teaching and cultivation of the French language in England during Tudor and Stuart times. Manchester, the University Press, 1920. 438 p. (PMFS, no. 3). *See* 578. 2799

Complete and thorough investigation of extent to which French language was understood and used in England during Tudor and Stuart periods and of methods whereby it was taught. Wide cultivation of the language, preparation and circulation of texts and dictionaries, pedagogical methods employed, more famous teachers and other related matters treated at length, with excellent illustrative details. Useful bibliographies of contemporaneous pedagogical manuals.

Lee, Sidney. The French renaissance in England. *See* 662.   2800

Very thorough and comprehensive survey of influence of the French on English renaissance, tracing influence both of trends of thought and literary movements and that of individual writers or groups of writers. Shows that this French influence was very large within itself; also that influences commonly considered Italian tended to come into England through France, with a French coloring. Supplemented with useful tables and charts illustrating parallel dates, personages, and movements in the two countries. *See* 1148, 1658.

Review : J. Lux in RPL 48:670-72, Nov. 19, 1910.

Michel, F. X. Les Écossais en France. Les Français en Écosse. London, Trubner, 1862. 2 v.   2801

A history of cultural relations between France and Scotland which interprets culture in its widest sense, and so treats of matters political, diplomatic, and military as well as of those philosophical, literary and social. Considers also interrelations of French and Scotch in their knowledge and cultivation of each other's language and in literary influences which one exerted upon other, latter thesis being illustrated by citations of related or parallel works.

Schoell, Franck L. L'hellénisme français en Angleterre à la fin de la renaissance. RLC 5:193-238, 1925.   2802

Surveys the state of Greek learning in England under Elizabeth and James I; shows that French influence through dictionaries, grammars, translations and commentaries was heavy; special analysis of influence of Jean de Sponde's Homer on Chapman's Homer.

Upham, A. H. The French influence in English literature from the accession of

Elisabeth to the Restoration. New York, Columbia University Press, 1908. 560 p. (Diss., Columbia)   2803

Well-documented account of influence of French literary forms and ideas on literature of England from accession of Elizabeth to the Restoration (1558-1660). Finds such influence originating in the Areopagus group, extending through vogue of sonnet, classical play, long religious epic, prose romance, and heroic poem; reflecting among many others especially influence of French Pléiade, Du Bartas, Rabelais, Montaigne, and French version of Platonism. Contains useful bibliography and three useful appendices, chief among them being a list of English translations of French works during period covered.

Some English Influences upon France

(Nos. 2805-2815)

Clement, N. H. The influence of the Arthurian romances on the five books of Rabelais. *See* 855.   2805

Argues that Rabelais' work constitutes a burlesque imitation of French medieval romances, chiefly romances of Round Table; Books I and II imitation of Arthurian Romances in general, and Books III, IV, and V of Grail-quest romances specifically. Interprets Rabelais' technique as medieval; his purpose, however, as renaissance; and his work, in spirit, a burlesque satire on medieval quest for truth through mysticism and intuition, and an attempt to replace such with the renaissance quest for truth through knowledge and reason.

Fabre, Frédéric. Le collège anglais de Douai : son histoire héroïque. RLC 10:201-229, 1930.   2806

Historical survey of the English college at Douai from its founding in 1568 until its end in 1793; with chief emphasis on its heroic struggles, its Catholic missionary work in England, and its services as an English center in France. Brief discussion also of references to it to be found in Elizabethan and Jacobean drama.

Hainsworth, George. L'Arcadie de Sidney en France. RLC 10:470-71, 1930.   2807

Cites from French literature of early 17th century three new evidences of popularity of Sidney's *Arcadia* in 16th century France.

Jirmounsky, M. M. La survivance littéraire des matières de France et de Bretagne au delà du moyen âge. RLC 9:209-22, 1929.   2808

Begins with thesis that poetry more fully than other arts reflects spiritual and intellectual temper of an age; proceeds then to show how medieval subjects and themes in " matters of France and Britain " evolved from a medieval into an early renaissance medium.

Jusserand, J. J. French ignorance of English literature in Tudor times. NC 43:590-603, Apr., 1898.   2809

While in 16th century the culture and literature of France were well known in England, on the contrary the culture, language and literature of England were almost entirely unknown in France. Although English players appeared in Paris, the French literary world seems to have ignored Shakespeare and his contemporaries.

— Shakespeare in France under the ancien régime. London, Unwin, 1899. 496 p.
                                                  2810

Study in French dramatic taste and theatrical history from time of Shakespeare to time of French Revolution. Attempts to explain why Shakespeare was so long ignored in France, and why so misinterpreted and underrated even after he was known. General ignorance of English literature in France, French insistence on the dramatic unities, and French horror of romantic extravagance seen as main reasons.

Chambrun, Clara (Longworth) comtesse de. Shakespeare across the Channel. AMS, p. 97-100.   2811

Argues for a contemporary 17th century interest in Shakespeare in France, as illustrated by comedies and tragedies of Alexandre Hardy, references to English players in Paris, and interest of Queen Henriette Marie in poet's works.

Morand, Paul. Les personnages anglais dans la littérature d'imagination en France, du douzième à la fin du dix-huitième siècle. AFR 4:134-46, 1920.   2812

Superficial causerie with sweeping statement for 16th century : " Jamais l'imagination ne fut plus pauvre qu'au seizième siècle " (p. 138).

Potez, Henri. Le premier roman anglais traduit en français. RHL 11:42-55, 1904.
                                                  2813

Deals with a French translation of Robert Greene's *Pandosta* published by L. Reynault in 1615, some nine years earlier than first publication of the French version of Sidney's *Arcadia*, hitherto regarded as earliest English romance to appear in French. This translation discovered in Bodleian Library by author of article.

Yates, F. A. English actors in Paris during the life time of Shakespeare. RES 1:392-403, 1925.   2814

Summarizes what has formerly been known of English actors in Paris between 1598 and 1604 from the papers of Hôtel de Bourgogne and *Journal* of Jean Héroard; adds some new light to this information through two newly discovered letters to Dudley Carleton which are preserved in the Foreign State Papers at the Public Record Office.

— Some new light on L'Écossaise of A. de Montchrétien. MLR 22:285-97, 1927.
                                        2815

Holds that Antoine de Montchrétien's *L'Ecossaise* follows in plan a suggestion derived from Pierre Matthieu's *Histoire des derniers troubles de France* (1597) of presenting death of Mary Stuart from both the English and French viewpoints; that such a plan accounts for apparent lack of unity in the tragedy; and that Montchrétien's interpretation alarmed both the English and the French and precipitated political fears on part of both.

English Authors Indebted to France
(Nos. 2816-2825)

Bastide, Charles. La France et les Français dans le théâtre de Shakespeare. Edda 6:112-23, 1916.   2816

Deals with Shakespeare's knowledge of French, his judgments on Frenchmen, his French sources and his possible knowledge of French poetry (Ronsard).

Berdan, John M. Wyatt and the French sonneteers. MLR 4:240-49, 1908-09.   2817

Minimizes Petrarchism of Marot and Saint-Gelais. Rebutted by L. E. Kastner, MLR 4:249-53, 1908-09.

Kastner, L. E. Drummond of Hawthornden and the poets of the Pléiade. MLR 4:329-341, 1908-09.   2818

Argues that Drummond of Hawthornden borrowed not only from French poet Desportes but also from several members

of Pléiade. This essay concerned chiefly with showing his borrowings from Ronsard and Tyard.

Keller, W. Die Franzosen in Shakespeares Dramen. DSGJ 76:34-56, 1940.   2819

Attempts to analyze Shakespeare's portrayal and evaluation of the French character; holds that he regarded Gascoigne as typical Frenchman and that his portrayals of the French were in general unfavorable, though at times tempered by his Huguenot sympathies. Largely impressionistic.

Chambrun, Clara (Longworth) *comtesse* **de.** Influences françaises dans la Tempête de Shakespeare. RLC 5:37-59, 1925.   2820

General discussion of *The tempest* as play of Shakespeare which is most classical in form, most philosophical in mood, most deeply influenced by Montaigne; sees also an influence of Rabelais. Argument not very convincing.

Maxwell, Ian Colin Marfrey. French farce and John Heywood. Melbourne, University Press, 1946. 175 p.   2821

Follows up thesis proposed in an article by Karl Young, *The influence of French farce upon the plays of John Heywood*, (no. 2825); develops this thesis into a general study of influence of French farce on Heywood's dramatic work as a whole.

Osborn, A. W. Sir Philip Sidney en France. Champion, 1932. 163 p.   2822

Short biography of Sidney with special emphasis on his visits to France, his relations with eminent Frenchmen, his devotion to French culture; analysis and criticism of French and classical quality of his mind and works, and of French and classical influences which he exerted on Elizabethan England.

Lambley, Kathleen Rebillon. Shakespeare's French. MisLK, p. 403-08.   2823

From his use of French in plays and his known association with French Huguenots in London, concludes that Shakespeare had a colloquial and perhaps fluent speaking knowledge of the language and a ready reading knowledge of easier French authors; for more difficult authors he turned to translations.

Thornton, Frances C. The French element in Spenser's poetical works. Toulouse, Lion, 1938. 379 p. (Diss., Toulouse)
                                        2824

Linguistic rather than literary study, culminating in a list of 4032 words °of French derivations in Spenser's vocabulary and a list of 457 verbs and nouns proved as French by their etymology.

Young, Karl. The influence of French farce upon the plays of John Heywood. MP 2:97-124, 1904-05.   2825

Concludes that Heywood was indebted to French farces both for his plots and for his characters. The three examples here discussed are : *John* derived from the French farce *Pernet*, *The pardoner and friar* from *Farce d'un pardonneur*, and *Wit and folly* from *Dialogue du fou et du sage*.

French Authors
(Nos. 2826-2850)

Atkinson, Dorothy F. The source of Two gentlemen of Verona. *See* 1010.   2826

Proposes the fifth tale of d'Yver's *Le printemps d'Yver* (1572) in English translation of Henry Wotton *A courtlie controversie of Cupid's cautels* as the basic source of plot and characterization in Shakespeare's *Two gentlemen of Verona*. Argues that Jorge de Montemayor's *Diana*, hitherto regarded as the basic source, is merely supplementary.

Bourgeois, A. F. Rabelais en Angleterre. RER 3:80-83, 1905.   2827

Supplements W. F. Smith's list of Shakespearean passages which have a Rabelaisian savor (2841), and effects a kind of synthesis of all such passages, as these have been agreed upon by critics.

Brown, Huntington. Rabelais in English literature. *See* 849.   2828

General examination of influence of Rabelais on thought, language, and literature of England from time of John Eliot (1593) through 18th century novel. While admitting a certain incompatibility between spirit of Rabelais and English temperament, it shows through well-documented evidence that such influence was extensive and continuous over the period under consideration and manifested in most realms of literary activity (poetry, drama, treatise, and novel).

Campbell, O. J. The earliest English reference to Rabelais's work (1533). HLQ 2:53-58, 1938-39.   2829

Finds in *The booke of marchauntes* (printed at London by Thomas Godfray

in 1533), which is a translation of Antoine de Marcourt's *Le livre des marchands*, a reference to Pantalope and Patagrule; that is, a reference to Rabelais which is earlier by twenty years than any known reference in an English-printed book.

Deutschbein, Max. Shakespeares Hamlet und Montaigne. DGSJ 80-31:70-107, 1946.   2830

Argues a general Montaigne influence on Shakespeare, insists on a special influence on *Hamlet*. Interprets innermost personality of Hamlet as shaped by tenets of Montaigne's philosophy; illustrates this thesis with quotations from the play and from Montaigne.

Feis, Jacob. Shakespeare and Montaigne. *See* 1609.   2831

Argues the thesis that Shakespeare was thoroughly familiar with philosophy of Montaigne, that he deeply disliked it, and wrote *Hamlet* to discredit it. According to this interpretation, Hamlet's delay in action is seen as a kind of vice resulting from his absorption in Montaigne's scepticism; his tragedy a result of this delay in action. Follows same general line of reasoning as Stedefeld in his *Hamlet : ein Tendenzdrama Shakespeares* (2842).

Harmon, Alice. How great was Shakespeare's debt to Montaigne? *See* 1629. 2832

Admits that Shakespeare knew something of Montaigne, but regards claims of recent scholars as to his indebtedness to French writer as greatly exaggerated. Points out that most of the parallel passages in thought are expressions of ideas common among renaissance writers.

Hooker, E. R. The relation of Shakespeare to Montaigne. *See* 1609. 1633.   2833

Carries on controversy initiated by Stedefeld (2842), Feis (2831), and Robertson (2839) as to scope and nature of Shakespeare's indebtedness to Montaigne. Argues with citation of many parallel passages from the two authors that scope of this indebtedness was large and came through the Florio translation; that *Essays* were used, however, as a " mere store-house of material " and Shakespeare never became a philosophic disciple of Montaigne. Valuable appendix of parallel passages.

Kastner, L. E. Spenser's Amoretti and Desportes. MLR 4:65-69, 1908-09.   2834

Argues that the Petrarchan element in

Spenser's *Amoretti* comes not directly from Petrarch but rather through the medium of French sonneteers, especially Desportes. Argument illustrated with parallel passages from the two poets.

Koenig, W. Ueber die Entlehnungen Shakespeares, insbesondere aus Rabelais und einigen italienischen Dramatikern. DSGJ 9:195-232, 1874.   2835

Chief purpose of this study is to discredit the wild and spontaneous genius and replace it with a Shakespeare who was a widely read and learned man, and who was familiar with and borrowed freely from the works of other writers.

Law, R. A. Belleforest, Shakespeare and Kyd. AMS, p. 279-94.   2836

While not denying that Shakespeare may have used an Ur-Hamlet ascribed to Kyd and now lost, Law questions the validity of accepting this explanation of plot source too readily, and proposes the counter suggestion that he may have gone for his plot directly to Belleforest's *Histoires tragiques*.

Legge, M. Dominica. An English allusion to Montaigne before 1595. RES ns 1:341-344, 1950.   2837

Suggests a possible allusion to Montaigne in *Gray's Inn Christmas revels* of 1594-95. Suggestion based chiefly on use of word " conference "; does not seem convincing.

Padelford, F. M. Sidney's indebtedness to Sibilet. JEGP 7:81-84, 1907-08.   2838

Argues that Sidney's *Defense of poesy* is indebted to Thomas Sibilet's *Art poétique français* as well as to Minturno's *De poeta*.

Robertson, J. M. Montaigne and Shakespeare. *See* 1609, 1723.   2839

Continues discussion of Montaigne's influence on Shakespeare. Reacts against view taken by such scholars as Stedefeld and Feis that Shakespeare was antagonistic to Montaigne's system of thought, and wrote *Hamlet* to discredit it. Holds rather that growth of his mind was deeply influenced by his study of Montaigne, that he accepted much of Montaigne view of things as his own, and that Montaigne coloring of his mind is reflected in his plays from *Hamlet* and *Macbeth* on.

Schmid, E. E. Shakespeare, Montaigne und die schauspielerische Formel. DGSJ 82-83:103-35, 1948.   2840

Develops thesis that fundamental to Shakespeare's drama and to Montaigne's philosophy alike is conception of man as a *Doppelnatur*, with all the paradoxes and seeming contradictions that such implies. Holds that whereas Shakespeare may have been confirmed in this concept by his reading of Montaigne, he did not necessarily derive such from him.

Smith, W. F. Rabelais et Shakespeare. RER 1:217-21, 1903.   2841

Though not convinced that Shakespeare ever read Rabelais, author cites and assimilates those Shakespearean lines or passages which seem to have a Rabelaisian savor, and which he had collected as notes to his edition of Rabelais.

Stedefeld, G. F. Hamlet : ein Tendenzdrama Shakespeares. Berlin, 1871. 94 p.   2842

Earliest extended study of relationship between Shakespeare and Montaigne. Centers around *Hamlet*, which it interprets as a drama designed for purpose of opposing the sceptical and cosmopolitan view of things taken by Montaigne. Argues that this tragedy is an apotheosis of practical Christianity, which shows that one devoid of Christian principles and lacking in Christian piety must end as Hamlet did in disaster.

Strathmann, Ernest Albert. The 1595 translation of Du Bartas' First day. HLQ 8:185-91, 1944-45.   2843

Points out that, although *Short-title catalogue's* description of 1595 translation of Du Bartas' *First day* assigns this translation to Sylvester, the actual title-page of 1595 edition leaves it anonymous. Result of the study is to add another anonymous translator to already impressive list of translators of Du Bartas.

Taylor, George C. Milton's use of Du Bartas. *See* 1368.   2844

Through citation of phraseological similarities, parallel ideas and passages, likenesses in rhetorical figures, etc. in the two poets, this work attempts to show that Milton's *Paradise lost* is deeply indebted to the epics of French poet Du Bartas. Puritanical atmosphere of elder Milton's household, known interest of young Milton in Du Bartas, his early translations or paraphrases in the Du Bartas style, and other biographical data are used to support thesis.

— Shakespeare's debt to Montaigne. *See* 1759. 2845

Through citation of parallel passages and phraseological similarities in the two writers, this continues work begun by Stedefeld (2842), Feis (2831), and Robertson (2839) on influence of Montaigne on Shakespeare; seems to carry it as near completion as such a work can be carried. While arguing that both verbal and thought influence were large, does not insist that Montaigne shaped Shakespeare into either a philosophical opponent or disciple. Attempts to distinguish between renaissance commonplaces and direct borrowings. *See also* 1609.

— The strange case of Du Bartas in The taming of the shrew. PQ 20:373-76, 1941. 2846

Holds that Katherine's speech at end of the old play *The taming of a shrew* (not Shakespeare's play) is a paraphrase from a passage of Du Bartas' *The divine weekes*, II, 195 ff.

Türck, Susanne. Shakespeare und Montaigne : ein Beitrag zur Hamlet-Frage. *See* 1773. 2847

Study begins with a rather strong defense of authenticity of alleged Shakespeare autograph in what is supposed by some to have been the poet's copy of Florio's translation of Montaigne. With this as background material, Türck then assimilates two types of parallel passages from the two authors : 1) *sinngemässe Parallelen* and 2) *Parallelen dem Gehalt nach.*

Villey, Pierre. Montaigne et les poètes dramatiques anglais du temps de Shakespeare. *See* 1790. 2848

Reviews evidence to show great and immediate popularity of Florio's translation of Montaigne in England; proceeds then to cite passages from various contemporary English dramatists who echo or reflect Montaigne ideas. Dramatists cited include Jonson, Marston, Webster, and Shakespeare, with chief emphasis on Marston.

Witherspoon, A. M. The influence of Robert Garnier on Elizabethan drama. *See* 2372. 2849

Investigates with thoroughness attempt to establish a school of classical drama in renaissance England that centered around Lady Pembroke and her literary coterie; differentiates between influences exerted on this group by Seneca and by French

dramatist Robert Garnier; concludes that influence of Garnier was dominant one. Twelve English dramas of the period are analysed to illustrate and prove this thesis; study is concluded with an analysis of causes which made the movement a failure.

Zeitlin, J. The development of Bacon's essays with special reference to the question of Montaigne's influence upon them. *See* 1806. 2850

Well developed argument against influence of Montaigne on Bacon, showing that Bacon developed his essay independently of Montaigne and that essays of the two men have little in common except the accidental and superficial.

Franco-Spanish Relations

(Nos. 2851-2875)

STERLING A. STOUDEMIRE

General Spanish Influences upon France

(Nos. 2851-2858)

Espiner, Mrs. Janet Girvan (Scott). Quelques érudits français du XVIᵉ siècle et l'Espagne. RLC 20:203-09, 1940-46. 2851

Short article indicating influence of *Silva* of Pedro Mejía, and Guevara's *Marco Aurelio* on French letters. Also indicates connection of Fauchet, François de Belleforest, Papire Masson with Italian and Spanish writers.

Hanotaux, Gabriel. De l'influence espagnole en France à propos de Brantôme. *In his:* Études historiques sur le XVIᵉ et le XVIIᵉ siècle en France. Hachette, 1886. p. 61-75. 2852

Brantôme as a Périgourdin close to Spain was one of the first to initiate a movement of Spanish imitation competing with Italian style in vogue at his time and leading to a wholesale hispanism in Corneille.

Hazard, Paul. Ce que les lettres françaises doivent à l'Espagne. RLC 16:5-22, 1936. 2853

Excellent article on Spain's contributions to French literature. First, the picturesque, indicating the influence upon Hugo, Gautier. Second, the "sentiments" and third, literary form, such as *Romancero*, the picaresque novel and other lesser contacts between France and Spain.

Martinenche, E. La comedia espagnole en France de Hardy à Racine. Hachette, 1900. 434 p. 2854

Full study traces in some detail influence of Spanish *comedia* upon French drama from time of Hardy, including works of Pierre and Thomas Corneille, Rotrou, Scarron, and others. Indicates great popularity and influence down to reaction against *comedia*, especially on part of Racine.

Reviews : G. Lanson in RHL 8:332-334, 1901; A. L. Stiefel in ZFSL 26:30-49, 1904.

Mathorez, J. Notes sur la pénétration des Espagnols en France du XIIe au XVIe siècle. BH 24:41-66, 1922. 2855

Short article indicating contacts between France and Spain as early as 812. In 15th century many Spaniards visited France, encouraged by close bonds of relationship in reigning families. Many Spaniards established themselves there and did their work there, notably Ignatius Loyola.

Michaud, G. L. The Spanish sources of certain sixteenth century French writers. *See* 942. 2856

Author takes from Foulché-Delbosc's *Bibliographie* and from Brunet the figure of 625 editions of French translations of Spanish works in 16th century. A preliminary survey, he says, shows that the essayistes and not the conteurs were those most influenced. Indicated that Montaigne was influenced by Mejía, Gómara, and perhaps Guevara. Also presents Spanish sources for Cholières and Jean Bouchet.

Morel-Fatio, A. Comment la France a connu l'Espagne depuis le moyen âge. *In his:* Études sur l'Espagne. Vieweg, 1888. p. 1-114. 2857

General study with not much detail on how France came to know Spain and Spanish literature, beginning with monks of Cluny in 12th century, intervention of French in civil wars of 14th century, Spain's rise in prestige with conquest of Granada and discovery of America, introduction of Spanish literature in 16th and 17th centuries, and close connections during first years of 19th century.

Rogers, P. P. Spanish influences on the literature of France. Hisp 9:205-35, 1926. 2858

Beginning with Middle Ages, points out certain areas of Spain's influence on France, finding high peak to be in 16th century with *Amadís* and *Diana*. Lists without comment imitations of picaresque novel and *comedia*. Important features are 1) a list (22 pages) of French authors whose works show Spanish influences, and 2) a well selected bibliography on influence of Spanish upon French literature.

Spanish Authors and Works

(Nos. 2859-2871)

Baret, Eugène. De l'Amadis de Gaule et de son influence sur les mœurs et la littérature au XVIe et au XVIIe siècle. Durand, 1853 & 1873. 203 p. 2859

Rather interesting, albeit at times debatable, study of influence of literature, particularly *Amadís de Gaula*, upon customs and manners of renaissance Europe. Even though there is no absolute measuring rod for such conclusions, it appears evident that some of the gentility of 16th century must have been at first in imitation, and later an established code.

Daele, Rose Marie. Nicolas de Montreulx (Ollenix du Mont-Sacré), arbiter of European literary vogues of the late renaissance. *See* 1016. 2860

Rich bibliography (p. 285-334) and elaborate index (p. 335-60). Author practically unearths a rather important though unknown writer, a forerunner of French classicism, who shows Spanish influences in novels like *Le seizième livre d'Amadis* (1577) and *Les bergeries de Juliette* (1585) and in dramas like *Diane* (1594). His *Amadis* is an original work, not a translation like that of Chappuys. *See* 1039, 2385.

Crooks, Esther. Translations of Cervantes into French. *In:* Cervantes across the centuries. Ed. by Angel Flores and M. J. Benardete. New York, 1947. p. 294-304. 2861

Ten-page description of French translations of Cervantes' works, from early 17th century, with consideration of chief French titles which were influenced by the Spaniard. Excellent short study. Also consult Maurice Bardon, " *Don Quichotte* " *en France au XVIIe et au XVIIIe siècle 1605-1815*. Champion, 1931. 2 v.

Hainsworth, Georges. Une ramification curieuse dans la bibliographie cervantesque :

la fortune de la première traduction française des Novelas ejemplares. BH 32:259-
267, 1930. 2862

Short article concerned with popularity
of first French translation of *Novelas
ejemplares*. French critical opinion of
Novelas from 1614 to 1664 is cited;
reference made to praise of Camus,
Scarron and others.

Neumann, M. H. Cervantes in Frankreich,
1582-1910. Rhisp 78:1-309, Feb., 1930.
2863

Long, excellent study listing translations of *Don Quijote*, *Novelas ejemplares*,
and *Persiles y Sigismunda*, their vogue and
influence upon French literature.

Matulka, Barbara. The Cid as a courtly
hero from the Amadís to Corneille. New
York, Columbia University, Institute of
French studies, 1928. 54 p. 2864

Study traces the Cid ideal from *Amadís*
to Corneille, taking into account themes
and motifs : " love versus hatred," " the
head motif," " the vanquished champion,"
" the love test," " the sword motif," and
others. *Mocedades* regarded as juncture
of Cid legend and Amadís theme. Also
some consideration of sources of *Mocedades
del Cid*, and Cid-Amadís theme in France
before Corneille.

Van Roosbroeck, G. L. The Cid theme in
France in 1600. Minneapolis, Pioneer
printers, 1920. 16 p. 2865

Traces the Cid theme from Corneille,
but points out that a modification of the
theme had appeared in a novel—*La hayne
et l'amour de Arnoue et de Clayremonde*—
as early as 1600, and that the novel, more
than Guillén de Castro's *Mocedades del
Cid*, stresses psychological analysis of
character.

Matulka, Barbara. The novels of Juan de
Flores and their European diffusion. New
York, 1931. 475 p. (Diss., Columbia)
2866

Excellent and long treatment on European diffusion of works of Juan de Flores.
In connection with study of *Grisel y
Mirabella*, there is a background analysis
of feminism in 15th century Spain, the
debt to Boccaccio, an analysis of the
motives, translations into other languages,
and influence upon European literature.
Grimalte y Gradissa treated in same fashion.
Full appendix lists all editions in all languages.

Clement, L. Antoine de Guevara, ses
lecteurs et ses imitateurs français au XVIe
siècle. *See* 1562. 2867

Antonio de Guevara's moral treatises
were pretty well known and read in France.
Article suggests influence of *El monosprecio
de corte y alabanza de aldea* upon Jean de
La Taille and possible influence of *Epistolas*
on Montaigne.

Laplane, Gabriel. Les anciennes traductions françaises de Lazarillo de Tormes.
HomEM, p. 143-55. 2868

Chiefly statistical, listing translations
into French of *Lazarillo de Tormes*, from
1560 to 1700. Twenty French editions
appeared in 120 years, and in whole
period there was a constant fair popularity.

Hainsworth, G. Quelques notes pour la
fortune de Lope de Vega en France. BH
33:199-213, 1931. 2869

Study on the fortune of Lope de Vega's
non-dramatic works in France. *Arcadia*
was known as early as 1610; translated in
1622. *Peregrino en su patria* was translated
in 1614. Vogue of other works is also
considered.

Coppin, Joseph. Montaigne traducteur de
Raymon Sebon. *See* 2504. 2870

A consideration of the vogue of *Liber
creaturarum* in France, 1500-40. Studies
exactness of Montaigne's translation of
Sebon's work, with several parallel passages as evidence. Conclusion reached that
Montaigne owes something to Sebon, in
style and diction, and that *Livre des créatures* is " une source assez importante des
Essais."

Vaganay, Hugues. Amadis en français,
essai de bibliographie. Florence, Champion, 1906. 151 p. 2871

Calls attention to the many French
translations of *Amadís* from 1540 to 161;
and to their rarity. Notes that Brunet'
bibliography in *Manuel du libraire*, I : 214
218 is very detailed and just as confusing
A very minute description of first twelve
books of the fine copy of *Bibliothèque d'
l'Académie de Lyon* is given, accompanie
by many illustrations.

Some French Influences upon Spain
(Nos. 2872-2875)

Faure, Elie. Montaigne et ses trois pre
miers-nés. *See* 1608. 287

General introduction to Montaigne and three essays concerning possible influences on Shakespeare, Cervantes, and Pascal. Points of contact are slight and influence negligible.

Gebhart, Emile. De Panurge à Sancho Pança. Bloud, 1911. 320 p.   2873
Discussion of French satire of 16th century rather than a study of Rabelais' influence on Cervantes. Rabelais represented as an Erasmian; other authors included are Calvin, La Boëtie and d'Aubigné.

Gillet, J. E. Note sur Rabelais en Espagne. RLC 16:140-44, 1936.   2874
Takes exception to statement of Élie Faure that Sancho Panza is a sort of Panurge. Gillet indicates that Rabelais was not known in Spain and that he was not translated until 20th century.

Hilton, Ronald. Four studies in Franco-Spanish relations. Toronto, University of Toronto Press, 1943. 57 p.   2875
Well-documented study on spiritual conflict between Old Spain and New Spain, with an investigation of the role that France has played in the struggle. Four essays treat 1) *North versus South, France versus Spain,* 2) *Auvergne and Spain,* 3) *Spaniards in Avignon in the 18th century,* 4) *L'Abbé Béliardi, a mysterious Italian intriguer in Franco-Spanish 18th century diplomacy.*

Other Countries
(Nos. 2876-2897)

W. B. FLEISCHMANN and L. N. GOULD

Germany
(Nos. 2876-2890)

Reynaud, Louis. Histoire générale de l'influence française en Allemagne. Hachette, 1915. 554 p.   2876
A nationalistic work which defeats its purpose of tracing most of German culture back to France. Author begins study in time of Celts; ends with cessation of hostilities between the two nations in 1918. Reynaud finds that German culture is always the culture of France a generation or so in the past. Whenever Germany is enjoying a (French-inspired) cultural supremacy, France is at a low point gathering strength for another cultural domination of Europe. Most of the good

things that Germany has produced in literature, art or politics have their roots in France; everything deplorable in Germany is *echt germanisch* and has no cultural connection with France. Cultural rather than a literary investigation of the two nations; chapter on renaissance (p. 157-91) deals with French reaction to German Reformation.

Rossel, Virgile. Histoire des relations littéraires entre la France et l'Allemagne. Fischbacher, 1897. 531 p.   2877
Impartial treatment of Franco-German literary relations by an unprejudiced Swiss. First half concerns itself with role of German literature in France, second half with role of French literature in Germany. Author finds themes in Rabelais which seem to come from Till Eulenspiegel and *Narrenschiff;* he neither affirms nor negates an influence here, but simply suggests various parts of the three works which need closer study to arrive at an answer. With regard to later centuries the part of Switzerland as literary mediator between Germany and France is also stressed.

Süpfle, Theodor. Geschichte des deutschen Kultureinflusses auf Frankreich, mit besonderer Berücksichtigung der literarischen Einwirkung. Gotha, Thienemann, 1885-90. 3 v.   2878
Three volume work bound in one. First volume concerns itself with historical influence of Gauls on their Teutonic neighbors and then deals with German influences up through time of Klopstock, with emphasis on reception given in France to works of better known German writers such as Brant, Reuchlin, Luther, Haller, Gessner, Gellert. Volume two deals with period from Lessing to end of Romanticism, with special stress on influence of Schiller's dramas; volume three treats period from Louis Philippe to 1890. Role of Alsace as a mediator between the two nations frequently stressed. Reference made throughout the three volumes to various other German influences, political, military, philosophical, scientific, on France.

Fraustadt, Fedor. Ueber das Verhältnis von Barclays Ship of fools zur lateinischen, französischen und deutschen Quelle. Breslau, Michkowsky, 1894. 50 p.   2879
Detailed analysis of relationship of text of Barclay's work to German original text, Latin translation by Jakob Locher, and French translation by Pierre Rivière.

Fraustadt, by very thorough textual comparisons, establishes without doubt that Locher's translation was the principal source for *Ship of fools*. Rivière's translation does, however, find some specific echoes in Barclay, while the original text (despite Barclay's assertion) seems to have been hardly used at all. Fraustadt also makes it clear how largely Barclay drew on scenes from contemporary English life to enhance his translation.

Moore, W. G. The evolution of a sixteenth century satire. MisLK, p. 351-60.   2880

A study in the international evolution of renaissance satire with France as its centre : traces shaping of Robert de Balsac's *Le chemin de l'ospital* from Brant's *Narrenschiff* with its shift to the French tradition, and evolution of Balsac's *Le chemin* into Robert Copland's English adaptation, *Hye way to the Spyttel Hous*.

Pompen, Aurelius Cornelius Gerard. The English versions of The ship of fools ; a contribution to the history of the early French renaissance in England. London, Longmans, Green, 1925. 345 p.   2881

Through analysis and comparison of all texts and versions of *The ship of fools* from Brant's original German edition (1494) through the two English versions of 1509 (that of Watson and that of Barclay respectively), author shows that neither of English versions was translated directly from German original; but rather that both derived indirectly from the Jakob Locher Latin version (1497), which was more nearly a paraphrase than a translation, largely stripped of its German characteristics, and more in the classical French than in the German tradition. Thus the Henry Watson version shown to be based on French versions that stem from the Locher first edition, and the Barclay version on French translations that go back through others.

Reviews : R. Mohl in MP 23:379-82, 1925-26; F. M. Padelford in MLN 41: 344-346, 1926.

Leube, Hans. Die Anfänge der französischen Lutherauffassung. ZKG 56:515-549, 1937.   2882

Essay consists of two parts. One, *Preisaufgabe* of 1802 of *Institut national* in Paris : *Quelle a été l'influence de la réformation de Luther sur les lumières et la situation politique des différens états de l'Europe?* This was won by Charles Villers, the great Franco-German inter-

mediary (p. 515-26). Second part, *Deutsche Reformation-französische Aufklärungfranzösische Revolution* (p. 526-49), concludes that French representatives of Enlightenment saw no spiritual relationship with the German reformers. Mme de Staël and Benjamin Constant substantiated Villers' concept; however, they were Protestant, not Catholic, and they were Swiss by birth.

Moore, Will Grayburn. La réforme allemande et la littérature française; recherches sur la notoriété de Luther en France. *See* 164.   2882A

See also : 772, 1931.

French Authors in Germany and Switzerland

(Nos. 2883-2890)

Marichal, Robert. Antoine d'Oraison, premier traducteur français de Luther. BHren 9:78-106, 1947.   2883

Critical first edition of MS 117-*Bibliothèque Inguimbertine de Carpentras*, a French translation of Luther's essay on preparation for death. Marichal proves by epigraphical means that this manuscript dates from ca. 1520, is therefore most certainly the second and very likely first French Luther translation. Points of interest concerning MS. are that it is dedicated to Marguerite de France, and that its first owner was Antoine-Honorat de Aqua, a gentleman who was translator's uncle and also a judge in the inquisition. Marichal reprints MS. in entirety, stressing literal quality of the translation and youth of translator by way of apology for an item that has only historical interest.

Droz, E. Le premier séjour d'Agrippa d'Aubigné à Genève. BHren 9:169-73, 1947.   2884

Miss Droz takes up problem of Agrippa d'Aubigné's sudden departure from Geneva in 1566. Traditionally, the rigid and demanding studies in Théodore de Bèze's college have been blamed for it. Also, d'Aubigné makes it clear in *Sa vie et ses enfants*, that he had decided disciplinary problems in his adolescence. Miss Droz has uncovered a criminal record of the time which, she believes, throws light on the issue. It seems that d'Aubigné was second-hand witness to a homosexual school scandal which led to intimidation of the witnesses questioned and to death by drowning for the offender; Miss Droz believes that these frightening proceedings constitute more plausible grounds for d'Aubigné's sudden flight than those assumed traditionally.

François, Alexis. Les sonnets suisses de Joachim du Bellay, expliqués et commentés. Trois tableaux de la Suisse vue par les écrivains français du seizième siècle. See 1242. 2885

Reproduces Sonnets CXXXIV *(Les Grisons)*, CXXXV *(Les Suisses)*, CXXXVI *(Genève)* and *La réponse de l'auteur au Quidam* (I-V). These are followed by a detailed commentary on the sonnets as well as by documentary appendices.

Bouillier, V. La renommée de Montaigne en Allemagne. See 1543. 2886

Author wants to show that Montaigne found more favor and a larger reading public in Germany than his past commentators have supposed. He does not concern himself with authors, periodicals and historical-literary works which simply mention or briefly quote the author of the *Essays* without commenting thereon : instead, he cites translations or lengthier quotations from Montaigne found in works of Moscherosch, Bodmer, Lessing, Goethe, C. F. Meyer, and others. These translations or quotations are all followed by commentaries favorable to the French thinker and they tend to show that his reception in Germany was larger than in Italy and Spain, and second only to England.

Frantzen, J. J. A. A. Kritische Bemerkungen zu Fischarts Übersetzung von Rabelais' Gargantua. Strassburg, Trübner, 1892. 86 p. (Diss., Strassburg). 2887

Frantzen does not share either Vilmar's or Ganghofer's unqualified praise for Fischart as a translator. He bases his conclusions on detailed examination of text used, individual words or expressions, sentence structure, proverbial expressions, Gallicisms, misunderstanding of individual words, etc.

Gebhart, Emile. Rabelais, la renaissance et la réforme. See 867. 2888

Gebhart writes a lively biography of Rabelais, together with an interpretation of *Gargantua* and *Pantagruel*. A short comparison of Rabelais, Aristophanes, Cervantes, and Swift is added as an afterthought. Gebhart shows Rabelais as a forerunner of the rationalistic spirit in France. Medieval form of Rabelais' work is only a kind of " mythe platonique " for Gebhart, whereby unenlightened 16th century public could be led to more essential rationalistic truths within the work. In his effort to make an enlightener out of Rabelais, Gebhart goes as far as to explain Rabelais' rejection of both the contemporary Church and Calvinism on a purely rationalistic basis. Comparative essay at end makes Rabelais superior to the three other comic authors through " warmth " of his spirit. This book is not recommended reading for beginning students of Rabelais. It does, however, offer valuable comment on Rabelais' rationalism.

Sainéan, L. L'influence et la réputation de Rabelais. See 896. 2889

Well-known book; embraces whole Rabelaisian tradition. First part deals with reaction of Rabelais' own literary milieu to his writings, and with Rabelais exegesis, criticism, editions, and translations both in France and abroad. Second part deals with prominent readers and imitators of Rabelais and appends portrait of Marnix de Sainte-Aldegonde, a 16th century French Rabelaisian. Sainéan's gift for precision serves him well when he deals with the French tradition. Reader will be somewhat disappointed by the brief *aperçus* in discussion of the tradition in other European countries and in America. Sainéan is always careful, however, to indicate studies where these aspects are treated at greater length.

Schwarz, Gottlieb. Rabelais und Fischart. Vergleichung des Gargantua und der Geschichtsklitterung von Pantagrueline Prognostication und Aller Practick Grossmutter. Diss., Zürich, 1885. 96 p. 2890

Compares texts from point of view of style, names of places and persons, composition, additions and changes, artistic and satiric as well as moral; compares both authors ethically and ideologically (religion, politics, education, and attitude towards women); compares 1572 and 1574 editions of *Pantagrueline Prognostication* and *Aller Practick Grossmutter*.

Holland

(Nos. 2891-2894)

Mathorez, J. Rapports intellectuels de la France et de la Hollande, du XIIIᵉ au XVIIIᵉ siècle. JS ns 19:157-68, 1921. 2891

Review article; deals with K. J. Riemens' *Esquisse historique de l'enseignement du français en Hollande* (1919), Gustave

Cohen's *Ecrivains français en Hollande* (1920) and A. Germain's *Les Néerlandais en Bourgogne* (1909).

Franchet, Henri. Erasme et Ronsard : la lettre Contra quosdam qui se falso jactant evangelicos et les Discours de misères de ce temps. *See* 1120.   2892

Source study of Ronsard's *Discours des misères de ce temps.* Franchet shows that Erasmus' letter *Contra quosdam qui se falso jactant* constitutes the most important source. Ronsard uses all of Erasmus' apologetic arguments, he borrows expressions, phrases, and even sentences from the letter. Franchet shows the correspondence in the description of ecclesiastical vices by Erasmus and Ronsard. He does not, however, enlarge on its significance for the general perspective of either Ronsard's thought or Erasmus' influence in France.

Mann, Margaret. Erasme et les débuts de la réforme française. Champion, 1934. 227 p.   2893

Painstakingly neat attempt to delineate Erasmus' early influence and critical reputation in France. Very thorough study of relationship of Erasmus and Lefèvre d'Étaples serves as starting-point for an essay of early Protestant view of Erasmus. Textual criticism of Louis de Berquin's translations from Erasmus is interposed, rather disappointingly, between foregoing discussion and a diffuse chapter on Erasmus and Calvin. Not a study in history of ideas, nor is it a theological work, nor has it much to do with Erasmus' influence on French literature. Yet this book contains a sufficiency of material reflecting on all of these aspects so that many researchers cannot afford to pass it by.

Schönfeld, Hermann. Die Beziehung der Satire Rabelais' zu Erasmus' Encoïnium Moriae und Colloquia. PMLA 8:1-76, 1893.   2894

Rambling article of 76 pages; deals with parallelisms in lives, ideas, and writings of these two great humanists. Attempt made to place gleanings from works of each side by side and to draw analogies between biographical details of each writer to explain similarity of ideas. Unfortunately, article is so riddled with digressions, ranging from a discussion of Rabelais' influence on Swift to Victor Hugo's

description of monastic life, that reader is doomed to lose sight of central argument.

Other Items

(Nos. 2895-2897)

Atkinson, Geoffroy. The extraordinary voyage in French literature before 1700. New York, Columbia University Press, 1920. 189 p.   2895

La littérature géographique française de la renaissance; répertoire bibliographique. *See* 380.

Les nouveaux horizons de la renaissance française. *See* 381.

The extraordinary voyage surveys the realistic novels of Bergeron, Foigny, Vairasse, and Fénelon. Atkinson places these stories of travel in a category apart from pastoral, adventurous, or burlesque 17th century French novels because of their realistic setting and didactic content. He poses interest in newly discovered lands and growth of rationalism in France as grounds for popularity of the extraordinary voyage novel. Even though Atkinson identifies certain aspects of these novels with growth of deistic and primitivistic concepts, he definitively, disclaims their influence on Defoe, or on European Robinsonade in next century.

Atkinson's bibliographical repertory contains descriptions of 524 works in French language which deal with description of non-European peoples and countries. Facsimile pages from almost every work are reproduced in a large appendix. Concise index by countries, authors, and libraries may be found in back. *Les nouveaux horizons* is a partial attempt to treat of historical and philosophical significance of these works.

Costa Coutinho, Bernardo Xavier da. Bibliographie franco-portugaise; essai d'une bibliographie chronologique de livres français sur le Portugal. Porto, Lopes da Silva, 1939. 409 p.   2896

2912 titles concerning all types of works and arranged strictly chronologically. Titles 2-75 concern 16th century.

Rouillard, C. D. The Turk in French history, thought and literature (1520-1660). Boivin, 1941. 700 p.   2897

Introduction gives an excellent historical background of late medieval Turkey along with a survey of official relations existing between France and Ottoman Empire. French concept of Turks is gleaned from travel accounts, historical works, geographical works, illustrations in books, dramas, prose fiction, verse and ballet. Often Turk also served as a mirror for self-criticism; for Montaigne, for instance, Turkish virtues and vices became a means of exemplifying faults of French moral and political practices. Of special interest is part IV, which gives a detailed account especially of French tragedies during the period under discussion which were based upon Turkish history.

APPENDIX

The Translators, Greek

Although it is contrary to the policy of the Editors to include unannotated material, the following list seemed important enough to call for an exception. Since the General Index had been completed before this decision was reached, proper names and subject headings in the following list which are not found in Dr. Hutton's main contribution (nos. 2514-2594G) are not included in it.

GENERAL EDITOR

Amyot

Histoire éthiopique de Heliodorus, 1547, 1585; *Diodore de Sicile* (Books 11-17), 1554, 1559; *Les amours pastorales de Daphnis et Chloe*, 1559, 1578; *Vies des hommes illustres de Plutarque*, 1559, 1565, 1567, 1619; *Œuvres morales de Plutarque*, 1572, 1574, 1618; *Œuvres de Plutarque, traduites du grec par Amyot*, ed., with the Notes of Brotier and Vauvilliers, by E. Clavier, Cussac, 1801-1806, 26 v.

Aesop

Les fables (from Steinhöwel's Latin), by Frère Julien Macho des Augustins de Lyon, Lyons, ca. 1480; 1540. *Apologues d'Ésope* (from L. Valla's Latin), by Guillaume Tardif, ca. 1490. *Les fables* (in verse), by Gilles Corrozet, 1542; with a *Vie d'Esope* tr. by Antoine du Moulin, Lyons, 1547; *Le second livre* (in verse), by Corrozet, 1548. *Les fables ... selon la vérité grec*, anon., Lyons and Paris, 1547. *Trois cent soixante et six apologues* (in verse), by Guillaume Haudent, Rouen, 1547.

Gnomic Verses, etc.

Naumachius, by J.-A. de Baïf *(in his: Etrenes de poésie françoise)*, 1574; by Clovis Hesteau *(in his: Œuvres poétiques*, 1578; by Pierre Tamisier *(in his: Anthologie)*, Lyons, 1589; by Vauquelin de La Fresnaye *(in his: Diverses poésies)*, Caen, 1605. Oracles. *Les oracles des douze Sibylles* (with Dorat's Latin), by Claude Binet, 1586. *Phocylides*, by J.-A. de Baïf *(in his: Etrenes)*, 1574; by Barthélemy Fournier, Lyons, 1577; by Pierre Tamisier *(in his: Anthologie)*, Lyons, 1589. Pythagoras, *Golden verses*, by J.-A. de Baïf *(in his: Etrenes)*, 1574; by Barthélemy Fournier (with

Phocylides), Lyons, 1577; by Catherine des Roches *(in: Les secondes œuvres des Mmes des Roches)*, Poitiers, 1583; by Pierre Tamisier *(in his: Anthologie)*, Lyons, 1589; by R.L. M.T. *(Les sages enseignemens)*, Lyons, 1596. Sentences. *Les très-élégantes sentences*, by Gilles Corrozet, 1546 (cf. *also* his *Hecatomgraphie*, 1541); *Sentences illustres des poètes lyriques, comiques et autres poètes grecs et latins*, by G.L.D.T., 1579. Seven sages. *Le Conseil des sept sages*, by Gilles Corrozet, 1544; *Les dicts des sept sages*, by François Habert, Lyons, 1549. *See also* Solon and Theognis.

Homer

Iliad, by Jean Samxon, 1530; Books 1-2, by Hugues Salel, Lyons, 1542; Books 1-10, by Salel, 1545; Books 11-12 and the beginning of 13, by Salel, 1554; Books 12-16, by Amadis Jamyn, 1574; Books 12-24, by Jamyn, 1577. *Odyssey*, Books 1-2, by Jacques Peletier, 1547; Book 14, by Antoine de Cotel, 1578; Books 1-3, by Amadis Jamyn, 1584; Books 1-24, by Salomon Certon, 1603; *Batrachomyomachia*, by Antoine Macault, 1540; by G. Royhier, Lyons, 1554; anon. imitation *(Bataille des rats et des grenouilles)*, La Jeune, 1580. *Œuvres d'Homère*, by Salomon Certon, 1615.

Drama

Aristophanes, *Plutus* (frgs. in Ronsard, *Œuvres*, 1617- Blanchemain's ed. 7.281-305, no. 1066). Euripides, *Hecuba*, by (Guillaume Bochetel), 1544, 1550; *Helen* (Prologue only), by J.-A. de Baïf *(in his: Euvres)*, 1572-73; *Iphigenia at Aulis*, by Thomas Sebillet, 1549; [unpublished : *Iphigenia at Aulis* (B.N. MS. Fr. 22505); *Troades* (Musée Condé MS. 1688)]. Sophocles, *Electra*, by Lazare de

Baïf, 1537; *Antigone*, by J.-A. de Baïf *(in his: Euvres)*, 1572-73; [unpublished : *Antigone*, by Calvy de La Fontaine (Bibl. de Soissons MS. 189 B)].

Other Greek Poets

Anacreon, twenty-nine paraphrases by Ronsard *(in his: Bocage and Meslanges)*, 1554; *Les odes d'Anacréon*, by Remy Belleau, 1556; *Quelques Odes d'Anacréon mises en musique*, by Richard Renvoisy, 1559. The Greek anthology, thirty-four epigrams, by Ronsard between 1553 and 1569 in various works; others by J.-A. de Baïf *(in his: Euvres)*, 1572-73; Pierre Tamisier, *Anthologie*, Lyons, 1589 (786 epigrams). Aratus, *Phaenomena* and *Prognostica* (incomplete), by Remy Belleau *(in his: Œuvres poétiques)*, 1578 (frgs. of *Prognostica in his: Bergerie*, 1565). Bion, *Lament for Adonis*, imit. by Mellin de Saint-Gelais *(in his: Œuvres)*, 1547; *Amour oyseau*, by J.-A. de Baïf *(in his: Euvres)* 1572-1573; several imitations by Ronsard *(see* Laumonier, *Ronsard poète lyrique*, 1143, p. 161). Hesiod, *Works and days*, by Richard Le Blanc, Lyons, 1547; by Lambert d'Aneau, 1571; by J.-A. de Baïf *(in his: Etrenes)*, 1574; by Jacques Le Gras, 1586. Moschus, *Amor fugitivus*, by Clément Marot *(in: La suite de l'Adolescence)*, 1534. Musaeus, *Hero and Leander*, by Clément Marot, 1541. Nicander, *Les œuvres*, by Jacques Grévin, Antwerp, 1567. Oppian, *Cynegetica*, by Florent Chrestien, 1575. Solon, frg. by Pardoux du Prat (with Marcus Aurelius), 1570; by Pierre Tamisier *(in his: Anthologie)*, 1589. Theocritus, *Idyll* 24, by J.-A. de Baïf *(in: Traductions de Latin en françoys)*, 1549; *Dialogue rustique et amoureux*, by Etienne Forcadel *(in his: Chant des sereines)*, 1548; *Idyll* 3, by Claude Turrin *(in his: Œuvres poétiques)*, 1572; paraphrases of several idylls, by J.-A. de Baïf *(in his: Euvres)*, 1572-73; *Bergerie pris de Théocrite*, by Antoine de Cotel *(in his: Mignardes et gaies poésies)*, 1578; *Idyll* 21 (imit.) by Jean de Vitel *(in his: Premiers exercices poétiques)*, 1588; translations of Theocritus' *Honey-stealer* are listed in (2561). Theognis, by Nicolas Pavillon, 1578.

Historians

Agathias, *History* (with Procopius), by Mart. Fumée, 1587. Appian, *Roman history*, by Claude de Seyssel, Lyons, 1544; *Iberica and Hannibal*, by Philippe des Avenelles, 1558; *Hannibal*, by B. Tagault, 1559. Arrian,

Anabasis, by Claude Witart, 1581. Cassius Dio, by Claude des Rosiers, 1542. Diodorus, *(see* Amyot, above); Books 18-20, by Claude de Seyssel, 1530; Books 1-3, by Antoine Macault, 1535. Eusebius, *Ecclesiastical history*, by Claude de Seyssel, 1532. Herodian, by Jean Colin, 1541; by Jacques de Vintimille, Lyons, 1554. Herodotus, by Pierre Saliat, 1556 (in part publ. 1552). Josephus, *Works*, by François Bourgoing, 1558; by Jean Le Frère, 1569; by Gilbert Génébrard, 1578; by Antoine de La Faye, 1597; *Antiquities*, by Guillaume Michel, 1534; *Jewish wars*, by Nicolas d' Herberay des Essars, 1553 (Book I publ. 1550). Polybius, Books 1-5, by Louis Meigret, 1542; portions of Books 6 and 16, by the same, 1545. Procopius, *Vandalica* and *Gothica* (with Agathias), by Mart. Fumée, 1587. Thucydides, by Claude de Seyssel, 1527. Xenophon, *Agesilaus*, by Loys Le Roy *(in his: Trois livres d'Isocrate)*, 1551; *Anabasis*, by Claude de Seyssel, 1529; *Cyropaedia*, by Jacques de Vintimille, 1547; Book I, by Loys Le Roy, 1551; *Economics*, by Geoffroy Tory, 1531; by F. de Ferris, 1562; by Etienne de La Boëtie, 1571; *Hiero*, by Jacques Miffant, 1550; *Memorabilia*, by Jean Doublet, 1582; *Resp. Lacedaem. et Athen.*, by Claude Pinart, 1579. Zonaras, by Jean de Maumont, 1561; by Jean Millet, 1583.

Orators

Demosthenes. *Philippics*, by Jean Lalemant, 1549; by Loys Le Roy, 1555; by Jean Papon *(Phil.* 2 and 3 only), Lyons, 1554. *Olynthiacs*, by Loys Le Roy, 1551. *Oraisons et harangues*, by Gervais de Tournay, 1579. Dio Chrysostomus. *Louange de la Loy*, by Fédéric Morel, 1598. Isocrates. *Demonicus*, by Calvy de La Fontaine, 1543; by Pierre Adam de Wassigny, Lyons, 1549; by Loys Le Roy, 1551. *Epistles*, by Loys de Matha, 1547. *Ad Nicoclem*, by Jean Brèche *(in his: Manuel royal)*, Tours, 1541; by Antoine Macault, 1544; by Pierre Adam de Wassigny, Lyons, 1549; by Loys Le Roy, 1551. *Nicocles*, by Louis Meigret, 1544; by Loys Le Roy, 1551. *De pace*, by Philippes Robert, Lyons, 1579. *Panegyricus*, by Pierre Adam de Wassigny, Lyons, 1548. Lysias. *Sur le meurtre d'Eratosthène*, by Jacques de Vintimille (with notes by Philibert Bugnyon), Lyons, 1576. *Contre les marchands de bleds*, by Philibert Bugnyon (with Isocrates' *De pace* by Ph. Robert), Lyons, 1579. Extracts. *Harangues militaires et concions* (from Herodotus, Thucydides, etc.), by François de Belleforest, 2nd ed., 1588.

*Medical Writers ; Miscellaneous
(A Selection)*

Apollodorus, *La bibliothèque*, by Jean Passerat (publ. by Rougevalet), 1605. Archimedes, *Des choses tombantes en l'humide* by Pierre Forcadel, 1565. Artemidorus, *Epitome ... traictant des songes*, by Charles Fontaine, Lyons, 1546. Dioscorides, *La matière médicinale*, by Martin Mathée, Lyons, 1553. Euclid, *Les neuf livres des eléments*, by Pierre Forcadel, 1564; *Du léger et du pésant*, by Forcadel (with Archimedes), 1565; *La musique*, by Forcadel, 1566. Galen, *Thérapeutique* (Bk. 14), by Jean Canape, Lyons, 1538 (Bk. 2, ibid., 1538 or 1539; Bks. 3-6 and 13, ibid., 1539); *Opuscules*, by Pierre Tolet (with Paulus Aegineta), Lyons, 1540; *Mouvement des muscles* and *Anatomie des os*, by Jean Canape, Lyons, 1541; *Des simples* (Bks. 5 and 9), by Jean Canape, Lyons, 1542; Book 5, by Jean de Bauhin, Antwerp, 1544; 3 Books, by Jean Brèche, Tours, 1545; 4 books, by Ervé Fayard, Limoges, 1548; 4 books, by Martin Grégoire, 1549; *Exhortation ... aux estudes*, by Michel Nostradamus, Lyons, 1557; *De l'usage des parties du corps*, by Claude Delachamps, Lyons, 1566. Hippocrates, *Présaiges ... item La protestation*, by Pierre Verney, Lyons, 1539; *De la nature humaine*, by Jean de Bourges, 1548; *Aphorismes*, by Jean Brèche, Pavia (Paris ?), 1550; by Jean Cassel (in verse), Lyons, 1592; *De l'enfant au ventre de la mère*, by Guillaume Chrestien, Reims, 1553; *Des ulcères, fistules, playes de teste*, by François Le Fèvre, 1555; *De la génération de l'homme*, by Guillaume Chrestien, 1559; *Le Médecin-chirurgien d'H.*, by François Le Fèvre, 1560; *La composition du corps humain*, by J. de La Fargue, Lyons, 1580. Julian, *Caesars*, by B. Grangier, 1580. Paulus Aegineta, *La chirurgie* (Book 6), by Pierre Tolet (with Galen), Lyons, 1540. Phalaris, *Les epistres*, by Claude Gruget, 1550. Philostratus, *Les images*, by Blaise de Vigenère, 1578; *La suite de Ph., avec les Statues de Callistrate*, by Blaise de Vigenère, 1596; *Vie de Apollonius*, by Blaise de Vigenère, 1599, (unpublished tr. by Thomas Sebillet, MS. B.N. f. fr. 1108).

Church Fathers (A Selection)

Ammonius of Alexandria, *Histoire ... des quatre évangélistes*, anon. (from the Latin of Nachtigall), Lyons, 1526. Athanasius, *Epistre ... aux catholiques*, by " un religieux de S. Denys," 1563. Athenagoras of Athens, *Apologie pour les Chrétiens and Traité de la Résurrection*, by Arnauld du Ferrier, Bordeaux, 1577. Basil, *A ses jeunes disciples et neveux*, by Claude de Pontoux, 1561; *Sermons*, by Christophle Hébrard, 1580; various treatises by Fédéric Morel, 1583-1608. Cyprian, *Œuvres*, by Jacques Tigeou, 1574. Cyril, *Sermons*, by F. de Belleforest, 1565. Dionysius the Areopagite, *Théologie*, by " un vénérable religieux de l'ordre des frères mineurs de l'Observance," s.d. Gregory Nazianzen, *Quatrains*, by Jacques de Billy, 1576. John Chrysostom, *Traicté ... que nulle n'est offensé sinon par soymesme*, by Pierre Pesselière, 1543; two homilies, by Jean de Billy, Lyons, 1544; *Cinq opuscules*, anon., 1557; *De la dignité sacerdotale*, by Richard Le Blanc, 1553; various tracts by Fédéric Morel, 1591-1615. Justin Martyr, *Œuvres*, by Jean de Maumont, 1554. Theodoret, *Histoire*, by M. Mathée, Poitiers, 1544; *Sermons* 9-10, by Claude d'Espence, Lyons, 1547. Synesius, *Hymnes*, by Jacques Courtin de Cissé, 1581.

Plato

Apology, by François Hotman, Lyons, 1549. *Axiochus*, by Etienne Dolet, Lyons, 1544; by Guillaume Postel (acc. to La Croix du Maine; doubtful), 1547. *Crito*, by Simon Vallambert, 1542; by Pierre du Val, 1547. *Euthyphro*, by Jean Martin, 1579. *Gorgias*, extracts by Loys Le Roy (with *Phaedo*, etc.), 1553. *Hipparchus*, by Etienne Dolet (with *Axiochus*), Lyons, 1544. *Ion*, by Richard Le Blanc, 1546. *Laws*, part of Book 3, by Loys Le Roy, 1562. *Lysis*, by Bonaventure des Périers, Lyons, 1544; by Blaise de Vigenère (with Cicero's *Laelius* and Lucian's *Toxaris*), 1579. *Phaedo*, by Loys Le Roy (with *Repub.* 10 and passages from *Gorgias* and *Phaedrus*), 1553; (MS. tr. by Jean de Luxembourg, B.N., fonds fr. 1081). *Phaedrus*, extracts by Loys Le Roy (with *Phaedo*, etc.), 1553. *Republic*, Book 10, by Loys Le Roy (with *Phaedo*, etc.), 1553; Books 1-2, 10, by Le Roy, 1555; entire, by Le Roy, 1600. *Symposium*, by Mathurin Heret, 1556; by Loys Le Roy, 1558; extracts by Antoine Heroët (*L'Androgyne*, in verse), Lyons, 1542, and by Guy Le Fèvre de La Boderie (*Discours de l'honneste amour*), 1578. *Theages*, by Pierre Trédéhan (in verse), Lyons, 1564. *Timaeus*, by Loys Le Roy, 1551.

Other Philosophers

Agapetus, by Jean Picot, 1563; by Pardoux du Prat (with Marcus Aurelius), 1570, by Pontus de Tyard, Rouen, 1604. Alexandre of Aphrodisias, *Problems*, anon. (with Aristotle's *Problems*), 1554; by Mathurin Heret, 1555. Aristeas, by E. B. L. G. Rouen,

1604, (With Tyard's Agapetus). Aristotle. *Nicomachean ethics*, by Nicolas Oresme, 1488, 1511; by Le Plessis, 1553. *Economics*, by Sibert de Lowenborch, 1532; by Gabriel Bounin, 1554 (repr. in 1600 as the work of La Boëtie; see 2576). *De mundo*, by Louis Meigret, 1541; by Pierre Saliat, Lyons, 1542. *Physiognomica*, by J. Bien, 1553. *Politics*, by Nicolas Oresme, 1489; by Loys Le Roy, 1568 (part of Book 5 had appeared in 1566). *Problems*, by anon., 1554. (earlier undated ed.); sec. 30, by Meury Riflant *(Le miroir des mélancholiques)*, 1543. *Secreta secretorum*, by (Guillaume de Tignonville), 1497, 1517, 1531. Cebes, *Tabula*, by Geoffroy Tory (with 30 *Dialogues* of Lucian), 1529; by Gilles Corrozet (in verse), 1543. Diogenes of Sinope, *Epistles*, by Louis Dupuys, Poitiers, 1546. Epictetus, *Manual*, by Antoine du Moulin, Lyons, 1544; by André de Rivaudeau, Poitiers, 1567; by Guillaume du Vair, 1591 (repr. by "Soc. Litt. de France," Paris, 1921). Hermes Trismegistus, *Deux livres (Puissance et sapience de Dieu; Volonté de Dieu)*, by Gabriel de Preau, 1549; *La table d'esmeraude*, by (Guillaume Rabot?) *(in: Le miroir d'alquimie de Rogier Bacon)*, Lyons, 1557; *Le Pimandre*, by François de Foix de la famille de Candalie, Bordeaux, 1579. Marcus Aurelius, by Pardoux du Prat (with Agapetus and an elegy of Solon), Lyons, 1570. Philo Judaeus, *Les œuvres*, by Pierre Bellier, 1575; *Du monde* (with Aristotle, *De mundo*, and Cicero, *Somnium Scipionis*), by Pierre Saliat, Lyons, 1542. Proclus *La sphère*, by Elie Vinet, Poitiers, 1544; *Deux livres du mouvement*, by Pierre Forcadel, 1565.

Lucian

Trente dialogues, by Geoffroy Tory *(in: La table de Cebès)*, 1529. *La mouche*, by Geoffroy Tory, (1533?). *La colomnie*, by Simon Bougouyn, 1529; by Jean Des Gouttes, Lyons, 1536; by Antoine Crappier, Lyons, 1551; by François Blaisot, Toulouse, 1559. *Des vraies narrations* (with the *Calumny*), by Simon Bougouyn, 1529. *De ceulx qui servent à gaiges* (with the *Calumny*), by Jean Des Gouttes, Lyons, 1536. *Hercules de Gaule*, by Gilles d'Aurigny, Poitiers, 1545. *Dialogue de l'amitié* (Toxaris), by Jacques de Rozières, 1546 or 1547; by Blaise de Vigenère (with Plato's *Lysis* and Cicero's *Laelius*), 1579. *Le menteur, ou l'incredule*, by Louis Meigret, 1548. *Louanges de l'astrologie*, by Antoine Mizauld, 1563. *Devis des dieux pris de Lucian* (in verse), by J.-A. de Baïf *(in his: Euvres)*,

1572-73. *Dialogue pris de L.* (in verse), by Etienne Forcadel *(in his: Œuvres poétiques)*, 1579. *Diogène et Alexandre* (in verse), by Jean Le Masle *(in his: Nouv. récréations poétiques)*, 1580. *Le martire de vérité*, by D.V.Z., (1585?). *Les œuvres de Lucian*, by Filbert Bretin, 1582.

Plutarch

Lives: (*See* Amyot, above). *Demetrius*, by Claude de Seyssel (with Diodorus), 1530. *Vies de huict excellens et renommez personnages* (Themistocles, Camillus, Pericles, Fabius, Alcibiades, Coriolanus, Timoleon, P. Aemilius), by George de ʽSelve, 1543. *Caton le jeune*, by Loys Marchant, 1554. *Epitome ou abrégé des vies de LIV personnages*, by Philippe des Avenelles, 1558. *Le trésor des vies de P.*, anon., Antwerp, 1567. *Avis ... sur les affaires d'état, tiré des Vies de P.*, by Girard du Haillan, 1578. *Moralia:* (*See* Amyot, above). *Pour discerner ung vray amy*, by François Sauvaige, 1521. *Politiques ... pour bien régir la chose publique*, by Geoffroy Tory, 1532. *Du gouvernement en mariage*, by Jean Lodé, 1535. *Touche naïfve pour esprouver l'amy et le flateur* and *L'art de faire son proffit de ses ennemys*, by Antoine du Saix, Lyons (Arnoullet), n.d.; Paris, 1537. *Education et nourriture des enfans*, by Jean Colin, 1537. *Recueil des ... nobles faicts de plusieurs femmes, " Ou là ou non,"* 1538. *De la tranquillité ... de l'esprit*, by Jean Colin, 1538. *La doctrine du prince*, by Jean Colin *(in his Manuel royal)*, Tours, 1541. *Narrations d'amour*, by Jean Fournier (with *Parthenius*), 1543. *Apophthegmes*, by Antoine Macault, 1543. *De la honte vicieuse*, by François Legrand, 1544. *Cinq opuscules (Si les bestes ont usage de la raison; Utilité des ennemis; Moyen de garder santé; Quels animaux ont le plus de raison; Commentaire de vice et vertu)*, by Estienne Pasquier, recteur des écoles de Louhans, 1546. *Deux opuscules (De non se courroucer; De curiosité; also, Si les maladies de l'âme tourmentent plus fort que celles du corps)*, by Pierre de Saint-Julien de Balleure, Lyons, 1546. *De ne prendre à l'usure*, by Antoine du Moulin (with E. Pasquier's *Cinq opuscules*), Lyons, 1546. *Vertus et nobles faictz des femmes*, by Denys Sauvage, Lyons, 1546. *De la cure familière ... préceptes de mariage*, anon., Lyons, 1546. *De l'industrie des animaux* and *Moyens de contregarder la santé*, by Arnault Pasquet de La Rocheffoucault (with *Pictorius*, *Les sept Dialogues)*, 1557. *La manière de se gouverner en mariage*, by Jacques Grévin, 1558. *Que les bestes usent de la raison*, by Adrien de la Planche, 1558. *Préceptes nuptieux* (in verse), by Jacques de La Tapie, 1559. *La tardive vengeance de Dieu*, by Jean de Marconville, 1563. *Lois connubiales*, by Jean de Marconville *(in his: L'heur et malheur de mariage)*, 1564. *Apophthegmes*, by Guillaume Haudent, Rouen, 1571. *Règles de mariage* and *Consolation de P. à sa femme*, by Estienne de la Boëtie *(in his: Mesnagerie)*, 1571-72. *Que la doctrine est req. à un prince*, by Claude d'Espence, 1575. *Le trésor des morales*, by François Le Tort, 1577. *De la création de l'âme*, by Loys Le Roy *(in his: Timée* of Plato, 2nd ed.), 1581. *De l'amour et de ses effects*, extr. de P., anon., 1595.

Romances

Achilles Tatius, frgs. *in : Les devis amoureux*, by Claude Colet, 1545; Books 5-8, by Jacques de Rochemaure, 1556; complete tr. by François de Belleforest, 1568. Aristaenetus, by Cyre Foucault, Poitiers, 1597. Eustathius (or Eumathius), by Jean de Louveau, Lyons, 1559; by Jérôme d'Avost, 1582. Heliodorus. *(See* Amyot, above). Parthenius, by Jean Fournier (with Plutarch, *Les narrations),* Lyons, 1543. *Histoires prodigieuses extraites de plusieurs auteurs grecs, latins, sacrez et profanes*, by P. Boaistuau, C. de Tesserant, F. de Belleforest, R. Hoyer, and J. de Marconville, 6 v., 1597-98.

ADDENDA

NOTE. — Because the following items were received after the Index was completed, they could not be serialized nor could the proper names in them be included in the Index. This section has been prepared in a further attempt to bring the Bibliography up to the end of 1954, with a few important titles of 1955.　　　　　D. C. CABEEN, GENERAL EDITOR.

SCIENCE AND TRAVEL

(Nos. 312-488)

ALBERT DOUGLAS MENUT

Architecture

Delorme, Philibert. Nouvelles inventions pour bien bastir et a petits fraiz. Morel, 1561. 61 ff.

Practical directions for erecting framework of buildings, according to new method invented by author, famous builder of châteaux, fortifications and supervisor of construction of the Tuileries.

— Le premier tome de l'architecture. Morel, 1567. 283 ff.

Opponent of Italian renaissance style, Delorme sought a return to Greek and Roman design. Reprinted together with *Les nouvelles inventions,* 1568, 1576; separately, 1626, 1648. Facsimile reproduction of both works, ed. C. Nizet. Librairies-imprimeries réunies, 1894. 702 p. *See* H. Clouzot, *Philibert de l'Orme,* Plon, 1910. 198 p.

Economics

Garrault, François, *sieur des Gorges.* Des mines d'argent trouvees en France, ouvrage et police d'icelles. Dalier et Roffet, 1579. 21 ff.

Director of royal treasury, author surveyed resources of country and established controls over coinage.

— Paradoxe sur le faict des monnoyes. Dupuys, 1578. 16 ff.

Published together with Bodin's *Discours* (*see above*).

— Les recherches des monnoyes, poix et maniere de nombrer des premieres et plus renommees nations du monde. Le Jeune, 1576. 128 p.

First French study of numismatics. Woodcuts of coins of several countries. Method derived from Budé's *De asse.*

Geography, Exploration and Travel

Girault, Simon. Globe du monde contenant un bref traité du ciel et de la terre. Langres, Des Preyz, 1572. 92 ff.

With numerous maps and charts, designed for education of children. Author wrote other works designed to facilitate children's learning. *See Dictionnaire des lettres françaises, XVIe siècle,* p. 348.

MISCELLANEOUS WRITERS

(Nos. 697-731)

HÉLÈNE HARVITT

Saulnier, V. L. Le sens du Cymbalum mundi de Bonaventure des Périers. BHren 13:43-69, 137-71, 1951.

Reviews in some detail the various studies of the *Cymbalum,* during the last 30 years, and then proceeds to his own

311

interpretation of Des Périers—this " Erasmien français." Des Périers preached " hesuchisme," that is to say, the taste for thinking for oneself, without saying anything. Silence, and hence immunity, before all spies, inquisitors and troublemakers. Hence an absolute hatred of words ; one book is sufficient : the Gospel,

one faith : absolute trust in Christ. This also was the belief of Marguerite de Navarre, and the *Cymbalum*, far from separating Des Périers from his princess, brought him closer to her. He wrote no more : his task was done. All that should now be done was to withdraw into the serenity of mystic love.

FRANÇOIS RABELAIS

(Nos. 817-916)

ALEXANDER H. SCHUTZ

Association Guillaume Budé. Congrès de Tours et Poitiers. Les belles lettres, 1954. 422 p.

Several major articles : M. Roques, *Aspects de Panurge* (p. 61-74) ; L. Febvre (no title), being no more than an allocution (p. 74-82) ; a top-class, richly documented discussion by Robert Marichal, *Le dernier séjour de Rabelais à Rome* (p. 104-32), designed to show R., in entourage of Cardinal Du Bellay, less as doctor than political " attaché de presse "; P. Jourda, *Rabelais, peintre de la France de son temps* (p. 132-36), showing him more interested in " les monuments et les curiosités " than landscapes, more attracted to peasant than other classes. Not much new, but skillful condensation. Most useful for us in this country : V. L. Saulnier, *Position actuelle des problèmes rabelaisiennes* (p. 83-104), relating progress since last report, 1948. First part (to p. 90) bibliographic; second part *Orientation présente*, focusing on desiderata.

Many talks at Congrès recorded in résumé : A. Huon, *Les hiéroglyphes dans les derniers livres de Rabelais* (p. 137-40) ; O. Jodogne, *Rabelais et Pathelin* (p. 141-42); C. A. Mayer, *A propos du réalisme de Rabelais* (p. 143) ; F. C. Roe, *Urquhart traducteur de Rabelais* (p. 143-45) ; S. F. Will, *Rabelais en Amérique* (p. 145-47).

Cohen, Marcel. Comment Rabelais a écrit. *In his :* Grammaire et style, 1450-1950. Éditions sociales [1954]. 237 p.

Articles had appeared in various journals. Have originality and some of the freshness of the spoken word. Like others of Cohen's writings, colored by political bias. Worth reading for comparisons with R.'s contemporaries.

Pons, Roger. La pensée religieuse de Rabelais. Et 279:299-317, Dec., 1953.

Anniversary appraisal of the literature on R.'s religious ideas, evaluating Lefranc, Febvre and others. Not only is R. an Erasmian, but one " ... dépassé par les événements, n'ayant rien à cacher, surtout pas de machinations athées..." (p. 316). The best point made in this article is that we get nothing out of continuing to appreciate R. primarily as thinker, where, in fact, he has little originality. It is how he says things, seriously or in the vein of medieval " folastrie " which removes the barriers of the centuries and makes him come alive for the modern reader. In the future " ... on exploitera moins le prestige de Rabelais, on jouira mieux de lui " (p. 317).

CONTEURS AND NOVELISTS

(Nos. 917-1045)

J. W. HASSELL, JR. AND W. L. WILEY

Hassell, J. Woodrow, Jr. Des Périers' *Nouvelle* XIII and the legend of St. Margaret. Renaissance papers, 1955, p. 19-31.

Study of origins, development and dissemination of version of story of imprisoned demons used by Des Périers.

Conclusion : D.'s assertion that he took the story from an alchemical treatise ascribed to Mary the Prophetess is not necessarily to be taken seriously; the St. Margaret legend was certainly one of the sources, probably the sole source, of the plot of *nouvelle* XIII.

— Des Périers' indebtedness to Castiglione. SP 50:566-72, 1953.

Discussion of Castiglione's influence on the *Joyeux devis*, especially on *nouvelle* 90.

— An Elizabethan translation of the tales of Des Périers : The mirrour of mirth, 1583 and 1592. SP 52:172-85, 1955.

Article includes detailed description of 1583 and 1592 editions of *The mirrour of mirth*, a comparison of their content with each other and with the French text, a commentary upon the quality of the translation, and the results of the author's inquiry into question of identity of translator. Concludes that the translator may have been Thomas Deloney.

Ilsley, Marjorie Henry. New light on the Proumenoir de M. de Montaigne. MP 52:1-11, 1954.

Comparison of the *Proumenoir* with its source. Concludes that Marie de Gournay's little novel " combines an intelligent imitation of an earlier work with an exact and sincere observation of reality " and that it " must be placed as one of the first and best ' romans d'analyse ' written in France." Article contains much useful bibliographical material.

Ritter, Raymond. Les solitudes de Marguerite de Navarre (1527-1549). Champion, 1953. 223 p.

Study of Marguerite's life in southern France. Beautifully illustrated. Valuable notes. No general index ; badly proofread. Of special interest to students of *Heptaméron* are p. 85-87, 113-32, 167, 172-73, 178-81, 210-11 (note 170).

Woledge, Brian. Bibliographie des romans et nouvelles en prose antérieurs à 1500. Geneva, Droz, 1954. 150 p.

Important for the medieval period.

PIERRE DE RONSARD
(Nos. 1061-1195)

MORRIS BISHOP

Ronsard, Pierre de. Les Bacchanales, ou Le folastrissime voyage d'Hercueil. Ed. André Desguine. Geneva, Droz, 1953. 367 p. (TLF)

The 642 lines of poem occupy 26 pages ; the introduction, commentary, variants, imitations, bibliography. Awe-inspiringly erudite ; but what an aftermath to R.'s picnic party!

— Le second livre des amours, éd. Alexandre Micha. Geneva : Droz ; Lille : Giard. 1951. 227 p. (TLF)

Excellent *édition critique*, with ample variants and notes. Introduction sensible, penetrating, circumspect.

— Les odes. Texte définitif publié pour la première fois avec complément et variantes par Charles Guérin. Éditions du Cèdre, 1952. 531 p.

Pleasant scholarly edition, following 1587 text ; with selection of sources and variants from Laumonier (1068) and with lexical and other notes by editor.

Hallowell, Robert Edward. Ronsard and the conventional Roman elegy. Urbana, University of Illinois Press, 1954. 176 p. (ISLL, v. 37, no. 4).

" Ronsard regarded himself as a successor to the Roman elegists, consciously struck their poses and adopted their mannerisms without always imitating them directly." Rich, judicious, well-informed study of difficult subject.

Lebègue, Raymond. Ronsard, l'homme et l'œuvre. Boivin, 1950. 173 p.

Excellent little book by eminent scholar, more concerned with analysis and appreciation of R.'s poems than with biography. In *Connaissance des lettres* series number 29 ; designed first for students, but serves as well for general reader seeking understanding.

Lesure, François, and Geneviève Thibault. Bibliographie des éditions musicales publiées par Nicolas du Chemin (1549-1576). Annales musicologiques 1:269-374, 1953.

Largely on R. Excellent full bibliographical descriptions.

Silver, Isidore. Pierre de Ronsard : panegyrist, pensioner, and satirist of the French court. RR 45:89-108, 1954.

Need, money motive, prompted much of R.'s court poetry. But he proved to be incomparable satirist.

— Ronsard in European literature. Hren 16:241-54, 1954.

Excellent résumé of studies of R.'s rayonnement in England, Scotland, Germany, Belgium, Holland, Italy, Poland.

MICHEL EYQUEM DE MONTAIGNE

(Nos. 1488-1806)

RICHARD R. STRAWN AND SAMUEL FREDERIC WILL

Frame, Donald M. Montaigne's discovery of man. The humanization of a humanist. Columbia University Press, 1955. 202 p.

A sound and well-written study of the evolution of M.'s thought, achieved through coordinated study of all available materials: literary, biographical, and historical. The best book on M. in English, and one of the best in any language.

TRANSLATORS: GREEK

(Nos. 2514-2594G)

JAMES HUTTON

Coyecque, Ernest. Josse Bade et les traductions de Claude de Seyssel. BEC 55:509-14, 1894.

Presents Seyssel's contract with Badius for printing his translations; interesting remarks and inferences, e.g., that the Thucydides was not a commercial success.

TRANSLATORS: ITALIAN (EXCEPT MACHIAVELLI)

(Nos. 2595-2639)

OLIN H. MOORE

Chamard, Henri. La traduction. In : Dictionnaire des lettres françaises, le seizième siècle (éd. Monseigneur Georges Grente), Fayard, 1951, p. 669-73.

A satisfactory outline of the history of translations in France during the sixteenth century. In spite of limitations of space, Chamard succeeds in making a clear exposition of the rival theories of the art of translating.

Giraldi Cinthio, G. B. Dialogues philosophiques... touchant la vie civile, translated by Gabriel Chappuys. L'Angelier, 1583. 474 ff.

With Italian text of the three philosophical dialogues in the Hecatommithi facing the French version.

Petrarca, Francesco. Six sonnetz de Pétrarque. Trans. by Clément Marot, Corrozet, n.d. 4 ff.

Marot translated also one of Petrarca's canzoni. See H. Hauvette, Les poésies lyriques de Pétrarque, Malfère, 1931, p. 142, and Marcel Françon, Sur l'influence de Pétrarque en France, Ital, 19:106-10, 1942.

INDEX

NOTE. — When entries in this Index are followed by more than three serial numbers, these serial numbers are identified as to content, as briefly as possible.
When the subject of the Index entry is the author of the item represented by the serial number, the number is given in italics.

1338, 2697-2700, 2756, 2793; Lataille : 1254; Latin : 1210, 1249, 1255-56, 1266, 1269, 1291, 1297, 1302, 1324, 1325; Lemaire : 1265; Lucanus : 1233, 1331; Lucianus : 1266; Lucretius Carus : 1218; Malestroit : 1222; Malherbe : 1257; Middle Ages : 1340; Military eloquence : 2198; Mulcaster : 1288; Ode : 1229, 1328; Olive : 1221, 1267, 1313, 1316, 1326, 1329, 1335-1336, 2698-99; Pater : 134, 1057, 1281; *Patrie :* 1223, 1293; Petrarquisme : 1245, 2730 ; Pindarus : 1179, 1319, 1321-22 ; Platonism : 741, 1268, 2574; Pléiade : 864, 1047, 1052, 1056-58, 1228, 1231, 1240, 1276, 1290, 1332 ; Poetic technique : 1341; Poitiers : 1231; Rabelais : 864; RLC : 91; Ronsard : 864, 1058, 1096, 1115, 1172, 1179, 1229, 1237, 1259-60, 1276, 1285, 1287, 1290, 1322-23; Saint-Quentin : 1294; Sannazaro : 1301 ; Sebillet : 1261, 1278; Sonnet : 1283; Spenser : 1262; Strowski : 1058; Switzerland : 1242, 2885; Tragedy : 2317, 2378; Vauquelin de La Fresnaye : 1400; Véron : 1279; Virgil : 1249, 1252-53 ; Works : *Amours:* 1263; *Antiquitez de Rome : 1202,* 1211, 1214-15, 1233, 1244, 1306-07, 1331; *Deffence et illustration:* 1203-06, 1213, 1215, 1227, 1232, 1236, 1247, 1252, 1261, 1278, 1298-99, 1338, 2793; *Discours:* 1224; *Divers jeux rustiques:* 1207-08, 1310; *Heureux qui comme Ulisse:* 1258, 1324; 1400, *Lettres:* 1209; *Œuvres: 1198-99,* 1304 ; *Œuvres choisies : 1200* ; *Œuvres poétiques: 1201, 1210* ; *Poète courtisan:* 1235; *Regrets: 1211,* 1215, 1222, 1238, 1251, 1269, 1273-74, 1286, 1293, 1333-34, 1337; *Superbi colli:* 1241, 1270; *Vanneur de blé:* 1057

Du Bellay, Martin, *sieur de Langey,* 2210
Du Bellay, René, 1220, 1222
Du Bellay family, 872, 1311, 2707
Dubois, Jacques, Grammar : 550, 553, 555, 579
Dubois, Jean, 1814, 2057
Dubosc, Georges, 672
Dubouchet, A., *861*
Du Bourg, Anne, 1452, 1848
Du Breil, André, *433*
Du Breuil, Catherine, 1305
Duchesne, Léger, 1266, 1347
Du Duc, Fronton, 2395
Duentzer, Heinrich, *2251*
Du Fail, Noël, section on : 958-65; Biography and criticism : 964; Italy : 193, 2672; Style and language : 965; Works : *Baliverneries: 958,* 960; *Contes d'Eutrapel: 958,* 963; *Propos rustiques: 959-62*
Dufay, Pierre, *1111*
Dufayard, Charles, *2565*
Du Fouilloux, Jacques, 1173
Dufour, Théophile, 1887

Dugast, Robert, 1297
Du Guez, Giles, *see* Giles du Guez
Du Guillet, Pernette, section on : 801-06; Biography and criticism : 785, 803, 806; Scève : 804-05; Works : *Poésies:* 801
Du Haillan, Bernard de Girard, *seigneur,* (BN entry), *see* Girard, Bernard de, *seigneur du Haillan*
Du Hamel, Jacques, *2360*
Duhamel, Pierre Albert, *238*
Duhem, Jules, *1237*
Duhem, Pierre Maurice Marie, *316, 317*
Du Méril, Édéléstand Pontas, 2313
Du Mesnil, Nicolas, 336
Dumolin, Guillaume, 164
Du Monin, Jean Edouard, 1347
Du Moulin, Antoine, section on : 701; Bibliography and biography : 701, 2577; Du Guillet : 801; Epictetus : 2582; Marguerite de Navarre : 701, 2577; Works : *Physiomonie:* 345
Dumoulin, Charles, section on : 2114-18; Biography and criticism : 2116-17; Legislation : 2114; *Prêt à intérêt:* 2118; *Promesses de vente:* 2115
Dumoulin, Joseph, 59
Du Périer, Antoine, *sieur de La Salargue,* 1037, 2360
Du Perron, Jacques Davy, *cardinal,* Biography : 1820-21; Italy : 2786; Mornay : 1810; *Prédication:* 1814, 1822; Ronsard : 1066, 1819; Works : *1818-19*
Dupeyrat, Guillaume, 2688
Dupleix, Joseph François, *marquis,* 1532
Dupleix, Scipion, 2786
Du Plessis-Marly, Philippe de Mornay, *seigneur, see* Mornay, Philippe de, *seigneur de Plessis-Marly, called* du Plessis-Mornay
Duportal, Jeanne, 1488, 1493
Duprat, François Antoine Brutus, *60*
Dupré, Galliot, 86
Du Puis, Guillaume, *434*
Dupuy, Ernest, 487, *2160*
Duras, *Mme* de, *see* Dufort-Duras, Marguerite (de Grammont) de
Dürer, Albrecht, *2485*
Du Roc Sort Manne, anagram of Romannet du Cros, *which see*
Du Souhait, *sieur,* 2361
Du Taillan family (Montaigne), 1675
Dutch, *see* Holland
Du Tillet, Jean, *sieur de la Bussière,* 2199
Du Vair, Guillaume, section on : 2256-83; Bibliography : 2270, 2279, 2579, 2581; Biography and criticism : 1538, 1846, 2269-70, 2276, 2280-83; Charron: 2277; Correspondence : 2260-62, 2272, 2581; Epictetus : 2266-67, 2578, 2580; *Ligue:* 2278; Lipsius : 2271; Magistrate : 2280-81; Malherbe : 2268, 2273; Marguerite de Valois : 2274; Orator : 2278; Stoicism: 198, 1847, 2275, 2282-83, 2580; Works : *Actions et traitez:*